COGNITIVE BEHAVIOR THERAPY

COGNITIVE BEHAVIOR THERAPY:

Applying Empirically Supported Techniques in Your Practice

Edited by
William O'Donohue
Jane E. Fisher
Steven C. Hayes

WILEY

John Wiley & Sons, Inc.

Library of Congress Cataloging-in-Publication Data:

O'Donohue, William T.
    Cognitive behavior therapy : applying empirically supported techniques in your practice /
William O'Donohue, Jane E. Fisher, Steven C. Hayes.
        p. cm.
    Includes bibliographical references and index.
    ISBN 0-471-23614-4 (cloth : alk. paper)
    1. Cognitive therapy.   2. Behavior therapy.   3. Psychotherapy. I. Fisher, Jane E. (Jane Ellen), 1957–
II. Hayes, Steven C.   III. Title.
    RC489.C63 O35 2003
    616.89'142—dc21   2002034201

Printed in the United States of America

10 9 8 7 6 5 4 3 2 1

This book is dedicated to our mentors:

Nicholas Cummings

James Geer

Noretta Koertge

Leonard Krasner

Sister Margaret Ann White, C.S.J.

Michael G. H. Coles

Laura Carstensen

Richard McFall

David Barlow

John Cone

CONTENTS

CONTRIBUTORS

Jonathan S. Abramowitz
Mayo Clinic
Rochester, MN

Amanda Nicolson Adams
Fitness Evolution
Reno, NV

Jennifer H. Adams
University of Houston
Houston, TX

Mark A. Adams
Fitness Evolution
Reno, NV

K. Angeleque Akin-Little
University at Albany, SUNY
Albany, NY

Claudia Avina
University of Nevada
Reno, NV

Anjali Barretto
The University of Iowa
Iowa City, IA

Stephen K. Bell
University of Florida
Gainesville, FL

Wendy Berg
The University of Iowa
Iowa City, IA

Jennifer L. Best
University of Southern California
Los Angeles, CA

Arthur W. Blume
University of Texas at El Paso
El Paso, TX

Stephen R. Boggs
University of Florida
Gainesville, FL

Stephanie Both
University of Amsterdam
Amsterdam, The Netherlands

Adrian H. Bowers
University of Nevada
Reno, NV

Thomas E. Boyce
University of Nevada
Reno, NV

Kirk A. Brunswig
University of Nevada
Reno, NV

Eric Burkholder
University of Nevada
Reno, NV

James E. Carr
Western Michigan University
Kalamazoo, MI

Nicole Cavenagh
University of Nevada
Las Vegas, NV

Daniel Cervone
University of Illinois at Chicago
Chicago, IL

Linda J. Cooper-Brown
The University of Iowa
Iowa City, IA

Michelle G. Craske
University of California
Los Angeles, CA

Gerald C. Davidson
University of Southern California
Los Angeles, CA

Sona Dimidjian
University of Washington
Seattle, WA

Keith S. Dobson
University of Calgary
Calgary, Alberta, Canada

Brad Donohue
University of Nevada
Reno, NV

Melanie P. Duckworth
University of Nevada
Reno, NV

V. Mark Durand
University of Albany
Albany, NY

Albert Ellis
The Albert Ellis Institute
New York, NY

Sheila M. Eyberg
University of Florida
Gainesville, FL

Kyle E. Ferguson
University of Nevada
Reno, NV

Jack W. Finney
Virginia Tech University
Blacksburg, VA

Jane E. Fisher
University of Nevada
Reno, NV

Edna B. Foa
University of Pennsylvania
Philadelphia, PA

John P. Forsyth
University of Albany, SUNY
Albany, NY

Maxwell R. Frank
University of Hawaii
Manoa, Hawaii

Martin E. Franklin
University of Pennsylvania
Philadelphia, PA

Patrick C. Friman
University of Nevada
Reno, NV

Alan E. Fruzzetti
University of Nevada
Reno, NV

Armida R. Fruzzetti
Truckee Meadows Community College
Reno, NV

Tiffany Fusé
University at Albany, SUNY
Albany, NY

Robert J. Gatchel
The University of Texas Southwestern Medical
    Center at Dallas
Dallas, TX

Scott T. Gaynor
Western Michigan University
Kalamazoo, MI

Patrick M. Ghezzi
University of Nevada
Reno, NV

Elizabeth V. Gifford
University of Nevada
Reno, NV

Alan M. Gross
University of Mississippi
University, MS

Kate E. Hamilton
University of Calgary
Calgary, Alberta, Canada

Jay Harding
The University of Iowa
Iowa City, IA

Cathi D. Harris
University of Arizona
Tucson, AZ

Linda J. Hayes
University of Nevada
Reno, NV

Steven C. Hayes
University of Nevada
Reno, NV

Holly Hazlett-Stevens
University of Nevada
Reno, NV

Lara S. Head
University of Mississippi
University, MS

Elaine M. Heiby
University of Hawaii
Manoa, Hawaii

Jennifer M. Heidt
Temple University
Philadelphia, PA

Ramona Houmanfar
University of Nevada
Reno, NV

Carl Jungquist
University of Rochester
Rochester, NY

Aaron Kaplan
Waikiki Health Center
Honolulu, HI

Kimberly Keller
University of Illinois at Champaign-Urbana
Champaign, IL

Mary Lou Kelley
Louisiana State University
Baton Rouge, LA

Kelly Koerner
Behavioral Technology Transfer Group
Seattle, WA

Adam R. Krantweiss
Binghamton University
Binghamton, NY

Ellen T. M. Laan
University of Amsterdam
Amsterdam, The Netherlands

Rebecca S. Laird
Anxiety, Stress, & Depression Center
Appleton, WI

Ranilo Laygo
University of Hawaii
Manoa, HI

Arnold A. Lazarus
Rutgers, The State University of New Jersey
Piscataway, NJ

Linda A. LeBlanc
Western Michigan University
Kalamazoo, MI

Eric Levensky
University of Nevada
Reno, NV

Donald J. Levis
Binghamton University
Binghamton, NY

Marsha M. Linehan
University of Washington
Seattle, WA

Steven G. Little
Hofstra University
Hempstead, NY

Andy Lloyd
University of Nevada
Reno, NV

Elizabeth Lombardo
Drexel University
Philadelphia, PA

Kristen Lowry
University of Nevada
Reno, NV

Jason B. Luoma
University of Nevada
Reno, NV

Kenneth R. MacAleese
University of Nevada
Reno, NV

Kristen A. Maglieri
University of Nevada
Reno, NV

Sherrie Maher
Western Michigan University
Kalamazoo, MI

Gayla Margolin
University of Southern California
Los Angeles, CA

G. Alan Marlatt
University of Washington
Seattle, WA

Christopher R. Martell
University of Washington and Independent
    Practice
Seattle, WA

Brian P. Marx
Louisiana State University
Baton Rouge, LA

Donald Meichenbaum
University of Waterloo
Waterloo, Ontario, Canada

Gerald I. Metalsky
Lawrence University
Appleton, WI

Raymond G. Miltenberger
North Dakota State University
Fargo, ND

Kevin J. Moore
Oregon Social Learning Center
Eugene, OR

Sally A. Moore
University of Washington
Seattle, WA

Elizabeth Mosco
University of Nevada
Reno, NV

Amy E. Naugle
Western Michigan University
Kalamazoo, MI

Cory F. Newman
University of Pennsylvania
Philadelphia, PA

Arthur M. Nezu
Drexel University
Philadelphia, PA

Christine Maguth Nezu
Drexel University
Philadelphia, PA

William O'Donohue
University of Nevada
Reno, NV

Pamella H. Oliver
California State University
Fullerton, CA

Henry J. Orff
University of Rochester
Rochester, NY

Julieann Pankey
University of Nevada
Reno, NV

Gerald R. Patterson
Oregon Social Learning Center
Eugene, OR

Michael L. Perlis
University of Rochester
Rochester, NY

Alan Poling
Western Michigan University
Kalamazoo, MI

Lisa G. Regev
University of Nevada
Reno, NV

Lynn P. Rehm
University of Houston
Houston, TX

Patricia Robinson
Mountainview Consulting Group, Inc.
Moxee, WA

Richard C. Robinson
The University of Texas Southwestern Medical
  Center at Dallas
Dallas, TX

Adel C. Robles
University of Nevada
Reno, NV

Horacio R. Roman
University of Nevada
Reno, NV

Gerald M. Rosen
Private Practice
Seattle, WA

Frederick Rotgers
Rutgers, The State University of New Jersey
Piscataway, NJ

Deborah A. Roth
University of Pennsylvania
Philadelphia, PA

Frank R. Rusch
University of Illinois at Champaign-Urbana
Champaign, IL

Tamara Penix Sbraga
Central Michigan University
Mount Pleasant, MI

Walter D. Scott
University of Wyoming
Laramie, WY

Chris Segrin
University of Arizona
Tucson, AZ

Chad Shenk
University of Nevada
Reno, NV

Deacon Shoenberger
University of Nevada
Reno, NV

Michael T. Smith
Johns Hopkins University School of Medicine
Baltimore, MD

Jonathan Tarbox
University of Nevada
Reno, NV

Rachal S. F. Tarbox
University of Nevada
Reno, NV

Timothy R. Vollmer
University of Florida
Gainesville, FL

David P. Wacker
The University of Iowa
Iowa City, IA

Michelle D. Wallace
University of Nevada
Reno, NV

W. Larry Williams
University of Nevada
Reno, NV

Ginger R. Wilson
University of Nevada
Reno, NV

Carrie S. Wright
University of Florida
Gainesville, FL

Lori A. Zoellner
University of Washington
Seattle, WA

PREFACE

Over the last three decades there has been a significant increase in interest in cognitive behavior therapy. This has occurred for several reasons: 1) Mounting experimental evidence supports the effectiveness of cognitive behavioral therapy for certain psychological problems including high incidence problems such as depression and the anxiety disorders. The well-known Chambless report, for example, identifies many cognitive behavioral therapies as being empirically supported. In fact, cognitive behavioral techniques comprise most of the list. 2) Cognitive behavior therapy tends to be relatively brief and often can be delivered in groups. Therefore it can be more cost-effective than some alternatives and be seen to offer good value. These qualities have become particularly important in the era of managed care with its emphasis upon cost containment. 3) Cognitive behavior therapy has been applied with varying success to a wide variety of problems. Thus, it has considerable scope and utility for the practitioner in general practice or the professional involved in the training of therapists. 4) Cognitive behavior therapy is a relatively straight forward and clearly operationalized approach to psychotherapy. 5) Cognitive behavioral therapy is a therapy system comprised of many individual techniques, with researchers and practitioners constantly adding to this inventory. A given behavior therapist, because of his or her specialty, may know or use only a small subset of these. A clinician or clinical researcher may want to creatively combine individual techniques to treat some intransigent problem or an unfamiliar or complicated clinical presentation.

This volume attempts to bring together all of the specific techniques of cognitive behavior therapy. It does this in an ecumenical fashion. Currently, there are divisions inside behavior therapy that this book attempts to ignore. For example, cognitive and more traditionally behavioral techniques are included. This offended some prospective authors who were clearly warriors in the cognitive-behavioral battle. We wanted to be inclusive, particularly because pragmatically the outcome research favors both sides of this particular battle.

Our major interest in compiling this book was twofold: First we noted the lack of a volume that provides detailed descriptions of the techniques of cognitive behavioral therapy. Many books talked about these but few described the techniques in detail. The absence of a comprehensive collection of the methods of cognitive-behavior therapy creates a gap in the training of students and in the faithful practice of cognitive behavior therapy. Second, with the increased interest in cognitive behavior therapy, particularly by the payers in managed care, there has been an increasing bastardization of behavior therapy. Some therapists are claiming they are administering some technique (e.g., relapse prevention or contingency management) when they clearly are not. This phenomenon, in our experience, rarely involves intentional deception but instead reflects an ignorance of the complexities of faithfully implementing these techniques. This book is aimed at reducing this problem.

There is an important question regarding the extent to which a clinician can faithfully implement these techniques without a deeper understanding of behavior therapy. The evidence is not clear and of course the question is actually more complicated. Perhaps a generically skilled therapist with certain kinds of clients and certain kinds of techniques can implement the techniques well. On the other hand, a less skilled therapist dealing with a complicated clinical presentation utilizing a more subtle technique might not do so well. There is certainly a Gordon Paul type question lurking here. Something like: "What kind of therapist, with what type of problem, using what kind of cognitive behavior therapy technique, can have what kinds of effects. . . ." With the risk of being seen as self-promoting the reader can learn about the learning and conditioning underpinnings of many of these techniques in O'Donohue (1998); and more of the theories associated with these techniques in O'Donohue and Krasner (1995).

Finally, we wish to thank all the chapter authors. They uniformly wrote excellent chapters and completed these quickly. We'd also like to thank our editor at John Wiley, Jennifer Simon. She shared our vision for this book, gave us some excellent suggestions for improvement, and has been wonderful to work with. We'd also like to thank Nanci Fowler and Sara Ashby for all their secretarial assistance. She was invaluable. Finally, we'd like to thank our families for their support, especially our children, Katie, Annie, Camille, Charlie, and Essie.

References

O'Donohue, W., & Krasner, L. (Eds.). (1995). *Theories of behavior therapy.* Washington: APA Books

O'Donohue, W. (Ed.). (1998). *Learning and behavior therapy.* Boston: Allyn & Bacon.

COGNITIVE
BEHAVIOR
THERAPY

1 INTRODUCTION

William O'Donohue and Jane E. Fisher

Cognitive behavior therapy (CBT) is an approach to human problems that can be viewed from several interrelated perspectives: philosophical, theoretical, methodological, assessment-oriented, and technological. This book focuses on the last aspect, so crucial to clinical practice, but situated in the other four, much as any one of a cube's six sides is situated among all of the others.

Philosophically, CBT can be viewed as being associated (or, according to some who put it more strongly, derived) with one or another variety of behaviorism. The behaviorisms are generally philosophies of science and philosophies of mind—that is, ways of defining and approaching the understanding of the problems traditionally associated with psychology.

There are at least two broad issues at the philosophical level: (1) What particular form of behaviorism is being embraced (O'Donohue & Kitchener, 1999, have identified at least fourteen), and (2) What is the nature of the relationship or association between this philosophy and the practice of CBT? Some have argued that behaviorism is irrelevant to behavior therapy—that one can practice behavior therapy and either reject behaviorism or be agnostic with regard to all forms of it. While an individual practitioner can behave in this way, some of the deeper structure that can be generative and guiding is lost. One can drive a car without an understanding of its workings, but one probably can't design a better car or modify an existing car without such an understanding. Similarly, a knowledge of behaviorism allows greater understanding of the choice points implicit in any technology. For example, why not view the client's problem as a neurological difficulty and intervene at this level? Behaviorism often provides possible answers to this kind of general challenge.

The second aspect of behavior therapy is its theoretical structure. Here the issues are less philosophical—less about general epistemic issues—and more about substantive assertions regarding more specific problems as well as the principles appealed to in making these assertions. What is panic? What are its causes? What is the role of operant conditioning in children's oppositional behavior?

There are also a wide variety of theories associated with behavior therapy (O'Donohue & Krasner, 1995), including

- Reciprocal inhibition
- Response deprivation
- Molar regulatory theory
- Two-factor fear theory
- Implosion theory
- Learned alarms
- Bioinformational theory
- Self-control theory
- Developmental theories
- Coercion theory

- Self-efficacy theory
- Attribution theory
- Information processing theory
- Relational frame theory
- Relapse prevention
- Evolutionary theory
- Marxist theory
- Feminist theory
- Dialectical theory
- Acceptance theory
- Functional analytic theory
- Interbehavioral theory

Theories can provide answers or at least testable hypotheses for questions regarding more specific problems, such as these: What is the basic nature of this kind of clinical problem? How does this problem develop? What maintains this problem? What are its associated features and why? How is this problem possibly modified?

The third aspect of CBT is its program for knowledge generation. In the main, CBT is experimental and relies on a mixture of group experimental designs (e.g., the randomized controlled trial) and single-subject experimental designs (although in the largest perspective it can be seen to include correlational designs and even case studies). Methodologically, CBT generally embraces constructs such as social validity, clinical significance, follow-up measurements, manualized treatment, adherence and competence checks, the measurement of process variables, independent replications, and real-world effectiveness research. This tool box is complex, but one can discern a few distinct styles—such as that of the applied behavior analyst and that of the cognitive therapist (O'Donohue & Houts, 1985). Other styles can be seen when the nature of the question differs—for example, when the interest is in measurement development and validation or in the questions typically associated with experimental psychopathology.

The fourth aspect of CBT is its approach to measurement. Here a key issue is how to accurately detect and quantify variables of interest. Cognitive behavior therapy is associated with both a distinctive delineation of the domain of interest and distinct methods for measuring this. In general, behavioral assessment can be distinguished from more traditional measurement approaches by its focus on sampling of behavior rather than looking for signs of more abstract constructs. There are diverse streams of thought within the CBT tradition, however, from the embrace of traditional psychometric standards to the radically functional (e.g., Hayes, Nelson, & Jarrett, 1987). Some of the chapters in this volume deal with assessment techniques either because they are central to therapy or because assessment methods themselves are so reactive that they may be seen, in part, as treatment. However, in the main this book does not focus on the measurement aspect, leaving that task to other fine anthologies (e.g., Haynes & Heiby, in press).

The final aspect of CBT is *technique*—skilled practice. No amount of philosophy or theory will relieve clinicians from this level of analysis. A surgeon may be a biological determinist philosophically and may hold to certain theories of cancer and cancer treatment, but to help patients the surgeon still needs to implement surgical technique in a skilled manner. Similarly, cognitive behavior therapists need to be skilled in the execution of their techniques. In fact, an interesting set of research questions involves the relationship between the degree of skill (e.g., poor, novice, experienced, master) and therapy outcome. For example, if a clinician arranges potential positive reinforcers that are too distal in contingency manager it will be less effective. Similarly, if a clinician conducts systematic desensitization with only a few steps in a fear hierarchy, with weakly trained progressive muscle relaxation skills, and pairings that are few and of very short duration, it is unlikely to be as effective as it could otherwise be.

We've identified approximately 70 distinct techniques in CBT, covering both standard behavior therapy and cognitive therapy techniques, and relatively recently developed procedures such as acceptance strategies and mindfulness. This number has to qualify CBT as one of the most variegated therapy systems. This diversity no doubt derives from an interplay of complex factors: (1) the multiple learning theories upon which traditional behavior therapy is based (O'Donohue, 1998); (2) the multielemental nature of each of these theories (e.g., setting events, discrimination training, schedules of reinforcement, generalization processes, fading, etc.); (3) the influence of other elements of experimental psychology such as experimental cognitive science; (4) the influence of other branches of psychology such as social psychology; (5) the influences of other intellectual domains (dialectics) or other fields of inquiry (mindfulness); (6) the interface of these with a particular kind of clinical problem (e.g., Borderline Personality Disorder); and finally (7) the creativity of the developers. But whatever the source of this tremendous variety, the presence of such a large number of major distinctive techniques leaves no doubt as to the multifactorial nature of contemporary CBT.

We've asked each of the chapter authors to follow a standard format, because we thought these main topics would delineate a bit of the context and all of the essential features needed to competently execute these techniques. We wanted them to describe who might benefit from this technique, contraindications, other factors relevant to making the decision to use or not to use the technique, how the technique might work (i.e., what process or pathway it may be associated with), and some of the evidence for its effectiveness. The major section of the chapter is a step-by-step guide that explains exactly how to implement the technique. Finally, we asked authors to include a brief table outlining the major elements of the technique.

The very number and diversity of CBT techniques place a significant burden on any practitioner of CBT and, even more so, on the student. It is our hope that this volume, by clearly and concisely describing these techniques, will ease this burden. We also hope that precision about techniques can help the field continue to keep its eye on Gordon Paul's (1969) classic question: What techniques, delivered by what type of therapist, for what kind of client, with what kind of clinical problem, in what kind of setting, produces what kind of result, by what kind of process?

References

Haynes, S., & Heiby, E. (in press). *The encyclopedia of behavioral assessment.*

Hayes, S. C., Nelson, R. O., & Jarrett, R. (1987). Treatment utility of assessment: A functional approach to evaluating the quality of assessment. *American Psychologist, 42*, 963–974.

O'Donohue, W. (Ed.). (1998). *Learning and behavior therapy.* Boston: Allyn & Bacon.

O'Donohue, W., & Houts, A. C. (1985). The two disciplines of behavior therapy. *Psychological Record, 35*(2), 155–163.

O'Donohue, W., & Kitchener, R. (1999). *Handbook of behaviorism.* San Diego: Academic Press.

O'Donohue, W., & Krasner, L. (Eds.). (1995). *Theories of behavior therapy.* Washington: APA Books.

Paul, G. L. (1969). Behavior modification research: Design and tactics. In C. M. Franks (Ed.), *Behavior therapy: Appraisal and status* (pp. 29–62). New York: McGraw-Hill.

2 ACCEPTANCE

Steven C. Hayes and Julieann Pankey

Psychological acceptance has been variously described as allowing, tolerating, embracing, experiencing, or making contact with a source of stimulation, particularly private experiences, that previously evoked escape, avoidance, or aggression (Cordova, 2001). To some degree, the importance both of therapeutic acceptance of the client and of helping the client accept him- or herself is recognized by all therapy approaches (Linehan, 1994). Acceptance, viewed broadly, is a critical component through which change strategies are engaged and is itself a significant mechanism of change (Greenberg, 1994; Hayes, Jacobson, Follette, & Dougher, 1994; Jacobson, Christensen, Prince, Cordova, & Eldridge, 2000). Wide differences exist, however, in conceptual definitions, the techniques employed to elicit acceptance, in the mechanism of change thought to be important (client focused or therapist stance), and in a focus on acceptance as a process and acceptance as an outcome.

Acceptance has a long history in behavioral health areas. Freud (1920) delineated psychopathological processes based on unconscious repression and avoidance of unwanted thoughts and emotions. Rogers (1961) focused on acceptance in terms of the therapist's relationship with the client. Here, acceptance was both a goal for the therapist to undertake in providing an unconditional, consistent, genuine, and noncritical psychotherapeutic context, and a client target for acceptance of self. Rogers posited that a genuine, interested, tolerant therapeutic stance known as *unconditional positive regard* was the critical ingredient in the therapeutic process. The therapist sets the context by providing a noncritical place in which the client may recognize and clarify his or her emotions, and the client may then achieve acceptance of self through openness to experience and recognition of his or her "spontaneous self" (Rogers, 1992).

Acceptance has also been part of the tradition of humanistic/existential psychotherapy (Greenberg, 1994). Fritz Perls (1973) discussed acceptance in terms of allowing oneself an awareness of and openness to experiencing emotion genuinely.

What is new about acceptance approaches is their manualization, systematic conceptualization, and inclusion in empirically supported therapies. Behavioral and cognitive behavioral researchers and clinicians have been particularly important in this change. From a behavioral point of view, acceptance is a function rather than a form or topography, and it is an action rather than the content of cognition or emotion (Dougher, 1994). Modern research agrees that acceptance applies primarily to the domain of private subjective events and experiences (Greenberg, 1994). For example, Cordova and Kohlenberg (1994) define acceptance as the toleration of the emotions evoked by aversive stimuli. Here, experiential avoidance is orthogonal to acceptance. For example, behaviors that function to limit interpersonal closeness are often avoidance maintained; therefore, tolerance of aversive situations manifested by not engaging behaviors to avoid, escape, or limit interpersonal contact is considered acceptance.

Linehan (1994) posits that acceptance and change highlight the synthesis of polarities in psychotherapy. A key component to Dialectical Behavior Therapy (DBT) (Linehan, 1993a) is the balance of acceptance and change in the treatment of mental disorder. Linehan defines acceptance as an active process of orienting to private experience moment by moment. It is entering reality just as it is at any given moment by noticing and describing without judgment. This sense of engaging acceptance over and over within any given moment is known as *radical acceptance.*

Hayes (1994) has defined psychological acceptance as one of the most important contextual change strategies. Here, acceptance refers to the conscious abandonment of a direct change agenda in the key domains of private events, self, and history, and an openness to experiencing thoughts and emotions as they are, not as they say they are. In this same vein, Dougher (1994) suggests that the key component of acceptance is letting go of one's control agenda and orienting toward valued actions. Defined that way, acceptance is not a goal in and of itself but a method of empowering the achievement of life goals.

EVIDENCE FOR THE IMPACT OF
ACCEPTANCE PROCEDURES

Acceptance plays a key role in many empirically supported therapies (Hayes et al., 1994). One such therapy is Integrative Behavioral Couple Therapy (IBCT; Christensen, Jacobson, & Babcock, 1995). This is an acceptance-based treatment for couple discord. A recent comparison study between IBCT and traditional behavioral couple therapy indicated that IBCT resulted in greater increases in marital satisfaction than traditional behavioral therapy (Jacobson et al., 2000).

Psychological acceptance is a vital component of Acceptance and Commitment Therapy (ACT; Hayes, Strosahl, & Wilson, 1999), a behavior analytically based psychotherapy approach. An ACT model attempts to undermine emotional avoidance and increase the capacity for behavior change. Research from a randomized, controlled trial of ACT in the workplace (Bond & Bunce, 2000) found that by increasing acceptance, ACT reduced stress and anxiety and increased behavior change in the workplace. Recent data from a randomized controlled trial using ACT to treat chronic, hospitalized seriously mentally ill patients experiencing hallucinations or delusions (Bach & Hayes, in press) found that acceptance of unwanted hallucinations resulted in higher reporting of positive psychotic symptoms. However, these individuals were nearly 4 times more likely to remain out of the hospital than were subjects not taught to accept these symptoms. These data suggest that symptom reporting reflected lower levels of denial and higher levels of psychological acceptance (Hayes, Pankey, Gifford, Batten, & Quinones, 2002).

Dialectial Behavior Therapy (DBT; Linehan, 1994) is an acceptance- and change-based cognitive behavioral treatment for chronically parasuicidal borderline patients. Data from a randomized controlled trial of DBT demonstrated that subjects who received DBT for 1 year had fewer incidences of parasuicide and less medically severe parasuicides, were more likely to stay in individual therapy, and had fewer inpatient psychiatric days (Linehan, Armstrong, Suarez, Allmon, & Heard, 1991). A follow-up randomized trial of DBT as compared with treatment as usual in the community at 1 year post-treatment found that during the initial 6 months of the follow-up, DBT subjects had significantly less parasuicidal behavior, less anger, and better self-reported social adjustment. During the final 6 months, DBT subjects had significantly fewer psychiatric inpatient days and better interviewer-rated social adjustment.

Process Evidence

The thought suppression literature provides insight into some of the processes underlying the deleterious effects of avoidance and the positive effects of acceptance (Hayes et al., 2002). Wegner, Schneider, Carter, and White (1987) found that active attempts to suppress targeted thoughts increased the occurrence of these thoughts, suggesting that active attempts to avoid private experience may have an ironic, paradoxical effect in that the attempts themselves increase the likelihood of the thought. Further research (Wenz-laff, Wegner, & Klein, 1991) demonstrated that individuals who try to suppress thoughts experience a reinstatement of the mood state that existed during the initial period of suppression.

A meta-analysis of coping strategies (Suls & Fletcher, 1985) found that avoidance strategies (denial, distraction, repression and suppression) were more adaptive in the short-run; but that nonavoidant strategies (attention, noticing, and focusing) had more positive long-term outcomes. Avoidance is omnipresent by nature in all its overt and covert iterations. Contrasted with the beneficial health outcomes related to reductions in emotional avoidance (McCurry, 1991), it seems clear that acceptance in some form may be widely beneficial across the continuum of more benign forms of psychological unrest to more overt psychopathology (see Hayes, Wilson, Gifford, Follette, & Strosahl, 1996, for a review).

THOSE WHO BENEFIT AND CONTRAINDICATIONS

Acceptance is particularly helpful with clients facing problems that are not amenable to the instrumental change strategies (Cordova, 2001), such as a difficult childhood history, automatic thoughts, or conditioned emotions. In some areas (e.g., acceptance of the continuity of consciousness or of self) acceptance is the only healthy alternative available.

Acceptance procedures are contraindicated, however, when they are applied to external situations or behaviors that can and should be controlled. For example, a pedophile might be encouraged to accept the presence of urges to molest children, but should not be encouraged to accept molesting behaviors; an abused spouse might be encouraged to accept angry reactions or feelings of shame, but should not be encouraged to accept abusive behavior or an abusive environment; a trichotillomanic might be encouraged to accept thoughts about pulling hair or the urge to do so, but should not be encouraged to accept hair pulling; a person with self-loathing thoughts would be encouraged to accept these thoughts as an ongoing process (e.g., "now I am having the thought that I am bad") but would not be en-

TABLE 2.1   Steps in the Use of Acceptance Methods

1. Detect and challenge experiential avoidance.
2. Encourage aware, flexible, open exposure to previously avoided events.
3. Encourage the development of new response functions in the presence of previously avoided events.
4. Use defusion techniques when exposure to private verbal events leads to verbal entanglement.

couraged to accept their literal content (e.g., "and in fact I am bad"). The evidence is not yet clear on this distinction in some areas, however. For example, it is not known if it is better to accept thoughts as thoughts (see Chapter 13 on cognitive defusion) or to dispute their content.

ACCEPTANCE TECHNOLOGY

Acceptance is not a specific technique per se, in relation to other techniques or treatment technologies, but rather a stance or posture from which to conduct therapy and from which a client can conduct life. It is a context.

The techniques that foster this context (see Table 2.1) are

1. Detecting and challenging experiential avoidance
2. Encouraging aware, flexible, open exposure to previously avoided events
3. Encouraging the development of new response functions in the presence of previously avoided events, and
4. Using defusion techniques when exposure to private verbal events leads to verbal entanglement.

Detecting and Challenging Experiential Avoidance

It is not possible to foster acceptance unless the logical alternative is challenged and reduced. Clients arrive in therapy convinced that they need to reduce or eliminate various private events (e.g., fear, sadness, self-doubt, etc.) in order to live a powerful and vital life. This stance is usually simply assumed—it is more a metacognition than a cognition. If this control-focused stance is not challenged, the client will view acceptance as a new, more sophisticated way to manipulate or control negative private experience (e.g., "if I stop trying to control my fear, it will go away"). There is little evidence that this is useful, and in functional terms it represents nothing new.

A wide variety of techniques can be helpful in challenging an ingrained control- and avoidance-focused agenda. Previous internally focused change efforts can be explored in depth, and the client can be asked if each was an ultimate, final, and fully satisfactory solution. The answer is always "no," or else the client would not still be seeking services. When a full set of control-focused efforts are developed, the therapist can point out the obvious: The client's own experience suggests that internally focused change efforts have provided no ultimate, final, and fully satisfactory solution. A client might be asked, "Which are you going to believe: your mind or your experience?"

Specific commonsense metaphors can be used to show that sometimes deliberate change efforts are doomed to failure. Acceptance and Commitment Therapy (Hayes et al., 1999) uses the following metaphor as one of several designed to make this point:

> The situation here is something like those "Chinese handcuffs" we played with as kids. Have you ever seen them? It is a tube of woven straw about as big as your index finger. You push both index fingers in, one into each end, and as you pull them back out the straw catches and tightens. The harder you pull, the smaller the tube gets and the stronger it holds your finger. You'd have to pull your fingers out of their sockets to get them out by pulling them out once they've been caught. Maybe this situation is something like that. Maybe these tubes are like life itself. Maybe there is no healthy way to deliberately get out of certain aspects of your life, like your history, your memories, or your automatic feelings and any attempt to do so just restricts the room you have to move. With this little tube, the only way to get some room is to push your fingers in, which makes the tube bigger. Maybe this situation is like that. Pushing in may be hard at first to do because everything your mind tells you to do casts the issue in terms of "in and out" not "tight and loose." But your experience is telling you that if what you are struggling with is cast in terms of "in and out," then

life will be tight. And your life has gotten tighter and tighter, has it not? Isn't that really part of why you came to see me? Well, maybe we need to come at this situation from a whole different angle than what your mind tells you to do with your painful experiences.

A variety of similar metaphors can be used to make the same point (e.g., struggling with anxiety is like struggling in quicksand; trying to push away experiences is like trying to push away flypaper; etc).

Encouraging Aware, Flexible, Open Exposure to Previously Avoided Events

Acceptance is not merely passive—it involves directly contacting the previously avoided functions or events. For example, acceptance of anxiety involves detecting its presence and deliberately exploring how it feels to be anxious. The methods of interoceptive exposure can be thought of in this way, as can many methods drawn from Gestalt and more experiential traditions.

An example of an acceptance technique of this kind is the "tin can monster" exercise used in ACT. The idea is that many experiences are difficult to experience because they are multifaceted. Like a huge monster made up of many less threatening pieces (e.g., bubble gum, bailing wire, and tin cans) it might be easier to deal with the pieces rather than the entire monster all at once. The client is asked to close his or her eyes and get into contact with a private experience he or she is trying to avoid or escape (e.g., anxiety). The client is then directed to notice, one at a time, specific bodily sensations that are occasioned by this overall experience. As each sensation is identified, the client is encouraged to see where the sensation begins and ends, what it feels like, and whether it is possible to feel that one sensation without avoidance. After several sensations are examined, the same approach is used with other response dimensions, such as emotions, urges to act, memories, and thoughts. Within each domain individual experiences are identified, examined, deliberately produced, and ultimately no longer avoided.

Marlatt and Gordon (1985) have presented a metaphor for this stage of acceptance from their work on addiction: "urge surfing." Cravings ebb and flow throughout our lives. At the peak of the wave (crest), individuals are most vulnerable to giving in to an urge because they fear that it will only get worse. The urge surfing metaphor is employed to help clients understand that individuals can become skilled at experiencing the rising and passing of urges without allowing themselves to be thrown off balance.

Encouraging the Development of New Response Functions in the Presence of Previously Avoided Events

Acceptance allows the response functions of previously avoided events to be more varied. Etymologically, *acceptance* means "to take in." Taking in what a situation affords is not merely a matter of feeling, sensing, or thinking what one has always felt, sensed, or thought. It also means developing *new* functions. Acceptance procedures can thus include any technique that multiplies and variegates the functions of previously avoided events. For example, suppose a panic disordered person is taken to a mall. Deliberately and with awareness, the therapist and client might spend time guessing the careers of the people walking by, or find the ugliest storefront in the mall, or see how long it takes to walk from one end of the mall to the other, or see how long they can balance on one foot, or together agree to do something silly (e.g., if the person is worried that panic will lead to social humiliation, the client and therapist might go into a women's clothing store and order a hamburger). The nature of the new functions that are established is not as important as the process of expanding a constricted repertoire.

Using Defusion Techniques When Exposure to Private Verbal Events Leads to Verbal Entanglement

Acceptance of thoughts is a difficult process, because what is being accepted is not their content but the process of thinking that content. Defusion techniques (see Chapter 13) are very helpful in allowing acceptance of private events.

Mindfulness techniques (see Chapter 35, this volume), such as those used in DBT (Linehan, 1993a, 1993b), involve all four of these steps. Mind-

fulness has to do with the quality of awareness that one brings to activities and requires for its practice acceptance of the moment (Linehan, 1994). These skills are taught to individuals in an effort to help them focus on one task or activity at a time, engaging in it with alertness, awareness, and wakefulness. Dialectical Behavior Therapy also offers skills training in *distress tolerance*, which promotes tolerating distress rather than acting from a place to ameliorate the pain. These skills include distraction, self-soothing, improving the moment, and learning pros and cons, which focuses on the pros of tolerating versus the cons of not tolerating. These skills are the mechanism by which one can *radically accept*, or enter reality as it is in the moment, accepting of total allowance now.

CONCLUSION

It is a paradox that acceptance is one of the more powerful forms of clinical change, because it involves a change in the purpose of change efforts themselves. There is a growing evidence base that acceptance skills are central to psychological well-being and can increase the impact of psychotherapy with a broad variety of clients.

Further Reading

Cordova, J. V. (2001). Acceptance in behavior therapy: Understanding the process of change. *The Behavior Analyst, 24,* 213–26.

Hayes, S. C., Strosahl, K., & Wilson, K. G. (1999). *Acceptance and commitment therapy: An experiential approach to behavior change.* New York: Guildford Press.

Linehan, M. M. (1994). Acceptance and change: The central dialectic in psychotherapy. In S. C. Hayes, N. S. Jacobson, V. M. Follette, & M. J. Dougher (Eds.), *Acceptance and change: Content and context in psychotherapy* (pp. 73–86). Reno, NV: Context Press.

References

Bach, P. A., & Hayes, S. C. (in press). The use of acceptance and commitment therapy to prevent the rehospitalization of psychotic patients: A randomized controlled trial. *Journal of Consulting and Clinical Psychology.*

Bond, F. W., & Bunce, D. (2000). Mediators of change in emotion-focused and problem-focused worksite stress management interventions. *Journal of Occupational Health Psychology, 5,* 156–163.

Christensen, A., Jacobson, N. S., & Babcock, J. C. (1995). Integrative behavioral couple therapy. In N. S. Jacobson & A. S. Gurman (Eds.), *Clinical handbook of couples therapy* (pp. 31–64). New York: Guilford Press.

Cordova, J. V. (2001). Acceptance in behavior therapy: Understanding the process of change. *The Behavior Analyst, 24,* 213–226.

Cordova, J. V., & Kohlenberg, R. J. (1994). Acceptance and the therapeutic relationship. In S. C. Hayes, N. S. Jacobson, V. M. Follette, & M. J. Dougher (Eds.), *Acceptance and change: Content and context in psychotherapy* (pp. 125–142). Reno, NV: Context Press.

Dougher, M. J. (1994). The act of acceptance. In S. C. Hayes, N. S. Jacobson, V. M. Follette, & M. J. Dougher (Eds.), *Acceptance and change: Content and context in psychotherapy* (pp. 37–50). Reno, NV: Context Press.

Freud, S. (1920). *Introductory lectures on psychoanalysis.* New York: Norton.

Greenberg, L. (1994). Acceptance in experiential therapy. In S. C. Hayes, N. S. Jacobson, V. M. Follette, & M. J. Dougher (Eds.), *Acceptance and change: Content and context in psychotherapy* (pp. 53–67). Reno, NV: Context Press.

Hayes, S. C. (1994). Content, context, and the types of psychological acceptance. In S. C. Hayes, N. S. Jacobson, V. M. Follette, & M. J. Dougher (Eds.), *Acceptance and change: Content and context in psychotherapy* (pp. 13–32). Reno, NV: Context Press.

Hayes, S. C., Jacobson, N. S., Follette, V. M., & Dougher, M. J. (Eds.) (1994). *Acceptance and change: Content and context in psychotherapy.* Reno, NV: Context Press.

Hayes, S. C., Pankey, J., Gifford, E. V., Batten, S. V., & Quinones, R. (2002). Acceptance and commitment therapy in experiential avoidance disorders. In F. W. Kaslow & T. Patterson (Eds.), *Comprehensive handbook of psychotherapy: Volume 2* (pp. 319–351). New York: Wiley.

Hayes, S. C., Strosahl, K., & Wilson, K. G. (1999). *Acceptance and commitment therapy: An experiential approach to behavior change.* New York: Guilford Press.

Hayes, S. C., Wilson, K. W., Gifford, E. V., Follette, V. M., & Strosahl, K. (1996). Emotional avoidance and behavioral disorders: A functional dimensional approach to diagnosis and treatment. *Journal of Consulting and Clinical Psychology, 64,* 1152–1168.

Jacobson, N. S., Christensen, A., Prince, S. E., Cordova, J., & Eldridge, K. (2000). Integrative behavioral couple therapy: An acceptance based, promising new treatment for couple discord. *Journal of Consulting and Clinical Psychology, 68,* 351–355.

Linehan. M. M. (1993a). *Cognitive behavioral treatment of borderline personality disorder.* New York: Guilford Press.

Linehan, M. M. (1993b). *Skills training manual for treating borderline personality disorder.* New York: Guilford Press.

Linehan, M. M. (1994). Acceptance and change: The central dialectic in psychotherapy. In S. C. Hayes, N. S. Jacobson, V. M. Follette, & M. J. Dougher (Eds.), *Acceptance and change: Content and context in psychotherapy* (pp. 73–86). Reno, NV: Context Press.

Linehan, M. M., Armstrong, H. E., Suarez, A., Allmon, D., & Heard, H. L. (1991). Cognitive-behavioral treatment of chronically parasuicidal borderline patients. *Archives of General Psychiatry, 48,* 1060–1064.

Marlatt, G. A., & Gordon, J. R. (1985). *Relapse prevention: Maintenance strategies in the treatment of addictive behaviors.* New York: Guilford Press.

McCurry, S. M. (1991). Client metaphor use in a contextual form of therapy. Unpublished doctoral dissertation, University of Nevada, Reno.

Perls, F. P. (1973). *The Gestalt approach and eye-witness to therapy.* Palo Alto, CA: Science and Behavior Books.

Rogers, C. R. (1961). *On becoming a person: A therapist's view of psychotherapy.* Boston: Houghton Mifflin.

Rogers, C. R. (1992). The processes of therapy. *Journal of Consulting and Clinical Psychology, 60,* 163–164.

Suls, J., & Fletcher, B. (1985). The relative efficacy of avoidant and nonavoidant coping strategies: A meta-analysis. *Health Psychology, 4,* 249–288.

Wegner, D. M., Schneider, D. J., Carter, S. R., & White, T. (1987). Paradoxical effects of thought suppression. *Personality and Social Psychology, 53,* 5–13.

Wenzlaff, R. M., Wegner, D. M., & Klein, S. B. (1991). The role of thought suppression in the bonding of thought and mood. *Journal of Personality and Social Psychology, 60,* 500–508.

3 ANGER (NEGATIVE IMPULSE) MANAGEMENT

Brad Donohue and Nicole Cavenagh

Anger is an internal affective experience that varies in its intensity and chronicity (Deffenbacher, 1996). It may be experienced as a negative impulsive reaction to a specific stimulus in the environment (e.g., aggression in response to being kicked; swearing consequent to being struck in the thumb with a hammer; urges to use drugs in response to an argument) or may persist over time and across situations. Problem-solving skill deficits, maladaptive withdrawal, child and spousal abuse, and increased risk for health problems such as essential hypertension and cardiovascular disease are all examples of problems often strongly influenced by ineffective management of anger (see, e.g., Deffenbacher, Demm, & Brandon, 1986; Gentry, Chesney, Gary, Hall, & Harburg, 1982; Krantz, Contrada, Hill, & Friedler, 1988; Novaco, 1979).

To assist in the remediation of anger and other negative impulsive behaviors, several cognitive behavior methods have been developed, including thought stopping, relaxation training, problem solving, and self-reward for performance of non-anger-associated behaviors. We will briefly delineate each of these methods, including their theoretical rationale and empirical support. We will conclude by describing an urge control intervention that combines these methods in the effective management of negative impulses that are associated with behavioral misconduct and impulsive urges to use illicit drugs.

RESPONSIVE POPULATIONS AND CONTRAINDICATIONS

The state of the literature in anger management does not allow clear guidance for specific populations who might or might not benefit. Anger and aggression can sometimes be a side effect of various biological processes, however, so these factors should be considered before focusing entirely on psychological approaches.

THOUGHT STOPPING

Thought stopping is a method that may be utilized to interrupt undesirable or unproductive thoughts that often lead to anger. The method is particularly effective when the level of arousal is relatively weak (i.e., first recognition of the stimulus eliciting anger). As exemplified by Wolpe (1990), the procedure begins with the patient closing his or her eyes and verbalizing a thought that has been associated with negative arousal or anger. The therapist consequently shouts, "stop!" and then points out to the patient that the thought has actually stopped. After practicing the termination of similar thoughts in separate trials, the patient is encouraged to practice the termination of thoughts subvocally. Other phrases or visual images (e.g., "cut it out," image of red stop sign) may be used instead of "stop!" to mentally disrupt anger (Deffenbacher, 1996). Thought stopping is conceptualized to work because thought inhibition is reinforced by the arousal reduction that occurs each time the individual successfully stops a thought. The procedure has demonstrated effectiveness in decreasing negative thinking (see Pedens, Rayens, Hall, & Beebe, 2001). However, it is important to note that thought stopping is not a primary method of intervention. Rather, the procedure is used as an initial component (Deffenbacher, 1996) because it does not alter the situation or environment, or teach coping skills.

RELAXATION TRAINING

Since anger is accompanied by physiological and emotional arousal (Suinn, 1990), relaxation training may be initiated to teach individuals to become aware of bodily tensions that often precede anger and may be used as cues to elicit relaxation (Kendall et al., 1991). Relaxation procedures vary, but they usually include some aspect of progressive muscle relaxation to assist in the early recognition of tension and subsequent regulation to a calm state of arousal (see Chapter 49, this volume). In this method, the individual is taught to tense and relax each of the major muscle groups, thus allowing him- or herself to focus on feelings distinguishing tension from relaxation. After reviewing all muscles, the individual is often instructed to imagine a relaxing scenario (e.g., resting on a warm beach, sitting in a remote forest). Tension-releasing exercises (e.g., instructing the individual to imagine tension leaving each of the major muscle groups; King, Hamilton, & Ollendick, 1988) and focused breathing (e.g., practicing slow and rhythmic diaphragmatic breathing; Kendall et al., 1991) are also popular relaxation exercise components that may be used in the reduction of anger.

PROBLEM-SOLVING SKILLS TRAINING

Anger can be an intrapersonal problem, an interpersonal problem, a community or societal problem, or some combination of these, and problem solving can be implemented in all of these cases (Chapter 45, this volume; D'Zurilla & Nezu, 2001). Problem solving is a conscious, rational, and pur-

poseful activity directed at finding one or more solutions to a specific problem (D'Zurilla & Nezu, 2001). For each problem scenario, the individual is taught to (1) make a brief summative statement of the problem, (2) generate potential solutions without critique, (3) evaluate the good and bad aspects of each solution, (4) choose one or more of the solutions, and (5) attempt the chosen solution(s). Self-instruction should be considered in the implementation of problem-solving strategies to help the individual initiate, implement, and evaluate potential solutions (Deffenbacher, 1996; Meichenbaum & Deffenbacher, 1988). Social problem-solving methods have demonstrated efficacy in reducing anger (Feindler, 1991), perhaps because in attempting to review options available, the individual is focused on solving the problem and is thus distracted from thoughts that are associated with anger.

SELF-REINFORCEMENT

Individuals who have difficulties in the management of their anger (as well as other negative impulsive behaviors) can be taught to reinforce themselves consequent to their performing behaviors that terminate or reduce anger (negative impulses), or that are incompatible with anger (Meichenbaum & Deffenbacher, 1988). Indeed, positive reinforcement is commonly employed in the management of anger, and self-praise has been shown to improve self-efficacy—that is, belief that anger can be sufficiently reduced (Meichenbaum & Deffenbacher 1988; Deffenbacher, 1996). Moreover, Bandura, Reese, and Adams (1982) found self-efficacy was related to physiological arousal such that tasks regarded with high self-efficacy resulted in no visceral reaction. Thus, it follows that if an individual has a strong belief in the ability to manage arousal, the physiological arousal will also be controlled.

URGE CONTROL

The urge control procedure employs components of each of the preceding anger control methods in sequence (see Chapter 67). The procedure was originally developed to assist adults and adoles-

TABLE 3.1   Steps in Urge Control

First Session:

1. Provide rationale.

   a. "Earlier, you had said that you have done some spontaneous things that resulted in trouble for you, such as getting angry and yelling at others. Anger often starts out as a casual thought and grows in intensity. As the intensity of anger grows, it becomes harder to prevent oneself from acting on negative impulses, such as aggressive behavior. The following technique is called the urge control procedure, and it will help you learn to control impulsive thoughts and feelings."

2. Identify most recent situation involving anger.

3. Model the following components of urge control.

   a. Stop!

   b. One negative consequence for self and one for others

   c. Relaxation, deep breaths

   d. State four or more behavioral alternatives that are incompatible with anger

   e. Imagine doing a behavior that is incompatible with anger

   f. Imagine telling friends or family about doing the behavior, and person responding positively

   g. State positive things that will happen because the selected behavior was performed

4. Reveal step(s) that helped decrease anger the most.

5. Reveal pre- and post-anger ratings.

6. Instruct client to perform urge control procedure for a recent anger situation.

7. Instruct client to reveal the component that helped decrease anger the most.

8. Instruct client to provide pre- and post-anger ratings.

9. Instruct client to provide ratings for each of the component steps that were role-played.

10. Instruct client to continue to role-play urge control trials, as needed.

Future Sessions

1. Instruct youth to use urge control in response to a situation involving anger.

2. Elicit youth's pre- and post-anger ratings.

3. Elicit component step that was most useful.

4. Elicit or provide feedback regarding trial.

---

cents in preventing urges to use drugs and alcohol (Azrin, McMahon, et al., 1994) and was later modified to address all impulsive behaviors that result in troublesome behavior, including those elicited from anger (Azrin, Donohue, et al., in press).

A step-by-step guide is provided in Table 3.1. Consistent with the format of behavioral therapy, a rationale for treatment is first provided to the client who is evidencing problems associated with impulsive behaviors or anger. For example, "earlier you told me that you often do impulsive things that have resulted in trouble for you, such as getting angry and punching other kids. Many people say they do things like this because they react before they've had a chance to think about how the action will affect themselves or others. They also say anger makes it harder to prevent them from doing impulsive behaviors that will

get them in trouble. Tell me some impulsive things you've done that later led to trouble for you or someone else [provide empathy]. The technique you are about to learn is called urge control because you will learn to control impulsive thoughts and feelings, such as anger, that usually lead to trouble for you. You will learn to recognize these feelings and thoughts early, when they are not as strong. This should enable you to do other behaviors that will keep you out of trouble. Do you have any questions?"

The client is informed that recognizing and stopping impulsive thoughts or anger when these thoughts first occur will greatly decrease the likelihood of engaging in negative impulsive behaviors. The client is instructed to disclose a situation in which he or she experienced a negative impulsive behavior subsequent anger and to identify the first thought associated with anger in that situation. As the following vignette demonstrates, the therapist must sometimes assist the client in determining his or her first thought related to anger.

> *Therapist:* Tell me about the last time your anger led to your doing an impulsive and troublesome behavior. I'm especially interested in knowing about the thought that you had before you made plans to engage in the impulsive behavior.
>
> *Youth:* I was arguing with this guy, and I thought it would feel good to let him have it, so I hit him.
>
> *Therapist:* You did a good job of identifying a thought that eventually led to hitting the boy in this situation. However, I want you to think hard. I'm sure you had a thought that brought you to the argument.
>
> *Youth:* I started to think of what a jerk he was for asking my girlfriend if she'd like to talk with him on the patio.
>
> *Therapist:* Excellent!

The therapist then models an urge control. The first step of the urge control procedure is to catch the anger-associated thought or image that preceded the troublesome impulsive behavior early in the response chain, and consequently terminate this thought or image by firmly stating "stop" while muscles are tensed. Background information associated with the situation should be stated with just enough detail to illuminate the situation (e.g., "I'm in front of the mailbox. My friend tells me to give the old man's mailbox a bash with the bat. I can feel the hatred for the old man because he got me in trouble last week.").

The second step is to state at least one negative consequence for getting angry and/or doing the undesired impulsive behavior, and at least one negative consequence for friends, loved ones, or others who care about the client. Negative consequences should be stated with affect reflecting despair, and muscles should remain tense. Consequences may be rotated (or added) as trials progress. Therapists should prompt detail regarding negative consequences.

Stating the last negative consequence should signal the performance of a muscle review to assure that negative feeling states, and tension in muscles, are not present. Major muscles should be reviewed from head to toe. During this review, if a muscle is tense, the client should use relaxing cue words until the muscle is no longer tense (e.g., "My arms are getting more and more relaxed. I am imagining a band of relaxation around my arms. They feel relaxed, calm, more and more relaxed."). Deep, rhythmic breaths should occur throughout the trial. Body weight should be evenly distributed and positioned in a relaxed state. Statements referring to the relaxed state of the body are acceptable throughout the relaxation period, which should continue until all muscle groups feel relaxed (ideally about 5 to 10 seconds). If no tension or negative feeling states are present, the client may be instructed only to breathe deeply.

The next step involves stating several behaviors that may be performed instead of getting angry or engaging in negative impulsive behaviors. These steps may include (1) stating several alternative actions that do not include anger or negative impulsive behaviors, (2) briefly checking to make sure the response is unlikely to bring about anger or negative impulsive behaviors for self or others, or (3) reviewing positive consequences for self and others that may occur consequent to behaviors that are not associated with anger or negative impulsive behaviors. During this exercise, it is important to provide prompts to the client regarding additional alternative behaviors, how self and others would be positively affected by alternative behaviors, what others would do for the client if alternative behaviors were performed, and how problem behaviors may continue to have negative consequences.

After stating several behaviors that are incompatible with the behaviors associated with anger or impulsiveness, the client is encouraged to choose one option and describe doing the behavior (e.g., "I'm imagining myself walking toward Jackie and telling her that I'd like to take her to get something to eat. I'm walking away from the guy and toward my car with Jackie. She is smiling and telling me that she'd love to get a big salad, and that she's glad I didn't start a fight with the guy."). When the client performs this step, the therapist should provide prompts to elicit detail, including questions as to how the client will successfully resolve difficult situations that are likely to occur. Sometimes the client may be instructed to practice getting out of difficult interpersonal situations (e.g., "Show me how you would ask your girlfriend to leave. I'll be her.").

The next step is to imagine telling a friend and/or family member about having performed the trouble-free alternative behavior. The recipient should respond in a favorable manner, and positive feelings should be delineated. For example, "I'm telling my mom that I could have fought the guy at the party, but instead I went to get something to eat with my girlfriend. As I'm telling her this I feel good about myself. My mom looks at me and says that I'm doing a great job, and that she's proud of me. She also tells me that she's been thinking about letting me have a curfew extension because I've been acting very responsible."

The trial concludes when the client describes several pleasant outcomes and positive character attributes. For example, "I'm really proud of myself for choosing to go out and eat with my girlfriend instead of fighting that guy. I'm going to have a great time with her and improve our relationship. I also liked how I avoided going near that guy. That says a lot about the kind of person I am. I can usually hold my own in a fight, but can also avoid them when I want. If I can keep my anger under control, I'm going to make my girlfriend and my parents proud, and I'll be able to get more privileges at home and school."

When clients practice the urge control procedure for the first time, it may be necessary to state the situation and prompt the client to subsequently state "stop" (e.g., "You're at the party. You hear the guy at the party ask your girlfriend to go out on the patio. Go ahead and yell 'stop!'"). Similarly, it may be necessary to prompt the client to perform each component initially, and later decrease this assistance.

After the client completes each trial, the therapist asks the client to provide his or her rating (0=no anger, 100=completely angry) of anger or desire to engage in the impulsive behavior prior to performing the trial, and after the trial is performed (i.e., pre- and posttrial urge level). The client is prompted to critique his or her performance, and the therapist subsequently praises the client for making statements during the trial that reflected protocol adherence, including suggestions or prompts to client regarding improve-

ment of future sessions. The number of trials performed depends on the extent of troublesome behavior since last contact. Poor performance during trials necessitates additional trials per session.

CONCLUSION

Of all of the negative emotions examined in behavioral health, anger is perhaps the most understudied. Techniques do exist, however, to help manage this emotion and the behavioral impulses it occasions that can cause so many destructive effects.

References

Azrin, N. H., Donohue, B., Teichner, G., Crum, T., Howell, J., & DeCato, L. (in press). A controlled evaluation and description of individual-cognitive problem solving and family-behavioral therapies in conduct-disordered and substance dependent youth. *Journal of Child and Adolescent Substance Abuse.*

Azrin, N. H., McMahon, P., Donohue, B., Besalel, V., Lapinski, K., Kogan, E., et al. (1994). Behavior therapy of drug abuse: A controlled outcome study. *Behaviour Research and Therapy, 32,* 857–866.

Bandura, A. (1986). *Social foundations of thought and action.* Englewood Cliffs, NJ: Prentice-Hall.

Bandura, A., Reese, L., & Adams, N.E. (1982). Microanalysis of action and fear arousal as a function of different levels of perceived self-efficacy. *Journal of Personality and Social Psychology, 43,* 5–21.

Deffenbacher, J. L. (1996). Cognitive-behavioral approaches to anger reduction. In K. S. Dobson & K. D. Craig (Eds.), *Advances in cognitive-behavioral therapy.* Thousand Oaks, CA: Sage.

Deffenbacher, J. L., Demm, P. M., & Brandon, A. D. (1986). Higher general anger: Correlates and treatment. *Behaviour Research and Therapy, 24,* 481–489.

D'Zurilla, T. J., & Nezu, A. M. (2001). Problem-solving therapies. In K.S. Dobson (Ed.), *Handbook of cognitive-behavioral therapies* (pp. 211–245). New York: Guilford Press.

Feindler, E. L. (1991). Cognitive strategies in anger control interventions for children and adolescents. In P.C. Kendall (Ed.), *Child and adolescent therapy: Cognitive-behavioral procedures* (pp. 66–97). New York: Guilford Press.

Gentry, W., Chesney, A., Gary, H., Hall, R., & Harburg,

E. (1982). Habitual anger-coping styles: I. Effect on mean blood pressure and risk for essential hypertension. *Psychosomatic Medicine, 44,* 195–202.

Kendall, P. C., Chansky, T. E., Freidman, M., Kim, R., Kortlander, E., Sessa, F. M., et al. (1991). Treating anxiety disorders in children and adolescents. In P. C. Kendall (Ed.), *Child and adolescent therapy: Cognitive-behavioral procedures.* New York: Guilford Press.

King, N. J., Hamilton, D. I., & Ollendick, T. H. (1988). *Children's phobias: A behavioral perspective.* Chichester, England: Wiley.

Krantz, D., Contrada, R., Hill, D., & Friedler, E. (1988). Environmental stress and biobehavioral antecedents of coronary heart disease. *Journal of Consulting and Clinical Psychology, 56,* 333–341.

Meichenbaum, D. H., & Deffenbacher, J. L. (1988). Stress inoculation training. *The Counseling Psychologist, 16,* 69–90.

Novaco, R. (1979). The cognitive regulation of anger and stress. In P. C. Kendall & S. Hollon (Eds.), *Cognitive-behavioral interventions: Theory, research, and procedures.* New York: Academic.

Pedens, A. R., Rayens, M. K., Hall, L. A., & Beebe, L. H. (2001). Preventing depression in high-risk college women: A report of an 18-month follow-up. *Journal of American College Health, 49,* 299–306.

Suinn, R. M. (1990). *Anxiety management training: A behavior therapy.* New York: Plenum.

Wolpe, J. (1990). *The practice of behavior therapy* (4th ed). Elmsford, NY: Pergamon.

4 ASSERTIVENESS SKILLS AND THE MANAGEMENT OF RELATED FACTORS

Melanie P. Duckworth

Assertive behavior usually centers on making requests of others and refusing requests made by others that have been judged to be unreasonable. Assertive behavior also captures the communication of strong opinions and feelings. Assertive communication of personal opinions, needs, and boundaries has been defined as communication that diminishes none of the individuals involved in the interaction, with emphasis on communication accuracy and respect for all persons engaged in the exchange.

Assertiveness is conceptualized as the behavioral middle ground, lying between ineffective passive and aggressive responses. Passiveness is characterized by an over-attention to the opinions and needs of others and the masking or restraining of personal opinions and needs. This over-attention to and compliance with the opinions and needs of others may serve as a strategy for conflict avoidance and/or maintenance of particular sources of social reinforcement. Aggressiveness often involves the imposition of one's opinions and requirements on another individual. Implicit in the discussion of assertiveness is the suggestion that assertive behavior is the universally preferred behavioral alternative and that assertive behavior necessarily leads to preferred outcomes. The degree to which assertive behaviors are to be considered superior to either a pas-

sive or an aggressive stance is determined by the situational context. The success of assertiveness does not always lie in tangible outcomes (e.g., request fulfillment). The success of assertiveness sometimes lies in the degree of personal control and personal respect that is achieved and maintained throughout the assertive exchange.

BEHAVIORAL AND COGNITIVE-AFFECTIVE FACTORS INFLUENCING ASSERTIVENESS

Given that assertive behavior occurs as a part of a broader interaction complex, the likelihood that an individual will engage in assertive behavior is a function of skill and performance competencies, reinforcement contingencies, and motivational-affective and cognitive-evaluative factors. Behavioral explanations for the use of passive or aggressive strategies rather than assertive strategies emphasize opportunities for skills acquisition and mastery and reinforcement contingencies that have supported the use of passive or aggressive behaviors over time. Behavioral conceptualizations for passivity often emphasize early learning environments in which passive responding may have been modeled (e.g., caregivers who were themselves anxious, shy, or in some other way less than assertive) or more assertive behavior punished (e.g., overly protective or dominating care givers). In the absence of opportunities for acquisition and reinforcement of other interaction strategies, passive behavior persists.

Important to any complete behavioral conceptualization of passive behavior would be an evaluation of the reinforcement that is associated with current displays of passive behavior; that is, how is passivity currently working for the individual? Behaviors that are reinforced are repeated. Repeated engagement in passive behavior suggests repeated reinforcement of such behavior. Passive responding may be reinforced through the avoidance of responsibility and decision making. With what amount of attention, positive or negative, are passive responses met? The individual employing passive strategies may need to reconcile his or her active influence on situations with the alleged passivity.

Aggressive behaviors can be learned through the observation of aggressive models and reinforced through their instrumental effects. Even in the absence of overt goal attainment, aggressive behaviors may be experienced as intrinsically reinforcing by virtue of the autonomic discharge associated with such behaviors. Aggressive behavior may serve as a socially sanctioned interaction style (Tedeschi & Felson, 1994). Aggressive behavior may also be a consequence of the absence of opportunities to acquire alternative social interaction strategies.

Motivational-affective factors are important to patterned displays of passive and aggressive behavior. Although the affective experience of anger is not sufficient to explain aggressive behavior, feelings of anger do increase the likelihood that the actions of others will be experienced as aggressive and will thereby elicit aggressive behavior. Cognitive explanations for passive and aggressive responding would posit that outcome expectations are primary in determining the passive or aggressive response. The passive individual may look to his or her history of failures in making and/or refusing requests in deciding whether to attempt the recommended assertive behavior. Outcome expectations may interfere with adoption of the new assertiveness. Such outcome expectations must be managed if the likelihood of assertive responding is to increase. The passive individual needs to be cautioned regard-

ing the imperfect relationship between assertive responding and desired outcomes. Initially, assertive responses may not meet with desired outcomes. It is the *persistence* of the assertive response that will ensure that the probability of the desired outcome increases over time. In the short run, then, the measure of successful assertion may not be the occurrence of a desired outcome but the mere assertive communication of one's opinions, needs, and/or limits.

ASSESSMENT

Assessment of assertiveness skills and performance abilities should be broad enough to capture and distinguish among various explanations for performance failure. Traditionally, a hierarchical task analysis is used to determine the causal variable that accounts for the skill or performance deficit (Dow, 1994). Initially, assertiveness skills are evaluated in a nonthreatening (or less threatening) environment. Given that the client demonstrates adequate assertiveness skills in the nonthreatening environment, assertiveness skills are evaluated in the context of more clinically relevant social situations. Given that skills are adequately demonstrated in clinically relevant social situations, other contributions to response failure are evaluated, including affective and cognitive variables that might mediate the skill-performance relation. Behavioral models of depression suggest that the pursuit of social interaction (and, thus, experience of reinforcement) may be limited by negative affective experiences that are present throughout the interaction (Lewinsohn, 1974). For example, anxiety that is experienced during an assertive interaction may be insufficient to impair performance but may be sufficient to render the interaction a punishing rather than reinforcing event.

PRECONDITIONS FOR ASSERTIVENESS

Assertive behaviors presuppose the existence of adequate social skills. An assertive communication is measured not only by the content of the verbalization but also by the accompanying nonverbal behaviors. Appropriate posture and eye contact are essential in executing an appropriately assertive response. An appropriately assertive posture would convey relaxed but focused attention, in contrast to an overly rigid posture, which might convey either anxiety or obstinacy. Other important nonverbal behaviors include facial expression and body movements and gestures. Affective displays should be congruent with the content of the assertive communication, not suggesting anxiety, false gaiety, or anger. Body movements that indicate nervousness and uncertainty (e.g. hand-wringing) should be avoided. Movements that convey anger or dominance (e.g., invasion of the other's personal space) should also be avoided. These nonverbal behaviors are included among behaviors identified by Dow (1985) as relevant to socially skilled behaving.

The content of the assertive communication is important in its clarity and form. The tone and fluidity of the request or refusal are also important. Generally, the assertive request is characterized by its reasonableness, its specificity regarding actions required to fulfill the request, and its inclusion of statements that convey the potential impact(s) of request fulfillment for both the individual making the request and the request recipient. The tone in which the request is delivered should convey the importance of the request; however, the tone should not imply some obligation on the part of the request recipient to comply with the request. Dow (1994) suggests that, in the context of a request for behavior change, the potential for a satisfactory outcome is maximized when the assertive communicator refrains from making assumptions about the motivations driving others' behaviors, refrains from questioning others regarding their motives, and interjects something positive about the individual with whom they are interacting. The content and tone of assertive refusals share the quality of being evenhanded and unwavering.

ASSESSMENT OF ASSERTIVENESS SKILLS AND PERFORMANCE ABILITIES

Assessment of skill sets and performance competencies is necessary prior to skills training and throughout the skills acquisition and practice process. Skills for behaving assertively are evaluated through the use of self-report instruments as well as behavioral observation in simulated and natural settings.

Questionnaires

Assertiveness skill evaluation and training often occur in the broader context of social skills and social competence. The self-report instruments that purport to measure assertiveness range from actual measures of assertive behaviors to instruments that assess related constructs such as social avoidance, self-esteem, and locus of control. The most commonly used measure of assertiveness skills is the Rathus Assertiveness Scale (Rathus, 1973).

Self-Monitoring Assignments

Self-monitoring of social behaviors performed in the client's natural environment is essential to both assessment and treatment of potential skills and performance deficits. Monitoring instructions usually require that the client describe his or her social interactions with others along a number of dimensions. The client may be instructed to briefly describe interactions with males versus females, acquaintances versus intimate others, peers versus persons in authority, and in structured versus unstructured interactions. Although real-world evaluation of skills is preferable, the clinician's office is the most common arena for skills evaluation and practice. Therefore, it is essential that the client provide detailed accounts of problem interactions and that the content and cues of the experimental arena be as consistent with that real world as possible.

BEHAVIORAL OBSERVATION

Behavioral observation is considered the preferred strategy for evaluating assertiveness skills and performance competencies. Usually observations and evaluations of assertive performances are made in clinical or research settings rather than real-world settings. Clinic and laboratory settings provide contexts for informal observation (waiting room behaviors and behaviors engaged in by the client during the clinical interview) and formal observation (social interaction tasks and role-playing) of an individual's behavior.

Clinical Interview

In the clinical setting, the client's waiting room behavior (i.e., his or her interactions with other persons in the waiting room and with clinic staff) is available for observation. Exchanges during initial assessment sessions also serve as data to be used in establishing the presence or absence of verbal and nonverbal communication skills considered essential to assertive displays as well as contextual factors that may influence the likelihood of assertive behaving and the mastery with which assertive behaviors are performed.

Social Interaction Tasks in Analogue Settings

In evaluating a client's social skill and comfort, the therapist may enlist confederates to engage the client in interactions that test the client's ability to initiate and participate in casual exchanges. These tasks are considered low-demand tasks: usually, they do not contain any of the elements of identified problematic interactions.

Social Interaction Tasks in Real-World Settings

Of course, the optimal arena for evaluating assertive behavior is the client's natural environment. As often as possible, the real-world context should be captured. For example, a male client reporting difficulty initiating social interactions with female peers might be observed in real-world settings that are familiar to him and that present opportunities for contact with female peers (e.g., the college library; an undergraduate seminar; a scheduled, on-campus extracurricular event). Other local contact arenas are also acceptable for evaluation of skills, including coffee houses, dance clubs, and the like.

Role-Playing

In the clinical context, a true observation of assertive behaviors is made through the use of role-playing. Based on the client's report of difficult interpersonal interactions, interaction opportunities that mimic these difficult interpersonal interactions (to a lesser or greater degree) are engineered and the client's use of assertive behaviors observed. Typically, the therapist serves as the relevant other in such role-play situations.

Research participants or clients are asked to display their skills repertoire in the context of contrived interactions with the researcher or therapist or some confederate. In structuring the role-playing, the therapist aims to lessen the artificial quality of the exercise and to strengthen the correspondence between the client's performance in artificial and natural settings. This is best achieved through the use of dialogue and contextual cues that closely approximate the naturally occurring problematic interactions. Role-playing confederates and scenarios are often selected with relevant contextual factors in mind.

ASSERTIVENESS TRAINING

When it has been established that a skills deficit explains performance failure, it is often useful to begin at the beginning. Table 4.1 presents a detailed, step-by-step guide to the conduct of assertiveness skills training. Assertiveness training usually begins with a didactic presentation of (1) definitions of assertiveness, passiveness, and aggressiveness; (2) the rationale for the use of assertive behavior; and (3) the basic content and procedural guidelines that govern assertive behavior. In starting the practice of assertiveness skills, the therapist always begins with a review of the more basic elements of assertive communication and continues along a graded hierarchy of skills sets essential to assertive communication across contexts. Traditionally, assertiveness training packages have identified several skill sets as essential to assertive behaving, including using nonverbal behavior as communication, giving and receiving compliments, giving and receiving criticism, and making and refusing requests. In addressing each of these skills sets, the therapist wishes to establish three things: (1) the presence and strength of a particular skill in the client's behavioral repertoire; (2) the situations in which the client competently and reliably displays the particular skill; and (3) the situations in which the client may be called upon to competently display the particular skill.

The presence and strength of a particular assertive skill or skill set may be established formally or informally. A client's nonverbal behaviors are immediately observable by the therapist. In the context of the therapeutic exchange, the therapist

TABLE 4.1   Key Components of an Assertiveness Training Protocol

1. *Presenting the rationale for assertiveness skills training.* Assertive communication of personal opinions, needs, and boundaries has been defined as communication that diminishes none of the individuals involved in the interaction, with emphasis on communication accuracy and respect for all persons engaged in the exchange. The success of assertiveness does not always lie in tangible outcomes (e.g., request fulfillment). The success of assertiveness sometimes lies in the degree of personal control and personal respect that is achieved and maintained throughout the assertive exchange. Assertive communication maximizes the potential for achievement of relationship goals in both professional and intimate contexts.

2. *Defining aggressive, passive, and assertive behaviors.* The therapist follows the presentation of the rationale with descriptions of each of the three common forms of communication: aggressive, passive, and assertive communication.

   a. Aggressive communication of needs usually pursues the goal of getting one's needs met or having one's opinion endorsed no matter the cost to the other individual or individuals participating in the exchange. Aggressive communication is often characterized by the words *should* or *must* or other language that suggests that the recipient is bound or required to meet the expressed need or agree with the expressed opinion. Aggressive communication is also characterized by nonverbal behaviors that are of an in-your-face quality. Aggressive communicators may ignore the boundaries of personal space, standing overly close to another individual. They may speak in loud, angry tones and in a number of other ways convey subtle pressure or even a threat to the other individual or individuals participating in the communication exchange.

   b. Passive communication is problematic, not because of obvious demands placed on the recipient, but because passive communications often do not reflect the true needs or preferences of the speaker. Passive communications involve the use of acquiescent language. The passive communicator often responds to others' statements of preferences and opinions with statements such as "if you think so" or "whatever you want is fine" or "no problem, I can take care of that." In the short term, the passive communicator may be seen as ensuring the pleasure and happiness of the recipients of such behavior. The problems with passive communications are usually experienced over time. The passive communicator begins to resent the fact that his or her true needs and opinions aren't being honored within these relationships. The recipient of passive communications may feel that the passive individual is only halfheartedly participating in the relationship and is avoiding responsibility for making important decisions within the relationship.

   c. Assertive communication ensures that the needs and opinions of the speaker are honestly expressed and owned by the speaker. Opinions are expressed as opinions rather than as statements of inarguable fact. This allows other participants in the exchange to comfortably express similar or opposing opinions. The communicator presents the request in a manner that is at the same time clear but respectful of the recipient's right to refuse such a request. In refusing requests, the assertive communicator states the refusal clearly and unwaveringly while at the same time indicating appreciation for the other individual's circumstances. Again, assertive communication has the goal of mutual respect.

3. *Reviewing content and procedural guidelines governing assertive behavior.* The assertive request is characterized by its reasonableness, its specificity regarding actions required to fulfill the request, and its inclusion of statements that convey the potential impact(s) of request fulfillment for both the individual making the request and the request recipient. Imbedding a request for behavior change between impact statements is referred to as *sandwiching*. In making a request for behavior change, then, the client would begin with a statement regarding the negative impact of the other's current behavior, then suggest a specific and reasonable behavioral alternative, and end with a statement suggesting the positive impact of the proposed behavioral alternative for both parties. The behavior change request is sandwiched between the two impact statements.

4. *Provision of overview of assertiveness skills training package.* Provide the client with an overview of the skill sets that comprise assertiveness skills training (i.e., nonverbal behavior as communication, giving and receiving compliments, giving and receiving criticism, and making and refusing requests). Suggest that the skill sets lie on a hierarchy, with practice of lower-level skill sets being critical to the successful acquisition and performance of higher-level skill sets. Explain that these general skills can be successfully applied across a variety of contexts.

5. *Specifying in-session tasks and homework assignments.* In-session tasks will center on the introduction of particular skill sets, modeling of the behaviors important to the particular skill set being targeted, and practice of those skills in the context of role-playing exercises. The client should be informed that self-monitoring of day-to-day interpersonal interactions will continue throughout assertiveness skills training. These real-world interactions will eventually serve as the setting for practice of assertive behavior.

6. *Modeling of assertive behavior.* For the particular skill set being targeted, the verbal content of a sufficiently assertive response is delineated and the appropriately assertive delivery of that verbal communication is modeled by the therapist or confederate.

7. *In-session practice of assertive behavior.* The client practices assertive behaviors in the context of in-session role-playing exercises that are (increasingly) similar to the identified problematic interactions.

TABLE 4.1 *Continued*

8. *Providing reinforcement and corrective feedback.* The evaluation of the role-playing performance should always begin with the solicitation of comments from the client. This strategy allows the therapist to (1) evaluate the client's understanding of the verbal and nonverbal behaviors that comprise the assertive response, and (2) evaluate the accuracy and objectivity with which the client evaluates his or her performance. The client's efforts and performance successes (however approximate) should be roundly reinforced by the therapist. Corrective feedback is provided by the therapist and/or confederate, and instructions for further refinement of the assertive performance are provided. Videotaping role-playing exercises is recommended in order to reduce recall burden and to provide specific, visual evidence for performance problems and performance gains over time.

9. *Real-world practice of assertive behavior.* Having practiced assertive behavior in the context of role-playing designed to simulate interpersonal interactions occurring in the client's natural environment, the client begins to practice assertive behavior in the context of naturally occurring interpersonal interactions. The client provides a technical and affective evaluation of the assertive performance in the real-world situation.

10. *Establishing realistic performance expectations and acceptable schedules of reinforcement.* Reinforcement and reiteration of reasonable performance goals are essential throughout the assertiveness skills training process. As the natural environment becomes the practice arena, realistic expectations for performance success are outlined, and obvious and regular self-reinforcement of successive approximations of the goal performance is mandated.

may observe nonverbal behaviors that are not at all consistent with the goals of assertive communication. This would signal that, at least within the context of the therapeutic exchange, direct training and practice of assertive nonverbal behavior are justified. When nonverbal behaviors have been observed to be sufficient in this context, the therapist may feel uncomfortable reviewing these more basic elements of assertive communication. In such situations the therapist is encouraged to (1) acknowledge the appropriateness of the client's nonverbal behavior in the therapeutic context, and (2) suggest that the display of appropriately assertive nonverbal behavior is sometimes bound by context—that is, assertive nonverbal behaviors sometimes depend on how comfortable the person feels in a given situation or with a given individual. A review of nonverbal behaviors would be completed, and instructions would be given that the client monitor and evaluate displays of appropriately assertive nonverbal behaviors in the natural environment.

The skills that characterize each level of the assertiveness hierarchy should be approached in a similar manner. For example, if in the ongoing context of therapy the client has evidenced skill in assertively requesting something of the therapist, this instance would be pointed to by the therapist and reinforced through praise. The therapist would then suggest that the display of even well-established skills can be influenced by situations and persons. The various aspects of request making would be reviewed, real-world

instances of successful and unsuccessful request-making attempts would be solicited, and the client would be instructed to monitor and practice assertive request making in the natural environment. The therapist will structure in-session role-playing exercises and homework assignments so that both more common and less common request making situations are encountered over the course of such practice. Table 4.1 presents a 10-step guide to assertiveness skills training.

When the absence of assertive behavior is explained by affective or cognitive factors rather than a skills deficit, other strategies are recommended as adjuncts to behavioral rehearsal of assertive behavior. Examples of such strategies include relaxation training to reduce performance inhibiting anxiety or anger, cognitive restructuring to challenge negative performance predictions and overgeneralizations regarding performance errors, and cognitive reframing with respect to performance goals and measures of performance success.

ASSERTIVENESS IN SPECIFIC CONTEXTS

When assertive behavior is routinely absent in the context of a particular relationship or relationship set, an evaluation of the relationship history and implicit or explicit rules of the relationship is appropriate. This information may provide the therapist with clues as to the habit strength associated with the nonassertive behavior and the extent to which the pattern of habitual responding is reinforced by others. A realistic appraisal of the benefits and deficits of the relationship may need to be delineated along with an emphasis on the sufficiency of the self.

Intimate Relationships

In the context of intimate relationships the greatest challenge to assertive behaving is often the long interaction history that has been established. Nonverbal and verbal components of intimate exchanges may have become habitual and less subject to immediate reinforcement contingencies. Intimate relationships are also unique with respect to the sensitivity of topics that may need to be addressed. The assertiveness skills forwarded for nonintimate interactions are applicable to intimate interactions. Particular attention may need to be given to acknowledging the degree to which a new interaction style is being forwarded. Sensitive behavior change requests (or request refusals) may involve family traditions, sexual behavior, or lifestyle behaviors. Sensitive topics such as changes in the frequency or type of sexual activities should be addressed in a manner that suggests an interest in experimentation rather than a permanent change to the couple's repertoire. Also, in such situations the emphasis placed on overt reinforcement of satisfying aspects of current interactions cannot be too strong.

Business Situations

Business situations are often replete with individuals skilled in the art of persuasion. Because of the high level of assertiveness that often characterizes business interactions, specific techniques have been forwarded as helpful when making or refusing some business request. These include the use of self-disclosure (suggestions of similarity in personal experiences or preferences are influential in selling an individual); repetition of request or request refusal (assuming a finite number of arguments for or against a given position, simple repetition of one's position suggests commitment to that stance and may wear down the resolve of the other individual); and singular focus (discussion of unrelated or tangentially related topics may serve to distract the participants from the critical topic).

CONCLUSION

In establishing the effectiveness of an assertive response, we often consider the outcome that is achieved. Although the ultimate goal of assertive communication may be to influence the behavior of others, the measure of assertiveness is the extent to which personal opinions, needs, and boundaries have been accurately and respectfully communicated and received. Competent performance of appropriately assertive behavior is best predicted when sufficient attention has been given to the interpersonal context in which the behavior is planned to occur. Very often, treating professionals fail to acknowledge the consequences of assertive behavior that the client would consider negative (e.g., loss of perceived control for the formerly aggressive individual and loss of attachment figures for the formerly passive individual). In adopting an assertive stance, individuals are not merely engaging in a simple display of a new behavior set; they are often realigning and reordering relationship priorities.

References

Dow, M. G. (1985). Peer validation and idiographic analysis of social skill deficits. *Behavior Therapy, 16,* 76–86.

Dow, M. G. (1994). Social inadequacy and social skill. In L. W. Craighead, W. E. Craighead, A. E. Kazdin, & M. J. Mahoney (Eds.), *Cognitive and behavioral interventions: An empirical approach to mental health problems* (pp. 123–140). Boston: Allyn and Bacon.

Lewinsohn, P. M. (1974). A behavioral approach to depression. In R. J. Friedman & M. M. Katz (Eds.), *The psychology of aggression: Contemporary theory and research* (pp. 157–178). Washington, DC: Wiley.

Rathus, S. A. (1973). A 30-item schedule for assessing assertive behavior. *Behavior Therapy, 4,* 398–406.

Tedeschi, J. T., & Felson, R. B. (1994). *Violence, aggression, and coercive actions.* Washington, DC: American Psychological Association.

5 ATTRIBUTION CHANGE

Rebecca S. Laird and Gerald I. Metalsky

Since Beck first introduced cognitive behavior therapy (CBT) for depression (1967; Beck, Rush, Shaw, & Emery, 1979), there have been numerous studies demonstrating its efficacy (for reviews see Dobson, 1989; Evans et al., 1992; Hollon, Evans, & DeRubeis, 1990; Jacobson & Hollon, 1996). Beck's CBT is based on the underlying theoretical rationale that an individual's emotions, motivations, and behavior are largely determined by the way in which he or she constructs the world. Subjective thoughts, images, and feelings are rooted in the enduring attitudes and assumptions, or schemas, that the individual develops from prior experience. Human experience is automatically filtered through these cognitive structures, by which input is categorized and evaluated.

According to Beck et al. (1979), some individuals develop maladaptive schemas that serve as vulnerability factors predisposing them to depression and other clinical disorders (Beck, Emery, & Greenberg, 1985). Many subsequent studies have found compelling evidence for attributional style (Abramson, Seligman, & Teasdale, 1978; Metalsky & Abramson, 1981; Nolen-Hoeksema, Girgus, & Seligman, 1992) as one such risk factor for depression in children, adolescents, and adults

The authors wish to acknowledge Tina Baeten, Eileen Diller, Marvel Herlache, Holly Husting, Kris Hutchison, and Carolyn Martin-Johnson for their invaluable contributions.

(for reviews see Andrews, 1989; Harvey & Galvin, 1984; Metalsky, Laird, Heck, & Joiner, 1995; and Peterson & Seligman, 1984). A depressogenic attributional style is the generalized tendency to attribute negative life events to internal, stable, global factors.

Unfortunately, there is a dearth of research that attempts to dismantle and evaluate the components of a cognitive behavior program in order to identify the active ingredients of successful treatment outcome for depression (Harvey & Galvin, 1984; Whisman, 1993). However, one impressive attempt to do this has been undertaken by Jacobson, Dobson, Gortner, and colleagues (Jacobson et al., 1996; Gortner, Gollan, Dobson, & Jacobson, 1998). These investigators compared behavioral therapy with two cognitive behavior treatment packages that were based on Beck et al.'s (1979) CBT for depression. Their partial CBT program was designed to identify and modify automatic thoughts, including maladaptive attributions for negative life events. The complete CBT program included the techniques utilized in the partial CBT program and added several specific interventions that were designed to identify and modify core schemas underlying the kinds of cognitive distortions that were targeted in the partial CBT condition. This complete CBT condition included interventions designed to modify attributional style (Peterson & Villanova, 1988). Both CBT conditions included a behavioral activation component and consisted of 12 to 20 sessions. Individuals receiving treatment met criteria for Major Depression according to the *Diagnostic and Statistical Manual of Mental Disorders* (3rd edition, revised [*DSM-III-R*]; American Psychiatric Association, 1987).

Upon completion of either CBT condition, depressed participants showed a significant improvement in depressive symptoms. Analyses revealed that clinical improvement was accompanied by a significant decrease in depressogenic attributions as well as a significant change in attributional style. The results persisted at 6-month and 2-year follow-ups (Gortner et al., 1998). It should be noted, however, that these studies did not include complete tests of whether attributional style served as a mediator of the effect of CBT on improvement in symptoms (see Teasdale et al., 2001, for a discussion of this issue).

WHO MIGHT BENEFIT

Cognitive behavior therapy that specifically included an attribution change component has been used successfully to treat depression in both individual and group outpatient settings (Nixon & Singer, 1993), with children (Carlyon, 1997), adolescents (Reynolds & Stark, 1987), adults (Goldberg, Gask, & O'Dowd, 1989), and married couples (Birchler, 1986). It may be used in conjunction with pharmacological treatment.

CONTRAINDICATIONS

Research on therapeutic attribution retraining for depression has not studied the efficacy of this technique with hospital inpatients or thought-disordered individuals. This technique is not recommended for implementation with depressed patients who are actively psychotic.

Interestingly, Addis and Jacobson (1996) found that the number and types of explanations clients gave for their depression were significantly associated with treatment outcome. Depressed subjects who attributed their depression to negative childhood experiences failed to respond to CBT, whereas subjects with external attributions for their depression appeared to benefit from CBT.

HOW TO APPLY ATTRIBUTION CHANGE TECHNIQUES: OVERVIEW

Beck et al. (1979) note that CBT ought to take place in the context of a therapeutic *relationship* characterized by warmth, accurate empathy, and genuineness. Building trust and rapport are crucial ingredients when treating depressed clients with CBT. It is also important to elicit client feedback regularly in order to check the client's understanding of the therapy and to assess for any averse reactions that may impede the therapy process.

Cognitive behavior therapy for depression is conducted within a framework of collaborative empiricism. The therapist assumes an active, directive stance, joining with the client in a logical and empirical investigation of the client's beliefs, attitudes, inferences, and assumptions. Therapy focuses on the present, examining the client's thoughts and feelings as they occur during the session as well as in the client's everyday life. Therapist and client work together to establish specific treatment goals designed to ameliorate depressive symptoms and any other problems that they agree to address.

The therapist begins treatment by educating the depressed client about the theoretical rationale behind CBT, which Beck notes is a very important foundation for this therapeutic approach (Beck et al., 1979). Early therapy sessions focus on two major areas: (1) teaching the client to recognize and understand the connections between his or her thoughts, feelings, and behavior; and (2) training the client to identify the automatic thoughts that accompany negative feelings and problematic behaviors. In particular, the client begins to observe the kinds of attributions that he or she makes for negative life events.

The next phase of therapy involves teaching the depressed client how to evaluate the evidence for and against these maladaptive attributions and other associated automatic thoughts. The therapist teaches the client how to challenge his or her cognitive distortions, and to substitute more rational and reality-based ways of thinking. In particular, the patient is encouraged to shift from making internal, stable global attributions for negative life events to making more adaptive attributions. The client is encouraged to practice self-observation, hypothesis-testing techniques, and logical challenges to cognitive distortions in daily life, and to bring these data in for further examination during therapy sessions.

The final phase of therapy, conducted over eight sessions, involves helping the depressed client identify the maladaptive assumptions and attitudes (schemas) underlying his or her cognitive distortions. The client and therapist together examine and evaluate his or her depressogenic attributional style. Alternative core beliefs are considered and the advantages and disadvantages of each are evaluated. The client is encouraged to practice evaluating his or her experience according to the new attributional schemas that have been consciously selected.

Step-by-Step Procedures: Step One

As can be seen in Table 5.1, the therapist must make a thorough assessment of the client's depressive and other symptoms. Other information gathered may include the client's ability to identify and label feelings, the specific kinds of situations that are problematic, the link between presenting complaints and depressive symptoms, and the kinds of thinking distortions to which the client is subject. In particular, the clinician is attuned to any of the client's statements that illustrate a tendency to blame himself or herself or to assume personal responsibility for adverse events, whether or not those events are under personal control.

TABLE 5.1   Attribution Change Step by Step

1. Perform client assessment.
2. Educate the client about the rationale and techniques of CBT for depression.
3. Teach the client to understand the connections between his or her thoughts, feelings, and behavior.
4. Train the client to identify depressogenic attributions that are associated with negative feelings.
5. Examine the evidence for and against those attributions. Substitute more rational, realistic thoughts for depressogenic attributions and other cognitive distortions.
6. Identify underlying assumptions and core beliefs that compose the client's depressogenic attributional style.
7. Evaluate, challenge, and modify the client's depressogenic attributional style.

Questionnaire data can supplement information gathered in a clinical interview. Jacobson et al. (1996) administered the Beck Depression Inventory (BDI; Beck, 1967; Beck, Steer, & Garbin, 1988), the Automatic Thoughts Questionnaire (ATQ; Hollon & Kendall, 1980), and the Expanded Attributional Style Questionnaire (EASQ; Peterson & Villanova, 1988) to each client before and after treatment. Information is also gathered about the client's understanding of the therapy process and his or her therapy goals.

Step Two

The therapist explains the theoretical rationale behind CBT. The client learns about Beck's (1967) cognitive theory of depression as well as the way in which CBT will be used to treat it.

Step Three

The client is encouraged to begin to apply the cognitive theory to his or her own situation. The therapist encourages the client to make connections between his or her own thoughts, feelings, and behaviors.

Step Four

The client learns to identify automatic thoughts and images that are associated with negative feelings and depressed behaviors. In particular, the client learns to identify and observe attributions that he or she makes for negative life events. The client is encouraged to keep a daily record of attributions and other automatic thoughts together with the feelings, problematic behaviors, and situations in which they occur outside of therapy. The therapist is active in eliciting client attributions for the negative events he or she experiences.

Step Five

The client learns to evaluate the logical and empirical validity of his or her attributions. Together the therapist and client identify an attribution associated with negative affect. They review the situation that gave rise to this automatic thought, gathering and defining all of the factors associated with that event that would be relevant in making a realistic and accurate attribution of responsibility. These factors may include a review of the relevant information available to the client at the time of the event, the possible role of others in contributing to the adverse occurrence, the controllability of the event, and its significance to the client and others. The client is encouraged to come up with alternative attributions and to consider the evidence for and against each of these competing hypotheses. Homework assignments may be given in order for the client to gather more information and to evaluate the empirical evidence for and against depressogenic and more adaptive attributions.

The therapist may question the client about the types of attributions that he or she would make if someone other than the client were in the client's place. Does the client exhibit a double standard when assigning blame to self, but make more realistic attributions for others? The therapist may also challenge the client to consider whether responsibility in this situation is an absolute 100%, or whether it is more logical to view responsibility as shared or partial (known as *deresponsibilitizing*).

The client is thus enabled to gain a more objective, balanced, and realistic view of his or her own responsibility in causing a negative event. The client is then encouraged to generalize this reattribution process to other negative life situations with the therapist's continued support.

Step Six

The therapist goes on to identify more general patterns in the client's depressogenic attributions, identifying the attributional schemas underlying the client's habitual way of construing negative life events. The downward arrow technique is useful here, wherein the therapist elicits the client's explanations for his or her problems, then generates hypotheses about various kinds of general patterns and concerns, ultimately leading to the identification of the core beliefs comprising the client's depressogenic attributional style. Homework assignments enable the client to see whether these core beliefs do in fact characterize his or her everyday experience.

Therapist and client then consider alternative

attributional core beliefs and discuss the immediate and long-term advantages and disadvantages of holding each kind of belief. The client is then encouraged to explore how alternative core attributions might be applied to life situations. The therapist and client also subject these underlying attributional assumptions to the same kind of logical and empirical scrutiny that they did the automatic thoughts and attributions in Step Five.

Further Reading

Beck, A. T., Rush, A. J., Shaw, B. F., & Emery, G. (1979). *Cognitive therapy of depression.* New York: Guilford Press.

Jacobson, N. S., Dobson, K. S., Truax, P. A., Addis, M. E., Koerner, K., Gollan, J. K., Gortner, E., & Prince, S. E. (1996). A component analysis of cognitive-behavioral treatment for depression. *Journal of Consulting and Clinical Psychology, 64,* 295–304.

Metalsky, G. I., Laird, R. S., Heck, P. M., & Joiner, T. E. Jr. (1995). Attribution theory: Clinical implications. In W. O'Donohue & L. Krasner (Eds.), *Theories of behavior therapy: Exploring behavior change* (pp. 385–413). Washington, DC: American Psychological Association.

References

Abramson, L. Y., Seligman, M. E. P., & Teasdale, J. (1978). Learned helplessness in humans: Critique and reformulation. *Journal of Abnormal Psychology, 87,* 49–74.

Addis, M. E., & Jacobson, N. S. (1996). Reasons for depression and the process and outcome of cognitive-behavioral psychotherapies. *Journal of Consulting and Clinical Psychology, 64,* 1417–1424.

American Psychiatric Association. (1987). *Diagnostic and statistical manual of mental disorders* (Rev. 3rd ed.). Washington, DC: Author.

Andrews, J. D. W. (1989). Psychotherapy of depression: A self-confirmation model. *Psychological Review, 96,* 576–607.

Beck, A. T. (1967). *Depression: Clinical, experimental, and theoretical aspects.* New York: Hoeber.

Beck, A. T. (1976). *Cognitive therapy and the emotional disorders.* New York: Meridian.

Beck, A. T., Emery, G., & Greenberg, R. L. (1985). *Anxiety disorders and phobias: A cognitive perspective.* New York: Basic Books.

Beck, A. T., Rush, A. J., Shaw, B. F., & Emery, G. (1979). *Cognitive therapy of depression.* New York: Guilford Press.

Beck, A. T., Steer, R. A., & Garbin, M. G. (1988). Psychometric properties of the Beck Depression Inventory: Twenty-five years of evaluation. *Clinical Psychology Review, 8*, 77–100.

Birchler, G. R. (1986). Alleviating depression with "marital" intervention. *Journal of Psychotherapy and the Family, 2*, 101–116.

Carlyon, W. D. (1997). Attribution training: Implications for its integration into prescriptive social skills training. *School Psychology Review, 26*, 61–73.

Dobson, K. S. (1989). A meta-analysis of the efficacy of cognitive-behavioral therapy for depression. *Journal of Consulting and Clinical Psychology, 57*, 414–419.

Evans, M. D., Hollon, S. D., DeRubeis, R. J., Piasecki, J. M., Grove, W. M., Garvey, M. J., & Tuason, V. B. (1992). Differential relapse following cognitive therapy and pharmacotherapy for depression. *Archives of General Psychiatry, 49*, 802–808.

Goldberg, D., Gask, L., & O'Dowd, T. (1989). The treatment of somatization: Teaching techniques of reattribution. *Journal of Psychosomatic Research, 33*, 689–695.

Gortner, E. T., Gollan, J. K., Dobson, K. S., & Jacobson, N. S. (1998). Cognitive-behavioral treatment for depression: Relapse prevention. *Journal of Consulting and Clinical Psychology, 66*, 377–384.

Harvey, J. H., & Galvin, K. S. (1984). Clinical implications of attribution theory and research. *Clinical Psychology Review, 4*, 15–33.

Hollon, S. D., Evans, M. D., & DeRubeis, R. J. (1990). Cognitive mediation of relapse prevention following treatment for depression: Implications of differential risk. In R. E. Ingram (Ed.), *Contemporary psychological approaches to depression* (pp. 117–136). New York: Guilford Press.

Hollon, S. D., & Kendall, P. E. (1980). Cognitive self-statements in depression: Development of an automatic thoughts questionnaire. *Cognitive Therapy and Research, 4*, 383–396.

Jacobson, N. S., Dobson, K. S., Truax, P. A., Addis, M. E., Koerner, K., Gollan, J. K., et al. (1996). A component analysis of cognitive-behavioral treatment for depression. *Journal of Consulting and Clinical Psychology, 64*, 295–304.

Jacobson, N. S., & Hollon, S. D. (1996). Cognitive behavior therapy vs. pharmacotherapy: Now that the jury's returned its verdict, it's time to present the rest of the evidence. *Journal of Consulting and Clinical Psychology, 64*, 74–80.

Metalsky, G. I., & Abramson, L. Y. (1981). Attributional style: Toward a framework for conceptualization and assessment. In P. C. Kendall & S. D. Hollon (Eds.), *Assessment strategies for cognitive-behavioral interventions* (pp. 13–58). San Diego, CA: Academic Press.

Metalsky, G. I., Laird, R. S., Heck, P. M., & Joiner, T. E. Jr. (1995). Attribution theory: Clinical implications. In W. O'Donohue & L. Krasner (Eds.), *Theories of behavior therapy: Exploring behavior change* (pp. 385–413). Washington, DC: American Psychological Association.

Nixon, C. D., & Singer, G. H. (1993). Group cognitive behavioral treatment for excessive parental self-blame and guilt. *American Journal on Mental Retardation, 97*, 665–672.

Nolen-Hoeksema, S., Girgus, J. S., & Seligman, M. E. P. (1992). Predictors and consequences of childhood depressive symptoms: A 5-year longitudinal study. *Journal of Abnormal Psychology, 101*, 405–422.

Peterson, C., & Seligman, M. E. P. (1984). Causal explanations as a risk factor for depression: Theory and evidence. *Psychological Review, 91*, 347–374.

Peterson, C., & Villanova, P. (1988). An expanded attributional style questionnaire. *Journal of Abnormal Psychology, 97*, 87–89.

Reynolds, W. M., & Stark, K. D. (1987). School-based intervention strategies for the treatment of depression in children and adolescents. *Special Services in the Schools, 3*, 69–88.

Teasdale, J. D., Scott, J., Moore, R. G., Hayhurst, H., Pope, M., & Paykel, E. (2001). How does cognitive therapy prevent relapse in residual depression? Evidence from a controlled trial. *Journal of Consulting and Clinical Psychology, 69*, 347–357.

Whisman, M. A. (1993). Mediators and moderators of change in cognitive therapy of depression. *Psychological Bulletin, 114*, 248–265.

6 BEHAVIORAL ACTIVATION TREATMENT FOR DEPRESSION

Christopher R. Martell

Behavioral treatment for depression dates back to the early 1970s with the theoretical formulations of C. B. Ferster (1973, 1981) and the applied work of Peter Lewinsohn and colleagues (Lewinsohn, 1974; Lewinsohn, Biglan, & Zeiss, 1976; Lewinsohn & Graf, 1973). The basic idea of the behavioral theory of depression was that individuals become depressed when there is an imbalance of punishment to positive reinforcement in their lives. According to Ferster (1981), when an individual responds primarily to deprivation and the removal of an aversive, deprived state, he or she develops behaviors that function primarily as avoidance behaviors and there is little access to positive reinforcement built into the behavioral repertoire of the individual. Treatment for depression would, therefore, consist of a process that would increase the individual's access to positive reinforcers.

Following the analysis of Ferster, Lewinsohn and colleagues focused on increasing pleasant events and pleasurable activities in order to treat depression (Lewinsohn & Graf, 1973). These researchers developed the use of activity logs and activity scheduling to help depressed patients increase positive activities that would combat their lethargy and bring them into contact with positive reinforcers. Contemporaries of Lewinsohn were formulating theories of depression that were more cognitive than behavioral (Beck, 1976;

Ellis, 1973). Beck's cognitive therapy for depression utilized the activity scheduling elements of Lewinsohn's approach but focused on changing the negative content of depressed patients' beliefs. Cognitive therapy was studied extensively and empirically validated as a treatment for depression, and the field of behavior therapy took on a distinctively cognitive profile throughout much of the 1980s and 1990s. The idea of increasing pleasant events alone, without cognitive interventions, was questioned (Hammen & Glass, 1975), and cognitive behavior therapy was seen as a psychosocial treatment of choice for depression.

In the 1990s, Neil S. Jacobson and colleagues began a dismantling study of cognitive therapy for depression, hypothesizing that the activation elements of the treatment were necessary and sufficient. Their component analysis study (Jacobson et al., 1996) demonstrated that depressed subjects treated with behavioral activation alone improved as well as those subjects treated with a full cognitive therapy treatment. Their results were maintained at follow-up (Gortner, Gollan, Dobson, & Jacobson, 1998). A detailed accounting of the process and controversies that followed this project has been published elsewhere (Jacobson & Gortner, 2000). The results of the component analysis study opened the door for a larger study of the treatment of depression, which compared cognitive therapy, behavioral activation, Paxil plus clinical management, Paxil alone, and pill placebo. The results of this study are currently being evaluated, but preliminary results are promising for psychosocial treatments of depression, cognitive therapy, and behavioral activation.

Jacobson and colleagues took an idiographic, behavior analytic approach to behavioral activation (Jacobson, Martell, & Dimidjian, 2001; Martell, Addis, & Jacobson, 2001). In their approach, therapists are encouraged not to assume that any particular behaviors will be positively reinforced or result in a client's feeling better when the behaviors occur. In other words, every behavior is analyzed according to its setting and consequences rather than the particular form it takes. Going for a walk, for example, may or may not be positively reinforced depending on a variety of contextual factors. The treatment is theory driven rather than protocol driven. A particularly new addition to the treatment from Jacobson's lab is the focus on targeting avoidance behavior as a primary treatment goal with depressed clients.

WHO MIGHT BENEFIT FROM THIS TECHNIQUE

Behavioral activation (BA) is currently a treatment for depression and has undergone evaluation in that arena. Although there are current projects underway using the BA approach for prevention of Post-Traumatic Stress Disorder (PTSD), for combined major depression and PTSD, and for the treatment of PTSD, no substantial data are available for use of this therapy with other problems. The BA focus on avoidance places it in the realm of other exposure-based treatments that have been used for the treatment of anxiety and other disorders. However, no data are yet available to demonstrate the utility of the approach in these areas. Participants in Jacobson's lab met criteria for Major Depressive Disorder and were screened out only if there was presence of a thought disorder or of active substance or chemical dependence. No other comorbid disorders were excluded. Therefore, the participant pool on which the treatment was tested had at least an Axis I major depressive disorder, but could have had comorbid Axis I or Axis II disorders (other than psychosis or substance dependence).

CONTRAINDICATIONS OF THE TREATMENT

Understanding the possible contraindications of this treatment requires clinical hypothesis rather than hard data. The treatment does not seem to be contraindicated for most people suffering from major depression. Although it is a context-based, nonpharmachological treatment that encourages clients to look outward at their life context rather than at hypothesized internal defects, it has even been used with clients who maintain a need for psychotropic medication (implying a flaw in the machine). We would caution clinicians, however, from using this technique with depressed individuals who may be involved in a domestic violence situation, where activating may expose them to greater harm from an abusive partner. Clinicians should be cautious not to encourage a client to engage in behavior that could result in any such harmful interpersonal interaction.

OTHER DECISIONS IN DECIDING TO USE OR NOT TO USE BEHAVIORAL ACTIVATION

Workshop presentations of examples of therapists using behavioral activation receive typical criticisms that therapists do not attend to client cognitions. The data suggest that BA alone, without evaluation of the content of clients' thinking, works well in the treatment of a major depressive episode. However, outside of the research setting, there is no prohibition against using cognitive restructuring. Some clients maintain strong beliefs that their thinking is the problem. We would recommend that, rather than arguing with a client, the therapist incorporate the very behavioral aspects of BA with a cognitive conceptualization. The two treatments are complementary and provide a bridge for some clients (and therapists). For example, the context and consequences of clients' thinking (where and when it occurs, and what effect it has on how the client feels and what he or she does next) can be incorporated into BA without focusing on the content.

HOW DOES THE TECHNIQUE WORK?

At this time, we can only make assumptions about the factors that make BA work. Primarily, the therapist takes the role of a coach, encouraging clients to become active even when they feel as if they cannot possibly complete tasks or get any pleasure from life. Because BA works to help clients establish a regular routine, it breaks the destructive process of routine disruption that often accompanies depression (Ehlers, Frank, & Kupfer, 1988). Activity in BA means getting engaged rather than just doing something for the sake of being busy or living under a Calvinist work ethic.

STEP-BY-STEP PROCEDURES

The treatment is based on the theory, described earlier, that depression often results from changes in a vulnerable individual's life that decrease the person's access to positive reinforcement. Basically, the treatment consists of strategies that increase activity and block avoidance so that the client can come in contact with natural reinforcers in his or her environment. In order to do this in a manner that is idiographic and not merely applying broad classes of pleasant activities that may or may not actually be reinforcing, the therapist needs to do a good functional analysis.

Conducting a Functional Analysis

Whereas the laboratory provides much control over conditions that can lead to accurate understanding of contingencies at work in the behavior of organisms under study, the clinical setting does not provide the same level of control. When we speak of functional analysis we are speaking of the best hypotheses that the therapist and client can develop about the antecedents, behaviors, and consequences that form elements of the client's repertoire contributing to depression. In BA we are interested in the function of the behavior and not the form of the behavior. Therefore, we are less concerned with what popular opinion may be about a certain behavior (e.g., people may think that going for a run early in the morning is a good and healthy thing to do) than with the function of a particular behavior for a particular person (e.g., the runner may actually be out early in the morning because she does not want to remain at home to have a discussion with her partner about having neglected to pay an expensive bill). Functional analysis is the heart of BA, and it will be conducted throughout the treatment. The first step, however, is to develop a general case conceptualization from a behavior analytic perspective.

There are several questions that the therapist needs to ask about the depressive episode that the client is experiencing. First, the therapist must understand the client's history and gather information about significant life events, positive or negative, that influence the client's current life context. To do this, the therapist simply need ask the client to recount such events, as with questions like "What is your family like? What kinds of things have been good in your life? What has hurt you or has been distressing?" It is also important, second, to understand how the client's behavior during a depressive episode is different from his behavior at other times. Asking the client "What is your life like when you are not depressed? Are there things that you are not doing now that you typically do when you are not depressed? What do you hope to accomplish in your life? Are you taking steps toward accomplishing these things?" can help to gather a picture of what problems the client may be experiencing.

Gathering this information helps the therapist to develop a case conceptualization of the client's depression. We express the case conceptualization in terms of the life events that may have contributed to the depression by making the client's life less rewarding, and we then look at how the client has tried to cope with the symptoms of depression. Often the client's attempts at coping become problems in themselves, and we refer to these as *secondary problem behaviors*. For example, the runner mentioned earlier might be coping with feelings of hopelessness and inadequacy by engaging in a fervent exercise program that enables her to avoid dealing with issues with her significant other. We would call her exercise regime a secondary problem. Even though we know exercise is good for depressed people in general, with this particular client we would want to help her to address her issues with her partner and then institute exercise that is not avoidance.

Day-by-Day Analysis

Since its earliest conception by Lewinsohn and others, BA has made ample use of activity charts to help therapists understand the level of a client's activity and to schedule pleasant events. We continue to rely heavily on activity charts in our work. We use activity charts for several reasons. The therapist can use an activity chart to understand the following:

1. The client's current level of activity
2. Restriction of the client's affect
3. Connections between the client's activity and mood
4. Mastery and pleasure ratings
5. How to help the client monitor avoidance behaviors
6. Guided activity
7. Steps the client is taking toward stated life goals

It does not matter what type of activity chart a therapist chooses to use with his or her clients. All that is important is that the chart include all the hours in the day and provide room enough for the client to record what he or she did and felt, and the intensity of the feeling, in each hour block.

Techniques for Dealing with Client Avoidance

We find it most important that clients continually be vigilant of their avoidance behaviors. It is also a basic tenet in BA that clients can choose to engage in activities that will possibly help them to feel better, or they can choose to continue to avoid and possibly remain depressed. Although we never tell clients that they are choosing to be depressed, we do indeed suggest to clients that choices made about specific behaviors can lead to certain consequences.

Three acronyms illustrate the concept of avoidance to clients and help them to be aware of their patterns and to modify behaviors. The first is the word ACTION, which stands for the following:

- *Assess* my behavior: Is my current behavior avoidant? How does this behavior serve me?

- *Choose* whether to activate myself and engage in behaviors that could help my depression in the long run, or to continue to avoid this experience.
- *Try* the behavior that I've chosen.
- *Integrate* any new activity into a regular routine, remembering that trying a new behavior only once is unlikely to lead to significant change.
- *Observe* the outcome of the behavior: Does it affect mood, or does it improve a life situation?
- *Never* give up. Counteracting depression and avoidance takes continued work, and tenacity in the face of frequent disappointments.

The second acronym we use is TRAP, which stands for *trigger,* or some happening or event; *response,* usually the client's emotional response to the trigger; and *avoidance pattern,* which is the typical avoidance response to the trigger. Once the client has identified a TRAP, we use the third acronym to help him or her get back on TRAC (*trigger, response, alternative coping*). The strategies of using activity charts and helping clients to recognize avoidance patterns and modify their behavior make up the bulk of BA treatment.

Conceptualized as a contextual treatment, BA focuses on helping clients to change behavior in such a way as to bring them into contact with positive reinforcers in their natural environment. There is much less emphasis on skills training than in other behavioral therapies. The model in BA is that therapists *may* conduct skills training, but they are not *required* to. Whether or not to conduct skills training such as problem-solving training will depend on the behavioral analysis of each client. In clinical outcome trials of BA, therapists have used problem-solving training or assertiveness training, but they have done so in a fashion that anchors the training in the context of the client's life. In other words, even in skills training, the BA therapist tries not to teach a broad class of skills that can be applied by following rules; rather, the therapist debriefs specific incidents in the client's life and helps the client understand how he or she might have changed an outcome by behaving differently. In some cases the client may be planning a particular encounter, and the therapist would discuss options for achieving particular outcomes.

FINAL CONSIDERATIONS

The therapeutic stance in BA is always collaborative. The therapist serves as a coach for the client. When the therapist is trying to help a client develop a new skill the therapist takes the position that his or her suggestions are hypotheses to be tested rather than prescriptions from an authority figure. Behavioral activation therapists are working within a model that is quite different from a medical model. Clients are seen as individuals whose lives have somehow gone awry rather than as patients with some defect or flaw that must be modified. The therapist works to help the client understand the areas of his or her life that are not working and to make adjustments in behavior to enhance the workable aspects of life.

In the treatment outcome studies conducted on BA to date from Jacobson's laboratory, the therapy has consisted of a 16-week protocol, with clients allowed up to 24 therapy sessions. Many clients begin to show improvement in depression scores within the first 10 sessions. However, there are no clear data to suggest an optimal length of treatment. Researchers in a different setting, conducting BA that primarily focused on activity scheduling, had successful results with a 10-session protocol (Lejuez, Hopko, LePage, Hopko, & McNeil, 2001). This would suggest that the treatment may be successful over a shorter time period.

Further Reading

Jacobson, N. S., Martell, C. R., & Dimidjian, S. (2001). Behavioral activation treatment for depression: Returning to contextual roots. *Clinical Psychology: Science and Practice, 8*(3), 255–270.

Martell, C. R., Addis, M. E., & Jacobson, N. S. (2001). *Depression in context: Strategies for guided action.* New York: W. W. Norton.

References

Beck, A. T. (1976). *Cognitive therapy and the emotional disorders.* New York: New American Library.

Ehlers, C. L., Frank, E., & Kupfer, D. J. (1988). Social zeitgebers and biological rhythms: A unified approach to understanding the etiology of depression. *Archives of General Psychiatry, 45,* 948–952.

Ellis, A. (1973). *Humanistic psychotherapy: The rational-emotive approach.* New York: McGraw-Hill.

Ferster, C. B. (1973). A functional analysis of depression. *American Psychologist, 28,* 857–870.

Ferster, C. B. (1981). A functional analysis of behavior therapy. In L. P. Rehm (Ed.), *Behavior therapy for depression: Present status and future directions* (pp. 181–196). New York: Academic Press.

Gortner, E. T., Gollan, J. K., Dobson, K. S., & Jacobson, N. S. (1998). Cognitive-behavioral treatment for depression: Relapse prevention. *Journal of Consulting and Clinical Psychology, 66*(2), 377–384.

Hammen, C. L., & Glass, D. R. (1975). Depression, activity, and evaluation of reinforcement. *Journal of Abnormal Psychology, 54*(6), 718–721.

Jacobson, N. S., Dobson, K., Truax, P. A., Addis, M. E., Koerner, K., Gollan, J. K., et al. (1996). A component analysis of cognitive-behavioral treatment for depression. *Journal of Consulting and Clinical Psychology, 64*(2), 295–304.

Jacobson, N. S., & Gortner, E. (2000). Can depression be de-medicalized in the 21st century? Scientific revolutions, counter-revolutions and the magnetic field of normal science. *Behaviour Research and Therapy, 38,* 103–117.

Jacobson, N. S., Martell, C. R., & Dimidjian, S. (2001). Behavioral activation treatment for depression: Returning to contextual roots. *Clinical Psychology: Science and Practice, 8*(3), 255–270.

Lejuez, C. W., Hopko, D. R., LePage, J. P., Hopko, S. D., & McNeil, D. W. (2001). A brief behavioral activation treatment for depression. *Cognitive and Behavioral Practice, 8,* 164–175.

Lewinsohn, P. M. (1974). A behavioral approach to depression. In R. M. Friedman & M. M. Katz (Eds.), *The psychology of depression: Contemporary theory and research* (pp. 157–185). New York: Wiley.

Lewinsohn, P. M., Biglan, A., & Zeiss, A. S. (1976). Behavioral treatment of depression. In P. O. Davidson (Ed.), *The behavioral management of anxiety, depression and pain* (pp. 91–146). New York: Brunner/Mazel.

Lewinsohn, P. M., & Graf, M. (1973). Pleasant activities and depression. *Journal of Consulting and Clinical Psychology, 41,* 261–268.

Martell, C. R., Addis, M. E., & Jacobson, N. S. (2001). *Depression in context: Strategies for guided action.* New York: W. W. Norton.

7   BEHAVIORAL CHAINING

W. Larry Williams and Eric Burkholder

Chaining refers to a set of procedures used to teach a task that consists of an ordered series of specific responses that must occur in a predetermined order to produce reinforcement. In the behavioral account each step of this series produces an outcome that serves as a reinforcer for the response that produced it and serves as a discriminative stimulus for the next response in the sequence (Martin & Pear, 1999). The chain terminates with some principal outcome, product, or reinforcer.

Chaining has been used by trainers in a myriad of professions dating back well over a hundred years (Crafts, 1929; Mountjoy & Lewandowski, 1984). In the basic literature, chaining has been used to study such fundamental processes as the nature of conditioned reinforcement (Boren, 1969; Boren & Devine, 1968; Fantino, 1965; Jwaideh, 1973; Kelleher & Fry, 1962; Pisacreta, 1982; Thvedt, Zane, & Walls, 1984; Weiss, 1978). In the applied literature, chaining has been shown to be a procedurally sound method of producing a broad range of complex behaviors in a variety of populations, from teaching college students to play golf (Simek, O'Brien, & Figlerski, 1994) to teaching disabled individuals how to engage in activities of daily living (Spooner, 1984). The work in developmental disabilities is particularly well elaborated, where chaining has been used to teach assembly-line tasks (Martin, Koop, Turner, & Hanel, 1981; Spooner, 1984; Spooner, Spooner, & Ulicny, 1986; Weber, 1978) family-style dining (Wilson, Reid, Phillips, & Burgio, 1984), responding to a fire alarm (Cohen, 1984), reducing escape behavior (Lalli, Casey, & Kates, 1995), picture naming (Olenick & Pear, 1980), treatment for total liquid refusal (Hagopian, Farrell, & Amari, 1996), community skills (McDonnell & Laughlin, 1989), and other complex skills (McWilliams, Nietupski, & Hamre-Nietupski, 1990). Other issues bearing on chaining have also been examined, including trainer preference for chaining procedure (Walls, Zane, & Thvedt, 1980), effects of conditions of reinforcement on chaining (Talkington, 1971), and teaching the effects of prompting and guiding procedures (Zane, Walls, & Thvedt, 1981).

Three conventional methods have evolved for teaching chains (see Table 7.1). *Total task presentation* involves teaching all of a chain's component responses on each teaching trial. *Forward chaining* teaches the first response in the chain to some criterion, then the first and second response, then the first three responses, and so on until the total chain is acquired. *Backward chaining* teaches the last response in the sequence first; then the second-to-last and the last responses; then the third-to-last, the second-to-last, and the last responses; and so on until the total chain is acquired. Which one of these three variants has the highest level of efficacy has not been satisfactorily answered, due to contradictory findings (Martin et al., 1981). It does seem clear that all three variants can be effective for teaching skills to a wide range of populations.

TABLE 7.1   Response Chaining

Response Chaining

1. A chain is an ordered series of specific responses that must occur in a predetermined order to produce its related functional reinforcement.

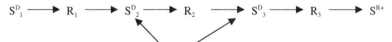

$$S^D_1 \longrightarrow R_1 \longrightarrow S^D_2 \longrightarrow R_2 \longrightarrow S^D_3 \longrightarrow R_3 \longrightarrow S^{R+}$$

2. Each response produces an outcome that serves as (a) a conditioned reinforcer for that response, (b) a discriminative stimulus (S^D) for the next response, and (c) a discriminative stimulus (S^V) for not engaging in that response

3. A *task analysis* is conducted for the task to be taught. This consists of breaking the task down into component response units based on the apparent or natural sequences that make up the task. Once produced, it is important to validate the task analysis for accuracy, completeness, and detail according to the skill level of the learner to be taught the chain.

Forward chaining teaches the components separately and in the order they occur in the chain. As each response is learned it is added to the others.	R_1 $R_1 \longrightarrow R_2$ $R_1 \longrightarrow R_2 \longrightarrow R_3 \longrightarrow S^{R+}$
Backward chaining teaches the last response in the chain first, then the second last, and so on. Each teaching trial involves the current response being taught and then the rest of the sequence already learned, and ends with the chain's natural reinforcer.	$R_3 \longrightarrow S^{R+}$ $R_2 \longrightarrow R_3 \longrightarrow S^{R+}$ $R_1 \longrightarrow R_2 \longrightarrow R_3 \longrightarrow S^{R+}$
Total task presentation is a variation of forward chaining and teaches all of the component responses on every teaching trial. That is, the whole chain is performed on every trial.	$R_1 \longrightarrow R_2 \longrightarrow R_3 \longrightarrow S^{R+}$

WHO MIGHT BENEFIT FROM THIS TECHNIQUE?

Professionals and educators who work with populations that need to learn complex activities, or populations that have displayed deficits in their ability to learn, may benefit from the systematic application of this technique. As described above, this technique has been widely used to teach a variety of skills to people with developmental disabilities. The use of this technique is appropriate for teaching any task that can be broken into smaller steps, such as making coffee, tying shoes, making a bed, assembling a bicycle brake, or engaging in any of a wide variety of crafts, hobbies, sports, exercises, and vocational and habilitation skills. Chaining may also be used for acquisition of complex verbal performances or for generating rules or strategies to guide other performances.

HOW DOES THIS TECHNIQUE WORK?

Chaining works by systematically establishing a specific response in the presence of a specific discriminative stimulus, itself the result of a specific prior response. As specific response units are established, they are put together into an ever-increasing string of responses until the final task is achieved. The final task is itself associated with a more significant functional reinforcer, typically the functional outcome of the task being taught (e.g., a prepared sandwich, a loaded dishwasher, completion of a preflight check, etc.) The arrangement of the responses and their outcomes is determined by a *task analysis*. The task analysis should be validated (walked through and tried) and prompting procedures (additional material; instructional, gestural, or physical aides) determined and specified as well as reinforcement criterion before starting the teaching procedure. Chaining works because each link in the chain (i.e., each discrete response), has a clear discriminative stimulus and either is directly reinforced by the trainer or leads to conditioned reinforcement, or both.

Completing and Validating a Task Analysis

A task analysis is breaking a complex activity into its component parts or units so that they can be individually shaped if they are not already in the subject's repertoire, or brought under appropriate stimulus control within the chain if they already are present. Any task that results in a typical outcome (e.g., taking a shower, making a bed) can be broken into the essential response components rather easily. Consider, for example, the task analyses in Figures 7.1 and 7.2.

Once a task has been broken into its component parts it needs to be validated prior to the start of the teaching procedure. There are many ways of validating a task analysis (Cooper, Heron, & Heward, 1987) including observing and piloting out the procedure, consulting experts or people who are fluent in performing the task, or performing the task repeatedly. Regardless of what method is used for the validation of the task analysis, each behavior to be taught should be discrete and follow a clear discriminative stimulus produced either by the initial instruction or by the previous link in the chain.

The number of steps can be increasingly refined until they are (1) small and easily taught, and (2) at the appropriate level for our learner. The ability of the learner, the behavioral characteristics of the learner, and the exact environment the skill will be taught in must be taken into consideration when conducting a task analysis. In the examples shown in the figures, our learner would have to have the ability to use both arms and discriminate bedding materials from other materials, in order to make use of the task analyses presented. For this reason, the exact steps and order of the steps in a task analysis may be different for two different learners, depending on the constraints of the environment and the task.

Figure 7.1. The sequence of chained responses in taking a shower. Each of the general responses below results in a specific outcome, which signals the next response. The necessary order is also well illustrated. Indeed, because of necessary pre-requisite conditions (being wet, being lathered up) this chain would be best taught in a forward chaining or whole task presentation method.

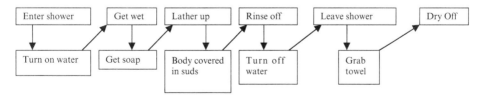

Note that each general response can itself be broken down into smaller responses each of which produce their own specific stimulus outcomes that signal another response. (For example there are many ways to "turn on water" such that some form of "getting wet" is the outcome resulting as a prompt to pick up soap, resulting in prompting soap application, etc.) Indeed these are the individual differences in how we shower, but no one applies soap before being wet, nor dries off before turning off the water, etc.

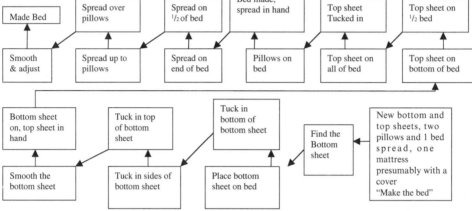

Figure 7.2. Making a bed. Although a certain sequence of responses is involved, this task can be easily arranged to be totally, partially, or not at all complete. As such, it is teachable in a backward chaining format, where the final product of a "made bed" always is the product of a training session. In a backward chaining format training would start with simply smoothing and adjusting the bed spread over the pillows. The rest of the bed would be already made.

Note that as with the shower example, many variations and component responses can be added, depending on the learning level and abilities of the learner. Nevertheless, a definite sequence of events can be observed each resulting in a situation or stimulus array that should prompt the next response (or set of component responses).

Determine What Chaining Procedure to Use

The trainer at this point has several different options as to how to chain the behavior. Selecting among the most commonly used chaining procedures depends upon the exact training situation.

Forward Chaining

A forward chaining procedure teaches each behavior sequenced from the first to the final skill in a forward sequential manner. For example, chaining the skills from the validated task analysis for taking a shower, our subject would be taught to turn on the water and would be reinforced for doing so until he or she displayed mastery (for example, three consecutive correct responses). Once our learner has demonstrated mastery of step one, the second step of getting oneself all wet would be introduced. Once the second step is introduced, simply turning on the water would no longer be reinforced: The learner would now have to turn on the water and get appropriately wet to be reinforced by our trainer. The other behaviors in our chain would then be added systematically

upon mastery until all steps in our validated task analysis have been performed.

An advantage of forward chaining is that teaching trainers to use a forward chain is relatively simple, and most people are taught to engage in new tasks in a forward manner. These advantages can lead to staff use of forward chaining and can decrease the need for staff supervision with this method of chaining (Wilson et al., 1984).

Backward Chaining

Backward chaining involves teaching a learner the final link in the chain first. For example, from our task analysis of bed making, smoothing the bedspread over the pillows is the final link. The trainer could engage in all the behaviors leading up to the smoothing of the bedspread over the pillows. The learner would then be required to do that last step. Upon mastery of smoothing, the next-to-last step (pulling the spread up to the pillows) would be added as a task, and so on until our learner is engaging in the entire task of making the entire bed independently.

One advantage of backward chaining is that right from the beginning of training, the learner ends up with the natural reinforcer for engaging in the chain, the made bed in our example. By association the preceding step produces a change in the environment (the S^D for the last step), which has already been followed by the ultimate reinforcer. Because of this repeated pairing, conditioned reinforcement should occur (Skinner, 1938), and this additional reinforcing function should aid in the acquisition of the chain. There are practical concerns, however, since the learner is passive in all steps up to the final link initially (Cooper et al., 1987). Staff also sometimes have trouble avoiding confusion in using backward conditioning.

Total Task Presentation

Total task presentation is a variant of forward chaining. This variant has the learner perform every step in the chain on every trial. The trainer assists the learner on any step that he or she cannot perform independently. This training continues until the learner can perform the entire task independently at the mastery criterion. This is accomplished by prespecifying prompts, including time between prompts, prior to the beginning of the training. For example, the trainer would initially use verbal prompts and hand-over-hand assistance for each step in making coffee, waiting 5 seconds between prompts until the learner either independently responds or is prompted to engage in the next behavior in the chain. As the learner begins to perform the task more independently the prompts are faded until the learner is engaging in the entire task independently. This procedure has been shown to facilitate fast chain acquisition (Martin et al., 1981; Spooner, 1984). Spooner (1984) suggests that the fast rate of acquisition may be accounted for by the presentation of every stimulus on every training trial and may be worth the effort and training time needed to engage in all steps during each trial.

Factors Related to the Effectiveness of Chaining

Research and experience have shown that several factors can influence the success of a chaining program.

1. *Conduct a task analysis.* Although there are numerous ways to break down a task into component responses of differing sizes, one should first conduct an analysis that leads to a series of responses that break along natural lines of the task steps and that produce characteristic clear situations or products. Then, depending on the discrimination skill level of the learner (Martin & Yu, 2000; Yu, Martin, & Williams, 1989) as well as other factors such as motor dexterity, one might further break down component steps into even smaller units. The final components, however, must maintain clear stimulus and response relationships with no single stimulus presentations controlling different component responses.

2. *Determine the types and arrangement of prompts.* The final response chain must be trained to occur in the presence of a specific instruction or cue and then be performed such that each response sets the occasion for the next, until the entire chain is completed. This requires arranging for the fading of initial interim instructions and prompts as the component responses are acquired as larger and larger units. For learners with language and rule-governed skills (Ellen & Pate, 1986; Hayes, 1989; Skinner, 1953) spoken, written, self-reported, or pictorial aides can effectively guide the learner through the sequence in an independent fashion. For nonverbal learners, interim instructions and prompts (gestural, physical, etc.) may be required to establish component responses and then gradually be eliminated as the main overall instruction gains control over the ever-expanding chain.

3. *Use a modeling demonstration.* Demonstration of the entire task to the learner will often result in much quicker acquisition of a chain and reduce cumbersome training involving establishment of partial chains and the gradual removal of the interim instructions for them as the appropriate sequence is established.

4. *Training sequence and corrections.* Begin training by providing the final instruction. If the learner errs or stops responding, provide a *momentum* cue such as "keep going" that is not specific to the behavior to be engaged in but that will cue the learner to continue to complete the chain. If an error occurs, intervene with a cor-

rection procedure such as modeling the step or instructional or gestural assistance until the learner completes the step. Then proceed to the next step by providing the final chain instruction again.

5. *Reinforcement.* As in any behavior change activity, one should use ample social praise for progress toward the final target behavior. Praise should be given for completion of individual responses and some larger reinforcer (such as an edible) provided when the whole chain is completed, or when larger units of the final chain are learned. Be cautious not to distract the learner from completing component responses because of well-intentioned but unnecessary reinforcing statements or provision of reinforcers that stop the engagement in completing the task (Gold, 1972). A stimulus preference assessment (see Chapter 59, this volume; DeLeong & Iwata, 1996) should be conducted to increase the chance that supposed reinforcers are indeed reinforcers. Choice among several demonstrated reinforcers is a preferred method.

6. *Prompt Fading.* Once a learner is engaging in a component response, and especially when component responses are beginning to occur in their desired sequence, it is crucial not to provide unnecessary additional instructions or cues. The objective is to have the naturally occurring cues from the task itself guide performance. Failure to remove instructions and interim prompts or assistance early on in training can result in the learner's waiting for assistance and not trying to complete the task independently.

Further Reading

Cooper, J. O., Heron, T. E., & Heward, W. L. (1987). *Applied Behavior Analysis.* Englewood Cliffs, NJ: Prentice Hall.

Martin, G., Koop, S., Turner, G., & Hanel, F. (1981). Backward chaining versus total task presentation to teach assembly line tasks to severely retarded persons. *Behavior Research of Severe Developmental Disabilities, 2,* 117–136.

References

Boren, J. (1969). Some variables affecting the superstitious chaining of responses. *Journal of the Experimental Analysis of Behavior, 12,* 959–969.

Boren, J., & Devine, D. (1968). The repeated acquisition of behavior chains. *Journal of the Experimental Analysis of Behavior, 11,* 651–660.

Cohen, I. (1984). Establishment of independent responding to a fire alarm in a blind, profoundly retarded adult. *Journal of Behavior Therapy and Experimental Psychiatry, 15,* 365–367.

Cooper, J. O., Heron, T. E., & Heward, W. L. (1987). *Applied behavior analysis.* Englewood Cliffs, NJ: Prentice Hall.

Crafts, L. (1929). Whole and part methods with nonserial reactions. *American Journal of Psychology, 41,* 543–563.

DeLeong, I. G., & Iwata, B. A. (1996). Evaluation of a multiple stimulus presentation format for assessing reinforcer preferences. *Journal of Applied Behavior Analysis, 29,* 519–533.

Ellen, P., & Pate, J. (1986). Is insight merely chaining? A reply to Epstein. *The Psychological Record, 36,* 155–160.

Fantino, E. (1965). Some data on the discriminative stimulus hypothesis of secondary reinforcement. *Psychological Record, 15,* 409–415.

Gold, M. (1972). Stimulus factors in skill training of retarded adolescents on a complex assembly task: Acquisition, transfer, and retention. *American Journal on Mental Deficiency, 5,* 517–526.

Hagopian, L., Farrell, D., & Amari, A. (1996). Treating total liquid refusal with backward chaining and fading. *Journal of Applied Behavior Analysis, 29,* 573–575.

Hayes, S. (1989). *Rule governed behavior: Cognition, contingencies, and instructional control.* New York: Plenum.

Jwaideh, A. (1973). Responding under chained and tandem fixed-ratio schedules. *Journal of the Experimental Analysis of Behavior, 19,* 259–267.

Kelleher, R., & Fry, W. (1962). Stimulus functions in chained fixed-interval schedules. *Journal of the Experimental Analysis of Behavior, 5,* 167–173.

Lalli, J., Casey, S., & Kates, K. (1995). Reducing escape behavior and increasing task completion with functional communication training, extinction, and response chaining. *Journal of Applied Behavior Analysis, 28,* 261–268.

Martin, G., Koop, S., Turner, G., & Hanel, F. (1981). Backward chaining versus total task presentation to teach assembly line tasks to severely retarded persons. *Behavior Research of Severe Developmental Disabilities, 2,* 117–136.

Martin, G. L., & Pear, J. J. (1999). *Behavior modification: What it is and how to do it* (6th ed). Upper Saddle River, NJ: Prentice Hall.

Martin, G. L., & Yu, D. (2000). Overview of research on

The Assessment of Basic Learning Abilities. *Journal on Developmental Disabilities 7*(2), 10–36.

McDonnell, J., & Laughlin, B. (1989). A comparison of backward and concurrent chaining strategies in teaching community skills. *Education and Training in Mental Retardation, 24*(3), 230–238.

McWilliams, R., Nietupski, J., & Hamre-Nietupski, S. (1990). Teaching complex activities to students with moderate handicaps through the forward chaining of shorter total cycle response sequences. *Education and Training in Mental Retardation, 25*(3), 292–298.

Mountjoy, P., & Lewandowski, A. (1984). The dancing horse, a learned pig, and muscle twitches. *The Psychological Record, 34*, 25–38.

Olenick, D. L., & Pear, J. J. (1980). Differential reinforcement of correct responses to probes and prompts in picture-naming training with severely retarded children. *Journal of Applied Behavior Analysis, 13*, 77–89.

Pisacreta, R. (1982). A comparison of forward and backward procedures for the acquisition of response chains in pigeons. *Bulletin of the Psychometric Society, 20*, 233–236.

Simek, T., O'Brien, R., & Figlerski, L. (1994). Contracting and chaining to improve the performance of a college golf team: Improvement and deterioration. *Perceptual and Motor Skills, 78*, 1099–1105.

Skinner, B. F. (1938). *The behavior of organisms.* New York: Appleton-Century-Crofts.

Skinner, B. F. (1953). *Science and human behavior.* New York: Free Press.

Spooner, F. (1984). Comparisons of backward chaining and total task presentation in training severely handicapped persons. *Education and Training of the Mentally Retarded, 19*(1), 75–121.

Spooner, F., Spooner, D., & Ulicny, G. (1986). Comparisons of modified backward chaining: Backward chaining with leap-aheads and reverse chaining with leap-aheads. *Education and Treatment of Children, 9*, 122–134.

Talkington, L. (1971). Response-chain learning of mentally retarded adolescents under four conditions of reinforcement. *American Journal of Mental Deficiency, 3*, 337–340.

Thvedt, J., Zane, T., & Walls, R. (1984). Stimulus functions in response chaining. *American Journal on Mental Deficiency, 88*, 661–667.

Walls, R., Zane, T., & Thvedt, J. (1980). Trainers' personal methods compared to two structured training strategies. *American Journal of Mental Deficiency, 3*, 495–507.

Weber, N. (1978). Chaining strategies for teaching sequenced motor tasks to mentally retarded adults. *The American Journal of Occupational Therapy, 32*, 385–389.

Weiss, K. (1978). A comparison of forward and backward procedures for the acquisition of response chains in humans. *Journal of the Experimental Analysis of Behavior, 29*, 255–259.

Wilson, P., Reid, D., Phillips, J., & Burgio, L. (1984). Normalization of institutional mealtimes for profoundly retarded persons: Effects and non-effects of teaching family-style dining. *Journal of Applied Behavior Analysis, 17*, 189–201.

Yu, D., Martin, G., & Williams, W. L. (1989). Expanded assessment for discrimination learning with the mentally retarded. *American Journal on Mental Retardation, 94*, 61–169.

Zane, T., Walls, R., & Thvedt, J. (1981). Prompting and fading guidance procedure: Their effect on chaining and whole task teaching strategies. *Education and Training of the Mentally Retarded, 16*(2), 125–130.

8 BEHAVIORAL CONTRACTING

Ramona Houmanfar, Kristen A. Maglieri, and Horacio R. Roman

A behavioral contract is a written or oral agreement between a client or clients and a clinician, a consultant, or an instructor that specifies expectations, plans, and/or contingencies for the behavior(s) to be changed (Martin & Pear, 1999; Kirschenbaum & Flanery, 1984). In their classic form, behavioral contracts (sometimes also called *contingency contracts*) are written, and specify a set of terms (i.e., the treatment plan) to be followed by the client, and related positive or negative consequences (Kidd & Saudargas, 1988) to be carried out conditionally on compliance or noncompliance with the plan (Homme, 1970; Kidd & Saudargas, 1988; Mann, 1972; Murphy, 1988; Petry, 2000; Welch & Holborn, 1988). Behavioral contracting has been applied to a wide variety of areas and settings, such as classroom behavior problems (Carns & Carns, 1994; De Martini-Scully, Bray, & Kehle, 2000; Homme, 1970; Ruth, 1996), instructional design (Brooks & Ruthven, 1984), addictive behaviors (Bigelow, Sticker, Liebson, & Griffiths, 1976; Mann, 1972), staff management (Azrin & Pye, 1989; Welch & Holborn, 1988), delinquency (Stuart & Lott, 1972), self-injurious behaviors (Heinssen, Levendusky, & Hunter, 1995), family relationships (Blechman, Olson, & Hellman, 1976; Jacobson, 1978), anorexia (Solanto, Jacobson, Heller, Golden, & Hertz, 1994), and weight loss programs (Anderson, Mavis, Robinson, & Stoffelmayr, 1993).

The clear and mutually negotiated guidelines in behavioral contracts serve four primary functions (Martin & Pear, 1999): (1) They provide an agreement of goals; (2) they ensure that all involved individuals have an accessible reference to monitor progress toward goals; (3) they outline specific responsibilities of the individuals involved (e.g., cost of the program to each individual in terms of time, effort, and money); and (4) they ensure that all individuals are committed to the project in that signatures are obtained.

The conceptual foundations of behavioral contracts are based on the basic principles of operant psychology (Murphy, 1988). Most behavioral contracts are based on the A-B-C approach to identifying and modifying *antecedents* to the target behavior (A), the target *behaviors* (B), and the *consequences* or reinforcers that shape and maintain behaviors (C). Since behavior is a function of its consequences, behaviors followed by positive or pleasant consequences are more likely to recur than behaviors followed by negative consequences. Behaviors that are influenced by a set of consequences can be changed by either withholding those consequences or imposing a new set of consequences. Accordingly, once problem behaviors (e.g., noncompliance with medication regime; drug or alcohol abuse) and their controlling consequences are identified, additional incentives (e.g., store vouchers, prizes, cash) and loss of privileges can be implemented through behavioral contracting to change the existing contingencies.

Behavioral contracting has particular utility for clinicians in dealing with compliance with treatment plans. Treatment noncompliance poses a major challenge to clinicians. Treatment plans that are more acceptable to clients are more likely to be followed than less acceptable plans (Kolko & Milan, 1983), and thus treatment acceptability is a critical dimension of the efficacy of a treatment plan (Kazdin, 1980; Yeaton & Sechrest, 1981). The negotiation process involved in behavioral contracting can increase treatment acceptability and compliance, and for that reason the use of negotiated contingencies and a focus on treatment process, not just outcome, are important participatory factors in design and implementation of behavioral contracts (Kirschenbaum & Flanery, 1984). Since how well the client does is directly related to how well he or she follows the contract-related contingencies, a behavioral contract should be viewed as a *tool* (Boudin, 1972) that facilitates treatment compliance and treatment efficacy.

With regard to the consequential aspect of a behavioral contract, the extent to which new consequences compete with and prevail over existing consequences is a function of three parameters: relative magnitude or size, schedule of delivery, and latency (Petry, 2000). For instance, a consequence that immediately follows a behavior may be more effective than a delayed consequence. Likewise, consequences that are delivered consistently and in small amounts tend to produce desirable change. Thus, the construction of contract terms should be preceded by an identification of reinforcers. Although one can hypothesize about the effectiveness of consequences in advance, change in behavior is the ultimate determinant of their influence. Accordingly, development and implementation of a monitoring system are essential in evaluating compliance with treatment contingencies.

WHO MIGHT BENEFIT FROM THIS TECHNIQUE?

Behavioral contracting is a treatment that is utilized in a variety of settings and for an even greater number of target behaviors, including classroom behavior, family-marital therapy, substance abuse, weight loss, smoking cessation, and physical exercise, to name a few. However, as mentioned earlier, treatment noncompliance poses a major challenge for the success of behavioral contracts, and in the selection of clients for use of behavioral contracting variables such as a client's skills and repertoire need to be considered. For example, a developmentally delayed or severely mentally ill client must be able to monitor the relevant contexts and his or her performances in them to make use of behavioral contracts as a treatment tool. Additionally, clients who exhibit behaviors that can be monitored directly through observations (e.g., attendance at meetings) or by their permanent products (e.g., urine samples) are better suited to benefit from behavioral contracts.

ASSOCIATED CHALLENGES

According to Miller (1990), difficulties with behavioral contracts develop when contracts (1) are too restrictive or parental, (2) appear to be punishing or rejecting, (3) substitute for therapy rather than enhancing therapy, and (4) are too rigid and do not allow for client determination or client input. Further, variables such as vagueness of the contract and the therapist's lack of vigilance to observe and monitor the client's compliance with the contract and implement the associated contingencies may participate in a contract's ineffective implementation.

STEP-BY-STEP PROCEDURES

This section outlines a scenario that may be experienced by a mental health professional who provides services in the area of family and marriage counseling. The example is used to illustrate the construction of an appropriate contract for a family receiving professional services.

Mr. and Mrs. Philbrick, who have been married for a little over 15 years, have sought out professional advice regarding their marital problems in addition to problems they are experiencing with their daughter. Recently, Mike (the father) has been spending more time at work and less time with the family. Rachel (the mother) feels that Mike isn't home enough and that he would rather be spending time with his friends than with his family on the weekends. Consequently, because Mike is not home during the week, communication between Mike and Rachel has declined considerably. Mike complains that the time he does spend at home is spent arguing about family matters, specifically about money. Rachel feels that she is the only one managing the household and never has time to do things for herself.

Mike and Rachel are also having trouble with their 14-year-old daughter, Katy. She frequently ignores her 10:00 curfew, sometimes coming home around 1:00 in the morning. Katy has always been a good student, but recently her grades have been starting to slip. Mike suspects that Katy may be drinking or, worse, getting into drugs. Mike and Rachel have tried to discipline Katy, but they report that nothing seems to be working. Rachel would like to spend more quality time with Katy and would like to see Mike do the same. Katy complains that her parents are always arguing and she doesn't want to be around them. Both Mike and Rachel would like to improve their marriage and their relationship with their daughter as well.

The first step in suggesting the most appropriate treatment is determining the family's or client's needs. Without a full assessment of the client's needs, determining the most appropriate course of action will be difficult and may result in targeting the wrong problem behaviors. Equally important in determining the appropriate course of treatment is identifying the client's willingness to change his or her behavior (Kirschenbaum & Flanery, 1984). Returning to the example under discussion, both Mike and Rachel have expressed an interest in improving their current situation; however, it is unclear whether Katy is committed to change as well. The initial decision to seek professional help is typically a good indicator of willingness to change; however, identifying which behavior the individual is willing to change must be determined during the interview or assessment process.

Once it has been determined that a behavioral contract is an appropriate technique to facilitate treatment, the therapist should begin to construct the written document. A well-written contract

TABLE 8.1   Key Steps in Constructing a Well-Written Behavioral Contract

1. Clearly specify the goals of the treatment and use language that is geared to the client's reading level.
2. Specify short-term as well as long-term goals.
3. Identify specific target behaviors for change.
4. Include a monitoring system to ensure that the client is meeting his or her goals.
5. Specify reward contingencies for compliance with treatment goals in addition to consequences for noncompliance.
6. Be agreed upon and signed by all involved parties.

must contain several essential pieces of information (see Table 8.1). The necessary components for constructing a behavioral contract are as follows:

1. The behavioral contract must clearly specify the goals of the treatment and use language that is geared to the client's reading level. If the client does not understand what is expected of him or her, the treatment will certainly not be followed.

2. The behavioral contract should specify short-term goals as well a long-term goal (Kirschenbaum & Flanery, 1984). The client's participation in setting his or her goals is essential in determining reasonable and obtainable goals (Locke, Shaw, Saari, & Latham, 1981; Ludwig & Geller, 1997). If treatment goals are too difficult, they will not be achieved, and subsequently any attempts to obtain the goals will not be reinforced. This may result in noncompliance with the treatment or termination of services altogether. Thus, providing reinforcing consequences for the completion of each small step toward the end goal will increase treatment success. For those individuals who do not possess the behavioral repertoire that is necessary to complete the end goal, the principle of *shaping* may be utilized (Skinner, 1953). In other words, the contract should specify relatively simple goals, initially ensuring that the client comes into contact with reinforcement. Once the client has achieved the desired level of behavior, systematic increase of goal difficulty should be implemented. For example, it may be better to set a goal for a decrease in the number of arguments between the couple (e.g., decrease by

two) that gradually becomes bigger than to start out with a very big goal at the beginning (e.g., decrease by 10).

3. The behavioral contract must identify specific target behaviors for change, and ones that will be supported in the natural environment once change occurs. It is also important that the contract specify the conditions under which target behaviors occur, including times and dates. The more specific the contract, the easier it will be to follow. This step is perhaps the most import aspect of the treatment process, but it can also be the most challenging. Identifying target behaviors in some situations may be relatively obvious (e.g., weight loss), but in others, such as family-marital interactions, it may be more difficult to pinpoint critical behaviors that will result in treatment success. For example, if the goal is to decrease arguments about money, the defining conditions of that target (topographically and situationally) should be clear.

4. Behavioral contracts should include a monitoring system to ensure that the client is meeting his or her goals. Target behaviors that are selected should be objectively quantifiable, that is, sufficiently clear that another individual can verify the completion of assigned goals. The contract should also specify the person responsible for monitoring treatment progress, how often the monitoring should occur, and by what method. Self-monitoring (the client records his or her own behavior) may be utilized in some situations, but reliability is a known problem, particularly in areas, such as drug addiction, that are difficult for the therapist to monitor (Petry, 2000). Clients are particularly likely to lie when self-report is linked to important consequences; thus, in these area reinforcers should be delivered based on the verification of products of behavior. In the area of drug use, for example, it is better to reward screened clean urinalysis data than to reward claims of abstinence. In some conditions self-monitoring can be less intrusive, less expensive, and more productive of consistent behavior change than external monitoring, particularly when the goal is personally relevant and important (Kirschenbaum & Flanery, 1984).

5. The behavioral contract must specify reward contingencies for compliance with treatment goals in addition to consequences for noncompliance. The contingencies should focus on the positive. That is, the contract should focus on what the client should do, rather than what he or she should avoid doing. The most effective contracts should specify both the reward for compliance and the consequence for noncompliance (Homme, 1970; Clark, Leukefeld, & Godlaski, 1999). Drawing from the previous example, an appropriate contract contingency for Katy would be "I agree to come home by my curfew for 3 weeks in a row. In the event that I do come home by my curfew for 3 weeks in a row, I will spend one Saturday a month shopping with my mother. In the event that I do not come home by my curfew, I will not be allowed to go shopping with my mother, and I will not be allowed to go out the following weekend." An inappropriate contingency for Katy would be "If I do not come home by my curfew, I will not be able to go out the following weekend and I will not spend one Saturday a month with my Mom shopping."

To maximize the effects of rewards, they should be delivered immediately, in frequent small amounts, and only when the desired behavior is achieved. The delivery of rewards can be systematically faded over time to lessen the amount of effort and any additional monetary costs associated with implementing the contract. For example, a reward may initially be delivered each time the desired behavior occurs and eventually decreased according to a more manageable schedule over time. If the desired behavior has not been maintained after the reinforcement schedule has been modified, the therapist should return to a reinforcement schedule that has previously produced successful performance.

6. Finally, the negotiated behavioral contract should be agreed upon and signed by all involved parties.

BEHAVIORAL CONTRACT EXAMPLE

The following example illustrates a family contract between the Philbrick family and Dr. Evans.

Mike Philbrick (father):

a. I agree to spend one family night a week with the

entire family. I agree not to argue with Rachel or Katy during this time.

b. I agree to help Katy with her homework every week on Tuesday and Thursday.

c. I agree to spend 1 hour a week on Sunday nights with Rachel discussing a topic that she chooses that is not related to work, the house, or the kids.

d. I agree to talk to Rachel about financial matters for 1 hour on Monday nights only.

e. In the event that I do a through d, I will spend one Sunday a month watching football with my friends. In the event that I do not accomplish a through d, I will not be allowed to watch football.

Rachel Philbrick (mother):

a. I agree to spend one family night a week with the entire family. I agree not to argue with Mike or Katy during this time.

b. I agree to take Katy shopping one Saturday afternoon per month. In the event that Katy does not come home by her curfew, she will not be allowed to go shopping.

c. I agree to spend 1 hour a week on Sunday nights with Mike discussing a topic that I choose that is not related to work, the house, or the kids.

d. I agree to talk to Mike about financial matters for 1 hour on Monday nights only.

e. In the event that I do a through d, I will spend one Saturday a month out of the house doing an activity that I choose.

Katy Philbrick (daughter):

a. I agree to come home by my curfew 3 weeks in a row.

b. I agree to spend one family night a week with the entire family. I agree not to argue with my Mom or Dad during this time.

c. I agree to spend the evening two days a week, Tuesday and Thursday, doing my homework with my dad.

d. In the event that I do a through c, I will spend one Saturday a month shopping with my Mom. In the event that I do not do a through c, I will not spend one Saturday a month shopping with my Mom.

By signing below, you indicate that you agree to the terms stated above and agree to monitor the completion of your treatment goals. A written record of accomplished treatment goals must be turned in to Dr. Evans every month during therapy sessions.

The behavioral contract will be monitored and revised by Dr. Evans as treatment goals are achieved.

Date _____
Family members   Negotiator
Mike Philbrick _____   Dr. Evans _____
Rachel Philbrick _____
Katy Philbrick _____

The behavioral contracting example utilized in this chapter is designed to build structure and predictability into the family system. Many families tend to highlight the negative behaviors of other family members and are often unclear about the reciprocal interaction of members' behaviors in the family unit. Consequently, behavioral contracting provides initial restructuring of the family behaviors and their antecedents and consequences. In this context, the role of the family therapist is to help the family design, initiate, and negotiate contracts; to assist in the identification and monitoring of specific problem behaviors and contingencies that are included in the contract; and eventually to facilitate the development of less formal verbal contracts in the later stages of therapy as written formal agreements become less necessary.

Further Reading

Homme, L. (1970). *How to use contingency contracting in the classroom* (revised ed.). Champaign, IL: Research Press.

Kirschenbaum, D. S., & Flanery, R. C. (1984). Toward a psychology of behavioral contracting. *Clinical Psychology Review, 4,* 597–618.

Miller, L. J. (1990). The formal treatment contract in the inpatient management of borderline personality disorder. *Hospital and Community Psychiatry, 41,* 985–987.

References

Anderson, J. V., Mavis, B. E., Robinson, J. I., & Stoffelmayr, B. E. (1993). A work-site weight management program to reinforce behavior. *Journal of Occupational Medicine, 35,* 800–804.

Azrin, N. H., & Pye, G. E. (1989). Staff management by behavioral contracting. *Behavioral Residential Treatment, 4*(2), 89–98.

Bigelow, G., Sticker, O., Liebson, I., & Griffiths, R. (1976). Maintaining disulfiram ingestion among outpatient alcoholics: A security deposit contingency contracting program. *Behavior Research and Therapy, 14*, 378–580.

Blechman, E. A., Olson, D. H. L., & Hellman, I. D. (1976). Stimulus control over family problem-solving behavior: The family contract game. *Behavior Therapy, 7*, 686–692.

Boudin, H. M. (1972). Contingency contracting as a therapeutic tool in the deceleration of amphetamine use. *Behavior Therapy, 3*, 604–608.

Brooks, R. R., & Ruthven, A. J. (1984). The effects of contingency contracting on student performance in a PSI class. *Teaching of Psychology, 11*(2), 87–89.

Carns, A. W., & Carns, M. R. (1994). Making behavioral contracts successful. *School Counseling, 42*(2), 155–160.

Clark, J. J., Leukefeld, C., & Godlaski, T. (1999). Case management and behavioral contracting: Components of rural substance abuse treatment. *Journal of Substance Abuse Treatment, 17*(4), 293–304.

De Martini-Scully, D., Bray, M. A., & Kehle, T. J. (2000). A packaged intervention to reduce disruptive behaviors in general education students. *Psychology in the Schools, 37*(2), 149–156.

Heinssen, R. K., Levendusky, P. G., & Hunter, R. H. (1995). Client as colleague: Therapeutic contracting with the seriously mentally ill. *American Psychology, 50*, 522–532.

Homme, L. (1970). *How to use contingency contracting in the classroom* (revised ed.). Champaign, IL: Research Press.

Jacobson, N. S. (1978). Specific and nonspecific factors in the effectiveness of a behavioral approach to the treatment of marital discord. *Journal of Consulting and Clinical Psychology, 46*, 442–452.

Kazdin, A. E. (1980). Acceptability of alternative treatments for deviant child behavior. *Journal of Applied Behavior Analysis, 13*, 259–273.

Kidd, T. A., & Saudargas, R. A. (1988). Positive and negative consequences in contingency contracts: Their relative effectiveness on arithmetic performance. *Education and Treatment of Children, 11*(2), 118–126.

Kirschenbaum, D. S., & Flanery, R. C. (1984). Toward a psychology of behavioral contracting. *Clinical Psychology Review, 4*, 597–618.

Kolko, D. J., & Milan, M. A. (1983). Reframing and paradoxical instruction to overcome "resistance" in the treatment of delinquent youths: A multiple baseline analysis. *Journal of Consulting and Clinical Psychology, 51*(5), 655–660.

Locke, E. A., Shaw, K. N., Saari, L. M., & Latham, G. P. (1981). Goal setting and task performance 1969–1980. *Psychological Bulletin, 90*, 125–152.

Ludwig, T. D., & Geller, E. S. (1997). Assigned versus participative goal setting and response generalization: Managing injury control among professional pizza deliverers. *Journal of Applied Psychology, 82*, 253–261.

Mann, R. A. (1972). The behavior therapeutic use of contingency contracting to control an adult behavior problem: Weight control. *Journal of Applied Behavior Analysis, 5*, 99–109.

Martin, G., & Pear, J. (1999). *Behavior modification: What is it and how to do it.* Upper Saddle River, NJ: Prentice-Hall Inc.

Miller, L. J. (1990). The formal treatment contract in the inpatient management of borderline personality disorder. *Hospital and Community Psychiatry, 41*, 985–987.

Murphy, J. J. (1988) Contingency contracting in schools: A review. *Education and Treatment of Children, 11*(3), 257–269.

Petry, N. M. (2000). A comprehensive guide to the application of contingency management procedures in clinical settings. *Drug and Alcohol Dependence, 58*, 9–25.

Ruth, W. J. (1996). Goal setting and behavior contracting for students with emotional and behavioral difficulties: Analysis of daily, weekly, and total goal attainment. *Psychology in the Schools, 33*, 153–158.

Skinner, B. F. (1953). *Science and human behavior.* New York: Free Press.

Solanto, M. V., Jacobson, M. S., Heller, L., Golden, N. H., & Hertz, S. (1994). Rate of weight gain of inpatients with anorexia nervosa under two behavioral contracts. *Pediatrics, 93*, 989–991.

Stuart, R. B., & Lott, L. A. (1972). Behavioral contracting with delinquents: A cautionary note. *Journal of Behavioral Therapy and Experimental Psychiatry, 3*, 161–169.

Welch, S. J., & Holborn, S. W. (1988). Contingency contracting with delinquents: Effects of a brief training manual on staff contract negotiation and writing skills. *Journal of Applied Behavior Analysis, 21*, 357–368.

Yeaton, W. H., & Sechrest, L. (1981). Critical dimensions in the choice and maintenance of successful treatments: Strength, integrity, and effectiveness. *Journal of Consulting and Clinical Psychology, 49*(2), 156–167.

9 BIBLIOTHERAPY

Gerald M. Rosen

The term *bibliotherapy,* in its broadest sense, refers to the use of any literary work, including fiction, in the treatment of physical or emotional problems (Alston, 1962; Tews, 1970). This definition applies when librarians recommend a book on grieving, or suggest the right existential novel for a teenager's angst. Narrowing one's focus, there exists among the wide-ranging selection of self-help books a subset of texts that can be characterized as do-it-yourself treatments. These texts present readers with specific therapeutic procedures, the content of which varies with the particular persuasions of the times. Dumont (1913), for example, published a do-it-yourself treatment book that intended to teach readers the methods of personal magnetism. More recently, during the 1970s, a sizable group of leading academic psychologists translated various behavior therapies into do-it-yourself instructional formats. Lewinsohn wrote on depression (Lewinsohn, Munoz, Zeiss, & Youngren, 1979), Brownell (1980) on weight loss, Zimbardo on shyness (Zimbardo, 1977), and Azrin on habit control (Azrin & Foxx, 1974), to name just a few.

The present chapter considers the status of today's do-it-yourself treatment books, realizing full well that this focus encompasses but a small slice of bibliotherapy and the ever-expanding universe of self-help products, which now includes computerized (Newman, Consoli, & Talor, 1997) and internet-based (Jerome & Zaylor, 2000) programs.

THE LIMITS OF SELF-HELP

At first glance, the involvement of psychologists in the development of self-help materials would appear to advance the goal of "learning how to help people help themselves." Miller (1969) had used this phrase in his 1969 presidential address to the American Psychological Association while urging psychologists to "give psychology away" (p. 1074). Consistent with Miller's goals, psychologists not only published self-help programs in the 1970s, but they also conducted a considerable amount of research on the efficacy of these programs. Glasgow and Rosen (1978, 1982) located within this time period 117 studies or case reports that evaluated behaviorally oriented self-help instructional materials. Unfortunately, findings from studies in the 1970s demonstrated that the task of "giving psychology away" was more complex than initially thought. Matson and Ollendick (1977) evaluated a book entitled *Toilet Training in Less Than a Day* (Azrin & Foxx, 1974) and found that four of five mothers in a therapist-administered condition could successfully toilet train a child, whereas only one of five mothers who self-administered the book was successful. Zeiss (1978) conducted a controlled-outcome study on the treatment of premature ejaculation. Couples were randomly assigned to receive either self-administered treatment, minimal therapist contact, or therapist-directed treatment. As in an earlier reports by Zeiss (1977) and Lowe and

Mikulas (1975), treatment with only minimal therapist contact was effective. But of six couples who self-administered treatment in Zeiss' 1978 study, none successfully completed the program.

The same pattern of findings was demonstrated more recently when Gould and Clum (1995) found a self-help book with minimal therapist contact helpful in the treatment of panic disorder (Clum, 1990), while Febbararo, Clum, Roodman, and Wright (1999) found that a totally self-administered application of the program was not effective. Febarro and colleagues questioned "the efficacy of bibliotherapy and self-monitoring interventions when utilized absent from contact with a professional who conducts the assessment and monitors treatment compliance" (p. 209). Consistent with this conclusion, a meta-analysis of bibliotherapy studies by Marrs (1995) found that the amount of therapist contact moderated outcome for individuals with anxiety problems.

The other major finding that emerges from a review of research on do-it-yourself treatment books is that too little research has been conducted. Glasgow and Rosen (1978, 1982) conducted two reviews of the literature on behavioral self-help programs in the late 1970s and noted that the overall ratio of studies to books dropped from .86 to .59 from the time of the first review to the writing of the second. A recent PsychInfo search conducted in the year 2001 (Rosen, Glasgow, & Moore, 2002) gives the initial impression that this situation may have improved. Use of the key word *bibliotherapy* turned up 205 records for the 1990s. This finding suggests a continuing and active interest in self-help materials with psychologists actively studying and advancing the development of these programs. Unfortunately, a more detailed inspection of the records was not so encouraging. If one excludes from the 205 listed references all dissertations, chapters, commentaries, and review articles, and includes only controlled studies that assessed an individual self-help book, the actual number of references for the entire decade of the 1990s dwindles to 15. This finding is particularly sobering if one considers that a book publisher once estimated that more than 2,000 self-help books were published each year (Doheny, 1988).

A more recent article in *Newsweek* (McGinn, 2000) provided this assessment of the self-help industry: "Books are just one avenue to a brand-new you. From seminars to CDs to 'personal coaching,' the self-improvement industry rakes in $2.48 billion a year, according to the research firm Marketdata Enterprises, which predicts double-digit annual growth through 2003."

Current findings on the limits of self-help raise significant concerns for the consumer who considers a self-administered approach to the treatment of psychological problems. In addition to risks attendant on self-diagnosing a problem, there is the matter of choosing among a variety of mostly untested programs, possibly developing unrealistic expectations based on the promotional blurbs that accompany these books, and dealing with negative self-attributions that may accompany program failure (Barrera, Rosen, & Glasgow, 1981). Given these concerns, the developers of do-it-yourself treatment books have an ethical responsibility to properly develop, test, and market their programs (Rosen, 1987, 1993).

SELF-HELP MATERIALS IN CLINICAL PRACTICE

Although research findings on do-it-yourself treatment books strike a cautionary note for consumers who want to totally self-administer a program, it should be remembered that this is but one side of the empirical coin. Although research demonstrates that some programs fail when self-administered, these same studies generally support self-help efforts when therapist assistance is provided. Consider for example the previously cited studies by Zeiss, who found that couples were successful when treating premature ejaculation with minimal therapist assistance but unsuccessful when they applied the same methods on a totally self-administered basis (Zeiss, 1977, 1978). Zeiss handled this issue when he published a self-help book (Zeiss & Zeiss, 1978) by providing this cautionary statement to consumers:

> Research we have done with an earlier version of this program suggests . . . that couples have a lot of difficulty following through with the program on

their own. In our research, minimal contact with a therapist averaging only 6 minutes a week makes a tremendous difference in couples' abilities to complete treatment. . . . You may wish to make similar arrangements for yourselves. (pp. 36–37)

Here Zeiss observed that research provided strong support for the use of bibliotherapeutic materials when minimal therapist assistance was provided. Six minutes a week of a therapist's time along with an inexpensive book is a compelling alternative to costly weekly meetings at a sex therapy clinic.

Numerous publications have encouraged clinicians to consider the benefits of self-help therapies (e.g., Quackenbush, 1992; Warner, 1992). Starker (1988) demonstrated that clinicians held a positive view of self-help materials and frequently prescribed them to clients. A more detailed analysis of the uses of self-help materials was provided by Barrera, Rosen, and Glasgow (1981). These authors observed that self-help therapies can be used at the front end of an intervention, prior to actually commencing therapy, as a means to educate a prospective client and assist in the structuring of accurate expectations. One of the earliest illustrations of this use of self-help materials was provided by Patterson, who used programmed texts, such as *Living with Children* (Patterson & Gullion, 1968), to teach parents the basic principles of child management before beginning more intensive therapist-directed work (Patterson, Reid, Jones, & Conger, 1975). Isaac Marks (1978) understood this point as well when he provided this advice to readers of his self-help fear reduction program: "Severe problems are best handled by professional therapists, but you can help them help you if you understand your difficulty a bit better and get some idea of how to cope with it" (pp. x–xi).

There are numerous ways self-help materials can be used during therapeutic interventions (Barrera, Rosen, & Glasgow, 1981) once clinicians shift their thinking from therapist-directed efforts to the flexible possibilities of therapist-assisted approaches. *Therapist-directed* refers to a traditional approach to treatment wherein the therapist and patient meet for regular sessions with minimal or no use of supplemental instructional materials. *Therapist-assisted,* on the other hand, refers to a collaborative relationship between the client and therapist in which self-directed efforts are conducted by the client with varying levels of involvement from the professional. Variations on therapist-assisted approaches are nearly limitless, allowing therapists to economically monitor a client's efforts with telephone contacts, e-mail communications, or infrequent sessions.

A properly chosen bibliotherapy program can expand the range of services available to the public by allowing the consumer to self-direct his or her own treatment under varying levels of professional supervision. This approach can reduce time demands on a therapist, thereby reducing treatment costs while allowing the professional to serve more clients. Client-therapist collaborative efforts that use self-help programs can reach individuals who live in remote areas and are unable to make weekly appointments in cities where practitioners tend to locate. Self-help instructional materials can also be used at the end of a treatment intervention to increase a client's involvement in maintenance strategies.

CHOOSING THE RIGHT MATERIALS

Because there is little research on the effectiveness of self-help materials, consumers and clinicians have little direction for picking a program. Norcross and colleagues have attempted to provide some guidance by polling psychologists and rating available self-help books in a treatise entitled *The Authoritative Guide to Self-Help Resources in Mental Health* (Norcross et al., 2000). This type of review is not based on actual outcome studies; instead, recommendations are based on personal preferences and/or surveys that poll psychologists on the materials they like to use. Popularity polls among psychologists who use self-help materials in therapist-assisted contexts provide no useful information on the public's ability to self-administer a program at home. They also provide limited information to an empirically minded behavior therapist, who would be unimpressed if a Gallup poll showed that the majority of colleagues liked the Rorschach. A 1 to 5 star popularity rating provided by opinion surveys falls short of good

TABLE 9.1   Key Points Regarding Bibliotherapy

- Untested bibliotherapy materials in the form of do-it-yourself treatments can pose risks to consumers.

- The provision of minimal therapist assistance has been shown to greatly enhance the effectiveness of some self-help programs.

- Therapist-assisted therapy can be provided with great flexibility, using phone contacts, e-mail consultations, in-office sessions, or any combination of these as needed.

- One day it may be unethical not to inform consumers that a tested bibliotherapy provides an effective alternative to therapist-directed interventions.

science and does not provide a sound basis for consumer or clinician confidence.

Unfortunately, general surveys, recommendations of colleagues, and personal preferences remain the primary basis for deciding which instructional materials are likely to facilitate therapist-assisted treatment efforts. In truth, we are no better off than psychologists back in the 1970s. There are few studies, no practice guidelines, no data on optimal levels of contact that should be maintained with a client, and no rules for determining which patients are most likely to benefit from therapist-assisted treatments. Perhaps one day this will change and systematic research programs will lead to the development of effective do-it-yourself programs and practice guidelines (Rosen, Glasgow, & Moore, 2002). Until that day arrives, clinicians are on their own with one nagging concern to keep in mind. If studies like those conducted by Clum on panic disorder or Zeiss on sexual dysfunction demonstrate that a book with minimal therapist assistance does as well as therapist-directed treatment, is it incumbent upon psychologists to tell this to clients as part of informed consent? An answer to this question will be more pressing once a greater empirical basis is established for the use of bibliotherapy as an adjunct to clinician-administered treatments. (See Table 9.1 for key points in the use of bibliotherapy.)

Further Reading

Rosen, G. M., Glasgow, R. E., & Moore, T. E. (in press). Self-help therapy: The science and business of giving psychology away. In S. O. Lilienfeld, J. M. Lohr, & S. J. Lynn (Eds.), *Science and pseudoscience in contemporary clinical psychology* (pp. 399–424). New York: Guilford Press.

Starker, S. (1989). *Oracle at the supermarket: The American preoccupation with self-help books.* New Brunswick, NJ: Transaction.

References

Alston, E. F. (1962). Bibliotherapy and psychotherapy. *Library Trends, 11,* 159–176.

Azrin, N. H., & Foxx, R. M. (1974). *Toilet training in less than a day.* New York: Simon & Schuster.

Barrera, M., Jr., Rosen, G. M., & Glasgow, R. E. (1981). Rights, risks, and responsibilities in the use of self-help psychotherapy. In G. T. Hannah, W. P. Christian, & H. B. Clark (Eds.), *Preservation of client rights* (pp. 204–220). New York: The Free Press.

Brownell, K. D. (1980). *The partnership diet program.* New York: Rawon.

Clum, G. A. (1990). *Coping with panic.* Pacific Grove, CA: Brooks/Cole Publishing.

Doheny, K. (1988). Self-help. *Los Angeles Times,* 2 October, part VI, 1.

Dumont, T. Q. (1913). *The art and science of personal magnetism.* Chicago: Advance Thought.

Febbraro, G. A. R., Clum, G. A., Roodman, A. A., & Wright, J. H. (1999). The limits of bibliotherapy: A study of the differential effectiveness of self-administered interventions in individuals with panic attacks. *Behavior Therapy, 30,* 209–222.

Glasgow, R. E., & Rosen, G. M. (1978). Behavioral bibliotherapy: A review of self-help behavior therapy manuals. *Psychological Bulletin, 85,* 1–23.

Glasgow, R. E., & Rosen, G. M. (1982). Self-help behavior therapy manuals: Recent development and clinical usage. *Clinical Behavior Therapy Review, 1,* 1–20.

Gould, R. A., & Clum, G. A. (1995). Self-help plus minimal therapist contact in the treatment of panic disorder: A replication and extension. *Behavior Therapy, 26,* 533–546.

Jerome, L. W., & Zaylor, C. (2000). Cyberspace: Creating a therapeutic environment for telehealth applications. *Professional Psychology: Research and Practice, 31,* 478–483.

Lewinsohn, P., Munoz, R. F., Zeiss, A., & Youngren, M. A. (1979). *Control your depression.* Englewood Cliffs, NJ: Prentice-Hall.

Lowe, J. C., & Mikulas, W. L. (1975). Use of written material in learning self-control of premature ejaculation. *Psychological Reports, 37,* 295–298.

Marks, I. M. (1978). *Living with fear: Understanding and coping with anxiety.* New York: McGraw-Hill.

Marrs, R. W. (1995). A meta-analysis of bibliotherapy studies. *American Journal of Community Psychology, 23,* 843–870.

Matson, J. L., & Ollendick, T. H. (1977). Issues in toilet training normal children. *Behavior Therapy, 8,* 549–553.

McGinn, D. (2000). Self-help U.S.A. *Newsweek,* 10 February, 43–47.

Miller, G. A. (1969). Psychology as a means of promoting human welfare. *American Psychologist, 24,* 1063–1075.

Newman, M. G., Consoli, A., & Talor, C. B. (1997). Computers in assessment and cognitive behavioral treatment of clinical disorders: Anxiety as a case in point. *Behavior Therapy, 28,* 211–235.

Norcross, J. C., Santrock, J. W., Campbell, L. F., Smith, T. P., Sommer, R., & Zuckerman, E. L. (2000). *Authoritative guide to self-help resources in mental health.* New York: Guilford Press.

Patterson, G. R., & Gullion, M. E. (1968). *Living with children.* Champaign, IL: Research Press.

Patterson, G. R., Reid, J. B., Jones, R. R., & Conger, R. E. (1975). *A social learning approach to family interventions: Families with aggressive children* (vol. 1). Eugene, OR: Castalia Publishing.

Quackenbush, R. L. (1992). The prescription of self-help books by psychologists: A bibliography of selected bibliotherapy resources. *Psychotherapy, 28,* 671–677.

Rosen, G. M. (1987). Self-help treatment books and the commercialization of psychotherapy. *American Psychologist, 42,* 46–51.

Rosen, G. M. (1993). Self-help or hype? Comments on psychology's failure to advance self-care. *Professional Psychology: Research and Practice, 24,* 340–345.

Rosen, G. M., Glasgow, R. E., & Moore, T. E. (2002). Self-help therapy: The science and business of giving psychology away. In S. O. Lilienfeld, J. M. Lohr, & S. J. Lynn (Eds.), *Science and pseudoscience in contemporary clinical psychology* (pp. 399–424). New York: Guilford Press.

Starker, S. (1988). Do-it-yourself therapy: The prescription of self-help books by psychologists. *Psychotherapy, 25,* 142–146.

Tews, R. M. (1970). Progress in bibliotherapy. In M. J. Voigt (Ed.), *Advances in librarianship* (vol. 1). New York: Academic Press.

Warner, R. E. (1992). Bibliotherapy: A comparison of the prescription practices of Canadian and American psychologists. *Canadian Psychology, 32,* 529–530.

Zeiss, R. A. (1977). Self-directed treatment for premature ejaculation: Preliminary case reports. *Journal of Behavior Therapy and Experimental Psychiatry, 8,* 87–91.

Zeiss, R. A. (1978). Self-directed treatment for premature ejaculation. *Journal of Consulting and clinical Psychology, 46,* 1234–1241.

Zeiss, R. A., & Zeiss, A. (1978). *Prolong your pleasure.* New York: Pocket Books.

Zimbardo, P. G. (1977). *Shyness.* New York: Jove.

10 BIOBEHAVIORAL APPROACH TO BOWEL AND TOILET TRAINING TREATMENT

Patrick C. Friman

INTRODUCTION

Functional encopresis (FE) is a common, undertreated, and often overinterpreted form of fecal incontinence. Although all forms of incontinence require evaluation and treatment, when left untreated FE is more likely than other forms such as enuresis to lead to serious and potentially life-threatening medical sequelae and seriously impaired social acceptance, relations, and development. The reasons for the medical sequelae will be summarized briefly later. The primary reason for the social impairment is that soiling evokes more revulsion from peers, parents, and important others than other forms of incontinence (and most other behavior problems). As an example, severe corporal punishment for fecal accidents was still recommended by professionals in the late nineteenth century (Henoch, 1889). The professional approach to FE has evolved substantially since then, but the approaches by laypersons (and still some professionals) are not keeping pace. Children with FE are still frequently shamed, blamed, and punished for a condition that is almost totally beyond their control (Friman & Jones, 1998; Levine, 1982).

The definition of FE has remained relatively consistent across versions of the *Diagnostic and Statistical Manual of Mental Disorders* (*DSM*); the fourth edition of the *Manual* (*DSM-IV;* American Psychiatric Association, 1994) lists four criteria for FE: (1) There is repeated passage of feces into inappropriate places, whether involuntary or intentional; (2) at least one such event occurs per month for at least 3 months; (3) chronological age is at least 4 years (or equivalent developmental level); and (4) the behavior is not due exclusively to the direct physiological effects of a substance or a general medical condition except through a mechanism involving constipation. The *DSM-IV* describes two types: primary, in which the child has never had fecal continence, and secondary, in which incontinence returns after at least 6 months of continence. Approximately 3 percent of the general pediatric population meets these criteria.

UNDERLYING PROCESS

Successful treatment for FE targets the processes that cause the condition, and 90–95 percent of cases occur as a function of, or in conjunction with, reduced colonic motility, constipation, and fecal retention, and the various behavioral or dietary factors contributing to these conditions, which include (1) insufficient roughage or bulk in the diet; (2) irregular diet; (3) insufficient oral intake of fluids; (4) medications that may have a side effect of constipation; (5) unstructured, inconsistent, and/or punitive approaches to toilet training; and (6) toileting avoidance by the child. Any of these factors, singly or in combination, puts the child at risk for reduced colonic motility, actual constipation, and corresponding uncomfortable or painful bowel movements. Uncomfortable or painful bowel movements, in turn, negatively reinforce fecal retention, and retention leads to a regressive reciprocal cycle, which often results in regular fecal accidents. When the constipation is severe or the cycle is chronic, the child may develop fecal impaction, a large blockage caused by the collection of hard dry stool. Not infrequently, liquid fecal matter will seep around the fecal mass, producing what is known as *paradoxical diarrhea.* Although the child is actually constipated, he or she appears to have diarrhea. Some parents will attempt to treat this type of apparent diarrhea with the over-the-counter antidiarrheal agents, which only worsen the problem.

Of note is that a small minority of cases do not involve any problems with colonic motility or constipation; they involve regular, well-formed, soft bowel movements that occur somewhere other than the toilet. The process underlying these cases is not well understood; it is known, however, that they tend to be treatment resistant (Friman & Jones, 1998; also see Landman & Rappaport, 1985).

EVALUATION

The therapist faced with an encopretic child should essentially go no further with treatment until the child has received a medical evaluation. Two primary reasons for this cautionary dictate are the possibility of organic disease (see the "Contraindications" section) and the medical risk posed by fecal matter inexorably accumulating in an organ with a limited amount of space. An unfortunately all too frequent presenting problem in medical clinics is an encopretic child who has been in extended therapy with a nonmedical professional whose initial evaluation did not include referral for a medical evaluation and whose treatment did not address the etiology of FE (see the "Underlying Process" section). As a result, the children's colonic systems can become painfully and dangerously distended, some-

times to the point of being life-threatening (e.g., McGuire, Rothenberg, & Tyler, 1983).

The medical evaluation will typically involve a thorough medical, dietary, and bowel history. In addition, abdominal palpation and rectal examination are used to check for large amounts of fecal matter, very dry fecal matter in the rectal vault, and poor sphincter tone. Approximately 70 percent of constipation can be determined on physical exam, and detection can be increased to above 90 percent with an x-ray of kidneys, ureter, and bladder (KUB; Barr, Levine, Wilkinson, & Mulvihill, 1979).

Despite the emphasis on diet and behavior here, gleaned from the most empirical parts of literature, some psychologists and psychiatrists persist in viewing FE as a psychological problem. Yet over the past 15 years, several studies have concluded that, although some children with FE also have psychological problems, the incidence is simply not high enough to suggest a causal relationship between the two conditions (Friman & Jones, 1998). Thus, targeting psychological problems in order to obtain fecal continence would seem imprudent from the perspective of the scientific literature. Rather, when FE and behavioral or psychological problems co-occur, they often have to be treated separately. For example, children who have poorly developed instructional control skills are at risk for being noncompliant with treatment, and thus instructional control training may need to precede or accompany treatment for FE.

CONTRAINDICATIONS

Some medical conditions (e.g., Hirschprung's disease, hypothyroidism), if identified, may preclude referral to a therapist. The most common organic cause of bowel dysfunction is Hirschprung's disease, a condition involving segments of nonenervated tissue in the colon. To become familiar with the differential presentation of Hirschprung's and FE, therapists may wish to consult publications that compare and contrast the symptoms of the two disorders (e.g., Christophersen & Mortweet, 2001; Levine, 1982). Additionally, slow or absent weight gain in children who are below expected weight levels for their age may indicate a malabsorption syndrome and

TABLE 10.1 Sample Biobehavioral Treatment Plan

1. Refer to appropriately trained physician for evaluation.

2. Demystify bowel movements and problems and eliminate all punishment.

3. Completely evacuate bowel. Evacuation procedures are prescribed and overseen by physician.

4. Establish regular toileting schedule. Ensure that child's feet are on a flat surface during toileting.

5. Establish monitoring and motivational system.

6. Require child participation in cleanup.

7. Teach appropriate wiping and flushing.

8. Implement dietary changes that include regularity of meals and increases in fluid and fiber intake.

9. Utilize facilitative medication. What, when, and how much are to be established by physician.

10. Establish method for fading facilitative medication.

thus require specialized medical treatment (see Barr et al., 1979). Lastly, in a small percentage of cases FE is secondary to extraordinary emotional disturbance and thus resistant to behavioral or medical treatment focused primarily on FE (e.g., Landman & Rappaport, 1985). In such cases, the emotional condition may be a treatment priority, especially when there is no evidence of constipation or fecal retention. (See Table 10.1, "Sample Biobehavioral Treatment Plan," for an overview.)

TREATMENT: RETENTIVE FE

Although the child is the target of treatment, the parent (or primary caregiver) is the delivery agent and thus the primary recipient of the information about treatment. Discussing treatment in general terms with the child while expressing optimism about outcome is good practice. Additionally, any punitive parental responses toward fecal accidents, both intentional and unintentional, are to be terminated immediately. Requesting a related promise from the parent in the presence of the child can increase child interest in participation. Treatment is then laid out in a series of steps.

Demystifying FE

During or immediately following the evaluation, the entire elimination process, including its disordered manifestations, should be demystified (Levine, 1982). The belief, born of longstanding

characterological and psychopathological perspectives on FE, that bowel retention and bowel accidents are generally associated with personality development, and specifically with such characteristics as stubbornness, immaturity, or laziness, can result in parents' shaming and blaming their children into the bathroom. But a disordered process of elimination such as FE should no more be a target for censure and blame than should a disordered process of respiration, digestion, or motor movement. As indicated above, the literature does not reflect a significant association between psychological profiles and child bowel problems.

Bowel Evacuation

The primary goal of FE treatment is the establishment of regular bowel movements in the toilet, and the first step is to cleanse the bowel completely of resident fecal matter. A variety of methods are used, the most common of which involve enemas, laxatives, or a combination of the two. Although the therapist can assist with the prescription of these (e.g., with suggestions about timing, interactional style, behavioral management, etc.) the evacuation procedure must be prescribed and overseen by the child's physician. Typically, evacuation procedures are conducted in the child's home, but severe resistance can necessitate medical assistance, in which case the procedures must be completed in a medical setting. The ultimate goal, however, is complete parent management of evacuation procedures because they are to be used whenever the child's eliminational pattern suggests excessive fecal retention.

Toileting Schedule

The parent and therapist should choose a regular time for the child to attempt bowel movements. The time should not be during school hours, because unpleasant social responses to bowel movements in the school setting can cause regressive responses to treatment (e.g., retention). The choice among the times that remain (morning, afternoon, or evening) should be guided by the child's typical habits and child-parent time constraints. Establishing a time shortly after food intake can increase chances of success through the influence of the gastrocolonic reflex. In the early stages of treatment or in difficult cases, two scheduled attempts a day (e.g., after breakfast and dinner) may be necessary. The time the child is required to sit on the toilet should be limited to 10 or fewer minutes in order to avoid unnecessarily increasing the aversive properties of the toileting experience. The child's feet should be supported by a flat surface (e.g., the floor or a small stool) to increase comfort, maintain circulation in the extremities, and facilitate the abdominal push necessary to expel fecal matter from the body. The time should also be unhurried and free from distraction or observation by anyone other than the managing parent. Allowing children to listen to music, read, or talk with the parent can improve child attitude toward toileting requirements. Generally, toileting should be a relaxed, pleasant, and ultimately private affair.

Response to Toileting Efforts

If the child has a bowel movement in the toilet, he or she should be praised. In the early stages of treatment it is also helpful to have a reward system in place. An easy system involves a dot-to-dot drawing and a grab bag. The child identifies an affordable and desirable prize and the parent draws (or traces) a picture of it using a dot-to-dot format with every third or fourth dot bigger than the rest. The child connects two dots for each bowel movement in the toilet, and when the line reaches a larger dot, he or she earns access to a grab bag with small rewards (e.g., small toys, edibles, money, privileges). When all the dots are connected, the child earns the prize (Friman & Jones, 1998). A less elaborate and more naturalistic, but also more time-intensive, procedure involves the provision of special time. For example, following successful toileting a child might be allowed 10 to 15 minutes of special time with a parent during which the child is allowed to choose the activity (Christophersen & Mortweet, 2001). If the child does not have a bowel movement his or her effort should be praised, and another session should be scheduled for later in the day.

Response to Accidents

Accidents should not be the object of punishment or criticism. However, the child should partici-pate in cleaning up the mess that has been made. With younger children this may merely mean bringing soiled clothing to the laundry area and allowing themselves to be cleaned by the parent. With older children it may mean managing the entire mess themselves, including doing the laundry and cleaning their person. Children should earn praise and rewards for any bowel movements in the toilet, even if they had a prior accident.

In treatment-resistant cases, however, mild aversive consequences are sometimes used. Although there is little documentation of their effects, there is ample evidence of their use. One example, a procedure called *positive practice*, involves intensive practice of appropriate toileting behaviors following detection of an accident (e.g., a series of dry run trips to the bathroom from locations near detection of the accident; see Christophersen & Mortweet, 2001). Another example for which a small amount of data has been published involves a response cost procedure: using small tokens to reward toileting success and withdrawal of tokens (i.e., small fines) for accidents (Reimers, 1996).

Cleanliness Training

Successful toileting is a complex arrangement of small tasks, and two that are critical to overall success but often overlooked in fecal incontinence programs are wiping and flushing. The therapist should provide the parents instructions on how to motivate and teach children to complete these tasks.

Monitoring

Frequent monitoring accomplishes at least three goals: early detection of accidents, assessment of progress, and multiple opportunities for praise. Two levels of monitoring are usually employed. The first involves regular pants checks, which result in praise when pants are accident free and the procedure for accidents previously described when they are not. The second involves a record completed by the parent that documents toileting successes and accidents and the size and consistency of both. The therapist can make the latter record easier to keep by providing the parent with a user-friendly data sheet.

Dietary Changes

As discussed in the section on underlying processes, diet often plays a causal role in FE, and dietary changes are almost always part of treatment. One of the keys to establishing full fecal continence is a regular diet with a high level of dietary fiber. Fiber increases colonic motility and the moisture in colonic contents and thus facilitates easier and more regular bowel movements. To aid the parents in increasing the fiber content in their child's diet, an educational handout can be helpful (see Christophersen & Mortweet, 2001, for an example). Dietary changes can also be enhanced with over-the-counter preparations with dense fiber content (e.g., Metamucil, Perdiem).

Facilitating Medication

Successful treatment for FE will almost always require inclusion of medications that soften fecal matter, ease its migration through the colon, and/or aid its expulsion from the rectum. It is the consulting physician's decision whether to use medication (and, if so, what type); however, the therapist can inform the decision and educate the parent about its use. Generally it is best to avoid interfering with the sensitive biochemistry of the alimentary system, the colonic portion of it in particular, and thus inert substances are usually used. The most frequently used substance is mineral oil, used alone or in combination with other ingredients, such as magnesium. As indicated, prescription of the substance is the physician's prerogative, but ensuring compliance with the prescription is typically the therapist's task. Children will often resist ingesting substances with odd tastes and textures, and thus to gain their cooperation it is often necessary to mix the substances with a preferred liquid (e.g., orange juice) and follow ingestion with praise and appreciation.

A more invasive substance involves glycerin suppositories. Some physicians prescribe these because their use increases the predictability of bowel movements and reduces the likelihood of an out-of-home accident. When prescribed, suppositories should be used in the following sequence. Prior to the meal closest in time to the regularly scheduled toileting, the child should attempt a bowel movement. If the attempt is suc-cessful, regular procedures are followed and no suppository is given. If it is unsuccessful, a suppository should be inserted by the parent, the meal eaten by the child, and another attempt made after the meal. The combination of the gastrocolonic reflex initiated by the meal and the lubrication and mechanical stimulation provided by the suppository is usually sufficient to inaugurate a bowel movement. These advantages notwithstanding, inserting suppositories into a child's body can engender resistance, and in such cases the therapist can assist the process by teaching the child how to relax under stressful circumstances and by teaching the parent how to use instructional and motivational procedures to enhance compliance.

Fading Facilitative Medication

Ever cognizant that medication is the province of the physician, therapists can assist with its use by establishing methods to ensure it is taken (as described) and to design systematic steps for its ultimate withdrawal. Obviously partnership with the consulting physician is necessary in both cases. A frequently used withdrawal method is to eliminate the medication on one day a week contingent upon a series of consecutive accident-free, toileting success days (e.g., 14). The child is allowed to choose the day. If another similar series occurs, another day is chosen. If the child has an accident, the medication is replaced on one day. The parent and child go back and forth inside this system until the medication is completed faded out.

Treatment Resistance

As indicated above, in some cases direct FE treatment may be forestalled by, or conducted in conjunction with, treatment for the resistance (e.g., with instructional control training or psychotherapy). Some treatment-resistant cases, however, involve abnormal defecation dynamics (e.g., rectal distension, decreased sensitivity) much more than abnormal externalizing or internalizing behavior problems. For these cases various forms of biofeedback have been used to increase awareness and establish bowel habits (e.g., Loening-Baucke, 1990).

Evidence of Effectiveness

The first treatment-based break with characterological (punishment) and psychopathological (psychotherapy) perspectives on FE was provided by Murray Davidson, who described what has come to be called the pediatric approach (Davidson, 1958). The regimen involved starting a child on a daily dose of mineral oil and increasing the dosage until regular bowel functioning was established. The mineral oil regimen was often accompanied by reductions in dairy products and increases in fruits and vegetables and its initial evaluation yielded a high rate of success (90 percent; Davidson, Kugler, & Bauer, 1963).

Over the past 20 years, several descriptive and controlled experimental studies have supported the incorporation of Davidson's pediatric regimen into the multicomponent biobehavioral approach recommended here (Christophersen & Mortweet, 2001; Friman & Jones, 1998), and numerous documentations of success have led to the listing of this approach as an empirically supported treatment by the *Journal of Pediatric Psychology* (McGrath, Mellon, & Murphy, 2000). In fact, the literature on this comprehensive approach has progressed sufficiently to lead to group implementation. In the initial evaluation of group treatment, 18 encopretic children between the ages of 4 and 11 years and their parents were seen in groups of three to five families for six sessions. It is noteworthy that all of these children had previously failed a solely medical regimen. Soiling accidents decreased by 84 percent across the groups, and these results were maintained or improved at 6-month follow-up (Stark, Owens-Stively, Spirito, Lewis, & Guevremont, 1990).

Targeting Only the Symptom?

An occasionally voiced concern with the comprehensive direct treatment approach is that targeting only the symptoms of FE may produce behavioral or psychological side effects (e.g., symptom substitution). At least two large studies have undermined this concern. The first used a behavioral inventory to compare (before and after treatment and at 3-year follow-up) a group of encopretic children who were cured with a group who were not cured to determine whether any significant symptom substitution occurred in children cured of FE (Levine, Mazonson, & Bakow, 1980). The conclusion of the first study, that successful treatment was not accompanied by any problematic behavioral side effects, was replicated in the second, which used even more measures and analytic methods (e.g., Young, Brennen, Baker, & Baker, 1995).

FE without Constipation

Treatment of nonretentive FE is not well established; thus, recommending an optimal course of treatment is premature. Perhaps the best approach would begin with a comprehensive psychological evaluation that includes behavioral assessment techniques. Virtually all investigators who have described this subsample of children report emotional and behavioral problems and treatment resistance (e.g., Landman & Rappaport, 1985), and it is possible that some of these children's soiling is related to modifiable aspects of their social ecology. Some investigators have employed versions of the approach outlined previously and have included supportive verbal therapy (Landman & Rappaport, 1985) or have specifically taught parents how to manage their children's misbehavior (Stark et al., 1990). Clearly the various problems, other than soiling, exhibited by this subsample require some form of treatment (but the soiling itself needs direct treatment too).

PREVENTION

Functional encopresis can be a preventable condition. There are known risk factors and often a predictable developmental course. In his discussion of the causes of FE, Levine (1982) described three stages of its development. Such descriptions would aid the identification of children who would be most likely to benefit from preventive interventions.

According to Levine, in stage one (infants and toddlers) the primary causal variables are simple constipation and parental overreaction. In this stage a provider (probably a pediatrician but possibly a psychologist) should use demystification (described earlier) to initiate a preventive intervention. The general demystified instructions for parents should emphasize consistent, nonaggressive, well-informed management of any or all bowel problems, especially constipation. Parents should also be provided information on toileting readiness (e.g., Christophersen & Mortweet, 2001; Friman & Jones, 1998) before setting up a bowel training program. In general, no reaction at all to a bowel problem is better than an overreaction (Levine, 1982).

During stage two (3 to 5 years of age) the various stresses associated with toilet training are of paramount concern. Preventive efforts should include continued demystification, which at this stage involves gentle assistance with all toileting tasks, and encouragement to work on, and to talk about, toileting tasks. During stage two such aids as toilet seats and small stools for foot leverage may be helpful. Also, increased dietary fiber will loosen and moisten stools and help to prevent painful passage of hard stools. Most important is the avoidance of coercion, negative feedback, and inducements to rush the toileting process. The child should be encouraged to sit on the toilet at least once a day but for not longer than 5 minutes. The time for this toileting episode should be consistent across days, and the child should be praised for adherence to the schedule (Christoherson & Mortweet, 2001; Friman & Jones, 1998; Levine, 1982).

During stage three (early school years) scheduling toileting episodes becomes the primary concern. Toileting schedules at this stage are particularly critical for children whose risk of FE has increased because of problems during stages one and two. The psychosocial reactions to bowel movements at school, especially schools without doors on toilets stalls, can be a problem for the child at risk (Levine, 1982). For such children, a preventive effort should involve the regulation of bowel movements so that they occur in the children's home either before or after school. Perhaps the best method of increasing adherence to a home schedule is the use of suppositories (although potential problems with their use were noted earlier). In addition to regulation of bowel movements, the preventive intervention for the school-aged child at risk should include increased dietary fiber, elevated activity levels, increased fluid intake, continued demystification, and praise for the absence of accidents (Levine, 1982).

The preventive intervention recommended here is, however, at its most burdensome a mild treatment procedure and at its least burdensome a mild toilet training procedure. Thus, implementation of the intervention may not require a great deal of extra effort from the parents or the therapist. In fact, with the exception of those cases where suppositories are needed, prevention is equivalent to ordinary toilet training conducted at an appropriate age level. Therefore, the best preventive maneuver would be to provide all children with the intervention recommended for children at risk. Bowel training is, after all, a human experience that is often fraught with complications (Levine, 1982). It is difficult to ascertain how the interventions used to ease those complications in children at risk for FE would cause problems when used with children whose risk is lower. Conversely, the procedure might simplify the entire bowel training process for everyone concerned.

CONCLUSION

Functional encopresis has been misunderstood, misinterpreted, and mistreated for centuries. During the last half of the twentieth century, however, and particularly toward its end, a fuller, biobehavioral understanding of FE's causal conditions was obtained and an empirically supported approach to its treatment established. The biobehavioral understanding and approach to FE are dramatically different from the psychogenic understanding and approach of history. The biobehavioral approach addresses the physiology of defecation primarily and addresses the psychology of the child as a set of variables that are not causal but can be critical to active participation in treatment. The psychogenic approach, however, addressed the psychology of child primarily, especially insofar as causal variables were of interest, and gave minimal attention to the physiology of defecation. Although evaluation and treatment of FE absolutely require the direct involvement of a physician, ideal management involves a partnership between the physician, therapist, and family. In simple terms, the physician prescribes the treatment for FE, especially the parts pertaining to defection dynamics in general and evacuating the colon, changing the texture of fecal matter, and increasing colonic motility in particular. In an alliance with the physician (and family), the therapist addresses the educational, behavioral, and motivational variables that are critical to the implementation of treatment and a successful outcome. This united, biobehavioral approach can eliminate or at least minimize the possibility of the damaging overinterpretation and dangerous forms of treatment that blemished the approach to FE from antiquity through most of the twentieth century.

Further Readings

Christophersen, E. R., & Mortweet, S. (2001). *Treatments that work with children.* Washington, DC: American Psychological Association.

Friman, P. C., & Jones, K. M. (1998). Elimination disorders in children. In S. Watson & F. Gresham (Eds.), *Handbook of child behavior therapy* (pp. 239–260). New York: Plenum.

Levine, M. D. (1982). FE: Its potentiation, evaluation, and alleviation. *Pediatric Clinics of North America, 29,* 315–330.

References

American Psychiatric Association (1994). *Diagnostic and statistical manual of mental disorders* (4th ed.). Washington, DC: Author.

Barr, R. G., Levine, M. D., Wilkinson, R. H., & Mulvihill, D. (1979). Chronic and occult stool retention: A clinical tool for its evaluation in school aged children. *Clinical Pediatrics, 18,* 674–686.

Christophersen, E. R., & Mortweet, S. (2001). *Treatments that work with children.* Washington, DC: American Psychological Association. Davidson, M. (1958). Constipation and fecal incontinence. *Pediatric Clinics of North America, 5,* 749–757.

Davidson, M., Kugler, M. M., & Bauer, C. H. (1963). Diagnosis and management in children with severe and protracted constipation and obstipation. *Journal of Pediatrics, 62,* 261–275.

Friman, P. C., & Jones, K. M. (1998). Elimination disorders in children. In S. Watson & F. Gresham (Eds.), *Handbook of child behavior therapy* (pp. 239–260). New York: Plenum.

Henoch, E. H. (1889). *Lectures on children's diseases* (vol. 2; J. Thompson, Trans.). London: New Syndenham Society.

Landman, G. B., & Rappaport, L. (1985). Pediatric management of severe treatment resistant FE. *Journal of Developmental and Behavioral Pediatrics, 6,* 349–351.

Levine, M. D. (1982). FE: Its potentiation, evaluation, and alleviation. *Pediatric Clinics of North America, 29,* 315–330.

Levine, M. D., & Bakow, H. (1976). Children with FE: A study of treatment outcome. *Pediatrics, 58,* 845–852.

Levine, M. D., Mazonson, P., & Bakow, H. (1980). Behavioral symptom substitution in children cured of encopresis. *American Journal of Diseases of Children, 134,* 663–667.

Loening-Baucke, V. A. (1990). Modulation of abnormal defecation dynamics by biofeedback treatment in chronically constipated children with FE. *Journal of Pediatrics, 116,* 214–221.

McGrath, M. L., Mellon, M. W., & Murphy, L. (2000). Empirically supported treatments in pediatric psychology: Constipation and encopresis. *Journal of Pediatric Psychology, 25,* 225–254.

McGuire, T., Rothenberg, M., & Tyler, D. (1983). Profound shock following interventions for chronic untreated stool retention. *Clinical Pediatrics, 23,* 459–461.

Reimers, T. M. (1996). A biobehavioral approach toward managing encopresis. *Behavior Modification, 20,* 469–479.

Stark, L., Owens-Stively, J., Spirito, A., Lewis, A., & Guevremont, D. (1990). Group behavioral treatment of retentive FE. *Journal of Pediatric Psychology, 15,* 659–671.

Young, M. H., Brennen, L. C., Baker, R. D., & Baker, S. S. (1995). Functional FE: Symptom reduction and behavioral improvement. *Developmental and Behavioral Pediatrics, 16,* 226–232.

11 BREATHING RETRAINING AND DIAPHRAGMATIC BREATHING TECHNIQUES

Holly Hazlett-Stevens and Michelle G. Craske

Breathing retraining is a widely used technique in a number of anxiety and stress reduction therapies. Slow and deep breathing from the diaphragm (i.e., the abdominal muscle located underneath the lungs near the base of the ribs) promotes a subjective state of relaxation as well as physiological effects that are contrary to hyperventilation and autonomic nervous system arousal. As a result, breathing retraining often is used to counteract the chronic anxiety seen in Generalized Anxiety Disorder (GAD) and the hyperventilation associated with sudden, unexpected fight-or-flight activation in Panic Disorder. In addition to these specific anxiety reduction applications, breathing retraining is useful as a general relaxation strategy for individuals interested in learning stress management techniques (Fried, 1993).

Breathing retraining techniques typically begin with a demonstration of hyperventilation, which is followed by education about the physiology of overbreathing. The physiological effects experienced during initial hyperventilation induction are then contrasted with the slower heart rate, physical muscle relaxation, and other sensations that result from slow-paced abdominal breathing. Sometimes a cognitive meditation component is added to promote attentional focus on the deep breathing exercise. As individuals learn to engage in diaphragmatic breathing with repeated practice, they are encouraged to apply this skill whenever they detect signs of anxiety or worry or when they encounter stressful situations.

Breathing retraining has been investigated empirically as part of the larger cognitive behavior treatment packages for Panic Disorder (with or without agoraphobia) and for GAD. In the treatment of Panic Disorder, breathing retraining is combined with psychoeducation, cognitive restructuring, and interoceptive exposure (as well as in vivo exposure in the case of agoraphobia) treatment components (Craske & Barlow, 2001). In these cases, breathing retraining is presented early in treatment as an alternative coping response to behavioral avoidance. Its utility is attributed to the reduction of hyperventilation sensations and symptoms that contribute to a vicious cycle of fear responding found during panic attacks. In the treatment of GAD, breathing retraining is taught as a useful coping response whenever anxiety symptoms or worries are detected in the course of regular and frequent anxiety level monitoring. Thus, breathing retraining is presented in the context of psychoeducation and frequent monitoring of general anxiety symptoms, and it is combined with progressive and applied relaxation training, cognitive restructuring, and imaginal exposure techniques (Borkovec & Ruscio, 2001; Newman, 2000).

WHO MIGHT BENEFIT FROM THIS TECHNIQUE

Individuals with chronic anxiety symptoms, such as Panic Disorder and GAD, are most likely to benefit from breathing retraining. Individuals with these particular anxiety disorder diagnoses may chronically hyperventilate, thereby contributing to somatic anxiety symptoms. Thus, breathing retraining is used in Panic Disorder treatment to counteract hyperventilation, which can trigger a panic attack, and therefore is used to help control and prevent panic attacks in this population. In GAD cases, diaphragmatic breathing is taught in order to promote a general state of relaxation as well as a coping response to deploy when increased anxiety or worry is detected.

However, individuals suffering from other anxiety disorders or from subclinical anxiety symptoms may also benefit from the generalized relaxation and decreased arousal this technique provides. Some research has suggested that breathing retraining can be effective when it does not target physiology by providing a subjective sense of relaxation and feelings of control (Garssen, de Ruiter, & Van Dyck, 1992). Furthermore, Fried (1993) suggested that a variety of stress-related behavioral medicine conditions, such as insomnia, hypertension, noncardiac chest pain, headache, and gastrointestinal distress, may also benefit from breathing retraining intervention. Finally, breathing retraining may be a useful stress management tool for severely mentally ill psychiatric populations seeking ways to reduce general tension and anxiety (Key, Craske, & Reno, 2003).

CONTRAINDICATIONS OF THE TECHNIQUE

Individuals with medical conditions affecting the respiratory system, such as chronic obstructive pulmonary disease (COPD) or asthma, should first consult with their physician before breathing retraining is attempted. This caveat is particularly relevant because induced hyperventilation is conducted to demonstrate the physiological effects of overbreathing. However, the technique described presently is the same breathing technique used by physicians to teach respiratory patients how to breathe more effectively and therefore is not always contraindicated for respiratory patients.

OTHER DECISION FACTORS WHEN DECIDING TO USE THE TECHNIQUE

Certain individuals with Panic Disorder who enter treatment with strong convictions that panic attack symptoms represent physical harm may use breathing retraining to avoid feared panic sensations. This practice can undermine exposure-related treatment efforts by maintaining irrational fears that such hyperventilation sensations are harmful. Therefore, such clients are discouraged from using their breathing retraining skills in this way and are instructed to use diaphragmatic breathing only as a general relaxation strategy rather than as a response to panic attack episodes. Experienced therapists working with clients reporting high anxiety sensitivity (i.e., fear of anxiety-related sensations) sometimes refrain from teaching such clients breathing retraining for this reason.

HOW DOES BREATHING RETRAINING WORK?

Breathing retraining teaches individuals how to reduce the shallow chest breathing associated with chronic hyperventilation by engaging in deep diaphragmatic breathing. This intentional shift to slower and deeper breaths produces a host of physiological effects consistent with a state of relaxation. Learning to breathe properly allows for optimal levels of oxygen intake, thereby preventing an imbalance of oxygen and carbon dioxide in the blood and the myriad of resulting physical sensations resulting from the body's attempt to compensate for such an imbalance. An alternative view offered by Garssen et al. (1992) posits that breathing retraining induces a subjective relaxation response by presenting a credible explanation for threatening anxiety symptoms and promoting feelings of self-control.

STEP-BY-STEP PROCEDURES[1]

See Tables 11.1 and 11.2 for an overview of key elements. Breathing retraining typically begins with a demonstration of how hyperventilation affects physiology. The client is asked to stand and to voluntarily hyperventilate by breathing very quickly and deeply as if blowing up a balloon. Exhalations should be very hard and forced so that the air is taken all the way down to the lungs. The therapist first demonstrates this for the client by taking three to four deep breaths while exhaling as forcefully as possible at approximately 3 times the normal rate. The client then begins to overbreathe with the therapist. Oftentimes, the therapist will need to encourage the client to maintain speed and to exhale hard, because the client may reduce the level of effort after a few breaths. The client should try to continue for 60 to 90 seconds, but should be allowed to stop in the case of excessive distress.

After this demonstration, the client is asked to sit down, close his or her eyes, and breathe very slowly, pausing at the end of each breath. After the client begins to relax, this exercise is discussed in detail, beginning by asking the client to identify each physical sensation brought on by the voluntary hyperventilation. When treating clients with anxiety, such symptoms are discussed regarding their similarity with familiar anxiety-related sensations. In the case of Panic Disorder or recurrent panic attacks, similarity to the physical symptoms of a panic attack is highlighted even if the emotional aspects of the exercise differ because the client can identify the cause of the sensations. This exercise can then be used to launch a discussion of the role of hyperventilation in panic attacks.

The therapist then provides the rationale for breathing retraining and a brief explanation of the physiology resulting from hyperventilation. This information is crucial when treating Panic Disorder because it will help correct mistaken beliefs that such symptoms are harmful. This presentation of information should be explained in terms that the client can understand, and the amount of

---

1. These procedures are based on the manual entitled *Mastery of Your Anxiety and Panic*, 3rd ed. (Craske & Barlow, 2000).

TABLE 11.1   Key Elements of Breathing Retraining

- Conduct the voluntary hyperventilation exercise to demonstrate the effects of overbreathing.
- Describe the physiology of hyperventilation and explain the rationale for deep, diaphragmatic breathing.
- Teach the client how to engage in deep breathing and give corrective feedback.
- Assign homework practice exercises.
- Review client's progress with the home practice, giving feedback to help overcome any difficulties.

TABLE 11.2   Key Elements Specific to Panic Disorder

- After the voluntary hyperventilation exercise, these effects are systematically compared to feared panic attack sensations.
- Discussion of hyperventilation physiology includes identification of which effects might be misinterpreted as dangerous during a panic attack.
- Initial breathing practices are only conducted at scheduled times and in a relaxed setting.
- After breathing retraining skills have been developed in the relaxed practice setting, brief practice sessions are conducted in stressful settings.
- After breathing retraining skills are mastered in stressful settings, brief practice sessions are conducted in response to physical anxiety cues.
- Clients are reminded not to use breathing retraining skills when purposefully confronting feared sensations or situations during exposure-based treatment exercises.

detail should be tailored to each client's individual needs. Typically, the therapist begins by explaining that the body needs oxygen in order to survive. Whenever a person inhales, oxygen is taken into the lungs and then carried around the body, where it is released for use by the body's cells. The cells use the oxygen in their energy reactions and then release carbon dioxide (CO_2) back to the blood, where it is transported to the lungs and eventually exhaled. The balance between oxygen and carbon dioxide is very important and is maintained chiefly through an appropriate rate and depth of breathing. The appropriate rate of breathing, at rest, is usually around 10–14 breaths per minute. Hyperventilation is defined as a rate and depth of breathing that is too much for the body's needs at a particular point in time. Although breathing is controlled automatically, breathing can also be put under voluntary control. Consequently, the nonautomatic factors of fear and stress cause increased breathing because the muscles need more oxygen in order to fight or flee from danger. If the extra amount of oxygen is not used up at the rate at which it is brought in (as when there is no actual running or fighting going on), then the state of hyperventilation results.

The most important effect of hyperventilation is to produce a drop in carbon dioxide such that the amount of carbon dioxide is low in proportion to the amount of oxygen. This imbalance leads to constriction of certain blood vessels around the body, and the blood going to the brain is slightly decreased. Not only does less blood reach certain areas of the body, but the oxygen carried by this blood is less likely to be released to the tissues. Hence, although overbreathing means we are taking in more oxygen than necessary, less oxygen actually gets to certain areas of our brain and body. This causes two groups of symptoms. First are symptoms produced by the slight reduction in oxygen to certain parts of the brain, including dizziness, lightheadedness, confusion, breathlessness, blurred vision, and feelings of unreality. Second are symptoms produced by the slight reduction in oxygen to certain parts of the body, including increase in heartbeat to pump more blood around, numbness and tingling in the extremities, cold and clammy hands, and sometimes stiff muscles. Also, hyperventilating can produce a feeling of breathlessness, sometimes extending to feelings of choking or smothering, so that it actually feels as if there is not enough air.

Hyperventilation also causes other effects. First, the act of overbreathing is hard physical work. Hence, the person may feel hot, flushed, and sweaty. Because it is hard work, prolonged periods of hyperventilating will often cause tiredness and exhaustion. In addition, people who overbreathe often breathe from their chest rather than their abdomen; it is the latter that is really intended for breathing, as the diaphragm muscle serves this purpose and is located underneath the lungs. When chest muscles are primarily used for breathing, they become tired and tense because they are not well equipped for breathing, resulting in chest tightness or even severe chest pains. However, hyperventilation is not always obvious, especially with mild overbreathing for a long period of time. Therefore, many people are chronic hyperventilators but are unaware that such sensations may be the result of their breathing. Learning to breathe at an appropriate rate and depth can therefore reduce these sensations and promote feelings of relaxation. When treating clients with Panic Disorder, it is important to emphasize that hyperventilation is not dangerous. Increased respiration is central to the fight-or-flight fear response, and thus its purpose is to protect the body from danger. Hyperventilation is merely the body's natural way of compensating for such increased respiration in the absence of the physical exertion normally involved with behavioral fight or flight.

The next step is to teach a specific exercise to learn control over breathing. Typically, the therapist will model diaphragmatic breathing by placing one hand on his or her chest and the other hand on his or her abdomen and monitoring the movement of each. The client also attempts this while attending to the movement of each hand. The client should try to isolate breathing from the abdomen such that only that hand moves. During this process, the therapist encourages the client and gives corrective feedback until the client learns to breathe slowly (8–10 breaths per minute) yet smoothly and easily from the abdomen.

In the case of Panic Disorder or other chronic hyperventilators, the therapist may first instruct the client to breathe at his or her normal pace. The client would then attempt to reduce the rate of his or her breathing after one to two weeks of regular practice. This can be accomplished by matching the pace or breathing to counting and gradually slowing the counting to a rate near 10 breaths per minute. Sometimes it is helpful to pause between each step, before exhaling and before inhaling.

The therapist then explains that regular home practice is crucial to learning breathing retraining skills, and this exercise should be practiced at least twice a day for at least 10 minutes each time. The following instructions are given:

1. Find a quiet, comfortable spot where you will not be disturbed, and allow yourself a few seconds to calm down.

2. Concentrate on taking breaths right down to your stomach. There should be an expansion of the abdomen with every breath in (inhalation). The abdomen is sucked back in with every breath out (exhalation). If you are having trouble taking the air down to your stomach, try to push your stomach out just before you inhale so that there is a space for the air to fill. Be sure to place one hand on your chest and the other hand on your stomach, as the movement should come almost entirely from the lower (abdominal) hand. Try to limit the amount of movement from the upper (chest) hand. If you are normally a chest breather, this may feel artificial and cause feelings of breathlessness. That is a natural response; just remember that you are getting enough oxygen and the feelings of breathlessness will decrease the more you practice. If you find it very hard to keep your chest still, lie on the floor, flat on your stomach (that is, facing the floor) with your hands clasped under your head. This will make it easier to breathe from the abdomen. Once you have done that several times and feel comfortable breathing from the abdomen, practice the exercise again while in a seated position.

3. Keep your breathing smooth and fluid. Don't gulp in a big breath and then let it out all at once. When you breathe out, let the air escape equally over the whole time you are breathing out. Think of the air as oozing and escaping from your nose or mouth rather than being suddenly released. It does not matter whether you breathe through your nose or your mouth as long as you breathe slowly and smoothly. The nose is easier for this because it is a smaller opening.

4. Start to count on your inhalations. That is, when you breathe in, think the word "one" to yourself, and as you breathe out, think the word "relax." Think "two" on your next breath in and "relax" on the breath out. Think "three" on your next breath in and "relax" on the breath out. Continue this up to around "ten" and then go backwards to "one."

5. Focus only on your breathing and the words. This can be very difficult, and you may never be able to do it perfectly. You may not get past the first number without other thoughts coming into your mind. When this happens, do not get angry or give up. Simply allow the thoughts to pass through your mind and bring your attention back to the numbers.

6. When you first begin to count your breaths, you may become breathless or a little dizzy and begin to speed up your breathing. This should subside once you get used to the exercise. If it becomes too uncomfortable, stop for a short while and calm down, then begin again.

Individuals with Panic Disorder are reminded that they are learning to decrease physical feelings that may trigger panic attacks and that occur during panic attacks. These clients are warned against using this technique to cope with anxiety early on to avoid frustration. These clients may also benefit from tracking levels of concentration on the breathing and counting and the ease of breathing using a practice journal.

In subsequent therapy sessions, the therapist reviews the home practices with the client. Potential problems are identified and corrected. For example, was the client getting enough air into the abdomen? If not, the stomach can be pushed out slightly before inhaling. Were symptoms of anxiety experienced during practice? This is probably due to breathing a little fast or becoming anxious about breathing while attending to it. This reaction usually diminishes with practice. If the client expresses difficulty concentrating on the counting after frequent practice, then it may help to make an audio tape on which the client records his or her voice counting at the appropriate rate. Some clients will say that they have no trouble breathing at 8–10 breaths per minute and this is how fast they usually breathe. In this case, they may not be chronic hyperventilators but may still overbreathe during times of stress or panic. This technique may still be of benefit as a method of somatic control. Panic Disorder clients may use breathing retraining out of desperation as a method of avoiding the experience of panic. This fear of panicking should be subjected to cognitive restructuring or reminders that panic is not harmful. However, Panic Disorder clients should be strongly discouraged from using breathing retraining skills to avoid panic sensations during the course of interoceptive or in vivo exposure treatment.

Further Reading

Craske, M. G., & Barlow, D. H. (2000). *Mastery of your anxiety and panic* (3rd ed.). San Antonio, TX: Psychological Corporation.

Fried, R. (1987). *The hyperventilation syndrome: Research and clinical treatment.* Baltimore, MD: Johns Hopkins University Press.

Fried, R. (1993). The role of respiration in stress and stress control: Toward a theory of stress as a hypoxic phenomenon. In P. M. Lehrer & R. L. Woolfolk (Eds.), *Principles and practices of stress management* (pp. 301–331). New York: Guilford Press.

References

Borkovec, T. D., & Ruscio, A. M. (2001). Psychotherapy for generalized anxiety disorder. *The Journal of Clinical Psychiatry, 62,* 37–45.

Craske, M. G., & Barlow, D. H. (2000). *Mastery of your anxiety and panic* (3rd ed.). San Antonio, TX: Psychological Corporation.

Craske, M. G., & Barlow, D. H. (2001). Panic disorder and agoraphobia. In D. H. Barlow (Ed.), *Clinical handbook of psychological disorders: A step-by-step treatment manual* (3rd ed; pp. 1–59). New York: Guilford Press.

Fried, R. (1993). The role of respiration in stress and stress control: Toward a theory of stress as a hypoxic phenomenon. In P. M. Lehrer & R. L. Woolfolk (Eds.), *Principles and practices of stress management* (pp. 301–331). New York: Guilford Press.

Garssen, B., de Ruiter, C., & Van Dyck, R. (1992). Breathing retraining: A rational placebo? *Clinical Psychology Review, 12,* 141–153.

Key, F., Craske, M. G., & Reno, R. M. (2003). Anxiety-based cognitive-behavioral therapy for paranoid beliefs. *Behavior Therapy, 34,* 97–115.

Newman, M. G. (2000). Generalized anxiety disorder. In M. Hersen & M. Biaggio (Eds.), *Effective brief therapies: A clinician's guide* (pp. 157–178). San Diego, CA: Academic Press.

12 CLASSROOM MANAGEMENT

Steven G. Little

Managing behavior in the classroom in order to increase student learning has always been of concern to teachers and education personnel. Additionally, recent years have witnessed an increased focus on children's behavior in school as a result of the tragic events in locations such as Littleton, Colorado; Paducah, Kentucky; and Jonesboro, Arkansas. In spite of the fact that little reported violence involving children and youth is reported in schools (Heaviside, Rowand, Williams, & Farris, 1998) student classroom behavior is still of great concern to teachers, parents, and the general public. In fact, the number one concern of educators today involves students' emotional and behavioral problems in the classroom (Macciomei, 1999). Behaviors that are disruptive to the classroom, such as inattention, overactivity, and noncompliance, are currently the most common complaint of teachers (Goldstein, 1995). With prevalence rates of Attention-Deficit/ Hyperactivity Disorder (ADHD) estimated to be as high as 20% of the population (Coleman & Webber, 2002), rates of conduct disorder and Oppositional Defiant Disorder both as high as 16% (American Psychiatric Association, 1994), and the growing trend toward educating all children in the regular classroom (Little & Akin-Little, 1999), the need for empirically validated approaches to classroom management is evident.

There is no one specific technique that can be called classroom management. Rather, there are a number of techniques and procedures that can be followed to help teachers better manage the classroom. The exact techniques that are implemented depend on the ecology of the classroom, the level of involvement of the psychologist in the school and classroom, the type of disruptive behavior, and the severity of the problem behaviors. For the purpose of this chapter, classroom management is defined as a set of procedures that, if followed, should help the teacher maintain order in the classroom (see Table 12.1 for key elements of classroom management). The chapter is written for teachers, classroom consultants such as school psychologists, child clinical psychologists, social workers, behavioral specialists, and so on, and assumes a basic understanding of the principles of applied behavior analysis and behavior modification. The chapter will present both proactive and reactive procedures that can be combined to provide a comprehensive approach to classroom management.

CLASSROOM RULES

An essential element of any classroom management program is a set of firm, but fair, classroom rules (Malone & Tietjens, 2000; McGinnis, Frederick, & Edwards, 1995; Rademacher, Callahan, & Pederson-Seelye, 1998). Although rules are necessary for effective classroom management, they

TABLE 12.1 Key Elements of Classroom Management

1. Rules
2. Classroom structure
3. Positive reinforcement
4. Effective command giving
5. Response cost procedures
6. Group contingencies

alone are not sufficient to reduce rates of problem behavior in the classroom (Gettinger, 1988). Classroom rules must be integrated with a comprehensive behavior management plan. However, rules are the first place to start in effective classroom management.

In helping a teacher develop a set of classroom rules there are certain assumptions that need to be conveyed to the teacher. First and foremost is the idea that good classroom rules are the backbone of classroom management. With rules in place, other classroom management techniques will be much easier to implement. There should also be a minimum expectation for behavior for every student in the classroom. All students should be expected to follow the rules, even special education students. Once rule exceptions are made, a double standard exists and rules become worthless. Next, it is essential that students understand the resulting consequences (both positive and relating to privilege loss) of the rules. To accomplish this, it is advisable to have the teacher, during the first 2 weeks of school, randomly select students to read a rule, discuss why the rule is important, and explain what will happen if the rule is followed or not followed. To demonstrate that the teacher is fair, students should be allowed to question the utility or fairness of a rule during these discussion periods. It is also important that students know that rules cannot be questioned at other times, especially when a rule is broken. Further, the teacher makes the final decision, and that should be clearly stated at the onset. Finally, the teacher should post the classroom rules in a visible spot in the classroom before the first day of school.

There are a number of characteristics that have been found associated with good rules (McGinnis et al., 1995; Rhode, Jenson, & Reavis, 1993). These include the following:

- The *number* of rules should be kept to a minimum, with five rules considered the maximum. Compliance is greatest when students can readily recall all of the rules.
- The wording of rules should be kept as *simple* as possible and should convey exactly what behavior is expected. Pictures or icons depicting the rules may help younger students understand the rules.
- Keep the wording of the rules *positive* if at all possible. Most rules can be stated in a positive manner; some rules cannot. However, the majority of classroom rules should be positive. It is much better to have rules that convey the behavior that is expected of the students than a list of don'ts.
- The rules should be very *specific*. The more ambiguous the rules are, the more difficult they are to understand. If there are loopholes in the rules, students will find them. Operational definitions of expected behavior are the best.
- The rules should describe behavior that is *observable*. The behavior must be observable so that the teacher can make an unequivocal decision as to whether or not the rule has been followed.
- Rules describe behavior that is *measurable*. That is, behavior must be able to be counted or quantified in some way for monitoring purposes.
- The rules should be publicly *posted* in a prominent place in the classroom (e.g., in front of the classroom, near the door). The lettering should be large and block printed.
- Following the rules should be connected to *consequences*. Spell out what happens positively if students follow the rules and what they lose if they do not follow the rules.
- A *compliance* rule should always be included. Classroom behavior will correspond to the posted rules. If you want to improve compliance in the classroom, a rule such as "Do what your teacher asks immediately" should be included.

ENHANCING THE CLASSROOM ENVIRONMENT

Keeping with the initial focus of this chapter on proactive classroom management techniques, a number of factors dealing with the classroom environment need to be considered. Although consequent stimuli are frequently the focus of classroom management techniques, antecedent stimuli are equally important and need to be considered. Recognize that unstructured time in the classroom makes disruptive behavior more likely. If possible, 70% of classroom time should be devoted to academic activities. If students are engaged in interesting academic activities, disruptive behavior will be less likely. This does not mean, however, that the teacher needs to be actively teaching 70% of the day. The utilization of strategies such as peer tutoring and cooperative learning helps make this a more realistic goal. In addition, consider the following suggestions regarding structuring the classroom space:

- Place disruptive students in the front of the classroom near the teacher, but not separated from rest of class. Do *not* place a disruptive student next to the teacher's desk facing the classroom. That is placing a major source of positive reinforcement (peer attention) directly in front of the disruptive student.
- Do not let two disruptive students sit next to each other.
- Disruptive students need more frequent reinforcement for appropriate behavior than other students. Having them close to the teacher makes this easier to accomplish.
- If there is a group of difficult students in the classroom, have the most difficult ones sit close to the teacher and spread the others out. It is best to place students who tend to behave appropriately next to disruptive students.
- Students should have only relevant materials on their desk. Relevant material includes only the material necessary for completion of the current assignment.
- Do *not* place easily distracted students near the window or in other locations where distraction is likely.
- Moving around the classroom frequently is one of the best proactive strategies for a teacher. Walking around lets the teacher more easily detect problems before they escalate. It also allows the teacher to subtly reinforce students (e.g., touching students on the shoulder, leaning down to look at their work, saying "good job") and check on academic progress.

REINFORCEMENT STRATEGIES

Appropriate classroom behavior is maintained for many students in the classroom by naturally occurring reinforcers, such as positive attention from the teacher, grades, or self-reinforcement that results from task completion. These naturally occurring reinforcers may not be sufficient to maintain all desirable behaviors in all students, however. It is frequently necessary to look for more powerful reinforcers. Alberto and Troutman (1999) summarize categories and examples of positive reinforcers. These include

1. Edible reinforcers, such as foods and liquids. There are a number of drawbacks (e.g., lack of nutritional value) to using these in the school environment, however, and they should be avoided if possible.
2. Sensory reinforcers, such as exposure to visual, auditory, tactile, olfactory, or kinesthetic stimuli.
3. Tangible (material) reinforcers, such as certificates, badges, stickers, posters, and the like.
4. (a) Privilege reinforcers, such as being able to monitor other students, being captain of a team, or being excused from homework, and (b) activity reinforcers, such as being allowed playtime, special projects, or access to media.
5. Generalized reinforcers, such as tokens, points, or credits.
6. Social reinforcers, such as facial expressions, proximity, contact, feedback, or praise.

Caution should be used in selecting and using positive reinforcement. First of all, select reinforcement that is age appropriate and use natural reinforcement whenever it is possible (see Table 12.2). You should also recognize the student's level of functioning when selecting reinforcement (e.g., don't send a student for unsupervised free time in the library when he or she usually gets into trouble when unsupervised). Make certain you have parental and administrative support for the reinforcement you plan on using. Involvement of the parents in the administration of the reinforcement can also help in generalization efforts. It is very important to make sure the teacher does not use partial praise statements such as "I'm glad you finished your work—finally!" because statements such as these are self-defeating. Fi-

TABLE 12.2   Suggestions for Natural Positive Reinforcement

• Access to lunchroom snack machines (student supplies money)	• Omission of certain assignments
• A place at the head of the line (to anything)	• Job of running film projector or video player for class
• Position of team captain	• Position of class or office messenger or aide
• Care of class pets	• Job of sharpening class pencils
• Choice of activity or game for class	• Seat by a friend
• Job of passing out paper	• Time with favorite adult or peer
• Opportunity to decorate the classroom	• Position as tutor in class, or with younger students
• Extra portion at lunch	• Use of class walkman or tape recorder
• Extra recess or break time	• Use of magic markers and/or art supplies
• Free time to use specific equipment or supplies	• A visit to the school library (individual or group)
• A place for the student to display work	• Job of watering class plants
• Job of helping custodian	

nally, do not confuse positive reinforcement or privileges with a student's basic rights (e.g., depriving a student of lunch or reasonable access to the bathroom is probably illegal).

GIVING EFFECTIVE COMMANDS

Barkley (1997) provides guideline to parents in the area of effective command giving. Changing the manner in which commands are given may effectively reduce the frequency of problem behaviors and increase student compliant behavior. Although Barkley's list was designed for parents, it can easily be adapted for use with teachers in the classroom. The following list summarizes effective command-giving strategies for teachers and is adapted from those given by Barkley (1997) and Forehand and McMahon (1981).

- *Mean it.* Never issue a command you do not intend to follow through to its completion.
- *Never issue a command as a question or favor.* The command should be stated simply, directly, and in an unemotional manner.
- *Do not yell.* Getting upset may be reinforcing to the student. Try to maintain your composure.
- *Give the student time.* When giving a command, allow 5 to 10 seconds for the student to respond before (1) giving the command again or (2) giving a new command.
- *Avoid nagging.* Issue a command only twice, then follow through on the preplanned conse-

quence. The more you ask, the less likely the student is to comply.
- *Give only one or two commands at a time.* Too many commands can confuse the student.
- *Deliver the command while maintaining eye contact.* This helps ensure that the student is paying attention to you.
- *Be descriptive.* Telling the student specifically to "pick up the paper around your desk and stack your books" is much better than giving a vague instruction such as "clean up your desk."
- *Make more start requests than stop requests.* "Do" requests are better than "Don't" requests.
- *Verbally reinforce compliance.* It is easy to forget to socially reward a student when he or she complies with your request, but it is important to do so.

REDUCTIVE PROCEDURES

There are times when even the most proactive teacher must follow through with a negative consequence for an inappropriate behavior. Remember, however, that the worst time to select a punishment is during an episode with a student. In instances such as these the teacher may be tempted to use a punishment that is too severe for the behavior. Punishments that are too severe for the behavior are not likely to be effective. Teachers must also be concerned about ethical and legal issues involving the implementation of punishment procedures. Even in those localities where corporal punishment is legal, it is not recommended as an effective behavior management technique. For a detailed discussion of this and other important concerns regarding this issue, see Hyman and Snook (1999). Alberto and Troutman (1999, p. 279) offer the following hierarchy of procedure for behavior reduction from least intrusive to most intrusive.

Level I   Strategies of differential reinforcement
   a.   Differential reinforcement of low rates of behavior (DRL)
   b.   Differential reinforcement of other behavior(s) (DRO)
   c.   Differential reinforcement of incompatible behavior (DRI)
   d.   Differential reinforcement of alternative behavior(s) (DRA)
Level II   Extinction (terminating reinforcement)
Level III Removal of desirable stimuli
   a.   Response-cost procedures
   b.   Time-out procedures
Level IV   Presentation of aversive stimuli
   a.   Unconditioned aversive stimuli
   b.   Conditioned aversive stimuli
   c.   Overcorrection procedures

The most logical reductive techniques from this list for classroom use include response cost and overcorrection. Response cost is defined as the removal of a positive reinforcer contingent on inappropriate behavior. An example would include the loss of an enjoyable activity (e.g., computer time, recess) in response to an inappropriate behavior. In particular, response cost can be used to increase the effectiveness of a token economy. There are two basic types of overcorrection: restitutional (i.e., the individual must return the environment to a state better than it was before the misbehavior) and positive practice (i.e., the individual must engage in an overly correct form of the behavior). Restitutional overcorrection is the form most adaptable for the classroom. An example would include having a student pick up all of the garbage in the classroom after being caught throwing a paper on the floor.

GROUP CONTINGENCIES

A final consideration in developing classroom behavior management programs is interdependent group contingencies. When interdependent group contingencies are used, reinforcers are distributed to every member of the group contingent upon the group's meeting some criterion (Litow & Pumroy, 1975). They have several advantages. Teachers can implement one program for the entire class rather than an individual program for each member of the class. The entire group either earns or doesn't earn the reinforcement; therefore teachers do not have to monitor each student's performance and give reinforcers to some students and not to others. This not only makes the program easier to manage (Gresham & Gresham, 1982) but also should reduce backlash because classmates are not separated into reinforcer "haves" and "have-nots" (Cashwell, Skinner, Dunn, & Lewis, 1998). Because students are attempting to earn reinforcers as opposed to avoiding punishment, these programs can also be fun (Skinner & Watson, 2000).

Further Reading

Alberto, P. A., & Troutman, A. C. (1999). *Applied behavior analysis for teachers.* Upper Saddle River, NJ: Prentice-Hall.
Rhode, G., Jenson, W. R., & Reavis, H. K. (1993). *The tough kid book: Practical classroom management strategies.* Longmont, CO: Sopris West.

References

Alberto, P. A., & Troutman, A. C. (1999). *Applied behavior analysis for teachers.* Upper Saddle River, NJ: Prentice-Hall.
American Psychiatric Association (1994). *Diagnostic and statistical manual of mental disorders* (4th ed.). Washington, DC: Author.
Barkley, R. A. (1997). *Defiant children: A clinician's manual for assessment and parent training* (2nd ed.). New York: Guilford Press.
Cashwell, C. S., Skinner, C. H., Dunn, M. S., & Lewis, J. (1998). Group reward programs: A humanistic approach. *Humanistic Education and Development, 37,* 47–53.
Coleman, M. C., & Webber, J. (2002). *Emotional and behavioral disorders: Theory and practice* (4th ed.). Boston: Allyn and Bacon.

Forehand, R. L., & McMahon, R. J. (1981). *Helping the noncompliant child: A clinician's guide to parent training*. New York: Guilford Press.

Gettinger, M. (1988). Methods of proactive classroom management. *School Psychology Review, 17*, 227–242.

Goldstein, S. (1995). *Understanding and managing children's classroom behavior*. New York: Wiley.

Gresham, F. M., & Gresham, G. N. (1982). Interdependent, dependent, and independent group contingencies for controlling disruptive behaviors. *The Journal of Special Education, 16*, 101–110.

Heaviside, S., Rowand, C, Williams, C., & Farris, E. (1998). *Violence and discipline problems in U. S. public schools: 1996–1997* (NCES 98-030). Washington, DC: U.S. Department of Education, National Center for Education Statistics.

Hyman, I. A., & Snook, P. A. (1999). *Dangerous schools: What we can do about the physical and emotional abuse of our children*. San Francisco,CA: Jossey-Bass.

Litow, L., & Pumroy, D. K. (1975). A brief review of classroom group oriented contingencies. *Journal of Applied Behavior Analysis, 8*, 431–447.

Little, S. G., & Akin-Little, K. A. (1999). Legal and ethical issues of inclusion. *Special Services in the Schools, 15*, 125–143.

Macciomei, N. R. (1999). Behavior problems in urban schoolchildren. In N. R. Macciomei & D. H. Ruben (Eds.), *Behavior management in the public schools: An urban approach* (pp. 1–17). Westport, CT: Praeger.

Malone, B. G., & Tietjens, C. L. (2000). Re-examination of classroom rules: The need for clarity and specified behavior. *Special Services in the Schools, 16*, 159–170.

McGinnis, J. C., Frederick, B. P., & Edwards, R. (1995). Enhancing classroom management through proactive rules and procedures. *Psychology in the Schools, 32*, 220–224.

Rademacher, J. A., Callahan, K., & Pederson-Seelye, V. A. (1998). How do your classroom rules measure up? Guidelines for developing an effective rule management routine. *Interventions in School and Clinic, 33*, 284–289.

Rhode, G., Jenson, W. R., & Reavis, H. K. (1993). *The tough kid book: Practical classroom management strategies*. Longmont, CO: Sopris West.

Skinner, C. S., & Watson, T. S. (2000). Randomized group contingencies: Lotteries in the classroom. *The School Psychologist, 54*, 21, 24, 32, 36–38.

13 COGNITIVE DEFUSION

Jason B. Luoma and Steven C. Hayes

Cognitive defusion involves a change in the normal use of language and cognition such that the ongoing *process* of thinking is more evident and the normal functions of the *products* of thinking are broadened. Cognitive defusion is a descendant of *cognitive distancing,* a technique that dates back to the origins of cognitive therapy. Cognitive distancing consists of encouraging clients to detect their thoughts and to see them as hypotheses rather than objective facts about the world. It has long been described as a "first, critical step in cognitive therapy" (Hollon & Beck, 1979, p. 189) because it enables clinicians to teach clients to analyze, test, dispute, and alter negative thoughts through traditional cognitive techniques. Thus, cognitive distancing is conceptualized as a preparatory step: necessary but not sufficient to produce profound change.

A contextual treatment originally termed *Comprehensive Distancing* (Hayes, 1987) was one of the first to attempt to alter the functions of negative thoughts by the use of extended and elaborated forms of cognitive distancing. Now termed *Acceptance and Commitment Therapy* (ACT; Hayes, Strosahl, & Wilson, 1999), this treatment attempted to reduce the believability and behavioral impact of negative thoughts, not by disputation and test, but by the relentless emphasis on seeing thoughts as thoughts. Thus, thoughts are not so much hypotheses to be tested (as in traditional cognitive distancing) as they are habitual

constructions to be noticed and integrated into a wide variety of actions. This expanded technique was named *cognitive defusion* (it is also referred to by its difficult-to-pronounce synonym *deliteralization*) in order both to avoid the dissociative connotations of the original term and to emphasize the more comprehensive character of the process involved.

The purpose of cognitive defusion is to help clients who are caught up in the content of their own cognitive activity to *defuse,* or separate themselves, from the literal meaning of thoughts and instead become more aware of thinking as an active, ongoing, relational process that is situated both historically and situationally. Cognitive defusion is based on a functional contextual theory of language and cognition called relational frame theory (Hayes, Barnes-Holmes, & Roche, 2001). According to this view, thoughts acquire their literal meaning and much of their focused emotive and behavior regulatory functions only because the social/verbal community establishes a context in which symbols relate mutually to other events and have functions based on these relations.

In recent years a number of related concepts and procedures have emerged within empirical clinical traditions that have similar goals, such as mindfulness procedures (e.g., Linehan, 1993; Segal, Williams, & Teasdale, 2001; see also Chapter 35 in this volume) and the use of metacognitive strategies (Wells, 2000). Although it is clear that these concepts are closely related, the exact dividing lines are unclear. In this chapter the use of cognitive defusion in ACT will be emphasized.

EVIDENCE OF THE EFFECTIVENESS OF COGNITIVE DEFUSION

Data on the impact of cognitive defusion come from several sources. Some indirect evidence comes from that fact that clinical improvement in traditional cognitive therapy tends to occur early, often before the disputative components of the treatment are deployed but after cognitive distancing is used (Ilardi & Craighead, 1994). More direct evidence comes from the processes of change seen in outcome research on ACT, particularly with shortened forms of the treatment that have greatly emphasized the defusion component. Two small randomized controlled trials with depression, one of individual psychotherapy and another of group psychotherapy for depression (Zettle & Hayes, 1987; Zettle & Raines, 1989), compared ACT to a complete cognitive therapy package. Data demonstrated that ACT clients displayed equivalent or superior clinical improvement in depression, but through different processes. Cognitive defusion reduced the believability of depressogenic thoughts more quickly than traditional cognitive methods, but not the occurrence of these thoughts.

A more recent randomized controlled trial is particularly relevant. It compared a 3-hour-long version of ACT that greatly emphasized cognitive defusion to treatment as usual in the prevention of rehospitalization among psychotic individuals with active hallucinations or delusions (Bach & Hayes, 2002). This very focused and brief version of ACT decreased rehospitalization by 50 percent over 4 months of follow-up. The process of change once again involved a rapid decrease in the believability of symptoms but not in their frequency. Similar results have been shown for pain (Geiser, 1992; Hayes et al., 1999), workplace stress (Bond & Bunce, 2000), and a wide variety of other problems, including Panic Disorder, social anxiety, anorexia, alcoholism, bereavement, exhibitionism, and Generalized Anxiety Disorder (e.g., see Luciano, 2001).

WHO MIGHT BENEFIT FROM THIS TECHNIQUE

Cognitive defusion can be applied to any client problems that are exacerbated by entanglement with cognitive events. The preliminary data show that these procedures can rapidly alter the functions of these events. For treatment-resistant clients who have failed in previous courses of cognitive behavior therapy, cognitive defusion hold out the promise of reducing the negative impact of harmful thoughts without having first to alter the form, frequency, or situational sensitivity of those thoughts.

CONTRAINDICATIONS OF THE TECHNIQUE

The primary contraindication is treatment inconsistency. Cognitive defusion is aimed at undermining the excessive literality of thinking itself. Cognitive defusion thus does not combine well with approaches specifically aimed at testing, disputing, arguing, suppressing, or controlling cognitive events, since all of these are heavily focused on the literal meaning of thoughts (e.g., the adequacy of evidence for truth claims). Clients with brittle cognitive systems can be agitated by the very idea of simply noticing thoughts without agreement or disagreement. Such clients (e.g., those with some obsessive disorders) tend to present difficulties for most forms of therapy, however, including traditional forms of cognitive therapy, and furthermore can sometimes improve through the use of defusion procedures.

OTHER DECISIONS IN DECIDING TO USE OR NOT TO USE COGNITIVE DEFUSION

Cognitive defusion can be an important supplement to a number of other therapy approaches and techniques. It may be particularly well combined with more experiential and relational approaches that rely upon such techniques as behavioral activation (see Chapter 7 in this volume), acceptance (see Chapter 2 in this volume) and mindfulness (see Chapter 35 in this volume). It should be used when the clinician has determined that intervention is needed to reduce the impact of a client's thoughts, but the more lengthy and perhaps difficult process of cognitive disputation and correction is not desirable due to time constraints, past treatment failures with these approaches, or comparative data.

HOW DOES THE TECHNIQUE WORK?

When we think a thought, the functions of the current situations are usually altered by the content of that thought because symbols are mutually related to other events. For example, when one thinks of a lemon, some of the reactions produced by an actual lemon occur, at least in weakened form. For example, one may visualize a lemon and one's mouth may water. This process is helpful in most contexts. For example, a person thinking about how to fix a car can usefully go through the steps cognitively, seeing each step in his or her mind, before actually dismantling the car. Because many contexts are of this kind, people can come to interact with the world as cognitively organized without noticing that they are constantly organizing it. Verbal or cognitive constructions come to substitute for direct contact with events.

In clinical situations, however, this kind of cognitive fusion is often unhelpful and confining. When a panic-disordered client imagines how he or she might be trapped and socially humiliated in a particular situation, the client is seemingly dealing with the problem of being trapped, just as the mechanic is seemingly dealing with a car. If the literal functions of that thought dominate over all other possible functions, the issue may become how to avoid public situations so as to avoid being trapped, and not any of a thousand other possible responses. Commonly, considerable clinical attention is given to such negative thoughts and experiences with the intent of getting rid of them. However, a number of studies demonstrate that attempts to suppress, eliminate, or alter negative thoughts and feelings may result in paradoxical effects, at times actually increasing the frequency, intensity, and behavioral regulatory powers of these experiences. Furthermore, because these thoughts can be automatic and well established, altering them can be painstaking even when successful. Finally, this process can narrow the behavioral focus even more to the undesirable thought, when that very narrowness is part of the problem.

Emotions and thoughts achieve their power not only by their form or frequency but also by the context in which they occur. In cognitive defusion, rather than trying to directly change the content or frequency of these private events, the therapist targets the context that relates them to undesirable overt behavior so as to induce greater response flexibility. An example of a specific defusion technique will clarify this point. If a client rapidly says a word or phrase over and over again for a minute or two, two things will happen: The word will temporarily lose most of its meaning, and the sound of the word itself will emerge more dominantly (it is common for clients to say that they never realized the word sounded like that). The technique works best with one-syllable words (e.g., *milk*), but also works with two- or three-word phrases (e.g., "I'm bad") if more time is spent repeating them. In this example, as in all examples of defusion techniques, the word or phrase is still present but a nonliteral context is created that diminishes its normal symbolic functions and increases its more direct functions (in this example, its auditory functions). Stated another way, defusion techniques teach clients to think thoughts as thoughts, not so much through logical argument or direct instruction as through changes in the context of language and cognition itself, so as to make responding more fluid and functional.

As a result, the literal functions of problematic thoughts are less likely to dominate as a source of influence over behavior, and more helpful, direct, and varied sources of control over action can gain ground. A large body of literature shows that when individuals respond to stimuli in the environment based on verbal rules, insensitivity to the direct contingencies in the environment may result and the range of behaviors available may be excessively narrowed. Individuals may continue to apply the same logical solution even when that solution is not working in a particular context.

The contexts that are targeted by defusion techniques include those that establish literal meaning itself, such as in the repeated word example, but also contexts that encourage people to generate verbal reasons to justify their behavior, to control private events, or to be right about their explanations for actions. Cognitive defusion acts in part through establishing contexts in which sense-making is not supported, such as paradox, confusion, meditative exercises, experiential exercises, metaphor, and undermining sense-making language conventions. Instead, clients are encouraged to focus on opportunities that the current environment affords and the workability of specific cognitive events in fostering effective action in that environment.

STEP-BY-STEP PROCEDURES

Cognitive defusion techniques can be broken down into three major groups. First, clients are introduced to the concept that language may not hold all the answers: There may be other, more flexible ways of knowing that are beyond verbal knowing. Second, thoughts and emotions are objectified through various metaphors, leading to greater distinction between thought and thinker, emotion and feeler. Third, various language conventions and experiential exercises are introduced to differentiate buying a thought, as it were, from having a thought, with the goal of teaching clients to evaluate thoughts based on their functional utility rather than their literal truth. (See Table 13.1 for some examples of cognitive defusion techniques.)

THINKING VERSUS EXPERIENCE

"Verbal knowing rests atop non-verbal knowing so completely that an illusion is created that all knowledge is verbal" (Hayes et al., 1999, pp. 153–154). Cognitive defusion begins the attack on clients' confidence in conscious thought by demonstrating its limits. The repeated word exercise (usual at first done with an arbitrary word, such as *milk*) is often one of the earliest. Clients are encouraged first to notice all of the perceptual functions of the word (e.g., what milk tastes like) and then, after a minute or two of saying the word rapidly out loud, to notice how these functions have changed. This exercise quickly pulls back the curtain of literality and reveals the illusion language and cognition create. Metaphors and examples

can be used to demonstrate further the limits of conscious thought. A sample defusion metaphor is called *finding a place to sit* (Hayes, et al., 1999):

> *Therapist:* It's as if you needed a place to sit, and so you began describing a chair. Let's say you gave a really detailed description of a chair. It's a grey chair, and it has a metal frame, and it's covered in fabric, and it's a very sturdy chair. OK. Now can you sit in that description?
>
> *Client:* Well, no.
>
> *Therapist:* Hmmm. Maybe the description wasn't detailed enough. What if I were able to describe the chair all the way down to the atomic level? Then could you sit in the description?
>
> *Client:* No.
>
> *Therapist:* Here's the thing, and check your own experience: Hasn't your mind been telling you things like "The world is this way, and that way and your problem is this and that, et cetera?" Describe, describe. Evaluate, evaluate, evaluate. And all the while, you're getting tired. You need a place to sit. And your mind keeps handing you ever more elaborate descriptions of chair. Then it says to you, "Have a seat." Descriptions are fine, but what we are looking for here is an experience, not a description of an experience. Minds can't deliver experience, they only blab to us about our experience elsewhere. So we'll let your mind describe away, and in the meantime you and I will look for a place to sit. (p. 153)

The importance of experience can be revisited throughout therapy, as a way of cutting through excessive literal thinking. Comments such as "I don't want you to see this as a matter of belief, but to examine it against your experience" or "what does your experience say?" may help accomplish this end.

The limits of language can also be illustrated by examining how one learns any new skilled activity, such as a sport or hobby. For example, one could listen to a description of all the mechanics of how to swim, down the minutest detail of how exactly to hold one's hand, how to kick one's feet, and so on. However, in order to actually learn how to swim, one needs to get in the water and practice. This can be shown by asking the client to instruct the therapist in a motor behavior (e.g., "tell

TABLE 13.1   Some Examples of Cognitive Defusion (Deliteralization) Techniques

Technique	Example
The Mind	Treat the mind as an external event, almost as a separate person.
Mental appreciation	Thank your mind; show aesthetic appreciation for its products.
Cubbyholing	Label private events as to kind or function in a back channel communication.
"I'm having the thought that . . ."	Include category labels in descriptions of private events.
Commitment to openness	Ask if the content is acceptable when negative content shows up.
Just noticing	Use the language of observation (e.g., noticing) when talking about thoughts.
Titchener's repetition	Repeat the difficult thought until you can hear it.
Physicalizing	Label the physical dimensions of thoughts.
Put them out there	Sit next to the client and put each thought and experience out in front of you both as an object.
Open mindfulness	Watch thoughts as external objects without use or involvement.
Focused mindfulness	Direct attention to nonliteral dimensions of experience.
Sound it out	Say difficult thoughts very, very slowly.
Arrogance of word	Try to instruct nonverbal behavior and respond to each attempt with "how do I do that?"
Thoughts are not causes	Ask: "Is it possible to think that thought, as a thought, *and* do X?"
Choose being right or choose being alive	Ask: "If you have to pay with one to play for the other, which do you choose?"
There are four people in here	Open strategize how to connect when minds are listening.
Monsters on the bus	Treat scary private events as monsters on a bus you are driving.
Who is in charge here?	Treat thoughts as bullies; use colorful language.
Take your mind for a walk	Walk behind the client chattering like minds do, while client chooses where to walk.
And what is that in the service of?	Step out of content and ask this question.
Okay, you are right. Now what?	Take "right" as a given and focus on action.
Why, why, why?	Show the shallowness of causal explanations by repeatedly asking "why?"
Create a new story	Write down the normal life story, then repeatedly integrate those facts into other stories.
Carry cards	Write difficult thoughts on 3 x 5 cards and carry them with you.
Carry your keys	Assign difficult thoughts and experiences to the client's keys. Ask the client to think the thought as a thought each time the keys are handled, and then carry them from there.

me how I can get out of this chair") and following each instruction generated by the client (e.g., "bend your arms and put your hands on the seat and push") with the question "how do I do that?"

OBJECTIFYING THOUGHT

The natural sense of distance between self and object often disappears when those objects are thoughts because the literal functions of thought become so dominant. People tend to act as if a thought is an adequate substitute for experience.

Objectifying thoughts can help people handle their thoughts in more flexible and practical ways, in much the same way that external objects can be handled in multiple ways, depending on the purpose present in the moment.

Certain language conventions are helpful in that regard. Therapists using ACT often react to thoughts in playful ways, such as by saying "Well, thank your mind for that thought" or by congratulating clients for making dismal cognitive connections (e.g., Client: "So then I thought I'd completely blown it." Therapist: "Ah, very nice. Beautiful.") as if in appreciation of how creative minds can be. Another verbal convention has to do with labeling the type of talk clients are engaged in, rather than responding to the content of what the thought is literally about. The therapist can, as an unelaborated aside, simply label client talk by type (e.g., "Evaluation. Very good" or "Okay. Feeling."). Eventually clients can be taught to do this with their own talk, labeling evaluations as evaluations and feelings as feelings. For example, a client might verbalize the thought "I'm worthless." The client may be taught to say, "I'm having the evaluation that I'm worthless."

More extended metaphors can objectify thoughts as well. An ACT metaphor is the *passengers on the bus metaphor*, which compares the relationship between a person and his or her thoughts to that of a person and the bullies he or she has to fight against in order to live his or her life (Hayes et al., 1999):

> Suppose there is a bus and you're the driver. On this bus we've got a bunch of passengers. The passengers are thoughts, feelings, bodily states, memories, and other aspects of experience. Some of them are scary, and they're dressed up in black leather jackets and they have switchblade knives. What happens is that you're driving along and the passengers start threatening you, telling you what you have to do, where you have to go. . . . The threat they have over you is that if you don't do what they say, they're going to come up from the back of the bus.
>
> It's as if you've made deals with these passengers, and the deal is, "You sit in the back of the bus and scrunch down so that I can't see you very often, and I'll do what you say pretty much." Now, what if one day you get tired of that. . . . You stop the bus, and you go back to deal with the mean-looking passengers. But you notice that the very first thing you had to do was stop. Notice now, you're not driving anywhere, you're just dealing with these passengers. And they're very strong. They don't intend to leave, and you wrestle with them, but it just doesn't turn out very successfully.
>
> Eventually, you go back to placating the passengers, trying to get them to sit way in the back again where you can't see them. . . . Pretty soon, they don't have to tell you, "turn left"—you know as soon as you get near a left turn that the passengers are going to crawl all over you. In time you may get good enough that you can almost pretend that they're not

> on the bus at all. . . . However, when they eventually do show up, it's with the added power of the deals that you've made with them in the past.
>
> Now the trick about the whole thing is that the power the passengers have over you is 100% based on this: "If you don't do what we say, we're coming up and we're making you look at us." That's it. It's true that when they come up from they look as if they could do a whole lot more. They have knives, chains, and so forth. It looks as though you could be destroyed. The deal you make is you do what they say so they won't come up and stand next to you and make you look at them. The driver (you) has control of the bus, but you trade off the control in these secret deals with the passengers. In other words, by trying to get control, you've actually given up control! Now notice that even though your passengers claim they can destroy you if you don't turn left, it has never actually happened. These passengers can't make you do something . . . you are just making deals with them. (pp. 157–158)

Later in therapy, this metaphor can be reintroduced when clients bring up troubling thoughts, feelings, or behaviors that they feel are getting in the way of moving toward their valued goals. A therapist might say, "so what passenger is bothering you now?"

Another defusion exercise that can help clients distinguish between themselves and the content of their minds is to have clients write personally troubling thoughts cards. These cards can then be carried around by clients as homework, literally allowing them to carry their troubling thoughts as objects and still perform their daily activities.

A THOUGHT IS A THOUGHT IS A THOUGHT

Cognitive defusion presents clients experientially with the distinction between looking *at* a world as thought presents it (i.e., buying a thought) and looking at the world while simultaneously being aware of the process of thinking, being aware of the response alternatives present, and choosing one of many alternatives (i.e., having a thought). This is often done through a variety of meditative and mindfulness exercises, such as by having clients, eyes closed, imagine a stream with leaves floating by on it and placing each new thought that comes up on one of the leaves. Inevitably the stream stops, or people lose the exercise, when a thought comes along (e.g., "Am I doing this right?") that is not being looked *at* but is being looked *from*.

FOCUS ON THE FUNCTIONAL UTILITY OF THOUGHTS

All of the techniques in cognitive defusion are tied together by a common focus on the functional utility of thinking. Thoughts are not to be evaluated according to their literal truth or coherence with a network of understanding, but rather by their workability. In any given situation, the primary question the therapist and client should ask is whether buying a thought would move the client toward a life in line with his or her chosen values, or whether it moves the client in some other direction.

Various language practices and verbal conventions can serve to keep the client aware of the difference between the process of thinking and the products of thinking. When a client begins to describe reasons to justify behavior, the therapist can focus on the functional utility of these reasons through questions like these (Hayes et al., 1999, p. 164): "And what is that story in the service of? Is this helpful, or is this what your mind does to you? Have you told these kinds of things to yourself or to others before? Is this old? If God told you that your explanation is 100% correct, how would this help you? OK, let's all have a vote and vote that you are correct. Now what?"

CONCLUSION

Verbal understanding is very adaptive in many situations. However, the tendency for people to become fused with thoughts, to see them as being literally true, as well as the tendency for people to cling to and defend their own verbal constructions, can serve to restrict and narrow behavior and inhibit movement toward valued life goals. Cognitive defusion loosens the grip that excessive literality can hold on behavior so that more flexible and functional behaviors can emerge.

Cognitive defusion can open up a world of possible behaviors that may allow an individual to move in a direction that is more in line with his or her chosen values.

Further Reading

Hayes, S. C., Barnes-Holmes, D., & Roche, B. (Eds.) (2001). *Relational Frame Theory: A post-Skinnerian account of human language and cognition.* New York: Plenum Press.

Hayes, S. C., Strosahl, K. D., & Wilson, K. G. (1999). *Acceptance and Commitment Therapy: An experiential approach to behavior change.* New York: Guilford Press.

References

Bach, P., & Hayes, Steven C. (2002). The use of Acceptance and Commitment Therapy to prevent the rehospitalization of psychotic patients: A randomized controlled trial. *Journal of Consulting and Clinical Psychology, 70,* 1129–1139.

Bond, F. W., & Bunce, D. (2000). Mediators of change in emotion-focused and problem-focused worksite stress management interventions. *Journal of Occupational Health Psychology, 5,* 156–163.

Geiser, D. S. (1992). *A comparison of acceptance-focused and control-focused psychological treatments in a chronic pain treatment center.* Unpublished dissertation, University of Nevada, Reno.

Hayes, S. C. (1987). A contextual approach to therapeutic change. In N. Jacobson (Ed.), *Psychotherapists in clinical practice: Cognitive and behavioral perspectives* (pp. 327–387). New York: Guilford Press.

Hayes, S. C., Barnes-Holmes, D., & Roche, B. (2001). *Relational Frame Theory: A post-Skinnerian account of human language and cognition.* New York: Kluwer Academic/Plenum Publishers.

Hayes, S. C., Bissett, R., Korn, Z., Zettle, R. D., Rosenfarb, I., Cooper, L., et al. (1999). The impact of acceptance versus control rationales on pain tolerance. *The Psychological Record, 49,* 33–47.

Hayes, S. C., Strosahl, K. D., & Wilson, K. G. (1999). *Acceptance and Commitment Therapy: An experiential approach to behavior change.* New York: Guilford Press.

Hollon, S. D., & Beck, A. T. (1979). Cognitive therapy of depression. In P. C. Kendall & S. D. Barlow (Eds.), *Cognitive-behavioral intervention: Theory, research, and procedures* (pp. 153–203). New York: Academic Press.

Ilardi, S. S., & Craighead, W. E. (1994). The role of nonspecific factors in cognitive-behavior therapy for depression. *Clinical Psychology: Science & Practice, 1,* 138–156.

Linehan, M. M. (1993). *Cognitive-behavioral treatment of borderline personality disorder.* New York: Guilford Press.

Luciano, C. (Ed.) (2001). *Terapia de Aceptación y Compromiso (ACT) y el traastorno de evitación experiencial: Un síntesis de casos clínicos* [Acceptance and Commitment Therapy and experiential avoidance disorders: A synthesis of clinical cases]. Valencia: Promolibro.

Segal, Z. V., Williams, J. M. G., & Teasdale, J. D. (2001). *Mindfulness-based cognitive therapy for depression: A new approach to preventing relapse.* New York: Guilford Press.

Wells, A. (2000). *Emotional disorders and metacognition: Innovative cognitive therapy.* New York: Wiley.

Zettle, R. D., & Hayes, S. C. (1987). Component and process analysis of cognitive therapy. *Psychological Reports, 64,* 939–953.

Zettle, R. D., & Raines, J. C. (1989). Group cognitive and contextual therapies in treatment of depression. *Journal of Clinical Psychology, 45,* 438–445.

14 COGNITIVE RESTRUCTURING OF THE DISPUTING OF IRRATIONAL BELIEFS

Albert Ellis

Cognitive restructuring and the disputing of dysfunctional or irrational beliefs of people who have emotional and behavioral disturbances date back to ancient times, particularly to early Asian, Greek, and Roman philosophers, who took a constructivist view of humans. Several of these thinkers held that people have a considerable degree of agency or free will and that therefore, when their main goals and desires are thwarted by adverse conditions, they have some *choice* of reacting in a rational (self-helping) or irrational (self-defeating) manner. The idea that people's emotions are significantly connected with their modes of thinking was nicely summed up by Epictetus, a stoic philosopher, in the first century A.D. He succinctly stated that people are disturbed not by the events that happen to them but by their *view* of these events.

Nineteenth- and early twentieth-century psychologists largely based their treatment methods on this constructivist theory, as shown in the writings of Janet (1898), Dubois (1907), Coué (1923), and Adler (1927). Even Freud (1922/1960) pointed out that the small voice of reason can ultimately overcome the powerful voice of irrationality. His emphasis, however, on the overpowering influence on unconscious, often repressed, thinking and feeling led therapists to largely abandon dealing with their clients' irra-

tional thinking; by the time the 1950s arrived they were replacing cognitive restructuring with emotional and behavioral techniques of therapy.

In 1955, however, I started to do Rational Emotive Behavior Therapy (REBT) and to forcefully favor cognitive restructuring and the disputing of irrational client beliefs. At the same time, I pointed out that thinking, feeling, and behaving are holistically integrated and interactionally influence each other. Therefore, I hypothesized that effective therapy includes many techniques and had better be—as Arnold Lazarus indicated 15 years later—multimodal (Ellis, 1957, 1958, 1962; Lazarus, 1971). I was not the first therapist to use what became known as cognitive behavior therapy (CBT), since a few practitioners—such as Herzberg (1945) and Salter (1949)—had employed aspects of it previously. But I seem to have been the main therapist to create systematic cognitive restructuring, which I called disputing irrational beliefs, and which I will describe in this chapter. After I had promoted its use in several articles and books, it also began to be employed by several other therapists who presented their own versions of it—such as Beck (1967) and Meichenbaum (1977)—so that now it has become one of the most popular techniques of CBT.

Today, important aspects of cognitive assessment and cognitive restructuring are used, overtly or tacitly, by a great many different kinds of therapists. Thus, psychoanalysis delves into clients' unrealistic and illogical beliefs and somehow induces them to change these for healthier ideas and feelings. A few analysts, especially Karen Horney (1950), have clearly demonstrated the "tyranny of the shoulds," and some philosophers—especially Alfred Korzybski (1933/1991) described the self-defeating overgeneralizing and other thinking difficulties that people use to make themselves, as Korzybski said, "unsane." Rational Emotive Behavior Therapy and CBT pioneered in specifically showing clients their dysfunctional beliefs and how to dispute them and replace them with healthier philosophies.

Rational Emotive Behavior Therapy and CBT present an ABC theory of neurotic disturbance. When people are confronted with *adversities* (As) that interfere with their goals and purposes they can choose to have functional or rational *beliefs* (RBs) that will encourage them to create healthy emotional and behavioral *consequences* (Cs). But they can also choose to have irrational beliefs (IBs) that help produce unhealthy feelings and behaviors (Cs). Being constructivists (both innately and by social learning), and having language to help them, they are also able to think about their thinking, and even think about thinking about their thinking. Therefore, they can therapeutically choose to change their IBs to more rational (self-helping) beliefs.

Since people's thoughts, feelings, and actions reciprocally and sometimes powerfully affect each other, people can also simultaneously use— by themselves and with therapists' direction—a number of emotional and behavioral methods to improve their disturbed functioning. Therefore, REBT and CBT practitioners emphasize techniques of helping clients to change their dysfunctional cognitions, but at the same time they encourage clients to modify their handicapping feelings and desires. Only the main aspects of cognitive restructuring and the disputing of IBs that I largely use in my own practice of individual and group therapy will be described in this chapter (see Table 14.1 for the key elements of cognitive restructuring). I have described many of the emotional and behavioral techniques elsewhere and have emphasized how they are to be integrated with REBT's cognitive methods (Ellis, 2001a, 2001b, 2002).

WHO MIGHT BENEFIT FROM THIS TECHNIQUE?

Cognitive restructuring or the disputing of IBs may help psychotherapy clients who are convinced by their therapist or by themselves that (1) their emotional-behavioral dysfunctioning is partly the result of their irrational, unrealistic, and illogical thinking; (2) they can constructively change their irrational beliefs (IBs) to rational beliefs (RBs) and will then function significantly better; (3) their irrational and dysfunctional thinking includes strong emotional and behavioral components; (4) if they persist in emotionally (strongly) feeling against and behaviorally (actively) acting against their dysfunctional beliefs, they will automatically and unconsciously create an effective new philosophy that will tend to make them less disturbed and keep them from seriously disturbing themselves in the future.

TABLE 14.1   Key Elements of Cognitive Restructuring

- Show clients the ABCs of REBT and CBT. Show them how As alone do not lead to their disturbed Cs, but that they personally contribute to their Cs by engaging in strong and persistent beliefs (Bs) about their As. Thus, $A \times B = C$.

- Particularly show clients that when they disturb themselves (at point C) they have powerful RBs that largely consist of flexible preferences as well as strong IBs that largely consist of absolutistic, rigid musts, shoulds, and other demands.

- Show clients how to think, feel, and act against their rigid IBs with a number of cognitive, emotive, and behavioral techniques, which interrelate to each other.

- Show clients how to specifically dispute their IBs (1) realistically and empirically, (2) logically, and (3) juristically or pragmatically. Particularly show them how to change their rigid, absolutistic demands on themselves, other people, and world conditions to flexible, workable preferences.

- Show clients that when they actively and persistently dispute (D) their IBs they can create an effective new philosophy (E) that includes strong rational coping statements that can help them to feel better, get better, and stay better.

Most Axis I individuals can considerably benefit from this technique, and many Axis II individuals can obtain less, but still considerable, benefit from persistently and forcefully using it.

CONTRAINDICATIONS OF THE TREATMENT

Some individuals with Obsessive-Compulsive Disorder (OCD) and other severe thought disorders may take cognitive restructuring and the disputing of IBs to extremes and may become so absorbed in analyzing and changing their beliefs that they sidetrack themselves from other useful techniques of therapy. Individuals who are rigidly convinced that changing their IBs cannot have any effect on their feelings may refuse to try to do so or may waste their time and energy by trying only halfheartedly. People with abysmal self-deprecation may severely blame themselves for trying to use this technique and failing. Clients with abysmal low frustration tolerance may find it too hard to try and may give up on it.

OTHER DECISION FACTORS IN USING OR NOT USING THIS TECHNIQUE

Even when it appears that clients are unlikely to benefit from cognitive restructuring, it can be used if the therapist thinks that they will not be harmed or too sidetracked when they try it. When the disputing of IBs is not very effective, therapists may still find that it provides useful information on how else their resistant clients may benefit. Clients may be able to distract themselves from their problems and obtain palliative relief, even when cognitive restructuring itself is not very effective.

HOW DOES THIS TREATMENT WORK?

First, clients are educated by their therapist to acknowledge the four requisites mentioned above: that dysfunctional thinking significantly contributes to emotional disturbance; that they can constructively change this thinking and function better; that their IBs include strong emotional and behavioral elements; and that they can, by cogni-

tive restructuring, distinctly improve themselves and make themselves less disturbable.

Second, clients are specifically shown the differences between rational (self-helping) and irrational (self-defeating) beliefs. According to the theory of REBT, IBs that accompany disturbances are

1. Rigid and extreme, instead of flexible.
2. Inconsistent instead of consistent with social reality.
3. Illogical or nonsensical instead of logical.
4. Prone to produce dysfunctional feelings (e.g., depression, panic, and rage) rather than functional feelings (e.g., disappointment, concern, and frustration) when the client's goals and purposes are thwarted.
5. Prone to lead to dysfunctional behavioral consequences (e.g., serious avoidances and compulsions) instead of functional consequences (e.g., not avoiding or compulsively dealing with adversities).
6. Demanding and musturbatory philosophies, especially (a) "I absolutely must do well at all times!" (b) "You absolutely must treat me considerately and fairly at all times!" and (c) "Life conditions absolutely must be fair and favorable!"
7. Awfulizing and terribilizing beliefs, such as "I must do well at important tasks, and it's terrible—almost 100% bad—if I don't!" and "Living conditions must be satisfactory, and it's *awful* if they aren't!"
8. Beliefs that depreciate human worth, such as "If I don't perform well and please significant others, as I absolutely must, I am a total failure and am thoroughly unlovable!"

Clients are taught the ABCs of REBT theory and practice, which follow in the next section.

The ABCs of REBT

Clients are taught how to distinguish their RBs from their IBs, to find the specific IBs of their unhealthy feelings and behaviors (Cs), and then to actively and forcefully dispute (D) their IBs. Thus, their goal (G) is to lead a functional and reasonably happy life, in spite of the adversities (As) that occur, but their IBs about As help create their dysfunctional feelings (such as panic and depression) at C (consequences). They are also shown that they often have secondary symptoms of disturbance. Thus, when they feel depressed (C) about failing a test (A), they tend to have the IB that "I must not fail, and it shows that I am an inadequate person when I do!" But they secondarily take their depressed feeling (C) and make it into a new adversity (A): "Oh, I see that I am severely depressed." Then they have an RB about this secondary A ("I don't like being depressed; I wish I weren't"), which leads them to have the healthy C of feeling sorry and disappointed about A. But they also have an IB about A ("I must not be depressed!"), which produces a secondary disturbance, self-deprecation about their depression, at C.

The REBT of cognitive restructuring or disputing of clients' IBs shows them how to strongly (emotionally) and persistently (behaviorally) argue with their IBs in an empirical, logical, and pragmatic manner. Each of these argument types is illustrated in the following sections.

Empirical or Realistic Disputing of Irrational Beliefs

This technique proposes an answer or effective new philosophy (E) for each empirical question. For example, for the empirical question "Where is the evidence that I absolutely *must* perform well at all times and *must not* fail this test?" the answer or E might be "There is no evidence that I *must* not fail, although it would be *preferable* if I succeeded." Likewise, for the empirical question "Why must people like me for doing well at tests?" the answer might be "Obviously, they don't have to. I would like them to like me, but they can choose not to do so."

Logical Disputing of Irrational Beliefs

This technique calls IBs into dispute through logical questioning. For example, the logical query "Does it logically follow that, because I very much want to take tests well and win the approval of others, I absolutely have to do so?" might evoke this answer: "No, it doesn't follow that no matter how much I *want* to do well, I absolutely *have* to do so." Likewise, the logical question "Although it is highly preferable for people

to like me and for me to like myself for being a good test-taker, does it follow that this is *necessary*?" might lead to this answer: "No, it is great if they like me for that reason, but I can be happy and can always accept myself as a person *whether or not* I do well and *whether or not* people like me."

Pragmatic or Heuristic Disputing of Irrational Beliefs

Pragmatic questioning is another technique with which to dispute IBs. An example of a pragmatic question is "Where will it get me if I keep demanding, instead of preferring, that I absolutely must do well at test-taking and at winning people's approval for doing well?" The answer to this question might be "It will most probably get me anxious and depressed. Then I will hardly do well at test-taking or almost anything else!" Another pragmatic question could follow: "Also, where will it get me if I keep demanding that I not be depressed about test-taking? The answer might be "It will help make me depressed about my depression, and again less likely to do well at other tests."

Changing Musturbatory Demands To Preferences

Rational Emotive Behavior Therapy holds that when clients have goals, values, and preferences, they usually react to adversities by feeling healthily sorry and disappointed, but that when they have absolutistic, rigid insistences that they absolutely must do well, must be treated properly by others, and must live with conditions that are satisfactory, they then make themselves anxious, depressed, raging, compulsive, and avoiding. Thus, REBT shows clients how to keep their goals and desires but not raise them to unrealistic and illogical demands. In addition to empirically, logically, and pragmatically disputing clients' demands and helping them change them to preferences, it uses many other cognitive, emotional, and behavioral techniques. Some other forms of cognitive restructuring that clients learn through REBT include the following:

1. Working out rational coping statements—new RBs—and learning how to strongly (emotively) repeat them many times until they act on them.

2. Using positive visualization to hopefully envision their acting on efficacious and functional behaviors.

3. Working on cost-benefit analyses of their disturbed thoughts, feelings, and actions, to motivate them to see how harmful they are and how useful it will be to change them.

4. Doing cognitive homework, especially filling out regularly REBT self-help forms.

5. Modeling themselves after the therapist, after people they know, and after other people they learn about who have successfully changed their dysfunctional beliefs, feelings, and behaviors when assailed by grim As.

6. Reading and listening to REBT and CBT books, pamphlets, tapes, lectures, courses, and workshops.

7. Recording their own therapy sessions and playing them back several times.

8. Learning and using REBT's philosophy of unconditional self-acceptance, unconditional other-acceptance, and unconditional life-acceptance (Ellis, 2001a, 2001b, 2002, 2003).

9. Using practical problem-solving and self-management techniques when afflicted with As in their lives.

CONCLUSION

Rational Emotive Behavior Therapy and (to some extent) many forms of CBT hypothesize that if clients are made fully aware of their specific IBs and are strongly (emotively) and actively (behaviorally) helped to change their unrealistic, illogical, and disturbance-creating absolutistic demands into healthy preferences, they will often considerably reduce their disturbed feelings and behaviors. They can do this by empirically, logically, and heuristically doing cognitive restructuring, along with using various other emotionive-evocative and active-behavioral methods.

Further Reading

Ellis, A. (2001a). *Feeling better, getting better, staying better.* Atascadero, CA: Impact Publishers.

Ellis, A. (2001b). *Overcoming destructive thinking, feeling and behaving.* Amherst, NY: Prometheus Books.

Ellis, A. (2002). *Overcoming resistance: A Rational Emotive Behavior Therapy integrative approach.* New York: Springer Publishing.

References

Adler, A. (1927). *Understanding human nature.* New York: Greenberg.

Beck, A. T. (1967). *Depression.* New York: Hoeber-Harper.

Coué, E. (1923). *My method.* New York: Doubleday-Page.

Dubois, P. (1907). *The psychic treatment of nervous disorders.* New York: Funk and Wagnalls.

Ellis, A. (1957). Outcome of employing three techniques of psychotherapy. *Journal of Clinical Psychology, 13,* 334–350.

Ellis, A. (1958). Rational psychotherapy. *Journal of General Psychology, 59,* 35–49.

Ellis, A. (1962). *Reason and emotion in psychotherapy.* New York: Lyle Stuart.

Ellis, A. (2001a). *Feeling better, getting better, staying better.* Atascadero, CA: Impact Publishers.

Ellis, A. (2001b). *Overcoming destructive thinking, feeling and behaving.* Amherst, NY: Prometheus Books.

Ellis, A. (2002). *Overcoming resistance: A Rational Emotive Behavior Therapy integrative approach.* New York: Springer Publishing.

Ellis, A. (2003). *Anger: How to live with it and without it.* New York: Citadel Press.

Freud, S. (1960). *Jokes and their relation to the unconscious* (James Strachey, Ed. & Trans.). London: Routledge & Kegan Paul. (Original work published 1922)

Herzberg, A. (1945). *Active psychotherapy.* New York: Grune & Stratton.

Horney, K. (1950). *Neurosis and human growth.* New York: Norton.

Janet, P. (1898). *Neuroses et idea fixes* [Neuroses and fixed ideas]. Paris: Alcan.

Korzybski, A. (1991). *Science and sanity.* Concord, CA: International Society for General Semantics. (Original work published 1933)

Lazarus, A. A. (1971). *Behavior therapy and beyond.* New York: McGraw-Hill.

Meichenbaum, D. (1977). *Cognitive-behavior modification.* New York: Plenum.

Salter, A. (1949). *Conditioned reflex therapy.* New York: Creative Age.

15 COGNITIVE RESTRUCTURING: BEHAVIORAL TESTS OF NEGATIVE COGNITIONS

Keith S. Dobson and Kate E. Hamilton

Of the wide range of techniques to challenge negative thoughts in clinical practice, behavioral tests are no doubt one of the most potent. The power of self-observation of behavior has been recognized for a long time and has even formed the basis of developmental models of personality (Bem, 1970). Some have argued that the ability to behave, and to accurately perceive one's actions and consequences, is a hallmark feature of good mental health (Beck, Rush, Shaw, & Emery, 1979).

Negative cognitions have been recognized as features of many different forms of psychopathology, and cognitive behavior therapy has developed a large number of models and techniques to change these negative cognitions (Dobson, 2001). Behavioral tests are a significant part of this set of tools, and they can be widely applied to most problems that involve negative thinking. Negative cognitions that involve predictions about the future or statements about the self or others can be operationalized as hypotheses subject to empirical investigation. It is then possible to generate behavioral tests of these negative cognitions.

In this chapter we will describe the general process of conducting behavioral tests of negative cognitions, and then provide four clinical examples from the domains of anxiety, depression, marital dysfunction, and negative self-schemas more broadly.

The techniques of behavioral tests of negative cognition can be widely applied to a large number of negative cognitions (see Table 15.1 for the key techniques). The types of particular cognitions that are well suited to such tests, however, are those that involve negative predictions, negative attributions, negative conclusions and generalizations, and global self-assessments. Indeed, there are few cognitions that cannot be used to address this technique. Perhaps some of the more difficult types of cognitions put to a behavioral test are memories and delusions. Even in the former instance, however, it is sometimes possible to devise strategies to review historical phenomena, or to conduct interviews with significant figures from the past, to determine whether or not the client's memory accurately portrays what another person believes occurred.

Also, in the case of delusions, there is some evidence that even the process of developing behavioral tests of delusional thinking can significantly undermine the potency of those delusions (see Leeser & O'Donohue, 1999). In many respects, our perspective is that the flexibility of behavioral tests of negative cognitions is limited only by the clinician and the client's imagination.

The unique efficacy of behavioral tests of negative cognitions in cognitive behavior therapy has not been specifically evaluated. However, two dismantling studies have examined the com-

TABLE 15.1   Key Elements of Behavioral Tests of Negative Cognitions

1. Identify the negative cognition and its role in maintaining the problem behavior.

2. Operationalize the problem behavior and generate a behavior test.

3. Review the outcome of the behavior test with respect to the original negative cognition.

parative efficacy of cognitive behavior therapy and its two major components: (1) behavioral activation, and (2) behavioral activation with automatic thought modification. The results suggest that cognitive behavior therapy was no more effective, statistically, than its components either at termination or during a two-year follow-up period (Gortner, Gollan, Dobson, & Jacobson, 1998; Jacobson et al., 1996).

HOW TO USE BEHAVIORAL TESTS TO COUNTER NEGATIVE THINKING

Generally speaking, there are three main phases to the use of behavioral tests of negative thoughts. First, the client and therapist must agree that the negative thought in question is important and that it plays a contributing or maintaining role in the client's overall problem. For example, in anxiety-disordered patients, the tendency to perceive threat in many situations is clearly a negative cognition that perpetuates anxiety. A distressed wife who perceives that her husband only does those things that she wants because she nags him has a negative cognition that perpetuates marital distress. Thus, the first part of developing a behavioral test is working with the client sufficiently to enable him or her to become convinced that the negative cognition plays a critical role and that evaluating or changing this cognition is therapeutically important. In many instances, clients only get to this perspective when they have engaged in the examination of their negative thoughts over a period of time, or when other techniques, such as the dysfunctional thought record, are used (J. Beck, 1995).

Once a client has come to the perspective that his or her thought is worthy of evaluation, the therapist can suggest the possibility of a behav-

ioral test of that thought. Often, such suggestions are put in the form of experiments, assignments, or tasks, which the client and therapist can generate collaboratively, in the spirit of truly understanding the role of these thoughts. A critical factor in this process is ensuring that the patient agrees that this thought, at least in principle, can be modified through a behavioral test. If clients maintain that their particular cognition is absolute or incontestable, or that the therapist doesn't understand them if he or she suggests that it can be changed, clinical wisdom suggests that more preparatory work and data gathering about the role of the thought need to be conducted before the behavioral test is applied.

A second critical element of behavior tests of negative cognitions is the behavioral test itself. The behavior must be clearly specified in order for a behavior test to work well, and the cognition that is being targeted by the behavior test also needs to be well identified. In doing the behavior test itself, it is critical that the therapist and client agree as to what constitutes the behavior. This rule is important in reducing the possibility that the client will engage in a halfhearted attempt at the behavior and then draw the negative conclusion that this type of behavior test does not work. Behavior recordings in the form of audiotape, written description of the test, dysfunctional thought record, or other means might be employed by the therapist and client as aids to ensure that the behavior test is conducted in the way it was intended.

The third, and probably the most critical, aspect of the behavior test of cognitions is the review process. Having engaged in a behavior assignment or experiment, the therapist and client must evaluate the conclusions that the client draws about him- or herself or his or her previous cognitions. For example, if he or she had made a negative prediction, such as in the case of anxiety disorders, the actual experiences of the client need to be contrasted with those expectations in order to ensure that the next time these expectations are present the client can remember that these have been invalidated in the past. Likewise, the depressed patient who more realistically evaluates negative cognitions through behavior assignments needs to be able to see the role of his or her negative thinking in his or her previous higher levels of depression, in order to understand that behavior tests can meaningfully undermine negative cognitions and depression more generally. Thus, although simple behavioral activation in depression may have a salutary effect on depression, our perspective is that the client's perception of that behavior is the critical ingredient.

EXAMPLES OF BEHAVIORAL TESTS TO COUNTER NEGATIVE THINKING

After the patient and therapist are convinced that the cognition is clinically important, and the patient has accepted that the test of the thought may yield important clinical information, the therapist is in a position to actually accept a behavior test. The nature of the actual test will vary, depending on the clinical problem, and for this reason we provide four illustrative examples for the reader.

Panic Disorder

It is now fairly well accepted that panic-disordered patients generally have a critical cognition that involves the idea that if they experience the symptoms they associate with panic they may either be severely injured or even die. For example, a patient who monitors his heart rate may believe that if his heart rate and/or blood pressure exceed a certain value, he is likely to have a cardiac arrest or stroke and be critically injured or die. Therefore, the cognitive behavioral treatment of Panic Disorder typically involves a direct behavioral test of this critical negative cognition. The test is conducted by, first, inducing the patient to accept that this may only be a negative catastrophic prediction and that evaluation of this cognition's role in panic is warranted. Once the patient accepts these premises, the behavioral test begins: The patient engages in an activity that produces paniclike symptoms, but in a way that is structured so that the panic does not actually occur. For example, the patient may be instructed to engage in the exercise of walking up and down a flight of stairs in order to cause his or her heart rate to accelerate; however, when he or she stops the exercise, the heart rate quickly returns to normal without causing a panic attack or a myocardium infarct. Over time, the behavior test can be exaggerated to the point that the client is undertaking activities that he or she previously would have found too risky.

Behavioral tests of negative anxiety–related cognitions are extremely powerful in modifying those predictions (Barlow, 1988). It can be argued that without behavioral tests of these negative cognitions, successful treatment of most anxiety-related disorders is not possible. Contemporary behavior therapy of all the anxiety disorders involves exposure to the fear-provoking stimulus or situation, with cognitive restructuring attendant to behavioral tests (see Table 15.2 for the key elements of cognitive restructuring). Thus, this area probably represents the most widely accepted behavioral test of negative cognitions.

Depressive Cognitions

Depressed patients characteristically make negative assessments of themselves, others, and the world in general (Beck et al., 1979). These cognitive distortions can take many and varied forms, but their characteristic feature is that they typically reflect diminution of the client's self-worth or his or her status in the world. For example, a depressed homemaker may believe that she can never get her housework completed, and she may berate herself for her lack of accomplishment, while maintaining that even if she had been successful in completing her housework it would be of little consequence anyway. Behavioral tests are a potentially effective method to counter depressive cognitions, however. If the depressed homemaker can reach the perspective that her negative thoughts about her housework can be systematically evaluated, or comes to believe that completing her housework is of no particular benefit anyway, the therapist and the client can work together to develop a behavioral examination of these thoughts. Thus, the therapist and client can systematically consider the various tasks that are part of completing the housework, and they can develop a behavior plan for the successful completion of these various tasks. As the client gradually goes through these various areas, the effect of completing these tasks on her sense of accomplishment and mood can be evaluated. Depend-

TABLE 15.2   Key Elements of Cognitive Restructuring

- Show clients the ABCs of Rational Emotive Behavior Therapy (REBT) and cognitive behavior therapy (CBT). Show them that adversities (As) alone do not lead to their disturbed consequences (Cs) but that they personally contribute to their Cs by engaging in strong and persistent beliefs (Bs) about their As. $A \times B = C$.

- Particularly show clients that when they disturb themselves (at point C) they have powerful rational beliefs (RBs) that largely consist of flexible preferences *plus* strong irrational beliefs (IBs) that largely consist of absolutistic, rigid musts, shoulds, and other demands.

- Show clients how to think, feel, and act against their rigid IBs with a number of cognitive, emotive, and behavioral techniques, which interrelate to each other.

- Show clients how to specifically dispute their IBs (1) realistically and empirically, (2) logically, and (3) juristically or pragmatically. Particularly show them how to change their rigid, absolutistic demands on themselves, other people, and world conditions to flexible, workable preferences.

- Show clients that when they actively and persistently dispute (D) their IBs they can create an effective new philosophy (E) that includes strong rational coping statements that can help them to feel better, get better, and stay better.

ing on the client's current level of depression, it is possible to undertake such activities in a graduated fashion, so that the chances of the client's experiencing success in a gradual fashion are maximized.

Marital Distress

One of the characteristic negative thoughts in many distressed couples is that the partner is not truly committed to the success of the relationship and only engages in the positive activities because of the threat of negative consequences if the activity is not done. Thus, it is possible that in a given relationship the wife may believe that her husband only engages in social activities because she insists; if she did not mention these activities and did not remind him of the need to engage in them, they might never happen at all. The paradox is that such negative expectations for the partner may lead the wife to nag or to constantly remind her husband of social obligations and then to make such negative attributions as "he only did this because I nagged him" if he engages in the desired behavior. Thus, even if the husband was to honestly desire social relations, and even if he might engage in these without prompting, her behavior does not allow for this pattern to be recognized. If this pattern can be identified in a distressed relationship, it lends itself nicely to a behavior test of the negative cognition. In order to do a behavior test of this type of thought, it is first necessary for both the wife and the husband to see the pattern of negative thoughts that lead to

nagging behavior and that in effect are reinforced by either compliance or noncompliance with the social activity. The wife would be encouraged to elaborate her model of how her husband will not do these things unless he is nagged. The husband will be encouraged to discuss the effect nagging has on him, which is most likely that he resents it and feels that he does not get the credit he deserves when he actually engages in the things his wife wants. Both partners then need to agree that the wife will experiment with not nagging, on the understanding that if the husband cares for her and is honestly motivated to do these things, they will occur spontaneously. Hopefully, the husband will recognize his opportunity to reduce his partner's nagging and complaining, and will choose to engage in the desired activity without such prompting. In such a case, this behavior test of the effect of lack of complaining can provide powerful information that the husband is more motivated in contributing to the relationship than the wife first believed, can enhance the husband's sense of efficacy in the relationship, and can contribute to overall marital harmony.

Schema Change Therapy

A final example of behavior tests of negative cognitions can be seen in recent emphasis in cognitive behavior therapy on what is known as schema change therapy. Increasingly, therapists are interested in identifying general beliefs that clients have about themselves or how the world generally operates, and in putting these beliefs to behavior tests. For example, if a client comes to believe that he is a social loser, this general belief can be put to a behavior test. In order to perform such a test, the therapist and client must first agree that holding this belief is an important factor in restricting the client and limiting his social attainment. They need to agree that this thought is refutable, if sufficient evidence can be gathered to the contrary, and then they need to develop a behavior test. In order to carry out a test of general belief it is important to first operationalize the belief—"What is a social loser?"—and to work with the client to develop a method to potentially invalidate this self-construction. Often, the therapist will ask the client a question such as "What would it take for you not to believe you are a social loser?" or "How would you know you are no longer a social loser?" This question will help the client be concrete about the specific activities he or she associates with being a social loser, and will help to generate behavior tests of this construct. For example, if one of the criteria that the client enunciates is that he rarely has a date on the weekend evenings, the therapist and client could generate the assignment of getting the client a date, so that he can evaluate his social identity.

Another useful behavior test of a general belief is the as-if technique (J. Beck, 1995). In the as-if technique, a general self-schema that the client has adopted is identified, and some other more positive alternative is then developed. For example, if the client's self-schema is that he or she is unlovable, the alternative of being loved can be generated. The implications of holding the alternative belief can be discussed at length with the client, and then, if appropriate, the client can be encouraged to behave as if he or she is loved. Having done so, the client then evaluates how the adoption of this alternative way of being (both cognitively and behaviorally) affects his or her overall sense of self and emotional valuing. For many clients, such behavior tests are powerful methods to demonstrate to them that they have the potential to be different from their negative perceptions of themselves, and even if they are not fully successful in developing an alternative sense of self, these tests can be important milestones in the path to evaluating a range of possibilities that exist for them.

CONCLUSION

We have tried to demonstrate that behavior tests can be used to undermine a variety of negative cognitions seen in clinical practice, ranging from specific predictions to global negative self-assessments. We have emphasized three main phases of behavior test implementation. The first phase involves the identification of a negative cognition—in particular, the recognition of its importance and its role in maintaining the problem behavior. Having achieved this objective, the therapist and client collaboratively operationalize the problem behavior and generate an appropriate behavior test. Finally, the therapist and client engage in a review process to evaluate the conclusions that the client draws regarding the negative cognition. Clearly, self-observation through behavior tests offers a potent means of challenging and modifying maladaptive cognitions associated with a broad range of clinical problems.

References

Barlow, D. H. (1988). *Anxiety and its disorders: The nature and treatment of anxiety and panic.* New York: Guilford Press.

Beck, A. T., Rush, A. G., Shaw, B. F., & Emery, G. (1979). *Cognitive therapy of depression.* New York: Guilford Press.

Beck, J. (1995). *Cognitive therapy: Basics and beyond.* New York: Guilford Press.

Bem, D. (1970). *Beliefs, attitudes, and human affairs.* California: Brooks.

Dobson, K. S. (2001). *Handbook of cognitive-behavioral therapies* (2nd ed.). New York: Guilford Press.

Gortner, E. T., Gollan, J. K., Dobson, K. S., & Jacobson, N. S. (1998). Cognitive-behavioral treatment for depression: Relapse prevention. *Journal of Consulting and Clinical Psychology, 66,* 377–384.

Jacobson, N. S., Dobson, K. S., Truax, P. A., Addis, M. E., Koerner, K., Gollan, J. K., et al. (1996). A component analysis of cognitive-behavioral treatment for depression. *Journal of Consulting and Clinical Psychology, 64,* 295–304.

Leeser, J., & O'Donohue, W. (1999). What is a delusion? Epistemological dimensions. *Journal of Abnormal Psychology, 108,* 687–694.

16

COGNITIVE RESTRUCTURING: IDENTIFYING AND MODIFYING MALADAPTIVE SCHEMAS

Cory F. Newman

One of the central, identifying features of the cognitive theory of emotional disorders is its emphasis on the psychological significance of clients' beliefs about themselves, their personal world (e.g., other people), and the future (the "cognitive triad," in the words of A. T. Beck, 1976). As Aaron T. Beck formulated and developed cognitive therapy in the 1960s and 1970s, he postulated that much of the client's emotional distress—especially with regard to dysphoria and excessive anxiety—had to do with the problematic, inflexible ways they interpreted the events of their lives. Thus, even if the objective facts of the clients' lives were largely favorable, they might be prone to underestimate their resources and blessings and to overestimate their losses and threats to well-being (e.g., A. T. Beck, Rush, Shaw, & Emery, 1979; A. T. Beck, Emery, & Greenberg, 1985). In other words, even those individuals who behaved in such a way that they could elicit a good deal of positive reinforcement in everyday life, by dint of the negatively biased ways in which they would construe their experience, would not optimally incorporate their successes into their cognitive triad, thus setting themselves up for needless sadness, worry, low self-esteem, and other threats to a higher quality of life.

For those clients whose life situations were sufficiently aversive that others would agree that there were significant reasons to be dysphoric or anxious, the clients' negative beliefs were hypothesized to inhibit them from actively trying to improve their lot, owing to pervasive, ongoing feelings of helplessness and hopelessness (Alloy, Peterson, Abramson, & Seligman, 1984; A. T. Beck, 1976; A. T. Beck, Riskind, Brown, & Steer, 1988). Further, if life events were to become more favorable, an attributional style that did not allow the clients to take personal credit for such good fortune would continue to keep them low in self-esteem and self-efficacy, and thus at continued vulnerability to emotional disorders (Hollon, DeRubeis, & Seligman, 1992).

Various hypotheses have been put forth about the source of these dysfunctional thought processes, including modeling the cognitive style of emotionally troubled primary caregivers, and adverse life experiences, especially early life traumas and retraumatization (such as in the case of more severe personality disorders; see Layden, Newman, Freeman, & Morse, 1993). The problem worsens when individuals with dysfunctional thinking styles cognitively filter out (or minimize) information that would otherwise contradict their negative beliefs. Thus, they come to trust their biased perceptions and beliefs more than they trust their ongoing life experiences, and the negative schemas stubbornly remain in place.

Cognitive therapy endeavors to loosen and modify such troublesome schemas. (Note: The term *schemas* often denotes the most basic core dysfunctional beliefs that clients accept as fundamental truths in their lives. As this chapter focuses on changing clients' beliefs, including those deep enough to be termed schemas, the terms *beliefs* and *schemas* will be used interchangeably).

One of the earliest attempts by A. T. Beck and his colleagues to identify and measure the maladaptive beliefs hypothesized to be the most common culprits in clinical depression and anxiety disorders was their development of the Dysfunctional Attitudes Scale (DAS; Weissman & Beck, 1978). With this self-report questionnaire, clients were asked to endorse their degree of agreement (on a 7-point, Likert-type scale) with a wide range of beliefs, the extremes of which were hypothesized to be indicative of cognitive vulnerability to depression and anxiety. Sample items included the following:

- People will think less of me if I make a mistake.
- If I fail at work, then I am a failure as a person.
- I am nothing if a person I love does not love me.

There is evidence with unipolar depressive clients that changes in such negative beliefs are associated with positive outcome in treatment, as well as the reduction of symptomatic relapses in the future (Evans et al., 1992; Hollon et al., 1992; Parks & Hollon, 1988). Further, major improvements in clients' mood during the course of cognitive therapy have been found to follow sessions in which they made measurable cognitive changes (Tang & DeRubeis, 1999).

As cognitive therapy began to expand its application to additional clinical populations—most notably personality disorders (A. T. Beck, Freeman, & associates, 1990; Layden et al., 1993; Young, 1999)—new measures were developed to tap into the dysfunctional beliefs and schemas that were hypothesized to be salient for clients with long-standing, cross-situational disturbance. For example, the Personality Beliefs Questionnaire (PBQ; A. T. Beck et al., 2001) is a self-report measure that uses a Likert-type scale and comprises a clinically derived set of beliefs hypothesized to correspond to specific personality disorders. For

example, the item "If I ignore a problem, it will go away" is hypothesized to reflect a part of the cognitive style of clients who would meet the criteria outlined by the fourth edition of the *Diagnostic and Statistical Manual of Mental Disorders* (*DSM-IV*; American Psychiatric Association, 1994) for Avoidant Personality Disorder. In fact, early research on this instrument indicates that clients with personality disorders preferentially endorse PBQ items theoretically linked to their specific diagnosis (A. T. Beck et al., 2001).

Additionally, the Young Schema Questionnaire (YSQ; see Schmidt, Joiner, Young, & Telch, 1995) uses a similar self-report, Likert-type scale format as the PBQ, but for the purpose of identifying which of its 15 factor-analyzed schemas clients load on most heavily. These schemas include "mistrust," "defectiveness," "abandonment," "entitlement," and others, and they are hypothesized to be most prevalent in clients with the most severe personality disorders. A sample item is, "It is only a matter of time before someone betrays me" (mistrust schema). Future research on the above questionnaires will indicate their utility in identifying clients' schemas and personality disorders, highlighting targets for cognitive intervention, and measuring changes in beliefs and schemas as a result of treatment.

The major steps in changing cognitive schemas include (1) helping clients to self-monitor their thinking style so as to better understand their active role in creating their life views and emotions; (2), teaching clients the cognitive skills (e.g., self-applied Socratic questioning, rational responding) to be more flexible and adaptive in their attributional style, problem-solving skills, and hopefulness, and to modify and even abandon old ways of thinking; and (3) to create new behavioral repertoires and activities that would actively counteract their previously held (perhaps now outdated) maladaptive beliefs, and that would be more consistent with a broader, more flexible and constructive way of viewing oneself, one's world, and the future.

WHO MIGHT BENEFIT FROM THIS TECHNIQUE?

Any client can benefit from learning the skills of evaluating, testing, and reformulating their own thinking styles so that they become more functional in terms of good problem-solving, self-efficacy, and hopefulness. In fact, therapists themselves often are encouraged in their training and supervision to practice these methods, both as a way to empathize with their clients' trial-and-error learning process and as a way to perform spot checks on their own potentially problematic thinking styles (e.g., testing the belief that "If one of my clients has a depressive setback, it means that I have failed as a therapist").

However, the skills of self-monitoring, testing, and modifying one's beliefs can be particularly beneficial for clients who demonstrate one or both of the following clinical problems:

1. Those who have difficulty incorporating positive experiences into their overarching views of themselves, their lives, and their futures.
2. Those whose behavioral repertoire is based on faulty assumptions of personal failure and interpersonal rejection, such that they systematically inhibit themselves from trying to advance their lives, and expect (and then perhaps elicit) uncaring or conflictual interactions with others.

Clients such as those who exhibit these problems can improve their lives in an enduring way by learning to pay attention to, and to create, productive and constructive ways to use their time (without undue fear of failure), and to relate to others (without undue fear or mistrust).

CONTRAINDICATIONS OF THE TREATMENT

The drawbacks of the treatment fall into two categories, and they are readily avoided if the therapists are alert and diligent. The first category has to do with a suboptimal therapeutic relationship, and the second has to do with an incomplete or inaccurate case conceptualization.

Insufficient Rapport and/or Accurate Empathy

Regarding the first point, it is inadvisable for therapists to be too heavy-handed in their attempts to persuade clients to change their long-held beliefs. Cognitive therapy is a collaborative

therapy; thus, it is contraindicated to apply undue pressure on clients to relinquish their viewpoints. Therapists must demonstrate respect for the clients' ways of construing their worlds. Thus, when therapists suggest that clients consider testing the objectivity and functionality of their thinking, they would do well to point out how the clients may benefit from this self-reflective skill, especially in the long run. It is very important for therapists to try to understand how it is that the clients have developed their beliefs and how they are maintained. In doing so, therapists will be able to give sincere validation for their clients' ways of viewing their lives, as a prelude to trying to work together to find a better way to view them.

Similarly, the process of cognitive therapy loses its effectiveness and appeal if it is reduced to an arid, intellectual debate. The therapeutic relationship needs to involve empathy, warmth, and a little bit of appropriate humor. It is also important to insert some creativity into the process (cf. Rosen, 2000) so that there is stimulation and life in the therapeutic dialogue. These qualities in the therapeutic alliance help to ease the sometimes difficult and unfamiliar process of identifying and modifying maladaptive beliefs.

Inadequate Case Formulation

The second problem has to do with the therapist's insufficient attention to the client's unique phenomenology, including the client's personal history, current life situation (and its contingencies), and cultural factors. If therapists take a one-size-fits-all approach, such as by insisting that all clients need to relinquish a given belief, they will miss important, idiographic nuances that are vital to the understanding of the client. Thus, the therapist's interventions will seem off the mark, and the process of treatment will suffer (see J. S. Beck, 1995; Needleman, 1999; Persons, 1989).

STEP-BY-STEP PROCEDURES

The changing of dysfunctional schemas is neither a quick procedure nor a simple one. Accomplishing this difficult but worthy goal requires a combination of techniques, proffered in the spirit of a positive therapeutic alliance, and a well-formulated case conceptualization. There are a number of ways that cognitive therapists can help their clients in changing harmful beliefs into more healthy ones. Some of these methods are based on the structured, standard repertoire as demonstrated by A. T. Beck et al. (1979) and J. S. Beck (1995), such as the use of the daily thought records (DTRs). Other techniques stem from the principles inherent in using DTRs but may require some flexibility and creativity.

The following are some of the most commonly used techniques, often used as a package over numerous sessions. Although the sequence of usage is by no means etched in stone, the following methods are presented as representing a reasonable progression.

Let Emotions Be the Cue to Start the Process

It is very useful to demonstrate how clients' problematic moods can provide them with valuable information about their thought process. Specifically, clients are asked to notice their episodes of excessive anger, despair, fear, and the like, and to choose not to accept them at face value. Rather, clients are instructed to ask themselves, "What could be going through my mind right now that could be triggering or worsening how I'm feeling right now?" Clients are taught to write down their hypotheses.

Sometimes clients have a difficult time with this process, saying that they do not know what they are thinking coincidental to their upset. Therapists respond by saying, "You do not need to know *for certain*. It is sufficient if you take some educated guesses." If clients still demur, therapists can provide clients with a multiple-choice list of reasonable thoughts, and the client is asked, "Which of these thoughts rings a bell with you? Which of these *could* represent the way you view the situation?" At this point, it is usually possible to write down a list of plausible thoughts.

Many of these thoughts will hang together thematically. Patterns will emerge, such as expectations of abandonment, or mistrust of others, or the conviction of being unlovable, or certainty of being a failure, among other schemas. Further, therapists can utilize the clients' responses from questionnaires such as the DAS, PBQ, and YSQ to identify schemas that will need to be targets for intervention.

One of the most compelling ways clients can identify their schemas is by learning to spot when their emotional buttons, so to speak, have been pushed. In other words, therapists inform their clients that there will be times when their emotional reactions seem greatly disproportionate to the situation (at least in retrospect). Other people may say to the clients that they are being hypersensitive or are overreacting. Clients are taught that, rather than feeling angry or ashamed about this, they should ask themselves the question, "What *schema* just got activated?" For example, a woman became suicidal after getting what she thought was a bad haircut (see Layden et al., 1993). When the client asked herself this question, she concluded that she expected that her boyfriend would now leave her, thus activating both her "defectiveness" and "abandonment" schemas. This self-assessment paved the way for some cognitive modifications, along with emotional de-escalation.

Use Socratic Questions

Clients learn that they are prone to have systematic biases in the way they perceive and interpret their experiences. Thus, they are encouraged to question their own reactions—not in a self-denigrating way, but rather in a spirit of self-enhancing inquiry. Therapists use Socratic questions throughout the course of therapy in order to highlight the clients' need to re-evaluate their schemas. Additionally, clients are taught a standard series of Socratic questions they can use themselves, usually as part of their efforts to generate "rational responses" on their DTRs (see J. S. Beck, 1995).

Therapist-Generated Socratic Questions

Given that one of the main characteristics of dysfunctional schemas is their rigidity, it is unproductive for therapists to try to argue their clients out of their beliefs. If clients believe that "There is no point in getting close to others, because they will always leave me and I'll be devastated," the therapists will make little headway if they simply exhort the clients to believe that people will *not* always abandon them, and they will *not* always be devastated. Instead, therapists use open-ended, Socratic questions with the goal of helping clients expand their ability to consider other ways of looking at the situation. Therapists should take the following, general approaches in order to maximize this method: (1) Listen carefully to all of the clients' statements that (in passing) go against their own beliefs, and compile a mental or written list of such utterances; (2) ask clients for examples from their own life experience that seem to offer evidence against a rote acceptance of their negative schemas; and (3) if clients can succeed in generating such examples, ask the clients to reconcile this with their belief, and to consider the possibility that there may be exceptions to the rule that need to be considered; whereas (4) if the clients cannot offer such examples from their personal history, the therapist can tactfully report from the list they have generated (see step 1) as evidence for modifying the belief. Further, it should be noted that examples of ongoing, positive interactions in the therapeutic relationship often are excellent examples of data that go against clients' most pernicious schemas, most notably "mistrust" and "defectiveness."

Clients' Socratic Questions for Themselves

Clients are also taught to use the following Socratic (or *guided discovery*) questions for themselves, often as part of their between-sessions homework. After they have identified some of the thoughts and deeper schemas that may be responsible for their dysphoria or excessive anxiety, clients are asked to subject them to the following questions (adapted from J. S. Beck, 1995):

1. What other plausible perspective(s) can I take about this matter?
2. What factual evidence supports or refutes my beliefs?
3. What are the pros and cons of continuing to see things the way I see them, and what are the pros and cons of trying to see things differently?
4. What constructive action can I take to deal with my beliefs or schemas?
5. What sincere advice would I give to a good friend with the same beliefs?

Again, this exercise, performed repetitively across many situations and beliefs, has the power to loosen old, dysfunctional beliefs, and perhaps to prime them to be modified by new, more hopeful experiences.

Behavioral Experiments

Purely verbal techniques sometimes lack sufficient experiential power to provide clients with the necessary "aha!" reaction that can help them see things in a new and better way. Thus, behavioral experiments are used in order to provide in vivo evidence in support of the revised, more functional (i.e., less extreme, more flexible) beliefs.

In-Session Role Playing

Here, therapists ask clients to adopt the role of someone who sees life options outside the confines of the negative schemas, while the therapist takes the role of the supporter of the maladaptive schemas. The challenge is to stay in the role and to perform the negative part of the dialogue with respect—not as a caricature of the client. After the role-playing exercise is completed, the client is asked for feedback on the experience. Many repetitions of this process may be needed over the course of a number of sessions.

Homework between Sessions

In order to generalize the above process to the client's natural environment, clients are asked to test their beliefs between sessions. For example, the client who believes that everyone will abandon her may be asked to telephone three friends, or perhaps even to invite one or more to lunch (or another activity). Although the client may predict that she will be ignored, rejected, or stood up, she is encouraged nonetheless to take the chance of joining her friends and to pay close attention to *what actually happens.* If it happens that the client reports that her negative beliefs have been borne out, the therapist will turn the client's attention to a post hoc evaluation of what may have gone wrong, so as to make behavioral corrections in the future. More often than not, the outcome will go against the client's beliefs, but she will have a difficult time relinquishing the beliefs anyway. This is a standard outcome, because beliefs are difficult to change with any one intervention. Multiple interventions, with numerous repetitions, are required.

TABLE 16.1 Summary of Procedures

1. Use instruments such as the DAS, PBQ, and YSQ to identify problematic schemas, or assess them in response to clients' emotional reactions that are greatly disproportionate to the situation (an indicator of *schema activation*).

2. Provide the clients with validation and accurate empathy, based on a well-constructed case conceptualization.

3. Teach the clients to use their magnified, problematic emotional responses as cues to ask themselves what they are thinking and what schemas may have been activated.

4. Use Socratic questions to loosen the beliefs or schemas, and teach the clients to use these questions for themselves. Look closely at evidence from life experiences.

5. Use behavioral enactments, both in the form of in-session role playing and between-sessions experiments, so clients gain experience in acting on new beliefs.

6. In cases of early life traumas that have etiological significance, use a combination of relaxation, guided imagery, and rational reevaluation to counteract the negative beliefs and schemas that the clients have derived from these salient historical experiences.

7. Be prepared to have to use combinations of these techniques, numerous times, over the course of many sessions.

Imagery Reconstruction

A full description of the technique of imagery reconstruction is beyond the scope of this chapter; however, its importance warrants mention. Combining aspects of relaxation, guided imagery, and the use of rational reevaluation (as described earlier in this chapter) of past experiences salient to the client's schemas, imagery reconstruction is a highly evocative technique that should be used judiciously and with care. The rationale for this procedure includes the need for clients to be in an emotional state relevant to the activation of their schemas in order to best entertain alternative views to the schema, as well as the importance of revisiting key historical events that may have to do with the etiology of the schema.

For example, a client who believes he is a flawed and defective person owing to his experiences of childhood sexual abuse may be very resistant to changing this belief through standard methods of rational reevaluation in the here and now. However, in the context of a trusting therapeutic relationship, and under the calming influence of a relaxation induction, he may be more receptive to an imaginal revisiting of the scene of the abuse. The therapeutic guides the procedure cautiously and caringly, and the client's beliefs (pertinent to the memory) are elicited. Most importantly, the client is asked to talk to himself, as he remembers himself at the critical time in question, in order to give support and offer alternative, benevolent, compassionate, rational reinterpretations about his perceived defectiveness.

Similar procedures are described in great detail in Foa and Rothbaum (1998), Layden et al. (1993), and Resick and Schnicke (1993). See Table 16.1 for a summary of procedures.

Further Reading

Emery, G. (2000). *Overcoming depression: A cognitive-behavioral protocol for the treatment of depression.* Oakland, CA: New Harbinger.

Newman, C. F., & Haaga, D. A. F. (1995). Cognitive skills training. In W. O'Donohue & L. Krasner (Eds.), *Handbook of Psychological Skills Training* (pp. 119–143). Needham Heights, MA: Allyn & Bacon.

References

Alloy, L. B., Peterson, C., Abramson, L. Y., & Seligman, M. E. P. (1984). Attributional style and the generality of learned helplessness. *Journal of Personality and Social Psychology, 46*(3), 681–687.

American Psychiatric Association (1994). *Diagnostic and statistical manual of mental disorders* (4th ed.). Washington, DC: Author.

Beck, A. T. (1976). *Cognitive therapy and the emotional disorders.* New York: International Universities Press.

Beck, A. T., Butler, A. C., Brown, G. K., Dahlsgaard, K. K., Newman, C. F., & Beck, J. S. (2001). Dysfunctional beliefs discriminate personality disorders. *Behaviour Research and Therapy, 39*(10), 1213–1225.

Beck, A. T., Emery, G., & Greenberg, R. L. (1985). *Anxiety disorders and phobias: A cognitive perspective.* New York: Basic Books.

Beck, A. T., Freeman, A., & Associates. (1990). *Cognitive*

therapy of personality disorders. New York: Guilford Press.

Beck, A. T., Riskind, J. H., Brown, G., & Steer, R. A. (1988). Levels of hopelessness in DSM-III disorders: A partial test of content specificity in depression. *Cognitive Therapy and Research, 12*(5), 459–469.

Beck, A. T., Rush, A. J., Shaw, B., & Emery, G. (1979). *Cognitive therapy of depression.* New York: Guilford Press.

Beck, J. S. (1995). *Cognitive therapy: Basics and beyond.* New York: Guilford Press.

Evans, M. D., Hollon, S. D., DeRubeis, R. J., Piasecki, J. M., Grove, W. M., Garvey, M. J., et al. (1992). Differential relapse following cognitive therapy and pharmacology for depression. *Archives of General Psychiatry, 49,* 802–808.

Foa, E. B., & Rothbaum, B. O. (1998). *Treating the trauma of rape: Cognitive-behavioral therapy for PTSD.* New York: Guilford Press.

Greenberger, D., & Padesky, C. (1995). *Mind over mood.* New York: Guilford Press.

Hollon, S. D., DeRubeis, R. J., & Seligman, M. E. P. (1992). Cognitive therapy and the prevention of depression. *Applied and Preventive Psychiatry, 95,* 52–59.

Layden, M. A., Newman, C. F., Freeman, A., & Morse, S. B. (1993). *Cognitive therapy of borderline personality disorder.* Boston, MA: Allyn & Bacon.

Needleman, L. (1999). *Cognitive case conceptualization: A guide for practitioners.* Mahwah, NJ: Erlbaum.

Parks, C. W., Jr., & Hollon, S. D. (1988). Cognitive assessment. In A. S. Bellack & M. Hersen (Eds.), *Behavioral assessment: A practical handbook* (3rd ed., pp. 161–212). Elmsford, NY: Pergamon Press.

Persons, J. (1989). *Cognitive therapy in practice: A case formulation approach.* New York: W. W. Norton.

Resick, P. A., & Schnicke, M. K. (1993). *Cognitive processing therapy for rape victims: A treatment manual.* London: Sage.

Rosen, H. (2000). The creative evolution of the theoretical foundation for cognitive therapy. *Journal of Cognitive Psychotherapy: An International Quarterly, 14*(2), 123–134.

Schmidt, N. B., Joiner, T. E., Jr., Young, J. E., & Telch, M. J. (1995). The Schema Questionnaire: Investigation of psychometric properties and the hierarchical structure of a measure of maladaptive schemas. *Cognitive Therapy and Research, 19*(3), 295–321.

Tang, T. Z., & DeRubeis, R. J. (1999). Sudden gains and critical sessions in cognitive-behavioral therapy for depression. *Journal of Consulting and Clinical Psychology, 67*(6), 894–904.

Weissman, A. N., & Beck, A. T. (1978). Development and validation of the Dysfunctional Attitudes Scale: A preliminary investigation. Paper presented at the annual meeting of the American Educational Research Association, Toronto, Canada.

Young, J. E. (1999). *Cognitive therapy for personality disorders: A schema-focused approach* (3rd edition). Sarasota, FL: Professional Resource Exchange.

17 COMMUNICATION/PROBLEM-SOLVING SKILLS TRAINING

Pamella H. Oliver and Gayla Margolin

Communication training historically has been an integral component of behavioral marital therapy and continues to be a fundamental procedure utilized in contemporary forms of therapy for marital or couple distress (Jacobson & Christensen, 1996). Communication training involves the practice and enactment of two sets of skills—speaker/listener skills and problem-solving skills. In behavioral marital therapy, communication training typically is paired with behavior exchange interventions. Based on social learning theory, behavior marital therapy focuses on improving couples' interaction through skills training and through changing conditions in the environment that establish and maintain behavioral patterns. Jacobson and Margolin (1979), the traditional treatment manual for behavior marital therapy, provides a detailed description of communication training plus other therapy techniques such as behavior exchange. The steps of communication training are also provided in other, generally more recent, manuals for therapists (Baucom & Epstein, 1990; Jacobson & Christensen, 1996) and for clients (Christensen & Jacobson, 2000; Gottman, Notarius, Gonso, & Markman, 1976; Notarius & Markman, 1993).

Preparation of this manuscript was supported in part by a grant from the David and Lucile Packard Foundation.

PROPOSED MECHANISMS OF EFFECT

Many therapeutic treatments for distressed couples include communication training. The rationale for the procedure is derived from two models. One is a skills deficit model, the other a stimulus-response model. Communication skills training is basically a skills-oriented approach. The training is sometimes prescribed because the distressed couple is assumed to lack basic interpersonal skills with which to negotiate conflict. In contrast, the stimulus-response model assumes that although partners possess communication skills in general, they do not use effective communication behavior in the particular context of relationship tension. From this perspective, communication training is used as a means of stimulus control. That is, communication training provides a structure to circumvent the couple's well-developed patterns that preclude using effective communication and problem-solving skills. Whether the destructive behavioral patterns are seen as etiologic or as maintaining the problems, the couple's task is twofold: to learn and practice any necessary skills, and to utilize the structured procedures in such a way that the context of conflict is fundamentally changed.

OUTCOME RESEARCH

Research on the efficacy and effectiveness of communication skills training is embedded in empirical research on behavioral marital therapy. Baucom and colleagues (Baucom, Shoham, Mueser, Daiuto, & Stickle, 1998) have determined, based on more than 20 published controlled-treatment-outcome investigations, that behavioral marital therapy is an "efficacious and specific intervention" (Chambless & Hollon, 1998) for maritally distressed couples. With respect to the long-term effects of communication skills training in particular, a component analysis of behavioral marital therapy indicated that after 6 months the communication skills training component showed superior maintenance of treatment gains over the behavioral exchange component (Jacobson, 1984). However, a subsequent 2-year follow-up indicated no differential benefit of either component, and approximately 30% of couples who had improved in therapy later relapsed (Jacobson, Schmaling, & Holtzworth-Munroe, 1987).

In addition to questions of efficacy, a limited number of studies also have investigated the effectiveness, or real-life generalizability, of behavioral marital therapy. These studies have reported positive consumer ratings (Baucom et al., 1998). Dropout rates are estimated to be low, as suggested by a 6% attrition rate found by Hahlweg and Markman in their meta-analysis of behavioral marital therapy studies (1988).

INDICATIONS FOR USE

Communication skills training is generally considered an essential part of couples therapy, and its application may be extended to preventing marital distress as well as treating depression in maritally distressed couples. Most spouses do not apply the basic listening and problem-solving skills presented here to the difficult, conflictual issues of their relationship. Many have never used such skills. Others, who may be skilled communicators in some situations, dispense with good listening and problem solving when such skills are most needed, that is, in moments of frustra-

tion and anger. Instead, these spouses either withdraw from the interaction or resort to bombarding the spouse with the same ill-stated point. Preventive programs for couples incorporate similar intervention steps (e.g., Floyd, Markman, Kelly, Blumberg, & Stanley, 1995; Hahlweg & Markman, 1988), and thus these procedures are recommended for a more general clientele than just distressed couples. In addition, behavioral marital therapy has been shown to be successful in the treatment of depression. Results indicate that it is as beneficial as cognitive therapy in relieving depressive symptoms of wives in distressed couples, and more effective in enhancing the marital satisfaction of these couples (Jacobson, Dobson, Fruzzetti, Schmaling, & Salusky, 1991).

COMMUNICATION SKILLS TRAINING PROCEDURES

Weiss (1978) was the first to clarify the two modes of communication, speaker/listener skills and problem-solving skills, and to identify the difficulties if one spouse wants to express emotions while the other starts to problem-solve. Speaker/listener skills result in understanding and validation of a partner's perspective. These skills are an important goal in themselves as well as a preliminary step to problem solving. Productive problem solving occurs only when partners fully understand one another's viewpoint. Problem-solving skills lead to changes in the way partners handle a given situation. However, issues that do not require an action-oriented response need not progress to the problem-solving phase.

Function of Speaker/Listener Skills

The goal of practicing speaker/listener skills is to facilitate the accurate sending and receiving of messages. A common pattern in distressed couples is that communication falls into highly ritualized patterns, characterized by rapidly escalating conflict or frustrated withdrawal. Such patterns generally are fueled when one partner, feeling misunderstood, repeats and reiterates the same information. The other partner, feeling attacked, defends or counterattacks by responding to one small segment of information. The goal of practicing speaker/listener skills is to interrupt such ritualized patterns by building in steps that guarantee that spouses accurately receive one another's messages. Instructions that insert additional steps in couples' communication dramatically slow down the communication process and thereby interrupt well-rehearsed patterns. The additional steps change the fundamental nature of the communication and promote different expectations about the purpose of the interaction. When successfully enacted, these changes allow participants to figure out and articulate what they truly want to say and to ensure that the partner has accurately received the message.

In addition to imparting new skills, speaker/listener skills training also creates a stimulus situation that triggers the enactment of constructive speaker and listener behaviors rather than angry or divisive behaviors (Margolin, 1987). The enactment of these behaviors results in a greater closeness and intimacy despite the fact that the partners do not necessarily resolve the problem. This process of using problem discussions to enhance closeness is similar to the processes of "empathic joining" (Jacobson & Christensen, 1996) or "building a joint platform" (Wile, 1993).

Step-by-Step Procedures for Speaker/Listener Skills

For the purposes of training and practice, the speaker and listener roles are clearly defined. One partner, the speaker, introduces a topic that she or he wants to discuss, and the other partner, the listener, is to demonstrate that she or he understands what is being said.

The Listener's Role

The therapist defines and demonstrates four separate skills of increasing complexity that demonstrate accurate listening (Jacobson & Christensen, 1996; Jacobson & Margolin, 1979). Parroting, the most straightforward skill, requires the listener simply to repeat back verbatim what the partner has said. Paraphrasing requires the listener to rephrase, in her or his own words, the content of the communication. Reflection requires the listener to discern the emotion behind the speaker's message and to verbally check out that emotional in-

terpretation with the speaker. Validation conveys to the speaker that her or his perspective is understandable. Thus, the speaker's statement "I can't believe you didn't call your mother to let her know we'd be late for dinner" could be repeated back in those exact words, paraphrased as "You wanted me to call my mother letting her know we'd be late," reflected as "You're angry at me for not calling my mother and maybe also embarrassed that we delayed her dinner party," or validated as "It makes sense that you'd be angry at me if you thought I had made the call." It is important to note that none of these responses requires the listener to agree with the speaker.

These four listener skills are introduced sequentially. A new skill is introduced only when the previous skill has been mastered. The therapist actively directs the back-and-forth communication, prompting the listener's restatement, and asking the speaker if the listener's statement was correct. If the listener was not correct, the entire process is repeated. The communication is thus slowed down considerably by building in checks for clarity and accuracy before a reply can be given.

The Speaker's Role

At the same time that one partner is practicing listening skills, the other is practicing expressive skills. Expressive skills are as important as listening skills in fostering productive communication. Frequently a speaker begins to present a concern without fully knowing or acknowledging what makes that situation upsetting. Accurate expressiveness, or being able to state what is truly on one's mind, often evolves through the communication process. Through clarification and feedback from the listener, be it the partner or the therapist, the speaker gains further understanding about why a given situation is particularly distressing. According to Wile (1993), spouses' seemingly disproportionate anger often stems from feeling unentitled to very reasonable and normal reactions. Different dimensions of the process of expressing the core underlying feelings associated with a problem have been described as leveling (e.g., Gottman et al., 1976) or as disclosing "soft" as opposed to "hard" emotions (Jacobson & Christensen, 1996).

For the listener to accurately restate the

speaker's message, that message needs to be stated succinctly. Thus, an important role for the therapist is to interrupt statements that are too long and to cue the listener to restate what has been said thus far. This process of chunking speaker statements into manageable units provides the speaker with essential feedback about what portions of her or his statement have been received, thereby reducing the tendency for speakers to repeat the same message. Moreover, listeners can be encouraged to restate part of the speaker's statement but to raise questions if another part is still confusing. Only when the speaker has finished stating her or his complete point and the listener has demonstrated understanding of the entire message does the listener present her or his perspective. At that point, speaker and listener roles reverse. There is no guarantee in this process that the new speaker will not come across as angry and defensive, but at least she or he has accurately heard the original speaker's point of view.

The Therapist's Role

As described previously, the therapist plays an active role in maximizing the likelihood of success in speaker/listener skills training. The therapist models both speaker and listener behaviors and encourages, prompts, and reinforces the partners' efforts in this process. Most importantly, the therapist monitors and interrupts the process when it is not working to bring it back to a more productive course. Some instructions for communication training include extensive lists of "do" and "don't" rules. Certainly it is important for the therapist to demonstrate and prompt ways for partners to express strong feelings without provoking an immediate counterattack. However, the primary objective of speaker/listener skills training should not be overshadowed by undue attention to a list of communication rules. The overriding goal is to create an atmosphere of mutual respect and openness so that spouses can get their most difficult and controversial points across to one another.

Function of Problem-Solving Skills

Problem-solving skills training is designed to provide spouses with a strategy for examining and responding to situations that they want to change but are in disagreement about how to change. Thus, problem-solving skills are used when the spouses feel "stuck" because each is entrenched in a position that is different from, if not diametrically opposed to, the other's position. Three steps are involved in problem-solving skills. The first is to define the problem in a manner that is noninflammatory and that incorporates the role of both partners, thereby increasing the motivation of both partners to want to solve the problem. The second is to generate a broad array of solutions to the problem, thereby increasing the likelihood that the partners will find some set of solutions upon which they can agree. The third is to craft a carefully considered plan of action that can be put into effect quickly and, in subsequent sessions, can be monitored and modified. Proposed solutions are construed as works in progress: That is, even if they are successful, they generally need to be updated and revised as the problem starts to be resolved and/or as circumstances change. The content of each phase of the problem-solving session should be documented in writing to help keep the process on track and to avoid disagreements about the specifics of the agreed-upon plan.

Step-by-Step Procedures for Problem Solving

Skilled problem solving consists of four main steps, which are described in the sections that follow.

Defining the Problem

Problem definition is the most important and most difficult step in problem solving. It is the most important because it sets up a framework for thinking about and approaching the problem. It is the most difficult because it requires translating one spouse's complaint into a nonblaming relationship issue. It also requires balancing the specificity and generality of the problem definition—specificity so that spouses know what problem is being addressed, and generality so that they do not solve a small manifestation of a larger issue.

Ideally, problem definition acknowledges the role of both spouses and the consequences of the problem for both spouses. When those components are included, spouses find it easier to collaborate with brainstorming solutions. However, in generating the problem definition, it is common for spouses to revert to a pattern in which one partner complains or criticizes and the other partner defends her or his behavior. This situation is best managed by (1) not defining problems when either spouse is angry; (2) reminding spouses to state the problem in a way that is easiest for the partner to hear; (3) employing speaker/listener skills as needed; and (4) making sure that spouses do not sidetrack each other from one problem to another (Jacobson & Margolin, 1979).

Particularly when couples are first learning problem-solving skills, the therapist needs to play an active role to ensure that spouses define the problem in a way that opens up creative and constructive possibilities for addressing the problematic issue. For example, the initial complaint of a wife who comanaged a business with her husband was that the husband was obsessed with the business. This complaint directed toward the spouse was translated into the mutual issue that the couple had no relationship time apart from their business dealings. The redefinition of this problem opened up possibilities for new solutions toward reserving special relationship time as well as making sure that mutual business issues were adequately dealt with in a timely fashion.

Brainstorming Solutions

Once the partners and the therapist have agreed on a problem definition, the brainstorming process begins. The primary rules of brainstorming are that (1) any idea, no matter how outrageous, is worthy of mention, and (2) no evaluation of ideas takes place until the entire list is generated and rated. As a result of these rules, spouses are less inhibited in presenting their ideas and they stay focused on the one problem under discussion (Jacobson & Margolin, 1979). Each solution is written down until a list of 10 to 20 solutions is generated.

Rating Brainstormed Solutions

Still without discussion, spouses independently rate each suggestion (1 = suggestion is good; 2 = suggestion may be worthy of consideration; 3 =

TABLE 17.1   Communication Training

Speaker/listener skills	
Listener behaviors	Repeat verbatim
	Paraphrase
	Reflect
	Validate
Speaker behaviors	Make succinct statements
	Clarify and express accurate feeling statements
Problem-solving skills	Define problem in mutual, nonblaming language
	Brainstorm and then rate problem solutions
	Develop plan to be enacted in stated time period
	Implement plan
	Review implementation and revise plan

suggestion is bad). Each item rated as a 3 by both spouses is immediately removed from the list. Each item with a 1-1 or a 1-2 combination is discussed to develop a plan based on one or more of these ideas.

Developing and Revising a Plan

The initial plan should incorporate suggestions that can be put into effect within the next week, with the possibility of incorporating other steps in future weeks. Thus, a problem solution is reevaluated and revised until the problem is solved or a long-range solution is in place. What makes this process of problem solving very rewarding to spouses is that they discover multiple mutually acceptable solutions to a problem that previously seemed unsolvable.

See Table 17.1 for a summary listing of important communication/problem-solving skills.

GENERALIZABILITY

Following each session of communication skills training, spouses are given a homework assignment with which to repeat and consolidate the behaviors practiced in session and extend the behaviors to a new topic. When learning speaking/listening behaviors, spouses typically are asked to set aside a half hour once or twice during the week with each spouse alternately taking the role as speaker and as listener. Similarly, once the spouses have practiced problem solving with the therapist on several different issues, they can be asked to try the same procedures at home. For the first such assignment, the therapist may want to complete the problem definition in the session and then have the couple do the brainstorming and problem solution at home.

It is generally advised that the topics selected for homework practice of speaker/listener skills or of problem-solving skills should be less conflictual than those addressed in the session. Having the couple tape-record their communication skills homework is a good way for the therapist and couple to review homework practices. As with all between-session assignments, the therapist must fully debrief the homework during the next session. Ultimately, the goal is for the couple, on their own, to recognize when they need to use communication skills and then to employ the skills on their own.

CONCLUSION

Communication skills training sets up the structure and expectation that spouses will listen to each other and approach problem solving in new ways. Interaction behaviors to be enacted are shaped, with the therapist initially doing much modeling and reinforcing and spouses gradually doing the steps more independently. Although the steps of communication skills training are spelled out in several manuals, the timing and sequencing are left to the therapist's judgment. In order to optimize each individual couple's likelihood of success at each therapeutic stage, the therapist uses her or his judgment with respect to when to introduce communication skills training, how to pace the training, whether to begin the training on more or less serious problems, whether to combine communication training with other intervention procedures, and whether to introduce communication skills in a formal, educational manner or to work them in seam-lessly as needed in the couple's discussion of their problems.

References

Baucom, D. H., & Epstein, N. (1990). *Cognitive-behavioral marital therapy*. New York: Brunner/Mazel.

Baucom, D. H., Shoham, V., Mueser, K. T., Daiuto, A. D., & Stickle, T. R. (1998). Empirically supported couple and family interventions for marital distress and adult mental health problems. *Journal of Consulting and Clinical Psychology, 66*, 53–88.

Chambless, D. L., & Hollon, S. D. (1998). Defining empirically supported therapies. *Journal of Consulting and Clinical Psychology, 66*, 7–18.

Christensen, A., & Jacobson, N. S. (2000). *Reconcilable differences*. New York: Guilford Press.

Floyd, F. J., Markman, H. J., Kelly, S., Blumberg, S. L., & Stanley, S. M. (1995). Preventive intervention and relationship enhancement. In N. S. Jacobson & A. S. Gurman (Eds.), *Clinical handbook of couple therapy* (pp. 212–226). New York: Guilford Press.

Gottman, J., Notarius, C., Gonso, J., & Markman, H. (1976). *A couple's guide to communication*. Champaign, IL: Research Press.

Hahlweg, K., & Markman, H. J. (1988). Effectiveness of behavioral marital therapy: Empirical status of behavioral techniques in preventing and alleviating marital distress. *Journal of Consulting and Clinical Psychology, 56*, 440–447.

Jacobson, N. S. (1984). A component analysis of behavioral marital therapy: The relative effectiveness of behavioral exchange and communication/problem-solving training. *Journal of Consulting and Clinical Psychology, 52*, 295–305.

Jacobson, N. S., & Christensen, A. (1996). *Integrative couple therapy: Promoting acceptance and change*. New York: W. W. Norton.

Jacobson, N. S., Dobson, K., Fruzzetti, A. E., Schmaling, D. B., & Salusky, S. (1991). Marital therapy as treatment for depression. *Journal of Consulting and Clinical Psychology, 59*, 547–557.

Jacobson, N. S., & Margolin, G. (1979). *Marital therapy: Strategies based on social learning and behavior exchange principles*. New York: Brunner/Mazel.

Jacobson, N. S., Schmaling, K. B., & Holtzworth-Munroe, A. (1987). Component analysis of behavioral martial therapy: 2-year follow-up and prediction of relapse. *Journal of Marital and Family Therapy, 13*, 187–195.

Margolin, G. (1987). Marital therapy: A cognitive-behavioral-affective approach. In N. S. Jacobson (Ed.), *Psychotherapists in clinical practice: Cognitive and behavioral perspectives* (pp. 232–285). New York: Guilford Press.

Notarius, C., & Markman, H. (1993). *We can work it out: Making sense of marital conflict.* New York: G. P. Putnam's Sons.

Weiss, R. L. (1978). The conceptualization of marriage from a behavioral perspective. In T. J. Paolino & B. S. McCrady (Eds.), *Marriage and marital therapy: Psychoanalytic behavioral and systems theory perspectives* (pp. 165–239). New York: Brunner/Mazel.

Wile, D. (1993). *After the fight: A night in the life of a couple.* New York: Guilford Press.

18 COMPLIANCE WITH MEDICAL REGIMENS

Elaine M. Heiby and Maxwell R. Frank

In past decades, many medical regimens and public health advisories have involved prescribing individuals to modify their daily habits. Research has suggested that more than one half of all deaths in the United States have behavioral determinants (McGinnis & Foege, 1993). Important health areas that have been emphasized within the context of prior intervention and research efforts have included diet, exercise, and plaque control regimens; use of safety helmets, seat belts, and safer sexual practices; and adoption of routine cancer screening habits (e.g., for testicular, cervical, and breast cancers). Additional important components of preventive health medicine include smoking cessation, medication compliance, and the various self-monitoring activities associated with diabetes management.

Less than half of the population is initially compliant with instructions to make a behavioral change—and this figure diminishes rapidly over time (Myers & Midence, 1998). Numerous theories have proposed situational and behavioral targets for enhancement of compliance, stimulating a large body of research identifying correlates of compliance. At this time, however, the theoretical literature is disunified and has failed to successfully integrate empirically supported aspects of prior theories. Consequently, no standardized assessment device for risk of noncompliance and no empirically supported treatment or prevention package have been developed (e.g., as ar-

gued by Cramer, 1991). Therefore, this chapter will provide guidelines for enhancement of compliance that are based on consideration of what situational factors and behavioral competencies have been related to compliance and are subject to established environmental engineering and to the behavior modification techniques that are described in other chapters of this volume. Variables correlated with compliance that are not subject to modification, such as demographics and personality considerations, are not addressed.

The prescription to modify health-related behavior commonly involves little more than a health care provider's verbal recommendation. It is self-evident that if such prescriptions are made without prior consideration of the individual's *capacity* to comply with the prescription, nonadherence is more likely to occur. For example, has the physician assessed the patient's practical understanding of the prescription being made? Do environmental conditions exist in the patient's life such as may be necessary to ensure the success of the recommended behavior change? It is variables such as these that may play a role in whether the patient is successful in following through with the behavior change after he or she leaves the doctor's office. Some prescribed changes seem fairly simple, such as taking a once-daily medication for hypertension that is inexpensive and free of troublesome side effects. Other health regimens, however, will involve the adoption of far more complex skills—for example, the newly diagnosed diabetic patient will have to learn how to make sweeping changes in his or her diet, engage in wide variety of routine monitoring behaviors (such as blood glucose testing), get regular physical exercise, and start taking self-administered injections that are not only frequent, but commonly painful as well.

MAJOR THEORIES OF COMPLIANCE

Two prominent theories of compliance are primarily descriptive, process-oriented approaches: the Transtheoretical Model of Behavior Change (e.g., DiClemente, 1993) and the Relapse Prevention Model (Marlatt, 1985). The former has encouraged the view that long-term strategies are needed to maintain healthy habits, and it examines the paths individuals may take in the behavior change process. The latter model recognizes that a range of coping skills are needed to maintain healthy habits and that these skills include unspecified cognitive, emotional, and instrumental behaviors. In addition, we have assessed four theories of compliance that are primarily explanatory models that have helped identify concrete targets for behavioral change: (1) the Theories of Reasoned Action and Planned Behavior (Fishbein & Ajzen, 1975; Ajzen, 1985); (2) Social Cognitive Theory (Bandura, 1991); (3) Modified Social Learning Theory (Wallston, 1992); and (4) the Health Belief Model (Rosenstock, 1991). Although each major compliance theory enjoys some empirical support, none provides a comprehensive framework to guide the clinician about what to assess in order to identify targets for enhancement of compliance.

Heiby (1986) articulated the Health Compliance Model (HCM; Heiby & Carlson, 1986) to be a cognitive behavioral approach to compliance prediction built upon the principles of psychological behaviorism (Staats, 1975, 1996). Rather than simply cataloging empirically supported correlates, the HCM integrated and classified important variables according to the functional relationships they hold with behavioral outcomes (e.g., compliance behavior). Our most recent review of the compliance literature led to the formulation of a revised HCM (HCM-II; Frank,

Heiby, & Lee, in press) by calling upon a principle heuristic of the model as an exhaustive and systematic classifier of functional compliance-related factors. Variables were assessed according to whether they represent *facilitating conditions*, *discriminative stimuli*, *consequences*, or one of four somewhat overlapping basic behavioral personality repertoires: *language-cognitive*, *verbal-emotional*, *emotional-motivational*, and *sensorimotor*. Each of these theory components has the heuristic value of indicating the type of prevention and intervention technique that is expected to enhance compliance.

Facilitating conditions, discriminative stimuli, and *consequences* have implications for techniques involving environmental engineering, such as contingency contracting and stimulus control. *Language-cognitive* variables are conducive to techniques involving changes in knowledge and information processing, such as bibliotherapy and cognitive restructuring. *Verbal-emotional* variables may respond best to techniques involving manipulation of cognitions that elicit affect, such as self-control and attribution change. *Emotional-motivational* variables are conducive to techniques that change affective conditioning, such as exposure and systematic desensitization. Finally, *sensorimotor* variables may respond best to operant techniques, such as shaping and social skills training. In total, assessment of a wide range of situational factors and the behavioral repertoires related to compliance would provide the clinician with additional direction regarding what intervention may be effective given the current environmental circumstances and prior learning history of a particular individual.

GUIDELINES FOR COMPLIANCE ENHANCEMENT

Noncompliance to a medical regimen can be identified based on the following information: (1) self-report (e.g., from rating scales or self-monitoring logs); (2) health care provider clinical assessments, such as from interviews, objective medical tests (e.g., weight, blood glucose level, and blood pressure), and previous history of adherence to scheduled appointments and prescription refill data; and (3) reports from significant others. Because each of these sources of information is subject to unique measurement error, the reliability of identifying noncompliance may be enhanced by use of multimodal assessment. Similarly, because compliance may vary across situations, a time-series approach to assessment may help identify a dynamic relation to causal and maintenance factors.

We have developed a Health Behavior Schedule-II (Frank et al., in press), which is a questionnaire designed to assess 45 correlates of compliance to 12 commonly prescribed healthy practices that are conducive to a self-report questionnaire. Space limitation prevents reproducing the schedule here, but the questionnaire and its psychometric properties are available from the first author. Table 18.1, however, presents 37 correlates of compliance to healthy behaviors derived from the HCM-II and for which interventions have been established for a range of behavioral problems. Although only some interventions have been evaluated with compliance to healthy behaviors, the table provides a guideline for the clinician while we await the development of a taxonomy of problem-specific interventions for medical regimens.

In addition to identifying noncompliance, it is important also to ascertain causal and maintenance factors, which vary not only across individuals but also by the type of medical regimen prescribed. Some medical regimens involve sensorimotor skills most people have already learned, such as swallowing a pill. In such cases, the targets for compliance enhancement would more likely include facilitating conditions and discriminative stimuli (e.g., prompts, instructions), consequences (e.g., cost of the medication, symptom relief), language-cognitive skills (e.g., accurate understanding of instructions and the verbal expression of intention to take the medication), verbal-emotional skills (e.g., perception of being susceptible to severe disease if medication is not taken), and emotional-motivational characteristics (e.g., no fear of effects of medication). On the other hand, some medical regimens involve the acquisition of new sensorimotor skills, such as the use of a blood pressure cuff or the self-injection of medication with a hypodermic needle. Therefore, assessing a range of potential causal and maintenance factors is critical in identifying compliance enhancement programming

for a particular client and a particular medical regimen.

The complex and multivariate nature of the HCM-II addresses the overwhelming evidence that health behavior compliance is a truly heterogeneous construct (e.g., as argued by Norman & Conner, 1996; Marteau, 1993; Meichenbaum & Turk, 1987; Sobal, Ravicki, & DeForge, 1992). We believe that individuals do not exhibit uniform healthy lifestyles, but rather may be seen as incorporating a high degree of idiosyncrasy when their unique reasons for choosing to adhere to particular health behavior prescriptions are assessed. The task of promoting patients' successful behavior change must include components of assessment that are often overlooked in today's fast-paced, managed care–driven health care environment. A renewed emphasis must be placed on compliance promotional efforts that pay close attention to unique differences among the determinants of behavior for an array of health practices, populations, and environments.

AN EXAMPLE OF COMPLIANCE ENHANCEMENT

We will provide an example of how the clinician can consider the correlates of compliance to health behaviors and select the techniques of behavior change listed in Table 18.1. For each health behavior, it is important to assess situational factors and behavioral competencies. Please refer to other chapters in this volume for particular guidelines for implementation of the treatment and prevention techniques mentioned in the example.

Let's consider the example of an individual with arthritis who does not comply to a prescription by a rheumatologist to swim at least 30 to 45 minutes at least three times per week in order to prevent heart disease from being sedentary due to joint pain, to increase muscle strength around the joints to facilitate maintaining posture, to enhance joint flexibility, and to reduce joint pain.

First, it is important for the clinician to assess *facilitating conditions and discriminative stimuli.* These factors might include the patient's schedule; information about and understanding of the reasons to swim; access to a pool, lake, or ocean; reminders and prompts to go swimming; the availability of swimming partners; and so on. Sec-

TABLE 18.1   Compliance Correlates and Related Interventions

Correlates	Interventions
Facilitating conditions and discriminative stimuli	
Schedule permits time for regimen	Functional analysis; stimulus control; behavioral contracting
Pharmacist educates client with appropriate language and print	Bibliotherapy
Provider educates client	Bibliotherapy
Provider prompts client (phone calls, emails, letters)	Stimulus control
Physical prompts in everyday situations	Stimulus control
Social prompts from family and friends	Stimulus control
Prompts from support groups	Stimulus control
Minimal waiting time for appointments and distance to appointment	Functional analysis
Friendly office staff	Communication training
Provider answers client's questions	Communication training
Provider includes client in treatment decisions	Communication training
Provider assesses client's understanding of regimen	Communication training
Provider requests questions of client	Communication training
Provider contracts with client for compliance	Contingency contracting
Provider utilizes history of successful compliance	Generalization training
Consequences: punishments	
Minimize physical discomfort of regimen	Functional analysis
Minimize social embarrassment from regimen	Functional analysis
Minimize financial costs of regimen	Functional analysis
Consequences: reinforcements	
Material rewards for compliance	Contingency contracting; token economy
Symptom relief from regimen	Functional analysis
Social praise for compliance	Positive attention
Language-cognitive behavioral repertoire	
Self-prediction of compliance	Cognitive restructuring; self-efficacy enhancement
Knowledge about regimen	Bibliotherapy
Understands provider's instructions	Bibliotherapy
Verbal-emotional behavioral repertoire	
Perceives self as susceptible to severe disease	Attribution change; cognitive restructuring; harm reduction; problem solving; relapse prevention
Perceives benefits of compliance	Problem solving; cognitive restructuring
Does not avoid knowledge that health is in danger	Acceptance; systematic desensitization; cognitive distancing
Focuses on positive sensations	Mindfulness skills; self-monitoring; self-control
Does not focus on negative sensations	Thought stopping
Emotional-motivational behavioral repertoire	
Compliance elicits positive affect	Self-control; emotional regulation skills
Compliance elicits minimum fear and discomfort	Exposure; stress management; stress inoculation; systematic desensitization
Minimum anger over regimen	Anger management
Minimum depression	Self-control; cognitive restructuring; attribution change; assertiveness training
Sensorimotor behavioral repertoire	
Has instrumental skills for regimen	Modeling; behavior rehearsal; shaping
Uses reminders to comply	Self-control
Is assertive with others who interfere with compliance	Assertiveness training
Schedules time for regimen	Problem solving; self-monitoring; self-control

ond, it would be important to assess *consequences*. These might include *punishments* such as discomfort during and after swimming due to lack of endurance and poor form; embarrassment over one's appearance in a swimsuit; affordability (e.g., club membership and cost of a swimsuit and goggles); and the like. They might also include *negative and positive reinforcements,* such as joint pain reduction, relaxation, social praise, or more energy. Third, it would be important to assess *behavioral repertoires.* Assessment of behavioral competencies would include *language-cognitive characteristics* (self-prediction of compliance to regular swimming, knowledge of swimming techniques, and principles of successive approximation to goals), *verbal-emotional characteristics* (perception that swimming will lead to avoidance of muscle atrophy and heart disease, increase in joint flexibility, and reduction of joint pain), *emotional-motivational characteristics* (euphoric feelings during and after swimming, reduction in joint pain and greater joint flexibility during and after swimming, no fear of drowning or getting chlorinated or salt water in the eyes, ears, and nose during swimming), and *sensory-motor abilities* needed to swim comfortably (ability to stroke, kick, and breathe in the water; selection of goggles that fit; use of reminders to go swimming; assertiveness when one has scheduled a swim but faces pressure to do something else; managing one's schedule so that there is time for a swim).

These factors can be assessed through a semistructured interview, questionnaires, self-monitoring, and direct observation. The Health Behavior Schedule-II (Frank et al., in press) and self-monitoring could be used to assess behavioral competencies. An interview, self-monitoring, and direct observation could be used to assess situational factors. If any of these conditions are lacking, the clinician could enhance compliance by interventions listed in Table 18.1.

For improving *facilitating conditions* and *discriminative stimuli,* decreasing *punishments,* and increasing *reinforcement,* a functional analysis, stimulus control, behavioral contracting, bibliotherapy, generalization training, and a token economy are expected to be effective. The clinician could help identify what time is available for swimming given the client's other responsibilities

and engineer stimuli that prompt swimming at a scheduled time. The clinician could contract with the client to swim as scheduled, provide written information on the reasons and benefits for a person with arthritis to swim, identify past exercise skills that could facilitate the acquisition and successive approximation of a regular swimming schedule, and arrange for material reinforcement when successive goals are met (such as contingent gifts from a friend or spouse). If a swim coach is needed, the clinician could consult with the coach to ensure that the coach uses effective communication with the client (e.g., is friendly, answers questions, and assesses the client's understanding of information conveyed). The clinician could also consult with the rheumatologist to assure that he or she is communicating the prescription to swim regularly and hydrodynamically. If the client reports an increase in physical discomfort from swimming or a lack of symptom relief, the goals in successive approximation could be adjusted and immediate material and social awards enhanced by involvement of friends, family, the coach, and the physician. If the financial costs of the swimming regimen are burdensome for the client, the clinician could problem-solve how to budget these expenses or find an organization, such as the local chapter of the Arthritis Foundation, to fund them.

To improve behavioral competencies, the clinician could provide techniques that are effective for the deficient repertoire. For *language-cognitive deficiencies,* cognitive restructuring, self-efficacy training, and bibliotherapy could enhance self-prediction of one's ability to swim regularly and knowledge about how swimming can improve arthritic symptoms if approached in successive steps. For *verbal-emotional deficiencies,* attributional change, cognitive restructuring, and problem solving can enhance the perception that being sedentary increases the severity of the arthritic symptoms and that swimming reduces joint pain and enhances physical and mental energy and joint flexibility. For *emotional-motivational deficiencies,* self-control training can enhance the use of self-monitoring of the positive effects of swimming and self-reinforcement for attaining one's goals toward compliance. Exposure to swimming and systematic desensitization could reduce fears related to being in the water and the punishing consequences of being embarrassed of one's appearance in a swimsuit. *Sensorimotor deficiencies* can be addressed by involving a swim coach to provide praise, modeling, shaping, and behavioral rehearsal of swimming skills. Self-control skills could help the client use reminders to swim and engage in self-reinforcement for improvement of swimming skills and adherence to the regimen. Assertiveness training could help the client respond to requests to do something other than go swimming as scheduled. And problem-solving skills could help the client find the time to fit regular swimming into his or her schedule.

As with all interventions, it would be important to monitor the rate of compliance over time and evaluate the effect of treatment upon targeted situational and behavioral factors. Given that compliance tends to decrease over time for most individuals, periodic assessment of the need for further interventions is critical until the behavioral change has stabilized.

References

Ajzen, I. (1985). From intentions to actions: A theory of planned behavior. In J. Kuhl & J. Backmann (Eds.), *Action control: From cognition to behavior* (pp. 11–39). Berlin, Germany: Springer-Verlag.

Bandura, A. (1991). Self-efficacy mechanism in psychological activation and health-promoting behavior. In J. Madden (Ed.), *Neurobiology of learning, emotion and affect* (pp. 229–269). New York: Raven Press.

Cramer, J. A. (1991). Identifying and improving compliance patterns: A composite plan for health care providers. In J. A. Cramer & B. Spilker (Eds.), *Patient compliance in medical practice and clinical trials* (pp. 387–392). New York: Raven Press.

DiClemente, C. C. (1993). Changing addictive behaviors: A process perspective. *Current Directions in Psychological Science, 2,* 101–106.

Fishbein, M., & Ajzen, I. (1975). *Belief, attitude, intention, and behavior: An introduction to theory and research.* Reading, MA: Addison-Wesley.

Frank, M. R., Heiby, E. M., & Lee, J. H. (in press). Assessment of determinants of compliance to twelve health behaviors: Psychometric evaluation of the Health Behavior Schedule-II. *Psychological Reports.*

Heiby, E. M. (1986). A paradigmatic behavioral perspective of noncompliance to health regimens. Paper presented at the 94th Convention of the American Psychological Association, Washington, DC: August, 1986.

Heiby, E. M., & Carlson, J. G. (1986). The Health Compliance Model. *Journal of Compliance in Health Care, 1,* 135–152.

Marlatt, G. A. (1985). Relapse prevention: Theoretical rational and overview of the model. In G. A. Marlatt & J. R. Gordon (Eds.), *Relapse prevention: Maintenance strategies in the treatment of addictive behaviors* (pp. 3–70). New York: Guilford Publishing.

Marteau, T. M. (1993). Health-related screening: The psychological predictors of uptake and impact. *International Review of Health Psychology, 2,* 149–174.

McGinnis, J., & Foege, W. (1993). Actual causes of deaths in the United States. *Journal of the American Medical Association, 270,* 2207–2212.

Meichenbaum, D., & Turk, D. C. (1987). *Facilitating treatment adherence: A practitioners' guidebook.* New York: Plenum Press.

Myers, L. G., & Midence, K. (1998). Concepts and issues in adherence. In L. B. Myers & K. Midence (Eds.), *Adherence to treatment in medical conditions* (pp. 1–24). Amsterdam: Harwood Academic Publishers.

Norman, P., & Conner, M. (1996). The role of social cognition models in predicting health behaviors: Future directions. In M. Conner & P. Norman (Eds.), *Predicting health behavior: Research and practice with social cognition models* (pp. 197–225). Buckingham, UK: Open University Press.

Rosenstock, I. M. (1991). The health belief model: Explaining health behavior through expectancies. In K. Glanz, F. M., Lewis, & B. K. Rimer (Eds.), *Health behavior and health education* (pp. 39–62). San Francisco, CA: Jossey-Bass Publishers.

Sobal, J., Ravicki, D., & DeForge, B. R. (1992). Patterns of interrelationships among health-promotion behaviors. *American Journal of Preventive Medicine, 8,* 351–359.

Staats, A. W. (1975). *Social behaviorism.* Homewood, IL: Dorsey Press.

Staats, A. W. (1996). *Behavior and personality: Psychological behaviorism.* New York: Springer.

Wallston, K. A. (1992). Hocus-pocus, the focus isn't strictly on locus: Rotter's social learning theory modified for health. *Cognitive Therapy and Research, 16,* 183–199.

19 CONTINGENCY MANAGEMENT INTERVENTIONS

Thomas E. Boyce and Horacio R. Roman

Contingency management (CM) can be an important component of successful treatments for reducing substance abuse and increasing adherence to effective treatment goals (Chutuape, Silverman, & Stitzer, 2001; Higgins & Petry, 1999; Petry, 2000). However, clinical psychologists have not readily used this approach to manage other behavioral problems. Although initial reports of successful clinical applications of CM appeared in the early 1970s (cf. Bigelow & Silverman, 1999; Higgins & Petry, 1999), its evolution as a viable treatment alternative has been relatively slow, with the exception of some studies examining variations in the delivery of different reinforcers (Petry, 2000).

The artificial nature of CM (e.g., the notion of paying people to change their behavior) is often criticized (Andrzejewski, Kirby, Morral, & Iguchi, 2001; Rothfleisch, Ek, Rhoades, & Schmitz, 1999). As a result, psychologists and other human service professionals appear to have dismissed the usefulness of CM and its potential benefits. Nonetheless, this chapter (1) describes the basic tenets of CM; (2) reviews its historical foundations; (3) discusses the etiology of problems that may benefit from applications of CM; (4) outlines potential benefits, limitations, and special considerations; and (5) details the steps involved in designing and implementing CM as a primary intervention.

HISTORY AND DESCRIPTION OF CONTINGENCY MANAGEMENT

Contingency management can be described as the systematic supervision of behavior and the controlled delivery of rewards (i.e., conditioned reinforcers) to compete with powerful reinforcers (often primary) maintaining problem behaviors (Petry, 2000). Accordingly, CM treatment combines the delivery of incentives or rewards for increases in desired behaviors and the absence or reduction of problem behaviors while removing or withholding rewards or privileges when problem behavior is exhibited (Higgins & Petry, 1999; Petry, 2000). For example, a CM intervention to reduce overeating can include frequent weight measurements and delivery of rewards contingent on maintaining or attaining a prespecified weight. However, rewards would also be withheld when a person exceeds that weight. Alternatively, rewards could be made contingent on the selection and consumption of predefined healthy food choices and withheld for the selection of alternatives to these (Petry, Tedford, & Martin, 2001).

The fundamental concept underlying CM interventions is the assumption that (problem) behavior develops over time and is adaptive. Adaptive behavior is simply behavior that can be modified by its consequences (i.e., certain events strengthen [reinforce] or weaken [punish] behavior). Given this context, CM requires that a psychologist or other health care worker examine behavior as a function of its antecedents and consequences, and then systematically alter some dimension of the antecedent, the consequence, or both to promote desired behavior change. Put a different way, it may be said that antecedents direct behavior (they tell a person what to do) and consequences motivate behavior (people work to receive pleasant consequences or to avoid unpleasant consequences). However, not all consequences are equally effective. The characteristics believed to influence the effectiveness of a consequence to change behavior are its magnitude or size, time between behavior and the delivery of the consequence, and the likelihood that the consequence will follow the behavior on any given instance. In addition, establishing operations (i.e., motivational variables such as satiation and deprivation, etc.) play a significant role in determining the effectiveness (or lack thereof) of a consequence from moment to moment.

WHO CAN BENEFIT FROM CONTINGENCY MANAGEMENT INTERVENTIONS?

Over the past 30 years, contingency management has been used successfully to treat drug and alcohol abuse, to increase or maintain attendance at drug and alcohol group therapy meetings, and to increase completion of therapeutic goals (Petry, 2000). Although a review of these studies is beyond the scope of this chapter, they are described elsewhere (cf. Higgins & Silverman, 1999; Petry, 2000).

In general, CM has worked well for problem behaviors that are maintained by primary reinforcers (e.g., drugs, alcohol, nicotine, food, and sex), which, coincidentally, are extremely difficult to displace with alternative reinforcers. Intuitively, then, it is reasonable to assume that CM should also work well with behavior maintained by less powerful reinforcers (e.g., occupational safety). However, considering that CM interventions can be costly and effortful (Petry, 2000), CM may not be the primary mode of intervention. With this in mind, clients with severe behavior problems that have a significant cost to their families and society, such as chronic drug addictions, may benefit most from treatments involving CM.

Studies of CM interventions to treat substance abuse suggest that clients whose problem behaviors can be observed directly and objectively, or whose behaviors produce permanent and verifiable products, are best suited for these interventions. For example, a therapist can monitor the results of urine analyses to determine whether she or he should deliver rewards. However, it would be impractical and inconvenient to directly observe and monitor actual drug use. Furthermore, some behaviors cannot be observed directly, as is the case with clients who hear voices. For cases such as these, therapists may opt to observe behaviors that are correlated with improved outcomes, such as completing or staying on a drug regime. However, whether the client stops hearing voices remains an uncertainty. Put simply, CM interventions are most effective when therapists can observe or verify instances of desired behavior.

DESIGNING AN EFFECTIVE CM INTERVENTION: STEP-BY-STEP METHODS

Detailed descriptions of how to design an effective and practical CM program are provided elsewhere (e.g., Petry, 2000), and examples of settings in which CM interventions have been used and specific procedures are provided in several case studies (e.g., Petry, Martin, Cooney, & Kranzler, 2000; Petry, Petrakis, et al., 2001). The reader is encouraged to review the case studies for the practical applications of the step-by-step procedures summarized here.

Choose a Behavior and a Monitoring System

Contingency management works best with behaviors that are observable, recordable, and trackable over time. In short, self-reports should be avoided. When monitoring ongoing behaviors is not possible (e.g., in the case of someone who may have ingested narcotics the night before), a verifiable outcome of that behavior may be obtained (e.g., a urine sample for the presence of narcotics). Behaviors or outcomes that occur regularly and frequently work best in CM interventions because reinforcers can be applied contingently, consistently, and often. However, to ensure consistent application of CM procedures, one must have a good operational definition of the target on which the contingency is placed. Geller (1996) recommends following the SOON approach for defining critical behaviors. That is, a good behavioral definition is *specific* (unambiguous), *observable* (recordable and trackable), *objective* (leaving no room for interpretation; agreed upon by client and health care professional), and *naturalistic* (capable of occurring in the real world and necessary for desired outcomes).

Choose a Reinforcer

By definition, a reinforcer is a consequence produced by behavior that increases the probability of that behavior's being repeated in the future. Given that a CM program may have a limited budget, one may wish to select reinforcers that are just sufficient to produce desired behavior changes and that are adaptable to the settings in which one is working. One could start the selection process by first conducting a reinforcer preference assessment (cf. Pace, Ivanicic, Edwards, Iwata, & Page, 1985; see Chapter 59, this volume). When conducting a preference assessment, one is simply trying to identify which of the potential consequences available for use in a CM program that a client is most likely to work for. This can vary widely across individuals and from time to time. Pace et al. detail preference assessment procedures that may be adapted for use in a CM program. However, more often, CM programs make available a selection of prizes without assessing preference on the assumption that individuals will find something of value in the selections.

Petry and colleagues (Petry, Petrakis, et al., 2001) document two cases in which a prize lottery was used to promote drug and alcohol abstinence and completion of treatment goals in a clinic setting. In a third case, a portion of the pension monies of a drug-addicted paranoid schizophrenic were made available by a conservator contingent on attendance at meetings and adherence to treatment goals. In the lottery system, slips of paper indicating "good job," but not resulting in a prize, and other slips indicating a small prize (e.g., movie tickets, discount coupons, etc.) or a large prize (VCRs, televisions, radios, etc.) were placed in a bowl. The participant earned one draw from the bowl for every urine sample that was clean from cocaine or other drugs and four draws for samples that were completely clean. Each week of complete abstinence from drugs resulted in a number of bonus draws that increased with each week of complete abstinence.

Other reinforcers that have been used in CM programs include vouchers that can be exchanged at an on-site retail store, cash, methadone clinic privileges, employment and housing, and refunds and rebates of clinic costs. Although Reilly, Roll, and Downey (2000) demonstrated that when the magnitude of the reinforcers are equivalent, about equally as many participants preferred vouchers as did money, little research has been done to demonstrate the differential reinforcing effectiveness of various consequences (Petry, 2000). However, given that individuals respond differently to particular consequences, one can increase the likelihood of finding a suitable reinforcer if a preference assessment is first conducted. Additionally, this reinforcer will be most effective if it can be administered frequently and consistently based on verifiable behaviors and/or outcomes. Finally, it is noteworthy that in community-based applications of CM, contingencies are applied most consistently by counselors when they themselves receive graphical feedback on their CM performance and/or are rewarded with prize drawings for consistent applications of the contingencies (Andrzejewski et al., 2001).

To summarize, selection of consequences is an integral part of a successful CM intervention. The most effective consequences occur soon after a target behavior, are certain to occur, and are sizable enough to motivate behavior change. However, size is idiosyncratic. One can identify sizable reinforcers for a particular individual by assessing preference for available consequences. But little attention appears to have been given in the CM literature to assessing reinforcer preference.

Establish a Contingency Contract

In order to facilitate early improvements, one should formalize an agreement with the client. This agreement is called a *contingency contract* (see Chapter 8 in this volume). That is, one should specify what behaviors are expected, how they will be monitored, what consequences will occur given certain levels of performance, how the consequences will be administered, and for how long the program will apply. The contract should leave no room for interpretation and thus should specify exactly what the client will get for doing certain things. If one uses the SOON approach to defining critical behaviors and keeps the reinforcement schedule simple so that it can be consistently applied by whoever is administering it, then the contingency contract should be no problem to develop and maintain.

When establishing the contingency, it is best not set expectations too high (Petry, 2000), but rather to measure improvements relative to an individual's given baseline. That is, one may be most successful by reinforcing successive approximations toward a terminal goal, as when one starts an exercise regime by first walking for 15 minutes a day and later increasing this to 30 minutes, 1 hour, and so on.

Implement and Program for Generalization and Maintenance

Given the time and effort necessary to implement a CM program at the individual level, one must plan for the future. The long-term effectiveness of the CM program will be greater when one has identified sources of environmental control (i.e., antecedents and consequences) that are naturally occurring in the clients' environments. That is, the effect initially produced by the contrived reinforcers may be transferred to natural outcomes of behavior that will be sufficient to maintain the desired changes. For example, if a person first starting his or her walking program is rewarded for a walking session with 30 minutes of a preferred activity such as watching TV, TV watching as a consequence may not be necessary once the natural benefits of the walking program become available (e.g., the client starts to lose weight, clothes fit better, mood is improved, etc.). However, to ensure that these benefits are experienced and recognized as contingent on the newly acquired behavior (i.e., walking) one could explicitly help the client to make that connection.

Methods for programming natural consequences are discussed in detail by Stokes and Baer (1977). These techniques could be used to enhance the probability that successes initially achieved by the contrived contingencies of a CM program are brought under the control of the natural contingencies operating upon the individual. Programming for generalization and maintenance (cf. Boyce & Geller, 2001) should occur as early in the CM process as possible. That is, potential natural antecedents and consequences to direct and maintain desired behavior change in the absence of the contrived contingencies could be identified during the behavior selection process. Consequently, the contrived contingencies could be applied in a manner that maximizes the probability that these natural antecedents and consequences will eventually exert desired control over behavior.

CONCLUSION

Contingency management interventions have been used successfully primarily to treat substance abuse by promoting abstinence, increasing adherence to treatment regimes and attendance at counseling sessions, and promoting the selection and completion of treatment goals to improve quality of life. However, even though it is well suited to do so, CM has not been widely used in other areas of health promotion, such as weight control, safer sex, and prevention of cardiovascular disease.

The biopsychosocial approach to health psychology may in part explain a lighter emphasis on strategies that come out of the tradition of operant psychology. However, the more likely explanation is that CM programs can be costly. Furthermore, because of the need to focus on individuals in CM programs, effective community-based applications of CM are rare. Adaptation of CM techniques for large-scale application remains an area in need of investigation. Effective applications of CM on a large scale may increase the frequency at which they are used.

References

Andrzejewski, M. E., Kirby, K. C., Morral, A. R., & Iguchi, M. Y. (2001). Technology transfer through performance management: The effects of graphical feedback and positive reinforcement on drug treatment counselors' behavior. *Drug and Alcohol Dependence, 63,* 179–186.

Bigelow, G. E., & Silverman, K. (1999). Theoretical and empirical foundations of contingency management treatments for drug abuse. In S. T. Higgins & K. Silverman (Eds.), *Motivating behavior change among illicit-drug abusers: Research on contingency management interventions* (pp. 15–31). Washington, DC: American Psychological Association.

Boyce, T. E., & Geller, E. S. (2001). Applied behavior analysis and occupational safety: The challenge of programming response maintenance. *Journal of Organizational Behavior Management, 21,* 31–60.

Chutuape, M. A., Silverman, K., & Stitzer, M. L. (2001). Effects of urine testing frequency on outcome in a methadone take-home contingency program. *Drug and Alcohol Dependence, 62,* 69–76.

Geller, E. S. (1996). *The psychology of safety.* Boca Raton, FL: CRC Press.

Higgins, S. T., & Petry, N. M. (1999). Contingency management: Incentives for sobriety. *Alcohol Research and Health, 23,* 122–127.

Higgins, S. T., & Silverman, K. (Eds.). (1999). *Motivating behavior change among illicit-drug abusers: Research on contingency management interventions.* Washington, DC: American Psychological Association.

Pace, G. M., Ivanicic, M. T., Edwards, G. L., Iwata, B. A., & Page, T. J. (1985). Assessment of stimulus preference and reinforcer value with profoundly retarded individuals. *Journal of Applied Behavior Analysis, 18,* 249–255.

Petry, N. M. (2000). A comprehensive guide to the application of contingency management procedures in clinical settings. *Drug and Alcohol Dependence, 58,* 9–25.

Petry, N. M., Martin, B., Cooney, J. L., & Kranzler, H. R. (2000). Give them prizes and they will come: Contingency management for treatment of alcohol dependence. *Journal of Counseling and Clinical Psychology, 68,* 25–257.

Petry, N. M., Petrakis, I., Trevisan, L., Wiredu, G., Boutrols, N. N., Martin, B., et al. (2001). Contingency management interventions: From research to practice. *American Journal of Psychiatry, 158,* 694–702.

Petry, N. M., Tedford, J., & Martin, B. (2001). Reinforcing compliance with non-drug-related activities. *Journal of Substance Abuse Treatment, 20,* 33–44.

Reilly, M. P., Roll, J. M., & Downey, K. K. (2000). Impulsivity and voucher versus money preference in polydrug-dependent participants enrolled in a contingency-management-based substance abuse treatment program. *Journal of Substance Abuse Treatment, 19,* 253–257.

Rothfleisch, J., Ek, R., Rhoades, H., & Schmitz, J. (1999). Use of monetary reinforcers by cocaine-dependent outpatients. *Journal of Substance Abuse Treatment, 17,* 229–236.

Stokes, T. F., & Baer, D. M. (1977). An implicit technology of generalization. *Journal of Applied Behavior Analysis, 10,* 349–367.

20 DAILY REPORT CARDS: HOME-SCHOOL CONTINGENCY MANAGEMENT PROCEDURES

Mary Lou Kelley

Behavior therapists have long relied on parents and teachers to employ interventions with children. Parents and teachers have effectively used a variety of contingency management procedures for improving compliance, task engagement, and rule following, and for decreasing aggressive, disruptive, and disrespectful behavior. With regard to improving classroom behavior, the vast majority of studies have relied on teachers as the sole agent of change (Cohen & Fish, 1993). More recently, however, collaboration between parents and teachers to improve children's classroom behavior is increasingly seen in the literature (Kelley & McCain, 1995; Rhodes & Kratochwill, 1998; Rosen, Gabardi, Miller, & Miller, 1990). In part, increased parental involvement in promoting children's success in school is due to changing legal requirements and philosophical perspectives (Christenson, Hurley, Sheridan, & Fenstermacher, 1997). For example, P. L. 94-142 emphasizes teachers' legal and professional obligation to include parents in the educational process.

Although home-school collaboration is heralded in the literature, the natural environment presents many obstacles to establishing effective programs for improving academic behavior and classroom performance (Kelley, 1990). For example, a common practice is for parents to re-ceive intermittent, negative feedback about their children. This may lead parents to avoid involvement or to become discouraged about their ability to impact the child's school behavior. Teachers and parents often disagree on the causes and solutions to problems. They may see one another as indifferent, unresponsive, or just plain irresponsible. Finally, teachers may feel that they do not have the time for regular communication with parents given the demands of classroom instruction and management.

School-home notes or daily report cards require teachers to evaluate children daily and parents to provide consequences based on the resulting data. An example of a school-home note is seen in Table 20.1. The intervention often serves to improve parent-teacher communication and problem solving. Intervention effects are often quite substantial in spite of a great deal of variability in the specificity of target behaviors, evaluation methods, and reinforcement procedures. School-home notes have proven effective in reducing a variety of children's problematic behavior, including inattention, disruptive classroom behavior, lack of classwork or homework completion, and talking without permission; positive changes are often accompanied by improved grades. Home-based reinforcement of classroom behavior has been employed with chil-

TABLE 20.1   Example of a School Home Note

School-Home Note

Name: _____   Date: _____

Reading

Prepared for class	Yes	So-So	No
Used time wisely	Yes	So-So	No
Handed in homework	Yes	So-So	No
Comments:			

Math

Prepared for class	Yes	So-So	No
Used time wisely	Yes	So-So	No
Handed in homework	Yes	So-So	No
Comments:			

Recess

Played without hitting	Yes	No
Comments:		

Language arts

Prepared for class	Yes	So-So	No
Used time wisely	Yes	So-So	No
Participated in discussion	Yes	So-So	No
Handed in homework	Yes	So-So	No
Comments:			

Consequences provided by parents at home:

Parent questions/concerns:

dren of varied ages and abilities. For example, the procedure has been shown to be effective in increasing task engagement and decreasing disruptive behavior in a preschooler with Attention-Deficit/Hyperactivity Disorder (ADHD; McCain & Kelley, 1993), increasing attention and classwork accuracy and productivity in elementary school–aged children (Kelley & McCain, 1995); increasing academic performance and reducing disruptiveness in elementary school–aged children (Witt, Hannafin, & Martens, 1983); and reducing disruptive behavior in junior high school–aged students (Rosen et al., 1990). Some studies have shown that the behavior of high school students was improved through the use of daily report cards. The procedure has also been used successfully with entire classrooms of students (Lahey et al., 1977). Although the majority of studies targeted externalizing behavior prob-

lems or task engagement, they can be used as a treatment component for strengthening desired behaviors that are inhibited by anxiety; examples include working without crying in a school-phobic child and talking in a loud voice in a shy or selectively mute child.

In a typical school-home intervention, students are evaluated using fairly global categories that are not explicitly defined. For example, McCain and Kelley (1994) required teachers to evaluate whether the student's class work was completed correctly and whether they used class time well by circling "yes," "so-so," or "no" on the daily report card. The operational definition of each evaluative category was determined by the teacher's subjective perception. Although some studies evaluating school-home notes provided very specific evaluation criteria, most studies did not, and this appeared to be unrelated to outcome. However, some level of specificity of the target behavior and evaluation criteria are probably needed in order for the intervention to be effective (Kelley, 1990).

Most studies required teachers to evaluate children at the end of specific intervals of time by rating the level of the target behavior. However, two studies evaluated the additive effects of including response cost procedures to the effectiveness of a school-home note (Kelley & McCain, 1995; McCain & Kelley, 1994). On No Response Cost days, students were evaluated in the manner described above (McCain & Kelley, 1994). Report cards on Response Cost days had the addition of a series of happy faces. A face was crossed out each time the child was corrected or redirected. Using a reversal design with alternating treatments, the effect of adding response was equal to or greater than the impact of the traditional note alone.

The comprehensiveness of school-home notes has ranged considerably. Some studies evaluated student behavior during a specific time of day (e.g., nap time, lunchtime, math class). Other studies broke the day down into a number of intervals and evaluated student behavior throughout the day (Schumaker, Hovell, & Sherman, 1977).

Consequences earned by children for improved or satisfactory behavior have been varied. Consequences generally are positive and include tangible rewards and activities that children can enjoy that day after school. Praise alone is generally not an adequate consequence for increasing appropriate classroom behavior (Schumaker et al., 1977) although it has been effective in two studies that used nonclinical subjects (e.g. Lahey et al. 1977).

Although school-home notes typically are the source of data in determining rewards for desired classroom behavior, the information provided to parents on a daily basis can serve other valuable functions. School-home notes can also be used to inform parents about a child's progress in alternative therapies and programs. For example, the data from a school-home note are helpful in evaluating the effects and side effects of medication in children with ADHD. The communication of brief, specific information from teacher to parent can help parents and children plan for the next school day. For instance, a few comments on a note can facilitate test preparation or problem solving regarding an issue that occurred during the day. Thus, school-home notes often convey very useful information to parents and professionals involved with the child regarding behavior trends, ancillary intervention effects, and specific problem incidents.

FOR WHOM IS THE INTERVENTION APPROPRIATE?

School-home notes can be useful and effective treatment whenever children will benefit from home-based rewards for appropriate classroom behavior and increased parent involvement and parent-teacher collaboration. In order for the use of notes to be effective and appropriate, parents must be willing and able to provide positive consequences for appropriate behavior on a daily basis and in a consistent manner. The procedure works best with cooperative teachers who have a positive attitude, structured routines, and effective classroom management skills.

Children must be able to respond to delayed reinforcement and home-based consequences.

CONTRAINDICATIONS OF THE INTERVENTION

The procedure generally is not recommended with parents who have significant functional impairment or with parents who are likely to use the procedure in a negative, erratic, or abusive manner. For example, the procedure is unlikely to succeed with disorganized, unstructured, or lax parents. Likewise, school-home notes should not be used if a child's teacher is resistant or is likely to use the intervention negatively rather than in a supportive and positive manner. With regard to child characteristics, school-home notes will be ineffective if children do not have the skills to perform the desired behaviors or if the target behavior cannot be influenced by parental consequence. However, the note may be used along with school-based consequences when delay of reinforcement appears to impede effectiveness. The intervention also may not be effective with children who are depressed or who have serious emotional or behavior problems. However, information from a daily report card may be a useful component in a comprehensive treatment program when parental involvement helps children perform better in the classroom. Sometimes implementation of a daily report card may serve to accentuate the need for alternative placement, treatments, or services.

ASSESSMENT CONSIDERATIONS

As with any other behavioral procedure, an appropriate assessment of the child and his or her family and classroom setting must be conducted prior to using a school-home note. Assessment commonly begins with an initial interview with the parent or teacher who initiated the referral. Assessment procedures are detailed elsewhere (Kelley, 1990), and I will only briefly review them here. It is recommended that parents, teachers, and the child be interviewed where possible to develop a list of academic and behavioral strengths and weaknesses and to identify specific target behaviors. In addition, a thorough developmental history should be obtained from a parent or guardian that includes a history of physical, social, and academic skill development. Interviewees should be asked about any emotional or behavioral problems the child might be experiencing. Parents should be screened for psychopathology and family stressors during the interviews, and indications of such need to be considered.

Psychometrically sound, norm-referenced questionnaires should be obtained from the parents and the teacher(s) and the child when appropriate. Questionnaires should be used to screen for internalizing and externalizing behavior and emotional problems and for assessing the severity of symptoms. It is recommended that the clinician use a broadband, multi-informant measure such as the Child Behavior Checklist (Achenbach, 1991) or the Behavior Assessment System for Children (Kamphaus & Reynolds, 1998). Supplementary measures for assessing specific areas such as depression, anxiety, or ADHD may be administered when indicated. Finally, a review of the child's grades and achievement test scores should be conducted and any concerns about academic abilities addressed through norm-referenced or curriculum-based assessment.

It is very helpful to conduct a school observation in order to evaluate the child's placement in the classroom, his or her behavior, and the responses of others to the child's behavior. This information is very helpful in developing appropriate target behaviors to be included in the school-home note. The ultimate assessment question to be answered is whether a school-home note is likely to be an effective and appropriate treatment. This question can be answered by defining the specific behaviors to increase or decrease and by determining whether the child is able to perform the desired behaviors and respond to parent-based rewards, whether the teacher will provide feedback fairly and consistently, and whether the parents can reliably provide consequences that alter the frequency of target behaviors in desired ways.

HOW DOES THE INTERVENTION WORK?

Parents, teachers, and usually a consultant, such as a psychologist, collaboratively select target behaviors reflective of desired change in specific situations. The school-home note is constructed with the day divided into intervals of time or specific settings, such as recess, math class, English class, or center time. Teachers evaluate student behavior throughout the day on the note. Children are provided feedback from their teacher regarding their daily performance and bring the note home to review with their parents. Parents

discuss the data on the note with their children, with the emphasis on positive changes in behavior. Negative evaluations are discussed within a problem-solving context. For example, when a child brings home a "no" rating in an area such as "prepared for class," the parent is encouraged to discuss with the child possible solutions for preventing the problem in the future. Finally, predetermined consequences are provided by parents daily. Consequences are generated by parents with input from their child, usually with professional guidance.

STEPS TO DEVELOPING AND USING A SCHOOL-HOME NOTE

The following sections describe in detail the steps to developing and using a school-home note.

A summary of the steps to using a school-home note are shown in Table 20.2.

Step One: Discuss the Intervention with Parents and Teachers

When it is determined that a school-home note may be an effective intervention for improving a child's classroom behavior, the idea should be presented to the parents and teachers. During

TABLE 20.2 Key Points: Steps to Using a School-Home Note

1. Discuss the possible use of the intervention with parents and teachers.
2. Determine target behaviors to increase or decrease that are specific to the setting.
3. Divide the day into small units of time.
4. Determine anchors for evaluating behavior during the day.
5. Design an attractive, uncluttered, and developmentally appropriate note.
6. Discuss the intervention with the child prior to beginning the use of school-home notes.
7. Determine contingencies of reinforcement.
8. Begin using the note to establish baseline levels of behavior.
9. Review the completed note daily with the child.
10. Provide promised consequences.
11. Provide follow-up sessions to monitor effectiveness.

this meeting the overall procedure is presented along with the rationale for its use, and the likely outcomes are discussed. Concerns are addressed and the responsibilities of each involved person delineated. Children are usually responsible for remembering to get the note completed each day. However, I ask teachers to prompt children, especially in the beginning. Although it is often best to meet jointly with parents and teachers, separate meetings can be conducted, and sometimes telephone consultation with the teacher is adequate for developing the target behaviors. When parents and teachers have already established good, effective communication, parents can sometimes present the idea to the teacher along with sample school-home notes and handouts on use of the procedure.

Step Two: Determine Target Behaviors

Selecting relevant, socially valid target behaviors is critical to the success of school-home notes. Behaviors important to the child's academic and social success should be chosen. In general, academic products such as "completed classwork" or component behaviors such as "followed directions" or "prepared for class" should be chosen over process behaviors such as "paid attention." Although classroom conduct behaviors such as "talked only with permission" or "kept hands to self" are often included as target behaviors, it is recommended that academic-related behaviors always be included because increases in these behaviors often lead to improved conduct. Whenever possible, target behaviors should be defined in terms of behavior to increase rather than decrease. The written definition should be as specific as possible. Examples of common target behaviors in addition to those mentioned above include "used time wisely," "handed in homework," "participated in class discussion," "played nicely with peers," and "followed class rules." After target behaviors are determined, the behaviors should be defined and examples and nonexamples of the behavior discussed with the teacher, the parent, and eventually the child. Target behaviors may vary as a function of the specific setting. For example, young children may have group activities or independent seatwork at different times of the day, and appropriate targets vary across these settings.

Step Three: Determine Settings and Evaluative Criteria

Generally, school-home notes are used to evaluate children's behavior throughout the day. Like other behavioral interventions, school-home notes should provide information about specific behavior in specific settings. Thus, it is recommended that the child's school day be divided into relatively small, naturally occurring units of time. For example, the day may be divided into class periods such as math, reading, language arts, science, and social studies. For some children, the periods may include transition times such as walking in line to lunch or other activities and before- and after-school behavior. The intervals should include those in which it is important to improve behavior.

As seen in Table 20.1, each behavior is evaluated according to certain criteria. Although only a single word anchor is provided for different criteria on the school-home note, each possible rating (yes, so-so, no) is defined in more detail and later explained to the child.

Step Four: Design the Note

As seen in the example, the note should have a place for the child's name, the date, and each setting with the target behaviors and evaluation criteria listed. A place for the teacher's and parents' comments should be included. The note can be designed by the professional, the parents, or the teacher. It is recommended that numerous examples be provided, including definitions of target behaviors, to serve as a guide. In order to reduce the number of papers the child must handle daily, the child can be provided with a daily assignment book containing large squares for recording homework assignments. A teacher planner is ideal for this purpose. Target behaviors such as "handed in homework" are stamped in the square for the teacher to complete. Stamps can be made at most office supply stores. Many examples of school-home notes are available in Kelley (1990) and Barkley (1996). Handouts detailing the use of a daily report card are provided in Kelley (1990).

Step Five: Prepare the Child

Prior to beginning, the intervention should be thoroughly explained to the child. With some children it is helpful to include them in the selection of target behaviors and the design of the note. The child, parent, and teacher responsibilities should be determined and consequences discussed. The child should be told that the school-home note is to help the parent be more effective and that increased feedback will help the child learn about his teacher's perceptions of his behavior. By the time a school-home note is initiated, that parent-child relationship often is strained and quite negative with regard to discussions about school performance. It is recommended that professionals emphasize to parents that the school-home note will provide them with more complete and positive information on their child's daily behavior. This can help reduce parents' excessive questioning about school performance. Some children are embarrassed about being singled out. These concerns should be addressed and discussed. Methods of using the procedure discreetly can be arranged and the child's self-consciousness discussed with the teacher.

Step Six: Determine Rewards

The parent and child should discuss possible daily and weekly rewards. Often rewards include the activities that the child now enjoys in the evening, such as use of the computer, PlayStation, telephone, or television. In addition, it is recommended that an additional reward such as money, extra time watching TV, special time with Mom or Dad, or other desired consequences be included as well so children do not simply feel punished when they do not earn rewards. In many cases, use of a school-home note is well received by a child because activities that had been taken away for an extended period of time due to poor school performance are reinstated. Sometimes predetermined sanctions, such as writing an age-appropriate essay discussing how the child can avoid misbehaving the next day or performing an extra chore, are helpful when children appear to be motivated by escape from class demands. Sanctions should be planned well in advance and never added extemporaneously. Sanctions can be helpful with children who appear to be poorly motivated to put forth effort to improve their school performance. Specific criteria for earning consequences should be written in a contract and signed by the parent and child.

Step Seven: Begin Using the Note

When first beginning the daily report card program, thoroughly review the procedures with the child. The note can be provided by either the parent or the teacher. However, it is recommended that the professional working with the family and school or the parent make copies for two weeks and place the copies in a notebook. In this way parents, teachers, and assisting professionals can review previous notes and make comments on the note to be used the next day. Use of a colorful notebook makes it easy for all to find. In the beginning, children are rewarded simply for bringing the note home after it is completed by the teacher. In this way, baseline rates can be used to establish appropriate levels of behavior for earning rewards.

Step Eight: Review the Note with the Child

Parents should be encouraged to review the note with the child each day. Encourage the parent to begin at the beginning of the note and proceed through the sequence of the day. In this way all aspects of the child's day are reviewed, and parents will be discouraged from overly focusing on negative behavior. Recommend to parents that they spend equal amounts of time discussing positive and negative behavior. Children can learn as much from discussing what they did well and how to repeat the performance the next day as they can from discussing ways to improve their behavior in a specific situation. Because consequences for behavior are already determined, this does not need to be discussed on a nightly basis.

Step Nine: Provide Promised Consequences

Parents should be encouraged to provide consequences as promised. It is helpful to have the parents record the consequences provided on the school-home note so that teachers are reassured about parent follow-through and the therapist can review the notes and parent-delivered consequences with the family.

Step Ten: Provide Follow-Up to Assess Effectiveness

It is critical to review the completed notes with the parent and child to assess effectiveness. It is recommended that a follow-up session with the parent and the child be conducted within 2 weeks, and preferably within 1 week, of beginning the intervention. Trends in behavior should be discussed, and the methods that were used to improve behavior should be outlined. For example, the therapist should discuss with the child positive days or parts of days as well as days that were not so positive and any obstacles in the classroom that impeded behavior change. The therapist should also review whether the intervention has been implemented with integrity. The follow-up session is a good opportunity to determine criteria for earning rewards. Many times, the earning of no more than a specific number of "no" ratings on the school-home note is an easy-to-understand criterion.

Use of a school-home note frequently leads to improved behavior, more effective parent involvement, and reduced conflict. When ineffective, the therapist should reassess the appropriateness of the target behaviors and other factors, such as academic skill level, that may be impeding success. It may be that alternative or additional interventions are needed. For example, for children with ADHD, the school-home note may improve behavior but not to desired levels. Parents who had hoped to avoid medication may feel differently when they see the limitation of a behavioral intervention.

Step Eleven: Fade the Note as Behavior Improves

Notes can be faded as the child consistently demonstrates acceptable behavior. I recommend fading the amount of feedback per interval or the number of intervals before fading to a weekly note. Some children cannot be faded off the note without deterioration in the behavior. Children with ADHD may require the added parent involvement, structure, and external consequences provided by school-home notes in order to maintain appropriate behavior.

References

Achenbach, T. M. (1991). *Manual for the child behavior checklist (4-18) and 1991 profile*. Burlington, VT: University of Vermont, Department of Psychology.

Barkley, R. A. (1996). Using a daily school-behavior report card. *ADHD Report, 4*(6), 1–2 and 13–15.

Christenson, S. L., Hurley, C. M., Sheridan, S. M., & Fenstermacher, K. (1997). Parents' and school psychologists' perspectives on parent involvement activities. *School Psychology Review, 26*(1), 111–130.

Cohen, J. J., & Fish, M. C. (1993). *Handbook of school-based interventions: Resolving student problems and promoting healthy educational environments*. California: Jossey-Bass.

Kamphaus, R., & Reynolds, C. (1998). *Behavior assessment system for children manual*. Circle Pines, MN: American Guidance Service.

Kelley, M. L. (1990). *School-home notes: Promoting children's classroom success*. New York: Guilford Press.

Kelley, M. L., & McCain, A. P. (1995). Promoting academic performance in inattentive children: The relative efficacy of school-home notes with and without response cost. *Behavior Modification, 19*(3), 357–375.

Lahey, B. B., Gendrich, J. G., Gendrich, S. I., Schnelle, J. F., Gant, D. S., & McNees, M. P. (1977). *Behavior Modification, 1*(3), 381–394.

McCain, A. P., & Kelley, M. L. (1993). Managing the classroom behavior of an ADHD preschooler: The efficacy of a school-home note intervention. *Child & Family Behavior Therapy, 15*(3), 33–44.

McCain, A. P., & Kelley, M. L. (1994). Improving classroom performance in underachieving preadolescents: The additive effects of response cost to a school-home note system. *Child & Family Behavior Therapy, 16*(2), 27–41.

Rhodes, M. M., & Kratochwill, T. R. (1998). Parent training and consultation: An analysis of a homework intervention program. *School Psychology Quarterly, 13*(3), 241–264.

Rosen, L. A., Gabardi, C., Miller, D., & Miller, L. (1990). Home-based treatment of disruptive junior high school students: An analysis of the differential effects of positive and negative consequences. *Behavioral Disorders, 15*(4), 227–232.

Schumaker, J. B., Hovell, M. F., & Sherman, J. A. (1977). An analysis of daily report cards and parent-managed privileges in the improvement of adolescents' classroom performance. *Journal of Applied Behavior Analysis, 10*, 449–464.

Witt, J. C., Hannafin, M. J., & Martens, B. K. (1983). Home-based reinforcement: Behavioral covariation between academic performance and inappropriate behavior. *Journal of School Psychology, 21*, 337–348.

21 DIALECTICS IN COGNITIVE AND BEHAVIOR THERAPY

Armida R. Fruzzetti and Alan E. Fruzzetti

"All true thoughts come from the heart" —Chinese fortune cookie

The term *dialectics* has many meanings in philosophy, history, politics, and psychotherapy. For the purposes of this chapter, *dialectics* refers primarily to a set of interventions that instantiate modern cognitive and behavior therapy's embrace of both acceptance (see Chapter 2 in this volume) and change as important treatment strategies. Dialectical Behavior Therapy (Linehan, 1993), in particular, is predicated on both a dialectical worldview and on dialectical methods of persuasion, although other treatments also emphasize a synthesis of acceptance and change (cf. Christensen & Jacobson, 2000; Hayes, Stroshahl, & Wilson, 1999; Segal, Williams, & Teasdale, 2002; Wilson, 1996). This chapter will focus both on the broad acceptance and change dialectic discussed increasingly in cognitive and behavior therapies and on the specific dialectical strategies found in DBT.

DIALECTICS IN COGNITIVE AND BEHAVIOR THERAPY

In psychotherapy the primary dialectic is that of acceptance and change. Tension often occurs in psychotherapy between acceptance-oriented strategies and targets and change-oriented strategies and targets. Patients and therapists want to promote change (e.g., enhance potential, reduce suffering) and at the same time need to accept the suffering, difficulties, and potential limitations of the client. Therapies often align themselves along these apparent polarities. However, focusing only on change or acceptance may not be as helpful as integrating or synthesizing both. For example, a humanistic approach represents the acceptance polarity, and traditional behavior therapy represents the change polarity. A dialectical approach is not neutral or in the middle between these poles, but rather offers a synthesis of these polarities: Both acceptance and change are simultaneously employed as treatment strategies and as targets for client behavior.

Historically, dialectics provided a rationale for adding together and then synthesizing acceptance strategies (such as validating emotions, suffering, thoughts, etc.) with procedures to change behaviors and reduce problem behaviors (e.g., decreasing suicidal or crisis behaviors, panic, depression, etc., via skills training, stimulus control, exposure, cognitive restructuring, or contingency management). Ultimately, this synthesis resulted in a treatment theory and structure that we now call Dialectical Behavior Therapy (DBT). Dialectical principles in DBT were derived and adapted from both Western contemplative and Eastern meditative practices as well as from dialectical philosophy (Linehan, 1993; Pinkard, 1988). Theoretically, dialectics in DBT refers to an understanding of the nature of reality, the process of behavior change, and a method of engaging in persuasion (e.g., between therapist and client, therapist and consulting team), providing both an ontological and an epistemological framework for the theory and the treatment. The dialectical position informs specific applications or intervention strategies, as well as treatment targets. Thus, dialectical interventions may be beneficial to any cognitive behavioral therapist who seeks to utilize the full acceptance-change continuum.

Who Might Benefit from Dialectical Strategies

Dialectics have been utilized, in particular in DBT, with clients meeting criteria for Borderline Personality Disorder (who also have multiple co-occurring problems) and for other multiproblem difficult-to-treat populations (e.g., batterers, suicidal adolescents, or clients with chronic eating disorders, depression, or a history of substance abuse; see Koerner & Dimeff, 2000, or Fruzzetti, 2002, for brief reviews of DBT research). Similarly, a more dialectical approach (acceptance and change) has been developed specifically to augment cognitive and behavior therapy's emphasis on change. For example, acceptance strategies (mindfulness) have been added, with increasing success, to more traditional cognitive behavior therapy approaches to depression (e.g., Segal et al., 2002), eating disorders (Wilson, 1996), and chronic pain management (Kabat-Zinn, Lipworth, & Burney, 1985). Moreover, in a limited comparison to an acceptance-based approach DBT was shown to be more effective (Turner, 2000).

Cognitive and behavior therapy have long histories of empirical support. However, change-oriented treatment strategies are not perfect, and we know relatively little about why treatments fail when they do. Thus, a dialectical approach may be especially useful (1) when change-oriented or acceptance-oriented approaches are not successful, (2) when the treatment reaches a plateau short of its targets for improvement, (3) when clients and therapists get stuck in power struggles, or (4) for multiproblem clients in general.

Contraindications of the Treatment

At this time there are no known contraindications of utilizing dialectical strategies. Considerably more research is needed to understand when a dialectical assessment and intervention may not be a viable treatment option.

Other Decisions in Deciding to Use or Not to Use Dialectical Techniques

As previously indicated, utilizing a dialectical approach provides a framework for treatment, not just a specific set of techniques. Techniques from other therapies often illustrate one side of the dialectic. However, utilizing a dialectical approach requires the inclusion of both sides.

Theory or Mechanism by Which Dialectics Is Hypothesized to Work

Dialectical principles and strategies arise from a dialectical worldview, one in which wholeness and interrelatedness are emphasized over logical positivism and separateness. This is also consistent with a transactional model or contextual behavioral theory, which stresses the interrelated nature of the individual and the environment. Dialectics involves the synthesis of opposites (thesis and antithesis, proposition and counterproposition) in a variety of ways. The synthesis contains elements of both the thesis and the antithesis. A synthesis is not a compromise but rather a new position, proposition, idea, or explanation that recognizes and includes the essence or core value of each (previously apparently contradictory) side. For example, asking for less will get more, or creating more intimacy with another can foster one's independence. Examples of dialectical syntheses will be expanded upon throughout this chapter.

A dialectical therapeutic framework accepts change as an ongoing process and as a fundamental characteristic of reality. Therefore, as treatment progresses, it not only changes the client but also results in a change of the therapy and therapist. In addition, it recognizes that it may be more effective to balance attempts to help a client change with acceptance of the client and/or the client's behavior (actions, thoughts, emotions, etc.).

Dialectics may be like being lost in a very dangerous part of town. To get unlost, so to speak, one must first accept that one is lost, noticing exactly where one is (which may be very anxiety provoking) so that a plan of change (getting out) will be helpful. If one proceeds only to make change, perhaps by driving in many different direction, one is likely to stay lost, get more lost, and even run out of gas, endangering oneself even more. However, if one simply accepts that one is lost and does not move to change then one will remain lost, which may create even more misery. Thus, a therapist can be very soothing and reassuring toward clients ("of course you are scared when you're lost") while simultaneously pushing the clients to take action by getting into the car, with their thoughts and fears (not necessarily having to change them first), and beginning to drive, utilizing the directions that they have been given.

It is essential to recognize that, in a dialectical worldview, there is no right answer, strategy, or explanation of the causes of or solutions to behavior problems; rather, many reasonable and effective ones are possible. Furthermore, the most successful explanations are those that lead to successful interventions. De-emphasizing right and wrong may have salutary effects for the relationship between the therapist and client and for the relationship between the therapist and other members of a treatment or consultation team. Because there is no single truth to be found, it may be easier to work together toward specified goals, with many different approaches having merit, rather than arguing over the one correct answer or way to proceed. All parties to a discussion embrace the question "What is missing; what is being left out from our consideration?" and collaborate toward a fuller meaning or explanation, one with a new synthesis and new implications for intervention.

Finally, a dialectical approach informs the structure and the strategies of treatment when treatment becomes stuck and progress halted. From a dialectical point of view, failure to change suggests that something is missing from our understanding of the phenomenon (something is missing in the analysis), and/or that there is an imbalance between acceptance and change. The therapist may be placing too much emphasis on acceptance (feeling empathy for the client, pro-viding a lot of soothing) or too much on change (wanting client to "just do" the plan the two of them have come up with, etc.). A therapist who is pushing for change can become overly critical when progress stalls. This is likely to leave a client feeling shameful or angry and is likely to damage the therapeutic relationship. On the other hand, if a therapist is too accepting, he or she may contribute to the client's staying stuck in a situation rather than helping them move. Thus, clients may feel cared about but only make limited treatment gains. Similarly, therapists and clients may focus on client change to the exclusion of client self-acceptance, with less positive results.

SPECIFIC DIALECTICAL TREATMENT STRATEGIES

Dialectical strategies allow a therapist to help a client change by responding to the dialectical tensions that arise when the client tries to alter significant behavior patterns, either by highlighting both sides of these apparent polarities or by synthesizing them. Becoming stuck at one pole or the other can often lead to a power struggle in which each tries to convince the other, leading to impediments in the relationship and treatment, decreasing the likelihood that synthesis or progress will be achieved.

Dialectical Assessment

This is a conceptualization strategy that the therapist or treatment team employs for itself. Dialectics informs our clinical understanding about the causes of a given behavior. For example, for every proposition (or thesis) about the cause of a target behavior (e.g., excessive drinking, sad mood, emotional arousal), it is possible to generate one or more alternatives (antitheses) that expose the limitations of the original explanation and add potential explanatory power. This ongoing transaction of ideas (thesis and antithesis) forges new syntheses, which are in turn the next theses. Virtually any attribution about the cause of problem behavior has limitations, and recognizing these limitations allows for fuller understanding of the target problems and affords alternative avenues of intervention. For example, causality that focuses on learning histories neglects present factors; biological explanations neglect environmental factors; models that see the individuals as the host of the problem behavior miss the influence of family environment factors; approaches that see the problematic consequences miss the benefits, and so on. Of course, the reverse would similarly be true. In a dialectical analysis of causality, the process of exploring different factors continues until a more effective (not right or wrong) understanding or explanation is achieved, one from which an effective intervention is developed. Thus, dialectical assessment is not conducted only at the beginning of treatment, but is ongoing. This ensures that treatment targets and intervention strategies are being adequately identified and implemented.

In order to conduct a dialectical assessment, a therapist must evaluate all factors that are influencing a patient's behavior in the current environment. This may include past learning and larger systemic (e.g., social, familial, financial) factors. In developing this understanding, therapist and patient are constantly asking themselves, "What is being left out of our understanding?" until a workable intervention strategy is developed.

In developing a treatment plan for a client diagnosed with alcohol abuse, the therapist may utilize the dialectical assessment strategy in the following manner. Because the client's mother frequently drank alcohol as a means of emotional self-management, and the client was regularly exposed to this, it is reasonable to see the roots of the client's drinking historically, as learned through modeling. Whatever face validity this explanation may hold, this thesis naturally generates a critical idiographic question: "But why did the client drink on Thursday morning, not Wednesday evening or Thursday afternoon?" This question about current factors exposes the limitations of the first explanation or proposition. Arriving at some synthesis, one may conclude that both early learning and current emotional factors (e.g., the client had just been criticized in a phone conversation with a family member) were relevant in the present drinking behavior. This proposition may naturally generate another alternative proposition (antithesis) that exposes the limitations of the synthesis (new proposition): "When criticized, the client gets deeply ashamed and cannot tolerate this aversive arousal." This

new proposition leads the therapist and team to consider internal, not just external, factors. The team may then propose that the therapist teach the client ways to manage this sense of shame. If this assessment does not identify sufficient targets for intervention, the assessment will continue until such targets and intervention strategies were identified.

Dialectical Intervention Strategies

In the following sections, we will consider various strategies for dialectical intervention. These include the balancing of treatment strategies, the use of communication strategies, the encouragement of dialectical thinking, the examination of paradoxes, and the making of metaphorical lemonade from lemons. See Table 21.1 for a summary of these strategies.

Balanced Treatment Strategies

In order to maintain collaboration in session, the therapist may alternate between acceptance and change strategies. This requires integrating traditional, change-oriented behavior therapy strategies (skill training, contingency management, problem solving, etc.) with acceptance- or validation-based treatment strategies. The therapist maintains a stance of flexibility and stability, is nurturant and challenging, recognizes a client's limitations, and pushes the client to increase his or her capabilities. For example, a therapist and patient may have been practicing how the client will be assertive with her ex-husband, who has become increasingly hostile toward her. The patient is going to be seeing the ex-husband the next day, and the therapist is pushing the client concerning how she will be able to carry out her plan, highlighting for her all the pros of being able to do so. While pushing the patient to engage in this behavior, the therapist will need to ensure that he or she is being validating of the patient's fears of doing this behavior. The validation of these fears could take the form of helping her develop a safety plan or discussing another alternative to achieve her goals.

Balanced Treatment Targets

Clients typically have problem behaviors (e.g., panic, social withdrawal, aggression, disordered eating, substance abuse, suicidality) that are the

TABLE 21.1 Summary of Dialectical Strategies

Strategy	Description
Dialectical Assessment	Assessment of behavioral patterns seeking answer to question "What is left out of my understanding of this behavior?"
Balanced Treatment Strategies	Balancing acceptance and change strategies in session.
Balanced Treatment Targets	Balancing acceptance of some targets and the targeting of others for change.
Stylistic Strategies	Balance of acceptance-oriented (warmth, genuineness) and change-oriented (directive, offbeat style).
Dialectical Thinking and Behavior	Encouraging patient to move from either-or thinking to both-and thinking; encouraging patient to respond in balanced ways.
Metaphors	Using metaphors to help patients see alternative ways of thinking and responding.
Observing Paradoxes	Highlighting naturally occurring paradoxes in patient's life to facilitate letting go of extreme positions.
Lemonade out of Lemons	Encouraging patient to see that most problems afford opportunities as well. (Note that great care must be utilized when implementing this strategy.)

target of change in cognitive and behavior therapy. However, these problem behaviors occur in a complex cognitive-emotive-physiological-social context, and it is common for some of these contextual variables to become targeted for change along with the specific problem behavior. Disaggregating behaviors and focusing on acceptance of some while targeting change for others may be an effective alternative approach. For example, a client may binge and purge following awkward social interactions in which she feels a lot of shame about her body. It might be desirable simply to reduce her shame, binging, and purging all together. But because of the high levels of implicit criticism of her body from various media, and explicit criticisms from her family and peers, it may be extremely difficult to reduce her shame. Thus, it may be useful instead to help her learn to accept her shame as a normal emotional response to social criticism, then help her disaggregate her binging and purging from shame, and reduce or eliminate her disordered eating.

Stylistic Strategies: Acceptance-Oriented versus Change-Oriented Communication

Therapists can also use communication strategies to maintain balance in session by varying the intensity of emotion, communication, and speed in the session. Varying intensity conveys certainty, strength, and responsiveness to a client's movement such that the therapist is able to match the client, push the client to move faster, or slow the client down. Varying speed keeps the client

and therapist moving so that neither gets stuck maintaining a position. This can be akin to driving a car with a manual transmission. Varying intensity is similar to being attentive to when you must shift up or down to maintain a smooth ride and not create traffic flow difficulties. Sufficient speed allows for smooth changing of gears so that you do not grind the gears by taking too long in shifting.

Therapy at times can be like driving a car that needs a new drive shaft or that has a drive shaft that is very particular about how it gets shifted. Driving with the patient requires the therapist to become quite adept at how to drive that particular car without grinding the gears too often. With some cars and in different traffic circumstances you might have to shift quickly from gear to gear (strategy to strategy), gently at some times and forcefully at others.

Acceptance-oriented communication is more responsive, warm, and genuine. This type of communication is common in most therapies at some time. It generally communicates acceptance for the client and facilitates trust and respect in the therapeutic relationship. Change-oriented communication is often directive, but it can also include an offbeat style. This unorthodox communication must come from a place of caring and genuineness, lest it be seen simply as callous sarcasm or belittling of the patient's difficulties. When using change-oriented communication a therapist may present a style more extreme than or opposite to that of the patient, either being deadpan or highly emotional, responding to what a patient says but not in the manner the patient expects. Imagine the case of a patient in an inpatient setting who has recently attempted suicide on the ward. He expresses anger over his treatment by the staff (watching him, telling him when to shower, etc.). A therapist may respond by saying, "Well, what do you expect? If you act like a mental patient the staff are likely to treat you as one." Or the therapist may vary her or his tone intentionally to communicate to the client the dysfunctional nature of his behavior: "You aren't *really* thinking that's a good idea, are you?!" Acceptance-oriented and change-oriented communication must be used together to provide balance. Balance does not necessarily mean a fifty-fifty division; the balance is achieved in relation to what is occurring in the session in terms of what is needed to ensure movement and progress.

Increased Dialectical Thinking and Behavior as a Target for Clients

Encouraging dialectical thinking emphasizes patients' becoming aware of all-or-nothing thinking and challenging this type of thinking. However, as should be clear, dialectical thinking does not encourage finding absolute truths based on logic. Thus, therapist and patient are encouraged to move from either-or thinking to both-and thinking. For example, a patient may be angry with a therapist for "pushing [her] too much" and may want the therapist instead to "just be caring." The synthesis may be that in fact the therapist is doing the most caring thing possible by pushing her to do things that are difficult. In another example, synthesis can be used when a client proclaims that "If my girlfriend loved me she'd be willing to do X." The synthesis is for the client to recognize that his girlfriend can love him and not be willing to do what he wants.

Clients often become stuck making negative, critical, or judgmental self-statements or having negative or judgmental thoughts about themselves. It is common in cognitive therapy to attempt to refute or disprove these thoughts. However, research by Swan (1997) suggests when these kinds of thoughts are consistent with a person's self-view that such attempts may increase distress. Similarly, work on thought suppression

(e.g., Wegner, Schneider, Carter, & White, 1987) suggests that attempts to push out these kinds of thoughts may backfire and result in a rebound in which the negative thoughts or self-statements become even more distressing.

Dialectical thinking is an alternative to refutation. In a dialectical approach to critical or judgmental thoughts about themselves, clients are encouraged first to notice or observe the fact that they are having the thought (e.g., "She doesn't love me because I'm so awful"), thereby helping the clients to see thinking as another behavior and to decrease its literality and power. A therapist might say, "I know you think you're a bad person and undeserving of caring from your fiancé." The therapist might emphasize the legitimacy of this thought by noting, "You really did say some pretty awful things to her." Then, instead of trying to refute the self-judgment or directly block any catastrophizing, the therapist might attempt to provide another valid, albeit quite different, point of view: "Of course, at other times you have done other, nicer things. Let's see if there is some reparation you can make for when you were nasty. Repairing the damage would also be a nice thing." In dialectical thinking it is possible, even desirable, to notice both valued and problematic behaviors, along with their accompanying thoughts.

Encouraging dialectical behavior patterns involves having the patient learn to respond in a balanced way to situations. An unbalanced situation that patients often present occurs when they have had a major disagreement with someone. They perceive their position as right and the person with whom they are having a disagreement with as wrong, therefore justifying their displays of bitter anger. A dialectical stance is to not simply be a good therapist by supporting our clients against the world. It is instead to help the patients recognize that they may disagree with someone and that this does not make the other evil, a maltreater, or lesser than they are, just as they are not evil, bad, or lesser than; both sides have their validity and their value. This stance facilitates a client's responding in a more balanced way to the individual. The idea that neither is right or wrong at the level of absolute truth is very difficult to grasp for many patients and therapists. Most psychotherapy, and indeed western culture more generally, places values on behaviors as being either good behaviors or bad behaviors. A dialectical point of view is that behaviors simply are what they are: behaviors that are effective or ineffective in achieving goals.

Metaphors

Metaphors encourage dialectical thinking and balanced responding. The use of metaphors generates alternatives because the content of the metaphor does not elicit as big as a reaction as the actual situation, and the client may more easily take the observer's role. Thus, metaphors are generally easier for clients to hear because clients are less likely to feel that they are being persuaded or lectured to by their therapist.

Using metaphors as a strategy takes practice, but there are many examples of metaphors that can be used routinely in therapy. For example, when a client is not engaging in a particular behavior that would be effective for him or her to do in therapy (e.g., unwilling to engage in role-playing a situation), this can be compared to going to the dentist's office and not opening one's mouth. When describing the need for the patient to complete therapy homework, the therapist could employ a swimming metaphor: The therapist, who is the coach, can teach the swimmer (patient) to swim in a calm pool (therapist's office). But because the swimmer lives in the ocean, the swimmer needs to practice swimming there as well.

Observing Paradoxes

Sometimes people are in situations that are naturally paradoxical, and noticing or embracing these paradoxes may be more useful than attending to only one side of the paradox. Noticing or embracing a paradox is a completely different strategy from giving a paradoxical directive (e.g., prescribing or encouraging the problem behavior). Paradoxical interventions, such as prescribing the symptom, are by definition not done in a genuine manner because they are not meant to be executed literally. Paradoxical directives are not dialectical. Alternatively, observing paradoxes may be done dialectically. This is utilized with a client from a genuine place, and directives per se are not given. Instead, genuinely occurring paradoxes are noticed. This is not a strategy that uses logic or intellectualization to help a patient; instead, it is more experiential. Observing a paradox forces one to let go of extreme positions (thoughts, emotions, and behavior), thereby facilitating more flexible thinking and behaviors.

Embracing a paradox involves first noticing that attempts to solve a problem may be creating or exacerbating the problem. It follows naturally that stopping the previous method of trying to change (or accepting the situation) may paradoxically help to change it. For example, a person might desperately want another person to like her. In her attempts to have people like her she is pushy and demanding, which has the result of pushing people away. Noticing that "more gets you less" may help the person become more socially skilled as she realizes that "less is more."

Lemonade Out of Lemons

This strategy, when executed well, can be very helpful. However, when done poorly or misused it can lead to serious damage to the therapeutic relationship. Therefore, this strategy must be performed delicately. The therapist takes a problem and balances the problem with the opportunity the problem presents for something desirable. The therapist must be careful not to invalidate the difficulties the patient is having and must remember that making lemonade itself can be difficult. This must be done in the context of a caring relationship, lest it seem the therapist is being callous. For example, imagine a client who presented with difficulties with relationships and has been working on social skills with the therapist. All has been smooth for some time. Then one day he comes to session complaining that the new person, his supervisor, and he "don't get along" and that he is thinking of "just quitting," given all the problems he has had at work in the past. A possible response could be: "It makes sense that you might want to quit given all the past problems you've had and how hard it will be to manage this situation. But I need to point out to you that this is fantastic in another way. This is exactly the kind of opportunity we've needed so that now you can really practice!" Again, this tactic is not to take lightly the problem encountered, but to highlight that the problem may be balanced by the opportunity it brings. Remember that this is a strategy to be used with great care.

Misunderstanding dialectical strategies can lead to the question "Aren't you just playing games with your patients?" The answer is a clear "no." As previously indicated, these strategies must be employed within a context of caring, honesty, and commitment to what is being said and done. The therapist must maintain a stance in which she or he appreciates both sides of any apparent polarity or disagreement. The therapist must recognize that she or he does not have the monopoly on truth or answers but should be genuinely searching for what is left out, so that balance may be achieved.

Further Reading

Christensen, A., & Jacobson N. (2000). *Reconcilable differences.* New York: Guilford Press.

Linehan, M. M. (1993). *Cognitive behavioral treatment of borderline personality disorder.* New York: Guilford Press.

Wilson, G. T. (1996). Acceptance and change in the treatment of eating disorders and obesity. *Behavior Therapy, 27,* 417–439.

References

Christensen, A., & Jacobson N. (2000). *Reconcilable differences.* New York: Guilford Press.

Fruzzetti, A. E. (2002). Dialectical behavior therapy for borderline personality and related disorders. In T. Patterson (Ed.), *Comprehensive handbook of psychotherapy.* New York: Wiley.

Hayes, S. C., Stroshahl, K. D., & Wilson, K. E. (1999). *Acceptance and commitment therapy: An experiential approach to behavior change.* New York: Guilford Press.

Kabat-Zinn, J., Lipworth, L., & Burney, R. (1985). The clinical use of mindfulness meditation for the self-regulation of chronic pain. *Journal of Behavioral Medicine, 8,* 163–190.

Koerner, K., & Dimeff, L. (2000). Further data on dialectical behavior therapy. *Clinical Psychology: Science & Practice, 7,* 104–112.

Linehan, M. M. (1993). *Cognitive behavioral treatment of borderline personality disorder.* New York: Guilford Press.

Pinkard, T. (1988). *Hegel's dialectic: The explanation of possibility.* Philadelphia: Temple University.

Segal, Z. V., Williams, J. M. G., & Teasdale, J. D. (2002). *Mindfulness-based cognitive therapy for depression: A new approach to preventing relapse.* New York: Guilford Press.

Swan, W. B. (1997). The trouble with change: Self-verification and allegiance to the self. *Psychological Science, 8,* 177–180.

Turner, R. M. (2000). Naturalistic evaluation of Dialectical Behavior Therapy–oriented treatment for borderline personality disorder. *Cognitive and Behavioral Practice, 7,* 413–419.

Wegner, D. M., Schneider, D. J., Carter, S. R., & White, T. L. (1987). Paradoxical effects of thought suppression. *Journal of Personality and Social Psychology, 53,* 5–13.

Wilson, T. G. (1996). Acceptance and change in the treatment of eating disorders and obesity. *Behavior Therapy, 27,* 417–439.

22 DIFFERENTIAL REINFORCEMENT OF LOW-RATE BEHAVIOR

Jonathan Tarbox and Linda J. Hayes

Differential reinforcement of low-rate behavior (DRL) schedules are reinforcement schedules in which behavior is maintained at or below a specified rate. A DRL schedule can serve two purposes: (1) to reduce a behavioral excess to a more reasonable rate, and/or (2) to establish and maintain an adaptive behavior at or below a particular rate. Extensive research has been conducted on the effects of DRL schedules on the behavior of animals (Ferster & Skinner, 1957), but little research on clinical applications of DRL has been conducted. This chapter will review clinical research on treatments that have utilized DRL. In addition, basic research will be reviewed in an attempt to fill in the many gaps left by the paucity of clinical research. Treatment recommendations will be made based on existing empirical research.

As outlined by Deitz (1977), DRL schedules can be operationalized in two primary ways: (1) reinforcement can be delivered when less than a specified number of responses have occurred during a specified interval of time (henceforth referred to as the *full-session DRL*), or (2) reinforcement can be delivered contingent on the first response that occurs after a minimum interval of time has elapsed since the last response (i.e., after an interresponse time of a minimum duration has elapsed). This procedure will henceforth be referred to as the *spaced-responding DRL*.

In the little clinical research that has been conducted, DRL schedules have generally been implemented in cases in which a particular behavior occurs at a rate that is too high. Topographies have included stereotypy, bizarre speech, disruptive classroom behavior, and out-of-seat behavior in classrooms, among others (Deitz & Repp, 1973, 1974; Kostinas, Scandlen, & Luisellie, 2001; Lennox, Miltenberger, & Donnely, 1987; Singh, Dawson, & Manning, 1981).

The utility of DRL schedules is not restricted to behavioral excesses. They may be useful in situations in which a response is to be acquired, that is adaptive at low rates, but becomes problematic at high rates. Functional communication training provides an example. When functional communication training is implemented, a client is trained to communicate for reinforcement rather than engaging in problem behavior. This is a common treatment for destructive behaviors such as aggression and self-injury. However, the communication response itself may become problematic if emitted too often. For example, a client's requesting a break immediately upon being asked to work may result in the client's no longer completing work tasks. In cases such as these, a DRL schedule of reinforcement for communication may be prescribed. It would maintain the communicative behavior, but at rates that are deemed appropriate for achieving the goal of sustaining work activity.

Another possible target for DRL is stereotypy in individuals with autism. In cases where it is not deemed necessary to eliminate stereotypy completely, a DRL treatment may be warranted. A DRL treatment may also be useful in decreasing interrupting or irrelevant verbal behavior, where low rates may be tolerated. Finally, it is possible that placing a particularly intense problem behavior on a DRL might moderate the undesirable immediate effects of outright extinction. Whatever the application, DRL can be used to decrease behavioral excesses or to maintain appropriate behavior at low rates.

Contraindications of the Treatment

Treatment based on DRL necessarily maintains the behavior in question, albeit at a low rate. As mentioned above, DRL is only indicated when a behavior is problematic purely due to its excessive rate. Therefore, any time a particular behavior should be eliminated entirely, DRL is contraindicated. Examples of such situations might be self-injurious behavior, aggressive behavior, property destruction, and other destructive behaviors. In addition, it should be noted that DRL would be contraindicated as an acquisition procedure any time that it is desired that a skill be acquired rapidly and persist at a high rate.

HOW DOES THE TECHNIQUE WORK?

The DRL schedule works by providing reinforcement for a behavior only when it occurs at or below a specified rate. High rates of behavior do not result in reinforcement, and high rates thus decline. As rates meet or decline below the rate required for reinforcement, reinforcement is delivered, thus maintaining the behavior at or around the desired rate. The DRL technique is based on the general concept of differential reinforcement, which essentially states that one manifestation of behavior is reinforced and therefore persists (in this case low rates of behavior), while another manifestation of behavior is not reinforced and therefore does not persist (in this case high rates of behavior).

STEP-BY-STEP PROCEDURES FOR
IMPLEMENTING A FULL-SESSION DRL

One implements a full-session DRL schedule by first measuring the baseline rate of the behavior selected for reduction. A stable baseline should be observed before DRL is implemented. A terminal rate, consisting of the desired rate at the end of intervention (e.g., six responses per hour), should be specified prior to intervention. The value of the terminal rate should be determined in consultation with the client's caregivers. For example, some families may tolerate higher rates of particular behaviors than other families.

Next, an initial interval of time should be selected. No clinical research has evaluated specific guidelines for selecting initial interval length. The selection of interval length should be guided by convenience and by how often the therapist wants the client to contact the contingencies of the DRL schedule. The length of the interval selected will affect how often the individual comes in contact with the contingencies of reinforcement or nonreinforcement. For example, if the interval is 5 minutes, then the client would contact the relevant contingencies 12 times per hour. When nonreinforcement occurs, it is likely that some differential behavior on the part of caregivers will mark these events, even if it is not intended (or the therapist may specifically inform the client that he or she did not earn reinforcement because he or she responded too many times during that interval). This signal of nonreinforcement may be aversive and may therefore contribute to suppressing responding, therefore contributing to the success of the DRL intervention. However, the shorter the interval, the greater the effort required of the clinician in implementing the contingencies.

Next, an initial interim rate of the behavior should be selected. Little or no clinical research has evaluated what criteria should be used to select interim rates for DRL schedules in clinical treatment. The intervention is more likely to be effective if the initial interim rate is close to the average baseline rate; however, the specified schedule is then implemented by measuring the rate of occurrence of the behavior during the predetermined interval. If the behavior occurs at rates equal to or lower than the target rate for that interval, then reinforcement is delivered at the end of the interval and the next interval begins. If the behavior occurs at rates higher than the target rate, then reinforcement is omitted and the next interval begins.

Adjusting the Full-Session DRL Schedule

If the initial intervention is successful in controlling the rate of the behavior but the initial interim rate is higher than the terminal rate, then the interim rate must be adjusted until it reaches the terminal rate. The full-session DRL can be adjusted by decreasing the frequency of responses allowed during the interval for reinforcement or by decreasing the length of the interval. There is little or no research that has evaluated criteria for adjusting DRL schedules; however, it is probably safer to adjust the schedule slowly. Deitz and Repp (1973) used a full-session DRL and decreased the number of allowed responses from six to three, to two, and finally to zero. The schedule of thinning used in this study was successful, but it was not compared to any other possibility, so no criteria can be recommended reliably on empirical grounds. Nonetheless, the intervention is more likely to be successful if thinning is conducted gradually. If control of the target behavior is lost, then adjust the schedule back to the previously successful level.

STEP-BY-STEP PROCEDURES FOR IMPLEMENTING A SPACED-RESPONDING DRL INTERVENTION

A stable baseline rate of the target behavior should be observed. Next, select a terminal rate. For example, an average interresponse time (IRT) of 10 minutes can be selected. Next, an initial interim IRT must be selected (e.g., a minimum IRT of 8 seconds). The closer the initial interim IRT is to the average baseline IRT, the more successful the initial intervention is likely to be. The therapist then implements the intervention by observing the behavior and beginning a timer or stopwatch the first time the target behavior occurs. The therapist then waits until the behavior occurs again. If an IRT equal to or greater than the initial interim IRT has occurred (i.e., at least 8 sec-

onds have passed since the last occurrence of the behavior) then reinforcement is delivered. If the target behavior occurs before the interim IRT has occurred (i.e., the behavior occurred less than 8 seconds after the last occurrence) then the timer is reset. The timer is repeatedly reset, and reinforcement is not delivered, until responding occurs at or below the specified interim IRT.

Adjusting the Spaced-Responding DRL Schedule

Again, there is little or no clinical research on criteria for adjusting DRL schedules. The spaced-responding DRL schedule is adjusted by gradually increasing the IRT required for reinforcement. Singh et al. (1981) successfully reduced stereotypy in individuals with mental retardation using a spaced-responding DRL treatment and increased the length of the IRT from 12 seconds to 30 seconds, to 60 seconds, and finally to 180 seconds. In a basic study, Weisberg and Tragakis (1967) studied DRL responding in typically developing young children and lengthened the IRT from 10 to 18 seconds. Again, these progressions were successful, but they were not compared to any unsuccessful ones in order to determine the parameters of successful schedule thinning. All other things being equal, increasing the IRT gradually rather than abruptly is likely to contribute to the success of the intervention.

GENERAL ISSUES WITH DRL-BASED INTERVENTIONS

The remainder of this chapter focuses on various factors that may be relevant to clinical applications of DRL, including extinction, reinforcement, discriminative stimuli, collateral behavior, rules, and generalization. Each section will be further divided into discussions of existing clinical research, basic research with humans, and, when necessary, basic research with animals.

Extinction

Implementing extinction for behavior during the DRL interval will probably increase the effectiveness of the intervention. The therapist implements extinction by first determining what consequence is responsible for reinforcing the behavior. This consequence is then not delivered following the behavior. For example, if the client interrupts his parents and his parents inadvertently reinforce the behavior by delivering attention to the child, then implementing extinction would consist of the parents refraining from giving the child attention when he or she interrupts them. If extinction is not implemented, then the success of the DRL schedule will depend on the relative value of the reinforcers available in the DRL versus those available for engaging in the behavior. In other words, waiting to respond must result in a greater overall potency of reinforcement than responding immediately. Little or no clinical research has compared the presence and absence of extinction in DRL interventions, but several studies have been conducted that evaluate one or the other of these procedures, and the following section will be devoted to reviewing the results of these studies.

Early work on DRL has typically either not included extinction, or not reported the inclusion of extinction, during the DRL interval. Lennox et al. (1987) effectively decreased and controlled the rate of eating in an institutionalized adult. They prompted an incompatible response during the interval, effectively blocking attempts at eating from being successful, and indeed blocking was found to be necessary. If the maintaining reinforcer for attempts at eating was consumption of food, then it follows that preventing attempts at the response from producing food probably discontinued reinforcement of attempts, thus implementing extinction. It is also possible that blocking was aversive, thus punishing attempts at eating during the interval.

Singh et al. (1981) successfully utilized a spaced-responding DRL treatment to successfully decrease stereotypy in three teenagers with mental retardation. Attention was delivered contingent on the first response following a minimum IRT. Assuming that stereotypy was not maintained by attention, but rather by reinforcement from other sources, extinction was not implemented in conjunction with DRL. Kostinas et al. (2001) used a full-session DRL to successfully reduce perseverative vocalizations in an adult with mental retardation and Obsessive-Compulsive Disorder. The authors did not report what the consequence for the target behavior was during the interval, so it is not known whether extinction was implemented.

Deitz and Repp (1973) effectively decreased talking-out behavior in a single boy with mental retardation, with the use of a break from work as reinforcement. The authors reported that no differential consequences were programmed for occurrences of the target behavior, so it is reasonable to suspect that whatever source of reinforcement was responsible for maintaining the target behavior during baseline was still present during the DRL intervention. In a second experiment reported in the same study, the authors successfully decreased talking-out behavior in a classroom of children with mental retardation. Again, extinction was apparently not in effect, given that no particular change in consequence was programmed for the behaviors. In the third experiment of the same study, the authors successfully decreased the frequency of changes in discussion topic in a high school classroom. Once again, extinction was apparently not implemented. In a subsequent study, Deitz and Repp (1974) successfully reduced out-of-seat behavior and talking-out behavior in three typical fifth-grade children. Again, extinction was apparently not in effect.

The current behavioral approach to treating problem behavior involves identifying the reinforcement maintaining the problem behavior by way of a functional assessment. Extinction is then typically conducted through the elimination of the contingent relation between the target behavior and the reinforcing consequence. Interventions based on DRL will be more effective if extinction is implemented during the interval. However, the research just summarized clearly indicates that DRL can be effective without extinction. In addition, it may also be the case sometimes that extinction is difficult or impossible to implement. For example, in the case of disruptive classroom behavior, reinforcement in the form of attention may be mediated by other students and may not be under the direct control of the teacher.

In some cases, extinction might not be clinically indicated. For example, if the reinforcement for the behavior is negative, as in the removal of task demands, then placing this behavior on extinction may entail physical guidance to prevent the client from escaping or avoiding tasks. This may be too arduous and/or dangerous to implement. Similarly, ignoring attention-maintained destructive behavior may not be feasible, given that the client may do excessive physical damage to him- or herself, others, or the property of others. If it is not possible, or not feasible, to implement extinction, then it is suggested that far greater magnitudes of reinforcement be delivered contingent on meeting DRL criteria. For example, the client may still gain attention from displaying the target behavior, but the amount of attention earned from the DRL intervention could be made much greater than the amount that the target behavior naturally results in.

Selecting Reinforcers

The reinforcers used in DRL interventions will be among the most critical variables in the successful control of the behavior. Two categories of reinforcement may be used. The reinforcement that is already maintaining the target behavior prior to intervention, otherwise known as the *functional reinforcer*, may be used. The second category includes all other sources of reinforcement, referred to as *arbitrary reinforcement*. As stated earlier, the current trend in treatment for problem behavior is to take a functional approach. If sources of reinforcement for the target behavior have been identified, then the functional reinforcers can be used. If the functional reinforcer is used, it may be necessary to implement extinction or greatly increase the magnitude of reinforcement on the DRL schedule. If the client can emit the target behavior and receive reinforcement immediately, then he or she is unlikely to wait until the end of the interval for the same reinforcement.

If the reinforcer for the behavior has not been identified, then an arbitrary reinforcer must be used, and it may be equally effective. As has been mentioned, the reinforcement delivered in the DRL schedule must be more reinforcing than the reinforcement that the target behavior normally produces, if extinction is not implemented. A good approach to selecting powerful arbitrary reinforcers is to interview knowledgeable caregivers and conduct a preference assessment (see Chapter 59, "Stimulus Preference Assessment," in this volume). If the intervention is not success-

fully controlling the target response, increasing the magnitude or frequency of the reinforcement delivered may prove to be effective.

Discriminative Stimuli

Little or no clinical research has evaluated the effects of discriminative stimuli on the outcomes of DRL interventions. However, a small number of basic studies have. One such study on DRL responding in young children evaluated the effects of including a clock that signaled when reinforcement was available (Droit, 1994). The results clearly indicated an increase in DRL control when the clock was present. Marcucella (1974) reported results from a study on DRL responding in rats that demonstrated that adding discriminative stimuli increased the efficiency of responding. Both of these studies, in addition to making an appeal to well-known principles of discrimination, indicate that including stimuli that are discriminative for reinforcement and nonreinforcement enhances the effectiveness of interventions based on DRL.

Collateral Behavior

Collateral behavior is behavior other than the target behavior that tends to occur under DRL schedules. Little clinical research, but a significant amount of basic research, has evaluated the development of collateral behavior under DRL schedules. Clinically, collateral behaviors might constitute appropriate replacements for the target behavior. For example, if interrupting in a young child is the target behavior, then simply decreasing this response is probably less productive than decreasing it while simultaneously increasing appropriate behaviors such as independent play. In the Singh et al. (1981) study mentioned earlier, a spaced-responding DRL treatment was used to successfully decrease stereotypy in three teenagers with mental retardation. Large increases in untargeted appropriate social behavior were also observed as a result of the treatment.

Bruner and Revusky (1961), Kapostins (1963), Wasserman, Schroeder, and O'Hara (1988), and Stein and Landis (1973) reported significant amounts of collateral behavior under DRL schedules, despite the absence of programmed contingencies for collateral behavior. These studies provide significant support for the notion that DRL schedules increase collateral behavior. If this is the case, then clinicians would be wise to take advantage of this circumstance by ensuring that alternative appropriate behavior is increased. Moreover, these studies suggest that collateral behavior may actually increase the effectiveness of DRL schedules.

Rules

Rules are verbal descriptions of contingencies that may control behavior prior to its exposure to contingencies. Little or no clinical research has evaluated the effects of rules on DRL responding, but at least three basic studies are worth noting. Rosenfarb, Newland, Brannon, and Howey (1992) conducted a study that evaluated the effects of self-derived rules and rule following on analogue DRL and fixed-ratio responding in college students. The results demonstrated that the provision and derivation of rules greatly enhanced DRL responding. Two studies by Hayes and colleagues (Hayes, Brownstein, Haas, & Greenway, 1986; Hayes, Brownstein, Zettle, & Rosenfarb, 1986) assessed the effects of rules on schedule responding in college students. Both studies demonstrated that the provision of accurate rules greatly enhanced the efficiency of DRL responding. The results of these three studies suggest that rules describing DRL contingencies should be provided to clients capable of responding to them when one designs treatments based on DRL schedules.

Generalization

Little is known about generalization under DRL schedules; however, the initial results of basic studies are encouraging. Gray (1976) evaluated generalization of responding to novel stimuli (stimulus generalization) during extinction, following DRL training in pigeons, and generalization was directly related to efficiency in DRL responding. Landaburu, Williams, and Ghezzi (2001) reported results from an experiment on DRL and variable ratio (VR) schedules with college students that demonstrated that stimulus generalization occurred to a much greater extent following DRL training than following VR training. The results of these studies suggest that efficient use of DRL schedules of reinforcement may produce high levels of generalization, and thus treatments based on DRL may be especially indicated when generalization of treatment results is desired.

CONCLUSION

In summary, DRL is a procedure that has been the subject of a considerable volume of basic research but very little clinical research. This technique may be a useful procedure for decreasing problematic behavior that would be adaptive at lower rates. In addition, DRL may be useful for establishing new skills that will be appropriate at low rates. Further, DRL shows promise as a procedure that will foster generalization. The inclusion of extinction, rules, and discriminative stimuli is also to likely enhance the effectiveness of any DRL intervention.

Further Reading

Miltenberger, R. G. (Ed.). (2001). *Behavior modification: Principles and procedures.* Belmont, CA: Wadsworth.

References

Bruner, A., & Revusky, S. (1961). Collateral behavior in humans. *Journal of the Experimental Analysis of Behavior, 4,* 349–350.

Deitz, S. M. (1977). An analysis of programming DRL schedules in educational settings. *Behavior Research and Therapy, 15,* 103–111.

Deitz, S. M., & Repp, A. C. (1973). Decreasing classroom misbehavior through the use of DRL schedules of reinforcement. *Journal of Applied Behavior Analysis, 6,* 457–463.

Deitz, S. M., & Repp, A. C. (1974). Differentially reinforcing low rates of misbehavior with normal elementary schoolchildren. *Journal of Applied Behavior Analysis, 7,* 622.

Droit, S. (1994). Temporal regulation of behavior with an external clock in 3-year-old children: Differences between waiting and response duration tasks. *Journal of Experimental Child Psychology, 58,* 332–345.

Ferster, C. B., & Skinner, B. F. (1957). *Schedules of reinforcement.* New York: Appleton-Century-Crofts.

Gray, V. A. (1976). Stimulus control of differential reinforcement of low rate responding. *Journal of the Experimental Analysis of Behavior, 25,* 199–207.

Hayes, S. C., Brownstein, A. J., Haas, J. R., & Greenway, D. E. (1986). Instructions, multiple schedules, and extinction: Distinguishing rule-governed from schedule-controlled behavior. *Journal of the Experimental Analysis of Behavior, 46,* 137–147.

Hayes, S. C., Brownstein, A. J., Zettle, R. D., & Rosenfarb, I. (1986). Rule-governed behavior and sensitivity to changing consequences of responding. *Journal of the Experimental Analysis of Behavior, 45,* 237–256.

Kapostins, E. E. (1963). The effects of DRL schedules on some characteristics of word utterance. *Journal of the Experimental Analysis of Behavior, 6,* 281–290.

Kostinas, G., Scandlen, A., & Luisellie, J. K. (2001). Effects of DRL and DRL combined with response cost on perseverative verbal behavior on an adult with mental retardation and obsessive compulsive disorder. *Behavioral Interventions, 16,* 27–37.

Landaburu, H., Williams, W. L., & Ghezzi, P. M. (2001). *Examining the use of differential reinforcement of low rates of responding to promote generalization.* Unpublished masters thesis, University of Nevada, Reno.

Lennox, D. B., Miltenberger, R. G., & Donnely, D. R. (1987). Response interruption and DRL for the reduction of rapid eating. *Journal of Applied Behavior Analysis, 20.*

Marcucella, H. (1974). Signaled reinforcement in differential of low rate schedules. *Journal of the Experimental Analysis of Behavior, 22,* 381–390.

Rosenfarb, I. S., Newland, M. C., Brannon, S. E., & Howey, D. E. (1992). Effects of self-generated rules on schedule controlled behavior. *Journal of the Experimental Analysis of Behavior, 58,* 107–121.

Singh, N. N., Dawson, M. J., & Manning, P. (1981). Effects of spaced responding on the stereotyped behavior of profoundly retarded persons. *Journal of Applied Behavior Analysis, 14,* 521–526.

Stein, N., & Landis, R. (1973). Mediating role of human collateral behavior during spaced responding schedule of reinforcement. *Journal of Experimental Psychology, 97,* 28–33.

Wasserman, E. A., Schroeder, G. W., & O'Hara, M. W. (1988). Operant and alternative button pressing by college students on DRL and RR schedules of points reinforcement. *Bulletin of the Psychonomic Society, 26,* 319–322.

Weisberg, P., & Tragakis, C. J. (1967). Analysis of DRL behavior in young children. *Psychological Reports, 21,* 709–715.

23

DIFFERENTIAL REINFORCEMENT OF OTHER BEHAVIOR AND DIFFERENTIAL REINFORCEMENT OF ALTERNATIVE BEHAVIOR

Michele D. Wallace and Adel C. Robles

Differential reinforcement procedures, namely differential reinforcement of other behavior (DRO) and differential reinforcement of alternative behavior (DRA), have been repeatedly demonstrated to be relatively effective treatments for eliminating problem behavior (Poling & Ryan, 1982; Vollmer & Iwata, 1992). Specifically, DRO and DRA procedures have been used to treat a wide variety of behavior problems such as self-injurious behavior (Cowdery, Iwata, & Pace, 1990), aggression (Repp & Deitz, 1974), psychotic speech (Durand & Crimmins, 1987), disruption (Deitz, Repp, & Deitz, 1976), hyperactivity (Doubros & Daniels, 1986), stereotypy (Repp, Deitz, & Speir, 1974), pica (Donnelly & Olczak, 1990), thumb sucking (Knight & McKenzie, 1974), psychogenic coughing (Watson & Heindl, 1996), drug abuse (Iguchi, Belding, Morral, Lamb, & Husband, 1997), and severe vomiting and weight loss (Lockwood, Maenpaa, & Williams, 1997) to name a few. As such, both procedures represent effective alternatives to decrease undesirable behavior presented by a client. Thus, what follows is a step-by-step guideline for properly implementing each procedure (see Table 23.1).

CONSIDERATIONS PRIOR TO IMPLEMENTING A DIFFERENTIAL REINFORCEMENT PROCEDURE

Conducting a Functional Assessment

The most effective differential reinforcement procedures have been those conducted in combination with the use of extinction for problem behavior (Mazaleski, Iwata, Vollmer, Zarcone, & Smith, 1993). However, in order to use extinction for problem behavior, it is necessary to first determine the reinforcer maintaining such behavior. Therefore, a functional assessment of problem behavior (Iwata, Vollmer, & Zarcone, 1990) should be conducted to identify possible maintaining sources of reinforcement prior to implementing a differential reinforcement procedure (see Chapter 27, this volume).

Selecting Reinforcers to Deliver During Differential Reinforcement

Reinforcers scheduled to be delivered during differential reinforcement procedures should be chosen prior to implementation. The reinforcer can be either the reinforcer maintaining problem behavior or an arbitrarily chosen reinforcer. As previously mentioned, the most efficient treat-

TABLE 23.1   Steps in the Use of DRO and DRA to Reduce Problem Behavior

I. *Preparation*

   Step 1.   Conduct a functional assessment.

   Step 2.   Select reinforcers to deliver during differential reinforcement that fit the functional assessment.

II. *DRO procedures*

   Step 1.   Select the reinforcement interval length (e.g., use an interval slightly shorter than the mean interresponse time), focus (e.g., absence of the response during the whole interval or only at the end of an interval), and resetting feature (e.g., decide whether the time interval resets if problem behavior occurs at any point during the interval).

   Step 2.   Implement the DRO in a setting that is associated with the problem behavior.

   Step 3.   Thin the reinforcement schedule as problem behavior is reduced.

III. *DRA procedures*

   Step 1.   Select an alternative response (e.g. one that is functionally or literally incompatible with the behavior that needs to decrease).

   Step 2.   Select a reinforcement schedule (usually initially continuous reinforcement).

   Step 3.   Implement the DRA in a setting in which reinforcement can be immediate.

   Step 4.   Thin reinforcement schedule as behavior is acquired.

---

ments involve delivery of maintaining reinforcers. Thus, it should be noted that in order for arbitrarily chosen reinforcers to effectively reduce problem behavior, they must be more potent than the reinforcer maintaining problem behavior (Vollmer & Iwata, 1992).

If the item to be delivered during the differential reinforcement procedure is arbitrary, a stimulus preference assessment (SPA) should always be conducted to increase the likelihood that the item will function as a reinforcer (see Pace, Ivancic, Edwards, Iwata, & Page, 1985). Items approached most often during the SPA should subsequently be used during the differential reinforcement procedure.

DIFFERENTIAL REINFORCEMENT OF OTHER BEHAVIOR (DRO)

In DRO procedures, problem behavior is reduced by scheduling a reinforcer contingent upon the absence of problem behavior for a specific time interval. There are a number of mechanisms suggested to be responsible for the effectiveness of DRO procedures. First, because reinforcement is delivered only when problem behavior is absent, these behaviors are no longer reinforced. In this manner, problem behavior may be suppressed through the process of extinction. Second, because DRO procedures require scheduled rein-

forcement, individuals are less likely to experience deprivation from reinforcement. Third, scheduled reinforcement increases the probability of whatever response it follows. Thus, behavior other than problem behavior is likely to be strengthened (Miltenberger, 1997).

Advantages and Disadvantages of DRO

The advantages and disadvantages of DRO procedures should be considered prior to determining if DRO would be a suitable treatment. There are many advantages of using DRO to reduce problem behavior. First, the procedure is relatively easy to implement and capable of rapidly (Reynolds, 1961) and successfully (Poling & Ryan, 1982; Vollmer & Iwata, 1992) treating a multitude of behavior problems. Second, the procedure involves frequently scheduled reinforcement of many other behaviors. Third, the technique itself is nonaversive in that in does not rely on punishment.

Regardless of the benefits of DRO, there are a number of disadvantages that should be considered prior to implementation. First, the function of reinforcement delivery during DRO is to ensure relatively low levels of deprivation; however, if an individual engages in high rates of problem behavior he or she will probably fail to meet the schedule requirements for reinforcement and will become more and more deprived of the reinforcer. In this case, an individual may continue to engage in problem behavior or start engaging in other inappropriate behavior to ensure reinforcement. Second, because the procedure does not reinforce any replacement behavior in particular, it may unintentionally reinforce other inappropriate behavior. That is, DRO reinforces any behavior that is going on other than a specified problem behavior, and sometimes these behaviors may not be appropriate. For example, if one is using DRO to decrease aggression maintained by attention and one delivers reinforcement for not engaging in aggression just after the child swears, you would be delivering reinforcement for inappropriate vocalizations, which might subsequently increase swearing. Third, behavioral contrast may be another adverse side effect of a DRO procedure. Problem behavior may increase in other situations (in which DRO is not implemented) if reinforcement for problem behavior is still being provided in those situations, in part due to the contrast with the situation in which DRO contingencies apply. Fourth, DRO has been suggested to be less adequate in treating problem behavior maintained by automatic reinforcement (e.g., sensory reinforcement nonarbitrarily linked to some forms of responding), because the reinforcer delivered during the procedure must compete with reinforcers produced avoidably by problem behavior (Harris & Wolchik, 1979). Therefore, when choosing to use DRO with an individual who engages in problem behavior maintained by automatic reinforcement, it is advised that the reinforcer used in the DRO procedure compete with problem behavior as demonstrated in a competing item assessment (see Piazza, Adelinis, Hanley, Goh, & Delia, 2000).

Steps for Effective Usage of DRO

As previously mentioned, a functional assessment as well as careful reinforcer selection is advised prior to implementing any differential reinforcement procedure. Once these requirements for effective implementation of DRO have been met, there are a number of other important factors to consider, such as selecting reinforcement intervals, implementing the procedures, and thinning reinforcement schedules.

Selecting Reinforcement Intervals

In DRO, reinforcers are delivered following a period of time in which problem behavior is absent. Thus, time requirements for the absence of problem behavior are based on either fixed interval (FI) or variable interval (VI) schedules. Although FI schedules are most commonly used during DRO procedures, there are no rigid rules for choosing reinforcement intervals (Poling & Ryan, 1982).

An effective method for determining reinforcement intervals begins by measuring baseline rates of problem behavior, calculating the mean interresponse time (IRT), and subsequently using an interval slightly shorter than the mean IRT (Deitz & Repp, 1983). For example, if baseline responding occurs at a rate of 6 responses per minute (rpm), the mean IRT would be 10 seconds (s). Thus, the initial DRO schedule should be under 10 s. Moreover, it may be necessary to use even shorter time intervals if an extinction burst of problem behavior occurs during initial treatment sessions to ensure delivery of reinforcement.

Once the necessary time interval is chosen, within-interval requirements for reinforcer deliverance must also be considered. Whole-interval and momentary-interval requirements are two such possibilities. A whole-interval requirement involves the absence of problem behavior during an entire interval, and a momentary-interval requirement involves the absence of problem behavior only at the end of an interval. Both procedures have been shown to be effective in reducing problem behavior (Lindberg, Iwata, Kahng, & DeLeon, 1999; Repp, Barton, & Brulle, 1983).

Whether the interval will involve a resetting or non-resetting feature should also be considered. A resetting feature, whereby a time interval resets if problem behavior occurs at any point during the interval (Repp et al., 1974), is most common for DRO procedures (Vollmer & Iwata, 1992). Contrarily, a non-resetting feature involves a time interval, which is not reset if problem behavior occurs during the interval (Repp, Deitz, & Deitz, 1976). In the latter case, either the reinforcer would be delivered at the end of the interval (non-resetting in conjunction with momentary DRO) or the remainder of the interval would be added to the subsequent interval (non-resetting in conjunction with whole-interval DRO). Thus, the intervals may seemingly grow lengthier, and it is noteworthy that this could potentially lead to increased levels of deprivation when an individual continuously fails to meet the reinforcement requirement. A non-resetting DRO schedule might be useful, however, in a classroom or institutional setting where staff-client ratios are low and several clients are observed simultaneously.

Implementing DRO

Implementation of DRO should begin with the choice of a reasonable portion of the day in which it can consistently be implemented (Poling & Ryan, 1982). This may mean choosing the activity with which the problem behavior is interfering most. Because problem behavior decreases one setting at a time, subsequent settings should be systematically targeted.

Using a stopwatch, DRO intervals should be timed, and reinforcers should be delivered contingent upon the absence of problem behavior for a specified period of time (Miltenberger, 1997). If problem behavior occurs during a point at which reinforcement is scheduled to be delivered, the reinforcer should be withheld. Following reinforcement, the timer should be reset, and the steps we have outlined should be repeated. Once problem behavior begins to decrease to a specified criterion, it will be necessary to thin the reinforcement schedule. The criterion for thinning a reinforcement schedule should be that an individual is successfully receiving reinforcement for no problem behavior during most intervals (Miltenberger, 1997). An effective criterion for thinning reinforcement schedules is to increase schedule requirements following two consecutive sessions where problem behavior occurred at or less than 85% of baseline rates (Hanley, Iwata, & Thompson, 2001).

Thinning Reinforcement Schedules

Thinning reinforcement schedules can be achieved across sessions or within sessions (Repp & Slack, 1977). Either way, it involves increasing intervals by fixed increments, proportional increments, or IRT adjusting. Thinning schedules by fixed increments simply involves consistently increasing schedule requirements by a fixed length of time (Poling & Ryan, 1982). For example, using

a fixed 1-min increment would mean increasing a 2-min schedule to 3 minutes, 4 minutes, and 5 minutes, respectively. Thinning schedules by proportional increments involves consistently increasing schedule requirements by a percentage of time. For example, a 50% increment would involve increasing a 2-min schedule to 3 minutes, 4.5 minutes, and 6.75 minutes, respectively. Thinning schedules by IRT adjusting involves selecting an interval slightly lower than the mean IRT measured in the previous three to five sessions (Deitz & Repp, 1983; Vollmer, Iwata, Zarcone, Smith, & Mazaleski, 1993). For example, if the initial DRO schedule was 10 s and the rate of responding from the last five sessions was 3 rpm, the new mean IRT would be 20 s. Thus, one might increase the initial schedule to a DRO 15-s schedule.

Once again, the criterion adopted for thinning the reinforcement schedule should be met within each phase of the thinning process. In the event that an individual fails to meet the criterion for a number of sessions, the schedule requirement should be decreased in order to ensure that the individual successfully contacts reinforcement.

DIFFERENTIAL REINFORCEMENT OF ALTERNATIVE BEHAVIOR (DRA)

In DRA procedures, problem behavior is reduced through an increase in an alternative behavior that has been identified as a replacement for problem behavior. Thus, reinforcement is provided for alternative behavior while problem behavior is oftentimes (but not always) extinguished (Miltenberger, 1997). There are a number of mechanisms suggested to be responsible for the effectiveness of DRA procedures. First, when reinforcement is no longer delivered contingent upon problem behavior, suppression of problem behavior may occur through the process of extinction (Fisher et al., 1993). Second, alternative behavior is increased by deliverance of the reinforcer maintaining problem behavior. Thus, it is no longer necessary for an individual to engage in problem behavior to gain access to a specific reinforcer (Carr, 1988). Third, DRA procedures allow individuals to access reinforcement at whatever rate they choose to engage in alternative behavior. Thus, it has been suggested that DRA allows individuals to exert control over reinforcement (Carr & Durand, 1985).

Variations of DRA

Variations of DRA include differential reinforcement of incompatible behavior and functional communication training, which are described in the following sections.

Differential Reinforcement of Incompatible Behavior (DRI)

In DRI the topography of alternative behavior is incompatible with problem behavior. That is, problem behavior cannot occur while the individual is engaging in the alternative behavior. In this sense, incompatible behavior competes with problem behavior (Tarpley & Schroeder, 1979). For example, a child engaging in hand mouthing during a first grade "circle time" activity may be provided reinforcement for sitting with folded hands during the course of the activity. In this example, the child cannot physically fold his or her hands and simultaneously mouth his or her hands.

Functional Communication Training (FCT)

In another variation of DRA, FCT, the alternative behavior is a communicative response. Thus, the replacement behavior allows an individual to communicate or request access to the reinforcer maintaining problem behavior. For example, in the case that problem behavior is maintained by escape from demands, an individual would be taught to request a break. The FCT response (requesting a break) would be reinforced, while problem behavior (e.g., aggression, disruption, etc.) would be extinguished.

Advantages and Disadvantages of DRA

Consideration of the advantages and disadvantages associated with DRA procedures should be considered prior to implementation. There are many advantages to using DRA to treat problem behavior. As in the case of DRO, the first two involve the facts that (1) DRA has been demonstrated to successfully treat a multitude of behavior problems (Vollmer & Iwata, 1992) and (2) the procedure is a nonpunishing and non-aversive treatment because it occasions reinforcement regularly (Deitz & Repp, 1983). A third advantage is that DRA replaces problem behavior with more appropriate behavior (LaVigna & Donnellan, 1986), and as long as alternative behavior is reinforced and maintained, problem behavior is less likely to occur (Deitz & Repp, 1983).

Regardless of the benefits, there are at least two important disadvantages of DRA that should be addressed before implementation. First, results of the procedure are not necessarily achieved rapidly. Because DRA requires the acquisition of an alternative response, the target behavior may continue to occur until the alternative response has been strengthened. This means that decreases in the maladaptive behavior and increases in the adaptive behavior may occur slowly in some individuals. Second, individuals who have been taught an alternative response may use it at unmanageably high rates. For example, if you teach a child to request attention from his or her mother by saying "excuse me," the child might say "excuse me" 100+ times throughout dinner preparation. Consequently, until the reinforcement schedule is thinned, DRA may be a tedious and labor-intensive intervention unless the new behavior is extinguished by not reinforcing it. Thus, other problems (i.e., recovery of problem behavior or development of new problem behavior) may be promoted.

Steps for Effective Usage of DRA

Subsequent to the functional assessment and the careful selection of reinforcers, there are a number of other important steps to complete prior to implementation, such as selecting an alternative response, selecting reinforcement intervals, implementing DRA, and thinning reinforcement schedules.

Selecting an Alternative Response

Responses chosen to replace problem behavior should be responses that already occasionally occur in an individual's repertoire. These responses should be ones that natural contingencies are likely to reinforce, that is, ones that the social environment would naturally support. Additionally, an alternative response should require little response effort, such that an individual would be more likely to engage in alternative behavior than problem behavior (Miltenberger, 1997). Finally, it may also be beneficial to choose a number of alternative responses to reinforce (Kazdin, 1994). This might involve teaching an individual engaging in problem behavior maintained by attention not only to approach others but also to initiate conversation by saying "hello" or "let's talk." If it is not possible to choose an alternative response within the individual's repertoire, it will be necessary to devote time to shaping desired responses. This will involve providing differential reinforcement for successive approximations of a specified alternative behavior.

Selecting Reinforcement Intervals

Any reinforcement schedule, including fixed ratio (FR) and variable ratio (VR), may be used to reinforce an alternative response. However, an initial continuous reinforcement schedule (CRF) in which an alternative response is reinforced for every occurrence is recommended. A CRF schedule will allow the alternative response to increase more rapidly (Miltenberger, 1997).

Implementing DRA

During DRA implementation, reinforcement for alternative behavior should be delivered not only continuously, but also contingently and immediately. This means that contingent upon each occurrence of alternative behavior, reinforcement should be delivered without delay. Once problem behavior begins to decrease and alternative behavior has become efficient, it will be necessary to thin the reinforcement schedule (Miltenberger, 1997). The thinning criterion already outlined in the DRO section of this chapter is also recommended for DRA.

Thinning Reinforcement Schedule

Thinning reinforcement schedules involve either increasing response requirements by fixed or proportional ratios or arranging a multiple schedule requirement. To thin ratio schedules by fixed increments, consistently increase response requirements by a fixed number of responses. To thin ratio schedules by proportional increments, consistently increase ratio requirements by a percentage of responses (see DRO section for details on fixed and proportional methods).

One practical way of thinning reinforcement schedules by fixed or proportional increments involves response chaining. In response chaining, individuals are taught to complete a series of steps in a task before obtaining reinforcement. For example, individuals engaging in problem behavior to access escape may initially be taught to request a break. However, as individuals become efficient in requesting a break, they should be taught to complete one homework problem prior to requesting a break. In this manner, response chaining would ultimately lead to the completion of an entire worksheet of homework problems before a break is obtained (Lalli, Casey, & Kates, 1995).

Thinning reinforcement by arranging a multiple schedule would involve signaling periods of reinforcement and extinction for the alternative response by correlating each of these periods with a different stimulus. For example, a green card could be correlated with a period of reinforcement and a red card could be correlated with a period of extinction for alternative behavior. These periods would initially alternate in a fashion that would allow the reinforcement period to be greater than the extinction period. For example, it might be feasible to start by delivering continuous reinforcement for an alternative response for a period of 45 s followed by a period of 15 s in which no reinforcement is provided. Then, the multiple schedule could be further thinned (e.g., from 45/15 to 60/30, 60/45, 60/60, 60/90, 60/120, and so on) upon achieving decreases in problem behavior that reach the aforementioned criterion of 85% or lower than mean baseline rates for two consecutive sessions (Hanley et al., 2001).

CONCLUSION

Differential reinforcement, one of the most commonly used contingency-based procedures for the reduction of problem behavior, has been demonstrated to be easily implemented and an effective treatment strategy. When choosing to use DRO or DRA procedures, one should first identify the maintaining variables associated with the undesirable behavior. Moreover, when determining the suitability of differential reinforcement treatments, one should take into account possible advantages and disadvantages (previously outlined) prior to implementation. Finally, if the procedure is implemented in accordance with the above mentioned guidelines, one should be able to make lasting behavioral change with either DRO or DRA procedures.

References

Carr, E. G. (1988). Functional equivalence as a means of response generalization. In R. H. Horner, G. Dunlap, & R. L. Koegel (Eds.), *Generalization and maintenance: Life-style changes in applied settings* (pp. 221–241). Baltimore: Paul H. Brooks.

Carr, E. G., & Durand, V. M. (1985). Reducing behavior problems through functional communication training. *Journal of Applied Behavior Analysis, 18,* 111–126.

Cowdery, G. E., Iwata, B. A., & Pace, G. M. (1990). Effects and side effects of DRO as treatment for self-injurious behavior. *Journal of Applied Behavior Analysis, 23,* 497–506.

Deitz, D. E., & Repp, A. C. (1983). Reducing behavior through reinforcement. *Exceptional Education Quarterly, 3,* 34–46.

Deitz, S. M., Repp, A. C., & Deitz, D. E. D. (1976). Reducing inappropriate classroom behaviour of retarded students through three procedures of differential reinforcement. *Journal of Mental Deficiency Research, 20,* 155–226.

Donnelly, D. R., & Olczak, P. V. (1990). The effect of differential reinforcement of incompatible behaviors (DRI) on pica for cigarettes in persons with intellectual disability. *Behavior Modification, 14,* 81–96.

Doubros, S. G., & Daniels, G. J. (1986). An experimental approach to the reduction of overactive behavior. *Behaviour Research and Therapy, 4,* 251–258.

Durand, V. M., & Crimmins, D. B. (1987). Assessment and treatment of psychotic speech in an autistic child. *Journal of Autism and Developmental Disorders, 17,* 17–28.

Fisher, W., Piazza, C., Cataldo, M., Harrell, R., Jefferson, G., & Conner, R. (1993). Functional communication training with and without extinction and punishment. *Journal of Applied Behavior Analysis, 26,* 23–36.

Hanley, G. P., Iwata, B. A., & Thompson, R. H. (2001). Reinforcement schedule thinning following treatment with functional communication training. *Journal of Applied Behavior Analysis, 34,* 17–38.

Harris, S. L., & Wolchik, S. A. (1979). Suppression of self-stimulation: Three alternative strategies. *Journal of Applied Behavior Analysis, 12,* 199–210.

Iguchi, M. Y., Belding, M. A., Morral, A. R., Lamb, R., & Husband, S. D. (1997). Reinforcing operants other than abstinence in drug abuse treatment: An effective alternative for reducing drug use. *Journal of Consulting and Clinical Psychology, 65*(3), 421–428.

Iwata, B. A., Vollmer, T. R., & Zarcone, J. R. (1990). The experimental (functional) analysis of behavior disorders: Methodology, applications, and limitations. In A. C. Repp & N. N. Singh (Eds.), *Perspectives on the use of nonaversive and aversive interventions for persons with developmental disabilities* (pp. 301–330). Sycamore, IL: Sycamore Publishing Co.

Kazdin, A. E. (1994). *Behavior modification in applied settings* (5th ed.). Pacific Grove, CA: Brooks/Cole.

Knight, M. F., & McKenzie, H. S. (1974). Elimination of bedtime thumbsucking in home settings through contingent reading. *Journal of Applied Behavior Analysis, 7,* 33–38.

Lalli, J. S., Casey, S., & Kates, K. (1995). Reducing escape behavior and increasing task completion with functional communication training, extinction, and response chaining. *Journal of Applied Behavior Analysis, 28,* 261–268.

LaVigna, G. W., & Donnellan, A. M. (1986). *Alternatives to punishment: Solving behavior problems with nonaversive strategies.* New York: Irvington Publishers.

Lindberg, J. S., Iwata, B. A., Kahng, S., & DeLeon, I. G. (1999). DRO contingencies: An analysis of variable-momentary schedules. *Journal of Applied Behavior Analysis, 32,* 123–136.

Lockwood, K., Maenpaa, M., & Williams, D. E. (1997). Long-term maintenance of a behavioral alternative to surgery for severe vomiting and weight loss. *Journal of Behavior Therapy and Experimental Psychiatry, 28,* 105–112.

Mazaleski, J. L., Iwata, B. A., Vollmer, T. R., Zarcone, J. R., & Smith, R. G. (1993). Analysis of the reinforcement and extinction components in DRO contingencies with self-injury. *Journal of Applied Behavior Analysis, 26,* 143–156.

Miltenberger, R. (1997). *Behavior modification: Principles and procedures.* Pacific Grove: Brooks/Cole.

Pace, G. M., Ivancic, M. T., Edwards, G. L., Iwata, B. A., & Page, T. J. (1985). Assessment of stimulus preference and reinforcer value with profoundly retarded individuals. *Journal of Applied Behavior Analysis, 18,* 249–255.

Piazza, C. C., Adelinis, J. D., Hanley, G. P., Goh, H., & Delia, M. D. (2000). An evaluation of the effects of matched stimuli on behaviors maintained by automatic reinforcement. *Journal of Applied Behavior Analysis, 33,* 13–27.

Poling, A., & Ryan, C. (1982). Differential reinforcement of other behavior schedules: Therapeutic applications. *Behavior Modification, 6,* 3–21.

Repp, A. C., Barton, L. E., & Brulle, A. R. (1983). A comparison of two procedures for programming the differential reinforcement of other behavior. *Journal of Applied Behavior Analysis, 16,* 435–445.

Repp, A. C., & Deitz, S. M. (1974). Reducing aggressive and self-injurious behavior of institutionalized children through reinforcement of other behaviors. *Journal of Applied Behavior Analysis, 7,* 313–325.

Repp, A. C., Deitz, S. M., & Deitz, D. E. (1976). Reducing inappropriate behaviors in a classroom and in individual sessions through DRO schedules of reinforcement. *Mental Retardation, 14,* 11–15.

Repp, A. C., Deitz, S. M., & Speir, N. C. (1974). Reducing stereotypic responding of retarded persons by the differential reinforcement of other behavior. *American Journal of Mental Deficiency, 79,* 279–284.

Repp, A. C., & Slack, D. J. (1977). Reducing responding of retarded persons by DRO schedules following a history of low-rate responding: A comparison of ascending interval sizes. *Psychological Record, 3,* 581–588.

Reynolds, G. S. (1961). Behavioral contrast. *Journal of the Experimental Analysis of Behavior, 4,* 57–71.

Tarpley, H. D., & Schroeder, S. R. (1979). Comparison of DRO and DRI on rate suppression of self-injurious behavior. *American Journal of Mental Deficiency, 84,* 188–194.

Vollmer, T. R., & Iwata, B. A. (1992). Differential reinforcement as treatment for behavior disorders: Procedural and functional variations. *Research in Developmental Disabilities, 13,* 393–417.

Vollmer, T. R., Iwata, B. A., Zarcone, J. R., Smith, R. G., & Mazaleski, J. L. (1993). Within-session patterns of self-injury as indicators of behavioral function. *Research in Developmental Disabilities, 14,* 479–492.

Watson, T. S., & Heindl, B. (1996). Behavioral case consultation with parents and teachers: An example using differential reinforcement to treat psychogenic cough. *Journal of School Psychology, 34*(4), 365–378.

24 DIRECTED MASTURBATION: A TREATMENT OF FEMALE ORGASMIC DISORDER

Stephanie Both and Ellen Laan

INTRODUCTION

Directed masturbation, a behavioral treatment for female orgasmic disorder, was developed in the early 1970s. Like most sex therapy methods, directed masturbation is based on the sex therapy format introduced by Masters and Johnson. The pioneer laboratory work of Masters and Johnson (1966) showed that men and women are equally capable of responding sexually. In addition, their work in the field of treatment of sexual dysfunctions, described in their book *Human Sexual Inadequacy* (1970), showed that people with sexual dysfunctions could benefit substantially from a brief and directive treatment. The more liberal sexual climate of the 1960s and the increased liberation of women, together with the work of Masters and Johnson, initiated the assertion that for women it should be equally possible to experience sexual pleasure and orgasm as for men. The revolutionary Hite report (Hite, 1976) is an example of the increased attention in the 1970s to women's sexual experience.

Masters and Johnson already included specific interventions in their treatment method for making orgasms possible for women who never

or seldom experienced them. LoPicollo and Lobitz (1972) elaborated on the work of Masters and Johnson and designed a nine-step masturbation program for anorgasmic women. This program consisted of a number of basic elements: education, self-exploration and body awareness, directed masturbation, and sensate focus. Initially the program involved both partners of a couple, in an approach similar to that of Masters & Johnson. Two years later, Barbach (1974) transformed the masturbation program of LoPicollo and Lobitz to a format for group treatment for women without their partners, the so-called preorgasmic women's groups. The use of the word *preorgasmic* stressed the view that anorgasmia in women was thought to be mainly the result of an inadequate learning process. In this view, women who never experienced orgasm missed a history of discovery of their own sexuality. This omission is supposed to be repaired through learning of adequate masturbation skills that result in sexual arousal and orgasm. Eventually, these skills could be applied in interaction with a partner. In Barbach's approach there was an emphasis on facilitating women's autonomy and assertiveness in their sexual relationships. Later on, the masturbation program became available for a larger audience through the self-help books *For Yourself: The Fulfillment of Female Sexuality* (Barbach, 1975)

This chapter is an adaptation and extension of Both, de Groot, and Rossmark (2001).

and *Becoming Orgasmic* (Heiman, LoPicollo, & LoPicollo, 1976).

Directed masturbation is mainly based on operant and classical conditioning. Its starting point is the premise that a lack of association between sexual behaviors and positive feelings can lead to an absence of behaviors that might result in arousal and orgasm. The goal of the treatment is to replace inadequate behavior that prevents sexual arousal and orgasm with more appropriate behavior. Feelings of anxiety, shame, or guilt, which may prevent women from trying various kinds of sexual stimulation, are reduced by systematic desensitization.

More cognitive theories on sexual functioning stress the importance of anxiety and attention, and fear of losing control (Stock, 1993). Anxiety associated with sexual experiences can interfere with the ability to relax, and can lead to attention to a number of (nonsexual) concerns that result in inhibition of sexual arousal and orgasm (Barlow, 1986). Women who feel that they must remain in control, and who may have learned to fear the loss of control, are more likely to have problems in letting go, which is a necessary condition for orgasm to occur. The present method of directed masturbation is based on both learning and cognitive principles.

Directed masturbation is characterized by the prescription of behavioral exercises that are performed privately at home. The exercises focus initially on body awareness and body acceptance, and on visual and tactile exploration of the body. Secondly, women are encouraged to discover the areas of the body that produce pleasure when touched. After that, women are instructed in techniques of masturbation, and instructed to use fantasy and imaging to increase sexual excitement. Often Kegel exercises (contraction and relaxation of the pelvic floor muscles; Kegel, 1952) are prescribed, since they may increase women's awareness of sensations in the genitals, which may enhance sexual arousal (Messe & Geer, 1985). For those who become highly aroused but are inhibited in achieving orgasm, the use of role-play orgasm is recommended (Heiman & LoPicollo, 1986). In role-play orgasm a woman pretends she is losing control and is having an orgasm. This may help to overcome the fear of showing the uncontrolled behavior that may accompany orgasm.

The treatment has been applied in different settings, including group, individual, and couples therapy and bibliotherapy. Generally the treatment is brief, between 12 and 20 sessions. It is proven to be equally successful in different settings. Most outcome studies report high success rates, with greater than 80% of women being able to experience orgasm by masturbation, and a lower percentage, 20–60%, being able to experience orgasm with their partner (Heiman, 2000). Learning how to become orgasmic during masturbation does not necessarily generalize to being orgasmic during sexual activity with a partner (de Bruijn, 1982; Leff & Israel, 1983). However, most women report increased enjoyment in sex and increased acceptance of their bodies. Reviews of treatments for sexual dysfunctions in women that follow the criteria for validated or evidence-based practice (American Psychological Association [APA], 1994) conclude that directed masturbation treatments for primary anorgasmia fulfill the criteria for being "well-established" (Heiman & Meston, 1997) or at least "probably efficacious" (O'Donohue, Dopke & Swingen, 1997).

WHO MIGHT BENEFIT FROM THIS TREATMENT?

In clinical practice one comes across a variety of orgasmic problems. In the fourth edition of the *Diagnostic and Statistical Manual of Mental Disorders (DSM-IV)* Female Orgasmic Disorder is described as a persistent or recurrent delay in, or absence of, orgasm following a normal sexual excitement phase (APA, 1994). A distinction is made between lifelong and acquired orgasmic disorder and between global (never experiencing orgasm) and situational (reaching orgasm only with specific stimulation) orgasmic disorder.

Acknowledging the variability within and between women in the type or intensity of stimulation required to trigger orgasm, even in standardized conditions (Laan & van Lunsen, 2002; Levin & Wagner, 1985), the diagnosis of the disorder is based on "the clinician's judgment that the women's capacity to orgasm is less than would be reasonable for her age, sexual experience, and the adequacy of sexual stimulation she receives" (APA, 1994). However, a definition of orgasm and indications of what is "reasonable" are not provided by the *DSM-IV*.

Orgasm is usually defined as a combination of subjective experience and physiological changes. Generally the subjective experience of orgasm is described in terms of release of sexual tension and intense feelings of sexual pleasure. On the physiological level female orgasm is characterized by rhythmical contractions of the pelvic floor muscles and the uterus, and more general physiological changes in skeletal muscle tone and cardiovascular and respiratory responses.

Given the variance in type and intensity of stimulation needed to reach orgasm, and the two components of orgasm (subjective experience and physiological changes), it is not surprising that there exists a substantial variety in the orgasmic problems women report. Women seek help because they have never experienced orgasm, because they are capable of reaching orgasm by masturbation but not during sexual contact with a partner, because they can reach orgasm with a partner but not or seldom through intercourse, because they cannot reach orgasm except with a vibrator or through other specific types of sexual stimulation (for example, by lying face-down on the bed with legs pressed together while moving the pelvis), or because they experience orgasm physically but do not, or only weakly, experience feelings of pleasure or release of tension.

Directed masturbation is most effective in treating women with lifelong, global orgasmic disorder (Heiman and Meston, 1997; O'Donohue et al., 1997). However, the treatment may also be effective in women who can reach orgasm only through very specific masturbation manners. The focus in directed masturbation on discovery of various areas of the body that may produce pleasure when touched, and the encouragement to experiment with various techniques of masturbation, can expand a woman's skills to reach orgasm.

Following the definition of *DSM-IV*, orgasmic disorder is only diagnosed when there is a normal sexual excitement phase that is not followed by orgasm. But many women with lifelong, global anorgasmia experience only little sexual excitement or report problems in keeping a certain level of sexual excitement (Morokoff, 1989). Thus, in clinical practice, the diagnosis of orgasmic disorder may be made when, according to *DSM-IV* criteria, the diagnosis of Female Sexual Arousal Disorder may be more accurate. In fact, given its emphasis on learning behavior that makes sexual excitement and orgasm come about, directed masturbation is especially aimed at women who experience little sexual excitement. Some women with Hypoactive Sexual Desire Disorder have a history of sexual excitement problems and anorgasmia, combined with a lack of sexually rewarding experiences. Thus, orgasmic problems often involve sexual arousal problems, and desire problems can be caused by arousal and orgasmic problems. Not surprisingly, there is often comorbidity of anorgasmia, Sexual Arousal Disorder, and Sexual Desire Disorder (Segraves & Segraves, 1991). To summarize, given the overlap of sexual arousal, orgasmic, and desire problems, directed masturbation can be suitable for women with lifelong global orgasmic disorder, women with global sexual arousal problems, and women with Sexual Desire Disorder combined with arousal problems.

As noted before, orgasmic problems can be related to a lack of skills to achieve arousal and orgasm, or to inhibition of the orgasmic response due, for example, to fear of losing control, or both. Unfortunately, no clinical or epidemiological studies have examined the prevalence of these distinct forms of orgasmic disorder. Our clinical impression is that in a small percentage of cases of lifelong, global anorgasmia, fear of losing control is the major difficulty.

CONTRAINDICATIONS OF THE TREATMENT

Very little can be said about physical causes of inhibited female orgasm due to a lack of knowledge of the neurophysiological basis of orgasm. Damage to the central nervous system, the spinal cord, or the peripheral nerves caused by trauma or multiple sclerosis may lead to orgasmic difficulties (Sipski, 1998). There is no evidence of orgasmic difficulties as a result of estrogen or testosterone deficiencies (Bancroft, 1989). Psychotropic medications may impair orgasmic functioning. Selective serotonin reuptake inhibitors (SSRIs) and monoamine oxidase inhibitors (MAOI) are reported to delay or inhibit orgasm in women (Meston & Frohlich, 2000). Therefore, for an anorgasmic woman who is using psychotropic medication that is known to impair orgasm, it is recommended to start directed masturbation when the woman has reduced medication. However, in the presence of possible physical aetiology of the orgasmic problem, treatment may be started to see what improvements may be made.

Anorgasmic women may have had sexual abuse experiences (van Berlo & Ensink, 2000; Laumann, Paik, & Rosen, 1999). Although directed masturbation is not contraindicated for women with a history of sexual abuse, it is advisable to check carefully to determine if the woman is capable of coping with memories of the sexual abuse before a program is started. When the woman becomes substantially disordered by talking about the sexual abuse and reports post-traumatic stress symptoms, treatment for Post-Traumatic Stress Disorder is indicated. After treatment for post-traumatic stress a directed masturbation program can be considered. In cases of problems in the sexual relationship with a partner, we recommend that clinicians start couples therapy prior to an individual masturbation training program, or incorporate directed masturbation into couples therapy.

THE INITIAL INTERVIEW

The behavioral exercises that are used in directed masturbation have to be tailored to the individual needs of the client. Therefore, a thorough clinical interview is needed to get a full picture of the client and the nature of her orgasmic problem. The aim of the initial interview is to gather information concerning current sexual functioning, onset of the complaints, and the context in which the problem occurs. Specific attention should be given to the amount of subjective and physiological excitement the women experiences generally. In women who report high levels of excitement and who feel that they are almost reaching orgasm, fear of losing control may be an important factor.

An extensive sexual history should be taken, and the clinician should ask if the woman has ever experienced sexual abuse. To indicate to what extent the women has discovered her own sexuality it is necessary to ask about her feelings toward her body, masturbation experience, and familiarity with, and response to, different forms of sexual stimulation (e.g., erotic fantasy, sexual activity with partners). From this information an impression should be obtained of the woman's cognitions and feelings about sexuality and about masturbation specifically. For a detailed sexual history interview, refer to Heiman and LoPicollo (1988).

Besides sexual history, the psychiatric and medical history should be addressed. If a stable relationship exists, the nature of the general relationship should be examined. A conjoint partner interview is desirable to provide information concerning possible sexual problems of the partner.

STEP-BY-STEP PROCEDURES

The directed masturbation procedure described here is a fixed program of 10 sessions largely based on the programs described by LoPicollo and Lobitz (1972) and Barbach (1974), extended with more cognitive behavioral interventions (Both, de Groot, & Rossmark, 2001). Throughout the whole program there is a strong emphasis on increasing autonomy and assertiveness (see Table 24.1). The program can be applied in a group therapy setting, in individual therapy, and within couples therapy. Women differ in the speed with which they go through the program. To tailor the program to the individual needs of the client, the individual focus of the woman is explicitly discussed during the therapy.

The behavioral exercises that are assigned in each session have to be practiced at home for an hour each day. During each session the woman's

TABLE 24.1 Key Elements of the Directed Masturbation Program

1. Visual and tactile exploration of the body with a focus on body awareness and body acceptance

2. Education about spectatoring

3. Discussion of the impact of sexual upbringing

4. Emphasis on assertiveness and autonomy

5. Education about female sexual response

6. Education about the inhibiting or facilitating effects of cognitions

7. Masturbation instructions and exercises

8. Use of sexual fantasy or other sexual stimuli to increase sexual arousal

9. Introduction of the use of a vibrator

10. Dis-inhibition strategies (e.g., role-playing orgasm)

experiences with the assigned homework are extensively discussed. The woman is asked to keep a diary to record her behavior and feelings in response to the exercises.

We will now describe each session in more detail, including the exercises (homework) that are assigned.

Session 1

The rationale of the program is explained. After that, the woman is asked to formulate her personal goals: What does she want to achieve through the therapy? The woman is encouraged to formulate intermediate goals, and the therapist helps to phrase concrete goals and to express them in positive terms. Expressions like "I do not want to have so many negative feelings toward my body" are rephrased as "I want to accept my body as it is" or "I want to have more positive feelings toward my body."

The homework assignment is to take a shower and concentrate on the water touching the body. Afterwards, examine the nude body in a full-length mirror in minute detail.

Session 2

The discussion of the homework is tailored toward the client's creating time for herself and concentrating on bodily sensations. Negative and positive reactions to the body are discussed. Women who express mainly negative feelings toward their body are encouraged to name three parts they value positively the next time they examine their body.

The homework assignment is to take a shower and examine the body in the mirror, which is followed by touching the whole body, with an emphasis on experimenting and discovery of parts of the body that are nice to touch.

Session 3

The discussion of the exercise concentrates on *spectatoring* (watching yourself touching your body rather than feeling the sensations that you are experiencing) and on the discovery of sensitive areas of the body and pleasurable ways of touching. The subject of sexual upbringing is introduced. The impact of subtle messages regarding sexuality that may have been given by the client's family is discussed. Terminology for male and female genitals and sexual contact is discussed. The woman is asked to choose terms she wants to use for her genitals.

The homework assignment is a repetition of the previous exercise, extended by visual exploration of the genitals with the aid of a hand mirror. The client is also asked to write down the messages regarding sexuality given by her family (or other significant persons).

Session 4

Reactions toward the visual exploration of the genitals are discussed. The therapist shows pictures of female genitals and explains the anatomy. Common concerns regarding genital anatomy (e.g. too-big labia) are addressed. The impact of the messages regarding sexuality given by significant persons is discussed, and the woman is invited to formulate a new message for herself that will promote the achievement of her personal goals. Kegel exercises (contraction and relaxation of the pelvic floor muscles) are introduced (Kegel, 1952).

The homework assignment is a repetition of the previous exercise, extended with exploring the genitals by touching, and Kegel exercises.

Session 5

Discuss the feelings elicited by touching the genitals. Educate the client about the importance of relaxation during touching, and follow this with a progressive relaxation exercise (see Chapter 49 in this volume on relaxation training). Explain that the Kegel exercises can be used to enhance sexual arousal.

The homework assignment is the formerly assigned exploration and touching exercises and a visit to a female-oriented sex shop to look for erotic books or movies.

Session 6

The exploration and touching exercises are discussed with emphasis on attention to pleasurable and sexual feelings. The client is educated in the inhibiting or facilitating effect of cognitions: For example, the cognition "I should experience more arousal now; it doesn't work" is inhibiting, whereas the cognition "This feels nice; let's go on" is facilitating. With reference to the visit to the sex shop, material that may be sexually arousing, and how to use it, is discussed.

A female masturbation movie is shown (Liekens & Drenth, 1991). This movie is especially produced for use in sex therapy. Attitudes toward masturbation are explored, and myths about female sexual arousal and orgasm are discussed and refuted. Physical and subjective changes that occur during sexual arousal and orgasm are explained. Different stimulation techniques are described. The importance of the *solo-phase* (secluding oneself from the environment and concentrating completely on one's sexual sensations) to intensify arousal and to reach orgasm is explained.

The homework assignment consists of touching exercises combined with the intensification of arousal through experimenting with stimulation techniques and/or a lubricant.

Session 7

Exercises are discussed, with a focus on techniques that the woman can use to facilitate her arousal, such as teasing (suspending stimulation at the point that sexual excitement is high, waiting for a moment, and then continuing stimulation). The use of erotic fantasy and imagery to enhance sexual arousal is explained. Female sexual fantasy is discussed, and it is explained that fantasy is not necessarily about things a woman wants to experience in real life. In addition, the woman is asked to remember as vividly as possible a situation in which she enjoyed sexual arousal. She is encouraged to use this memory as an arousal-enhancing fantasy and to expand upon it.

The homework assignment is using a touching exercise and trying to enhance arousal by use of fantasy, erotic books or film, and/or teasing.

Session 8

The discussion of the exercises is tailored to the specific difficulties of each woman. The use of a

vibrator is brought up. The subject of fear of losing control is introduced. Different possible fears are discussed: for example, fear of behaving in an uncontrolled, unladylike fashion, or fear of losing urine during orgasm. Women may be afraid that during orgasm they will behave in a wild and uncontrolled manner, or that they will be completely unconscious for a period of time. To modify such irrational beliefs, physiological and psychological changes during orgasm are explained. Some women are inhibited sexually after experiencing an embarrassing situation in which they lost much fluid, probably during orgasm. The existence of female ejaculation is discussed to reassure the client that the losing of fluid, while not very common, is a recognized part of female sexual responses.

Sexual contact with a partner is discussed, with an emphasis on the wishes and expectations of the woman. Explicit attention is given to the insufficiency, for many women, of intercourse alone to bring about orgasm.

The homework assignment is the same as in session 7, plus experimenting with a vibrator and role-play orgasm.

Session 9

Discussion of the exercises is tailored to the woman's specific difficulties. Partner sex is discussed more extensively, with a focus on assertiveness and communication.

The homework is identical to that for session 8.

Session 10: Evaluation

The woman is asked to indicate to what extent she reached the goals she formulated in the first session. The therapist helps to describe the changes in behavior or subjective experience that appeared during the program. The woman formulates a plan for what she needs to do in the future to maintain the goals she has reached and to make further progress.

Session 11: Follow-Up Session After Three Months

The woman's specific experiences and difficulties during the follow-up period are discussed.

PROBLEMS TO DEAL WITH DURING THE TREATMENT PROGRAM

One of the problems that may occur during directed masturbation is resistance toward performing the assigned exercises. A woman may avoid the exercises from the start, or from the point that they involve masturbation. A lack of adherence to the exercises from the start can be related to resistance toward spending time to herself. The woman may believe that she is only allowed to spend time in activities that benefit others. Resistance to the assignments involving genital touching may be related to strong prohibitions against masturbation. In both cases the woman should be confronted with the question of how the avoidance behavior serves her. She has to choose whether to engage in the exercises that could help her or to continue the avoidance behavior. Limiting the number of sessions beforehand may prevent the avoidance from becoming prolonged. Incorporation of the homework into the woman's regular routine can also be helpful (for example, going to bed early to do the exercises).

A well-known pitfall in directed masturbation is becoming too goal-oriented. A strong focus on reaching orgasm may have a counterproductive effect. Throughout the treatment program, the therapist should help the woman pay attention to the pleasurable feelings she is experiencing during the exercises instead of paying attention to feelings she thinks she is expected to experience.

Directed masturbation is a highly directive therapeutic approach, and there is a risk that clients will place the responsibility for the achievement of orgasm on the therapist. The therapist has to make it clear that it is the client who is responsible for the discovery of her own sexuality. A coaching attitude, in which the therapist provides information, support, and permission, but confronts the client when necessary, is the most fruitful therapeutic approach.

DISCUSSION

During the evaluation and follow-up sessions of the directed masturbation program described in this chapter a majority of the clients report improvements in body awareness, body acceptance, sexual arousal, enjoyment in sex, and decreased feelings of shame or fear of being abnormal. Our clinical experience is that about 40% of clients are able to experience orgasm by masturbation at the end of the program. Nowadays, the results are not as good as those reported in the 1970s and 1980s. The difference in success can perhaps be explained by selection. The increased availability of information about female sexuality may help many anorgasmic women to find out by themselves how to reach orgasm. The women who seek help today may be a group with more complicated problems. Clearly, more recent treatment efficacy data are needed. Given the high comorbidity of orgasmic and arousal problems, it would be more meaningful for outcome studies to distinguish women with both orgasmic and arousal disorder from women with orgasmic disorder only.

It can be expected that during the upcoming years there will be more information on medications for treating sexual arousal and orgasm disorders in women. Possibly, a combination of directed masturbation and pharmacological treatments may lead to an even more efficacious treatment method for female orgasmic disorder in the future.

Further Reading

Everaerd, W., Laan, E., Both, S., & Velde, J. van der. (2000). Female sexuality. In L. T. Szuchman & F. Muscarella (Eds.), *Psychological perspectives on human sexuality* (pp. 101–146). New York: Wiley.

Heiman, J. R. (2000). Orgasmic disorders in women. In R. E. Leiblum & R. C. Rosen (Eds.), *Principles and practices of sex therapy* (3rd ed., pp. 118–153). New York: Guilford Press.

References

American Psychiatric Association (1994). *Diagnostic and statistical manual of mental disorders* (4th ed.). Washington, DC: Author.

Bancroft, D. H. (1989). *Human sexuality and its problems.* Edinburgh: Churchill Livingstone.

Barbach, L. G. (1974). Group treatment of preorgasmic women. *Journal of Sex and Marital Therapy, 1,* 139–145.

Barbach L. G. (1975). *For yourself.* New York: Doubleday.

Barlow, D. H. (1986). Causes of sexual dysfunction.

Journal of Consulting and Clinical Psychology, 54, 140–148.

Berlo, W. van, & Ensink, B. (2000). Problems with sexuality after sexual assault. *Annual Review of Sex Research, 11,* 235–285.

Both, S., de Groot, H. E., & Rossmark, M. (2001). Orgasmestoornissen bij de vrouw: Een cognitief-gedragstherapeutische groepsbehandeling [Orgasmic disorders in women: A cognitive-behavioral group treatment program]. In M. W. Hengeveld & A. Brewaeys (Eds.), *Behandelingsstrategieën bij seksuele dysfuncties [Treatment strategies for sexual dysfunctions]* (pp. 73–91). Houten, The Netherlands: Bohn Stafleu van Loghum.

Bruijn, G. de (1982). From masturbation to orgasm with a partner: How some women bridge the gap—and why others don't. *Journal of Sex & Marital Therapy, 8,* 151–167.

Heiman, J. R. (2000). Orgasmic disorders in women. In R. E. Leiblum & R.C. Rosen (Eds.), *Principles and practices of sex therapy* (3rd ed.). New York: Guilford Press.

Heiman, J. R., & LoPicollo, J. (1988). *Becoming orgasmic: A sexual and personal growth program for women* (rev. and expanded ed.). New York: Simon & Schuster.

Heiman, J. R., LoPicollo, L., & LoPicollo J. (1976). *Becoming orgasmic: A sexual growth program for women.* Englewood Cliffs, NJ: Prentice-Hall.

Heiman, J. R., & Meston, C. M. (1997). Evaluating sexual dysfunction in women. *Clinical Obstetrics and Gynecology, 40,* 616–629.

Hite, S. (1976). *The Hite report.* New York: Dell.

Kegel, A. H. (1952). Sexual function of the pubococcygeus muscle. *Western Journal of Surgery, Obstetrics, and Gynecology, 60,* 521–524.

Laan, E., & van Lunsen, R. H. W. (2002). Orgasm latency, orgasm duration and orgasm quality in women: Validation of a laboratory sexual stimulation technique combining vibrotactile and visual stimuli. Manuscript in preparation.

Laumann, E. O., Paik, A., & Rosen, R. C. (1999). Sexual dysfunction in the United States: Prevalence and predictors. *Journal of the American Medical Association, 281,* 537–544.

Leff, J. J., & Israel, M. (1983). The relation between mode of female masturbation and achievement of orgasm in coitus. *Archives of Sexual Behavior, 12,* 227–236.

Levin, R. J., & Wagner, G. (1985). Orgasm in women in the laboratory: Quantitative studies on duration, intensity, latency, and vaginal blood flow. *Archives of Sexual Behavior, 14,* 439–449.

Liekens, G., & Drenth, J. (1991). Het vrouwelijk orgasme [Female orgasm]. Amsterdam: Select Movies Video.

LoPicollo, J., & Lobitz, W.C. (1972). The role of masturbation in the treatment of orgasmic dysfunction. *Archives of Sexual Behavior, 2,* 163–171.

Masters, W., & Johnson, V. (1966). *Human sexual response.* Boston: Little, Brown.

Masters, W., & Johnson, V. (1970). *Human sexual inadequacy.* Boston: Little, Brown.

Messe, M. R., & Geer, J. H. (1985). Voluntary vaginal musculature contractions as an enhancer of sexual arousal. *Archives of Sexual Behavior, 14,* 13–28.

Meston, C. M., & Frohlich, M. A. (2000). The neurobiology of sexual function. *Archives of General Psychiatry, 57,* 1012–1030.

Morokoff, P. (1989). Sex bias and POD. *American Psychologist, 44,* 73–75.

O'Donohue, W. T., Dopke, C. A., & Swingen, D. N. (1997). Psychotherapy for female sexual dysfunction: A review. *Clinical Psychology Review, 17,* 537–566.

Segraves, K. B., & Segraves, R. T. (1991). Hypoactive sexual desire disorder: Prevalence and comorbidity in 906 subjects. *Journal of Sex and Marital Therapy, 17,* 55–58.

Sipski, M. L. (1998). Sexual functioning in the spinal cord injured. *International Journal of Impotence Research, 10,* S128–S130.

Stock, W. E. (1993). Inhibited female orgasm. In W. O'Donohue & J. H. Geer (Eds.), *Handbook of sexual dysfunctions: Assessment and treatment* (pp. 253–278). Boston: Allyn & Bacon.

25 EMOTION REGULATION

Alan E. Fruzzetti, Chad Shenk, Elizabeth Mosco, and Kirsten Lowry

Although emotions were often ignored in the early years of cognitive and behavior therapy, our understanding of emotion, its relationships with cognition and overt behaviors, and the factors that help regulate emotion have grown considerably in the past twenty-five years. Emotion often occupies center stage in current theoretical and empirical work in normative child development and developmental psychopathology (e.g., Southam-Gerow & Kendall, 2002), adult psychopathology (e.g., Keltner & Kring, 1998), and treatment of individuals (Linehan, 1993a, 1993b), couples (e.g., Fruzzetti & Fruzzetti, in press; Johnson & Whiffen, 1999) and families (e.g., Hoffman, Fruzzetti, & Swensen, 1999).

Although considerable disagreement remains among these burgeoning areas and different language is often employed within various subfields of psychology, there are still many commonalities in the concepts governing emotion and emotion regulation. In this chapter we will describe a basic model for the development of emotion dysregulation and explicate the core components of psychological interventions designed to help clients regulate their emotions, and describe the essential strategies that have been shown to be effective for these problems.

UNDERSTANDING EMOTION REGULATION AND DYSREGULATION

Prior to identifying a suitable definition of emotion regulation and dysregulation, it is important to note that understanding these processes fully is tantamount to resolving long-standing problems in defining emotions. Although psychologists have studied emotions at least since William James (1890), we continue to employ a lexicon that implies that an emotion is a thing inside a person. We should more accurately discuss emotions as processes or ongoing behaviors or as a system of behaviors that includes multiple inputs and outputs. Indeed, this has been the history of our understanding of emotions: As our knowledge of emotion has increased we have included physiological and sensory, cognitive, facial musculature, body posture, verbal, and other factors in our models of what influences emotions (e.g., Plutchik, 1994; Schacter & Singer, 1962; Zajonc, 1984).

Defining Emotion Regulation and Dysregulation

Definitions of emotion regulation typically include a variety of individual and environmental strategies that influence the experience and expression of emotion. For example, Gross (1998) writes that "emotion regulation refers to the processes by which individuals influence which emotions they have, when they have them, and how they experience and express these emotions" (p. 275). Conversely, others note that parents socialize their children and exert enormous influence in regulating their children's emotions (e.g., Eisenberg, Cumberland, & Spinrad, 1998; Saarni & Crowley, 1990). Still others emphasize both the individual's role and that of the social environment in the development of both emotion regulation skills and problems with emotion dysregulation. For example, Thompson (1994) described emotion regulation as both the "extrinsic and intrinsic processes responsible for monitoring, evaluating and modifying emotional reactions . . . to accomplish one's goals" (pp. 27–28). Linehan (1993a) similarly emphasizes both the role of the emotionally vulnerable individual and the role of an invalidating social environment in the development of emotion dysregulation in borderline personality and related disorders. Thus, re-regulating dysregulated emotion may provide a common target for a broad set of disorders, including Major Depressive Disorder and other affective disorders, Post-Traumatic Stress Disorder (PTSD) and other anxiety disorders, eating disorders, substance abuse disorders, and several personality disorders (Fruzzetti, 2002).

Southam-Gerow and Kendall (2002) note the dialectical nature of emotion regulation: Emotions are understood to regulate other (cognitive, physiological, and overt physical) behaviors of the individual, yet emotion is also the phenomenon to be regulated. Although regulating emotion per se is the more typical immediate target, this is often in the service of regulating other behaviors in turn, and understanding the dialectical role of emotion regulation helps one understand the multiple contexts and meanings of emotion regulation intervention strategies.

Emotion dysregulation may be understood to occur when a person's high emotional arousal disrupts her or his effective self-management. That is, a person should not be considered to be dysregulated emotionally when he or she is simply upset. Rather, the hallmark of dysregulation is negative emotional arousal of sufficient intensity or duration to interfere with the person's goals. This interference could be in the form of

dysfunctional behavior in which the person engages in order to regulate (lessen the intensity or duration of) the negative emotion or in the form of emotional pain or misery that inhibits the person from engaging in ordinary self-management.

Developing Dysregulated Emotions: Transactions between Person and Environment.

Most theories of emotion regulation and dysregulation employ a variant of a biosocial model to explain deficits in emotion regulation abilities in children and adults. Linehan (1993a) has perhaps been most explicit in identifying the individual and environmental factors that are likely to result in emotion dysregulation. Specifically, she has identified three *individual vulnerability* factors (dispositional, biological-mediated) that may be present from birth or conditioned over time: (1) high sensitivity to emotional stimuli, (2) high reactivity to emotional stimuli, and (3) difficulty returning to an emotional baseline after a prompting event. Linehan maintains that the combination of individual vulnerability and *invalidating responses* from the social or family environment results in pervasive problems of emotion dysregulation. An *invalidating social environment* is one in which the phenomenologically valid needs and behaviors (e.g., beliefs, emotions, expression of pain, wants, actions) of the individual are not understood and are invalidated by criticism, inattention, punishment, dismissal, blaming, or unresponsiveness, or by erratic, extreme, or otherwise socially and developmentally inappropriate responses.

The *transactional* nature of the development of emotion dysregulation is an important, if often overlooked, part of the development of these problems. That is, an emotionally vulnerable person (highly sensitive and reactive, and with a slow return to baseline) can exacerbate or create an invalidating social environment, which in turn can increase an individual's propensity for emotion dysregulation. Similarly, an invalidating social environment can exacerbate or create emotion dysregulation in an individual, which can further tax the social environment and make it more likely to be invalidating.

The consequences of the transaction between an emotionally vulnerable individual and her or his invalidating social or family environment include the following: (1) The individual does not learn to discriminate emotions and label them in a manner that is consistent with the social community; (2) the person has limited emotional understanding, which also results in little proactive emotion management activities, such as reducing vulnerability to negative emotion or increasing positive emotional experiences to buffer against negative experiences; (3) because the individual is usually instructed to control her or his emotions and suppress emotional displays but is not taught *how* to do so, the person does not learn to regulate emotional arousal, and in fact may rely on others for this function; (4) because of unresponsiveness to the communication of pain or misery, the person may develop very extreme responses to negative emotion (all-or-nothing emotional reactions); (5) because of inattention or punishing responses, the person is likely to have difficulty differentiating among some emotions, and in particular discriminating between *primary* and *secondary* emotions (primary emotions are those in response to the situation, whereas secondary emotions are those in response to the primary emotion); and (6) individuals may learn not to trust their own experience and may instead invalidate their own emotions, experiences, beliefs, reactions, and so on. Overall, redressing these deficits in emotion management are the goals of emotion regulation skills.

Empirical Support

Although a number of treatments have emotion regulation targets and employ emotion regulation strategies or skills, the most direct and comprehensive of these are studies utilizing Dialectical Behavior Therapy (DBT; Linehan, 1993a, 1993b). Although a comprehensive review is beyond the scope of this chapter, multiple studies have documented the effectiveness of DBT in promoting more effective emotion regulation in adults and adolescents with serious problems regulating emotion (e.g., Bohus et al., 2000; Koons et al., 2001; Linehan, Armstrong, Suarez, Allmon, & Heard, 1991; Linehan et al., 1999; Miller, Wyman, Huppert, Glassman, & Rathus, 2000; Rathus & Miller, 2002; Telch, Agras, & Linehan, 2000; Verheul et al.,

2003). These studies have typically included clients with Borderline Personality Disorder and seriously dysfunctional behavior such as suicidality and self-injury, chronic depression, chronic anxiety, PTSD, dissociative behaviors, eating disorders, substance abuse, and aggressive and violent behaviors (see also Koerner & Dimeff, 2000, and Fruzzetti, in press, for brief reviews). Thus, emotion regulation skills and interventions may be appropriate for anyone with deficits in these domains, in particular those who are not responsive to other, more typical, cognitive and behavioral interventions.

STRATEGIES FOR REGULATING EMOTION

Because emotion dysregulation can result from multiple deficits in emotion regulation skills, it may be useful to divide these skills into two groups: (1) those skills designed primarily to help individuals *accept* their emotions (understand, discriminate, label accurately, experience safely, validate, and express emotions), and (2) those skills designed primarily to help individuals change their emotions (change the type of emotion, its intensity, or its duration). Many of the strategies described in the following sections may be found in a variety of cognitive and behavior therapy applications. However, because of the comprehensive nature of DBT (Linehan, 1993a) and its significant body of empirical support, DBT strategies for emotion regulation are emphasized (see Linehan, 1993b, for further description and client handouts). Because different clients may have different levels of skill there is no formal protocol for implementing these strategies and facilitating these skills. Rather, the strategies that follow may be implemented sequentially, in an overlapping fashion, or according to a client's needs in a given situation.

Acceptance Strategies

Acceptance strategies (see Chapter 2, this volume) include understanding emotions, discriminating between and accurately labeling emotions, tolerating painful emotions, observing and describing emotions, allowing or participating in emotions, and validating emotions.

Understanding Emotions

Despite its complexity, it is often useful to provide basic psychoeducation in the functions of emotion (both in terms of evolution and in terms of individual self-awareness) and in the various factors that influence emotion (e.g., events, appraisals, biological functioning, learning history or emotional disposition, facial expression and body posture, other emotions, labels for events and emotional responses, availability of supportive vs. unsupportive others). Although it is obvious to many, some may not know that understanding the multiple determinants of ordinary emotion can provide a quick avenue toward assessment of the factors that are leading to dysregulated emotion.

Discriminating and Accurately Labeling Emotions

Before any specific treatment of problematic emotion can be attempted, the client's actual emotion must be identified (discriminated from among multiple sensory and environmental cues) and labeled accurately. There are several steps in discriminating or identifying emotions. First, it may be useful to notice the prompting event for the emotion. What was happening before the feeling began? Emotions may be elicited by events in a person's life, by a person's interpretation of an event, or by thoughts, memories, sensations, or other private events or behaviors. Thus, the second step is noticing interpretations about the event, and noticing that interpretations are not facts. There are often bodily responses that accompany emotional reactions. Noticing sensations in the stomach, sweating, dizziness, body language, facial expression, and so on can help to sort out the accurate emotion (cf. Eckman, 1993; Linehan, 1993b). It may be helpful for a confused client to imagine other people in their situation and describe how they might feel. This can be especially useful if the client has developed normative social emotional awareness but has high emotional reactivity that interferes with self-observations. This observing role is also a core skill in mindfulness skill training (discussed later).

Awareness of action urges is also important in identifying emotions. Does the person have the urge to run away, attack, cry, or hide? Certain action urges are associated fairly specifically with given emotions (e.g., fear: avoid or run; anger: attack; sadness: withdraw; shame: hide; love: approach), as are other forms of emotional expression. The person may be able to work backwards by noticing an action urge, then inferring the emotion, then confirming it by exploring recent events or triggers that are consonant with that particular emotion. Thus, awareness of interpretations or appraisals, prompting events, bodily sensations, expressive urges, and aftereffects of emotion can be utilized to identify and label emotions accurately.

It is important to discriminate between primary and secondary emotions. *Primary* emotions may be considered to be the normative emotional response in a given context. In contrast, *secondary* emotions are reactions to the primary emotion. For example, anger often may be a secondary emotional response to fear, sadness, or shame: The person has learned to escape from the primary emotion to anger, which may now be a conditioned emotional reaction in the situation (Fruzzetti & Levensky, 2000). If a person has a tendency to react with secondary emotions and be aware only of these, it is essential to use emotion identification skills to turn awareness toward primary emotional responses. Otherwise, the client will react in ways that are nonnormative and will be less likely to achieve his or her goals and/or will be invalidated by the social community, which will in turn make affect dysregulation more likely.

Tolerating Painful Emotion

Accurate labeling of emotion also requires that the person be able to tolerate the emotion until it subsides naturally or until the person can employ change strategies. The most common and effective strategies include distracting oneself from the stimulus for the negative emotion and/or distracting oneself from the experience of the emotion itself by engaging fully in some other activity; soothing oneself (or soliciting soothing by others); engaging in relaxation; or engaging in some sort of cognitive activity, such as imagery or prayer.

Observing and Describing Self and Emotion

The ability to discriminate, observe, and describe different aspects of ourselves, our internal experience, the physical world around us, or other people is another set of skills related to acceptance and regulation of emotion. These skills are often called *mindfulness* skills because of the pioneering work by Marsha Linehan (1993a, 1993b; see Chapter 35, this volume) that adapted the Eastern meditative tradition to Western psychological interventions. Thus, this subset of mindfulness skills includes (but is not limited to) learning to notice, observe, be aware of, and describe oneself (as observer) and one's private experiences (emotions, sensations, thoughts, etc.) as one is experiencing them in the moment, even if the experience, or part of the experience, is painful or distressing. These are part of what one does when practicing mindfulness (observe, describe). It is also important how one approaches this attention control tasks. That is, mindfulness also includes observing and describing things nonjudgmentally (without a positive or negative evaluation of the emotion), one at a time (concentrating on doing one thing at a time by letting go of distractions), and effectively (using what works or is necessary in the present situation; cf. Linehan, 1993b, pp. 111–113).

Allowing or Participating in the Emotion

Emotionally dysregulated clients often expend a great deal of effort trying to escape from or preempt negative emotions. However, it is a necessary part of living life to have regular negative emotional experiences. Rather than trying to suppress or avoid them, an alternative is to allow or embrace them, without becoming consumed or dysregulated by them. This involves the ability to simultaneously be aware of one's emotion and be aware of the context (whole person, situation, events) of the emotion. The skill involves titrating one's level of awareness between noticing the emotion itself and observing oneself as the person experiencing the emotion, while neither suppressing nor avoiding the emotion. The idea is that a person can have an emotion without acting on it and can actually feel alive and content while experiencing emotions, especially if they are not labeled negative, bad, or dangerous. For example,

following the death of a loved one it is healthy to feel sadness and grief. People mourn loved ones by going back and forth between noticing and experiencing the sadness, communicating about it (titrating away from the emotional intensity), soothing themselves, and engaging in other activities (ordinary ones like eating, driving, or sleeping).

Self-Validating Emotions

Clients who are emotionally dysregulated often invalidate their own experience, which in turn contributes to further dysregulation. For example, dysregulated individuals often become judgmental about their experience, delegitimize or pathologize their own suffering (e.g., "I deserve this pain" or "I should be able to do this without feeling so bad"), identify their emotions inaccurately, or do not even notice (for some time, anyway) that they have a particular emotion. In contrast, self-validation is the opposite of these behaviors. At the most basic level, self-validating skills start with interrupting those behaviors that are particularly dysregulating (self-judgments) and simply noticing and describing (without interpretation) the facts of the situation (what happened, how it feels, what the emotion is). At the next level, individuals can notice the legitimacy of their own emotional reaction, either because of their own history or disposition, or because their response is quite normative (cf. Hoffman et al., 1999; Linehan, 1998). For example, a person whose friend didn't show up for lunch might say, "I shouldn't have counted on this person anyway. I feel stupid and ashamed." Coaching in self-validation would help the person notice her or his actual emotion (e.g., disappointment) and notice that this feeling makes sense (is normative) in this particular situation. Consequently, the person might end up saying, "I'm disappointed. Of course I am; I was looking forward to lunch with my friend. I'll find out what happened to her." Thus, self-validation is predicated on accurate labeling and the ability to tolerate negative emotion. Moreover, not only does self-validation interrupt escalating individual emotional arousal, but it also promotes effective interpersonal behaviors and more regulated relationships, which in turn facilitate more effective emotion regulation.

Change Strategies

There are a number of different skills and strategies that may be instrumental in changing the experience of an emotion (its intensity or duration), or changing the emotion itself in a given situation. Some change strategies require a great deal of counterconditioning in a therapy session, followed up by in vivo practice (e.g., exposure and response prevention), whereas others follow more naturally from heightened emotional awareness and acceptance (e.g., reducing vulnerability to negative emotion).

Exposure and Response Prevention

At times, emotion dysregulation (hyperarousal or numbing) occurs in response to discrete stimuli (e.g., stimuli associated with trauma), and can be treated using formal exposure and response prevention strategies. However, at other times the stimuli associated with dysregulated emotion are many and diffuse, or the stimulus for dysregulation is itself another emotion (a secondary emotion in response to a primary one). When these situations occur, the same principles of exposure and response prevention are utilized, but the strategies may be altered so *acceptance* of the emotion becomes the target. Then the acceptance of emotion strategies above (e.g., observing, describing, or participating) may be utilized. For example, a client might have such a long history of being criticized and invalidated, in combination with a lot of emotion sensitivity, that countless stimuli elicit shame and sadness. However, she may have experienced shame and sadness as being more painful than anger, and anger as more effective in pushing away invalidating others. Consequently, she may experience and express anger quite consistently, neither noticing nor expressing sadness or shame. In this situation the therapist may try to help her ignore her feelings of anger (thoughts, labels, etc.) and block the action urges associated with anger (facially, verbally, etc.) and instead try to discriminate sadness or shame among her sensations, appraisals, experience, recent events or triggers, and so on. If she also has few invalidating social encounters she may be able to learn to (1) ignore her anger, (2) block her angry behaviors, (3) notice her sadness or shame, (4) attenuate her sadness and shame with repeated exposure to life situations that do not naturally elicit sadness or shame, and (5) build more effective relationships.

Reducing Vulnerability to Negative Emotion

It is possible to take advantage of the fact that so many other behaviors and events affect emotion to help reduce vulnerability to negative emotion. For example, individuals can minimize vulnerability by treating physical illnesses effectively (e.g., taking medication for disease, stretching or exercising for backache), balancing their eating (e.g., consuming healthy amounts of nutritional foods), not ingesting mood-altering drugs (e.g., alcohol, illicit drugs), practicing good sleep hygiene (e.g., getting enough sleep on a regular schedule; see Chapter 66 on the treatment of insomnia), and exercising regularly (cf. Linehan, 1993b).

Increasing Positive Emotions

This skill teaches individuals to minimize the risk of dysregulation by balancing negative emotions in their lives with increasing amounts of pleasurable experiences and positive emotions (see also Chapter 7 on behavioral activation). This involves increasing pleasurable activities and fully engaging in them. It is essential for this skill to be augmented by attention to (mindful observing, participating) any positive emotion that results from new or renewed activities, rather than reorienting attention back to preexisting negative emotions. Activities might include setting and achieving both shorter- (for today) and longer-term goals, repairing relationships, building new relationships, paying attention to activities that reflect client goals and values, and actively participating in ordinary daily activities.

Changing Emotions by Acting Opposite to Current Emotion

This skill bears similarity to exposure and response prevention in principle, but in practice it does not require formal exposure or therapist assistance. Acting opposite begins with accurate identification and labeling of a current negative emotion that the person wants to change (entirely alter or reduce the intensity or duration) and its associated action urge (see earlier discussion). Then the client can identify actions that are opposite to the present action urge or action tendency and try to engage in this opposite action (assuming it is safe to do so). For example, a person with a lot of social fears is likely to have a tendency to avoid social situations. The opposite action would be to engage mindfully in some social activity and notice other aspects of the experience (in particular that nothing dangerous occurs, and also any incipient positive emotional experience). Similar opposite actions could be approached for shame or guilt (talking to someone instead of avoiding), sadness (becoming active instead of withdrawing), or anger (gently avoiding instead of attacking). Again, opposite action is likely to be most successful when the client already has many of the other skills described (identifying and labeling emotions accurately, tolerating painful emotion, being mindful of less painful aspects of emotional experience, etc.).

Changing the Social and Family Environment

Although the focus of this chapter is on how individuals can learn to regulate their emotions, it would be incomplete without mention of the importance of having a supportive or validating social or family environment (or at least the absence of a critical or invalidating one). Delineating the many interventions that can be employed to help family members and friends become less invalidating and more validating is beyond the scope of this chapter. However, it is important to realize that when nascent emotion regulation skills learned in treatment are punished by the client's family or friends they are unlikely to develop successfully. Thus, assessing for the consequences when clients try out their newly learned skills in their family and social environment is an essential part of any skill training. Intervening to make family members and friends more receptive to and reinforcing of client emotion regulation skills may be the difference between success and failure.

References

Bohus, M., Haaf, B., Stiglmayr, C., Pohl, U., Bohme, R., & Linehan, M. (2000). Evaluation of inpatient Dialectical Behavioral Therapy for borderline personality disorder: A prospective study. *Behaviour Research and Therapy, 38*, 875–887.

Eisenberg, N., Cumberland, A., & Spinrad, T. L. (1998). Parental socialization of emotion. *Psychological Inquiry, 9*, 241–273.

Ekman, P. (1993). Facial expression and emotion. *American Psychologist, 48*, 384–392.

Fruzzetti, A. E. (2002). Dialectical Behavior Therapy for borderline personality and related disorders. In T. Patterson (Ed.), *Comprehensive Handbook of Psychotherapy* (Vol. 2, pp. 215–240). New York: Wiley.

Fruzzetti, A. E., & Fruzzetti, A. R. (2003). Borderline personality disorder: Dialectical Behavior Therapy with couples. In D. K. Snyder & M. A. Whisman (Eds.), *Treating difficult couples: Helping clients with coexisting mental and relationship disorders* (pp. 235–260). New York: Guilford Press.

Fruzzetti, A. E., & Levensky, E. R. (2000). Dialectical Behavior Therapy for domestic violence: Rationale and procedures. *Cognitive and Behavioral Practice, 7*, 435–447.

Gross, J. J. (1998). The emerging field of emotion regulation: An integrative review. *Review of General Psychology, 2*, 271–299.

Hoffman, P. D., Fruzzetti, A. E., & Swenson, C. R. (1999). Dialectical Behavior Therapy: Family skills training. *Family Process, 38*, 399–414.

James, W. (1890). *Principles of psychology*. New York: Holt, Rinehart, and Winston.

Johnson, S. M., & Whiffen, V. E. (1999). Made to measure: Adapting emotionally focused couple therapy to partners' attachment styles. *Clinical Psychology: Science and Practice, 6*, 366–381.

Koerner, K., & Dimeff, L. A. (2000). Further data on Dialectical Behavior Therapy. *Clinical Psychology: Science and Practice, 7*, 104–112.

Koons, C. R., Robins, C. J., Tweed, J. L., Lynch, T. R., Gonzalez, A. M., Morse, J. Q., et al. (2001). Efficacy of Dialectical Behavior Therapy in women veterans with borderline personality disorder. *Behavior Therapy, 32*, 371–390.

Keltner, D., & Kring, A. M. (1998). Emotion, social function, and psychopathology. *Review of General Psychology, 2*, 320–342.

Linehan, M. M. (1993a). *Cognitive behavioral treatment of borderline personality disorder*. New York: Guilford Press.

Linehan, M. M. (1993b). *Skills training manual for treating borderline personality disorder*. New York: Guilford Press.

Linehan, M. M. (1998). Validation and psychotherapy. In A. Bohart & L. S. Greenberg (Eds.), *Empathy and psychotherapy: New directions to theory, research, and practice*. Washington, DC: American Psychological Association.

Linehan, M. M., Armstrong, H. E., Suarez, A., Allmon, D., & Heard, H. (1991). Cognitive-behavioral treatment of chronically suicidal borderline patients. *Archives of General Psychiatry, 48,* 1060–1064.

Linehan, M. M., Schmidt III, H., Dimeff, L. A., Craft, J. C., Kanter, J., & Comtois, K. A. (1999). Dialectical Behavior Therapy for patients with borderline personality disorder and drug-dependence. *The American Journal on Addictions, 8,* 279–292.

Miller, A. L., Wyman, S. E., Huppert, J. D., Glassman, S. L., & Rathus, J. H. (2000). Analysis of behavioral skills utilized by adolescents receiving Dialectical Behavior Therapy. *Cognitive and Behavioral Practice, 7,* 183–187.

Plutchik, R. (1994). *The psychology and biology of emotion.* New York: Harper Collins.

Rathus, J. H., & Miller, A. L. (2002). DBT adapted for suicidal adolescents. *Suicide and Life-Threatening Behavior, 32,* 146–157.

Saarni, C., & Crowley, M. (1990). The development of emotion regulation: Effects on emotional state and expression. In E. A. Blechman (Ed.), *Emotions and the family: For better or for worse* (pp. 53–73). Hillsdale, NJ: Lawrence Erlbaum Associates.

Schacter, S., & Singer, J. (1962). Cognitive, social, and physiological determinants of emotional states. *Psychological Review, 69,* 379–399.

Southam-Gerow, M. A., & Kendall, P. C. (2002). Emotion regulation and understanding: Implications for child psychopathology and therapy. *Clinical Psychology Review, 22,* 189–222.

Telch, C. F., Agras, W. S., & Linehan, M. M. (2000). Group Dialectical Behavior Therapy for binge-eating disorder: A preliminary, uncontrolled trial. *Behavior Therapy, 31,* 569–582.

Thompson, R. A. (1994). Emotion regulation: A theme in search of definition. *Monographs of the Society for Research in Child Development, 59,* 24–52.

Verheul, R., van den Bosch, L. M., Koeter, M. W. J., de Ridder, M. A. J., Stijen, T., & van den Brink, W. (2003). Dialectical behavior therapy for women with borderline personality disorder: 12-month, randomised clinical trial in the Netherlands. *British Journal of Psychiatry, 182,* 135–140.

Zajonc, R. B. (1984). On the primacy of affect. *American Psychologist, 39,* 117–123.

26 FLOODING

Lori A. Zoellner, Jonathan S. Abramowitz, and Sally A. Moore

Flooding involves prolonged exposure to stimuli that evoke relatively high levels of excessive or inappropriate anxiety or fear. This procedure differs from other exposure-based procedures in that flooding begins with exposure to highly fear-evoking stimuli whereas other techniques employ graduated exposure, progressing from less anxiety-provoking stimuli. Flooding may be conducted in real life (*in vivo* exposure) or in fantasy (*imaginal* exposure). The basics of exposure-based procedures include systematic prolonged and repeated exposure to fear-arousing stimuli until the anxiety and fear associated with the situation have been greatly reduced.

WHEN ARE FLOODING PROCEDURES USED?

Clinicians are often reluctant to use flooding procedures since the client invariably experiences high levels of discomfort. However, flooding is a useful method for reducing fear and should be considered in several circumstances. In vivo flooding is often employed when a time-limited intervention is desired; for example, in the treatment of a hospital phobic whose spouse needs to spend time in the hospital or an airplane phobic who has an important business trip. Imaginal flooding is often useful in instances for which it is not possible to conduct in vivo exposure. For example, imaginal exposure may be used for intrusive fear-evoking memories of a traumatic event in individuals with Post-Traumatic Stress Disorder (PTSD) or feared consequences in individuals with Obsessive-Compulsive Disorder (OCD).

Although there is limited research examining who does or does not make a good candidate for flooding procedures, clinical experience provides some guidelines about when to pursue other treatment options. Clinical judgment should be used when deciding whether flooding procedures are appropriate for particular clients. The therapist should consider factors that could interfere with motivation to complete the intense therapy (e.g., severe depression) or contribute to a client's being unable to successfully tolerate extreme distress either before, during, or after exposure (e.g., psychosis, severe dissociative symptoms including prolonged dissociative episodes and flashbacks, substance dependence, and suicidality). Further, imaginal flooding procedures are not recommended for PTSD symptoms related to realistic guilt or shame (e.g., murdering or raping).

ARE FLOODING PROCEDURES EFFECTIVE IN REDUCING FEAR?

We will consider the two types of flooding (i.e., invivo and imaginal) separately as we discuss the effectiveness of flooding in reducing fear.

Flooding In Vivo

The efficacy of in vivo flooding is well documented for several anxiety disorders, including specific phobias (Mannion & Levine, 1984), Social Phobia (Turner, Beidel, & Jacob, 1994), and Panic Disorder and Agoraphobia (Emmelkamp & Wessels, 1975; Feigenbaum, 1988; as cited by Barlow, 2001). Perhaps its greatest use is in the treatment of specific phobias. Öst and colleagues (see Öst, Alm, Brandberg, & Breitholtz, 2001) have shown that a single 2- to 3-hour session of therapist-supervised in vivo flooding can lead to significant and lasting improvement for many phobias, including claustrophobia and fears of animals, blood, injections, and flying.

Flooding in Imagination

Imaginal flooding (in conjunction with other procedures) is also used in the treatment of many anxiety disorders, including OCD (e.g., Freeston et al., 1997), PTSD (e.g., Foa et al., 1999), Generalized Anxiety Disorder (e.g., Borkovec & Costello, 1993), and Social Phobia (e.g., Heimberg, Becker, Goldfinger, & Vermilyea, 1985). Although imaginal exposure has been shown to be an effective procedure for targeting specific feared situations and thoughts (e.g., fears of disastrous consequences in OCD; Foa, Steketee, & Grayson, 1985), research does not indicate that it is clearly more effective by itself than in vivo exposure as a monotherapy. Thus, imaginal exposure is frequently used as a treatment component (paired with in vivo exposure or cognitive therapy) rather than as a stand-alone treatment. Perhaps the most common usages of flooding in imagination as a treatment component are in the areas of PTSD and OCD.

WHY DOES FLOODING WORK?

Many theories have been proposed to explain the general process of anxiety reduction during exposure-based therapy, but none yet account for all of the data. We will describe the three theories that we use most often to discuss the fear reduction process with our clients. First, emotional processing theory (Rachman, 1980) proposes that exposure involves the modification of a pathological *fear structure,* defined by Lang (1977) as an underlying memory structure that contains excessive and distorted stimulus (e.g., quick movement in the grass), response (e.g., standing still, heart racing), and meaning (e.g., a snake is going to bite me) propositions. Foa and Kozak (1986) elaborated on this idea, suggesting that a fear structure can be modified by accessing it through fear evocation and then providing corrective information.

Second, Bouton (1988) proposed a context specificity hypothesis for fear reduction. In this theory, exposure can be viewed as an example of retroactive interference, in which new learning is introduced to interfere with information that was learned at an earlier point. Specifically, new learning during exposure helps make the meaning of a feared stimulus ambiguous because memories of both fear and fear reduction are retained. Bouton argued that context (e.g., internal or environmental backgrounds) serves to resolve this ambiguity by determining the meaning of the stimuli and the response. In illustrating this conceptualization, Bouton (1991, p. 436) noted "that the meaning of an ambiguous word, and the response it evokes, depends almost by definition on what the context retrieves. Your reaction to someone shouting 'Fire!' will be very different in the movie theater and in the shooting gallery."

Third, Bandura (1977, 1983) proposed a self-efficacy theory of fear reduction. He suggested that an *efficacy expectation* is the conviction that one can successfully execute the behavior required to produce an outcome. Therefore, a treatment reduces fear to the extent that a person's sense of self-efficacy has been elevated and strengthened (Bandura, 1983). Bandura further suggested that one of the best means for raising and strengthening self-efficacy is direct behavioral experience and accomplishment.

HOW TO CONDUCT FLOODING IN VIVO

Although the exact flooding procedures depend upon the patient's idiosyncratic fears, there are important common principles across all anxiety disorders (see Table 26.1). The procedures for in vivo flooding are largely similar to those used in

TABLE 26.1   Steps in Using Flooding

1. Form a strong therapeutic alliance.

2. Thoroughly assess the client's fears and related avoidance.

3. Provide an effective rationale.

4. Provide prolonged therapist-directed exposure to the most anxiety arousing situations.

   a. Therapist describes the situation.

   b. Therapist demonstrates how to perform the task.

   c. Therapist instructs the client to do the same.

5. During imaginal exposure, particularly, titrate the client's level of engagement and distress.

6. Stay in the fear-producing situation until there is at least a 50% reduction in fear.

7. Debrief client's reactions to exposure as therapy proceeds.

8. Repeat until fear has been significantly reduced and all relevant areas of avoidance have been addressed.

graduated in vivo exposure (see Chapter 34, this volume). The first step is to provide a foundation for the treatment by presenting a clear therapeutic rationale, forming a strong therapeutic alliance, and thoroughly assessing the client's fears and related avoidance. This foundation helps the client make more informed choices regarding treatment options (e.g., the choice of confronting the fear), increases commitment to the choice made, and provides a preview of what is to be expected during treatment.

Client understanding and acceptance of treatment rationales have been linked to positive therapeutic outcome (e.g., Addis & Jacobson, 1996, 2000). Initially, we clarify that therapy will be time limited and specific to the client's fears and related symptoms. A cognitive behavioral model of the maintenance of fear is presented, in which avoidance of fear-related thoughts, feelings, situations, and memories prolongs excessive, irrational fear responses by preventing the client from learning that his or her anticipated outcomes are not likely to occur. Thus, the goal of flooding is to help the client approach fear-eliciting stimuli, prevent avoidance behaviors, and disconfirm his or her overestimates of danger. Although this discussion is largely didactic, often the client can provide good examples of the role of avoidance in his or her life.

It is useful to explain that although an initial

increase in fear can be expected, this is temporary, and fear will eventually decline. Moreover, with repeated exposure the amount of fear evoked will continue to lessen. Often, we diagram the relationship between time and level of fear to illustrate how fear initially increases but then gradually decreases with continued exposure, and to show how the level of fear lessens with each successive repetition (see Figure 26.1). It may also be helpful to elicit an example from the patient's life when he or she overcame a fear (e.g., of riding a roller coaster) by facing the situation despite an initially high level of anxiety. Analogies can also be helpful in describing the process to patients. A good example to use is that of helping a child get comfortable diving off a high diving board. One approach, a graduated method, would start with the child getting comfortable diving into the water at the side of the pool, gradually starting to dive off a low diving board, and then eventually moving up to the high dive. Another approach, a flooding method, would be to simply have the child, despite his or her fear, repeatedly dive off the high dive. The point can be made that the results are similar; however, the process is different. Once the distinction is described, the client can help by generating the advantages and disadvantages of each method (e.g., distress, time, etc.).

An integral part of the initial sessions is forming a therapeutic relationship by discussing the collaborative nature of therapy. The client is informed that the treatment is conducted as teamwork, with both the therapist and the client taking responsibility for achieving good results. The therapist plays the role of coach and cheerleader and never forces the client into any situation. Moreover, all situations are discussed and demonstrated before the flooding session begins. Other elements of forming a good alliance include praising the client for coming into treatment, acknowledging his or her courage, communicating an understanding of the client's symptoms, validating the client's experience, and being nonjudgmental.

Next, a thorough assessment of fear-related cognitions and activities, situations, or places that are avoided is conducted. Attention must be paid not only to areas of actual avoidance but also to underlying reasons for avoidance. For example,

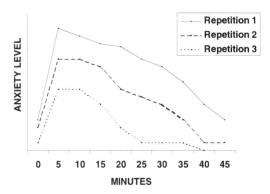

FIGURE 26.1   Relationship between time and the degree of anxiety/fear during flooding sessions.

there may be many reasons why someone is afraid of flying on an airplane: "I'm afraid that turbulence will cause the plane to crash," "I'm afraid of being in such a small, confined space," or "I'm afraid the plane will be hijacked." In this example, only in one case would flying alone on a bumpy flight be a target for treatment. Attention should also be paid to subtle forms of avoidance (e.g., distraction) and possible safety cues (e.g., carrying anti-anxiety medication). A list of activities and situations is generated, and a subjective unit of discomfort scale (SUDS), ranging from 0 to 100, is used to rank these activities or situations. With flooding in vivo, the top areas of avoidance are targeted for treatment at the onset of exposure.

Flooding in vivo consists of prolonged therapist-directed exposure to the most anxiety-arousing situations, selecting from key domains at the top of the list. For example, in the treatment of claustrophobia, situations or activities might include being in a small windowless room with the door locked, riding in elevators, and the like. As previously described, the therapist describes the situation, demonstrates how to perform the task, and then instructs the client to do the same. The SUDS levels are monitored throughout exposure, and the client is encouraged to stay in the fear-producing situation until there is at least a 50% reduction in fear or SUDS levels decline to around 20 or 30. Exposure is repeated until fear has significantly reduced and until all relevant areas of avoidance have been addressed.

HOW TO CONDUCT FLOODING IN IMAGINATION

How flooding in imagination, or imaginal exposure, is conducted also varies greatly across the anxiety disorders. For example, in OCD, imaginal exposure often focuses on a client's feared consequences; in PTSD, imaginal exposure often focuses on the memory of the traumatic event. In the following sections we present examples of how imaginal flooding is implemented in the treatment of OCD and PTSD. In both examples, imaginal exposure is only one component of a treatment package that usually includes in vivo exposure and/or cognitive therapy.

Procedures for Imaginal Exposure in the Treatment of OCD

Assessment of distressing obsessional thoughts, ideas, or images is necessary for effective imaginal exposure. Therefore, the clinician should inquire about patients' feared consequences associated with obsessional situations or stimuli. For example, a patient fearing the number 666 may be scared that as a result of confrontation with this number she will be possessed by the devil. Unacceptable anxiety-evoking intrusive thoughts, ideas, or urges should also be identified. Common examples include unacceptable sexual thoughts (e.g., incest) or ideas of accidents or illnesses occurring to loved ones. Clinicians should assess the degree of distress evoked by the obsessional thoughts and any behavioral or mental strategies used to control or neutralize the thoughts.

Appraisals of obsessional thoughts should also be assessed. In OCD, it is common for patients to ascribe undue significance to unwanted upsetting thoughts. For example, the assumption that having an immoral thought is tantamount to performing an immoral action is common. Patients may also mistakenly believe that their unwanted thoughts about disasters are equivalent to wishes for such disasters. Another misperception frequently observed in OCD patients is the belief that obsessional thoughts imply responsibility for harm or its prevention (e.g., "The plane may crash if I think about it"). It is beneficial to determine specific distorted beliefs about thoughts since imaginal exposure will be used as a tool to demonstrate that such upsetting thoughts or ideas do not, themselves, indicate or produce harmful consequences.

The next step is to present a rationale for imaginal exposure as a therapeutic tool. This may be accomplished by helping the patient to understand that most people normally experience upsetting thoughts (Rachman & de Silva, 1978), and thus such thoughts are quite normal. The problem, therefore, is not the thoughts per se, but the *misinterpretation* of such thoughts as highly significant. Specific information obtained in assessment should be used to illustrate how such misinterpretations evoke anxiety, preoccupation with the thought, and urges to control or dismiss the thought (e.g., compulsive rituals). Thus, one focus of treatment for OCD must be to modify the connection between essentially normal (harmless) thoughts and excessive anxiety. Repeated practice confronting (rather than avoiding or neutralizing) such thoughts will help patients to learn that these thoughts themselves do not pose any significant threat.

Imaginal exposure is often used as an adjunct to in vivo exposure and response prevention for OCD. For example, if in vivo exposure for a patient with contamination obsessions involves touching a bathroom door handle and then holding a baby (without washing his or her hands), imaginal exposure will include imagining the feared consequences of this exposure exercise. The patient and therapist together generate a script that incorporates all elements of the patient's obsessional fear. As a general rule, it is helpful to include *uncertainty* as a theme in imaginal exposure since obsessional fears often involve uncertainty about possible harm. The patient or therapist next reads the imaginal script into a tape recorder (it is useful to use loop-tapes, which repeat without being manually rewound). Here is an example of such a script:

> You usually go out of your way to avoid touching bathroom doors and always wash your hands if you do touch them. But this time you didn't wash, and instead held [baby] and touched her face and hands for a long time. Now you're thinking that she's contaminated and may become very sick. You desper-

ately want to wash both [baby] and yourself to be sure that there will be no illness. But you know that you must not ritualize if you are to beat your OCD. So you decide to risk it, remaining unsure of whether both of you will become sick from touching the door. You picture little [baby] in the infectious disease unit of the hospital and the doctors telling you that she may have become sick because someone forgot to wash their hands after using the bathroom. You should have known that little babies don't have fully developed immune systems. Perhaps you have caused your child to become deathly ill. The uncertainty is excruciating.

Patients are instructed to listen to the tape and fully engage in the upsetting imagery. Patients should resist urges to suppress the thought, engage in compulsive rituals, or obtain reassurances, although reminding themselves that obsessional thoughts are normal and harmless is acceptable.

Procedures for Imaginal Exposure in the Treatment of PTSD

Imaginal exposure is introduced after the therapist and the client have discussed posttrauma reactions and the rationale for exposure, and after a therapeutic alliance has been formed as part of a treatment package. See Foa and Rothbaum (1998) for a detailed discussion. In imaginal exposure for PTSD, the focus is on the trauma memory. Trauma survivors often try hard to push intrusive memories of the event out of their minds. However, by engaging in the memory rather than avoiding it, they learn that the memories of the trauma are not intrinsically dangerous. Consequently, the trauma can be remembered without intense or disruptive anxiety. During imaginal exposure, the client recalls the memory as vividly as possible, imagining the trauma as if it is happening at that moment. The client is encouraged to describe the trauma in the present tense and recount as many details as possible, including specific thoughts and feelings. The therapist monitors SUDS levels every 5 minutes during flooding and checks to ensure that the client maintains a vivid image of the events being recalled. The goal of imaginal exposure is to help the client to access important, fear-related elements of the trauma memory but also to remain firmly grounded in the present. Thus, the client relives the trauma knowing that he or she is safe, and that the memory, although upsetting, cannot hurt him or her.

Imaginal exposure during a therapy session typically continues for approximately 45 to 60 minutes, with the patient repeating the memory several times. Although details are helpful in enhancing vividness, the goal is not to recall as many details as possible or recover lost memories. As therapy proceeds, the imaginal exposure focuses on the most difficult parts of the trauma (so-called hot spots) to promote fear reduction. The therapist's key role is to help titrate the client's level of engagement and distress, either by encouraging more detail and affect (for underengagement) or by diminishing detail and affect (for overengagement). Clients who underengage may be able to describe the trauma in detail but may be unable to connect with the emotional content of the memory. Conversely, those who overengage may show visual signs of distress (e.g., making physical movements reminiscent of the trauma) and have difficulty maintaining their sense of grounding and safety. Several procedural modifications help to increase or decrease engagement with the memory. For underengagement, the client is encouraged keep his or her eyes closed and to use the present tense. Often it is helpful for the therapist to probe for details, sensory information (e.g., what the patient sees, hears, smells, touches), thoughts, and feelings. For overengagement, the client is encouraged to keep his or her eyes open or, if they are closed, to periodically open them to promote grounding. Often with overengagement, the therapist will increase verbal communication, focusing the client and communicating empathy (e.g., "You're doing a great job staying with the memory even though it's hard.")

Following imaginal exposure, time is allotted to discuss both the client's experience during the exposure and his or her reaction to it. The client is instructed to listen to the audiotape of the imaginal exposure daily and to record pre, peak, and post SUDS levels. The therapist monitors the imaginal exposure homework to make sure that the client is listening to the tape in a manner that will encourage full engagement with the trauma memory (e.g., the client is not listening to the tape in the car on the way to work). Imaginal exposure to the trauma memory and homework are repeated until fear regarding the trauma memory has been greatly reduced.

CONCLUSION: HELPING THE CLIENT HANDLE DISTRESS

Possibly more so than with other exposure-based therapies, flooding demands that both the therapist and client be able to tolerate distress. When a client is having problems tolerating exposures, we often fall back on the basics of the therapy to help the client (and ourselves) through the distress. One of the first things we do is reiterate the rationale for the therapy: reminding the client of the process of fear reduction, the efficacy of the therapy, and, if possible, their previous successes with the process. We also fall back on the therapeutic alliance. Here, we remind the client that the exposures are the client's choice and that we will support and work with them through the process. A therapist should convey a calm and relaxed manner when a client is distressed. Finally, even if the exposure itself (e.g., hearing about a particularly upsetting or frightening traumatic event) or the client's distress is distressing to you as a therapist, it is helpful to remember that you too will grow more comfortable with time and repetition.

References

Addis, M. E., & Jacobson, N. S. (1996). Reasons for depression and the process and outcome of cognitive-behavioral psychotherapies. *Journal of Consulting and Clinical Psychology, 64*, 1417–1424.

Addis, M. E., & Jacobson, N. S. (2000). A closer look at the treatment rationale and homework compliance in cognitive therapy for depression. *Cognitive Therapy and Research, 24*, 313–326.

Bandura, A. (1977). Self-efficacy: Toward a unifying theory of behavioral change. *Psychological Review, 84*, 191–215.

Bandura, A. (1983). Self-efficacy determinants of anticipated fears and calamities. *Journal of Personality and Social Psychology, 45*, 464–469.

Barlow, D. H. (2001). *Anxiety and its disorders: The nature and treatment of anxiety and panic* (2nd ed.). New York: Guilford Press.

Borkovec, T. D., & Costello, E. (1993). Efficacy of applied relaxation and cognitive-behavioral therapy in the treatment of generalized anxiety disorder. *Journal of Consulting & Clinical Psychology, 61*(4), 611–619.

Bouton, M. E. (1988). Context and ambiguity in the extinction of emotional learning: Implications for exposure therapy. *Behavior Research and Therapy, 26,* 137–149.

Bouton, M. E. (1991). A contextual analysis of fear extinction. In P. R. Martin (Ed.), *Handbook of behavior therapy and psychological science: An integrative approach* (pp. 435–453). New York: Pergamon General Psychology Series.

Emmelkamp, P. M. G., & Wessels, H. (1975). Flooding in imagination vs. flooding in vivo: A comparison with agoraphobics. *Behavioral Research & Therapy, 13,* 7–15.

Foa, E. B., Dancu, C. V., Hembree, E. A., Jaycox, L. H., Meadows, E. A., & Street, G. P. (1999). A comparison of exposure therapy, stress inoculation training, and their combination for reducing posttraumatic stress disorder in female assault victims. *Journal of Consulting and Clinical Psychology, 67,* 194–200.

Foa, E. B., & Kozak, M. S. (1986). Emotional processing of fear: Exposure to corrective information. *Psychology Bulletin, 99,* 20–35.

Foa, E. B., & Rothbaum, B. O. (1998). *Treating the trauma of rape.* New York: Guilford Press.

Foa, E. B., Steketee, G., & Grayson, J. B. (1985). Imaginal and in vivo exposure: A comparison with obsessive-compulsive checkers. *Behavior Therapy, 16,* 292–302.

Freeston, M. H., Ladouceur, R., Gagnon, F., Thibodeau, N., Rheaume, J., Letarte, H., et al. (1997). Cognitive-behavioral treatment of obsessive thoughts: A controlled study. *Journal of Consulting & Clinical Psychology, 65*(3), 405–413.

Heimberg, R. G., Becker, R. E., Goldfinger, K., & Vermilyea, J. A. (1985). Treatment of social phobia by exposure, cognitive restructuring, and homework assignments. *The Journal of Nervous and Mental Disease, 173*(4), 236–245.

Lang, P. J. (1977). Imagery in therapy: An information processing analysis of fear. *Behavior Therapy, 8,* 862–886.

Mannion, N. E., & Levine, B. A. (1984). Effects of stimulus representation and cue category level on exposure (flooding) therapy. *British Journal of Clinical Psychology, 23,* 17.

Öst, L. G., Alm, T., Brandberg, M., & Breitholtz, E. (2001). One vs. five sessions of exposure and five sessions of cognitive therapy in the treatment of claustrophobia. *Behaviour Research and Therapy, 39*(2), 167–183.

Rachman, S. (1980). Emotional processing. *Behaviour Research and Therapy, 18,* 51–60.

Rachman, S., & de Silva, P. (1978). Abnormal and normal obsessions. *Behaviour Research and Therapy, 16,* 233–238.

Turner, S. M., Beidel, D. C., & Jacob, R. G. (1994). Social phobia: A comparison of behavior therapy and atenolol. *Journal of Consulting & Clinical Psychology, 62*(2), 350–358.

27 FUNCTIONAL ANALYSIS OF PROBLEM BEHAVIOR

James E. Carr and Linda A. LeBlanc

BACKGROUND

In 1977, E. G. Carr proposed five hypotheses regarding the motivation of self-injury of individuals with developmental disabilities. Three of the hypotheses, and perhaps the most provocative, suggested that self-injury could be acquired and maintained by contingencies of reinforcement (i.e., self-injury could be operant behavior). These three sources of reinforcement were (1) attention from others, (2) escape from aversive situations, and (3) sensory stimulation. The practical implication of E. G. Carr's operant hypotheses was that, once identified, the reinforcer responsible for maintaining self-injury could be modified as a treatment.

Several years later, Iwata and colleagues (Iwata, Dorsey, Slifer, Bauman, & Richman, 1994/1982) developed the *functional analysis,* an experimental procedure used to determine whether self-injury was indeed maintained by the operant variables proposed by E. G. Carr (1977). The convergence of an operant framework for considering the motivation of problem behavior with a procedure to identify such functions resulted in a pervasive change in the way clinicians and researchers assess and treat problem behavior. Since the publication of these two seminal articles, the field has moved toward a function-based model of treatment selection and away from the previously endemic, topography-based model.

In other words, instead of selecting a treatment for a problem behavior based on its topographical classification (e.g., aggression), treatments are now generally selected based on the behavior's function (e.g., attention from others). This newer function-based approach to treatment selection is considered beneficial because it (1) directly addresses the individual's motivation for engaging in the behavior instead of ignoring or overpowering it, (2) facilitates the teaching of replacement behaviors, and (3) diminishes the reliance on aversive procedures (J. E. Carr, Coriaty, & Dozier, 2000).

The functional analysis is but one method within the broader *functional assessment*[1] process of which the ultimate purpose is the identification of the variables that maintain problem behavior. Functional assessment is often characterized as three distinct, but compatible, methods

---

1. In applied behavior analysis, especially as it pertains to developmental disabilities, the term *functional analysis* specifically refers to experimental methods for identifying behavioral function (Mace, 1994) because of the long-standing meaning of the term *analysis* within the field (Baer, Wolf, & Risley, 1968). The term *functional assessment* refers more broadly to all methods used to infer or identify behavioral function. However, in other areas, the term *functional analysis* has been used synonymously with functional assessment (e.g., see Chapter 6 in this volume).

(Lennox & Miltenberger, 1989). Informant assessments, often the first step in the functional assessment, involve the use of rating scales and interviews to generate hypotheses about behavioral function (i.e., what consequences the behavior produces). Descriptive assessments entail direct observation of the problem behavior in the natural environment to determine when the behavior occurs (e.g., with a scatter plot; Touchette, MacDonald, & Langer, 1985) and its immediate environmental antecedents and consequences (e.g., with an A-B-C assessment; Lerman & Iwata, 1993). The third method, the experimental functional analysis, involves brief experimentation to confirm hypotheses often generated by prior informant and descriptive assessments. In a functional analysis, the variables hypothesized to maintain problem behavior are delivered contingent on that behavior within brief sessions. When the problem behavior increases in rate (i.e., is reinforced) compared to a control condition, this can be indicative of a demonstrated behavioral function.

During the last 20 years, numerous studies have been conducted in an effort to improve the functional analysis (e.g., Neef & Iwata, 1994). Iwata and colleagues (e.g., Iwata, Duncan, Zarcone, Lerman, & Shore, 1994; Vollmer, Iwata, Duncan, & Lerman, 1993; Vollmer, Iwata, Zarcone, Smith, & Mazaleski, 1993) have developed several variations of and extensions to their original functional analysis, which was based on a multielement experimental design (i.e., rapidly alternating sessions of different conditions). These methodological variations have improved our ability to identify behavioral function in cases in which the original multielement functional analysis (described in the step-by-step instructions) has proved inconclusive. Similarly, Derby et al. (1992) made a significant contribution with the development of their brief functional analysis, which is capable of being conducted in a few hours. This was a significant achievement, especially in the current managed behavioral health care environment, given that the original functional analysis sometimes required several weeks to complete. Vollmer, Marcus, Ringdahl, and Roane (1995) further extended this line of research by providing a progressive model for conducting a functional analysis. The model began

with a brief functional analysis, and, if necessary, was followed by the more traditional multielement analysis along with additional analyses for clarifying ambiguous functional analysis data. As a result of 20 years of research and development, clinicians and researchers today have access to a number of functional analysis methods with which to identify the function of problem behavior.

WHO MIGHT BENEFIT FROM THE FUNCTIONAL ANALYSIS?

The functional analysis has proved remarkably general. In the 20 years since its introduction, the functional analysis has been effectively applied to a number of populations, including children and adults with developmental disabilities (e.g., Autism, Mental Retardation), children and adults with brain injuries, and preadolescents with and without clinical diagnoses (e.g., Attention-Deficit/Hyperactivity Disorder). The common feature of these groups of individuals is that they have relatively unsophisticated verbal repertoires. The functional analysis achieves its effects via contingency-shaped behavior. Therefore, any rules a verbally competent client might generate could interfere with the analysis. For example, if a client followed a rule such as "Each time I hit the therapist she lets me stop working," the functional analysis data would be indicative of rule-governed behavior instead of reinforcement contingencies. A client might also follow an incorrect rule during a session, which might produce data that would result in an erroneous interpretation of the data. In addition, verbally competent clients might experience the functional analysis as artificial, which could result in further interference. The functional analysis has also been successfully applied to a wide variety of problem behaviors, including self-injury (Iwata, Pace, Dorsey, et al., 1994), aggression (Marcus, Vollmer, Swanson, Roane, & Ringdahl, 2001), tantrums (Vollmer, Northup, Ringdahl, LeBlanc, & Chauvin, 1996), stereotypy (Kennedy, Meyer, Knowles, & Shukla, 2000), pica (Piazza et al., 1998), psychotic speech (Wilder, Masuda, O'Connor, & Baham, 2001), and vocal tics (J. E. Carr, Taylor, Wallander, & Reiss, 1996). Finally, and perhaps most important, the functional analysis has been shown to be successful across a wide variety of behavioral functions, including attention from others, access to tangible items, escape from instructional demands, escape from social interaction, escape from unpleasant noise, and automatic/sensory stimulation, among others.

POSSIBLE CONTRAINDICATIONS

Although the functional analysis has been successfully applied to a number of problem behaviors, there are at least three classes of behavior for which the functional analysis might not be appropriate.

Low-Rate Behavior

Since one of the requirements for a functional analysis is a moderate- to high-rate behavior (i.e., a behavior that is likely to occur at least once or twice during a 10- to 15-minute session), the functional analysis is generally inappropriate for low-rate problem behavior. When a functional analysis is attempted with a low-rate behavior, the behavior is unlikely to occur during sessions and therefore will not come into contact with the arranged contingencies. Instead, informant and descriptive assessments are typically used to assess the function of low-rate problem behavior (Radford & Ervin, 2002; Sprague & Horner, 1999).

Life-Threatening Behavior

An additional concern is the use of a functional analysis with life-threatening behaviors. Because the functional analysis achieves its outcome via the purposeful reinforcement of problem behavior during brief sessions, it may be unethical in some cases to apply this procedure with behavior that is potentially life threatening. Examples of such behavior include pica of dangerous objects (e.g., pushpins), suicidal behavior, and self-injury that occurs at a high intensity and/or involves a vulnerable area of the body (e.g., eye poking). However, it may be possible to conduct a functional analysis with such behaviors by using protective equipment (e.g., helmets, eye patches) for some forms of self-injury and simulated but safe pica objects (Piazza et al., 1998).

Covert Behavior

Functional analyses cannot be conducted with problem behaviors that only occur in private. For example, although operant variables may maintain trichotillomania (clinically problematic hair pulling), some individuals will not engage in this behavior in the presence of others (Elliott & Fuqua, 2000).

ADDITIONAL CONSIDERATIONS

Because functional analysis involves the deliberate, controlled reinforcement of problem behavior, the procedure should only be conducted by trained professionals who are properly supervised. In addition, it can be politically advantageous for the agency in which the analysis is conducted to support its use. It is also important to consider safety precautions for the client and staff when conducting a functional analysis for behavior such as self-injury or aggression. For some behaviors that might result in significant injury to the client or staff, it may be necessary to have medical staff available on site. Finally, termination criteria should always be established to inform the clinician when a session should be terminated due to excessive intensities or frequencies of problem behavior.

HOW DOES THE FUNCTIONAL ANALYSIS WORK?

The necessary components of a functional analysis test condition are as follows: (1) the relevant *establishing operation*[2] must be present (e.g., depri-

---

2. An establishing operation (EO) is an event that increases or decreases the reinforcing (or punishing) effect of a consequence (for further information, see McGill, 1999). In other words, it alters the client's motivation for a specific consequence. In a functional analysis test condition, the EO must be present in order for the delivered consequence to function as a reinforcer. For example, in a demand condition in which brief escape from a task is being evaluated, the task itself must be at least somewhat unpleasant. The unpleasantness of the task is an EO that increases escape from the task as a reinforcer.

vation of attention within the session); (2) discriminative stimuli must be present (e.g., the presence of a therapist); and (3) the putative reinforcer (e.g., staff attention) is delivered contingent on behavior. These three components work together to simulate the complete reinforcement contingency for a problem behavior. In other words, the functional analysis is effective because, within the session, problem behavior is evoked and is subsequently exposed to differential consequences that should result in increased levels of problem behavior when the maintaining reinforcer is delivered.

EMPIRICAL SUPPORT FOR THE FUNCTIONAL ANALYSIS

A number of studies (e.g., Iwata, Pace, Cowdery, & Miltenberger, 1994; Repp, Felce, & Barton, 1988) have demonstrated superior treatment effects with procedures prescribed by the outcome of a functional assessment compared to a default, non-function-based alternative. For example, Iwata, Pace, Cowdery, et al. demonstrated that only variations of extinction that were matched to behavioral function were effective in treating self-injury. For example, the attention-maintained head hitting of one individual was successfully treated using planned ignoring (i.e., attention extinction). However, having the individual wear a helmet to attenuate sensory stimulation (i.e., sensory extinction) for the same behavior was ineffective. Although the ultimate validity of a functional analysis is a successful treatment based on its results, additional empirical support can be found by examining the percentage of functional analysis cases that resulted in interpretable data from two recent experimental-epidemiological analyses. Iwata, Pace, Dorsey, et al. (1994) reported that, out of 152 functional analyses, 138 (91%) resulted in data clearly indicating a behavioral function. Similarly, Vollmer et al. (1995) reported the successful identification of behavioral function in 17 of 20 (85%) cases using several variations of the functional analysis.

STEP-BY-STEP INSTRUCTIONS

The following steps represent the standard procedure for conducting a functional analysis of problem behavior.

Preliminary Assessment

As mentioned previously, there are three types or levels of functional assessment: informant, descriptive, and experimental functional analysis. These three methods progress from less time- and labor-intensive to more time- and labor-intensive with an increasing degree of certainty about likely maintaining variables. Many clinicians begin the functional assessment process at the informant level, in which caregivers are interviewed or complete rating scales to provide preliminary information on the problem behavior. Some examples of structured informant assessments that researchers have developed include the Motivation Assessment Scale (Durand & Crimmins, 1988) and the Functional Analysis Interview (O'Neill et al., 1997). Sturmey (1994) reviewed the psychometric properties of several informant rating scales and suggested that additional demonstration of their reliability and validity is needed.

Next, the client is typically observed in the natural environment (a descriptive assessment) to further assess the problem. Typically when the problem behavior occurs the therapist should note that it occurred, as well as its immediate, observable antecedent and consequence. The therapist may also note the date, time, and location of the behavior as well as what activity was occurring and what persons were present. Data obtained using this method are summarized to examine potential patterns associated with the occurrence of behavior. A benefit of the descriptive assessment is that the therapist is actually observing the problem behavior in the natural setting (as opposed to an artificial one) and is not relying on the verbal information from others. Another benefit of the descriptive assessment is its ability to assess the function of behaviors that do not occur frequently but are nonetheless problematic. Unfortunately, all data collected using this method are correlational and cannot be considered definitive.

Finally, a functional analysis can be conducted to confirm findings produced by the informant and descriptive assessments. The purpose of the functional analysis is to conduct a brief experiment to test the effects of different antecedent conditions and reinforcers on problem behavior.

Setting and Session Features

Most functional analyses are conducted in analogue rather than naturalistic settings. The trade-off is that although the analogue setting is probably more likely to produce interpretable results (because extraneous variables are eliminated), the naturalistic setting may be more likely to evoke the problem behavior due to the presence of relevant idiosyncratic stimuli.

Wallace and Iwata (1999) determined that sessions 10 or 15 minutes in duration resulted in clearer results than 5-minute sessions. Sessions should be conducted using a rapidly alternating multielement design (Barlow & Hersen, 1984) with randomized presentation of experimental conditions. For example, a therapist might conduct a block of five 10-minute sessions in approximately 1 hour (e.g., attention → escape → alone → control → escape). Sessions should be separated from each other by at least a few minutes to (1) allow the therapist to prepare for the next session and (2) help the client differentiate between different conditions. Each condition should generally be conducted a minimum of three times, although Fisher, Hagopian, Sevin, and Piazza (1994) suggested that 10 sessions of each condition resulted in the clearest data. Although it is possible to conduct the entire functional analysis in one time period (e.g., 4 hours), sessions are generally conducted over at least several days, to accord with therapist availability and to prevent client fatigue.

As stated earlier, in each condition, the therapist creates specific antecedent situations, provides specific consequences for the problem behavior, and ultimately looks for a reinforcement effect. Each condition should have some physical aspect that serves a discriminative stimulus to help the client differentiate it from the others (Conners et al., 2000). The therapist can use different therapists, rooms, or areas; wear different-colored shirts; or place a different-colored poster board on the wall for each condition. In addition, if the behavior is potentially dangerous, safety guidelines that specify criteria for terminating a session should be set prior to beginning the analysis.

Common Test Conditions

The following are descriptions of the most commonly used functional analysis conditions.

Attention from Others

The purpose of this condition is to determine whether the behavior is maintained by attention from others (i.e., social positive reinforcement). The client should be seated and given a medium-preference item with which to interact. Each time the behavior occurs, the client should receive 3 to 5 seconds of attention for the behavior. The content of these attention deliveries typically involves social disapproval (e.g., "Please don't do that"). However, the type and specific content of attention (positive or negative) used should match what the therapist believes occurs in the client's environment (perhaps from a prior descriptive assessment).

Escape from Instructional Demands

The purpose of this condition is to determine whether the behavior is maintained by escape from or avoidance of instructional demands (i.e., social negative reinforcement). The therapist should provide a task (e.g., academic, habilitative) that has been demonstrated to be at least moderately difficult for the client. When the problem behavior occurs, give the client a 20- to 30-second break before resuming instruction. Always praise task compliance. Consider carefully the nature of the demands presented in this condition. The task demands should be similar to those delivered in the natural environment in terms of the type of task, rate of presentation of tasks, and level of task difficulty.

Access to Tangible Items

The purpose of this condition is to determine whether the behavior is maintained by access to preferred tangible items (e.g., toys, leisure materials). Before the session begins, give the client brief, free access to the preferred item. At the beginning of the session, remove the item and give it back for 20 to 30 seconds if the problem behavior occurs. This condition should only be conducted when there is strong evidence from prior functional assessment to indicate that access to preferred items may serve a likely maintaining function.

Alone/No Interaction

This condition is designed to determine whether the behavior is maintained by automatic reinforcement (i.e., sensory reinforcement or self-stimulation). In an alone-condition session, the client is typically left alone for the duration of the session. However, if this is not practically feasible, the therapist can be present, but he or she should not provide any social interaction throughout the session. In addition, there should be little stimulation in the environment (e.g., no radio, television, or other tangible items). High rates of behavior in this condition might be indicative of an automatic reinforcement function.

Control

The purpose of the control condition is to provide an ideal environment for the client so that we might never expect the problem behavior to occur. Therefore, the environment should be enriched with preferred items. The client should also be given frequent attention on a reasonable schedule (usually 3 to 5 seconds of attention every 30 seconds), and no demands should be presented. The function of this condition is to reduce the motivation to engage in the problem behavior because all of the potential maintaining reinforcers are freely available. The control condition should generally produce few problem behaviors; therefore, data from all other conditions should be compared with data from this condition.

Customized Test Conditions

Although the common conditions described above cover the majority of maintaining environmental variables for problem behavior, it may sometimes be necessary to customize test conditions to account for an idiosyncratic function. For example, McCord, Iwata, Galensky, Ellingson, and Thomson (2001) used functional analyses with problem behaviors whose function was escape from unpleasant noise (i.e., problem behav-

ior terminated the noise). Similarly, McCord, Thomson, and Iwata (2001) used a functional analysis to assess the function of problem behavior that occurred primarily during transitions, which could include multiple reinforcement sources. When developing a customized test condition, ensure that the relevant antecedent conditions are present (e.g., unpleasant noise, an adult who can terminate the noise) and that the hypothesized reinforcer (e.g., termination of noise) is delivered contingent on each problem behavior.

We recommend always including at least the control and alone/no-interaction conditions in the analysis, plus any additional test conditions that are deemed relevant from the preliminary assessment. Although the control condition should always be included, the alone condition could be eliminated in instances in which another person's presence is necessary for the problem behavior (e.g., aggression) to occur. The ability to customize the functional analysis by including only relevant conditions and by developing new conditions makes it particularly suitable for clinical practice.

Data Collection and Analysis

During each session, observational data should be collected on some measure of problem behavior such as frequency, duration, or percentage of intervals with occurrence (Cooper, Heron, & Heward, 1987). The nature of the behavior (e.g., whether each instance of the behavior is discrete, whether instances of the behavior occur for variable durations) will determine the appropriate measure. Data should be plotted on a line graph one session at a time. The data from all conditions should then be compared, with visual inspection, to identify those with the highest level(s) of behavior compared to the control condition. Hagopian et al. (1997) developed specific criteria that can be used during the visual inspection of functional analysis data. In general, the procedure requires one to compare each test condition to the control condition to determine if an important percentage of those sessions had rates of behavior at least 2 standard deviations above the average of the control condition sessions.

Although the standard, multielement-design functional analysis often results in interpretable data, additional analyses are needed when it does not. We refer the reader to the protocol developed by Vollmer et al. (1995) for conducting a series of follow-up analyses when functional analysis outcomes are ambiguous. One of the final phases of this protocol is a series of consecutive alone/no-interaction sessions. If problem behavior persists during these sessions, the common conclusion is that the behavior is maintained by automatic (i.e., sensory, self-stimulatory) reinforcement. We refer the reader to an article by LeBlanc, Patel, and J. E. Carr (2000) for a description of assessments that are designed to clarify the specific sensory consequences that may maintain problem behavior.

LINKING THE FUNCTIONAL ANALYSIS
TO TREATMENT

At the conclusion of the functional assessment process (i.e., informant assessment → descriptive assessment → functional analysis; see Figure 27.1), the therapist should have a more definitive understanding of the maintaining variable(s) of the client's problem behavior. It is then necessary to develop a treatment plan that incorporates this information. For example, if the functional analysis identified an attention function, this should be directly addressed in the subsequent treatment. Common interventions for an attention-maintained behavior include using planned ignoring of the problem behavior, providing noncontingent (free) attention to the client throughout the day, and teaching the client more appropriate ways to obtain attention (see Iwata, Vollmer, Zarcone, & Rodgers, 1993). However, regardless of the specific type of treatment that is selected, the therapist should ensure that it directly addresses the behavior's function, so that the information obtained with the functional analysis is best used and, most importantly, the client ultimately receives the most effective and relevant treatment possible.

Further Reading

Neef, N. A., & Iwata, B. A. (Eds.). (1994). Special issue on functional analysis approaches to behavioral assessment and treatment [Special issue]. *Journal of Applied Behavior Analysis, 27*(2).

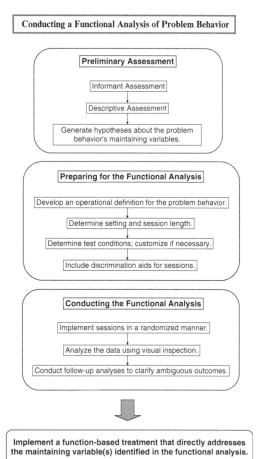

FIGURE 27.1   Key Steps in Conducting a Functional Analysis of Problem Behavior

O'Neill, R. E., Horner, R. H., Albin, R. W., Sprague, J. R., Storey, K., & Newton, J. S. (1997). *Functional assessment and program development for problem behavior: A practical handbook* (2nd ed.). Pacific Grove, CA: Brooks/Cole.

Repp, A. C., & Horner, R. H. (1999). *Functional analysis of problem behavior: From effective assessment to effective support.* Belmont, CA: Wadsworth.

References

Baer, D. M., Wolf, M. M., & Risley, T. R. (1968). Some current dimensions of applied behavior analysis. *Journal of Applied Behavior Analysis, 1,* 91–97.

Barlow, D. H., & Hersen, M. (1984). *Single case experimental designs: Strategies for studying behavior change* (2nd ed.). Boston: Allyn and Bacon.

Carr, E. G. (1977). The origins of self-injurious behavior:

A review of some hypotheses. *Psychological Bulletin, 84,* 800–816.

Carr, J. E., Coriaty, S., & Dozier, C. L. (2000). Current issues in the function-based treatment of aberrant behavior in individuals with developmental disabilities. In J. Austin & J. E. Carr (Eds.), *Handbook of applied behavior analysis* (pp. 91–112). Reno, NV: Context Press.

Carr, J. E., Taylor, C. C., Wallander, R. J., & Reiss, M. L. (1996). A functional-analytic approach to the diagnosis of a transient tic disorder. *Journal of Behavior Therapy and Experimental Psychiatry, 27,* 291–297.

Conners, J., Iwata, B. A., Kahng, S., Hanley, G. P., Worsdell, A. S., & Thompson, R. H. (2000). Differential responding in the presence and absence of discriminative stimuli during multielement functional analyses. *Journal of Applied Behavior Analysis, 33,* 299–308.

Cooper, J. O., Heron, T. E., & Heward, W. L. (1987). *Applied behavior analysis.* Columbus, OH: Merrill.

Derby, K. M., Wacker, D. P., Sasso, G., Steege, M., Northup, J., Cigrand, K., et al. (1992). Brief functional assessment techniques to evaluate aberrant behavior in an outpatient setting: A summary of 79 cases. *Journal of Applied Behavior Analysis, 25,* 713–721.

Durand, V. M., & Crimmins, D. B. (1988). Identifying the variables maintaining self-injurious behavior. *Journal of Autism and Developmental Disorders, 18,* 99–117.

Elliott, A. J., & Fuqua, R. W. (2000). Trichotillomania: Conceptualization, measurement, and treatment. *Behavior Therapy, 31,* 529–545.

Fisher, W., Hagopian, L., Sevin, J., & Piazza, C. (1994, May). Visual inspection and statistical interpretation of brief and extended functional analyses. In B. A. Iwata (Chair), *Current research on the functional analysis of severe behavior disorders.* Symposium conducted at the 20th Annual Convention of the Association for Behavior Analysis, Atlanta, GA.

Hagopian, L. P., Fisher, W. W., Thompson, R. H., Owen-DeSchryver, J., Iwata, B. A., & Wacker, D. P. (1997). Toward the development of structured criteria for interpretation of functional analysis data. *Journal of Applied Behavior Analysis, 30,* 313–326.

Iwata, B. A., Dorsey, M. F, Slifer, K. J., Bauman, K. E., & Richman, G. S. (1994). Toward a functional analysis of self-injury. *Journal of Applied Behavior Analysis, 27,* 197–209. (Reprinted from *Analysis and Intervention in Developmental Disabilities, 2,* 3–20, 1982)

Iwata, B. A., Duncan, B. A., Zarcone, J. R., Lerman, D. C., & Shore, B. A. (1994). A sequential, test-control methodology for conducting functional analyses of self-injurious behavior. *Behavior Modification, 18,* 289–306.

Iwata, B. A., Pace, G. M., Cowdery, G. E., & Miltenberger, R. G. (1994). What makes extinction work: An analysis of procedural form and function. *Journal of Applied Behavior Analysis, 27,* 131–144.

Iwata, B. A., Pace, G. M., Dorsey, M. F., Zarcone, J. R., Vollmer, T. R., Smith, R. G., et al. (1994). The functions of self-injurious behavior: An experimental-epidemiological analysis. *Journal of Applied Behavior Analysis, 27,* 215–240.

Iwata, B. A., Vollmer, T. R., Zarcone, J. R., & Rodgers, T. A. (1993). Treatment classification and selection based on behavioral function. In R. Van Houten & S. Axelrod (Eds.), *Behavior analysis and treatment* (pp. 101–125). New York: Plenum.

Kennedy, C. H., Meyer, K. A., Knowles, T., & Shukla, S. (2000). Analyzing the multiple functions of stereotypical behavior for students with autism: Implications for assessment and treatment. *Journal of Applied Behavior Analysis, 33,* 559–571.

LeBlanc, L. A., Patel, M. R., & Carr, J. E. (2000). Recent advances in the assessment of aberrant behavior maintained by automatic reinforcement in individuals with developmental disabilities. *Journal of Behavior Therapy and Experimental Psychiatry, 31,* 137–154.

Lennox, D. B., & Miltenberger, R. G. (1989). Conducting a functional assessment of problem behavior in applied settings. *Journal of The Association for Persons with Severe Handicaps, 14,* 304–311.

Lerman, D. C., & Iwata, B. A. (1993). Descriptive and experimental analyses of variables maintaining self-injurious behavior. *Journal of Applied Behavior Analysis, 26,* 293–319.

Mace, F. C. (1994). The significance and future of functional analysis methodologies. *Journal of Applied Behavior Analysis, 27,* 385–392.

Marcus, B. A., Vollmer, T. R., Swanson, V., Roane, H. R., & Ringdahl, J. E. (2001). An experimental analysis of aggression. *Behavior Modification, 25,* 189–213.

McCord, B. E., Iwata, B. A., Galensky, T. L., Ellingson, S. A., & Thomson, R. J. (2001). Functional analysis and treatment of problem behavior evoked by noise. *Journal of Applied Behavior Analysis, 34,* 447–462.

McCord, B. E., Thomson, R. J., & Iwata, B. A. (2001). Functional analysis and treatment of self-injury associated with transitions. *Journal of Applied Behavior Analysis, 34,* 195–210.

McGill, P. (1999). Establishing operations: Implications for the assessment, treatment, and prevention of problem behavior. *Journal of Applied Behavior Analysis, 32,* 393–418.

Neef, N. A., & Iwata, B. A. (Eds.). (1994). Special issue on functional analysis approaches to behavioral assessment and treatment [Special issue]. *Journal of Applied Behavior Analysis, 27*(2).

O'Neill, R. E., Horner, R. H., Albin, R. W., Sprague, J. R., Storey, K., & Newton, J. S. (1997). *Functional assessment and program development for problem behavior: A practical handbook* (2nd ed.). Pacific Grove, CA: Brooks/Cole.

Piazza, C. C., Fisher, W. W., Hanley, G. P., LeBlanc, L. A., Worsdell, A. S., Lindauer, S. E., et al. (1998). Treatment of pica through multiple analyses of its reinforcing functions. *Journal of Applied Behavior Analysis, 31,* 165–189.

Radford, P. M., & Ervin, R. A. (2002). Employing descriptive functional assessment methods to assess low-rate, high intensity behaviors: A case example. *Journal of Positive Behavior Interventions, 4,* 146–155.

Repp, A. C., Felce, D., & Barton, L. E. (1988). Basing the treatment of stereotypic and self-injurious behaviors on hypotheses of their causes. *Journal of Applied Behavior Analysis, 21,* 281–289.

Sprague, J. R., & Horner, R. H. (1999). Low-frequency high-intensity problem behavior: Toward an applied technology of functional assessment and intervention. In A. C. Repp & R. H. Horner (Eds.), *Functional analysis of problem behavior: From effective assessment to effective support* (pp. 98–116). Belmont, CA: Wadsworth.

Sturmey, P. (1994). Assessing the functions of aberrant behaviors: A review of psychometric instruments. *Journal of Autism and Developmental Disorders, 24,* 293–304.

Touchette, P. E., MacDonald, R. F., & Langer, S. N. (1985). A scatter plot for identifying stimulus control of problem behavior. *Journal of Applied Behavior Analysis, 18,* 343–351.

Vollmer, T. R., Iwata, B. A., Duncan, B. A., & Lerman, D. C. (1993). Extensions of multielement functional analysis using reversal-type designs. *Journal of Developmental and Physical Disabilities, 5,* 311–325.

Vollmer, T. R., Iwata, B. A., Zarcone, J. R., Smith, R. G., & Mazaleski, J. L. (1993). Within-session patterns of self-injury as indicators of behavioral function. *Research in Developmental Disabilities, 14,* 479–492.

Vollmer, T. R., Marcus, B. A., Ringdahl, J. E., & Roane, H. S. (1995). Progressing from brief assessments to extended experimental analyses in the evaluation of aberrant behavior. *Journal of Applied Behavior Analysis, 28,* 561–576.

Vollmer, T. R., Northup, J., Ringdahl, J. E., LeBlanc, L. A., & Chauvin, T. M. (1996). Functional analysis of severe tantrums displayed by children with language delays: An outclinic assessment. *Behavior Modification, 20,* 97–115.

Wallace, M. D., & Iwata, B. A. (1999). Effects of session duration on functional analysis outcomes. *Journal of Applied Behavior Analysis, 32,* 175–183.

Wilder, D. A., Masuda, A., O'Connor, C., & Baham, M. (2001). Brief functional analysis and treatment of bizarre vocalizations in an adult with schizophrenia. *Journal of Applied Behavior Analysis, 34,* 65–68.

28 FUNCTIONAL COMMUNICATION TRAINING TO TREAT CHALLENGING BEHAVIOR

V. Mark Durand

Children and adults with developmental disorders often engage in behaviors that are disturbing and, at times, dangerous to themselves and others. Aggression, self-injurious behavior, and other disruptive behaviors pose such a serious threat to efforts to help these individuals lead more independent lives that a great deal of research has focused on the treatment of these behaviors (Durand & Merges, 2001). A wide range of consequences have been tried in efforts to reduce the behavior problems exhibited by persons with disabilities, including time out from positive reinforcement (Wolf, Risley, & Mees, 1964), contingent restraint (Azrin, Besalel, & Wisotzek, 1982), overcorrection (Johnson, Baumeister, Penland, & Inwald, 1982), and contingent electric shock (Corte, Wolf, & Locke, 1971; Tate & Baroff, 1966). Although many of these interventions demonstrate effectiveness in the initial reduction of challenging behaviors, sustained and clinically relevant improvements are elusive (Durand & Carr, 1989).

An alternative behavioral approach to the traditional treatments for challenging behaviors was developed in the mid-1980s and has been referred to as Functional Communication Training (FCT; Carr & Durand, 1985). This approach specifically uses communication to reduce challenging behavior (Durand, 1990). This strategy includes assessing the variables maintaining the behavior to be reduced and providing the same consequences for a different behavior. It is assumed that if individuals can gain access to desired consequences more effectively with the new response, they will use this new response and will reduce their use of the undesirable response. Applying this logic to challenging behavior, one is able to teach individuals more acceptable behaviors that serve the same function as their problem behavior. So, for example, we could teach people to ask for attention by saying, "Am I doing good work?" This would allow them to gain teacher attention in this appropriate way rather than in an inappropriate way such as through slapping their faces.

WHO MIGHT BENEFIT FROM THIS TREATMENT

A variety of individuals with developmental disorders such as Autistic Disorder and Mental Retardation have been assisted with this approach. Research on FCT has focused on severe challenging behaviors such as aggression and self-injurious behavior (e.g., Bird, Dores, Moniz, & Robinson, 1989; Durand & Kishi, 1987), stereotyped behavior (e.g., Durand & Carr, 1987; Wacker et al., 1990), and a variety of communication disorders (e.g., Carr & Kemp, 1989; Durand & Crimmins, 1987). Intervention has been conducted in group homes (e.g., Durand & Kishi, 1987), schools (e.g., Hunt, Alwell, Goetz, & Sailor, 1990), and vocational settings (e.g., Bird et al., 1989).

CONTRAINDICATIONS OF THE TREATMENT

Because of its reliance on communication, those individuals who are in environments that are relatively unresponsive to their needs and requests will often be frustrated in their attempts to gain access to preferred reinforcers. Therefore, major environmental modifications are required prior to any attempt to implement FCT.

HOW DOES THE TREATMENT WORK?

The mechanism behind the success of FCT is assumed to rely on *functional equivalence* (Durand, 1990). In other words, behaviors maintained by a particular reinforcer (e.g., escape from work) are replaced by other behaviors if these new behaviors serve the same function and are more efficient at gaining the desired reinforcers. Using communication as the replacement behavior provides an added benefit because of its ability to recruit natural communities of the desired reinforcers (Durand, 1999). One effect of this view of behavior problems is that it suggests that these behaviors are not just responses that need to be reduced or eliminated. This perspective reminds us that attempting to eliminate these behaviors through some reductive technique would leave these individuals with no way of accessing their desired reinforcers, and therefore we could anticipate that other maladaptive behaviors would take their place (also called *symptom substitution* or *response covariation*).

EVIDENCE FOR THE EFFECTIVENESS OF FCT

Empirical support for the success of functional communication training in reducing challenging behavior is growing (Durand & Merges, 2001). Researchers are just beginning to explore the boundaries of this intervention approach through the study of maintenance (e.g., Bird et al., 1989; Durand, 1999; Durand & Carr, 1991; Durand & Carr, 1992), the role of response efficiency (Horner, Sprague, O'Brien, & Heathfield, 1990), and a variety of other important parameters (Brown et al., 2000; Kelley, Lerman, & Van Camp, 2002; Lerman, Kelley, Vorndran, Kuhn, & LaRue, 2002).

With growing evidence of the value of this intervention approach in reducing a variety of problem behaviors, it is important to evaluate how FCT compares with other interventions. Hanley and colleagues, for example, compared the effectiveness of FCT with noncontingent reinforcement (NCR) on the multiple behavior problems of two children (Hanley, Piazza, Fisher, Contrucci, & Maglieri, 1997) They found that both interventions initially reduced problem behaviors but that the participants demonstrated a preference for FCT.

An important aspect of FCT—its usefulness outside specially designed settings—has also been investigated. Durand and Carr (1992) and Durand (1999) have found that not only could individuals be taught to communicate to reduce their behavior problems, but their requests could be adapted (at times using alternative communication systems) so that they were effective outside school and with untrained community members. The research to date suggests that we can teach people with behavior problems ways of communicating that will be understood even by people who do not have training in the area of communication difficulties or intellectual disabilities.

STEP-BY-STEP PROCEDURES

Table 28.1 illustrates the basic steps used to assess behavior and conduct FCT. These steps can often be complicated, and readers are referred to the section on further reading for more detailed instructions.

Step 1: Assess the Function of Behavior

In order to assess the function of a problem behavior, the antecedents and consequences of that behavior need to be identified. Challenging behaviors are often found to serve one or more of the

TABLE 28.1   Step-By-Step Instructions for Functional Communication Training

Step	Description
1. Assess the function of behavior	Use two or more functional assessment techniques to determine what variables are maintaining the problem behavior.
2. Select the communication modality	Identify how you want the individual to communicate with others (e.g., verbally or through alternative communication strategies).
3. Create teaching situations	Identify situations in the environment that are triggers for problem behavior (e.g., difficult tasks) and use these as the settings for teaching the alternative responses.
4. Prompt communication	Prompt the alternative communication in the setting where you want it to occur. Use the least intrusive prompt necessary.
5. Fade prompts	Quickly fade the prompts, insuring that no problem behaviors occur during training.
6. Teach new communicative responses	When possible, teach a variety of alternative communicative responses that can serve the same function (e.g., saying "Help me" or "I don't understand").
7. Modify environment	When appropriate, implement changes in the environment, such as improving student-task match in school.

following functions: (1) to avoid or escape non-preferred stimuli (e.g., difficult demands, non-preferred staff); (2) to access preferred stimuli (e.g., toys, attention); or (3) to increase sensory stimulation. Once the purpose of a targeted behavior is understood, individuals can be taught to request the variables previously obtained by the challenging behavior.

There are a number of functional assessment strategies that are useful for determining the function of behavior, including ABC charts, functional analyses, and a variety of rating scales. We always begin with informal observations and interviews of significant others, but we continue the process using *multiple forms of assessment*, including the Motivation Assessment Scale (MAS) and structured observations in the individual's environment. The MAS is a questionnaire that we can give to teachers, paraprofessionals, family members, or anyone else who has a great deal of contact with the individual (Durand & Crimmins, 1988, 1992). The MAS asks questions that determine where, when, and under what conditions problem behaviors occur and determines their functions. Information from the MAS and from other forms of functional behavioral assessments is used to design plans for reducing the behavior problems.

A functional analysis—manipulation of aspects of the environment to assess behavior change—is frequently cited as the best method of determining the function of a behavior problem

(Mace, 1994) However, there are also a number of issues to consider prior to conducting this type of assessment (Durand, 1997). One issue is *accessibility to manipulation*. There are certain influences that you cannot or would not manipulate or change in order to perform a functional analysis. Factors such as some illnesses, disrupted family life, and chromosomal aberrations can certainly affect behavior problems, but they cannot or should not be turned on and off in order to assess their influence.

Another concern involves the *ethics* of conducting a functional analysis. There are other influences that you could manipulate but that you may not want to change if they will result in an increase in challenging behavior. In many instances, deliberately increasing a severe behavior problem in order to assess it (e.g., by reinforcing challenging behavior) can be questioned on ethical grounds. In these cases, assessment that does not involve manipulation (and subsequent increases in challenging behavior) would be recommended (for a more detailed discussion of these issues, see Durand, 1993).

Step 2: Select the Communication Modality

The type of response to encourage from the individual needs to be determined. If the individual already has some facility in one mode of communication (e.g., verbal, sign language), then that mode should be considered for functional communication training. Usually, if an individual has been unsuccessful in learning to communicate effectively after extensive verbal language training, then the communication modality to be used should be either signing or symbolic. If the person has also been unsuccessful with sign language training (e.g., has not learned to sign or uses sloppy and incomprehensible signs) we recommend symbolic communication training, at least initially. Symbolic communication training can involve the use of picture books, tokens with messages written on them, or other assistive devices (e.g., vocal output devices). This form of communication training has the advantage of being relatively easy to teach, and it is universally recognizable.

Step 3: Create Teaching Situations

The environment is arranged to create opportunities for communication (e.g., putting an obstacle in the way of a person trying to open a door and prompting him or her to ask for assistance). This use of *incidental teaching* (McGee, Morrier, & Daly, 1999)—arranging the environment to establish situations that elicit interest and that are used as teaching opportunities—is an important part of successful communication training. Using the person's interest in some interaction, whether it be a desire to stop working on a difficult task or a desire to elicit the attention of an adult, is a very powerful tool in teaching generalized communication. As soon as possible, training trials are interspersed throughout the individual's day where appropriate. Generalization and maintenance of intervention effects may be facilitated by using the criterion environment (i.e., where you want the person to communicate) as the training environment. With the typical model of teaching skills in a separate setting (e.g., in the speech therapist's office), once the response is learned you need to encourage the performance of that behavior in settings where you want it to occur (e.g., in the cafeteria). When training is begun in the natural or criterion setting, extensive programming for generalization is not necessary because it will be occurring where you want it to occur. In addition, obstacles to maintenance can be immediately identified (e.g., whether the consequences being provided in that setting going to maintain

the new response) when you are teaching in the criterion environment.

Step 4: Prompt Communication

Teaching individuals to communicate as a replacement for their challenging behavior requires a range of sophisticated language training techniques (Durand, Mapstone, & Youngblade, 1999). A multiphase prompting and prompt fading procedure is used to teach the new communicative response. Prompts are introduced as necessary, then faded as quickly as possible. Some learners negatively resist attempts to teach important skills (e.g., the individual screams and kicks), others positively resist (e.g., the individual laughs and giggles instead of working), and still others passively resist (e.g., the individual does not look at materials and makes no response). When an individual kicks, screams, and rips up work materials whenever they are presented, or passively ignores efforts to get him or her to attend to a task, teaching becomes a major challenge and learning becomes highly unlikely.

One procedure we have used for these types of problems is to teach the individual to request assistance (e.g., by saying, "Help me") or a brief break from work. Often the problem behaviors appear to be attempts to avoid or escape from unpleasant situations. It makes sense, then, that if the individual is taught to appropriately request assistance *and receives it,* then the task will seem easier and problem behaviors should be reduced. Similarly, if an individual has been working for some time on a task and is allowed to ask for a break *and receives it,* then this individual's problem behavior should also be reduced.

Step 5: Fade Prompts

We begin reducing the individual's reliance on prompts by fading back on the most intrusive assistance being used. In the case of teaching a student to point to a picture book to make a request, we do this by going from a full physical prompt to partial prompts (e.g., just touching his hand), to gestural prompts (e.g., motioning to prompt his hands), to finally only the verbal prompt "What do you want?" Throughout the training we rely heavily on delayed prompting. After several trials, we would intersperse a trial with a delayed prompt (i.e., we waited approximately 5 seconds), to see if the individual would respond without the next level of prompt. For example, if a student had been responding to just a touch of his hand to point to a picture, we would make a gesture as if we were going to prompt him, and then wait 5 seconds.

We do not wait until responding is extremely stable to move on to the next level of prompting. In other words, the person does not have to be correctly responding to, say, 9 out of 10 prompts for 2 weeks for us to move to the next step. We would attempt to move to the next step if the individual was successful at a step for 3–5 consecutive responses. We do this in order to prevent the person from becoming prompt dependent (i.e., too reliant on prompts to respond).

Training progresses quickly over several weeks to the point where the individual can communicate with no external prompting. As is typical in our training, behavior improves most dramatically as soon as the individual begins to make requests without prompts.

Step 6: Teach New Communicative Responses

Once successful, intervention continues by introducing new communicative forms (e.g., requests for food, music, work), reintroducing work demands, expanding the settings in which communication is encouraged to include the whole day, and introducing new staff into the training program.

Step 7: Environmental Modification

Recommendations are often made concerning environmental and curricular changes. For example, it can be useful to consider curricular changes for a student who is attempting to escape from academic tasks. However, we typically approach these types of changes with considerable caution. The fear is that we will create such an artificial environment that the student may not be able to adapt to new challenges or new environments. The goal of FCT is to teach the student a form of coping skill that will enable him or her to appropriately respond to new and unexpected situations (e.g., a new teacher, more difficult work).

Therefore, we view environmental modifications as a form of short-term prevention strategy rather than the main programmatic intervention.

PREDICTING SUCCESSFUL OUTCOMES

We have identified a number of factors that seem to influence the success or failure of functional communication training. These elements of training appear to be necessary conditions for initial reductions in behavior, generalization across people and stimulus conditions, and/or maintenance across time.

Response Match

This consists of matching the communicative behavior to the function of the challenging behavior. In other words, the new trained response should evoke the same consequences as the targeted challenging behavior.

Response Success

This refers to whether or not significant others respond to the trained communicative responses. Simply engaging in these communicative acts (i.e., making responses that match the function of challenging behavior) without a subsequent response by others will not result in reductions in challenging behavior.

Response Efficiency

Response efficiency refers to whether the response is more effective and efficient in getting the student the reinforcers he or she obtained with his or her problem behavior. In a series of studies, Horner and colleagues examined this aspect of functional communication training (Horner & Day, 1991; Horner et al., 1990).

Response Acceptability

This refers to whether the response is acceptable to significant others. If the new communicative response is seen as unacceptable in community settings, then others will not respond appropriately and the desired consequences will not be obtained.

Response Recognizability

This refers to whether the response can be recognized, especially by others who may not be highly trained. If the trained response is not easily recognizable by significant others in the environment, then these people will not respond and challenging behavior will not be reduced.

Further Reading

Carr, E. G., Levin, L, McConnachie, G., Carlson, J. I., Kemp, D. C., & Smith, C. E. (1994). *Communication-based intervention for problem behavior: A user's guide for producing positive change.* Baltimore, MD: Paul H. Brookes.

Durand, V. M. (1990). *Severe behavior problems: A functional communication training approach.* New York: Guilford Press.

Durand, V. M. (1999). Functional communication training using assistive devices: Recruiting natural communities of reinforcement. *Journal of Applied Behavior Analysis, 32,* 247–267.

References

Azrin, N. H., Besalel, V. A., & Wisotzek, I. E. (1982). Treatment of self-injury by a reinforcement plus interruption procedure. *Analysis and Intervention in Developmental Disabilities, 2,* 105–113.

Bird, F., Dores, P. A., Moniz, D., & Robinson, J. (1989). Reducing severe aggressive and self-injurious behaviors with functional communication training: Direct, collateral and generalized results. *American Journal on Mental Retardation, 94,* 37–48.

Brown, K. A., Wacker, D. P., Derby, K. M., Peck, S. M., Richman, D. M., Sasso, G. M., et al. (2000). Evaluating the effects of functional communication training in the presence and absence of establishing operations. *Journal of Applied Behavior Analysis, 33,* 53–71.

Carr, E. G., & Durand, V. M. (1985). Reducing behavior problems through functional communication training. *Journal of Applied Behavior Analysis, 18,* 111–126.

Carr, E. G., & Kemp, D. C. (1989). Functional equivalence of autistic leading and communicative pointing: Analysis and treatment. *Journal of Autism and Developmental Disorders, 19,* 561–578.

Corte, H. E., Wolf, M. M., & Locke, B. J. (1971). A comparison of procedures for eliminating self-injurious behavior of retarded adolescents. *Journal of Applied Behavior Analysis, 4,* 201–213.

Durand, V. M. (1990). *Severe behavior problems: A functional communication training approach.* New York: Guilford Press.

Durand, V. M. (1993). Functional assessment and functional analysis. In M. D. Smith (Ed.), *Behavior modification for exceptional children and youth* (pp. 38–60). Baltimore: Andover Medical Press.

Durand, V. M. (1997). Functional analysis: Should we? *Journal of Special Education, 31,* 105–106.

Durand, V. M. (1999). Functional communication training using assistive devices: Recruiting natural communities of reinforcement. *Journal of Applied Behavior Analysis, 32,* 247–267.

Durand, V. M., & Carr, E. G. (1987). Social influences on "self-stimulatory" behavior: Analysis and treatment application. *Journal of Applied Behavior Analysis, 20,* 119–132.

Durand, V. M., & Carr, E. G. (1989). Operant learning methods with chronic schizophrenia and autism: Aberrant behavior. In J. L. Matson (Ed.), *Chronic schizophrenia and autism: Issues in diagnosis, assessment, and treatment* (pp. 231–273). New York: Springer Publishing.

Durand, V. M., & Carr, E. G. (1991). Functional communication training to reduce challenging behavior: Maintenance and application in new settings. *Journal of Applied Behavior Analysis, 24,* 251–264.

Durand, V. M., & Carr, E. G. (1992). An analysis of maintenance following functional communication training. *Journal of Applied Behavior Analysis, 25,* 777–794.

Durand, V. M., & Crimmins, D. B. (1987). Assessment and treatment of psychotic speech in an autistic child. *Journal of Autism and Developmental Disorders, 17,* 17–28.

Durand, V. M., & Crimmins, D. B. (1988). Identifying the variables maintaining self-injurious behavior. *Journal of Autism and Developmental Disorders, 18,* 99–117.

Durand, V. M., & Crimmins, D. B. (1992). *The Motivation Assessment Scale (MAS) Administration Guide.* Topeka, KS: Monaco & Associates.

Durand, V. M., & Kishi, G. (1987). Reducing severe behavior problems among persons with dual sensory impairments: An evaluation of a technical assistance model. *Journal of The Association for Persons with Severe Handicaps, 12,* 2–10.

Durand, V. M., Mapstone, E., & Youngblade, L. (1999).

The role of communicative partners. In J. Downing (Ed.), *Teaching communication skills to students with severe disabilities within general education classrooms* (pp. 139–155). Baltimore, MD: Paul H. Brookes.

Durand, V. M., & Merges, E. (2001). Functional communication training: A contemporary behavior analytic intervention for problem behaviors. *Focus on Autism and Other Developmental Disabilities, 16,* 110–119.

Hanley, G. P., Piazza, C. C., Fisher, W. W., Contrucci, S. A., & Maglieri, K. A. (1997). Evaluation of client preference for function-based treatment packages. *Journal of Applied Behavior Analysis, 30,* 459–473.

Horner, R. H., & Day, H. M. (1991). The effects of response efficiency on functionally equivalent competing behaviors. *Journal of Applied Behavior Analysis, 24,* 719–732.

Horner, R. H., Sprague, J. R., O'Brien, M., & Heathfield, L. T. (1990). The role of response efficiency in the reduction of problem behaviors through functional equivalence training: A case study. *Journal of the Association for Persons with Severe Handicaps, 15,* 91–97.

Hunt, P., Alwell, M., Goetz, L., & Sailor W. (1990). Generalized effects of conversation skill training. *Journal of the Association for Persons with Severe Handicaps, 15,* 250–260.

Johnson, W. L., Baumeister, A. A., Penland, M. J., & Inwald, C. (1982). Experimental analysis of self-injurious, stereotypic, and collateral behavior of retarded persons: Effects of overcorrection and reinforcement of alternative responding. *Analysis and Intervention in Developmental Disabilities, 2,* 41–66.

Kelley, M. E., Lerman, D. C., & Van Camp, C. M. (2002). The effects of competing reinforcement schedules on the acquisition of functional communication. *Journal of Applied Behavior Analysis, 35,* 59–63.

Lerman, D. C., Kelley, M. E., Vorndran, C. M., Kuhn, S. A. C., & LaRue, R.H., Jr. (2002). Reinforcement magnitude and responding during treatment with differential reinforcement. *Journal of Applied Behavior Analysis, 35,* 29–48.

Mace, F. C. (1994). The significance and future of functional analysis methodologies. *Journal of Applied Behavior Analysis, 27,* 385–392.

McGee, G. G., Morrier, M. J., & Daly, T. (1999). An incidental teaching approach to early intervention for toddlers with autism. *Journal of the Association for Persons with Severe Handicaps, 24,* 133–146.

Tate, B. G., & Baroff, G. S. (1966). Aversive control of self-injurious behavior in a psychotic boy. *Behavior Research and Therapy, 4,* 281–287.

Wacker, D. P., Steege, M. W., Northup, J., Sasso, G., Berg, W., Reimers, T., et al. (1990). A component analysis of functional communication training across three topographies of severe behavior problems. *Journal of Applied Behavior Analysis, 23,* 417–429.

Wolf, M. M., Risley, T. R., & Mees, H. (1964). Application of operant conditioning procedures to the behavior problems of an autistic child. *Behavior Research and Therapy, 1,* 305–312.

29 GENERALIZATION PROMOTION

Frank R. Rusch and Kimberly Keller

Great progress has been made over the past 15 years in our ability to teach individuals with diverse levels of disabilities to use strategies that require them to rely upon their cognitive abilities to perform a variety of skills, as opposed to being directed by others. Such strategies are important because they possess the potential to promote the ability to perform new skills under new circumstances and at different points in time. Thus, such strategies more effectively promote generalization, because they allow the individual to make the decisions and act upon those decisions without being dependent on others.

Recent research suggests that traditional cognitive strategies possess a number of features that, when combined, promote a level of generalization that far exceeds what has typically been reported in the literature. Traditionally, cognitive strategies, such as antecedent cue regulation, self-instruction, self-monitoring, self-reinforcement, and correspondence training, include picture prompts, verbal instructions provided by a teacher, verbal instructions adopted by the student, and a self-evaluation component. These strategies typically incorporate single examples of the problem and consequently usually require additional training to promote the generalized use of the cognitive strategy. However, large gains have been reported when multiple, and different, examples are combined with these cognitive strategies (Rusch, Hughes, & Wilson, 1995).

A handful of investigations have reported using cognitive strategies with multiple examples. For example, Hughes (1992) introduced a cognitive-processing model that was successful in teaching four residents with severe mental retardation to solve typical problems that arose while completing daily residential chores. The approach consisted of combining a variation of traditional self-instructional strategies with multiple training examples that shared important stimulus properties. For example, when different objects are in the way of someone who is trying to sweep a floor or vacuum a rug, the objects (stimuli) share the property of being in the way of completing the task. Similarly, Hughes and Rusch (1989) studied a problem-solving strategy that required employees to find the similarity in a response required by a novel situation and past responses made by the employees. Examples included moving items that were in the way and finding missing items that were necessary to complete work assignments. All participants extended their problem-solving abilities to nontrained examples.

Use of multiple examples has also been reported in the applied literature to be an effective approach to producing task acquisition as well as generalized responding. For example, Horner, Jones, and Williams (1985) taught three individuals to cross streets independently by teaching them to cross different streets. The primary strategy included multiple examples of the problem that required a solution; in this instance, students were taught to cross more than one intersection, and their ability to cross untrained intersections was assessed as additional intersections were introduced. All three students in the Horner et al. study demonstrated that they could cross untrained intersections only after they were introduced to multiple intersections during training.

The primary difference between the approach introduced by Horner, Jones, and William versus the cognitive approach reported by Rusch and his colleagues is that the latter promotes self-mediation in that the student acquires the ability to guide current and future behavior given similar problem situations as opposed to orienting the student to the stimulus properties of the problem to be solved and relying upon the stimuli to mediate the solution. Clearly, teaching a person to rely upon and, in effect, develop his or her self-instructional verbal behavior has potential advantages that far exceed an approach that relies upon the stimulus properties of the problem alone to direct behavior, even given the positive outcomes historically associated with external mediation.

In response to an extensive review of the literature related to employment outcomes and cognitive strategies, Rusch et al. (1995) introduced a six-step problem-solving model that includes self-instruction combined with multiple examples. The major components of the cognitive-processing model comprise the following steps: (1) selecting an array of examples (responses) a student may be required to make in an environment; (2) classifying the multiple examples into teaching sets based upon a functional analysis of the response requirements; (3) dividing members of the teaching set into responses that will serve as training examples and responses that will function as generalization probes; (4) teaching self-instruction using training examples; (5) evaluating the effects of instruction using training and nontraining examples (i.e., generalization probes) as well as evaluating the student's ability to verbalize the self-instructional statements; and (6) withdrawing training based on performance (Rusch et al., 1995).

In this chapter, we update this model, drawing primarily upon our work related to transition from school to work (Rusch & Chadsey, 1998). We have learned that for a student to maintain employment after graduation, he or she must maintain acceptable social and vocational performance standards across a diverse range of conditions. Clearly, it is impractical and impossible to teach each and every appropriate response required by each and every stimulus situation that may arise in an employment setting. We believe that selecting an array of representative stimulus conditions and training the student to respond appropriately to these selected examples increases the likelihood that the student will make the appropriate responses and thus meet performance standards. We further contend that students will be able to respond to new situations that may arise at home, in social situations, and at different points in time if they have learned the cognitive model we will describe.

To illustrate our approach we provide an example of several situations that typically occur in a classroom environment. The situations are directly related to the experiences of a high school student who is required to make several transitions throughout the school day, including arriving at a new period (e.g., algebra, English literature, ceramics) and preparing him- or herself and/or materials associated with that period (e.g., arriving at the new period, preparing him- or herself for the lesson, putting educational material away, and departing the classroom) repeatedly throughout the day. These transitions are also typical of a work day, in which employees are required to make similar transitions. Table 29.1 provides a step-by-step review of the model.

STEP 1: SELECTING AN ARRAY OF EXAMPLES (RESPONSES)

Identifying typical situations that occur in schools requires the teacher to select potential examples for training. For example, when students enter classrooms, attendance is taken, students prepare themselves and/or the classroom for instruction, and at the end of the period they prepare to leave the classroom. Once the list of examples is known (the stimulus situations), the correct responses to each of the stimulus situations are identified (entering the room, walking to the desk, sitting down, answering roll call, locating classroom materials—notepads, pencils, books, or art supplies—cleaning the area at the

TABLE 29.1   Model for Teaching Self-Instruction Using Multiple Exemplars

1. *Step 1: Select an array of examples*

   a. Survey setting
   b. Determine range of situations (stimuli) that student is likely to encounter
   c. Determine the correct responses to stimuli
   d. Select representative examples

2. *Step 2: Classify examples into teaching sets*

   a. Conduct traditional functional analysis of response requirements
   b. Determine similarity among responses based on functional analysis
   c. Classify related responses into teaching sets based on common operations

3. *Step 3: Divide members of set into training and generalization probes*

   a. Equally divide members of each testing set
   b. Assign members to groups of responses to be trained or to serve as generalization probes (assignment should be random)

4. *Step 4: Teach self-instruction*

   a. Conduct training sequence
      i. Teacher provides rationale
      ii. Teacher models correct responses while self-instructing aloud
      iii. Student performs same responses while teacher instructs aloud
      iv. Student performs same responses while self-instructing aloud
      v. Teacher provides corrective feedback and/or prompting if student does not perform approximation of correct verbal or motor responses
      vi. Teacher reminds student to self-instruct when presented with a problem situation
   b. Teach self-instruction statements
      i. Statement of problem (e.g., "Where do I go?")
      ii. Statement of generic problem-solving response (e.g., "Go to class")
      iii. Statement of self-report (e.g., "I'm here")
      iv. Statement of self-reinforcement (e.g., "good job")
   c. Adjust training time
      i. Determine student's ability level
      ii. Adjust number and length of instructional sessions to student's ability level

5. *Step 5: Evaluate effect of instruction*

   a. Take measures of verbalized self-instruction steps and responses to multiple examples made during training
   b. Take measures of verbalized self-instruction steps and responses to multiple examples made during performance
   c. Take measures of responses to untrained problems (generalization probes)

6. *Step 6: Withdraw training*

   a. Establish acceptable performance criteria
   b. Assess generalization over time (response maintenance of problem-solving strategy)

end of the period, putting things away, and departing the classroom). These representative examples (multiple examples) serve as potential teaching sets.

STEP 2: CLASSIFYING MULTIPLE EXAMPLES INTO TEACHING SETS BASED UPON A FUNCTIONAL ANALYSIS

Identifying responses to specific stimulus situations (examples) requires a traditional functional analysis to determine which response operations are needed to produce an effect on the environment. Using traditional functional analysis, you may determine if the responses required to complete a task successfully are similar and can therefore be classified into teaching sets. Examples include entering the room, walking to a desk, sitting down, answering roll call, and finding classroom materials. Once the responses have been identified, they need to be categorized into teaching sets. For example, entering different classrooms, choosing different desks, and answering different roll calls comprise three different teaching sets.

STEP 3: DIVIDING MEMBERS OF EACH TEACHING SET INTO SEPARATE RESPONSE GROUPS

The third step of the cognitive strategy requires dividing members of each teaching set into responses that will serve as the training examples and those that will serve as the generalization probes. The skills to be taught are selected based on situations that students are likely to experience throughout the transitions in the school day. Responses to these situations are then assigned to functionally related teaching situations, including entering classrooms, walking to appropriate desks, sitting in a desk or chair, responding to attendance cues, locating materials, cleaning up the area, and leaving the classroom.

Members of each set are randomly assigned for training or generalization probes. The generalization probes serve to illustrate the extent to which the desired responses have been learned. It is critical to generalization for the novel situations to be similar to the situations to which the student is introduced during training (Stokes & Baer, 1977). Such similarity is important because it produces similar responding in both training and nontraining conditions. For example, the student may be instructed to enter two of the five classrooms, with three of the classrooms serving to evaluate generalized learning.

STEP 4: TEACHING SELF-INSTRUCTION USING TRAINING EXAMPLES

Self-instruction is designed to promote students' ability to guide their own responses to stimulus situations by stating verbal prompts. (Note that a student who is nonverbal may demonstrate self-instruction by using picture prompts, drawings, charts, and page turning [Copeland & Hughes, 2000; Gifford, Rusch, Martin, & White, 1984]. Self-instruction is taught by transferring teacher-produced verbal responses to the picture prompt with the student using the nonverbal prompt.) The student is able to gain independence in tasks because the prompting is reliant on internal rather than external cues (Hughes, 1992).

The success of self-instruction is related to three factors: (1) training sequence used, (2) self-

instructional statements (or visual cues) taught, and (3) length of training time (Rusch et al., 1995).

Conduct Training Sequence

The teacher provides a rationale for training, which he or she follows by modeling the correct response and self-instructing aloud using the training examples with the student. The student is then required to execute the same responses while the teacher instructs aloud. Opportunities are provided for practice, with the student performing the same responses while self-instructing aloud. The modeling and self-instructional strategies can be used with a student who is nonverbal by using a pointer, a page-turning device, or a checklist (Garff & Storey, 1998). Next, the teacher provides corrective feedback and/or additional prompting if the student does not execute the correct verbal or physical response. Finally, the teacher provides prompts to remind the student to self-instruct when presented with a new stimulus (Hughes, Hugo, & Blatt, 1996).

Teach Self-Instructional Statements

The actual verbal statements are used with the training examples. The verbal statements include (1) verbalization of the problem (e.g., "Where do I go?"); (2) a statement of the generic problem-solving response (e.g., "Go to class"); (3) a statement of self-report (e.g., "I'm here"); and (4) verbalization of self-reinforcement (e.g., "good job"). Another example of self-instructional statements is demonstrated by the student locating classroom materials: (1) verbalization of the problem (e.g., "What do I need?"); (2) a statement of the generic problem-solving response (e.g., "I need notebook, pencil, and book."); (3) a statement of self-report (e.g., "I have my materials"); and (4) verbalization of self-reinforcement (e.g., "good job.").

Adjust Length of Training Time

Students' self-instruction ability will dictate the number and length of instructional sessions required to teach self-instruction. To teach the student to use either a picture prompt or his or her own verbal behavior (Copeland & Hughes, 2000), we recommend that two examples of the stimulus situation be used prior to teaching. For example, we recommend teaching self-instructional statements while teaching the student to clean up two different work areas.

STEP 5: EVALUATE THE EFFECTS OF INSTRUCTION ON TRAINING AND NONTRAINING EXAMPLES

The student needs to evaluate his or her response by making a decision about the acceptability of that response and adjusting future responses accordingly. Self-evaluation is a critical component in successful acquisition of the self-instructional strategy. This evaluation places students in control of their present and future responses by teaching them to use internal cues rather than relying upon external cues provided by a teacher or employer for a job well done (Grossi & Heward, 1998). Teachers need to evaluate the four self-instruction verbalizations previously mentioned.

STEP 6: WITHDRAW TRAINING

When to withdraw training is determined by correct responses to untrained stimulus situations. That is, the student must make correct responses to new stimulus situations in settings where training did not occur before training can be withdrawn. For example, if five different situations represent "entering a room" and two of them are used for training, the remaining three examples are used to evaluate generalized learning of the cognitive strategy.

CONCLUSION

Generalized learning has been a fairly elusive, yet desired, outcome in education, especially for children and youths with disabilities. That we have demonstrated this population's ability to learn a specific task cannot be disputed—countless published books and articles attest to our ability to teach simple and complex responses. Teaching students to respond correctly outside the demands of specific instructional settings has not been as successful, however. In part, our failure to teach generalization may be due to our teaching approach, which typically intertwines the ability to learn a new response with invaluable teacher-provided external mediation (verbal and nonverbal). In this chapter, we suggest combining a proven behavioral approach with emerging strategies that rely upon guiding and reinforcing one's own behavior. Further, the approach requires that we select responses that are desired and teach them using more than one example to promote students' learning in diverse situations.

References

Copeland, S. R., & Hughes, C. (2000). Acquisition of a picture prompt strategy to increase independent performance. *Education and Training in Mental Retardation and Developmental Disabilities, 35,* 294–305.

Garff, J. T., & Storey, K. (1998). The use of self-management strategies for increasing the appropriate hygiene of persons with disabilities in supported employment setting. *Education and Training in Mental Retardation and Developmental Disabilities, 33,* 179–188.

Gifford, J. L., Rusch, F. R., Martin, J. E., & White, D. M. (1984). Autonomy and adaptability: A proposed technology for the study of work behavior. In N. R. Ellis & N. R. Bray (Eds.), *International review of research in mental retardation* (Vol. 12, pp. 285–318). New York: Academic Press.

Grossi, T. A., & Heward, W. L. (1998). Using self-evaluation to improve the work productivity in trainees in a community-based restaurant training program. *Education and Training in Mental Retardation and Developmental Disabilities, 33,* 248–263.

Horner, R. H., Jones, D. N., & Williams, J. A. (1985). General case programming for community activities. In B. Wilcox & G. T. Bellamy (Eds.), *Design of high school programs for severely handicapped students* (pp. 61–98). Baltimore: Paul H. Brookes.

Hughes, C. (1992). Teaching self-instruction utilizing multiple exemplars to produce generalized problem solving among individuals with severe mental retardation. *American Journal on Mental Retardation, 97,* 302–314.

Hughes, C., & Rusch, F. R. (1989). Teaching supported employees with severe mental retardation to solve problems. *Journal of Applied Behavior Analysis, 22,* 365–372.

Hughes, C., Hugo, K., & Blatt, J. (1996). Self-instructional intervention for teaching generalized problem-solving within a functional task sequence. *American Journal on Mental Retardation, 100,* 565–579.

Rusch, F. R., & Chadsey, J. C. (1998). *Beyond high school: Transition from school to work.* Boston: Wadsworth Publishing.

Rusch, F. R., Hughes, C., & Wilson, P. G. (1995). Utilizing cognitive strategies in the acquisition of employment skills. In W. O'Donohue & L. Krasner (Eds.), *Handbook of psychological skills training clinical techniques and applications* (pp. 363–382). New York: Pergamon Press.

Stokes, T., & Baer, D. M. (1977). An implicit technology of generalization. *Journal of Applied Behavior Analysis, 13,* 119–128.

30 HABIT REVERSAL

Amanda Nicolson Adams, Mark A. Adams, and Raymond G. Miltenberger

Habit reversal (HR) was developed by Nathan Azrin and his colleagues in the early 1970s as a treatment for nervous habits and tics. An article appearing in *Behaviour Research & Therapy* (Azrin & Nunn, 1974) and reprinted in Rachman (1997) theorized that nervous habits persist because of response chaining, limited awareness, excessive practice, and social tolerance. Habit reversal was designed to counteract these influences. Prior to the development of HR, negative practice (i.e., numerous forced repetitions; developed by Knight Dunlap in the 1930s) was a popular and validated method of treating tic disorders. Although it was ahead of its time in 1930, inconsistent results following from its application led to a decrease in both research in and application of negative practice for habit treatment. Habit reversal is not only a more effective treatment for tic disorders, but it also has efficacy for the treatment of many other so-called nervous habits or habit disorders as well.

WHO MIGHT BENEFIT FROM THIS TECHNIQUE

Along with tic disorders (Clarke, Bray, Kehle, & Truscott, 2001; Woods & Miltenberger, 1995), trichotillomania, or chronic hair pulling, has emerged as a second primary application area for HR procedures (Diefenbach, Reitman, & Williamson, 2000; Elliot & Fuqua, 2000; Rapp, Miltenberger, Long, Elliott, & Lumley, 1998; Rothbaum & Ninan, 1999). In addition to these two prominent disorders, other repetitive behavior disorders have been successfully treated using HR (Woods & Miltenberger, 2001), including stuttering (de Kinkelder & Boelens, 1998; Wagaman, Miltenberger, & Arndorfer, 1993; Woods, Fuqua, & Waltz, 1997), nail biting (Woods et al., 2001), oral habits such as lip or mouth biting and teeth grinding (Azrin, Nunn, & Frantz-Renshaw, 1982), oral-digital habits or thumb sucking (Woods et al., 1999; Long, Miltenberger, Ellingson, & Ott, 1999), pica (Woods et al., 1996), scratching (Rosenbaum & Ayllon, 1981), chronic skin-picking (Twohig & Woods, 2001b), self-choking (Higa, Chorpita, & Yim, 2001), social incompetence (Anderson & Allen, 2000), chronic facial pain including chronic headaches (Townsend, 2000), self-biting (Jones, Swearer, & Friman, 1997), and disruptive outbursts (Allen, 1998). In sum, there are data-based evaluations of HR treatment for tic disorders and a wide variety of habit behaviors or repetitive behavior disorders, as indicated here. Although not intended as an exhaustive list of behaviors treated using HR, this list speaks to the vast scope of applications for this technique.

CONTRAINDICATIONS OF THE TREATMENT

Habit reversal does not seem contraindicated for most people. There are some situations, however, that may present limitations. Applications of HR that include a pretreatment functional analysis component have recently appeared in the literature. It is interesting, but not surprising, to find that behaviors shown to be controlled by automatic reinforcement (i.e., self-stimulatory behaviors) tend to respond best to HR, whereas behaviors that function for escape, attention, or other social consequences respond less consistently to HR as treatment (Woods et al., 2001; Higa et al., 2001). Although this line of research is extremely limited in scope at this time, and the vast majority of studies show the effectiveness of HR independent of knowledge of behavioral function, this research does suggest that the function of the habit may be an important consideration when selecting a treatment for tics, habits, or repetitive behavior disorders.

Several studies have examined the particular components of HR. In one such study, Liberetto (1999) concluded that the competing response component seemed more effective than awareness training in the treatment of nail biting, and that increases in awareness seemed unrelated to treatment success. However, Wright and Miltenberger (1987) and Woods et al. (1996) found awareness training by itself to be an effective treatment for some individuals' tics. In what also could be considered a contrary finding, Long et al. (1999) found that limitations exist in the success of HR for individuals with mental retardation. Although the authors do not state that the inability to successfully train awareness was responsible for poor results with a developmentally delayed population, they found that more immediate and clear contingency procedures were needed. Nonetheless, different HR treatment components or other treatment procedures may be called for depending upon the client population, the particular habit being treated, and the function of the habit being treated.

HOW DOES THE TECHNIQUE WORK?

Azrin and Nunn (1974) developed HR with ten procedures grouped into four components: (1) motivation procedures, (2) awareness training, (3) competing response practice, and (4) generalization procedures. Relaxation training has been added as a component in a number of studies (Azrin & Nunn, 1974; Finney, Rapoff, Hall, & Christopherson, 1983). Given the multicomponent nature of HR, some research has focused on component analyses of HR (Miltenberger, Fuqua, & Woods, 1998; Twohig & Woods 2001a) and has implemented simplified procedures consisting of three steps: (1) awareness training, (2) competing response training, and (3) social support (Elliot, Miltenberger, Rapp, Long, & McDonald, 1998; Long, Miltenberger, & Rapp 1999; Rapp et al., 1998).

AWARENESS TRAINING

Awareness training involves extensive self-assessment to ensure that the client is aware of the individual responses that make up the habit and their environmental antecedents. Clients are asked to practice detecting the first signs of the particular behavior excess so that they will be able to stop the response early in the sequence.

COMPETING RESPONSE TRAINING

Clients practice performing a response that competes with the behavior excess. For example, a person who bites his or her nails may practice putting on hand lotion or squeezing a ball so that the hands are not available for nail biting. This response must be one that the client can sustain for several minutes, one that is compatible with everyday activities, and one that is inconspicuous to others.

Research on HR components has asserted that awareness training and competing response training (i.e., a planned, practiced alternate response) seem to be the critical components (Miltenberger & Fuqua, 1985; Miltenberger, Fuqua, & McKinley, 1985; Woods et al., 1996). Sharenow, Fuqua, and Miltenberger (1989) and Woods and colleagues (1999) have examined the competing response component by comparing a topographically similar response to a dissimilar competing response. Results were roughly comparable for the similar and dissimilar competing responses, leading to the possible conclusion that the competing response does not necessarily have to be a physically incompatible behavior.

MOTIVATION PROCEDURES

In an attempt to motivate the client to work at eliminating the habit, Azrin and Nunn (1974) used three procedures. First, they had clients review the inconveniences caused by the habit. Second, they enlisted significant others to provide social support, including reinforcement for using the competing response and refraining from engaging in the habit behavior. Third, they had the client publicly display control of the habit and solicit reinforcement from significant others.

GENERALIZATION PROCEDURES

The primary procedure used to enhance generalization was for the client to engage in symbolic rehearsal by imagining successful control of the habit in situations where the habit previously occurred. For example, one might imagine having to wait in line (an occasion that had previously prompted nail biting) and mentally rehearse engaging in alternative behaviors to nail biting.

STEP-BY-STEP PROCEDURES

Habit reversal is typically implemented in a small number of treatment sessions, which are followed by booster sessions as needed. The first session is devoted to assessment and the establishment of data collection. In the following sessions the therapist describes HR procedures and provides instructions for the client to use the procedures in the natural environment. (See Table 30.1 for the key elements of HR procedure.)

TABLE 30.1   Key Elements of Habit Reversal

1. Inconvenience review: Help the client see how the habit interferes with his or her life.
2. Awareness training: Make the client aware of each instance of the habit.
3. Competing response training: Teach the client to engage in one or more incompatible behaviors to replace the habit.
4. Social support: Involve the assistance of others to help the client use the competing response successfully.
5. Generalization procedure: Practice symbolic rehearsal and other steps to promote success in the client's everyday life.

Assessment and Data Collection

The therapist asks the client to describe the sequence of behaviors involved in each occurrence of the habit. For example, a client who engages in hair pulling might describe a sequence in which she strokes her hair, finds a strand, twirls it between her finger and thumb, reaches down to the root, pulls out the hair, looks at it, rubs it on her lips, and then drops it to the floor. The therapist also asks about antecedents and consequences related to the habit behavior to identify antecedents that may have stimulus control over the behavior and to determine whether any form of social reinforcement may be involved in the maintenance of the behavior. If the habit behavior serves a social function (e.g., the client receives attention for engaging in the habit), operant procedures may be used in place of, or in addition to, HR procedures. Information on antecedents is also valuable for proper use of HR procedures.

The therapist works with the client in the first session to develop a data collection plan. The client (or the parents in the case of a child) may record the occurrence of the habit behavior using frequency, duration, or time sample recording. For example, an adult may keep a simple tally of the number of times he bites his nail each day (frequency recording). Alternately, a parent may observe a child periodically while the child is studying or watching television and record whether hair pulling was observed during each observation (time sample recording). In addition to direct observation of the habit behavior, the client may record a permanent product of the habit behavior, such a nail length for a nail biter or number of hairs collected or the size of the depilated area for a hair puller.

Implementing Habit Reversal Components

Habit reversal procedures are implemented after the assessment and data collection plan are completed. Before implementing HR procedures, the therapist provides an overview of the procedures and a rationale for the treatment components.

Inconvenience Review

The purpose of this procedure is to have the client consider all of the ways in which the habit has caused inconvenience, embarrassment, or disruption in the client's life. After reviewing the various ways that the habit has had a negative impact on the client's life, the client may become more motivated to work at implementing the HR procedures. The therapist can conduct the inconvenience review by asking the client open-ended questions such as "How has your hair pulling caused difficulty in your life?" or "How has your hair pulling inconvenienced or embarrassed you?" The therapist may also use a checklist of possible negative consequences resulting from the habit. Keuthen, Stein, and Christenson (2001) developed a checklist for hair pullers that listed physical consequences (e.g., bald spots), emotional consequences (e.g., shame or embarrassment), economic consequences (e.g., cost of wigs), and interpersonal consequences (e.g., avoidance of intimate relationships). Whether the therapist uses open-ended questions or a checklist, the use of this procedure should help the client see the negative impact the habit has had and motivate the client to direct more substantial effort toward therapy.

Awareness Training

The goal of awareness training is for the client to become aware of each instance of the habit as it occurs and to become aware of antecedents to the habit. The client is told that he or she must be aware of each occurrence of the habit in order to be able to control the habit. Increased awareness is critical for the use of the competing response. The first step in awareness training is to have the client describe all of the behaviors involved in the occurrence of the habit (response description).

If they were clearly described in the initial interview, the therapist will review the information with the client at this time. The next step is response detection. For some target behaviors such as motor and vocal tics or stuttering the client is instructed to identify each occurrence of the habit in session. The therapist praises the client for detecting each instance of the habit and prompts the client when the client fails to identify an instance of the habit. With practice in session, the client should identify each occurrence of the habit behavior at close to 100% accuracy.

Some habit behaviors may not occur in session, such as nail biting, thumb sucking, hair pulling, and other nervous habits. For target behaviors such as these, the therapist asks the client to simulate the occurrence of the habit in session in order to facilitate awareness of the habit. The client attempts to simulate the sequence of behaviors involved in the habit exactly as the behaviors would occur in the natural environment. While the client is simulating the habit behavior, the therapist will tell the client to stop at various points in the sequence of behaviors and to notice how the behavior looks or feels in an attempt to enhance awareness. As the client is simulating the habit behavior, the client should also simulate the activities or situations during which the behavior occurs. For example, the client simulates sitting at a desk at school as he or she reaches up to pull his or her hair.

In addition to response description and detection procedures, the therapist will also help the client become more aware of antecedents to the habit, including overt environmental antecedents and covert antecedents. Questions about antecedents are asked in the first session and revisited during awareness training. Examples of overt antecedents may include specific activities, times of day, locations, or the client's own behavior. For example, hair stroking or twirling may be an antecedent to hair pulling. Children may be more likely to bite their nails when they are resting their faces on their hands while at their desks in school or while watching television. Covert antecedents may be relevant to a number of habit behaviors. For example, hair pulling may be more likely to occur when the client experiences tension or anxiety, and motor tics may be more likely to occur when the client experiences specific sensations in the area affected by the tic (e.g., itching, burning, tickling, etc.). Discussion of overt and covert antecedents should increase the client's awareness of the incipient occurrence of the habit in the natural environment. Such awareness should facilitate the proper use of the competing response.

Competing Response Training

The goal of competing response training is to teach the client to engage in one or more physically incompatible behaviors to replace the habit behavior. The client is told that he or she will learn to engage in a different behavior to replace the habit behavior and that with practice the new behavior will become a habit itself. The competing response should be inconspicuous, require little response effort, and compete physically with the habit. For a motor tic, the competing response would involve tensing the muscles involved in the tic. For a vocal tic, the competing response would involve diaphragmatic breathing with the mouth closed. For a hand-to-head habit such as hair pulling, nail biting, or thumb sucking, the competing response would involve an alternative use of the hand(s) such as clenching a fist, holding an object, folding the hands, sitting on the hands, putting hands in pockets, and so on. The client is instructed to engage in the competing response for about 1 minute contingent on the occurrence of the habit behavior or the antecedents to the habit behavior. In this way, the competing response will interrupt the habit or prevent its occurrence.

After providing a rationale for the use of the competing response, the therapist works with the client to choose a number of competing responses that the client could use in each of the situations in which the habit occurs. The client then practices the use of the competing responses in session. For habits that occur in session (e.g., tics, stuttering), the client uses the competing response immediately contingent on the occurrence of the habit or the antecedents to the habit. The therapist praises the client for proper use of the competing response and prompts the client to use the competing response if the client fails to do so at the appropriate time. Competing response practice should continue until the client is using the competing response consistently. For habits that do not occur in session, the therapist has the client simulate the habit behavior and practice the competing response. The client will simulate different situations in which the habit occurs and engage in the competing response contingent on the simulation of the habit. The therapist instructs the client to use the competing response when antecedents are present or early in the chain of behaviors so that the competing response prevents the occurrence of the habit.

Social Support

Social support involves the assistance of a significant other to help the client use the competing response successfully. A parent, a spouse, or a good friend may serve as the social support person. The social support person attends the treatment sessions and learns to assist the client in three ways. First, the social support person is told to praise the client for the absence of the habit in situations in which the habit typically occurs. Second, the support person is instructed to praise the client for using the competing response appropriately. Third, the support person is instructed to prompt the client to use the competing response when the habit occurs and the clients fails to use the competing response to control the habit. The social support person practices these three activities with the client in the presence of the therapist.

Generalization Procedures

A number of procedures are used to promote the use of the HR procedures outside of the session in the client's everyday life. First, the social support person provides prompts and reinforcement. Second, the client is instructed to engage in symbolic rehearsal in the session. The therapist has the client imagine using the competing response to successfully control the habit behavior in situations in which the habit behavior has been most likely to occur. Third, the therapist has the client enter into situations in which the habit has typically occurred, use the competing response, and solicit praise from the social support person. Fourth, the therapist gives specific instructions for the client and social support person to practice the use of the skills learned in session to control the habit in the natural environment. Practice in the natural environment may involve short daily practice sessions and the routine use of the procedures wherever and whenever the habit occurs.

Booster Sessions

Following the initial sessions during which the therapist describes the HR procedures to the client and instructs the client to use the procedures in the natural environment, the therapist will conduct a number of booster sessions as needed. In these sessions, the therapist reviews the data with the client to see if the habit behavior is decreasing and reviews the client's use of the treatment procedures. The therapist praises the client's efforts and discusses any difficulties the client may be having. In some cases, the initial treatment sessions and two or three booster sessions may be sufficient for success (e.g., Rapp et al., 1998). In other cases, a number of booster sessions may be needed to achieve success (e.g., Wagaman et al., 1993). Depending on the case, adjunct treatment procedures (including operant contingencies and other cognitive behavioral strategies) may be called for if the habit behavior is not decreasing as expected (e.g., Keuthen et al., 2001; Woods & Miltenberger, 2001).

Further Reading

Azrin, N. H., & Nunn, R. G. (1974). A rapid method of eliminating stuttering by a regulated breathing approach. *Behaviour Research and Therapy, 12,* 279–286.

Miltenberger, R., Fuqua, R.W., & Woods, D.W. (1998). Applying behavior analysis with clinical problems: Review and analysis of habit reversal. *Journal of Applied Behavior Analysis, 31,* 447–469.

Woods, D., & Miltenberger, R. (Eds.). (2001). *Tic disorders, trichotillomania, and other repetitive behavior disorders: Behavioral approaches to analysis and treatment.* Boston: Kluwer.

References

Allen, K. D. (1998). The use of an enhanced simplified habit-reversal procedure to reduce disruptive outbursts during athletic performance. *Journal of Applied Behavior Analysis, 31*(3), 489–492.

Anderson, C. M., & Allen, K. D. (2000). Making social competence a habit. *Cognitive & Behavioral Practice, 7*(2), 239–241.

Azrin, N. H., & Nunn, R. G. (1974). A rapid method of eliminating stuttering by a regulated breathing approach. *Behaviour Research and Therapy, 12,* 279–286.

Azrin, N. H., Nunn, R. G., & Frantz-Renshaw, S. E. (1982). Habit reversal versus negative practice treatment of self-destructive oral habits (biting, chewing, or licking of the lips, cheek, tongue, or palate). *Journal of Behavior Therapy and Experimental Psychiatry, 13,* 49–54.

Clarke, M. A., Bray, M. A., Kehle, T. J., & Truscott, S. D. (2001). A school-based intervention designed to reduce the frequency of tics in children with Tourette's syndrome. *School Psychology Review, 30*(1), 11–22.

De Kinkelder, M., & Boelens, H. (1998). Habit-reversal treatment for children's stuttering: Assessment in three settings. *Journal of Behavior Therapy & Experimental Psychiatry, 29*(3), 261–265.

Diefenbach, G. J., Reitman, D., & Williamson, D. A. (2000). Trichotillomania: A challenge to research and practice. *Clinical Psychology Review, 20*(3), 289–309.

Elliott, A. J., & Fuqua, R. W. (2000). Trichotillomania: Conceptualization, measurement, and treatment. *Behavior Therapy, 31,* 529–545.

Elliott, A. J., Miltenberger, R. G., Rapp, J. T., Long, E. S., & McDonald, R. (1998). Brief application of simplified habit reversal to treat stuttering in children. *Journal of Behavior Therapy & Experimental Psychiatry, 29*(4), 289–302.

Finney, J. W., Rapoff, M. A., Hall, C. L., & Christopherson, E. R. (1983). Replication and social validation of habit reversal treatment for tics. *Behavior Therapy, 14,* 116–126.

Higa, C. K., Chorpita, B. F., & Yim, L. M. (2001). Behavioral treatment of self-choking in a developmentally normal child. *Child & Family Behavior Therapy, 23*(2), 47–55.

Jones, K. M., Swearer, S. M., & Friman, P. C. (1997). Relax and try this instead: Abbreviated habit reversal for maladaptive self-biting. *Journal of Applied Behavior Analysis, 30*(4), 697–699.

Keuthen, N. J., Stein, D. J., & Christenson, G. A. (2001). *Help for hair pullers: Understanding and coping with trichotillomania.* Oakland, CA: New Harbinger.

Liberetto, S. V. (1999). Habit reversal treatment and nailbiting: Is awareness implicit in the competing response? *Dissertation Abstracts International, 60* (3-B), 1305.

Long, E. S., Miltenberger, R. G., Ellingson, S. A., & Ott, S. M. (1999). Augmenting simplified habit reversal in the treatment of oral-digit habits exhibited by individuals with mental retardation. *Journal of Applied Behavior Analysis, 32*(3), 353–365.

Long, E. S., Miltenberger, R. G., & Rapp, J. T. (1999). Simplified habit reversal plus adjunct contingencies in the treatment of thumb sucking and hair pulling in a young child. *Child & Family Behavior Therapy, 21*(4), 45–58.

Miltenberger, R., & Fuqua, W. (1985). Contingent vs. non-contingent competing response practice with nervous habits. *Journal of Behavior Therapy and Experimental Psychiatry, 16,* 195–200.

Miltenberger, R., Fuqua, W., & McKinley, T. (1985). Habit reversal with muscle tics: Replication and component analysis. *Behavior Therapy, 16,* 39–50.

Miltenberger, R., Fuqua, R. W., & Woods, D. W. (1998). Applying behavior analysis with clinical problems: Review and analysis of habit reversal. *Journal of Applied Behavior Analysis, 31,* 447–469.

Rachman, S. (Ed.) (1997). *Best of behavior research and therapy.* Amsterdam, The Netherlands: Pergamon/Elsevier Science.

Rapp, J., Miltenberger, R., Long, E., Elliott, A., & Lumley, V. (1998). Simplified habit reversal for chronic hair pulling in three adolescents: A clinical replication with direct observation. *Journal of Applied Behavior Analysis, 31,* 299–302.

Rosenbaum, M. S., & Ayllon, T. (1981). The behavioral treatment of neurodermatitis through habit reversal. *Behaviour Research and Therapy, 19,* 313–318.

Rothbaum, B. O., & Ninan, P. T. (1999). Manual for the cognitive-behavioral treatment of trichotillomania. In D. J. Stein, G. A. Christenson, et al. (Eds.), *Trichotillomania.* American Psychiatric Press.

Sharenow, E., Fuqua, R. W., & Miltenberger, R. (1989). The treatment of motor tics with dissimilar competing response practice. *Journal of Applied Behavior Analysis, 22,* 35–42.

Townsend, D. R. (2000). The use of a habit reversal treatment for chronic facial pain in a minimal therapist contact format. *Dissertation Abstracts International, 60*(12-B), 6387.

Twohig, M. P., & Woods, D. W. (2001a). Evaluating the duration of the competing response in habit reversal: A parametric analysis. *Journal of Applied Behavior Analysis, 34*(4), 517–520.

Twohig, M. P., & Woods, D. W. (2001b). Habit reversal as a treatment for chronic skin picking in typically developing adult male siblings. *Journal of Applied Behavior Analysis, 34*(2), 217–220.

Wagaman, J., Miltenberger, R., & Arndorfer, R. (1993). Analysis of a simplified treatment for stuttering in children. *Journal of Applied Behavior Analysis, 26,* 53–61.

Woods, D. W., Fuqua, R. W., Siah, A., Murray, L. K., Welch, M., Blackman, E., et al. (2001). Understanding habits: A preliminary investigation of nail biting function in children. *Education & Treatment of Children, 24*(2), 199–216.

Woods, D. W., Fuqua, R. W., & Waltz, T. J. (1997). Evaluation and elimination of an avoidance response in a child who stutters: A case study. *Journal of Fluency Disorders, 22*(4), 287–297.

Woods, D., & Miltenberger, R. (1995). Habit reversal: A review of applications and variations. *Journal of Behavior Therapy and Experimental Psychiatry, 26,* 123–131.

Woods, D., & Miltenberger, R. (Eds.). (2001). *Tic disorders, trichotillomania, and repetitive behavior disorders: Behavioral approaches to analysis and treatment.* Norwell, MA: Kluwer.

Woods, D., Miltenberger, R., & Lumley, V. (1996). Sequential application of major habit reversal components to treat motor tics in children. *Journal of Applied Behavior Analysis, 29,* 483–493.

Woods, D. W., Murray, L. K., Fuqua, R. W., Seif, T. A., Boyer, L. J., & Siah, A. (1999). Comparing the effectiveness of similar and dissimilar competing responses in evaluating the habit reversal treatment for oral-digital habits in children. *Journal of Behavior Therapy & Experimental Psychiatry, 30*(4), 289–300.

Wright, K., & Miltenberger, R. (1987). Awareness training in the treatment of head and facial tics. *Journal of Behavior Therapy and Experimental Psychiatry, 18,* 269–274.

31 HARM REDUCTION

Arthur W. Blume and G. Alan Marlatt

The principal goal of harm reduction is reduce the risk of harmful health consequences related to a targeted behavior. Unlike some behavior change strategies, the goal of harm reduction is not necessarily the extinction of the behavior (although it can be one of the goals) but instead the modification of the behavior in such a way as to reduce its risk to the person (Marlatt, 1998a).

Harm reduction strategies first developed in the area of addictive behaviors, for a couple of reasons. First, many substance-using clients felt marginalized by the strict abstinence requirements of traditional substance abuse treatment programs. Second, with the rapid spread of communicable and preventable diseases associated with substance use, such as HIV and hepatitis infection, it become critical to develop a new therapeutic approach that targeted the possible negative sequelae of substance use among those who were not willing or able to abstain (Marlatt, 1998b).

Although harm reduction often utilizes empirically supported cognitive behavioral strategies, some well-known harm reduction strategies are pharmacological. Methadone replacement as an alternative to heroin use may be the most common. The literature suggests that methadone replacement has been helpful in reducing the risks related to heroin usage in a very cost-effective way for many people over a number of years (Barnett, Zaric, & Brandeau, 2001; Yoast, Williams, Deitchman, & Champion, 2001).

More recently, other pharmacological harm reduction techniques have been used successfully in an effort to reduce the risks of substance abuse by controlling cravings (in an effort to reduce the amount used) or by reducing aversive consequences of other conditions to make substance use less attractive. Naltrexone and acamprosate may hold some promise for the reduction of cravings (Kranzier & Van Kirk, 2001). On the other hand, some pharmacological interventions may reduce the potential harm of substance use by reducing other comorbid aversive conditions. For instance, using medicines to control psychiatric symptoms or using therapeutic doses to properly medicate a person for pain may reduce specific factors that contribute to substance abuse via self-medication (Blume, Anderson, Fader, & Marlatt, 2001; Blume, Schmaling, & Marlatt, 2000).

Needle exchanges are perhaps the best-known nonpharmacological harm reduction programs and often use cognitive behavioral principles to modify injectable drug use behavior. Needle exchanges arose in order to reduce the risk of HIV and hepatitis infection among injectable drug users, who will often share syringes if unused or clean syringes are not easily accessible. With needle exchanges, clean syringes are distributed on the streets in easily accessible locations in neighborhoods of high substance use. The person using the injectable drugs is asked to trade used syringes for new ones, with the old syringes being properly disposed of to eliminate the possibility of reuse. At the exchanges, education is often provided on cleaning used syringes, and is accompanied by the distribution of condoms, another harm reduction technique. The use of needle exchanges has been shown to effectively reduce the spread of HIV and other communicable diseases (Gibson, 2001) and has been associated with ultimate reductions in substance use and increased treatment seeking in one study (Hagan et al., 2000); moreover, needle exchanges have been found to be very cost effective, since in terms of public money the cost of prevention is lower than the cost of treating HIV-positive patients (Kahn, 1998). Federal funding of needle exchanges has been recommended by a panel of scientists, but unfortunately the report has been ignored (Yoast et al., 2001).

WHO MIGHT BENEFIT FROM THIS TECHNIQUE

Harm reduction works well for people who are unable or unwilling to abstain from substances (Marlatt, 1998a) by reducing the consequences of a potentially risky behavior (e.g., Baer, Kivlahan, Blume, McKnight, & Marlatt, 2001; Hagan et al., 2000). Furthermore, harm reduction may be effective for those clients who have not done well with therapies that demand abstinence or cessation of the targeted behavior as a criterion for treatment (Marlatt, 1998a; Marlatt, Blume, & Parks, 2001), such as clients with co-occurring psychiatric disorders (Blume et al., 2001; Little, 2001) and clients who may have a history of multiple relapses (Marlatt et al., 2001). Harm reduction also works well in the secondary prevention of particular health problems when a person has already made the decision to engage in a particular behavior that has the capacity for harm (e.g., safe sex practices can reduce the potential for harm of high-risk sexual behavior).

CONTRAINDICATIONS OF THIS THERAPY

Harm reduction may not be the most appropriate choice if the person is willing and able to abstain from a potentially harmful behavior, such as substance abuse. Many people who use harm reduc-

tion therapy often believe that extinction of the target behavior may be a desirable ultimate goal for some clients and that harm reduction is a stepwise method for reaching that goal (e.g., Denning, 2001; Marlatt, 1998a). Furthermore, if harm reduction techniques have been unsuccessful in reducing risky behavior for a person, then other behavioral plans should be considered.

Finally, harm reduction relies upon a certain level of skills in the client. If those skills (e.g., cognitive skills) are not present, then self-directed harm reduction strategies should not be encouraged. However, for a great many people, any steps toward reducing the potential harmful consequences of a behavior would be in the client's best interest. In this context, harm reduction can be used with populations that are often underserved and excluded.

HOW DOES THE TECHNIQUE WORK?

The primary goal of harm reduction is to protect the client's health while respecting the goals for behavior change he or she has developed. In this respect, harm reduction is very client centered in its approach, with the client deciding what the goals of behavior change may be. The therapist is available to aid the client in reaching his or her goals for therapy by suggesting behavioral strategies for change and by encouraging the shaping of behavior in a way that validates client goals. Successive approximations toward reduced health risks are the measure of successful harm reduction therapy.

STEP-BY-STEP PROCEDURES

The following sections will elaborate on the procedures for harm reduction outlined in Table 31.1.

Step 1: Determination of Client's Behavior Change Goal

The first step is for the client and therapist to determine what the goals of the client are with regard to the target behavior. An assessment of personal motivation to change is made at that time, often utilizing the Transtheoretical Stages of

TABLE 31.1   Harm Reduction Step by Step

1. Determine the client's goal for behavior change.
2. Assess the behavior chain of the client's target behavior.
3. Educate the client about the target behavior and its consequences.
4. Develop a consensus with the client about the type of intervention strategies .
5. Provide continued assessment and, where necessary, reevaluation of goals and strategies.
6. Teach maintenance strategies.

Change Model (Prochaska & DiClemente, 1982). The therapist may decide to use motivational interviewing strategies (Miller & Rollnick, 2002) to enhance commitment to behavioral goals or to investigate whether the client is willing to change other behavior that the therapist perceives to be risky. Prompting the client to discuss the pros and cons of change versus no change may be utilized to enhance motivation to change. The therapist also may wish to mention potential health risks in a disarming fashion by sharing what has happened to other people in situations similar to that of the client, and then asking the client what he or she may think about those risks and if the client has concerns about specific aversive consequences of his or her behavior.

Step 2: Self-Monitoring and Other Assessment of Target Behavior Chain

The next step is to encourage behavioral monitoring via either self-monitoring forms or diaries in order to assess current behavior patterns. Monitoring will provide both the therapist and client with data concerning risky behavioral practices and will suggest points of intervention in behavior chains for the therapist. For example, among people abusing substances, self-monitoring is a very effective strategy to help them understand the scope and relationship of problems with the substance use. Clients keep daily diaries of time, type, amount, cues to use substances, and consequences of substance use, which can be quite helpful in clarifying what the change strategies and goals of modification should be (Blume et al., 2001; Dimeff, Baer, Kivlahan, & Marlatt, 1999). Assessment of a person's behavior and its

consequences via standardized measures with social norms also may be fruitful if the opportunity for such assessment exists. Assessment also allows clients to objectively reflect upon the consequences of substance use. Some research has found that assessment alone (without feedback) may contribute to reductions in substance use, presumably by increasing awareness of the desirability for behavior change through exploration of personal concerns about substance use (e.g., Miller, 1999). There are data that suggest that some people are unaware that their behavior deviates significantly from social norms, and providing evidence of this deviation can sometimes enhance contemplation of behavior change (e.g., Miller, Zweben, DiClemente, & Rychtarik, 1999).

Step 3: Education about the Target Behavior and Its Consequences

The next step is to educate the person about the potential consequences of the risky behavior. Education may include exposure to new information about the targeted behavior and its consequences, and challenges to positive expectancies and myths associated with the targeted behavior (Dimeff et al., 1999). For example, in the case of risky drinking behavior, a therapist may wish to challenge positive alcohol expectancies by walking a person through an episode of drinking, from first drink to the consequences of withdrawal. For high-risk sex, a therapist may wish to challenge the "that won't happen to me" myth with data related to infection rates.

Step 4: Agreed-upon Intervention Strategies

The client and the therapist develop a behavior modification plan utilizing agreed-upon strategies developed specifically to aid the client to reach his or her goals for behavior change, and the client begins to act upon the plan. During this time, the therapist uses sessions to reinforce successive approximations toward reduced health risks by the client. Several harm reduction strategies have been developed for substance use modification, and these techniques would be applicable for non-substance-related harm reduction as well.

Switching

An effective method for reducing the harm related to a target behavior is to have the client switch to a less harmful alternative behavior. For example, a therapist may suggest that someone who is attempting to reduce harmful substance use switch to a less harmful substance or alternate what he or she typically uses with something less harmful. One example of the former method would be to encourage beer drinkers to switch from high-alcohol-content beer to a less potent beer. In another example, switching people from harder drugs to marijuana has been used successfully in European countries to reduce the harmful consequences of substance abuse (Marlatt, 1998b). Alternating an alcoholic beverage with a nonalcoholic beverage, or eating while drinking, can effectively slow the rate of alcohol consumption.

Tapering

Tapering is a very important harm reduction strategy: A taper often begins with either alternating or switching to safer alternatives. Tapering involves setting goals for successive approximations toward cessation of the behavior. One strategy that may encourage tapering is to limit access. For example, therapists may find it helpful to have heavy-drinking clients buy less alcohol at a time and keep less on hand, rather than stocking up, in order to make it less convenient to engage in the target behavior. Furthermore, harm reduction emphasizes the practice of moderately engaging in the targeted behavior. Using substance use as an example, emphasizing that tolerance actually diminishes the positive effects of substance use is quite a powerful motivation for moderating use.

Pharmacotherapy

As previously mentioned, pharmacotherapy can be a particularly helpful harm reduction intervention. Pharmacotherapy can be used to help people in the tapering process by alleviating other uncomfortable symptoms (e.g., anxiety or depression). Furthermore, especially with consideration to clients who abuse substances, clients can be taught to improve nutritional habits (for example, by ingesting more thiamine), as well as to avoid potentially harmful over-the-counter medication (e.g., acetaminophen use combined with heavy drinking can harm the liver).

Structuring Time

If people engage in activities that are incompatible with the targeted behavior, then there is less potential to experience aversive consequences. We have found it important to encourage and offer access to exciting, interesting, and challenging alternative activities that diminish available free time in which to use substances. It is important to help clients fill their days with non-using structured activities. Furthermore, if clients choose to use, they should be taught where and when to do so more safely. Many research studies have shown that people are more likely to overdose in unfamiliar surroundings or when using unfamiliar substances, especially when they are alone. Harm reduction teaches clients to be smart and safe when using—to use familiar substances in familiar surroundings with familiar people who can provide help in case of emergency (e.g., drug overdose).

Distress Management

Other effective harm reduction strategies may address distress that occurs as a result of either engaging in or being on an extinction schedule for the targeted behavior. Distress management skills may include urge surfing (see Chapter 67 in this volume) and other distress tolerance strategies (Linehan, 1993; Marlatt, 1985), and meditation (Marlatt & Kristeller, 1999). Each of these strategies emphasizes that discomfort is transitory and that observing may be more useful than attempting to control the distress.

Trial Cessation

One interesting strategy is to ask a client to engage upon a trial period of voluntarily ceasing the behavior. In the area of substance abuse, clients are often asked to have a trial period of abstinence (called *sobriety sampling*), which can be useful for both the client and the therapist in understanding the persistent nature of the habit. Also, from the harm reduction perspective, any period of abstinence may allow cognitive abilities to improve, increasing clients' abilities to make better choices.

Skills Training

A final strategy to reduce the harm of the targeted behavior is skills training. With this strategy, the client's skills are assessed to see if they seem to be at an appropriate level to make it likely that the client will reach his or her goals for behavior change. If not, then the therapist will provide skills training specifically related to the behavior modification goals of the client.

Step 5: Continued Behavior Monitoring and Reevaluation of Behavior Change Goals

Continued monitoring of behavior assesses whether the client's goals are being reached. During this step, the therapist and client use sessions to discuss progress, and the therapist may suggest strategy changes if needed. Reevaluation of goals regarding the targeted behavior can be performed by the client, and a new behavioral plan can be developed and implemented to reach the revised goals for the targeted behavior.

Step 6: Maintenance of Changes

The final step is to teach the client to use maintenance strategies when the behavior modification goals have been reached. Relapse prevention strategies may work well for maintaining the behavioral changes even if the goals are not extinction of the behavior (Larimer & Marlatt, 1990).

CONCLUSION

Harm reduction has been useful for behavior modification that may not have extinction as its goal, and it may serve as a first step toward extinction for some clients. Harm reduction is very pragmatic and utilizes many different empirically validated cognitive behavioral change strategies. The therapy often involves grassroots participation in which the consumers of mental health care offer input into what kinds of behavior change goals and strategies may work for them. Harm reduction has produced good results in helping people change their behavior, and has shown promise in other areas of health behavior change.

One of the strengths of this technique is its attention to the client's goals for seeking help, and its collaborative approach in the therapeutic process. Because of this, harm reduction shows great promise in helping people from underserved populations who often do not do well in conventional treatment. Harm reduction is able to serve more clients because it attempts to serve the needs of clients along a continuum of change rather than employing a black and white, all-or-nothing abstinence approach. In this way, harm reduction applies a public health rather than moralistic model of treatment.

Further Reading

Marlatt, G. A. (Ed.). (1998). *Harm reduction: Pragmatic strategies for managing high risk behaviors.* New York: Guilford Press.

Denning, P. (2000). *Practicing harm reduction psychotherapy: An alternative approach to addictions.* New York: Guilford Press.

References

Baer, J. S., Kivlahan, D. R., Blume, A. W., McKnight, P., & Marlatt, G. A. (2001). Brief intervention for heavy drinking college students: Four-year follow-up and natural history. *American Journal of Public Health, 91,* 1310–1316.

Barnett, P. G., Zaric, G. S., & Brandeau, M. L. (2001). The cost-effectiveness of buprenorphine maintenance therapy for opiate addiction in the United States. *Addictions, 96,* 1267–1278.

Blume, A. W., Anderson, B. K., Fader, J. S., & Marlatt, G. A. (2001). Harm reduction programs: Progress rather than perfection. In R. H. Coombs (Ed.), *Addiction recovery tools: A practical handbook* (pp. 367–382). Thousand Oaks, CA: Sage Publications.

Blume, A. W., Schmaling, K. B., & Marlatt, G. A. (2000). Revisiting the self-medication hypothesis from a behavioral perspective. *Cognitive and Behavioral Practice, 7,* 379–384.

Denning, P. (2001). Strategies for implementation of harm reduction in treatment settings. *Journal of Psychoactive Drugs, 33,* 23–26.

Dimeff, L. A., Baer, J. S., Kivlahan, D. R., & Marlatt, G. A. (1999). *Brief alcohol screening and intervention for college students (BASICS): A harm reduction approach.* New York: Guilford Press.

Gibson, D. R. (2001). Effectiveness of syringe exchange

programs in reducing HIV risk behavior and HIV seroconversion among injecting drug users. *AIDS, 15*, 1329–1341.

Hagan, H., McGough, J. P., Thiede, H., Hopkins, S., Duchin, J., & Alexander, E. R. (2000). Reduced injection frequency and increased entry and retention in drug treatment associated with needle-exchange participants in Seattle drug injectors. *Journal of Substance Abuse Treatment, 19*, 247–252.

Kahn, J. G. (1998). Economic evaluation of primary HIV prevention in injection drug users. In D. R. Holtgrave (Ed.), *Handbook of economic evaluation of HIV prevention program, AIDS prevention, and mental health* (pp. 45–62). New York: Plenum Press.

Kranzier, H. R., & Van Kirk, J. (2001). Efficacy of naltrexone and acamprosate for alcoholism treatment: A meta-analysis. *Alcoholism: Clinical and Experimental Research, 25*, 1335–1341.

Larimer, M. E., & Marlatt, G. A. (1990). Applications of relapse prevention with moderation goals. *Journal of Psychoactive Drugs, 22*, 189–195.

Linehan, M. M. (1993). *Skills training manual for treating Borderline Personality Disorder.* New York: Guilford Press.

Little, J. (2001). Treatment of dually diagnosed clients. *Journal of Psychoactive Drugs, 33*, 27–31.

Marlatt, G. A. (1985). Cognitive assessment and intervention procedures for relapse prevention. In G. A. Marlatt & J. R. Gordon (Eds.), *Relapse prevention: Maintenance strategies in the treatment of addictive behaviors* (pp. 3–70). New York: Guilford Press.

Marlatt, G. A. (1998a). Basic principles and strategies of harm reduction. In G. A. Marlatt (Ed.), *Harm reduction: Pragmatic strategies for managing high risk behaviors* (pp. 49–66). New York: Guilford Press.

Marlatt, G. A. (1998b). Harm reduction around the world: A brief history. In G. A. Marlatt (Ed.), *Harm reduction: Pragmatic strategies for managing high risk behaviors* (pp. 30–48). New York: Guilford Press.

Marlatt, G. A., Blume, A. W., & Parks, G. A. (2001). Integrating harm reduction therapy and traditional substance abuse treatment. *Journal of Psychoactive Drugs, 33*, 13–21.

Marlatt, G. A., & Kristeller, J. (1999). Mindfulness and meditation. In W. R. Miller (Ed.), *Integrating spirituality into treatment* (pp. 67–84). Washington, DC: American Psychological Association.

Miller, E. T. (1999). *Preventing alcohol abuse and alcohol-related negative consequences among freshmen college students: Using emerging computer technology to deliver and evaluate the effectiveness of brief intervention efforts.* Unpublished doctoral dissertation, University of Washington, Seattle.

Miller, W. R., & Rollnick, S. (2002). *Motivational interviewing* (2nd ed.). New York: Guilford Press.

Miller, W. R., Zweben, A., DiClemente, C. C., & Rychtarik, R. G. (1999). *Motivational enhancement therapy manual: A clinical research guide for therapists treating individual with alcohol abuse and dependence* (Project MATCH Monograph Series, Vol. 2). Rockville, MD: National Institute on Alcohol Abuse and Alcoholism.

Prochaska, J. O., & DiClemente, C. C. (1982). Transtheoretical therapy: Toward a more integrative model of change. *Psychotherapy: Theory, Research, and Practice, 19*, 276–288.

Yoast, R., Williams, M. A., Deitchman, S. D., & Champion, H. C. (2001). Report of the Council on Scientific Affairs: Methadone maintenance and needle-exchange programs to reduce the medical and public health consequences of drug abuse. *Journal of Addictive Diseases, 20*, 15–40.

32 HOMEWORK IN COGNITIVE BEHAVIOR THERAPY

Patricia Robinson

Homework has been described as "the most generic of behavioral interventions" (Goisman, 1985, p. 676). Use of homework in psychotherapy was first documented in the literature over 60 years ago (Herzberg, 1941), and early developers of cognitive behavior therapy emphasized the importance of homework assignments (Beck, Rush, Shaw, & Emery, 1979). Shelton and Levy (1981) published a manual describing a systematic approach to use of homework in clinical practice that has been available for decades. Contemporary writers continue to emphasize homework in formulations of cognitive behavior therapy (Alford & Beck, 1994; Hollon & Beck, 1994) and to specify homework assignments in manualized, empirically supported treatments for specific disorders, such as Panic Disorder and Generalized Anxiety Disorder (Barlow & Craske, 1989; Craske, Barlow, & O'Leary, 1992). Homework is identified as an important treatment component in marital and family therapy (Carr, 1997; Hansen & MacMillan, 1990), solution-focused therapy (Beyebach, Morejon, Palenzuela, & Rodriguez-Arias, 1996), and addiction treatment (Annis, Schober, & Kelly, 1996), among many others.

Recently collected survey data suggest that most psychologists report (1) using homework in some, but not all, sessions and (2) employing a systematic approach to homework about a quarter of the time. Kazantzis and Deane (1999) found that 98% of a group of 221 New Zealand practicing psychologists used homework assignments. Within this group, cognitive behavioral therapists, in comparison with therapists practicing other models of treatment, were significantly more likely to use homework activities involving explicit recording (53% vs. 36%) and to recommend homework in more sessions (66% of sessions vs. 57%). Of concern is this survey's finding that that only one in four reported use of a systematic approach to homework, such as was recommended by Shelton and Levy (1981).

Given today's managed care context, therapists are probably more likely to use homework more often and more consistently when such use improves the rapidity and clinical effectiveness of treatment. It is likely that exposure to these desirable contingencies is enhanced when therapists take a systematic approach to homework. A systematic approach to homework includes (1) specification of the location and length of the homework assignment, (2) provision of a written note for the patient concerning the homework plan, and (3) completion of a written note in the treatment record indicating the extent or quality of homework completion for each session (Shelton & Levy, 1981). A step-by-step guide within such a systematic approach will be offered in this chapter.

EVIDENCE FOR EFFECTIVENESS OF HOMEWORK

In 1941, Herzberg reported that "short treatment of neuroses by graduated tasks" was effective with approximately 60% of his client sample (Herzberg, 1941). Studies have suggested a positive correlation between homework adherence and treatment outcome (Burns & Auerbach, 1992; Burns & Nolen-Hoeksema, 1991; Leung & Heimberg, 1996), and, most recently, a causal link between homework and outcome has been suggested in a study in which Burns and Spangler (2000) use structural equation modeling with a large group of clients. They report effect sizes in their two client samples that are similar in magnitude to those reported by Persons, Burns, and Perloff (1988). Persons and her colleagues found a mean reduction in Beck Depression Inventory scores of 16.6 points for patients who did homework in comparison to a 2.4 point reduction for patients who did little or no homework. An effect size of this magnitude is of a sufficient size to lead to nearly complete elimination of symptoms for patients with mild to moderate levels of depression.

Several studies indicate that completion of homework supports the maintenance of gains after treatment completion. Edelman and Chambless (1995) evaluated the relationship of homework completion and long-term change among social phobic clients in a cognitive behavioral group treatment. At the 6-month follow-up, clients who adhered more to homework instructions reported less anxiety during a behavioral task, greater decrements in anxiety, and more change in avoidant behavior. Thompson and Gallagher (1984) also found that homework during the later phase of treatment helped older depressed adults maintain gains following completion of treatment.

Future studies will need to identify the type of homework that actually leads to clinical improvement. Available information suggests that patients may be more likely to adhere when they are allowed to participate actively in the formulation of the plan. In a trial of two approaches to teaching parenting skills, participants in the coping modeling problem-solving group completed more homework and rated the program more

highly than participants in the master modeling approach (Cunningham, Davis, Bremner, & Dunn, 1993). Additionally, patient acceptance of treatment rationale, in addition to homework compliance, has been found to make an independent contribution to treatment outcome (Addis & Jacobson, 2000). It appears that collaborative development and providing an acceptable rationale for treatment and related homework are critical components of homework assignments that lead to clinical improvements.

HOW DOES THE TECHNIQUE WORK?

The causal structure that accounts for the positive association between homework compliance and degree of improvement is not understood. In the case of depression, Burns and Spangler (2000) have suggested four possibilities: (1) Homework has positive causal effects on changes in depression; (2) depression influences the amount of homework completed between sessions; (3) a positive feedback loop exists in which homework assignments lead to improvement in depression, and the uplift in mood increases the likelihood of homework compliance; or (4) homework compliance is only spuriously correlated with depression because of an unknown third variable with simultaneous casual effects on homework compliance and depression. In their study (Burns & Spangler, 2000) homework compliance had a causal effect on changes in depression, and the magnitude of this effect was large. Patients who did the most homework improved much more than patients who did little or no homework. Homework compliance did not appear to be a proxy for any other, unobserved variable, such as motivation.

WHO MIGHT BENEFIT FROM HOMEWORK ASSIGNMENTS

Homework provides critical information for the therapist and client to use in formulating and evaluating change plans, as well as opportunities for the client to practice new skills introduced in treatment sessions. Therefore, treatment outcome is presumably very closely linked to consistent development of high-quality homework and client and therapist adherence. Available literature suggests that depressed patients benefit from homework assignments (Burns & Nolen-Hoeksema, 1991; Persons et al., 1988; Neimeyer & Feixas, 1990; Startup & Edmonds, 1994; Addis & Jacobson, 2000; Burns & Spangler, 2000). Additionally, homework compliance has been related to a positive treatment outcome with social phobia (Leung & Heimberg, 1996) and agoraphobic men and women (Edelman & Chambless, 1993). The relative contribution of homework to treatment outcome has not been established for other disorders. Survey data suggest that 80% of psychologists believe homework is of great importance in the treatment of anxiety, nonassertiveness, and social skills, and 65% see homework as being of great importance in the treatment of depression, anxiety disorders, insomnia, obsessions and compulsions, and sexual dysfunction (Kazantzis & Deane, 1999). Data from the same survey suggest that 50% see homework being as of little or moderate importance for treatment of delusions and hallucinations, learning disorders, and sexual abuse.

Since there are many reports of the success of homework, and only speculations to the contrary it seems possible that the vast majority of patients benefit from completion of well-developed homework assignments. Critical issues for developing beneficial homework assignments include (1) accurate evaluation of the client's readiness for change, (2) the quality of the therapeutic alliance, (3) the level of collaboration in homework development, (4) the rationale given for homework, (5) the utilization of client strengths in formulation of the homework plan, and (6) the extent to which homework adherence is positively reinforced both inside and outside of the treatment session.

CONTRAINDICATIONS FOR HOMEWORK ASSIGNMENTS

Practitioners need to use homework systematically with almost all clients, but they should use it with caution with clients with cognitive and/or motivational deficits. Highly symptomatic clients with delusions and hallucinations may have

difficulty with written homework tasks (Nelson, 1997). This is because many of these patients may be unwilling or unable to complete written homework assignments and because they find it difficult to work at the abstract level of thinking about thinking. However, some of these clients may benefit from homework assignments involving completion of practical tasks between sessions and reporting back to the therapist from memory (Chadwick, Birchwood, & Trower, 1996). Obesity treatment clients who fail to comply with self-monitoring instructions at the beginning of therapy have been observed to be likely to fail to lose weight (Wadden & Letizia, 1992). Clinical experience suggests that obesity treatment clients who continue to not complete self-monitoring assignments despite the therapist's best efforts to collaborate, provide a rationale for self-monitoring, and positively reinforce any approximation toward completion of self-monitoring assignments do not do well in treatment (Wilson & Vitousek, 1999). This may be the case with clients with other complaints who do not intend to make a change within the next 6 months. Prochaska and DiClemente (1983) have proposed a Transtheoretical Model that applies to intentional change and individual decision making about health behavior, and this approach is often useful with less motivated psychotherapy clients. This model suggests specific strategies for working with clients to help them move from the precontemplation stage to the action stage of change (Prochaska, 1994). Miller and Rollnick (1991), developers of motivational interviewing, also offer ideas for working successfully with clients who are in the contemplation stage of change (see Chapter 38, this volume).

OTHER FACTORS IN DECIDING TO USE OR NOT TO USE HOMEWORK

If a client fails to adhere to a homework assignment, the therapist needs to avoid repeating assignment of the same homework and should share responsibility for the adherence failure. The therapist is the expert on behavior change and, hence, has ultimate responsibility for the feasibility of assigned homework. When a client fails to implement a homework plan, the therapist needs to take time to identify the specific obstacles to implementation and to address these thoughtfully in a new homework assignment. When motivation for change is lacking, the therapist will need to accommodate the willingness level of the patient and plan homework consistent with that level. It is important to scale client confidence in a homework plan developed immediately after a failed homework plan. This can be accomplished by asking the client to rate his or her confidence on a scale of 1 (no confidence) to 10 (total confidence). When client confidence is less than total, the therapist may want to revise the plan and/or offer additional support to the client. The therapist's offer of a brief phone call check-in may inspire more client confidence, particularly after a failed homework assignment. For the vast majority of client contacts, the therapist will develop homework assignments that are adjusted to the patient's level of organization and motivation and that are supported optimally by the client's social network, the client's own self-reinforcement plan, and/or the therapist.

STEP-BY-STEP PROCEDURES FOR USING HOMEWORK

Although homework is a potentially beneficial part of cognitive behavioral treatment with most disorders and in all phases, homework assignments are more likely to contribute to client improvement when they match the demands of the phase of treatment and are sensitive to process-of-care factors. Table 32.1 offers a conceptual

structure for systematic use of homework in cognitive behavior therapy. In Table 32.2, there are 12 questions that therapists can use as a quality check on homework. Applying these questions with one new client each week will help therapists become more systematic in developing and evaluating homework in their practice setting. In the initial contact, the most common assignment will involve some form of self-monitoring. Self-monitoring is the act of tracking the frequency, intensity, or duration of a clinical target behavior and recording this information in some type of written record. The process-of-care factor that is most critical in determining the success of self-monitoring assignments is the client's level of motivation for change. During the behavior change phase of treatment, self-efficacy and skills are important factors in homework design. Finally, the relationship of homework assignments to client values merits focus in tailoring homework assignments for the maintenance phase of treatment. Although all three of the suggested process-of-care variables may play a critical role at any phase of treatment, they are often more salient at the treatment phase suggested earlier and indicated in Table 32.1.

The M&Ms of Monitoring Assignments: Initial Homework Assignments

The M&Ms of monitoring assignments consist of (1) motivation for change and (2) monitoring method selection. Client level of motivation can change significantly even within a single session. A homework assignment that permits assess-

TABLE 32.1 Step-by-Step Procedures for Developing Homework Assignments

Phase of Treatment	Process-of-Care Target	Homework Target
Initial: the M&Ms of monitoring assignments	Motivation for change	Monitoring method selection
Middle: the six S's of successful behavior change assignments	Self-efficacy/strengths	• Soundness of rationale • Size and place of assignment • Skills required • Self-reinforcement • Support (social, therapist)
Conclusion: the four R's of effective maintenance assignments	Related to values	• Relapse prevention plans • Regular review • Revised to support lifestyle

TABLE 32.2   Questions to Use as a Quality Check for Use of Homework in Cognitive Behavioral Treatment

Phase of Treatment	Question
Initial	1. Does the client intend to change in the next 6 months?
	2. What is the most feasible method of self-monitoring?
Middle	3. What client strengths relate to the homework task, and how strong is the client's belief in his or her ability to complete the task?
	4. What are the client's beliefs about the cause of and solution for the problem?
	5. How much time will homework take, and where will it occur?
	6. What skills are required to implement the homework?
	7. What are the planned potential positive reinforcers for the homework assignment (self, others, therapist)?
	8. Is the homework plan in written form for the client (as a take-home) and for the therapist (in records)?
Conclusion	9. How are most beneficial homework tasks related to client values?
	10. What changes and/or new skills helped the client improve, how often and when will they continue to be performed, and who will support them?
	11. What is the emergency plan?
	12. How can the most beneficial homework assignments be integrated into the client's lifestyle?

ment of the level of motivation for change on an ongoing basis according to a structured method can open the door for later action-oriented psychotherapy. Of course, self-monitoring is at the heart of cognitive behavior therapy.

Motivation for Change

In introducing the concept of homework, the therapist may tell clients that research findings suggest that clients who commit themselves to developing and implementing homework assignments may experience significantly more benefit from treatment than patients who do little or no homework. The therapist can explain that most of the client's life happens between treatment sessions and that putting it on the street, so to speak, facilitates improvement.

Given encouragement, most clients will readily state their level of intention to change. When clients are sent to treatment by others, they may have not had the opportunity to sort out the pros and cons of behavior change. They may lack information about the options for change and the related benefits.

When a client indicates ambivalence, the therapist may offer assignments that increase the client's information level and/or help the client clarify costs and benefits of treatment at the present time. It is important to avoid strong-arming clients and to offer them a choice. This stance will help to keep the door open for treatment later.

Therapists may even offer phone call check-ins on a quarterly basis, particularly to patients at risk for poor outcomes. With this approach, there is the possibility that services will become available close to the time when the client's level of motivation increases. New models of care, such as the Primary Care Behavioral Health Model (Robinson, Wischman, & Del Vento, 1996; Strosahl, 1997) support strategic work with less motivated members of a population, because the mission of the model is to improve the health status of an entire population. In these therapeutic relationships, the client's homework is to participate in discussion of the pros and cons of change during quarterly telephone calls.

Monitoring Method Selection

Monitoring methods need to be feasible, meaning that the client has the necessary skills, time, and interest required to complete the monitoring. Many clients will have difficulties with monitoring assignments that require them to carry around workbooks or even large pieces of paper. A single half-sheet or a small pocket notebook (with the instructions written inside the cover) is often more feasible. Another option is to ask the client to record monitored information in his or her personal calendar, whether that is a monthly calendar in the bedroom, a daily appointment book, or a palm pilot. The nature of the monitoring assignment needs to be simple and straightforward, and the assignment should practiced in session, followed by a self-reinforcing activity, and acknowledged by the therapist in all follow-up sessions.

The Six S's of Successful Behavior Change Assignments: Homework in the Middle Phase

The six S's of successful behavior change homework assignments include self-efficacy/strengths, soundness of rationale, size of assignment, skills required, self-reinforcement, and support. In order for behavior change homework assignments to contribute their maximum impact to client improvement, both the therapist and client must be intentional and thorough in their development, implementation, and follow-up.

Self-Efficacy/Strengths

It is important to identify client strengths and to incorporate them into the homework assignment. Although this seems simple in principle, it can be deceptively difficult in practice. An example of working with a more challenging patient will illustrate this point. The client was a woman with substantial economic challenges, who reported moderate symptoms of depression, as well as marital, parent-child, occupational, and health problems. When asked, the client indicated that she had no strengths. When asked what brought her pleasure, she indicated that nothing brought her pleasure. When asked if she liked to go outside, she said that she did like to sit on the steps of her trailer, but that she often felt afraid there because neighbors of a different race had thrown rocks at her. Within a few minutes of questioning, the following homework assignment was developed: She would ask her 21-year-old daughter (the only licensed driver in the family) to drive her to a safe park twice weekly, where she would walk and enjoy the plants for 30 minutes. Her self-efficacy about this plan was high. She knew that she could ask her daughter, that she could walk, and that she would enjoy seeing the plants at the park.

Soundness of Rationale

Available findings suggest that depressed clients who give existential reasons for their depression had better outcomes with cognitive therapy. Clients who gave relationship-oriented reasons for

their depression had consistently more negative process (including homework) and treatment outcomes with cognitive therapy (Addis & Jacobson, 2000). This finding may be related in part to the acceptability of the rationale for treatment, including the nature of the homework assigned. Often, an understanding of the clients' beliefs about the cause of their problem helps the therapist to construct an acceptable rational for treatment. Because depression is a very common reason for seeking treatment, it will be used in illustrating this point. Some clients believe the cause of depression is biochemistry or bad genes. Others insist that it is due to life circumstances. Conceivably, a similar behavioral activation plan (e.g., going to a movie with a friend and evaluating the impact on mood) could be collaboratively developed for both clients. However, the rationale would need to be tailored to each client. In the case of the client who believes in biochemical causation, the rationale might be that this assignment made sense because the activity might facilitate a biochemical change that would improve brain chemistry and mood functioning. For the other client, the rationale might be that the assignment could provide a counterbalance to difficult situations, therefore reducing the overall impact of the life circumstance problems. When the therapist provides an acceptable rationale, the client is able to put the homework assignment into a framework that is consistent with his or her prevailing world view.

Size of Assignment

The size of the assignment depends upon the client's readiness for change, his or her self-efficacy, and his or her resources, including mastery of prerequisite skills and availability of potential positive reinforcers. Some clients come to the initial session with a great deal of motivation, self-efficacy, and resources. This type of client may participate collaboratively in developing a homework plan and require no follow-up beyond a brief phone check-in concerning implementation of the homework plan. By way of illustration, consider the case of a pregnant woman who came to therapy with the complaint that her best friend had died. She explained that she was experiencing a great deal of sadness and was worried about the impact on her unborn child. The planned homework assignment included development of a weekly schedule of health-related behaviors (e.g., exercise and relaxation activities) and social activities, along with scheduled times when she could experience her loss and her sadness. Although the size of the homework was huge (i.e., 6 hours of exercise, 7 hours of grieving, 5 hours of social activities, 4 hours of pleasurable activities, etc.), the client was completely confident because it matched her readiness to change, her self-efficacy, and her resources.

Skills Required

Many good homework assignments blow up because the client simply does not have the prerequisite skills necessary to succeed at the assignment. In one such case, a young therapist developed a homework assignment for an inpatient adolescent that involved independent laundry behavior. The therapist planned the time and location for the task and identified planned reinforcers. Unfortunately, the client came from a family that did not have an automatic washer and had never operated a washing machine. The client made an effort, but placed a bar of soap, rather than laundry detergent, in the machine, and the result was not a positive experience. A good way to identify specific skill requirements is to ask the client to visualize doing the homework assignment in session and to report on perceived obstacles. Then the therapist can help the client develop the skills needed to overcome the obstacles or change the homework assignment.

Self-Reinforcement

Since many homework assignments involve asking the patient to engage in different, more effective behaviors, it is important to reward these behaviors immediately after they occur. Many clients who are motivated to change behavior don't succeed because there are no immediately available reinforcements in their natural environment. They are forced to rely on an intrinsic sense of gratification, which may be absent, or they may receive negative feedback when they behave in more personally effective ways (e.g., a woman who asserts herself rather than submitting to a verbally aggressive husband). The therapist can explain that most people don't have someone to cheer them on during the difficult process of self-change. Therefore, learning to make and implement self-reinforcement plans is an important life skill. Self-reinforcement plans need to have all of the qualities of good homework plans (i.e., they should be specific, simple, etc.) and to be affordable. Examples of self-reinforcement following a desired homework assignment include going to a movie, watching a favorite television show, listening to a favorite CD, taking a long warm bath, and so forth.

Support (Therapist, Social)

Early in treatment, it is important to identify who the client can rely on to provide social support and social reinforcement for completing a homework assignment. Who cares about the changes she or he is trying to make? It is often useful to jot down the name of the identified social supporter and to suggest to the client that they give a brief report to the social supporter close to the time that they complete a homework assignment.

The therapist also needs to understand this his/her attention is a powerful secondary reinforcer. Because of this, the therapist must be entirely committed to monitoring homework assignments and providing praise and social reinforcement when the assignment has been completed. This can be accomplished in a number of ways and depends upon the needs of the client. All clients need to know that completion of homework is important, and the therapist demonstrates this by asking the client about homework completion in the first 5 minutes of the follow-up session. The therapist should be thorough in asking about all aspects of the homework experience and offer praise the client for effort, completion, and self-observation. At times, a client will need the therapist to provide this type of support between sessions. This can be offered when a client is planning a homework assignment that is particularly challenging. The therapist can provide support to enhance adherence by giving a 2-minute phone call: "Did you do it? good for you!" For single-session clients and for follow-up maintenance homework assignments, support of homework may be accomplished by mail, internet, or voice mail communications. Additionally, follow-up of homework assignments by other team members (e.g., primary care physicians, teachers) is an option for behavioral health providers who provide consultation services as part of a team or staff in primary care clinics or schools.

The Four R's of Effective Homework Assignments during the Maintenance Phase

The maintenance phase of treatment includes development of a large homework assignment— the relapse prevention plan. A strong plan will link the client's intention to maintain new changes to important values and thoughtfully integrate the continued shaping of new behaviors into the client's lifestyle.

Related to Values

As treatment concludes, whether at the second or twentieth contact, the client and therapist need to address the questions related to values, such as why it matters and what value the client will use at the moment when choice is required. Success in the maintenance phase of treatment requires the client to engage in independent committed action. Hayes, Strosahl, and Wilson (1999) suggest strategies for furthering client preparation for successful development of homework assignments in this phase of treatment.

Relapse Prevention Plans

Development of an effective relapse prevention plan involves identification of the skills that have contributed most to the client's improvement (many of which were discovered or fine-tuned in homework assignments) and packaging these into a feasible lifestyle plan. Because of the importance of providing positive reinforcement for newly acquired skills, the plan needs to specify self-reinforcement and social reinforcement strategies for newly learned behaviors. This may involve the client's participation in supportive group programs (e.g., attendance at Toastmasters after treatment for public speaking phobia), reports to buddies (e.g., calling a close friend to report completion of a monthly self-monitoring procedure), or follow-up by other professionals (teachers, spiritual leaders, primary care providers).

Regular Review

Clients vary in their personal organizational style, and some may prefer to plan a regular review of relapse prevention plans with a therapist or case manager. This review can be conducted in a brief phone call that targets the relapse prevention plan (Katon et al., 1996) or in a group booster session. Providing a generic, drop-in psychoeducational group, such as the Quality of Life Class, on a weekly basis at an accessible location, such as a primary care clinic, allows clients who need more direct support to receive it. Use of a curriculum that furthers development of self-management skills through structured, empirically supported homework assignments (see Robinson, 1996) allows the therapist to be more efficient in meeting the needs of clients who are in the process of creating stable change in chronic dysfunctional patterns.

Revised to Support Lifestyle

Many aspects of a client's life may change during the first 6 months after a successful episode of psychotherapy. A follow-up appointment 6 months after the completion of active treatment provides an opportunity for the client and therapist to revise the relapse prevention plan with better understanding of the person's more functional lifestyle. As more effective behaviors are developed and integrated into the client's native repertoire, it is only natural to see the relapse prevention plan evolve in content and complexity. These changes should be anticipated as part of a successful psychotherapy maintenance plan.

Further Reading

Robinson, P. (1996). *Living life well: New strategies for hard times*. Reno, NV: Context Press.

Shelton, J. L., & Levy, R. L. (1981). *Behavioral assignments and treatment compliance: A handbook of clinical strategies*. Champaign, IL: Research Press.

References

Addis, M., & Jacobson, N. S. (2000). A closer look at the treatment rationale and homework compliance in cognitive behavioral therapy for depression. *Cognitive Therapy and Research, 24*(3), 313–326.

Alford, B. A., & Beck, A. T. (1994). Cognitive therapy of delusional beliefs. *Behavioral Research and Therapy, 32*(3), 369–380.

Annis, H. M., Schober, R., & Kelly, E. (1996). Matching addiction outpatient counseling to client readiness for change: The role of structured relapse prevention counseling. *Experimental and Clinical Psychopharmacology, 4*(1), 37–45.

Barlow, D. H., & Craske, M. G. (1989). *Mastery of your anxiety and panic*. Albany, NY: Graywind Publications.

Beck, A. T., Rush, J. A., Shaw, B. F., & Emery, G. (1979). *Cognitive therapy of depression*. New York: Guilford Press.

Beyebach, M., Morejon, A. R., Palenzuela, D. L., & Rodriguez-Arias, J. L. (1996). Research on the process of solution-focused therapy. In S. D. Miller, M. A. Hubble, & B. L. Duncan (Eds.), *Handbook of solution-focused brief therapy* (pp. 299–334). San Francisco, CA: Jossey-Bass.

Burns, D. D., & Auerbach, A. H. (1992). Does homework compliance enhance recovery from depression? *Psychiatric Annals, 22*(9), 464–469.

Burns, D. D., & Nolen-Hoeksema, S. (1991). Coping styles, homework compliance, and the effectiveness of cognitive-behavioral therapy. *Journal of Consulting and Clinical Psychology, 59*(2), 305–311.

Burns, D. D., & Spangler, D. L. (2000). Does psychotherapy homework lead to improvements in depression in cognitive-behavioral therapy or does improvement lead to increased homework compliance? *Journal of Consulting and Clinical Psychology, 68*(1), 46–56.

Carr, A. (1997). Positive practice in family therapy. *Journal of Marital and Family Therapy, 23*(3), 271–293.

Chadwick, P., Birchwood, M., & Trower, P. (1996). *Cognitive therapy for delusions, voices and paranoia*. Chichester, England: Wiley.

Craske, M. G., Barlow, D. H., & O'Leary, T. (1992). *Mastery of your anxiety and worry*. Albany, NY: Graywind Publications.

Cunningham, C., Davis, J. R., Bremner, R., & Dunn, K. W. (1993). Coping modeling problem solving versus mastery modeling: Effects on adherence, in-session process, and skill acquisition in a residential parent-training program. *Journal of Consulting and Clinical Psychology, 61*(5), 871–877.

Edelman, R. E., & Chambless, D. L. (1995). Adherence during sessions and homework in cognitive-behavioral group treatment of social phobia. *Behaviour Research & Therapy, 33*(5), 573–577.

Goisman, R. M. (1985). The psychodynamics of prescribing in behavior therapy. *American Journal of Psychiatry, 142*, 675–679.

Hansen, D. J., & MacMillan, V. M. (1990). Behavioral assessment of child-abuse and neglectful families: Recent developments and current issues. *Behavior Modification, 14*(3), 255–278.

Hayes, S., Strosahl, K., & Wilson, K. (1999). *Acceptance and Commitment Therapy: An experiential approach to behavior change*. New York: Guilford Press.

Herzberg, A. (1941). Short treatment of neuroses by graduated tasks. *British Journal of Medical Psychology, 19*, 19–36.

Hollon, S. D., & Beck, A. T. (1994). Cognitive and cognitive-behavioral therapies. In A. E. Bergin & S. L. Garfield (Eds.), *Handbook of psychotherapy and behavior change* (4th ed., pp. 428–466). New York: Wiley.

Katon, W., Robinson, P., Von Korff, M., Lin, E., Bush, T., Ludman, E., et al. (1996). A multifaceted intervention to improve treatment of depression in primary care. *Archives of General Psychiatry, 53*, 924–932.

Kazantzis, N., & Deane, F. P. (1999). Psychologists' use of homework assignments in clinical practice. *Professional Psychology: Research and Practice, 30*(6), 581–585.

Leung, A. W., & Heimberg, R. G. (1996). Homework compliance, perceptions of control, and outcome of cognitive behavioral treatment of social phobia. *Behaviour Research & Therapy, 34*(5–6), 423–432.

Miller, W. R., & Rollnick, S. (1991). *Motivational interviewing*. New York: Guilford.

Neimeyer, R. A., & Feixas, G. (1990). The role of homework and skill acquisition in the outcome of group cognitive therapy for depression. *Behavior Therapy, 21*(3), 281–292.

Nelson, H. E. (1997). *Cognitive behavioural therapy with schizophrenia: A practice manual*. Cheltenham, England: Stanley Thorne.

Persons, J. B., Burns, D. D., & Perloff, J. M. (1988). Predictors of dropout and outcome in cognitive therapy for depression in a private practice setting. *Cognitive Therapy and Research, 12*(6), 557–575.

Prochaska, J. O. (1994). Strong and weak principles for progressing from precontemplation to action on the basis of twelve problem behaviors. *Health Psychology, 13*, 47–51.

Prochaska, J. O., & DiClemente, C. C. (1983). Stages and processes of self-change of smoking: Toward an integrative model of change. *Journal of Consulting and Clinical Psychology, 51*, 390–395.

Robinson, P. (1996). *Living life well: New strategies for hard times*. Reno, NV: Context Press.

Robinson, P., Wischman, C., & Del Vento, A. (1996). *Treating depression in primary care: A manual for primary care and mental health providers*. Reno, NV: Context Press.

Shelton, J. L., & Levy, R. L. (1981). *Behavioral assignments and treatment compliance: A handbook of clinical strategies*. Champaign, IL: Research Press.

Startup, M., & Edmonds, J. (1994). Compliance with homework assignments in cognitive-behavioral psychotherapy for depression: Relation to outcome and methods of enhancement. *Cognitive Therapy, 18*, 567–579.

Strosahl, K. (1997). Building integrated primary care behavioral health delivery systems that work: A compass and a horizon. In N. Cummings, J. Cummings, & J. Johnson (Eds.), *Behavioral health in primary care: A guide for clinical integration* (pp. 37–58). Madison, CN: Psychosocial Press.

Thompson, L. W., & Gallagher, D. (1984). Efficacy of psychotherapy in the treatment of late-life depression. *Advances in Behaviour Research and Therapy, 6*, 127–139.

Wadden, T. A., & Letizia, K. A. (1992). Predictors of attrition and weight loss in patients treated by moderate and severe caloric restriction. In T. A. Wadden & T. B. VanItallie (Eds.), *Treatment of the seriously obese patient* (pp. 383–410). New York: Guilford Press.

Wilson, G. T., & Vitousek, K. M. (1999). Self-monitoring in the assessment of eating disorders. *Psychological Assessment, 11*(4), 480–489.

33 INTEROCEPTIVE EXPOSURE FOR PANIC DISORDER

John P. Forsyth and Tiffany Fusé

Interoceptive exposure is at the core of most effi-cacious cognitive behavioral interventions for Panic Disorder (PD) and is based, in large part, on the biopsychosocial model of panic (Barlow, 2001). According to this model, PD results from an association between an unexpected false alarm (i.e., panic attack) and bodily or environ-mental cues that were present during the initial attack. This learning process results in bodily cues acquiring fear-evoking functions to elicit subsequent learned alarms or panic attacks (see Barlow, 2001; Bouton, Mineka, & Barlow, 2001; Forsyth & Eifert, 1996a, 1996b, 1998). This pro-cess, in turn, is thought to contribute to the de-velopment of hypervigilance and sensitivity to bodily and environmental cues that were associ-ated with panic in the past, and thus to a positive feedback spiral in which unexpected arousal evokes fear and is responded to as such, which further amplifies that arousal, leading to stronger negative emotional learning and further associa-tions between learned alarms and other bodily or environmental cues, including arbitrary verbal events (e.g., the statement "I am dying" contra-dicts the speaker who never died during prior panic attacks). Anxious apprehension is a feature of this cycle, and covert and overt forms of be-havioral avoidance are common. Cognitive be-havior therapy (CBT) is designed to modify several elements that are believed to maintain PD, whereas interoceptive exposure (IE) is used explicitly to modify learned relations between bodily cues and subsequent panic. Indeed, all ef-fective treatments for PD have IE as a component (Barlow, 2001; Craske & Barlow, 2000; Craske, Rowe, Lewin, & Noriega-Dimitri, 1997; Penava, Otto, Maki, & Pollack, 1998; Klosko, Barlow, Tassinari, & Cerny, 1990), and IE is also effective as a treatment for PD when used alone (e.g., Beck, Shipherd, & Zebb, 1997; Griez & van den Hout, 1986; van den Hout, van der Molen, Griez, Lous-berg, & Nansen, 1987). Therefore, IE represents the behavioral component of CBT for PD and, like other forms of exposure therapy (see Chapter 34 on in vivo exposure and Chapter 62 on systematic desensitization this volume), is designed to pro-vide a structured context that facilitates new corrective emotional learning. Interoceptive ex-posure differs from other forms of exposure ther-apy only in that it involves exercises designed to evoke feared bodily cues and sensations, with the goal being to reduce the tendency for bodily cues to evoke strong fear and, secondarily, the ten-dency for a client to respond fearfully to them.

WHO MIGHT BENEFIT FROM THIS TREATMENT

Interoceptive exposure, whether in an individual or group therapy format, is a brief (12–15 ses-sions) and highly effective intervention for prob-lems where panic attacks are a prominent feature (e.g., Craske, Brown, & Barlow, 1991; Craske et al., 1997; Zuercher-White, 1997). Approximately 70 to 90% of persons suffering from PD remain free from panic at 1- and 2-year follow-ups when IE is included as part of a comprehensive treatment package. Moreover, CBT for PD produces more durable long-term outcomes at 6 months compared to pharmacotherapy (e.g., imipramine) and has lower attrition rates (Barlow, Gorman, Shear, & Woods, 2000; see also Gould, Otto, & Pollack, 1995). Interoceptive exposure also appears to be effective as a treatment for nocturnal panic: Exercises are tailored to evoke sensations that accompany sleep and sudden waking from a sleeping state (e.g., relaxation and startle). Fears of gastrointestinal symptoms that accompany Irritable Bowel Syndrome—a condition that tends to co-occur with PD—also responds well to IE. Interoceptive exposure also may be appropriate for problems other than panic, and particularly cases in which (1) bodily signs and symptoms evoke distress, pain, or psychological suffering, and (2) responding to bodily signs and symptoms appears problematic. Examples of such problems include, but are not limited to, conditioned nausea resulting from chemotherapy, hypochondriacal symptoms, illness phobia (e.g., cardiophobia), chronic pain, and abuse of controlled substances that is motivated by avoidance or escape from unpleasant bodily symptoms and emotional events. However, it should be stressed that efficacy data are limited regarding the utility of IE for problems other than panic. Though IE does appear effective when included as part of routine CBT for individuals with panic and other comorbid conditions, most studies exclude persons with active substance abuse or dependence, psychosis, and suicidal or homicidal ideation or intent; additionally, data regarding the efficacy of IE in ethnic minority populations are limited at best (Chosak, Baker, Thorn, Spiegel, & Barlow, 1999).

CONTRAINDICATIONS OF THE TREATMENT

Interoceptive exposure is a structured, nonpharmacologic intervention that encourages clients to confront feared bodily sensations in a supportive therapeutic environment while resisting the natural tendency to engage in covert and overt avoidance or escape strategies. In many respects it can be thought of as an in vivo method of directly confronting the natural tendency toward experiential avoidance of unwanted private events (see Chapter 2 on acceptance in this volume)—events that are otherwise harmless and perfectly adaptive components of human emotional responding. Yet IE is certainly not to be used for all clients, and it is even contraindicated in some cases. For instance, IE exercises designed to elicit cardiorespiratory cues (e.g., jogging, running up a staircase, hyperventilation) are not appropriate for those suffering from certain cardiopulmonary medical conditions. Moreover, exercises such as breathing through a straw, rebreathing expired air, or inhaling enhanced concentrations of carbon dioxide–enriched air are contraindicated for clients with asthma, chronic obstructive lung disease, renal disease, seizure disorders, and certain blood disorders such as anemia. If the therapist is uncertain about whether a particular IE exercise is appropriate for a client, it is recommended that the therapist consult with the client's primary care physician or select an alternate exercise. When a particular exercise is not feasible for a client, the therapist may model the exercise so as to demonstrate both how ordinary activities may cause somatic sensations and that such sensations are not harmful. Moreover, some medications, particularly those that attenuate physical symptoms, such as benzodiazapines and some other anxiolytics, can interfere with the processes that IE is designed to target and change. For instance, medications that attenuate arousal may work against a client fully experiencing both conditioned and unconditioned autonomic arousal during exposure, and hence extinction processes. In fact, poorer long-term outcomes have been noted when IE is combined with benzodiazapines and other anxiolytic medications (e.g., Brown & Barlow, 1995; Klosko et al., 1990; Spiegel & Bruce, 1997). Moreover, there is the risk that patients may erroneously attribute any improvement to the medication and not to their efforts during IE. Severe cases of depression, including suicidal or homicidal ideation or intent, contradict IE as a first-line treatment, whereas the presence of Axis II disorders may simply result in some delayed therapeutic benefit (Tsao & Craske, 2000). Moreover, though elevated cortisol and plasma cate-cholamine levels are associated with panic at-tacks and may harm a developing fetus (Nonacs, Cohen, & Altshuler, 1998), therapists should be cautious about using IE to generate intense arousal in pregnant women, particularly during the third trimester, due to the risk of inducing false labor. Finally, noncompliance is a frequent concern with IE and can occur for several reasons (e.g., extremely fearful clients, lack of faith in the treatment, lack of social support and/or motivation). Noncompliance is not a contraindication for IE, but it should be addressed in a creative and supportive manner and may even require a slower pace of IE exercises and/or structuring of such exercises in a more graduated fashion.

OTHER CONSIDERATIONS IN DECIDING TO USE OR NOT TO USE INTEROCEPTIVE EXPOSURE

Whether IE alone is sufficient to result in changes in the way clients think about their bodily sensations and panicogenic responses is a source of continuing controversy and debate. In fact, IE is most often bundled with some form of cognitive restructuring intervention that is designed to challenge and replace the tendency of patients with PD to catastrophically misinterpret signs and symptoms of arousal. Such cognitive conceptualizations could, and probably should, be routinely integrated with IE. For instance, during exposure exercises, clients would be directly confronting feared bodily cues and symptoms of arousal and could be taught to simultaneously confront faulty misinterpretations or catastrophic patterns of consequential thinking (e.g., heart palpitations mean "I am having a heart attack"). Thus, IE could be conceived of as an experiential exercise to evoke both bodily cues and the associated verbal and symbolic catastrophic thoughts associated with them. The context and consequences of such thinking could then be incorporated into IE without necessarily focusing on the thought content. For instance, a therapist might focus on clients' tendencies to respond to their own responses and the strategies they use to reduce, escape from, or avoid such feelings, and then focus on the ways both contribute to other problems in living. The goal then would not be to eliminate or replace autonomic responses and associated thoughts, but to use IE to learn how to respond to them differently and how to behave differently when such private events occur.

HOW DOES INTEROCEPTIVE EXPOSURE WORK?

Interoceptive exposure, like other forms of exposure therapy, is predicated on two interrelated learning processes. The first of these is based on extensive laboratory research showing that stimuli can acquire fear-evoking functions via Pavlovian or respondent learning processes (see Bouton et al., 2001; Forsyth & Eifert, 1996a, 1996b) and that the capacity of such stimuli to evoke fearful responding can be attenuated via the controlled and systematic presentation of such fear-evoking cues without the anticipated aversive consequences. Such attenuation in fearful responding over repeated nonreinforced exposure trials, in turn, is based on the principle of extinction—a principle that should not be confused with elimination or habituation of responding. Indeed, no response is eliminated via exposure-based interventions, although this has become a common way to talk about extinction. Moreover, extinction is based on a learning process, whereas habituation is generally regarded as an unlearned process involving similar attenuation of responding to stimuli upon repeated presentation. Interoceptive exposure and the underlying principles driving its operation are fairly well worked out.

The second learning process, however, is not as well understood, particularly the factors that account for clients' tendency to respond fearfully to conditioned processes associated with otherwise normal bodily cues, and specifically how IE alone changes this tendency. This issue is critical when one considers that there is nothing inherently pathogenic about conditioned fearful responses. The responses themselves are quite adaptive, but become problematic when clients (1) respond to them in an effort to reduce their frequency, intensity, and duration, and (2) engage in behaviors that otherwise interfere with and restrict a full and valued life (see Chapter 2 in this volume; see also Hayes, Strosahl, & Wilson, 1999; Forsyth, 2000). The goal of IE is to expose clients to feared bodily sensations that are tailored to their unique concerns, thereby allowing clients to resist the natural tendency to avoid or escape from them. The result is that clients learn to respond to their responses differently, and this corrective emotional experience makes the natural tendency to avoid or escape nonsensical as a solution. This process will be accelerated initially to the extent that the exposure exercises are taught and repeated in a controlled systematic fashion with minimal variability. Later such exercises should be practiced by the client in a variety of settings to maximize generalization, and therapists and clients should be aware that generalization training will probably result in some reemergence of fearful responding based on what is known about spontaneous recovery and contextual control over behavior (e.g., exposure to racing heart sensations will likely evoke a different response in the safe confines of the therapist's office as opposed to driving on the interstate during rush hour traffic).

TABLE 33.1 Steps Involved in the Conduct of Interoceptive Exposure

1. Perform idiographic assessment and functional analysis.
2. Begin self-monitoring of panic attacks and associated behaviors.
3. Provide client with adequate rationale for using interoceptive exposure.
4. Construct fear hierarchy from self-monitoring and behavioral experiments.
5. Arrange exercises from least feared/easiest to most feared/most difficult.
6. Begin in-session exposure with client's least feared exercise and symptoms.
7. Assign in-session exposure exercises for homework between sessions.
8. Monitor and address subtle and overt forms of avoidance and escape behavior.
9. Arrange for generalization via naturalistic interoceptive exposure exercises.
10. Continuously review and plot data and use to guide treatment decisions.

STEP-BY-STEP GUIDE ON HOW TO IMPLEMENT INTEROCEPTIVE EXPOSURE

Interoceptive exposure is predicated on the conceptual learning framework previously described and consists of structured exposure exercises that are designed to elicit bodily sensations that are of primary concern to the client. Thus, the nature of IE exercises will vary from client to client depending on their principal complaints. The treatment consists of activities designed to evoke signs and symptoms of autonomic arousal so that the client can fully experience such sensations in a voluntary and deliberate manner while resisting any tendency toward avoidance or escape. The nature and structure of IE activities should be tailored idiographically to the client and should be derived from a thorough assessment. See Table 33.1 for a quick reference to the steps involved in conducting IE.

CONDUCTING AN IDIOGRAPHIC ASSESSMENT AND FUNCTIONAL ANALYSIS

It is important for the therapist to determine the appropriateness of IE for the client before begin-

ning. Prior to initiating IE, the therapist will want to conduct a thorough assessment of the client's medical history with respect to problematic signs and symptoms of autonomic arousal and the antecedents and consequences of such symptoms, including how the client normally responds to them. In this context, the therapist should have the client begin self-monitoring in his or her naturalistic environment. Self-monitoring data, in turn, will be used to develop a fear hierarchy and to select appropriate IE exercises in therapy. Self-monitoring of panic attacks, for instance, should be made immediately following each attack and should be structured to include prompts for the following information: (1) date and time of the attack; (2) the situation in which the attack occurred; (3) a self-rating of the distress and fear associated with the attack (e.g., 0 = no distress/fear to 9 = extreme distress/fear); (4) a list of signs and symptoms from the *Diagnostic and Statistical Manual of Mental Disorders,* fourth edition (*DSM-IV*), so that the client can indicate which symptoms occurred during the attack; (5) a place to indicate what was occurring before the panic attack (i.e., antecedents that could include environmental cues, thoughts, stressors, particular foods, drugs, or beverages consumed) and what the client did following the attack (i.e., consequences that may include self-mediation and overt and covert forms of escape and avoidance), including any accompanying self-statements; and (6) an estimate in minutes of how long the panic attack lasted at its peak.

Self-monitoring is important for several reasons. First, it provides the therapist with information about the nature and extent of the client's problems as they occur naturally (i.e., is the problem really a problem?). Second, it provides information about potential contextual factors that may maintain or exacerbate the problem, including information about contexts (e.g., people, places, times of day, behaviors) that are not problematic for the client (e.g., being at home vs. being in a crowd of people). Third, it provides the therapist and with information that can be used to better conceptualize the client's problem. For example, self-monitoring data are often useful as a means to identify overt and covert triggers for panic attacks, triggers that are often difficult for the client to identify early in therapy. Fourth, and most important for present purposes, self-monitoring provides data that will be used to construct a hierarchy of feared bodily signs and symptoms and to select appropriate IE exercises. Therapists should take great care to explain the nature and purposes of self-monitoring, including how it should be done properly. Usually self-monitoring begins at the outset of therapy in conjunction with basic psychoeducation about fear and panic and continues throughout therapy.

PROVIDING CLIENTS WITH AN ADEQUATE
RATIONALE FOR USING INTEROCEPTIVE
EXPOSURE

Inexperienced therapists often make the mistake of implementing IE too soon, before a good working therapist-client relationship has had time to develop, and without providing their clients with an easy-to-understand explanation of the procedure, the rationale underlying it, and anticipated costs and benefits. This is a mistake. Symptoms that will be evoked by IE are precisely those that the client wishes not to experience. After all, therapy is supposed to make clients feel better, not

worse. In the case of IE, however, there is some truth to the trite phrase "no pain, no gain." Clients need to be provided with an explanation of the nature of fear and anxiety as adaptive responses, and informed of how those same responses can become life constricting and debilitating. That is, clients need a tailored conceptualization regarding the role that learning plays in the development of their difficulties with panic, and particularly how subtle and overt forms of avoidance and escape behavior serve to maintain their difficulties. Interoceptive exposure can then be explained as a means for clients to do something different, namely, to face their fear in a gradual fashion so as to learn new ways of responding to their own responses. Therapists can guarantee their clients that as long as they respond the way they have been responding (i.e., attempting to avoid or escape from their own responses), they will continue to have the problems that they are presently having. At some level, most clients suffering from panic attacks know this already. Therefore, IE could be thought of an experiential strategy that is designed to assist the clients in mastering their ability to experience a full range of emotional responses, fully and without defense, for what they are and not for what clients they think they are (i.e., something dangerous and harmful). Interoceptive exposure is not a means to get rid of fear—an approach that would be maladaptive for humans and most nonhuman species as well. Providing a thorough rationale—a topic that has been discussed extensively by others in several places elsewhere—presents an opportunity for the therapist and client to develop a collaborative effort, to set expectations, and to prepare the client for exercises that will be somewhat difficult to do initially but will get easier with repeated practice (see Craske & Barlow, 2000).

STRUCTURE AND SELECTION OF
INTEROCEPTIVE EXPOSURE EXERCISES

Self-monitoring data should be reviewed prior to each session, and noncompliance or obstacles to successful self-monitoring should be addressed and corrected. The therapist and client should then begin the process of arranging the problematic symptoms gleaned from self-monitoring data in a hierarchy from least to most severe or distressing. The symptoms placed in the hierarchy should occur with sufficient frequency or intensity and be associated with significant life disruption to warrant their inclusion. Once the list is compiled, the therapist can then solicit in-session verbal ratings of distress from the client in response to each element of the hierarchy. This may be done so as to provide additional information about how the client currently responds to each element of the hierarchy. The next step involves selection of IE exercises, which should be selected for their ability to evoke problematic bodily sensations that the client is afraid of (Taylor, 2000). This process, in turn, should initially be conducted in session under careful therapist guidance. To the extent that it is feasible, the therapist should opt for using mini in-session behavioral experiments that involve exercises (to be described) designed to evoke the problematic symptoms from the hierarchy. While the client is completing the exercises, the therapist notes which exercises produce the highest level of anxiety for the client, regardless of their similarity to the client's most feared sensations. The therapist should also ask the client whether the sensations evoked by a particular IE exercise are similar to sensations that accompany naturally occurring panic, including any associated catastrophic and noncatastrophic thoughts. For example, a client who fears the sensation of dizziness may be asked to spin in an office chair for a minute, immediately after which a therapist will give a prompt for a rating of distress or fear, including a report of any catastrophic self-statements (e.g., "I feel like I'm losing control or going crazy"), and an assessment of the extent to which the induced sensations were similar to those that accompany the client's panic outside of therapy. Such mini behavioral experiments for each element of the hierarchy can be used to (1) confirm the ordering of the IE exercises that will follow, (2) test catastrophic beliefs and predictions, and (3) begin the process of helping the client to discover the likely noncatastrophic causes/consequences of the feared somatic cues. Moreover, such experiments provide important directly observable information about how the client responds to a wide array signs and symptoms of autonomic arousal, some of which may be unexpected (Zuercher-White, 1997). This kind of information is difficult to glean from paper-and-pencil self-monitoring alone.

TYPES OF INTEROCEPTIVE EXPOSURE EXERCISES

The universe of possible IE exercises is only limited by the therapist's creativity and available resources. The following is a partial list of commonly used in-session IE exercises, including information about their implementation and typical effects.

Breath Holding

Breath holding involves asking the client to hold his or her breath for a period of time. The duration of breath holding can be increased in a graduated fashion over exposure trials. This procedure typically evokes broadband symptoms of cardiorespiratory distress, specifically the feeling of suffocation or air hunger (see the earlier discussion of contraindications).

Breathing through a Straw

Several inexpensive small- and large-bore straws can be used for this IE exercise. The nose should be occluded while the client breathes through a straw for 30 seconds or more. This exercise evokes breathlessness and sensations of smothering, and it can be combined with other IE exercises, such as climbing stairs.

Climbing Steps

This exercise and its variants (e.g., fast walking, jogging in place) evoke cardiorespiratory sensations and more widespread sensations of autonomic arousal associated with physical exertion (see contraindications). Modifications to this procedure can range from climbing up and down one or two steps to climbing several flights of stairs. As appropriate, the pace can be graduated within different levels (e.g., 2 steps, 5 steps, 10 steps, and within each level, for varied durations).

Spinning

This IE exercise can also take several forms, and it is designed to evoke sensations of dizziness and vertigo. Such exercises may include therapist- and non-therapist-assisted spinning in an office chair, spinning while standing, and placing the head between the knees and suddenly moving into an upright sitting position.

Hyperventilation

This procedure involves voluntarily speeding up the pace of breathing and is capable of inducing panic attacks, including dissociative symptoms, in susceptible individuals. This occurs, in part, because carbon dioxide is expired at a rate greater than metabolic demand. The therapist demonstrates full exhalations and inhalations through the mouth at a pace of about one breath for every 2 seconds. This procedure may be extended for up to 3 to 5 minutes (see contraindications).

Rebreathing Expired Air

Rebreathing expired air into a bag is also capable of inducing wide-ranging bodily sensations similar to panic, which result from a rise in partial pressure carbon dioxide over and above metabolic demand. For this exercise a client may be provided with a brown lunch bag and asked to inhale and exhale directly into the bag. This procedure may be extended for up to 3 to 5 minutes, or longer in some cases, depending on how well the procedure is producing its intended effects for a given client (see also contraindications).

IMPLEMENTATION OF INTEROCEPTIVE EXPOSURE

Interoceptive exposure is typically utilized as an integral component of a larger CBT package in the treatment of PD and is often initiated after psychoeducation, breathing retraining, and cognitive restructuring. The sessions on cognitive restructuring focus on challenging automatic thoughts and changing core beliefs (Zuercher-White, 1997). In randomized controlled trials, the treatment is typically between 12 and 15 sessions (Otto & Deckersbach, 1998).

All IE exercises should be explained and modeled by the therapist prior to being attempted by the client. This does not mean, however, that all IE exercises are introduced in one session. As indicated, IE exercises are introduced and practiced in session in a graduated fashion. Typically, this means that a client will begin with the easiest-to-tolerate IE exercise from the hierarchy. The therapist, should first model the IE exercise and then carefully observe the client doing it him- or herself to ensure that it is completed correctly. Correct completion of the exercise depends largely on the approach one adopts. For instance, some argue that clients should simply be instructed to induce the feared somatic sensations, and then focus on simply experiencing the symptoms, without trying to change them (Otto & Deckersbach, 1998). Others, however, have suggested that to obtain the maximum benefit from IE, the therapist should instruct the client to attempt to intensify the sensations after inducing the somatic cues (Taylor, 2000). We see both approaches as complementary, because both are consistent with maximizing the process of corrective emotional learning and the general aim of teaching the client new ways of responding to his or her own responses. In either case, therapists will want to be particularly watchful for subtle and overt forms of escape or avoidance (e.g., distraction, taking fewer and more shallow breaths during hyperventilation), because such avoidance can retard the process of extinction.

It is important that the client practice each exercise a sufficient number of times during the therapy session, for two reasons. First, such practice provides the opportunity for the client to experience some therapeutic benefit; second, it ensures that the exercise is rehearsed well enough so that it can be performed willingly by the client outside of therapy. It is also important for the therapist to assess the client's ratings of distress, fear, and the presence and severity of physical and cognitive responses to each exercise. To the extent possible, this assessment should be quantitative, structured (e.g., using a 0 to 10 visual scale to solicit ratings of distress and fear), and ongoing throughout IE. Such data are critical for clinical decision making about the pace and structure of IE. Such data can also provide important information to the client regarding his or her improvement and can even help to facilitate compliance with therapy. In our work, we like to see that a client can show at least a 50% pre- to postexposure reduction in reported fear and anxiety in response to the same exercise. Moreover, we like to see that this reduction is stable over at least three repetitions of the same exercise in session before we assign the exercise for homework and, similarly, before we decide to move on to other exercises in the hierarchy. Some exercises for some clients will undoubtedly require several in-session exposure trials before any clinically meaningful reductions in anxious and fearful responding are observed. This is fine and to be expected. Interoceptive exposure exercises that are completed successfully in session should then be assigned as client homework outside of session.

EXPOSURE HOMEWORK

Completing homework (i.e., client practice of exposure exercises outside of therapy) is an integral component of the treatment. The simple metaphor of learning to ride a bicycle for the first time can be helpful to convey to the client the importance of practice. No one learns to ride a bike the first time he or she tries, and often the process can be painful. To make learning a bit easier, we add training wheels. Yet no one wants to ride a bicycle with training wheels for the rest of his or her life. With repeated practice and effort we expect to get to the point of being able to remove the training wheels and ride without them. At that point, there may be a few more bumps and bruises along the way. Even seasoned bicyclists fall once in a while, but they spend more time on the bike riding than they do falling on the ground. A similar process is at work with IE practice outside of therapy. Interoceptive exposure should start in a comfortable environment (e.g., the privacy of one's home) and be structured at regular (i.e., several times a day) clustered intervals so that the client masters the skill (Craske & Barlow, 2000; Craske, Barlow, & Meadows, 2000). Home practice is analogous to using training wheels to ride a bike in that the goal is to master the basic

skills first before applying those skills in other situations that are more challenging. Initially, such homework may simply include practice with the exposure exercises covered in session (e.g., practicing breath holding at home), and later it may progress to exposures in other contexts and settings. Such homework should be completed regardless of whether the client is feeling anxious or distressed about IE or other matters. In fact, it may be particularly valuable for the client to perform IE exercises when he or she is under stress (Taylor, 2000), although not initially. It is essential that the therapist convey to the client the importance of completing homework assignments and performing the IE exercises correctly. To facilitate compliance, the therapist should provide homework sheets with columns and spaces for the date, the setting, the start and end times of practice (i.e., duration), pre- and postpractice ratings of fear, distress (using some interval scale with anchor points), and extent of symptoms experienced, and a place to note associated catastrophic and noncatastrophic thoughts. Such homework should be routinely collected and reviewed by the therapist during each session, and the therapist should reinforce the client for successfully completing or attempting the homework exercises. The therapist should also routinely plot both in-session and outside session data and periodically review the data with the client. Reviewing client progress in this manner can be a powerful motivator and can also highlight areas that remain problematic or require additional clinical attention.

The therapist will want evidence that the client has shown clinically meaningful and stable attenuation of fearful responding to a given IE exercise in session and outside session before moving on to the next step: instructing the client to go about his or her usual activities while experiencing feared somatic sensations. The purpose here is to remove the training wheels and to start allowing the client to practice experiencing somatic symptoms while performing routine activities. Practice with IE exercises should continue several times during the day; however, now the practice will occur in those situations where the signs and symptoms of arousal are particularly disruptive or problematic (e.g., school, work, driving, walking, waiting in line). For example, IE exercises such as applying pressure to the throat or standing up suddenly can be performed at a desk while at work (Zuercher-White, 1997). To derive the maximum benefit from the treatment, clients should perform IE exercises in as many different contexts and situations as possible (Taylor, 2000). As before, the therapist should provide rating forms for the client to complete, and the resultant data should be plotted and reviewed regularly in therapy. Failure on the part of the therapist to review, discuss, and plot the homework assignments regularly, and to use such data to guide treatment decisions, sends the client the wrong message—namely, that the homework is really not important—so the client will start to wonder why he or she should bother doing it.

PROMOTING GENERALIZATION THROUGH NATURALISTIC INTEROCEPTIVE AND SITUATIONAL EXPOSURE

It is important for clients to perform IE exercises in a wide range of situations and under diverse circumstances, which promotes generalization while also helping clients learn that feared interoceptive cues are not harmful to them in general (Taylor, 2000). Naturalistic IE is a component of this process and involves a client exposing him- or herself to common daily activities or situations that produce feared somatic sensations. Prior to treatment, these situations and activities are typically avoided or else endured with great distress. With naturalistic IE, the focus shifts to structured exercises that are performed by the client in increasingly feared and less safe situations (Otto & Deckersbach, 1998). For example, the client may begin by performing IE homework exercises at home with his or her spouse present, then perform them at home without a safe person present, subsequently performing them in a shopping mall with a safe person present, and ultimately going to the mall alone. Other common examples of naturalistic IE include going to an amusement park and going on scary rides, or engaging in a workout program such as running, cycling, or aerobics. Swimming may be a viable option for clients with medical conditions that preclude their participation in other forms of exercise

(Taylor, 2000). Although naturalistic IE and situational exposure have common elements, they differ in that the goal of naturalistic IE is to induce symptoms of autonomic arousal, whereas the goal of situational exposure is to expose the client to the feared situations themselves, without regard for the somatic sensations they produce (Taylor, 2000).However, naturalistic IE and situational exposure may be combined in some exercises. For example, a client could join an aerobics class, so as to experience cardiac and respiratory cues in the presence of a group of people. Both the therapist and client should arrange for such exposures in a structured and deliberate fashion, preferably one that progresses from least to most difficult. Homework should be assigned and reviewed regularly in therapy as before.

STRATEGIES FOR DEALING WITH AVOIDANCE: ELIMINATING SAFETY SIGNALS AND BEHAVIORS

Safety signals (i.e., stimuli that the person associates with the absence of feared outcomes; e.g., reassurance, repeated checking, being with a significant other, carrying an empty pill bottle) and safety behaviors (i.e., actions designed to ward off fear events; e.g., escape and avoidance behavior) are problematic because they prevent fearful responses to interoceptive cues from being extinguished and block the process of corrective emotional learning. Here we briefly outline three strategies for eliminating safety signals and behaviors (cf. Taylor, 2000).

Identify Subtle and Obvious Safety Signals and Behaviors

First, the therapist and client work together to identify both subtle and obvious safety signals and behaviors. The therapist may also observe the client during in-session IE activities and then ask the client whether he or she did anything in order to prevent catastrophic outcomes or make the situation less frightening. The therapist and client should arrive at a list of safety signals and behaviors, and both domains should be continually assessed, particularly as IE is practiced by the client in other, more naturalistic contexts. Indeed, it is not uncommon to find that clients utilize different safety signals and behaviors in different situations, or even several different safety signals and behaviors across similar situations (Taylor, 2000).

Demonstrate That Safety Signals and Behaviors are Ineffective as a Solution

The second step involves demonstrating to the client that safety signals and behaviors are ineffective as a solution for his or her problems. This can be accomplished by doing mini in-session behavioral experiments in which the client first engages in an IE exercise while also engaging in a safety behavior, or in the presence of a safety signal, and then performs the IE exercise again but without the safety signals or behaviors (Taylor, 2000).

Assist the Client in Abandoning Safety Signals and Behaviors and in Developing Repertoire-Expanding Solutions

Finally, it is essential that the therapist educate the client about the functional role safety signals and avoidance behavior play in maintaining the client's problem, including the ways they may actually constrict the client's ability to live a full and valued life. Most clients will be reluctant to simply give up their tendency to use safety signals and behaviors; however, the therapist may assist the client to discard them in a gradual fashion over repeated exposure exercises (Taylor, 2000).

Further Reading

Barlow, D. H. (2001). *Anxiety and its disorders: The nature and treatment of anxiety and panic* (2nd ed.). New York: Guilford.

Bouton, M. E., Mineka, S., & Barlow, D. H. (2001). A modern learning theory perspective on the etiology of panic disorder. *Psychological Review, 108*(1), 4–32.

Carter, M. M., & Barlow, D. H. (1993). Interoceptive exposure in the treatment of panic disorder. In L. VandeCreek, S. Knapp, & T. L. Jackson (Eds.), *Innovations in clinical practice: A source book: Vol. 12.* (pp. 329–336). Sarasota, FL: Professional Resource Press/Professional Resource Exchange.

References

Barlow, D. H. (2001). *Anxiety and its disorders: The nature and treatment of anxiety and panic* (2nd ed.). New York: Guilford.

Barlow, D. H., Gorman, J. M., Shear, K., & Woods, S. W. (2000). Cognitive-behavioral therapy, imipramine, or their combination for Panic Disorder: A randomized controlled trial. *Journal of the American Medical Association, 283,* 2529–2536.

Beck, J. G., Shipherd, J. C., & Zebb, B. J. (1997). How does interoceptive exposure for Panic Disorder work? An uncontrolled case study. *Journal of Anxiety Disorders, 11,* 541–556.

Bouton, M. E., Mineka, S., & Barlow, D. H. (2001). A modern learning theory perspective on the etiology of Panic Disorder. *Psychological Review, 108,* 4–32.

Brown, T. A., & Barlow, D. H. (1995). Long-term outcome in cognitive behavioral treatment of Panic Disorder: Clinical predictors and alternative strategies for assessment. *Journal of Consulting and Clinical Psychology, 63,* 754–765.

Chosak, A., Baker, S. L., Thorn, G. R., Spiegel, D. A., & Barlow, D. H. (1999). Psychological treatment of Panic Disorder. In D. J. Nutt, J. C. Ballenger, & J. Lépine (Eds.), *Panic Disorder: Clinical diagnosis, management and mechanisms* (pp. 203–219). London: Martin Dunitz Ltd.

Craske, M. G., & Barlow, D. H. (2000). *Mastery of your anxiety and panic (MAP-3; 3rd ed.).* San Antonio, TX: The Psychological Corporation.

Craske, M. G., Barlow, D. H., & Meadows, E. A. (2000). *Mastery of your anxiety and panic (MAP-3): Therapist guide for anxiety, panic, and agoraphobia* (3rd ed.). San Antonio, TX: The Psychological Corporation.

Craske, M. G., Brown, T. A., & Barlow, D. H. (1991). Behavioral treatment of Panic Disorder: A two-year follow-up. *Behavior Therapy, 22,* 289–304.

Craske, M. G., Rowe, M., Lewin, M., & Noriega-Dimitri, R. (1997). Interoceptive exposure versus breathing retraining within cognitive-behavioural therapy for Panic Disorder with agoraphobia. *British Journal of Clinical Psychology, 36,* 85–99.

Forsyth, J. P. (2000). A process-oriented behavioral approach to the etiology, maintenance, and treatment of anxiety-related disorders. In M. J. Dougher (Ed.), *Clinical behavior analysis* (pp. 153–180). Reno, NV: Context Press.

Forsyth, J. P., & Eifert, G. H. (1996a). The language of feeling and the feeling of anxiety: Contributions of the behaviorisms toward understanding the function-altering effects of language. *The Psychological Record, 46,* 607–649.

Forsyth, J. P., & Eifert, G. H. (1996b). Systemic alarms in fear conditioning, volume I: A reappraisal of what is being conditioned. *Behavior Therapy, 27,* 441–462.

Forsyth, J. P., & Eifert, G. H. (1998). Phobic anxiety and panic: An integrative behavioral account of their origin and treatment. In J. J. Plaud & G. H. Eifert (Eds.), *From behavior theory to behavior therapy* (pp. 38–67). Needham, MA: Allyn & Bacon.

Gould, R. A., Otto, M. W., & Pollack, M. H. (1995). A meta-analysis of treatment outcome for Panic Disorder. *Clinical Psychology Review, 15,* 819–844.

Griez, E., & van den Hout, M.A. (1986). CO_2 inhalation in the treatment of panic attacks. *Behaviour Research and Therapy, 24,* 145–150.

Hayes, S. C., Strosahl, K. D., & Wilson, K. G. (1999). *Acceptance and commitment therapy: An experiential approach to behavior change.* New York: Guilford.

Klosko, J. S., Barlow, D. H., Tassinari, R., & Cerny, J. A. (1990). A comparison of alprazolam and behavior therapy in treatment of Panic Disorder. *Journal of Consulting and Clinical Psychology, 58,* 77–84.

Nonacs, R., Cohen, L. S., & Altshuler, L. L. (1998). Course and treatment of Panic Disorder during pregnancy and the postpartum period. In J. F. Rosenbaum & M. H. Pollack (Eds.), *Panic Disorder and its treatment* (pp. 229–246). New York: Marcel Dekker.

Otto, M. W., & Deckersbach, T. (1998). Cognitive-behavioral therapy for Panic Disorder: Theory, strategies, and outcome. In J. F. Rosenbaum & M. H. Pollack (Eds.), *Panic Disorder and its treatment* (pp. 181–204). New York: Marcel Dekker.

Penava, S. J., Otto, M. W., Maki, K. M., & Pollack, M. H. (1998). Rate of improvement during cognitive-behavioral group treatment for Panic Disorder. *Behavior Research and Therapy, 36,* 665–673.

Spiegel, D. A., & Bruce, T. J. (1997). Benzodiazepines and exposure-based cognitive behavior therapies for Panic Disorder: Conclusions from combined treatment trials. *American Journal of Psychiatry, 154,* 773–781.

Taylor, S. (2000). *Understanding and treating Panic Disorder.* Chichester: Wiley.

Tsao, J. C. I., & Craske, M. G. (2000). Panic Disorder. In M. Hersen & M. Biaggio (Eds.), *Effective brief therapies: A clinician's guide* (pp. 63–78). New York: Academic Press.

van den Hout, M., van der Molen, M., Griez, E., Lousberg, H., & Nansen, A. (1987). Reduction of CO_2-induced anxiety in patients with panic attacks after repeated CO_2 exposure. *American Journal of Psychiatry, 144,* 788–791.

Zuercher-White, E. (1997). *Treating Panic Disorder and agoraphobia: A step-by-step guide.* Oakland, CA: New Harbinger.

34 LIVE (IN VIVO) EXPOSURE

Holly Hazlett-Stevens and Michelle G. Craske

Live (in vivo) exposure to feared situations has been a cornerstone of behavior therapy for decades. Even psychoanalytic and Gestalt therapy techniques relied on the principle of exposure to treat neuroses (Foa & Kozak, 1986). Mary Cover Jones is credited with one of the earliest documented cases of in vivo exposure for treating a case of phobia in the 1920s (Barlow & Durand, 1999). After observing how fear could be classically conditioned by pairing presentations of aversive, unconditioned stimuli with neutral, innocuous objects, she successfully extinguished a young boy's fear response to furry animals by gradually and systematically exposing him to white rabbits (Jones, 1924). Thus, this therapeutic technique is historically linked to early experimental studies of classical conditioning and related principles of conditioned stimulus (CS)–unconditioned stimulus (UCS) extinction.

One of the most influential exposure techniques is the procedure of *systematic desensitization* developed by Salter (1949) and by Wolpe (1958). Systematic desensitization involves a series of exposure exercises presented in gradual steps of increased fear intensity. These exposures are conducted during relaxation, an emotional and physiological state considered incompatible with the conditioned anxiety or fear response. Systematic desensitization has received a wealth of empirical support for its efficacy (Leitenberg, 1976), but the role of relaxation in its effectiveness

has been the subject of much debate (Borkovec & O'Brien, 1976; Levin & Gross, 1985). In general, the incorporation of contiguous relaxation (i.e., systematic desensitization) is indicated when the therapist maintains control over the exposure (Borkovec & O'Brien) and when generalization of treatment effects to untreated phobias is desired (AuBuchon & Calhoun, 1990). However, in vivo exposure alone without relaxation training is widely used to treat a number of anxiety disorders and phobias, and much research supports this practice (see reviews by Foa & Kozak, 1985; Öst, 1996). Furthermore, in vivo exposure without relaxation training is a crucial component of effective psychological treatments for Panic Disorder with Agoraphobia (Craske & Barlow, 2001), Social Phobia (Heimberg et al., 1990), and Obsessive-Compulsive Disorder (Foa & Franklin, 2001).

In vivo exposure techniques are useful in the treatment of anxiety related to circumscribed objects or situations. Treatment typically begins with assessment of which objects or situations an individual fears and avoids as well as any contextual cues and features of the phobic stimuli that enhance this fear response. The therapist and client then work together to generate a hierarchy of situations or stimuli for the client to face in ascending order of difficulty. Finally, these exposures are conducted, often in a graded fashion such that the client moves up to the next hierarchical step only after mastering the previous one. The client is encouraged to experience the full fear response during exposures without engaging in subtle forms of avoidance, such as distraction or looking away from the stimulus. Depending on the nature of the fear, such exposure can produce therapeutic effects quickly, at times in only a single session (Öst, 1996).

WHO MIGHT BENEFIT FROM IN VIVO EXPOSURE

Most individuals with anxiety involving circumscribed, irrational fears of external objects or situations benefit from this technique. This applies to people diagnosed with Panic Disorder with Agoraphobia, Specific Phobia, or Agoraphobia without Panic (i.e., the situational avoidance associated with other anxiety-related bodily responses such as Generalized Anxiety Disorder or irritable bowel syndrome). In vivo exposure is equally important in the treatment of Social Phobia (Heimberg et al., 1990), Obsessive-Compulsive Disorder (Foa & Franklin, 2001), and situational avoidance resulting from traumatic events (Foa & Meadows, 1997).

CONTRAINDICATIONS

Individuals with cardiovascular medical conditions (e.g., arrhythmia, heart disease) may be physically unable to tolerate the fear activation associated with in vivo exposure and should seek medical advice before attempting this form of treatment. Individuals currently living in physically dangerous or volatile situations in which their behavioral avoidance serves a realistic self-protective function should not attempt this form of treatment until conditions of physical safety have been restored. For example, if a client currently involved in a domestic violence situation was afraid to shop at local stores, ride public transportation, and so on due to a realistic fear of encountering an abusive partner, this client should not attempt such exposure until this external threat has been addressed. In vivo exposure may also be inappropriate for individuals

suffering from psychosis, other thought disorders, or dementia, especially when behavioral avoidance of certain situations is considered adaptive for that individual.

ANY OTHER DECISION FACTORS IN DECIDING TO USE THE TECHNIQUE

Some clients may not be prepared or willing to engage in in vivo exposure when first presenting for psychological treatment. For example, a client with severe Panic Disorder with Agoraphobia convinced that a panic attack could result in a heart attack may not be willing to enter such situations at first. Treatment for this individual would first require psychoeducation to increase understanding of the harmless nature of the fight-or-flight panic attack response and/or cognitive restructuring to correct catastrophic misinterpretations about racing heart sensations before in vivo exposure to agoraphobic situations could be attempted.

Imaginal exposure can be done before in vivo exposure when a client's fear is so severe that the individual is unable to begin with live exposure items on the hierarchy, or if the situation cannot be recreated for live exposure. Another interesting alternative is the use of virtual reality equipment. This medium provides sensory exposure to stimuli resembling the actual feared situation, and may be particularly helpful when treating fear of heights (Rothbaum et al., 1995), spiders (Carlin, Hoffman, & Weghorst, 1997), or flying (Mühlberger, Herrmann, Wiedemann, Ellgring, & Pauli, 2001), or cases of claustrophobia (Botella et al., 1998).

In the special case of blood-injection-injury type specific phobias, the fear reaction usually involves a vasovagal physiological response, leading to a drop in blood pressure and the possibility of fainting (Öst, 1992). When treating this disorder, exposure exercises should be accompanied by applied muscle tension so that the client purposefully increases blood pressure to prevent the fainting response when confronting feared blood-, injection-, or injury-related stimuli (Öst, 1996).

HOW DOES IN VIVO EXPOSURE WORK?

In vivo exposure techniques originally were based on the behavioral principle of *extinction*. Thus, live exposure is believed to reduce anxiety because the CS is repeatedly presented in the absence of any accompanying aversive UCS. However, more recent accounts suggest that exposure also promotes cognitive restructuring because clients learn during exposure trials that the feared stimuli are in fact harmless (e.g., Craske & Barlow, 2001). In 1986, Foa and Kozak presented a neobehavioristic theory of emotional processing to explain how repeated exposure leads to fear reduction. Based on the work of Peter Lang, they conceptualized fear as a program for escape or avoidance and suggested two conditions needed for successful fear reduction. First, the full fear structure must be activated, in which fear-relevant information become available in a form sufficient to activate the fear memory. Second, new information incompatible with elements of the original fear structure must then be presented and processed in order to change the threat-related meanings contained within the fear structure. As a result, new cognitive, affective, physiological, and environmental information become integrated into memory, and this hypothetically leads to emotional change. In a recent review, Foa and Kozak (1998) examined the contributions of Peter Lang's work to fear reduction theory and suggested new applications of this theory to specific anxiety disorder groups. However, some aspects of this theory have not always been empirically supported. For example, A. J. Lang and Craske (2000) have shown that good long-term fear reduction is possible without short-term reduction of physiology.

STEP-BY-STEP PROCEDURES[1]

The first therapeutic step (see also Figure 34.1) involves a functional analysis of the avoidance behavior to determine exactly what the client fears.

Key Elements of In Vivo Exposure
Conduct a functional analysis of avoidance behavior.
Describe the purpose and value of exposure to feared situations or objects.
Generate a hierarchy of fear items.
Begin repeated, systematic exposure to fear items, beginning at the bottom of the hierarchy.
Continue with repeated exposure to the next fear hierarchy item when exposure to the previous item generates only mild fear.
Assign self-directed exposure exercises for home practice.
Review client's progress with the home practice, giving feedback to overcome any difficulties.

FIGURE 34.1   Key Elements of In Vivo Exposure

The therapist asks pointed questions to determine which aspects of the situation or object are responsible for the fear response. This ensures that a fear hierarchy relevant for that individual is generated, because certain context features that make the situation more or less fearful will be used to design subsequent exposure exercises. Assessment also is conducted for any safety signals or for other subtle avoidance behaviors (such as distraction or averting eyes) the client relies upon when overt behavioral avoidance is not an option; these behaviors can undermine the functional exposure experienced during the exposure exercises.

Next, the therapist provides a brief rationale so that the client understands the value and purpose of the exposure. This typically begins with a description of the nature of fear and avoidance and the principle of classical conditioning. The client's anxiety is conceptualized as a conditioned reaction of increased physiological arousal and subjective fear to certain external cues that were somehow associated with danger in the past. Exposure exercises are therefore considered necessary to break the CS-UCS association previously learned, and they allow the client's mind and body to learn that no danger actually exists. Oftentimes this will lead to a discussion of how the client acquired the fear originally, making the notion of classical fear conditioning more salient. In the case of panic disorder with agoraphobia, fears of interoceptive bodily sensations are also discussed, and ideally,

---

1. These procedures are based on the manuals of Craske, Antony, and Barlow (1997) and of Craske and Barlow (2000).

in vivo exposure is conducted in combination with interoceptive exposure (Craske & Barlow, 2001).

Once the client clearly understands the rationale, the therapist and client work together to generate a hierarchy of feared items. At this time, the value of gradual exposure is presented as a means for the client to develop a sense of mastery over manageable situations, preventing feelings of overwhelming fear and the risk of inadvertently strengthening the fear. Although in vivo exposure is typically done in this gradual fashion, some cases may warrant more the more intensive exposure procedure known as *flooding* (see Chapter 26 of this book). The exposure hierarchy is often generated by asking the client to list situations that would be anxiety provoking while ranking each for its anxiety level (this can be done using a 0-to-8-point Likert scale). The variety of situations generated will depend on how circumscribed the fear is. For example, if the client presents with a specific fear of heights, all hierarchy items will involve situations involving height. Conversely, if an individual experiences agoraphobia encompassing a number of situations, then these different places should be identified and ranked. Each item should include as specific detail as possible, and the same type of situation may be repeated in another step with the alteration of important stimulus features. For example, the first hierarchy step for an individual fearful of driving might involve simply sitting in a parked car while resting the hands on the steering wheel. Higher steps on the hierarchy may include pulling the car out of the driveway, followed by driving one loop around a block in the neighborhood, followed by driving the distance of one exit on the freeway, and so on. The anxiety levels assigned to each step can then be used to rank order the hierarchy items according to difficulty.

This step is followed by selection of exposure exercises to be done on a scheduled basis. The therapist can model the exposure exercise and then coach the client during in-session exposure to the first hierarchy item. This coaching includes encouraging the client to fully experience all aspects of the external situation as well as any internal anxiety response. The client is discouraged from simply stopping the exposure as soon as anxiety is detected. Rather, the client is instructed to monitor the anxiety level during the exposure and experience the habituation of anxiety before discontinuing the exercise. When an exposure trial has ended, the therapist asks the client to rate his or her current anxiety level and to describe the experience. If the client noticed anxiety-provoking thoughts during the exposure, these thoughts can be discussed and put into perspective with psychoeducation or with cognitive restructuring. If the client reports low anxiety during the exposure, the therapist queries for any reasons the client did not experience greater anxiety (e.g., if the client was using distraction and not attending to the stimulus) and try again. As a general rule, the client continues repeated exposure to that hierarchy item until exposure results in an anxiety level of only around 2 (on the 0-to-8-point scale). At that time, the next hierarchy item is selected for subsequent exposure.

If it is most important for the client also to engage in self-directed exposure exercises in between therapy sessions. If therapist-directed, in-session exposure is not feasible, clients can be instructed to ascend the hierarchy on their own. The following instructions should be given to guide clients in this homework:

1. Clients begin with the least feared items from the hierarchy list. In the case of agoraphobia in which the individual fears more than one situation, different types of exposures can be conducted over the same homework period.
2. Some items may require practice only a couple of times before mild levels of anxiety are reached. Other, more difficult items may require practice 5, 10, or 20 times. Practice is recommended at least 3 times per week, although the more the better.
3. A long, continuous practice is usually more helpful than shorter, interrupted practices. In other words, it is more helpful to do a solid hour of practice rather than four separate 15-min practices. Practices that are too short will only resemble current avoidance behavior (i.e., escaping from the phobic situation as soon as possible or remaining for a short while but with a sense of "holding on for dear life" until the practice is over). These attitudes only strengthen the mistaken belief that the exposure involves actual risk.

4. Exposure is most effective when all aspects of the task are attempted in the same manner as if there were no fear. For example, if the hierarchy item was to walk across a certain bridge, then walking very quickly across the bridge without ever looking over the edge would be much less effective than walking at a slower pace, stopping every now and then to look over the rail.

5. In the case of panic disorder with agoraphobia, the client might also be encouraged to identify and challenge anxiety-provoking thoughts associated with the feared situation before engaging in the exposure exercise.

6. If the client feels it's absolutely necessary to prematurely terminate an exposure exercise due to intense fear, the best strategy is to stop and allow the anxiety to reduce but then to resume the exposure, even if only for a few minutes longer. If not, another practice is scheduled soon afterward involving an item expected to generate significant anxiety levels that are less than that experienced during the previous exposure trial.

7. After each exposure trial, the client records his or her anxiety level. The previous exposure item is repeated until the fear response reduces to a mild level. Clients are encouraged to appreciate a sense of accomplishment after each exposure, rather than minimizing its significance.

In subsequent treatment sessions, the therapist reviews these exposure attempts with the client by reinforcing attempts, reassuring clients that progress is not always linear and more often fluctuates up and down, and giving corrective feedback. The therapist and client can collectively problem-solve any practical difficulties in conducting the exercises. If the client does not experience the expected fear reduction following repeated exposure, then further assessment of factors that could be maintaining the fear response should be conducted. For example, the client may be engaging in maladaptive coping styles during the exposure, such as holding onto a good luck charm or other safety signal believed to protect the client from danger, attempting the exposure with great caution (thereby reinforcing beliefs that the situation is harmful), or avoiding

aspects of the stimulus through mental distraction or by looking away from fearful stimuli. The therapist also assesses the length of exposures attempted, because exceedingly brief exposures do not allow for habituation of the anxiety response or for corrective learning. Finally, unsuccessful fear reduction can result from resisting the fear response during exposure. If clients try to "fight" the anxiety and suppress their fear response, this may paradoxically increase the anxious meaning of the situation. Such clients are encouraged to embrace and to closely monitor their anxiety responses so that they can experience decreases over time. The therapist continues to track the client's progress in this manner as the client ascends up his or her exposure hierarchy.

Depending on the nature and severity of the fear, some clients (especially specific phobia cases) may show dramatic fear reduction over only a few sessions. On the other hand, more generalized fears associated with social phobia and agoraphobia may involve much more complex hierarchies, including many steps spanning over several weeks.

Further Reading

Barlow, D. H. (Ed.). (2001). *Clinical handbook of psychological disorders: A step-by-step treatment manual* (3rd ed.). New York: Guilford.

Craske, M. G., Antony, M. M., & Barlow, D. H. (1997). *Mastery of your specific phobia.* San Antonio, TX: The Psychological Corporation.

Craske, M. G., & Barlow, D. H. (2000). *Mastery of your anxiety and panic (MAP-3)* (3rd ed.). San Antonio, TX: The Psychological Corporation.

References

AuBuchon, P. G., & Calhoun, K. S. (1990). The effects of therapist presence and relaxation training on the efficacy and generalizability of in vivo exposure. *Behavioural Psychotherapy, 18,* 169–185.

Barlow, D. H., & Durand, V. M. (1999). *Abnormal psychology* (2nd ed.). Pacific Grove, CA: Brooks/Cole Publishing.

Borkovec, T. D., & O'Brien, G. T. (1976). Methodological and target behavior issues in analogue therapy outcome research. *Progress in Behavior Modification, 3,* 133–172.

Botella, C., Banos, R. M., Perpina, C., Villa, H., Alcaniz, M., & Rey, A. (1998). Virtual reality treatment of claustrophobia: A case report. *Behaviour Research and Therapy, 36*, 239–246.

Carlin, A. S., Hoffman, H. G., & Weghorst, S. (1997). Virtual reality and tactile augmentation in the treatment of spider phobia: A case report. *Behaviour Research and Therapy, 35*, 153–158.

Craske, M. G., Antony, M. M., & Barlow, D. H. (1997). *Mastery of your specific phobia.* San Antonio, TX: The Psychological Corporation.

Craske, M. G., & Barlow, D. H. (2000). *Mastery of your anxiety and panic (MAP-3)* (3rd ed.). San Antonio, TX: The Psychological Corporation.

Craske, M. G., & Barlow, D. H. (2001). Panic disorder and agoraphobia. In D. H. Barlow (Ed.), *Clinical handbook of psychological disorders: A step-by-step treatment manual* (3rd ed., pp. 1–59). New York: Guilford Press.

Foa, E. B., & Franklin, M. E. (2001). Obsessive-compulsive disorder. In D. H. Barlow (Ed.), *Clinical handbook of psychological disorders: A step-by-step treatment manual* (3rd ed., pp. 209–263). New York: Guilford Press.

Foa, E. B., & Kozak, M. J. (1985). Treatment of anxiety disorders: Implications for psychopathology. In A. H. Tuma & J. D. Maser (Eds.), *Anxiety and the anxiety disorders* (pp. 421–452). Hillsdale, NJ: Erlbaum.

Foa, E. B., & Kozak, M. J. (1986). Emotional processing of fear: Exposure to corrective information. *Psychological Bulletin, 99*, 20–35.

Foa, E. B., & Kozak, M. J. (1998). Clinical applications of bioinformational theory: Understanding anxiety and its treatment. *Behavior Therapy, 29*, 675–690.

Foa, E. B., & Meadows, E. A. (1997). Psychosocial treatments for posttraumatic stress disorder: A critical review. *Annual Review of Psychology, 48*, 449–480.

Heimberg, R. G., Dodge, C. S., Hope, D. A., Kennedy, C. R., Zollo, L. J., & Becker, R. E. (1990). Cognitive behavioural group treatment for social phobia:

Comparison with a credible placebo control. *Cognitive Therapy and Research, 14*, 1–23.

Jones, M. C. (1924). A laboratory study of fear: The case of Peter. *Pedagogical Seminary, 31*, 308–315.

Lang, A. J., & Craske, M. G. (2000). Manipulations of exposure-based therapy to reduce return of fear: A replication. *Behaviour Research and Therapy, 38*, 1–12.

Leitenberg, H. (1976). Behavioral approaches to treatment of neuroses. In H. Leitenberg (Ed.), *Handbook of behavior modification and behavior therapy* (pp. 124–167). Englewood Cliffs, NJ: Prentice-Hall.

Levin, R. B., & Gross, A. M. (1985). The role of relaxation in systematic desensitization. *Behaviour Research and Therapy, 23*, 187–196.

Mühlberger, A., Herrmann, M. J., Wiedemann, G., Ellgring, H., & Pauli, P. (2001). Repeated exposure of flight phobics to flights in virtual reality. *Behaviour Research and Therapy, 39*, 1033–1050.

Öst, L.-G. (1992). Blood and injection phobia: Background and cognitive, physiological, and behavioral variables. *Journal of Abnormal Psychology, 101*, 68–74.

Öst, L.-G. (1996). Long-term effects of behavior therapy for specific phobia. In M. R. Mavissakalian & R. F. Prien (Eds.), *Long-term treatments of anxiety disorders* (pp. 171–199). Washington, DC: American Psychiatric Press.

Rothbaum, B. O., Hodges, L., Kooper, R., Opdyke, D., Williford, J. S., & North, M. (1995). Effectiveness of computer-generated (virtual reality) graded exposure in the treatment of acrophobia. *American Journal of Psychiatry, 152*, 626–628.

Salter, A. (1949). *Conditioned reflex therapy.* New York: Creative Age.

Wolpe, J. (1958). *Psychotherapy by reciprocal inhibition.* Stanford, CA: Stanford University Press.

35 MINDFULNESS PRACTICE

Sona Dimidjian and Marsha M. Linehan

In recent years, the practice of mindfulness has been increasingly applied to the clinical treatment of both physical and mental health problems. Although mindfulness practice has its roots in Eastern meditative and Western Christian contemplative traditions, the contemporary clinical use of mindfulness has focused on the core characteristics of mindfulness, independent of its spiritual origin and background. In this context, mindfulness is understood as awareness simply of what is, at the level of direct and immediate experience, separate from concepts, category, and expectations. It is a way of living awake, with your eyes wide open. Mindfulness as a practice is the act of repetitively directing your attention to only one thing. And that one thing is the one moment you are alive—allowing the moment, so to speak. As a set of skills, mindfulness practice is the intentional process of observing, describing, and participating in reality nonjudgmentally, in the moment, and with effectiveness (i.e., using skillful means). Mindfulness is thus the practice of willingness to be alive to the moment and radical acceptance of the entirety of moment. Mindfulness has as its goal only mindfulness. At the same time, it is the window to freedom, wisdom, and joy.

There are many ways of teaching and practicing mindfulness; in fact, methods of teaching and practicing mindfulness in the spiritual traditions noted previously have been evolving for centuries. In the clinical context, there exist three pri-

mary treatment models that employ the use of mindfulness strategies[1] and that have been subjected to empirical scrutiny; these include mindfulness-based stress reduction (MBSR) and the closely related mindfulness-based cognitive therapy (MBCT), mindfulness-based relapse prevention, and Dialectical Behavior Therapy (DBT).[2] This chapter draws from each of these models to provide a basic background in the clinical use of mindfulness and to highlight a general step-by-step procedure composed of common elements found in each of the various models.

---

1. It should also be noted that this chapter deals primarily with the teaching of mindfulness as a clinical *intervention* strategy. Mindfulness can also be discussed, however, as a therapeutic strategy, thus referring to particular qualities (e.g., being spontaneous, nonjudgmental, awake, etc.) that the therapist may bring to the clinical process. The value of the therapist's practice of mindfulness, independent of the teaching of mindfulness, has recently been discussed in the field of medicine (Epstein, 1999). Although this topic is highly relevant to the practice of cognitive behavioral therapies, a thorough discussion is beyond the scope of this chapter.
2. Although there is significant overlap between mindfulness and acceptance interventions, acceptance-based models that do not explicitly employ mindfulness practices (e.g., Acceptance and Commitment Therapy, Integrative Couple Therapy) are not included here.

PRIMARY MINDFULNESS STRATEGIES AND THEIR EMPIRICAL STATUS

Kabat-Zinn was the first to propose an empirically supported clinical application of mindfulness practice (Kabat-Zinn, 1990). This model, MBSR, was initially used for the treatment of chronic pain and was later applied to a diverse array of disorders. Recently, Segal, Williams, and Teasdale (2002) proposed an adaptation of Kabat-Zinn's model, MBCT, for use in the prevention of depressive relapse. Both MBSR and MBCT use a similar structure, which consists of an eight-week program of group sessions. Both models emphasize the importance of regular, formal mindfulness practices, which include sitting meditation, walking meditation, body scan meditation, and yoga. Clients are asked to commit to daily periods of formal practice, ranging between 30 and 45 min, as homework. Informal practice is also a focus of the program, as clients practice bringing mindfulness to daily activities such as eating, driving, washing the dishes, talking on the phone, and so on. MBSR also includes a 1-day-long mindfulness practice session during the course.

Marlatt (1994) has been a strong proponent of the utility of mindfulness practices in the treatment of addictive behaviors. In the mindfulness-based relapse prevention model developed by Marlatt and Gordon (1985), mindfulness skills are incorporated with particular emphasis on increasing awareness of cravings and urges to use substances. For instance, clients are taught the skill of *urge surfing* (see Chapter 67 in this volume), in which they "let go" of the urges and experience their transitory and impermanent nature (Marlatt). More recently, Marlatt has also proposed the application of a formal 10-day mindfulness meditation course for the treatment of addictive behaviors (MacPherson & Marlatt, 2001). The efficacy of the course, which includes extended periods of formal sitting meditation as well as instruction on meditation and Buddhist principles, is currently being investigated in a randomized clinical trial with incarcerated substance abusers.

Linehan (1993a, 1993b) pioneered the use of mindfulness strategies in the treatment of borderline personality disorder. Linehan's model, DBT, employs mindfulness strategies as part of a larger package of cognitive behavioral interventions. In contrast to other models, Linehan's DBT model does not teach formal mediation practices; instead, it breaks down the meditation process into its component parts, thus teaching clients the psychological and behavioral skills comprising most Eastern meditative and Western contemplative practices. Most DBT mindfulness exercises emphasize opportunities for using the mindfulness skills in everyday activities and situations. The specific mindfulness skills taught in DBT include "what" skills (i.e., observing, describing, and participating) and "how" skills (i.e., performing the "what" skills nonjudgmentally, one-mindfully, and effectively). The mindfulness skills are a core module of the treatment and are woven into a range of treatment procedures used in DBT. For instance, they are taught as "the vehicles for balancing 'emotion mind' and 'reasonable mind' to achieve 'wise mind'" (Linehan, 1993b, 63) and as elements of emotion regulation and distress tolerance. Mindfulness skills are taught as part of the weekly DBT skills groups and are also emphasized in individual therapy sessions. As homework, clients also monitor their daily use of the mindfulness skills on a written diary card.

Although the role of mindfulness interventions has been investigated across a broad range of clinical problems, most of the studies conducted to date have been uncontrolled. For instance, studies on MBSR in the treatment of the following disorders demonstrate promise, but all have lacked random assignment to control groups: chronic pain (Kabat-Zinn, 1982; Kabat-Zinn, Lipworth, & Burney, 1985; Kabat-Zinn, Lipworth, Burney, & Sellers, 1987; Randolph, Caldera, Tacone, & Greak, 1999); fibromyalgia (Kaplan, Goldenberg, & Galvin-Nadeau, 1993); anxiety and panic disorder (Kabat-Zinn et al., 1992; Miller, Fletcher, & Kabat-Zinn, 1995); mood and stress symptoms among cancer patients (Carlson, Ursuliak, Goodey, Angen, & Speca, 2001); binge eating disorder (Kristeller & Hallett, 1999); and multiple sclerosis (Mills & Allen, 2000). The few controlled trials that have been conducted do suggest that MBSR is efficacious in the treatment of psoriasis (Kabat-Zinn et al., 1998) and mood disturbance and stress symptoms among cancer patients (Speca, Carlson, Goodey, & Angen,

2000). A controlled trial also found MBCT to be efficacious in preventing relapse among recovered depressed patients with histories of recurrent depression (Teasdale et al., 2000). Finally, there is extensive research documenting the efficacy of DBT (cf. Koerner & Dimeff, 2000). In addition to the methodological problems discussed previously, it should also be noted that the practice of mindfulness is a component of the larger treatment packages that have been empirically tested; in each case other cognitive, behavioral, or psychoeducational interventions are also included. Therefore, no studies have independently investigated the role of mindfulness per se.

WHO MIGHT BENEFIT FROM MINDFULNESS STRATEGIES, AND CONTRAINDICATIONS OF THE TREATMENT

The research conducted to date suggests that mindfulness as a clinical intervention may have promise across a broad range of clinical problems; however, randomized controlled clinical trials are needed to document its efficacy. Although there is no evidence to date for any particular contraindications to the use of mindfulness interventions, investigators have suggested a number of cautions. Teasdale et al. (2000) caution therapists against using MBCT with clients currently in an acute depressive episode. Linehan (1994) also notes that extended formal practice is often not indicated for many seriously disturbed clients and instead suggests the use the component skills listed earlier or more abbreviated periods of formal practice (e.g., a few minutes).

OTHER FACTORS TO CONSIDER IN DECIDING TO USE MINDFULNESS STRATEGIES

One of the key questions under discussion among treatment developers is whether therapists and instructors should be required to have their own mindfulness practice (Dimidjian, Epstein, Linehan, MacPherson, & Segal, 2001). The MBSR and MBCT approaches require that therapists be engaged in a daily formal practice (i.e.,

sitting meditation, yoga) as part of the model (Kabat-Zinn, 1990; Segal et al., 2002). It is argued that this prerequisite ensures both that therapists will teach from an experiential as well as an intellectual knowledge base and that they will have direct understanding of the effort and discipline required of clients. In contrast, other models such as DBT do not prescribe a formal mindfulness practice for DBT therapists, although some mindfulness activities are required. For instance, formal mindfulness is practiced at the outset of every consultation team meeting, which is a requisite part of DBT, and therapists are required to practice particular mindfulness exercises prior to using them with clients. In this sense, although DBT therapists are not required to have a personal formal practice, they are members of a formal community of therapists learning mindfulness. Interestingly, Epstein (2001) suggests that, in some cases, a personal formal practice may actually be harmful to the clinical process if clinicians bring rigidity or pride about their practice into their clinical work. Linehan (2001) concurs with this position and has suggested that the most important factor in one's personal preparation may be having a mindfulness teacher (either in person or through books) or a community of fellow practitioners, or both.

Unfortunately, there are no empirical data to date that validate the importance of a therapist's personal practice for competent clinical practice; thus, the degree to which a therapist maintains a formal practice will, in part, be guided by the particular model used. For therapists interested in integrating mindfulness strategies as part of other treatment regimens, it will, at a minimum, be important to consider one's own degree of understanding and familiarity with mindfulness practices.

Another important consideration is the question: "is mindfulness practice a means to an end or an end in itself?" (Linehan, 2001). In the spiritual traditions from which they are derived, an essential quality of mindfulness practice is the act of nonstriving or nonattachment to outcome, and the models discussed earlier specifically emphasize this quality of mindfulness. Individuals seeking clinical care, however, are often expressly interested in a particular outcome (e.g., feeling better or less depressed, etc.). Therapists using mindfulness clinically must balance this inherent tension between the "end in itself" quality of mindfulness and the goal-directed quality of clinical care.

HOW DOES MINDFULNESS PRACTICE WORK?

There is no definitive evidence regarding mechanisms of change in the clinical use of mindfulness, although a number of theoretical models have been proposed. Specific hypothesized mechanisms include relaxation (Benson, 1984), metacognitive change (cf. Teasdale, Segal, & Williams, 1995), and replacement of a "negative addiction" with a "positive addiction" (Marlatt, 1994). It has also been suggested that the process of change in mindfulness parallels that of exposure interventions (Kabat-Zinn, 1982; Kabat-Zinn et al., 1992; Linehan, 1993a, 1993b) and acceptance interventions (Linehan, 1993a, 1993b, 1994; Marlatt, 1994). Mindfulness practice may also work by enhancing the use of other cognitive and behavioral procedures, such as problem solving (Linehan, 1993a). Finally, numerous studies have documented a range of physiological effects of meditation practice among nonclinical populations (see, e.g., Austin, 1998); it is likely, therefore, that some of the clinical benefits of mindfulness practice may be mediated by physiological effects. It is also probable that mindfulness does not operate via one single pathway but that its effects are mediated by numerous processes; clearly, further investigation of mechanisms of change will be an important next step for empirical inquiry.

STEP-BY-STEP GUIDELINES FOR THE CLINICAL USE OF MINDFULNESS PRACTICE

Although the primary clinical models utilizing mindfulness strategies are unique in many respects, they also share basic common elements. These common elements are distilled here and in Table 35.1 as a set of six steps to employ in the clinical application of mindfulness practice. This guideline is offered to acquaint the reader with the practice of mindfulness; however, clinicians should be cautioned to recall that these steps have not been empirically tested independently of the larger models from which they are derived.

Step 1: Preparation

Preparation consists of three main parts. First, the therapist must decide what activity the client will practice. It is important to recall that mindfulness is not a particular activity (e.g., sitting quietly with crossed legs on a cushion); it is the quality of awareness that one brings to any activity, to any internal or external stimulus. Therefore, the activities or experiences that can serve as targets for mindfulness practice are endless. Awareness of breathing is perhaps most commonly associated with mindfulness (and it is a core element of most traditions and clinical models), but other possibilities for mindfulness practice abound, includ-

TABLE 35.1 Six Major Steps of the Clinical Use of Mindfulness Practice

Step	Activity
1. Preparation	• Select a target activity or stimulus for mindfulness practice. • Determine how long it will be practiced. • Complete personal preparation.
2. Didactic instruction	• Introduce client to the rationale and goals of mindfulness practice. • Introduce to the client the main characteristics of mindfulness. • Instruct the client on the specific target practice.
3. In-session practice	• Lead and participate with the client in the selected practice activity.
4. Sharing	• Elicit description from the client of his or her direct experience of the practice. • Elicit commentary about the practice from the client.
5. Corrective feedback	• Provide corrective feedback, weaving in information outlined in step 2 as indicated.
6. Homework	• Review homework in manner consistent with procedures outlined in steps 4 and 5.

ing eating, walking, physical movement in yoga or dancing, laughing, singing, listening, seeing, driving, answering the telephone, and so forth.

Second, the therapist must decide how long the client will practice. Among the models discussed in this chapter, the duration of practice varies greatly, ranging from a single minute of practice to 10 days. Duration of practice also varies across different interventions within one model; for instance, MBCT assigns 3-min "breathing space" practices as well as 45-min sitting meditations. At present, no empirical data exist to guide the selection of target activity and/or practice duration; therefore, therapists should be guided by the sequencing guidelines of the treatment model employed and by their assessment of the individual needs, motivation, and capabilities of their clients.

Third, it is important for therapists to prepare personally for the use of mindfulness strategies. At a minimum, it is important for therapists to practice the target activities that will be used before teaching them to their clients. Beyond this, the extent of personal preparation suggested varies across the primary models, as noted previously. Most would agree, however, that preparation involves doing whatever is necessary to be mindful in one's interaction with the client. Toward this end, Segal et al. (2002) advise therapists to take the time necessary to begin sessions, not hurriedly, but with a balance of "openness and 'groundedness'" (84).

Step 2: Didactic Instruction and Orientation

There are three levels of didactic instruction and orientation that the therapist must provide: (1) instruction on the goals and rationale of mindfulness practice, (2) instruction on the key characteristics of mindfulness, and (3) instruction on the selected practice activity.

The first level of instruction requires the therapist to provide a rationale to clients for the use of mindfulness interventions. Although this should be specifically tailored to the client's presenting problems, most models incorporating mindfulness interventions also emphasize the general goal of helping the client to access a sense of wisdom and a corresponding experience of decreased struggle or suffering. In DBT, this is referred to as "wise mind" (Linehan, 1993a, 1993b); in MBCT, as "inherent wisdom" (Segal et al., 2002).

The second level of instruction involves the introduction of mindfulness and its key characteristics. Although each model uses slightly different language, there is considerable conceptual overlap in the key qualities of mindfulness that are emphasized. A brief summary of these qualities is outlined in the following paragraphs. The first three qualities refer to activities that one does when practicing mindfulness; the next three refer to the style in which the first three activities are undertaken.

- *Noticing/Observing/Bringing Awareness.* This is one of the core characteristics of what one does when practicing mindfulness. It is paying attention to direct experience, at the level of pure sensation, without concepts or categories. Therapists can explain that, most often, we move without awareness from the level of direct experience and sensation to conceptual description (and often from there quickly to judgment). For instance, we hear sounds from the tree above and think, "Ah, a bird, what a lovely song." Noticing, however, is hearing the bird's song as *just the elements of sound* (e.g., timbre, pitch, pace, melody, etc.) without classifying or categorizing the experience of hearing as "bird" (or judging it to be "lovely").
- *Labeling/Noting/Describing.* This refers to the activity of observing and then adding a descriptive label to the experience. Again, specific examples will be helpful in explaining this characteristic. For instance, if one is practicing mindfulness of washing the dishes and thinks, "I forgot to pay the phone bill!" labeling/noting/describing would be to say simply "thinking," or "remembering," or "a thought went through my mind." If pain in the shoulder arises, labeling/noting/describing would be to attend to the specific sensation and say, for instance, "tightness." It is important to understand and convey that labeling occurs at the level of process, and thus avoids getting stuck in content. Thus, labeling/noting/describing allows one to step back from experience with awareness, to "decenter" (Segal et al., 2002). It is this act of mindfulness that gives rise to the direct experience of "I am not my emotions," "thoughts are not facts," and so on.

- *Participating.* This refers to throwing oneself fully into an activity or experience. It is becoming one with experience without reservation; it is characterized by spontaneity. This quality is an important one for clients to learn, but it is also a critical quality for therapists to bring to the teaching of mindfulness.

- *Nonjudgmentally/with Acceptance and Allowing.* These refer to three closely related and central aspects of mindfulness practice. *Judgment* is the act of labeling things as good or bad. Most often, we live with great attachment to that which we judge as "good," great aversion to that which we judge as "bad." *Nonjudging* is bringing a gentle, open, and noncritical attitude to experience. It is "assuming the stance of an impartial witness to your own experience" (Kabat-Zinn, 1990, 33). Nonjudging also facilitates letting go or becoming nonattached, which means not trying to hold onto that which is "good" or push away that which is "bad" (e.g., difficult, painful, boring, etc.). Nonjudging is also a form of accepting. *Accepting* is seeing what is. It is not trying to be or get anywhere or anything else; it is not trying to be more relaxed, more joyful, less in pain, more enlightened, and so on. It is ceasing efforts to control or to make things other than they are.

It is important to explain to clients that we practice nonjudging/accepting/allowing with all aspects of mindfulness practice—even the act of judging (e.g., don't judge judging!). Asking clients to focus on the "facts" (e.g., who, what, when, and where) can be a helpful way of practicing nonjudgment (Linehan, 1993b). Therapists may also need to clarify that nonjudging does not mean replacing negative judgments with positive ones. Nonjudging means not making judgments at all, as opposed to being "Pollyanna-ish." It is also important to explain that nonjudging and accepting can be very difficult to do; in fact, Linehan (1993a, 1993b) uses the term *radical acceptance* to connote "that the acceptance has to come from deep within and has to be complete" (102). Therapists may need to address perceived obstacles to accepting; these often include thinking that acceptance confers approval and/or that acceptance will foreclose future opportunities for change (Linehan, 1993b; Kabat-Zinn, 1990). In DBT, the skills of "turning the mind" (or actively choosing to accept) and "willingness" as opposed to "willfulness" are presented as paths toward acceptance.

- *Effectively.* This refers to the quality of mindfulness that has as its chief emphasis "what works." Mindfulness is not concerned with opinions or ideas about right or wrong. A mindful approach is one that easily abandons being right in favor of being effective. This quality stems from the notion of "using skillful means" found in most Eastern meditative traditions.

- *In the Moment/with Beginner's Mind.* Being in the moment refers to being in *this* moment without reference to past or future; only this moment exists. Being in the moment also is the opposite of doing one thing while thinking about something else or attempting to do several activities at once. Kabat-Zinn (1990, 35) explains the quality of beginner's mind: "No moment is the same as any other. Each is unique and contains unique possibilities. Beginner's mind reminds us of this simple truth."

It should be noted that the presentation of the key characteristics is rarely completed in a single didactic session. Instead, certain characteristics may be emphasized in the instructions for specific mindfulness practices or woven into the process of sharing and corrective feedback. It is also often useful to adopt a Socratic style in explaining these qualities of mindfulness, asking clients to add examples from their own lives, generate questions, and so on. Also, stories, metaphors, poetry, and concrete examples are often useful methods of conveying the key characteristics of mindfulness.

At the third level of instruction, the therapist needs to instruct the client in the specific in-session or at-home practice activity. The instructions should be delivered before the practice and may also be repeated, in full or part, at several points during the practice. Instructions should be clear, specific, and simple. It is also common to begin many mindfulness instructions with an invitation to focus on body position or posture; specific instructions about whether to open or close the eyes should also be included if relevant to the activity. Instructions should also include information about the length of the practice and how the beginning and end will be identified; ringing a mindfulness bell may be useful for this purpose.

It is also often helpful, depending on the client's level of skill, to anticipate and provide instruction on common difficulties that may arise. Chief among these is the experience of wandering attention. Therefore, the therapist may anticipate the wandering of attention to thoughts (e.g., "I can't do this," "I forgot to put money in the parking meter," etc.), strong emotions (e.g., boredom, frustration, hopelessness, excitement, anxiety, etc.), physical sensations (e.g., an itch on the left foot, soreness in the shoulders, hearing noises in the hall, etc.), and/or action urges (e.g., the urge to end the practice, to distract, etc.). In each case, the therapist should reassure the client that the wandering of attention is normal—and perhaps even inevitable— for most practitioners of mindfulness. The therapist can also explain that the wandering of attention does not indicate that the client is doing the practice "wrong"; in contrast, responding to the wandering of attention is, itself, part of the practice of mindfulness. The instruction is simply to observe that attention has wandered and to bring it gently, without judgment, back to the target activity.

Step 3: In-Session Practice

Mindfulness is not something that can be taught (or learned) simply by talking about it. Mindfulness is an experientially based skill that needs to be developed over repeated trials of practice. Therefore, in-session practice is critical, as such practice provides the chief context for teaching and learning. Step three is, thus, leading the selected practice. In addition, it is important for the therapist to engage in the target practice with the client. Doing the practice with the client models the mindful behavior, decreases client self-consciousness (Marlatt & Kristeller, 1998), and helps to ensure that the therapist teaches from an immediate "moment to moment experience" (Segal et al., 2002, 89).

Step 4: Sharing

After the target activity has been completed, the therapist asks the client to share his or her experience, including any difficulties encountered. Segal et al. (2002) emphasize the importance of using open-ended questions and an attitude of curiosity in this process. Interestingly, the activity of sharing may itself present opportunities for further mindfulness practice. For instance, if clients report their experience with judgmental language (e.g., "I tried to be mindful of walking, but I did a terrible job"), therapists can guide them to describe their experience without judgmental terms, thereby creating an opportunity for practicing nonjudging (e.g., "I tried to be mindful of walking, but I kept thinking of other things"). MBCT formalizes this distinction by asking clients first "to describe their actual experience during the practice" and later to provide "comments on their experiences" (Segal et al., 89).

Step 5: Corrective Feedback

Although this step is discussed as a separate step for heuristic purposes, in actuality, client sharing and corrective feedback are often closely intertwined. In fact, the careful weaving of client sharing and therapist feedback presents one of the most powerful opportunities for the therapist to teach mindfulness. Therapists are typically able to address obstacles to learning most effectively when instruction is linked to immediate and specific client experiences.

A number of difficulties are frequently addressed during corrective feedback. For instance, being distracted (e.g., by thoughts, noises, emotions, urges, physical sensations, etc.) is a very common experience that clients describe during sharing. It is often helpful in corrective feedback to remind clients that the wandering of one's mind from the target activity is not a sign of failure, but part and parcel of the practice. Clients often report, "I couldn't do it" following a mindfulness practice. To this, therapists can inquire, "Were you aware of 'not doing it'"? Frequently the response is yes. At this point, therapists can explain, "You did it!" and again explain that the practice is to simply be aware of *whatever* arises during the practice.

Feelings of frustration or discouragement (and corresponding self-judgment) may also be common. Clients may feel frustrated that they do not see immediate results in reaching their therapeutic goals (e.g., "It didn't work; I don't feel any better"). Clients may feel that being mindful is too difficult and feel frustrated with the need to practice what is seemingly such a simple activity again and again. In response to both of these concerns, therapists can highlight the inherent dialectic of mindfulness practice between goal orientation and letting go. Therapists can also remind clients that repeated practice is also an inherent part of learning mindfulness. Clients should be cautioned at the outset that mindfulness rarely "just happens." It is simple, but not easy. As in the learning of all new skills, it requires rehearsal and overlearning to master. It thus demands intention, concentration, commitment, and discipline. It requires effort even when one may not feel like exerting effort. MBCT and MBSR both explain to clients, "You don't have to like it; you just have to do it" (Kabat-Zinn, 1990; Segal et al., 2002). It also requires repeated practice and a corresponding attitude of patience. It will often feel like one is starting over, again and again. Often, reference to stories and metaphors that illustrate other skills that require repeated practice and the ineffectiveness of self-judgment and criticism in the process can be useful.

Step 6: Homework

All models utilizing mindfulness strategies emphasize at-home practice. As in all cognitive and behavioral therapies, a heavy emphasis is placed on the generalization of skills learned in sessions and the role of homework toward this end. Specific homework practices can be structured as part of the treatment program, as in MBSR and MBCT, which use a combination of formal and informal practices as well as audiotaped instruction. Homework can also be individually tailored to particular clients, as in DBT. In general, homework assignments should be clear and specific, and potential obstacles to completion should be anticipated and discussed. The next session should include a review of homework that is conducted in a manner consistent with steps 4 and 5 (sharing and corrective feedback) discussed previously.

Further Reading

Kabat-Zinn, J. (1990). *Full catastrophe living: Using the wisdom of your body and mind to face stress, pain, and illness.* New York: Dell Publishing.

Linehan, M. M. (1993a). *Cognitive-behavioral treatment of borderline personality disorder.* New York: Guilford Press.

Linehan, M. M. (1993b). *Skills training manual for treating borderline personality disorder.* New York: Guilford Press.

Segal, Z., Williams, J. M. G., and Teasdale, J. D. (2002). *Mindfulness-based cognitive therapy for depression: A new approach to preventing relapse.* New York: Guilford Press.

References

Austin, J. H. (1998). *Zen and the brain: Toward an understanding of meditation and consciousness.* Cambridge, MA: MIT Press.

Benson, H. (1984). *Beyond the relaxation response: How to harness the healing power of your personal beliefs.* New York: Times Books.

Carlson, L. E., Ursuliak, Z., Goodey, E., Angen, M., & Speca, M. (2001). The effects of a mindfulness meditation-based stress reduction program on mood and symptoms of stress in cancer outpatients: 6-month follow-up results. *Supportive Care in Cancer, 9*, 112–123.

Dimidjian, S., Epstein, R., Linehan, M. M., MacPherson, L., & Segal, Z. (2001). The clinical application of mindfulness practice. Panel discussion conducted at the Association for the Advancement of Behavior Therapy 35th Annual Convention, Philadelphia.

Epstein, R. M. (1999). Mindful practice. *Journal of the American Medical Association, 282*, 833–839.

Kabat-Zinn, J. (1982). An outpatient program in behavioral medicine for chronic pain patients based on the practice of mindfulness meditation: Theoretical considerations and preliminary results. *General Hospital Psychiatry, 4*, 33–47.

Kabat-Zinn, J. (1990). *Full catastrophe living: Using the wisdom of your body and mind to face stress, pain, and illness.* New York: Dell Publishing.

Kabat-Zinn, J., Lipworth, L., & Burney, R. (1985). The clinical use of mindfulness meditation for the self-regulation of chronic pain. *Journal of Behavioral Medicine, 8*, 163–190.

Kabat-Zinn, J., Lipworth, L., Burney, R., & Sellers, W. (1987). Four-year follow-up of a meditation-based program for the self-regulation of chronic pain: Treatment outcomes and compliance. *Clinical Journal of Pain, 2*, 159–173.

Kabat-Zinn, J., Massion, A. O., Kristeller, J., Peterson, L. G., Fletcher, K. E., Pbert, L., Lenderking, W. R., & Santorelli, S. F. (1992). Effectiveness of a meditation-based stress reduction program in the treatment of anxiety disorders. *American Journal of Psychiatry, 149*, 936–943.

Kabat-Zinn, J., Wheeler, E., Light, T., Skillings, Z., Scharf, M. J., Cropley, T. G., Hosmer, D., & Bernhard, J. D. (1998). Influence of a mindfulness meditation-based stress reduction intervention on rates of skin clearing in patients with moderate to severe psoriasis undergoing phototherapy (UVB) and photochemotherapy (PUVA). *Psychosomatic Medicine, 50*, 625–632.

Kaplan, K. H., Goldenberg, D. L., & Galvin-Nadeau, M. (1993). The impact of a meditation-based stress reduction program on fibromyalgia. *General Hospital Psychiatry, 15*, 284–289.

Koerner, K., & Dimeff, L. (2000). Further data on dialectical behavior therapy. *Clinical Psychology: Science and Practice, 7*, 104–112.

Kristeller, J. L., & Hallett, C. B. (1999). An exploratory study of a meditation-based intervention for binge eating disorder. *Journal of Health Psychology, 4*, 357–363.

Linehan, M. M. (1993a). *Cognitive-behavioral treatment of borderline personality disorder.* New York: Guilford Press.

Linehan, M. M. (1993b). *Skills training manual for treating borderline personality disorder.* New York: Guilford Press.

Linehan, M. M. (1994). Acceptance and change: The central dialectic in psychotherapy. In S. C. Hayes, N. S. Jacobson, V. M. Follette, and M J. Dougher (Eds.), *Acceptance and change: Content and context in psychotherapy* (pp. 73–86). Reno, NV: Context Press.

Marlatt, G. A. (1994). Addiction and acceptance. In S. C. Hayes, N. S. Jacobson, V. M. Follette, and M. J. Dougher (Eds.), *Acceptance and change: Content and context in psychotherapy* (pp. 175–197). Reno, NV: Context Press.

Marlatt, G. A., & Gordon, J. R. (1985). *Relapse prevention: Maintenance strategies in the treatment of addictive behaviors.* New York: Guilford Press.

Marlatt, G. A., & Kristeller, J. A. (1998). Mindfulness and meditation. In W. R. Miller (Ed.), *Integrating spirituality in treatment: Resources for practitioners* (pp. 67–84). Washington, DC: APA Books.

Miller, J. J., Fletcher, K., & Kabat-Zinn, J. (1995). Three-year follow-up and clinical implications of a mindfulness meditation-based stress reduction intervention in the treatment of anxiety disorders. *General Hospital Psychiatry, 17*, 192–200.

Mills, N., & Allen, J. (2000). Mindfulness of movement as a coping strategy in multiple sclerosis: A pilot study. *General Hospital Psychiatry, 22*, 425–431.

Randolph, P. D., Caldera, Y. M., Tacone, A. M., & Greak, M. L. (1999). The long-term combined effects of medical treatment and a mindfulness-based behavioral program for the multidisciplinary management of chronic pain in west Texas. *Pain Digest, 9*, 103–112.

Segal, Z., Williams, J. M. G., & Teasdale, J. D. (2002). *Mindfulness-based cognitive therapy for depression: A new approach to preventing relapse.* New York: Guilford Press.

Speca, M., Carlson, L. E., Goodey, E., & Angen, M. (2000). A randomized, wait-list controlled clinical trial: The effect of a mindfulness meditation-based stress reduction program on mood and symptoms of stress in cancer outpatients. *Psychosomatic Medicine, 62*, 613–622.

Teasdale, J. D., Segal, Z., & Williams, J. M. (1995). How does cognitive therapy prevent depressive relapse and why should attentional control (mindfulness) training help? *Behaviour Research and Therapy, 33*, 25–39.

Teasdale, J. D., Segal, Z. V., Williams, J. M., Ridgeway, V. A., Soulsby, J. M., & Lau, M. A. (2000). Prevention of relapse/recurrence in major depression by mindfulness-based cognitive therapy. *Journal of Consulting and Clinical Psychology, 68*, 615–623.

36 MODELING AND BEHAVIORAL REHEARSAL

Amy E. Naugle and Sherrie Maher

Modeling and behavioral rehearsal procedures emerged as formal techniques for modifying behavior in the late 1950s and early 1960s. The rationale for the utility of these procedures is based on the premise that humans can acquire new behavior or decrease existing problem behaviors through observation and imitation. Early applications of modeling procedures were used primarily in two domains: (1) to facilitate the acquisition of behavioral skills, and (2) to eliminate phobias and other anxious and fearful behaviors (e.g., Bandura, Grusec, & Menlove, 1967). The encouraging findings regarding the efficacy of these procedures resulted in expanding modeling techniques to address a broad range of clinical phenomena.

Modeling and behavioral rehearsal techniques are included as a substantial component of skills training and are often combined with other therapeutic procedures to comprise treatment packages for a variety of different psychosocial problems. As one contemporary example, modeling and behavioral rehearsal strategies are becoming crucial elements of intervention and prevention programs for sexual assault. Recent literature in the area of sexual assault suggests that women do not benefit from educational programs alone (Yeater & O'Donohue, 1999). It is therefore recommended that direct behavioral instruction, and the modeling and practice of specific skills, are necessary to reduce risk of sexual assault (Naugle, 1999). While modeling procedures can be applied to diverse types of problems and behaviors, the general technology and terminology of modeling and behavioral rehearsal are relatively straightforward.

Modeling simply refers to the behavior of the *model,* or the individual(s) performing the target behavior. Models can either be present or "live" with the observer or *symbolic* in that they are observed from a videotape or book. Modeling can also be done *covertly* when an observer is asked to imagine a model performing the target behavior. For example, athletes may use covert modeling strategies to enhance their performance by imagining either themselves or someone else performing an athletic skill with mastery.

Imitation refers to the behavior of the *observer,* or the one who observes the model. This term refers to behavior on the part of the observer, but does not necessarily imply acquisition or learning of the target behavior. *Observational learning* refers to learning that occurs and is retained as the result of observing the behavior of a model. This learning can occur without direct imitation of the target behavior. In observational learning, the observer has access not only to the behavior of the model, but also to the reinforcing or punishing consequences that follow the modeled behavior. For example, a young sibling observes his older brother being punished for taking the family car without permission. Although the sibling has not learned to drive, he may retain this information, and use this information in the future to avoid negative consequences. Conversely, the observer may acquire a desirable behavior that is modeled and associated with positive consequences. A younger sister may observe her older sister diligently studying for an exam for which she receives an excellent grade and is praised by her parents. Such observational learning may then result in the development of similar study skills in the younger sister.

Behavioral rehearsal simply involves having the client practice or perform the desired or target behavior. Generally, behavioral rehearsal can be viewed as a shaping process. In order to facilitate the acquisition of a specific skill, behavioral rehearsal involves four subcomponents, including prompting, shaping, providing feedback, and delivering reinforcement (Spiegler & Guevremont, 1998).

FUNCTIONS OF MODELING

Modeling serves several functions or purposes. One function of modeling is to facilitate the acquisition of behaviors or skills. Therapists can use modeling to prompt clients to perform a behavior that is absent from their repertoire. Lovaas and his colleagues have effectively used modeling procedures combined with reinforcement to establish language in children with autism (e.g., Lovaas, Berberich, Perloff, & Schaeffer, 1966; Lovaas, Schreibman, & Koegel, 1974). Additionally, modeling and behavioral rehearsal have been effective at improving performance skills such as assertive-refusal behavior (e.g., McFall & Lillesand, 1971) and component social skills such as the ability to initiate and maintain conversations (e.g., Whitehill, Hersen, & Bellack, 1980). When teaching complex behavior or behavior patterns, it is necessary to break the skill down into more rudimentary and simple components. In addition, rehearsal and repeated practice will aid clients in becoming more proficient in the target skill. However, skills training and the acquisition of complex behavior require not only that individuals learn *what* to do, but that they know when and where to appropriately apply the skills as well as be motivated to execute the skill (Spiegler & Guevremont, 1998).

Modeling can also function to teach clients to perform certain behaviors at appropriate times and in appropriate settings. For example, it is often appropriate or acceptable to yell loudly and perform "the wave" at a football game; however, it is inappropriate to exhibit these same behaviors at the library. Motivation to apply a skill is largely, if not entirely, impacted by the contingencies associated with performing the behavior. Certainly client behavior can be shaped through the process of direct reinforcement. The therapist may contingently respond to the client by reinforcing approximations to the target behavior, or contact with natural contingencies outside of therapy may influence the client's behavior. However, client motivation can be enhanced through processes of vicarious reinforcement as well. While the data regarding the effectiveness of vicarious reinforcement are mixed, there is some evidence to suggest that reinforcement procedures can effectively increase the behavior of individuals who simply observe the reinforcement of another person's behavior (e.g., Kazdin, 1973; Maeda, 1985; Ollendick, Shapiro, & Barrett, 1982).

Modeling procedures can also function to disinhibit or reduce fear and anxiety through the process of vicarious extinction. In order to decrease avoidance behavior in response to feared objects or situations, fearful clients observe a model performing approach behaviors that are increasingly more threatening. Treatment packages targeting anxiety reduction generally involve both demonstration of approach behavior by a model as well as participation by the observer (e.g., desensitization or exposure). The inclusion of modeling procedures presumes that a client can be encouraged to face the feared object or animal if a model similar to the client can face the feared situation or phobic stimulus. A number of studies have demonstrated the effectiveness of vicarious extinction procedures in treating anxious or fearful behavior (e.g., Bandura & Menlove, 1968; Mattick & Peters, 1988; Silverman, 1986).

WHAT MAKES MODELING EFFECTIVE?

Bandura in 1969 and later in 1977 described four processes of how behavior is acquired from observational learning. These processes work together to render modeling more effective in modifying the behavior of an observer. The four processes that Bandura proposed mediate the effectiveness of modeling include attention to the modeled behavior, reproduction of the modeled behavior, retention of what is learned, and motivation to perform the behavior. Effective modeling requires that the observer have the ability to pay attention to the model as well as to attend to specific aspects of the context itself. Interference in attending to the behavior of the model does not allow the observer to learn the nuances of the behavior or to discriminate the conditions under which the behavior is appropriate (Masters, Burish, Hollon, & Rimm, 1987). Bandura (1977) advises that to enhance the effectiveness of observational learning, it is necessary for the model or the context in which the modeled behavior occurs to possess certain characteristics. The model/context should be "distinctive" in that the behavior of the model as well as the model itself captures the observer's *attention*. As such, the model(s) should be exemplary, but not so distinct that the observer does not identify with the model. Bandura suggests it is important to have the characteristics of the model and the scene/context match the observer as much as possible. Emotional arousal is an additional factor that may impact one's ability to pay attention to the modeled event. For example, if one is too sleepy or too agitated, attention and subsequent learning may be compromised.

Another aspect of effective modeling procedures concerns the ability of the observer to reproduce the modeled behavior and to retain learning in order to produce the behavior in the future. Reproduction and retention of modeled behavior is partially dependent on the given level of skill that the observer possesses. For example, it would be unrealistic to ask a beginning skater to perform a triple axel when even more remedial turns and jumps are not in his or her repertoire. Exposing the observer to multiple observations or repeated practice can enhance retention of learning. Overarching the entire process is that there must be a certain level of motivation for the observer to perform the target behavior. It is essential to determine whether the behavior to be learned possesses some intrinsic value or

requires externally mediated consequences to establish and maintain it. It is well known that utilizing rewards for performance can enhance motivation.

WHO IS LIKELY TO BENEFIT FROM MODELING PROCEDURES?

Modeling procedures have been used to treat a wide array of clinical problems across diverse types of clients and diverse types of settings. Modeling procedures have been effective for training communication skills and daily living skills in individuals with autism and mental retardation (e.g., Charlop & Milstein, 1989; Frea & Hughes, 1997; Goldstein & Mousetis, 1989; Matson, Smalls, Hampff, Smiroldo, & Anderson, 1998). The procedures have been used to promote social skills in individuals with schizophrenia and other severe emotional problems (e.g., Mueser, Levine, Bellack, & Douglas, 1990; Trower, 1995). Modeling and behavioral rehearsal are essential components of assertiveness training (e.g., Kazdin & Mascitelli, 1982; Kipper, 1992) and in improving interpersonal skills in depressed individuals (e.g., Hersen, Bellack, & Himmelhoch, 1980; Reed, 1994), as well as in clients with long-standing emotional and interpersonal difficulties (Linehan, 1993; Linehan, Tutek, Heard, & Armstrong, 1994). Components of treatments designed to improve problem-solving and coping skills also utilize modeling procedures. For example, many cognitive-behavioral interventions for substance abusers incorporate participant modeling and behavioral rehearsal techniques to teach individuals refusal skills as well as other coping behaviors (e.g., Corbin, Jones, & Schulman, 1993; Ingram & Salzberg, 1990; Longabaugh & Morganstern, 1999). Essentially, modeling procedures can be applied to almost any situation that calls for the development or refinement of a specific behavioral skill. The procedures enable clients to practice skills in which they are deficient or require additional remediation. Modeling/rehearsal may help by providing the client access to skilled modeling of the target behavior(s), as well as by providing sufficient opportunity to practice skills, to adopt and strengthen new behaviors, and to learn when, where, how the use of the behavior is appropriate. With the assistance of a therapist, clients will gain mastery of the skill as well as increase their confidence, which will facilitate performance of the desired behavior and maximize the likelihood that the behavior will be maintained.

In addition, modeling procedures have been shown to be effective at reducing or eliminating maladaptive behaviors, specifically at reducing avoidance behavior in fearful or anxious individuals. For example, participant modeling has been combined with other cognitive-behavioral techniques to effectively treat animal phobias (e.g., Bandura et al., 1967; Freeman, 1997; Smith, Kirkby, Montgomery, & Daniels, 1997) and other specific phobias (e.g., Osborn, 1986). Individuals with dental fears and injection phobias have also benefited from modeling procedures (e.g., Sanders & Jones, 1990; Trijsburg, Jelicic, van den Broek, & Plekker, 1996). Modeling and behavioral rehearsal may also be effective strategies for decreasing trauma-related anxiety among individuals diagnosed with post-traumatic stress disorder (e.g., Schwartz, Houlihan, Krueger, & Simon, 1997). Indeed, covert modeling is one recommended technique in cognitive-behavioral treatment packages for treating victims of sexual assault (Naugle, Resnick, Gray, & Acierno, 2002). Treatments for obsessive-compulsive disorder also have incorporated modeling and behavioral rehearsal techniques to effectively prevent compulsive responding (e.g., Silverman, 1986).

CONTRAINDICATIONS

There appear to be few contraindications for modeling and behavioral rehearsal techniques and there are no apparent dangers to using these procedures with clients. Modeling procedures can be very efficient and cost effective and can be used with even the most cognitively, socially, and emotionally challenged individuals. The procedures can be implemented across a wide variety of settings and contexts, in both the natural environment and more restrictive therapeutic or laboratory settings. Furthermore, the procedures are relatively easy to implement and can produce behavior change in only a few sessions. The main requisite skill appears to be simply that the individual is capable of observing the modeled behavior and of applying this observation to his or her own behavior. Any problems that emerge from the use of modeling procedures are likely the result of inappropriate application of the technique or the fidelity of the treatment delivery (Rosenthal & Steffek, 1991).

That being said, there are several types of clients for whom modeling and behavioral rehearsal may not be indicated. These include the following:

1. Individuals who are not capable of accepting or recognizing that they play a part in their behavior problems.
2. Individuals who are unwilling or fearful of risks because of perceived negative consequences (real or imagined).
3. Individuals who refuse to practice in the behavioral rehearsal component of training.
4. Individuals who do not complete homework assignments or who do so in a lackadaisical fashion.
5. Individuals undergoing severe crises in their daily lives.
6. Individuals who experience severe psychomotor agitation or retardation. These individuals may have problems focusing their attention or sustaining energy directed toward treatment.

MODELING AND BEHAVIORAL REHEARSAL SKILLS TRAINING PROCEDURES

The components of modeling procedures in skills training include assessment of skill deficits and identification of target behaviors, direct instruction, modeling, behavioral rehearsal, feedback and reinforcement, and between-session homework (see Table 36.1; Morrison, 1990; Speigler & Guevremont, 1998).

Assessment

During the assessment phase, the task of the therapist is to identify specific behavioral excesses or deficits to be targeted, as well as the conditions that maintain the problem. The ideal strategy for identifying targets for treatment is to observe the

TABLE 36.1   Components of Modeling and Behavioral Rehearsal Procedures

Component	General Goals	Specific Strategy
Assessment	• Identify target behaviors or skill deficits • Assess client's discrimination regarding appropriate use • Evaluate dimensions of behavior (e.g., latency, emotional expression, etc.)	• Clinical interview • Self-report questionnaires • Self-monitoring • Direct observation • Functional analysis • Behavioral inventories • Role-playing
Instruction	• Provide rationale for use of skill • Describe skill to be performed	• Make sure instruction is specific • Check client comprehension of instruction
Modeling	• In vivo modeling versus symbolic modeling • Coping models versus mastery models	• Clients can either observe modeled behavior live or watch video-tape of the model • Start with most simply behavior/skill first • Coping models may be helpful for clients who are hesitant/fearful
Behavioral rehearsal	• Prompt client practice of modeled behavior • Reinforce client efforts • Provide verbal feedback regarding execution of the skill • Shape behavioral approximations to desired behavior using contingent reinforcement	• Rehearsal can be done in naturalistic settings or using role-played scenarios • Start with most simply behavior/skill first • Reinforcing client efforts will enhance motivation to perform more complex behaviors • Make feedback concrete and specific

client in his or her natural environment. However, additional techniques for assessing clinical problems and formulating intervention strategies include clinical interviews, functional analyses, role-playing, self-monitoring, self-report questionnaires, or standard behavioral inventories (Spiegler & Guevremont, 1998). Given the subjective nature of self-report, errors or inaccuracies in a client's reports of problem situations can lead to implementing modeling procedures that are less relevant to the client's actual situation. Again, it is therefore advisable to incorporate either direct observation or role-play situations into assessment practices.

In addition to aiding in the identification of target behaviors, information gathered during the assessment phase is incorporated into actual modeling and behavioral rehearsal exercises to treat the target behavior. Therefore, information gathered from assessment practices should be as detailed and specific as possible. This will allow therapists to tailor modeling scenarios and other role-play or behavioral rehearsal exercises to the individual client. It has been suggested that clients are more easily engaged when role-play situations pertain specifically to them (Masters

et al., 1987). Using scenarios in which they are personally invested enhances the engagement of clients in the role-play or rehearsal exercises.

In using role-play situations, therapists may elect to utilize client-specific scenarios or more generic, standardized scenarios to assess and treat relevant behaviors. In either case the formats of these tests are quite similar. Once a rationale for the role-play exercise is provided, the client is presented with a typewritten description of each scene before engaging in the role-play. The therapist then reads the brief description and reads the opening line of the scenario. Following a prompt from the therapist, the client is required to respond to the scenario as though he or she were actually interacting in the role-play situation. The client responds, the therapist gives another prompt, and the interaction is recorded. Recording client responses and role-played interactions allows therapists to rate the effectiveness of client skills, plan appropriate interventions, and provide explicit feedback to clients regarding their skill fluency.

Not only does role-playing provide relevant behavioral samples when direct observation in the client's natural environment is not possible, it provides an opportunity to measure and provide feedback regarding a number of different dimensions of the behavior or interaction. These dimensions may include overall quality or effectiveness of the response, latency or timing of the response, speech fluency and volume, appropriateness of emotional expression, eye contact, body language and mannerisms, and so on. Any of these dimensions may be relevant factors in determining the competency or mastery of the skill being modeled.

Instruction

Once specific skill deficits or target behaviors have been identified from a thorough, comprehensive assessment, the therapist can move on to instructing the client with regard to the desired behavior or behaviors and implementing formal modeling and behavioral rehearsal techniques to modify behavior. In general it is useful for the therapist to present a rationale for learning the requisite skill before actual demonstration of that skill. For example, a therapist may say, "We have reason to believe that women with poor assertiveness skills may have a greater chance of being sexually assaulted. The literature has shown that firmly refusing advances from the opposite sex by clearly saying 'No' has been found to be effective in avoiding assaults. Clear and direct communication is an important strategy for avoiding misunderstandings between men and women in dating or social situations."

Modeling

Verbal instruction alone is generally not sufficient for bringing about behavior change. Modeling procedures are therefore necessary to demonstrate the skill to be learned. Continuing with the above example, in targeting sexual assertion skills the therapist may begin by stating, "Let's begin by practicing a couple of situations where you should say no. Imagine for a minute that you are out at a bar. A man whom you do not know approaches you and asks to buy you a drink. You do not know the man and do not think that drinking more in this situation is a good idea. In this situation it is important and appropriate to clearly convey to the man that you do not

want him to buy you a drink and are not interested in continuing the interaction with him." In order to aid the client in learning appropriate assertive behavior for this social situation, the therapist should first model assertive refusal behavior for the client. Modeling of this skill can be done in vivo (e.g., the client role-plays the man in the scenario and the therapist models the target skill) or through the use of a video in which the client watches a model perform the targeted behavior.

When using modeling to facilitate skills acquisition or to extinguish problem behaviors, the distinction is sometimes made between using coping models versus mastery models. It is the task of the therapist to determine which modeling approach is most appropriate. *Mastery models* perform the desired behavior or skill with confidence, competence, and without error from the outset. Alternatively, *coping models* are models who initially display some trepidation or hesitancy in performing a skill and at first execute the behavior with some flaws. Initial hesitancies by the model are then replaced by increasingly skillful demonstration of the behavior as the model copes with the demands of the situation (Masters et al., 1987). Coping models can be especially useful with clients who are somewhat hesitant, fearful, or incompetent themselves (e.g., Kazdin, 1974; Meichenbaum, 1971). Mastery models are better suited to situations that involve developing precise skills (e.g., refusing a ride from a stranger or physically defending oneself).

Behavioral Rehearsal

The next component of modeling procedures involves behavioral rehearsal of the modeled behavior by the client. Most applications of modeling require clients to participate by performing the behavior immediately after it is appropriately modeled for them. This allows the therapist to reinforce and subsequently shape client performance of the target skill. Again, rehearsal of modeled behavior can be done in the context of role-play scenarios or in more naturalistic settings. When modeling and rehearsal are used to reduce anxiety-related behaviors, in vivo modeling and rehearsal may be the most effective form of treatment delivery. For example, the client may be required to engage in modeled approach behavior with respect to a feared stimulus or situation (e.g., walk toward a cage containing a snake, handle the snake, etc.). As is illustrated in the snake phobia example, successful treatment in many cases requires clients to acquire a complex behavioral repertoire or to engage in increasingly difficult behaviors. Graduated modeling involves presenting modeling procedures in sequences that become progressively more difficult or demanding, much in the same tradition as systematic desensitization (Masters et al., 1987).

Throughout the practice session(s) the therapist must make sure he or she is providing adequate reinforcement and feedback for the client's efforts and approximations to the desired behavioral goal. Therapist-mediated social reinforcement of client attempts to perform the target behavior facilitates client efforts to perform increasingly difficult and demanding skills. Therefore, it is important for therapists to adequately praise client efforts prior to offering suggestions on how to improve the skill or before directly shaping approximations to the target behavior. When providing verbal feedback regarding the client's actual performance, it is crucial that the feedback be clear and behaviorally *specific* (e.g., "You held your posture quite nicely, now try keeping my eye contact a little longer").

Homework and Generalization

Repeated practice of requisite skills promotes retention of the learned behavior and also facilitates appropriate implementation of the skills in the client's natural environment. Modeling procedures require that clients learn basic skills and then move on to learning and practicing more advanced skills while also promoting appropriate generalization of the skills outside of therapy. Homework and out-of-session practice are essential components of modeling approaches to treatment in order to maximize generalization. Homework assignments need to be constructed in such a way as to maximize successful execution of extrasession practice. Repeated modeling trials and in-session practice will ensure that the client is capable of performing the behavior without the therapist present. In addition, accompa-

nying clients into real-world settings and using in vivo shaping is another way for the therapist to promote successful use of the skill and to ensure that additional homework assignments are carried out. It is essential that the therapist and client review between-session homework at the next session to identify any problems and review the modeled behavior if necessary.

In addition to using homework assignments to promote generalization, there are other strategies that can be used to transfer learning to real-world settings. The use of multiple models in role-playing or behavioral rehearsal exercises may increase the likelihood that clients are better prepared for applying newly learned skills to novel situations. Since it is difficult, if not impossible, to anticipate all possible variations in one's environment, instructing the client on general problem solving skills may be an additional way of circumventing difficulties in skill generalization. Finally, follow-up assessments or booster sessions are encouraged to maintain successful behavior change.

CONCLUSION

This chapter provides an introductory overview to the concepts and techniques of modeling and behavioral rehearsal procedures. Behavioral and cognitive-behavioral interventions have a long tradition of incorporating these strategies into comprehensive treatment packages for a wide range of behavioral and clinical problems. For more in-depth coverage of the principles of observational learning and modeling the reader is encouraged to utilize the following reading resources. In addition, the reader may benefit by referring to treatment protocols or descriptions for individual clinical problems to learn more about specific applications of the techniques.

Further Reading

Bandura, A. (1969). *Principles of behavior modification.* New York: Holt, Rinehart, & Winston.

Bandura, A. (1977). *Social learning theory.* Englewood Cliffs, NJ: Prentice Hall.

Masters, J. C., Burish, T. G., Hollon, S. D., & Rimm, D. C. (1987). *Behavior therapy: Techniques and empir-*

ical findings (3rd ed.). Orlando, FL: Harcourt Brace Jovanovich.

O'Donohue, W., & Krasner, L. (1995). *Handbook of psychological skills training: Clinical techniques and applications.* Needham Heights, MA: Allyn & Bacon.

References

Bandura, A. (1969). *Principles of behavior modification.* New York: Holt, Rinehart, & Winston.

Bandura, A. (1977). *Social learning theory.* Englewood Cliffs, NJ: Prentice Hall.

Bandura, A., Grusec, J. E., & Menlove, F. L. (1967). Vicarious extinction of avoidance behavior. *Journal of Personality and Social Psychology, 5,* 449–455.

Bandura, A., & Menlove, F. L. (1968). Factors determining vicarious extinction of avoidance behavior through symbolic modeling. *Journal of Personality and Social Psychology, 7,* 111–116.

Charlop, M. H., & Milstein, J. P. (1989). Teaching autistic children conversational speech using video modeling. *Journal of Applied Behavior Analysis, 22,* 275–285.

Corbin, S. K., Jones, R. T., & Schulman, R. S. (1993). Drug refusal behavior: The relative efficacy of skills-based and information-based treatment. *Journal of Pediatric Psychology, 18,* 769–784.

Frea, W. D., & Hughes, C. (1997). Functional analysis and treatment of social-communicative behavior of adolescents with developmental disabilities. *Journal of Applied Behavior Analysis, 30,* 701–704.

Freeman, S. (1997). Treating a dog phobia in a person with Down's syndrome by use of systematic desensitization and modelling. *British Journal of Learning Disabilities, 25,* 154–157.

Goldstein, H., & Mousetis, L. (1989). Generalized language learning by children with severe mental retardation: Effects of peers' expressive modeling. *Journal of Applied Behavior Analysis, 22,* 245–259.

Hersen, M., Bellack, A. S., & Himmelhoch, J. M. (1980). Treatment of unipolar depression with social skills training. *Behavior Modification, 4,* 547–556.

Ingram, J. A., & Salzberg, J. (1990). Effects of in vivo behavioral rehearsal on the learning of assertive behaviors with a substance abusing population. *Addictive Behaviors, 15,* 189–194.

Kazdin, A. E. (1973). The effect of vicarious reinforcement on attentive behavior in the classroom. *Journal of Applied Behavior Analysis, 6,* 71–78.

Kazdin, A. E. (1974). The effect of model identity and fear-relevant similarity on covert modeling. *Behavior Therapy, 5,* 624–635.

Kazdin, A. E., & Mascitelli, S. (1982). Behavioral rehearsal, self-instructions, and homework practice in developing assertiveness. *Behavior Therapy, 13,* 346–360.

Kipper, D. A. (1992). The effect of two kinds of role playing on self-evaluation of improved assertiveness. *Journal of Clinical Psychology, 48,* 246–250.

Linehan, M. M. (1993). *Cognitive-behavioral treatment of borderline personality disorder.* New York: Guilford Press.

Linehan, M. M., Tutek, D. A., Heard, H. L., & Armstrong, H. E. (1994). Interpersonal outcome of cognitive behavioral treatment for chronically suicidal borderline patients. *American Journal of Psychiatry, 151,* 1771–1776.

Longabaugh, R., & Morganstern, J. (1999). Cognitive-behavioral coping-skills therapy for alcohol dependence: Current status and future directions. *Alcohol Research and Health, 23,* 78–85.

Lovaas, O. I., Berberich, J. P., Perloff, B. F., & Schaeffer, B. (1966). Acquisition of imitative speech by schizophrenic children. *Science, 151,* 705–707.

Lovaas, O. I., Schreibman, L., & Koegel, R. L. (1974). A behavior modification approach to the treatment of autistic children. *Journal of Autism and Childhood Schizophrenia, 4,* 111–129.

Maeda, M. (1985). The effects of combinations of vicarious reinforcement on the formation of assertive behaviors in covert modeling. *Japanese Journal of Behavior Therapy, 10,* 34–44.

Masters, J. C., Burish, T. G., Hollon, S. D., & Rimm, D. C. (1987). *Behavior therapy: Techniques and empirical findings* (3rd ed.). Orlando, FL: Harcourt Brace Jovanovich.

Matson, J. L., Smalls, Y., Hampff, A., Smiroldo, B. B., & Anderson, S. J. (1998). A comparison of behavioral techniques to teach functional independent-living skills to individuals with severe and profound mental retardation. *Behavior Modification, 22,* 298–306.

Mattick, R. P., & Peters, L. (1988). Treatment of severe social phobia: Effects of guided exposure with and without cognitive restructuring. *Journal of Consulting and Clinical Psychology, 56,* 251–260.

McFall, R. M., & Lillesand, D. B. (1971). Behavioral rehearsal with modeling and coaching in assertion training. *Journal of Abnormal Behavior, 77,* 313–323.

Meichenbaum, D. H. (1971). Examination of model characteristics in reducing avoidance behavior. *Journal of Personality and Social Psychology, 17,* 298–307.

Morrison, R. L. (1990). Interpersonal dysfunction. In

A. S. Bellack, M. Hersen, & A. E. Kazdin (Eds.), *International handbook of behavior modification and therapy* (pp. 503–519). New York: Plenum Press.

Mueser, K. T., Levine, S., Bellack, A. S., & Douglas, M. S. (1990). Social skills training for acute psychiatric inpatients. *Hospital and Community Psychiatry, 41,* 1249–1251.

Naugle, A. E. (1999). *Identifying behavioral risk factors for repeated victimization using video-taped stimulus materials.* Unpublished doctoral dissertation, University of Nevada, Reno.

Naugle, A. E., Resnick, H. S., Gray, M., & Acierno, R. (2002). Treatment for acute stress and PTSD following rape. In J. Petrak & B. Hedge (Eds.), *The trauma of sexual assault: Treatment, prevention, and policy* (pp. 135–156). London: John Wiley & Sons.

Ollendick, T. H., Shapiro, E. S., & Barrett, R. P. (1982). Effects of vicarious reinforcement in normal and severely disturbed children. *Journal of Consulting and Clinical Psychology, 50,* 63–70.

Osborn, E. L. (1986). Effects of participant modeling and desensitization on childhood warm water phobia. *Journal of Behavior Therapy and Experimental Psychiatry, 17,* 117–119.

Reed, M. K. (1994). Social skills training to reduce depression in adolescents. *Adolescence, 29,* 293–302.

Rosenthal, T. L., & Steffek, B. D. (1991). Modeling methods. In F. H. Kanfer & A. P. Goldstein (Eds.), *Helping people change: A textbook of methods* (pp. 70–121). New York: Pergamon Press.

Sanders, M. R., & Jones, L. (1990). Behavioural treatment of injection, dental, and medical phobias in adolescents: A case study. *Behavioural Psychotherapy, 18,* 311–316.

Schwartz, C., Houlihan, D., Krueger, K. F., & Simon, D. A. (1997). The behavioral treatment of a young adult with post traumatic stress disorder and a fear of children. *Child and Family Behavior Therapy, 19,* 37–49.

Silverman, W. H. (1986). Client-therapist cooperation in the treatment of compulsive handwashing behavior. *Journal of Behavior Therapy and Experimental Psychiatry, 17,* 39–42.

Smith, K. L., Kirkby, K. C., Montgomery, I. M., & Daniels, B. A. (1997). Computer-delivered modeling of exposure for spider phobia: Relevant versus irrelevant exposure. *Journal of Anxiety Disorders, 11,* 489–497.

Spiegler, M. D., & Guevremont, D. C. (1998). *Contemporary behavior therapy* (3rd ed). Pacific Grove, CA: Brooks/Cole.

Trijsburg, R. W., Jelicic, M., van den Broek, W. W., & Plekker, A. E. M. (1996). Exposure and participant modelling in a case of injection phobia. *Psychotherapy and Psychosomatics, 65,* 57–61.

Trower, P. (1995). Adult social skills: State of the art and future directions. In W. O'Donohue & L. Krasner (Eds.), *Handbook of psychological skills training: Clinical techniques and applications* (pp. 54–80). Needham Heights, MA: Allyn & Bacon.

Whitehill, M. B., Hersen, M., & Bellack, A. S. (1980). Conversational skills training in socially isolated children. *Behaviour Research and Therapy, 18,* 217–225.

Yeater, E. A., & O'Donohue, W. (1999). Sexual assault prevention programs: Current issues, future directions, and the potential efficacy of intervention with women. *Clinical Psychology Review, 19,* 739–771.

37 MODERATE DRINKING TRAINING FOR PROBLEM DRINKERS

Frederick Rotgers

Ever since D. L. Davies (1962) published case reports of alcoholics who moderated their alcohol consumption, continuing controversy in the alcohol treatment field has centered on whether a return to moderate drinking is an appropriate treatment goal for problem drinkers. Fueled more by untested clinical lore than by data, those on the abstinence-only side of the controversy have largely ignored the substantial body of research demonstrating that many problem drinkers moderate their drinking to safe levels following treatment rather than becoming completely abstinent, and supporting the efficacy of moderation training for a large segment of problem drinkers (Heather & Robertson, 1997; Heather et al., 2000; Walters, 2000). In fact, this literature is now so extensive that Heather et al. described Behavioral Self-Control Training (one form of moderation-focused treatment) as "probably the most researched single treatment modality in the alcohol problems field with over 30 controlled trials devoted to it" (2000, p. 562), adding that it is "supported by the second largest number of positive studies of any treatment modality in the literature" (p. 562).

In some ways, the controversy over moderation is surprising. The idea that many problem drinkers may be able to moderate successfully, and that personal commitment to moderation may be a critical determinant of outcome, is hardly new. In fact, acknowledgment of the possibility of moderate drinking outcomes for some problem drinkers, as well as a personal "experiment" that an individual may use to determine if moderation is possible for that individual, both appear the "Big Book" of Alcoholics Anonymous.

It is not yet clear who is most likely to benefit from moderation training approaches but reviews of the literature suggest that most problem drinkers can derive some benefit, even those who demonstrate moderate to severe dependence on alcohol (Heather et al., 2000; Rosenberg, 1993; Walters, 2000). Research shows that allowing problem drinkers who enter treatment to select their own drinking goal enhances both retention and outcome (Ojehagen & Berglund, 1989; Sanchez-Craig & Lei, 1986) even though most problem drinkers who enter treatment choose abstinence over moderation (Rotgers, 1996). Considering the extensive research base, moderation approaches should now be a part of the overall armamentarium of treatment approaches available to clinicians working with problem drinkers.

MODERATION TRAINING APPROACHES

Two types of moderation training program have been reported in the literature. The most common, and the one to be discussed in detail here, is based on principles of cognitive-behavioral therapy and largely involves self-control training (Dimeff, Baer, Kivlahan, & Marlatt, 1999; Miller & Munoz, 1982; Sanchez-Craig, 1995; Sobell & Sobell, 1996). The other approach to moderation training is based on the principles of cue exposure treatment (Heather et al., 2000), but it will not be treated in detail here since there are few data supporting the efficacy of this approach as compared to self-control training.

Four manualized approaches to moderation training have received substantial empirical support: *Behavioral Self-Control Training* (BSCT; Miller & Munoz, 1982); *Saying When*, now known as *DrinkWise* (Sanchez-Craig, 1995); and *Guided Self Change* (GSC; Sobell & Sobell, 1996). All three are aimed at adults, rely heavily on client-guided (self-help) methodologies, and are typically of short duration, at least with respect to formal therapist involvement. A fourth program, the *Brief Alcohol Screening and Intervention for College Students* (BASICS; Dimeff et al., 1999) is aimed at college students whose drinking places them at high risk for alcohol-related consequences. A support group based loosely on principles of moderation training, Moderation Management (MM), has been found by one study to be attracting many problem drinkers who would otherwise not seek formal intervention (Humphreys & Klaw, 2001; Kishline, 1994; Rotgers & Kishline, 1999). Self-help materials based on a combination of MM principles and BSCT are also becoming available (Rotgers, Kern, & Hoeltzel, 2002).

All of these programs are brief in duration (as few as three sessions, but typically no more than six) and highly client driven. They all differ from traditional approaches to the treatment of problem drinkers in that the main goal is not to stop drinking (although some clients may choose this as their goal), but to reduce the harm and negative consequences associated with the client's particular drinking behavior. As such, all of these programs can be considered "harm-reduction" programs in which the goal is not necessarily to eliminate substance use, but rather to enhance client health and well-being even though substance use continues (Marlatt, 1998).

KEY ELEMENTS OF MODERATION TRAINING

Moderation training approaches share several common elements. These elements are outlined in Table 37.1. The context for delivering this material varies with the specific approach, but moderation training programs can be administered with only limited therapist assistance via books or other materials. For example, BSCT is now available in a computerized version that can be administered with or without therapist assistance (Hester & Delaney, 1997).

Self-Assessment

Prior to actual initiation of change efforts, clients are urged to do an objective self-assessment of their drinking (quantity and frequency), its effect on their lives, the extent to which changing their drinking will likely result in difficulty coping with situations and emotions for which drinking was a primary coping strategy, and identification of situations in which drinking is more or less likely to be excessive. Some programs recommend that the client initiate a short (30 days or less) period of abstinence following a period of self-monitoring of drinking behavior. The period of abstinence is designed to allow physiological recovery from the effects of alcohol, reduce tolerance to the effects of alcohol, and provide an opportunity for continued self-assessment of the role alcohol plays in day-to-day coping. When abstinence is initiated immediately, self-monitoring is focused on urges and temptations to drink and situations in which they occur (Sanchez-Craig, 1995).

Of critical importance during the initial abstinence period, or period of self-monitoring of

TABLE 37.1 Key Elements of Moderation Training for Problem Drinkers

- Self-assessment and self-monitoring of drinking behavior or urges to drink
- Initial period of 2–4 weeks abstinence
- Normative feedback
- Goal setting
- Development and implementation of behavioral coping strategies
- Maintenance planning and lifestyle changes

drinking if abstinence is eschewed, is the identi-fication of situations (including both emotional and cognitive states and environments) in which the client is likely to over-drink (i.e., exceed safe drinking limits). Identification of these high-risk situations is critical further along in treat-ment when the client, either by himself or herself or in conjunction with the therapist, will de-velop a set of coping strategies for managing drinking in those situations. Self-monitoring of urges and temptations to drink assists in this process.

Normative Feedback

Most drinkers have little idea of what "normal" or "safe" drinking practices consist, and tend to view their own drinking as the same as or less than that of the average drinker. Normative feed-back usually takes one or both of two forms: edu-cation about empirically derived "safe" drinking limits (Sanchez-Craig, Wilkinson, & Davila, 1995) or feedback from the therapist as to how the indi-vidual's reported drinking patterns compare with those of peers (Dimeff et al., 1999). For ex-ample, clients might be taught the empirically de-rived safe drinking limits of no more than 4 standard drinks daily for men, no more than 3 standard drinks daily for women, and no more than 16 and 12 standard drinks weekly for men and women respectively (Sanchez-Craig et al., 1995).

Normative feedback may also be provided in the form of education with respect to the rela-tionship between alcohol consumption and blood alcohol content (BAC). As with general norms about drinking patterns and safe drinking limits, clients typically have little awareness of how many drinks they can consume and still re-main below safe BAC levels (e.g., for operating a motor vehicle).

Goal Setting

Formal and explicit goal setting is a component of all of the well-developed moderation train-ing programs. Clients set goals for maximum numbers of drinks per drinking day, number of abstinent days (always a part of an effective mod-eration program), and maximum numbers of drinks per week. Goals may also be formulated in terms of maximum BAC to be achieved during a given week. Finally, goals may be formulated with respect to drinking situations that the client may wish to avoid, or in which the client may de-cide to remain abstinent due to a heightened risk of over-drinking in those situations (e.g., drinks after work with coworkers).

All moderation programs accept abstinence as a legitimate outcome goal for clients who choose it. Based as they are in the philosophy of "harm reduction" (Marlatt, 1998), all moderation pro-grams encourage movement toward the healthi-est possible life circumstances a given client is willing to pursue. For many clients, this may mean abstaining from alcohol altogether for a specified period of time, or indefinitely.

Behavioral Strategy Development and Implementation

Once self-assessment and goal setting are com-pleted, the next step in effective moderation is to develop specific strategies and techniques for coping with situations in which the client is at high risk to drink more than is safe. These strate-gies can be focused on either intrapersonal or ex-trapersonal (contextual) factors and should be made explicit and clear using an "if-then" strat-egy specification format. Various programs cate-gorize the stages of strategy development and implementation differently, but all urge clients to develop strategies that are as behaviorally spe-cific, and as easy to implement, as possible.

While the number and types of strategies available to clients to cope effectively with high-risk situations is large (and probably as varied as clients themselves) and limited only by client and therapist ingenuity, an example of a set of strategies and their focus will be helpful. A client might adopt a strategy of counting drinks by shifting coins from one pocket to another with each drink (focus on the drinking behavior it-self), or might insure that he or she doesn't drink alcohol to quench thirst; develop a pattern of pacing drinks over time; decide to not drink when angry, depressed, or anxious; and learn as-sertive drink refusal skills for use in situations in which the client feels strong social pressure to over-drink.

Maintenance of Behavior Change

All moderation programs contain an explicit focus on maintaining changes made during treatment. Specifically, developing healthy alternatives to drinking, continuing to monitor drinking even when the client feels he or she has achieved moderation successfully, changing social networks to include nondrinking peers, and addressing other psychological problems that may have contributed to over-drinking are all recommended components of moderation training programs.

WHO IS LIKELY TO BENEFIT FROM MODERATION TRAINING?

The research on moderation approaches initially suggested that persons who were younger, female, and socially stable, had shorter problem drinking histories, and had lower levels of dependence on alcohol were most likely to maintain moderate drinking levels following treatment (Rosenberg, 1993). Recent literature reviews have begun to conclude that even some alcohol-dependent persons may be able to moderate successfully. Walters (2000) found that some dependent drinkers may benefit from BSCT, and that it is effective for dependent drinkers as is abstinence-focused treatment. Similarly, Heather et al. (2000) found that more severely dependent drinkers in their sample actually responded better to moderation approaches on a variety of indicators than did less dependent drinkers.

It appears that client commitment to moderation as a goal, coupled with a willingness to carry out the behavioral procedures needed to achieve moderation, are the two most important initial indicators of possible success in moderation training. However, at present there is no touchstone available to determine with certainly which clients will succeed and which will not.

THE RISKS OF MODERATION

Moderation training has its failures. Oddly, the clinical lore often seems to lay the failure of absti-
nence-based treatments at the feet of clients (they were "in denial" and thus "unmotivated") and those of moderation treatments at the feet of the therapists who use them. Overall, having moderation training as an alternative treatment augments the success of treatment.

A major concern voiced by opponents of moderation is that failure will lead to increased hazard to the client, who probably should have stopped drinking altogether. Abstinence-only advocates are concerned that the mere availability of moderation approaches will tempt people who have successfully achieved prolonged abstinence to attempt to resume drinking, but no empirical evidence supports this contention. Similarly, there is a concern that most drinkers will choose moderation over abstinence if a choice is offered, when the data show the exact opposite to be true (Rotgers, 1996). Furthermore, several studies suggest that when clients are permitted to select and to change their drinking goals during treatment, the typical shift of goal is from moderation to abstinence (Ojehagen & Berglund, 1989; Parker, Winstead, Willi, & Fisher, 1979). Thus, moderation training, systematically applied with therapist assistance, in a therapeutic climate of experimental observation of outcomes, can become a significant stepping stone to abstinence for many clients.

Some in the alcohol-treatment field assert (see, e.g., Maltzman, 1987) that most people with drinking problems who enter treatment have made many prior, unsuccessful attempts to moderate their drinking and thus that moderation training is contraindicated as a waste of treatment resources. Moderation training, however, is a specific, systematic technology. It should not be confused with unsystematic attempts to moderate drinking. Furthermore, there are data showing that any a priori assumption about drinking goals is dangerous, since therapist preselection of such a goal, be it abstinence or moderation, is associated with poorer outcomes (Sanchez-Craig & Lei, 1986). Offering moderation training as an option in treatment, and allowing the client to choose whether to pursue it based on objective feedback of assessment results (as in Miller's "Drinker's Check Up" procedure; Miller & Sovereign, 1989) can enhance treatment retention and improve outcome.

CONCLUSION

Despite the objections of many traditionally oriented treatment providers in the alcohol field, moderation training for problem drinkers has garnered a significant level of empirical support. Moderation training is an important component of empirically based treatment for alcohol problems.

References

Davies, D. L. (1962). Normal drinking by recovered alcohol addicts. *Quarterly Journal of Studies on Alcohol, 23,* 94–104.

Dimeff, L. A., Baer, J. S., Kivlahan, D. R., & Marlatt, G. A. (1999). *Brief Alcohol Screening and Intervention for College Students (BASICS): A harm reduction approach.* New York: Guilford Press.

Heather, N., Brodie, J., Wale, S., Wilkinson, G., Luce, A., Webb, E., & McCarthy, S. (2000). A randomized controlled trial of Moderation-Oriented Cue Exposure. *Journal of Studies on Alcohol, 61,* 561–570.

Heather, N., & Robertson, I. (1997). *Problem drinking* (3rd ed.). Oxford, U.K.: Oxford University Press.

Hester, R. K., & Delaney, H. D. (1997). Behavioral Self-Control Program for Windows: Results of a controlled clinical trial. *Journal of Consulting and Clinical Psychology, 65,* 686–693.

Humphreys, K., & Klaw, E. (2001). Can targeting non-dependent problem drinkers and providing Internet-based services expand access to assistance for alcohol problems? A study of the Moderation Management self-help/mutual aid organization. *Journal of Studies on Alcohol, 62,* 528–532.

Kishline, A. (1994). *Moderate drinking: The moderation management guide for people who want to reduce their drinking.* New York: Crown.

Maltzmann, I. (1987). Controlled drinking and the treatment of alcoholism. *Journal of the American Medical Association, 257,* 927.

Marlatt, G. A. (Ed.). (1998). *Harm reduction: Pragmatic strategies for managing high-risk behaviors.* New York: Guilford Press.

Miller, W. R., & Munoz, R. F. (1982). *How to control your drinking: A practical guide to responsible drinking* (Rev. ed.). Albuquerque: University of New Mexico Press.

Miller, W. R., & Sovereign, G. (1989). The check-up: A model for early intervention in addictive behaviors. In T. Loberg, W. R. Miller, P. E. Nathan, & G. A. Marlatt (Eds.), *Addictive behaviors: Prevention and early intervention.* Amsterdam: Swets & Zeitlinger.

Ojehagen, A., & Berglund, M. (1989). Changes of drinking goals in a two-year out-patient alcoholic treatment program. *Addictive Behaviors, 14,* 1–9.

Parker, M., Winstead, D., Willi, F. & Fisher, P. (1979) Patient autonomy in alcohol rehabilitation: I. Literature review. *International Journal of the Addictions, 14,* 1015–1022.

Rosenberg, H. (1993). Prediction of controlled drinking by alcoholics and problem drinkers. *Psychological Bulletin, 113,* 129–139.

Rotgers, F. (1996). It's time to truly broaden the base of treatment for alcohol problems: Empowering clients with respect to drinking goals as a first step. *The Counselor, 14,* 33–36.

Rotgers, F., Kern, M. F., & Hoeltzel, R. (2002). *Responsible drinking: A moderation management approach for problem drinkers.* Oakland, CA: New Harbinger.

Rotgers, F., & Kishline, A. (1999). Moderation Management®: A support group for persons who want to reduce their drinking, but not necessarily abstain. *International Journal of Self Help and Self Care, 1,* 145–158.

Sanchez-Craig, M. (1995). *DrinkWise: How to quit drinking or cut down.* Toronto: Center for Addiction and Mental Health.

Sanchez-Craig, M., & Lei, H. (1986). Disadvantages of imposing the goal of abstinence on problem drinkers: An empirical study. *British Journal of Addiction, 81,* 505–512.

Sanchez-Craig, M., Wilkinson, D. A., & Davila, R. (1995). Empirically based guidelines for moderate drinking: One-year results from three studies with problem drinkers. *American Journal of Public Health, 85,* 823–828.

Sobell, L. C., & Sobell, M. R. (1996). *Problem drinkers: Guided self-change treatment.* New York: Guilford Press.

Walters, G. D. (2000). Behavioral self-control training for problem drinkers: A meta-analysis of randomized control studies. *Behavior Therapy, 31,* 135–149.

38 MOTIVATIONAL INTERVIEWING

Eric R. Levensky

A challenge clinicians frequently face when attempting to help clients make significant behavioral changes (e.g., stop smoking or using drugs or alcohol; start engaging in medication compliance, proper diet, or exercise), is getting the clients motivated to make these changes and committed to a particular course of therapeutic action. This challenge arises because behavioral changes of this nature are difficult to achieve, and client motivation is often considered to be an important ingredient in producing such changes. Furthermore, a lack of motivation is frequently thought to be implicated in unsuccessful attempts at behavior change (Garfield, 1994; Miller, 1985).

Motivational Interviewing (MI; Miller & Rollnick, 1991) is a relatively brief psychosocial intervention originally developed to increase individuals' motivation to reduce problematic alcohol consumption. Rollnick and Miller (1995) define MI as "a directive, client-centered counseling style for eliciting behavior change by helping clients to explore and resolve ambivalence" (p. 326). In recent years, MI has become a widely used treatment for problem drinking, and has also been adapted to promote behavior change in a number of other areas, including drug abuse, smoking, HIV risk, exercise, diet, sexual offending, diabetes, and chronic pain (see Dunn, Deroo, & Rivara, 2001, and Miller, 1996, for reviews of this literature). These adaptations have ranged

from as brief as 5- to 15-min interventions in medical settings (e.g., Rollnick, Heather, & Bell, 1992) to a manualized four-session therapy (e.g., Project MATCH Research Group, 1997).

RESEARCH ON THE EFFICACY OF MI

Outcome evaluations of MI have been conducted across a range of adaptations of the approach (see Dunn et al., 2001; Lawendowski, 1998; Miller, 1996; and Rollnick & Miller, 1995, for reviews of this literature). Most of these evaluations have examined the efficacy of MI as brief (one- to four-session) stand-alone or pretreatment interventions for problem drinking, and have generally found MI to produce significant reductions in alcohol use, as well as increased participation in treatment (Dunn et al.). The multisite Project MATCH (Project MATCH Research Group, 1997) found that a 4-session version of MI was as effective as were more intensive (12-session) cognitive-behavioral and 12-step treatments for problem drinkers. Dunn et al. conducted a systematic review of 29 randomized trials of brief interventions adapted from MI for the behavioral domains of substance abuse (17 studies), smoking (2 studies), HIV risk reduction (4 studies), and diet/exercise (6 studies). These authors found significant support for the effectiveness of MI, with 73% of the adaptations for substance abuse having significant effect sizes. Significant effects were also found in each of the other three behavioral domains; however, the authors concluded that the data were inadequate to evaluate the effect of MI in these areas.

WHO MIGHT BENEFIT FROM MI?

As mentioned previously, MI has been shown to be effective primarily for problem drinking, but has also been adapted to a number of other behavioral domains with some success. Theoretically, the basic principles and techniques of MI are applicable to any type of behavior change targets. What is required in successfully adapting MI to a new behavioral domain is faithfully applying the spirit of MI when using the approach's techniques and strategies (Rollnick & Miller, 1995). A goal of this chapter is to adequately convey this spirit such that MI may be applied in faithful manner.

EMPIRICAL AND THEORETICAL UNDERPINNINGS OF MI

Motivational Interviewing is strongly grounded in six treatment elements that have been found to be common across effective brief interventions for alcohol abuse (Bien, Miller, & Tonigan, 1993; Miller & Sanchez, 1993). These elements, summarized with the acronym "FRAMES," are (1) conducting an assessment of the client's risk or impairment status and providing the client *Feedback* regarding this status, (2) emphasizing the client's *Responsibility* for changing his or her behavior, (3) giving the client specific and direct *Advice* to make a behavioral change, (4) providing the client with a *Menu* of alternatives (as opposed to a single approach) for how he or she could go about making the recommended behavioral change, (5) communicating *Empathy* to the client regarding the client's situation, and (6) taking steps to increase the client's sense of *Self-efficacy* regarding his or her ability make a behavioral change. Motivational Interviewing was developed with a goal of incorporating these elements into a comprehensive and cohesive intervention.

In addition to being rooted in the FRAMES treatment elements, MI is also guided by the Transtheoretical Model of change (Prochaska & DiClemente, 1982; Prochaska, DiClemente, & Norcross, 1992). This model explains behavior change as a process in which individuals progress through a series of five stages of change: (1) the *precontemplation* stage, during which the client does not believe that the behavior is a problem and is not intending to change the behavior in the near future; (2) the *contemplation* stage, during which the client is considering changing the behavior but is ambivalent about doing so; (3) the *preparation* stage, during which the client has decided to change the behavior and has a specific plan for doing so in the near future; (4) the *action* stage, during which the client has actually made a behavioral change; and (5) the *maintenance* stage, during which the client takes actions to avoid a behavioral relapse. The Transtheoretical Model assumes that behavior change is a cyclical process, and that most people will relapse and progress through the stages several times before successfully maintaining the change. This model is an important component to MI in the sense that it orients the clinician first to understand the client's current level of readiness to change, and then to work accordingly at facilitating the client's successful movement through these stages. This idea of working with clients "where they're at" in terms of readiness for change is crucial in MI. Of particular concern is helping clients move successfully through the contemplation and preparation stages.

HOW DOES MI WORK?

Do date, research on MI has not identified the causal mechanisms of the approach. However, Miller and Rollnick (1991) suggest that MI produces behavioral change by creating an uncomfortable discrepancy for clients between how they would like to be living their lives (i.e., their values and goals) and how they are currently living (e.g., consequences of behavioral problem). These authors propose that clients are motivated to reduce this uncomfortable discrepancy and, in the context of a directive, reflective, supportive, and nonconfrontational therapeutic interaction, will do so by making behavioral changes that are consistent with their life goals and values. This perspective assumes both that client motivation must come from within the client (as opposed to coming from external forces) and that the clinician has an important role in eliciting and enhancing this motivation, as well as in producing change.

THE PRACTICE OF
MOTIVATIONAL INTERVIEWING

The purpose of this section is to describe MI such that clinicians can come to understand the fundamental principles and techniques of this approach. Motivational Interviewing can be a rather technically complex intervention, and a comprehensive description of its techniques is beyond the scope of this chapter. However, it is hoped that the information given here will provide the basis for faithful implementation of the basic approach. Readers are encouraged to refer to the more comprehensive descriptions of MI techniques listed in the "Suggestions for Further Reading" at the conclusion of this chapter.

Rollnick and Miller (1995) argue that it is essential for the clinicians delivering MI to fully understand, and act in accordance with, the "spirit" of the approach, rather than merely following the strategies and techniques the make up the treatment. A useful way to convey the spirit of MI is to contrast it with other common approaches to behavior change. Miller and Rollnick (1991) provide three tables contrasting the important elements (e.g., principles, strategies, and techniques) of MI with the elements of *confrontation-of-denial*, *skills training*, and *nondirective* approaches to behavior change. These contrasting elements are presented here in Table 38.1. Some important points about the nature of MI illustrated in Miller and Rollnick's tables are that MI is an inherently nonconfrontational, yet quite directive, approach that attempts to produce change through creating and mobilizing a client's intrinsic motivation rather than through external forces or skills training.

Basic Principles

As stated previously, MI is more of a stylistic approach to producing behavior change than a spe-

cific set of techniques. Therefore, what is most important in conducting MI is that the clinician keeps with the spirit of MI by adhering to its core therapeutic principles. Miller and Rollnick (1991) have described five principles that are core to MI:

1. *Express empathy.* Communicate acceptance of the client, use reflective listening, and normalize the client's ambivalence.
2. *Develop a discrepancy.* Increase the client's awareness of the consequences of the problematic behavior, orient the client to the discrepancy between his or her current behavior and his or her values and life goals, and have the client generate reasons for change.
3. *Avoid argumentation.* Switch therapeutic strategies in response to defensiveness, and avoid the use of judgmental labels.
4. *Roll with resistance.* Use the momentum of client resistance to foster change, invite the client to consider new points of view rather than having them imposed on him or her, and enlist the client to participate actively in problem solving.
5. *Support self-efficacy.* Increase the client's confidence in his or her ability to engage in the necessary change-related behaviors through emphasizing the client's personal responsibility for change and through orienting the client to successful models and to the wide range of possible approaches to behavior change.

Basic Method

The basic principles of MI can be instantiated in a number of different ways depending on setting, population, and resources. Descriptions of several methods of delivering MI are provided in Miller and Rollnick (1991), Miller, Zweben, DiClemente, and Rychtarik (1992), and Rollnick, Mason, and Butler (2000). The general method described here has been extracted from these sources.

The essential task of the clinician in MI is to engage in behaviors that will enhance clients' intrinsic motivation to make behavioral changes. Motivational Interviewing provides clinicians with a set of specific therapeutic behaviors thought to produce this motivation through helping the client to identify and resolve his or her

TABLE 38.1 Contrasts between Motivational Interviewing and Other Common Methods of Producing Behavior Change

Confrontation-of-Denial Approach	Motivational Interviewing Approach
Heavy emphasis on acceptance of self as having a problem; acceptance of diagnosis seen as essential for change	De-emphasis on labels; acceptance of "alcoholism" or other labels seen as unnecessary for change to occur
Emphasis on personality pathology, which reduces personal choice, judgment, and control	Emphasis on personal choice and responsibility for deciding future behavior
Therapist presents perceived evidence of problems in an attempt to convince the client to accept the diagnosis	Therapist conducts objective evaluation, but focuses on eliciting the client's own concerns
Resistance is seen as "denial," a trait characteristic requiring confrontation	Resistance is seen as an interpersonal behavior pattern influenced by the therapist's behavior
Resistance is met with argumentation and correction	Resistance is met with reflection
Goals of treatment and strategies for change are prescribed for the client by the therapist; client is seen as "in denial" and incapable of making sound decisions	Treatment goals and change strategies are negotiated between client and therapist, based on data and acceptability; client's involvement in and acceptance of goals are seen as vital

Skill-Training Approach	Motivational Interviewing Approach
Assumes that the client is motivated; no direct strategies are use for building motivation	Employs specific principles and strategies for building client motivation for change
Seeks to identify and modify maladaptive cognitions	Explores and reflects client perceptions without labeling or "correcting" them
Prescribes specific coping strategies	
Teaches coping behaviors through instruction, modeling, directed practice, and feedback	Elicits possible change strategies from the client and significant others
Specific problem-solving strategies are taught	Responsibility for change methods is left with the client; no training, modeling, or practice
	Natural problem-solving processes are elicited from the client and significant others

Nondirective Approach	Motivational Interviewing Approach
Allows the client to determine the content and direction of counseling	Systematically directs the client toward motivation for change
Avoids injecting the counselor's own advice and feedback	Offers the counselor's own advice and feedback where appropriate
Empathetic reflection is used noncontingently	Empathetic reflection is used selectively, to reinforce certain processes
Explores the client's conflicts and emotions as they exist currently	Seeks to create and amplify the client's discrepancy in order to enhance motivation for change

Source: Reprinted with permission from *Motivational interviewing: Preparing people for change,* by W. R. Miller and S. Rollnick, 1991 (New York: Guilford Press, pp. 53–55).

ambivalence about change. These behaviors typically include eliciting and reinforcing self-motivating statements through asking open-ended questions, providing feedback, listening with empathy, responding to resistance in a non-confrontational manner, affirming the client, and summarizing (Miller & Rollnick, 1991; Rollnick & Miller, 1995). Each of these is described in the following sections.

Eliciting Self-Motivational Statements

Motivational Interviewing assumes that (1) clients are ambivalent about changing their behavior, (2) it is this ambivalence that keeps clients immobilized, and (3) the primary task of the clinician is to help clients understand and resolve this ambivalence in a manner that produces behavioral change. *Ambivalence* is thought of as state in which clients have compelling reasons for both changing their behavior and not changing it. An example of such ambivalence would be an individual wanting to stop smoking to increase the quality of his health and spousal relationship and not wanting to stop because in doing so he would lose to the stress-reduction and weight-control benefits of cigarette use.

In MI, the clinician works to help the client identify his or her reasons for and against change, and to make the reasons for change more compelling to the client than the reasons against it. The *clinician* does not do this by presenting arguments to the client for the existence of a problem or for the need for change, but rather by having the *client* generate these arguments. Specifically, the clinician attempts to elicit self-motivational statements from the client by encouraging him or her to discuss the behavior and its consequences in the context of the client's values and goals. Miller and Rollnick (1991) describe several classes of such motivational statements:

- Recognizing the behavior (or lack of behavior) as a problem
- Expressing concern about the problem
- Willingness to consider changing the behavior
- Desire or intention to change the behavior
- Recognizing the benefits of changing the behavior
- Optimism about the ability to change behavior

The clinician elicits these statements by asking open-ended questions regarding the problem behavior (or the lack of behavior) and its consequences. These questions could include the following:

- What makes you think your drinking may be a problem?
- What have been some of the consequences of your smoking for you?
- What are some of your concerns about your diet?
- Why do you think you need to make a change in your amount of exercise?
- What makes you believe that you could take your medications as prescribed?

Miller and Rollnick (1991) suggest that it can often be useful to follow up these questions with further questions that may prompt the client to make additional self-motivational statements or to elaborate on these statements. Examples of such questions include, "Why else to you think your drinking may be a problem?" and "In what other ways has your smoking impacted your relationships?" Additionally, open questions about the client's goals for the future and the impact of the problem behavior on the client's ability to reach these goals can be useful.

Another method for eliciting self-motivational statements is to provide the client with information regarding the behavior of interest and its consequences. This information often includes assessment results regarding the severity of the behavior or the physical consequences that have resulted from it, or regarding the severity of current health problems that would likely be elevated by the client continuing to engage in a target behavior. The clinician then asks the client open-ended questions about his or her reactions to this feedback.

Empathic Listening

As the client responds to the open-ended questions and feedback, the clinician uses several empathic listening techniques to facilitate the exploration and resolution of the client's ambivalence. (The clinician also uses empathic listening as the primary mode of interacting with the client throughout the entire therapeutic process.) These techniques include (1) listening carefully to the content and meaning of what the client is saying; (2) listening reflectively, or repeating back what the client has said or summarizing it slightly; (3) "mind-reading," or reflecting back what the client may be feeling or thinking but has not said directly; and (4) validating the client, or communicating to the client that his or her thoughts and feelings (including ambivalence) are understandable. The primary functions of empathic listening are to highlight and reinforce the client's self-motivational statements and to reduce his or her resistance to change. Miller et al. (1992) point out several additional functions of these techniques, including (1) making the client feel respected, listened to, and understood; (2) ensuring that the clinician understands what the client is saying; (3) encouraging the client to discuss issues around his or her ambivalence; and (4) helping the clinician understand the nature of the client's ambivalence.

In order for the empathic listening techniques to have their intended functions, the clinician must follow several guidelines (Miller & Rollnick, 1991). First, the clinician should always reflect back and highlight to the client any self-motivational statement that the client makes. The goal of this reflection is to get the client to talk more about his or her reasons for changing. Second, the clinician's reflections should be accurate (match the meaning of the client's statement), or the client will likely feel misunderstood, and will likely become resistant to change. Third, it is important that the clinician's reflections do not include advice, agreement, or disagreement. Fourth, the reflections must not be biased. That is, if the client states his or her reasons both for changing and for not changing, both sides of this ambivalence should be reflected by the clinician. Related to this, the clinician should not appear to be confrontational, have an agenda of change, or be judgmental about the behavior. Any of these would likely result in client resistance. Fifth, although the clinician is not confrontational about change, the clinician is quite directive in that he or she systematically uses open-ended questions and empathic listening skills (particularly reflection) to highlight for the client the costs of inaction and the benefits of change. Sixth, an overarching goal is to form a discrepancy in the client between his or her life goals and values and his or her current behavior (and its consequences), but this must be done through reflecting the client's own statements.

The following is a brief example of the use of reflective listening in conjunction with the eliciting of self-motivational statements:

> Clinician: "What concerns you about your smoking?"
> Client: "Well, it's something that I enjoy, but I know it's also bad for my health."
> Clinician: "You enjoy smoking, but you're also concerned about its effects on your health. What are some of the specific concerns you have about the effects of smoking on your health?"

Responding to Resistance

Resistance is thought of as behaviors that interfere with behavior change or the therapeutic process. These can include arguing, not following through with therapy homework, denying that behavior change is needed, lying, not listening, and interrupting (Miller & Rollnick, 1991). In MI, resistance is not considered to be a pathological characteristic of the client, but rather is thought of as the result of the clinician misjudging the client's readiness to change and proceeding toward change faster than the client is ready to do so, or the result of the client feeling invalidated or misunderstood. Therefore, it is up to the clinician to continually monitor the client's readiness to change and act accordingly (see the later section on "Assessing Readiness to Change"). Motivational Interviewing assumes that a client's readiness to change will fluctuate throughout the change process.

Although it can be tempting, the clinician never responds to client resistance in a confrontational or change-focused manner (arguing, confronting, persuading, coercing, pathologizing, threatening, etc.). It is thought that this only strengthens client resistance. Rather, the clinician responds to resistance with a number of alternate responses (Miller & Rollnick, 1991). These responses include the following:

- *Simple reflection.* Reflecting the resistant statement.
  Client: "My diet is pretty much fine the way it is."
  Clinician: "You're fairly content with your diet as it is."
- *Reflection with amplification.* Amplifying the resistant statement.
  Client: "I don't think my smoking is a problem."
  Clinician: "Your smoking hasn't caused you any problems at all."
- *Double-sided reflection.* Highlighting both sides of the ambivalence in response to a resistant statement.
  Client: "If I stop smoking, I'm sure I will gain a ton of weight."
  Clinician: "On one hand, you're worried that

quitting will cause you to gain weight, and on the other, you are worried that continuing to smoke may harm your relationship."

• *Shifting the focus.* Shifting the topic away from the object of the resistant statement.

Client: "My life is way too chaotic right now for me to make a change in my diet."

Clinician: "It's entirely up to you whether you make a change in your diet. What I would like to talk about right now is how your current diet is affecting you."

• *Paradox.* Going along with the resistance to promote a shift to a direction of change.

Client: "I've been drinking for 20 years. I can't even imagine my life without it."

Clinician: "You have been drinking for a long time, it may be too hard to quit now."

• *Reframing.* Recasting resistant statements in a manner that favors change without challenging the content of the statement.

Client: "I can handle my cocaine much better these days. I rarely get too high anymore."

Clinician: "When people have used a lot of cocaine they will often build up a tolerance to it."

• *Emphasizing personal control.* Communicating that it is up to the client to decide whether he or she will change and what he or she will do to make the change.

Client: "I really don't think I need to stop smoking."

Clinician: "This is entirely your decision. You get to decide whether you will stop smoking."

Affirming the Client

Affirming the client is an important clinician behavior in MI. It involves the clinician making statements that communicate acceptance, respect, appreciation, and encouragement for the client. The function of affirming the client is to validate the client for his or her efforts, reinforce engagement in the therapeutic process, enhance the therapeutic relationship, and support self-efficacy. Affirming statements can be made throughout the therapeutic process.

Summarizing

The clinician should periodically summarize what the client has said during the session. Summarizing can be particularly useful at the end of a session to reinforce important points that have been made. It is crucial that the clinician include a summary of the client's self-motivational statements; however, the summary should also include other important elements of the client's ambivalence.

Making a Plan for Change

Motivational Interviewing typically concludes with the development of a specific plan for behavior change and a commitment from the client to follow through with it. Miller and Rollnick (1991) and Miller et al. (1992) discuss guidelines and considerations for arriving at such a plan, which are reviewed in the following sections.

Assessing Readiness to Change

Before moving into the behavior change–planning phase, the clinician must determine if the client is sufficiently motivated to make such a change. Miller and Rollnick (1991, p. 115) suggest several factors the clinician can look for as signs that the client is motivated for change:

• The client is less resistant (e.g., stops arguing, denying the problem, and raising objections).
• The client asks fewer questions about the problem.
• The client appears more resolved (e.g., peaceful and settled).
• The client asks questions or makes statements indicating that he or she is oriented toward or open to change (e.g., recognizing the need to change, asking about how to change, imagining life with behavior change, etc.).
• The client makes attempts at behavior change or takes steps to prepare for change (e.g., smokes slightly fewer cigarettes, looks into a membership at the gym, etc.).

Although these behaviors can indicate a client's readiness to move on to the change-planning phase, it is important to note that readiness to change is not a fixed client trait, but rather, is an ever-fluctuating state. Therefore, it is typically necessary for the clinician to take a step back and use the techniques described in the previous section when client resistance is observed.

Discussing a Plan

Once the clinician has determined that the client is sufficiently motivated to change, the clinician begins to facilitate the client's commitment to a course of action. The key here is to get the client to suggest a course of action. If the client does not do this on his or her own, the clinician can ask the client open-ended questions about what specific changes the client would like to make and how the client would like to go about making them. The clinician responds with reflection and emphasizes the client's free choice, and does not tell the client what changes to make or how to make them.

Providing Information and Advice

Although the clinician does not give the client unsolicited advice about behavior change, it is important that the clinician does provide clear and accurate information when it is requested. If the client does ask for advice, the clinician provides it as suggestions that the client can choose to do or not, rather than as prescriptions for what he or she should do. Additionally, when possible, the client should be presented with several options for change as opposed to just one.

The Nature of the Change Plan

It is important that the client specify exactly (1) what change the client wants to make, (2) why the client wants to make that change, (3) what specific steps the client will take to make the change, (4) what the barriers are to the client's making the change, (5) what things would help the client to carry out the change plan, and (6) how the client will know that the plan is working (Miller et al., 1992). The change plan can also involve follow-up sessions to refine the initial plan and to assess and reinforce client commitment to change.

Asking for a Commitment

After the behavior change plan has been clearly specified by the client, the task of the clinician is to get from the client a solid commitment to carrying out the change plan. The clinician can do this by asking the client, "Can you can commit doing this plan?" If the client declines to commit to the plan, the clinician should ask him or her to wait until later to make the commitment, and possibly continue to explore the client's ambivalence.

CONCLUSION

Motivational Interviewing (MI) is a directive, yet nonconfrontational, counseling approach to increasing clients' motivation to make significant behavioral changes. This approach assumes that clients have difficulty making such changes because they have compelling reasons for both changing and not changing. Motivational Interviewing provides clinicians with a set of guiding principles and specific techniques for helping clients to identify factors that contribute to their ambivalence about change, and to resolve this ambivalence in a manner that produces behavioral change. The therapeutic principles that guide MI are expressing empathy, developing a discrepancy, avoiding argumentation, rolling with resistance, and supporting self-efficacy. These principles are instantiated primarily through the techniques of eliciting self-motivational statements, listening reflectively, and responding to resistance with reflection and empathy rather than confrontation and argument.

Further Reading

Miller, W. R., & Rollnick, S. (1991). *Motivational interviewing: Preparing people for change.* New York: Guilford Press.

Miller, W. R., Zweben, A., DiClemente, C. C., & Rychtarik, R. G. (1992). *Motivational enhancement therapy manual: A clinical research guide for therapists treating individuals with alcohol abuse and dependence* (Project MATCH Monograph Series, Vol. 2). Rockville, MD: National Institute on Alcohol Abuse and Alcoholism.

Rollnick, S., Mason, P., & Butler, C. (2000). *Health behavior change: A guide for practitioners.* Edinburgh, Scotland: Churchill/Livingstone.

Rollnick, S., & Miller, B. (1995). What is motivational interviewing? *Behavioural and Cognitive Psychotherapy, 23,* 325–334.

Website: www.motivationalinterview.com

References

Bien, T. H., Miller, W. R., & Tonigan, J. S. (1993). Brief interventions for alcohol problems: A review. *Addiction, 88,* 315–336.

Dunn, C., Deroo, L., & Rivara, F. (2001). The use of brief interventions adapted from motivational interviewing across behavior domains: A systematic review. *Addiction, 96*(12), 1725–1742.

Garfield, S. L. (1994). Research on client variables in psychotherapy. In A. E. Bergin & S. L. Garfield (Eds.), *Handbook of psychotherapy and behavior change* (4th ed., pp. 190–228). New York: John Wiley & Sons.

Lawendowski, L. A. (1998). A motivational intervention for adolescent smokers. *Preventative Medicine, 27,* A39–A46.

Miller, W. R. (1985). Motivation for treatment: A review with special emphasis on alcoholism. *Psychological Bulletin, 9,* 84–107.

Miller, W. R. (1996). Motivational interviewing: Research, practice, and puzzles. *Addictive Behaviors, 21*(6), 835–842.

Miller, W. R., & Rollnick, S. (1991). *Motivational interviewing: Preparing people for change.* New York: Guilford Press.

Miller, W. R., & Sanchez, V. C. (1993). Motivating young adults for treatment in lifestyle change. In G. Howard (Ed.), *Issues in alcohol use and misuse by young adults* (pp. 55–82). Notre Dame, IN: University of Notre Dame Press.

Miller, W. R., Zweben, A., DiClemente, C. C., & Rychtarik, R. G. (1992). *Motivational enhancement therapy manual: A clinical research guide for therapists treating individuals with alcohol abuse and dependence* (Project MATCH Monograph Series, Vol. 2).

Rockville, MD: National Institute on Alcohol Abuse and Alcoholism.

Prochaska, J., & DiClemente, C. (1982). Transtheoretical therapy: Towards a more integrative model of change. *Psychotherapy: Theory, Research, and Practice, 19,* 279–288.

Prochaska, J., DiClemente, C., & Norcross, J. (1992). In search of how people change: Applications to addictive behaviors. *American Psychologist, 47,* 1102–1114.

Project MATCH Research Group. (1997). Matching alcohol treatment to client heterogeneity: Project MATCH post-treatment drinking outcomes. *Journal of Studies on Alcohol, 58,* 7–29.

Rollnick, S., & Allison, J. (2001). Motivational interviewing. In N. Heather, T. J. Peters, & T. Stockwell (Eds.), *International handbook of alcohol dependence and problems* (pp. 593–603). New York: John Wiley & Sons.

Rollnick, S., Heather, N., & Bell, A. (1992). Negotiating behaviour change in medical settings: The development of brief motivational interviewing. *Journal of Mental Health, 1,* 25–37.

Rollnick, S., Mason, P., & Butler, C. (2000). *Health behavior change: A guide for practitioners.* Edinburgh: Churchill/Livingstone.

Rollnick, S., & Miller, B. (1995). What is motivational interviewing? *Behavioural and Cognitive Psychotherapy, 23,* 325–334.

39 MULTIMODAL BEHAVIOR THERAPY

Arnold A. Lazarus

CONTEXT

When follow-ups on a variety of clients who had received standard behavior therapy revealed that many were apt to suffer setbacks within 6 months to a year (Lazarus, 1971), investigations into the reasons behind this lack of durability revealed that treatment omissions (leaving several response deficits untreated) lay behind most of the relapses. The treatment repertoire advocated by Wolpe (1958) and by Wolpe and Lazarus (1966) glossed over or completely disregarded many cognitive variables, sensory responses, mental images, and interpersonal factors. Thus, agoraphobic clients received relaxation training, imaginal and in vivo desensitization, and between-session homework assignments to consolidate and augment whatever gains ensued. Virtually no attention was paid to cognitive mediation (e.g., negative automatic thoughts, dichotomous reasoning, unrealistic expectations, and other self-defeating beliefs). Similarly, interpersonal processes (other than unassertive behaviors) were given short shrift (e.g., marital discord, familial tensions, the impact of authority figures, or sibling rivalry). Unaddressed and untreated, these issues, when triggered, retained the power to undermine whatever treatment gains had accrued.

ENTER COGNITIVE RESTRUCTURING AND MORE

The fact that Lazarus (1971) included an entire chapter on cognitive restructuring was met with strong disfavor by the mainstream behavior therapists who regarded it as a regressive return to "mentalism." Nevertheless, by the mid-1970s, *cognitive-behavior therapy* had replaced *behavior therapy* as the accepted designation, and the field became trimodal—emphasizing *A*ffect, *B*ehavior, and *C*ognition (ABC). This remains true to this day. Nevertheless, Lazarus (1976, 1989, 1997, 2000) has contended that equal weight should be given to imagery, sensation, interpersonal relationships, and biological considerations thus operating from a seven-point multimodal perspective (*B*ehavior, *A*ffect, *S*ensation, *I*magery, *C*ognition, *I*nterpersonal relationships, and *D*rugs/biological factors).

Using the easy-to-remember mnemonic acronym BASIC I.D. (taken from the initial letters of the foregoing modalities), the multimodal framework emphasizes the discrete and interactive impact of these seven modalities. (The *D* modality underscores that prescription drugs are the most commonly used biological intervention, but nonetheless one must not lose sight of the entire medical panoply.) Whenever feasible, multimodal therapists will employ empirically supported techniques, or refer out to an expert, when necessary, to implement a specific procedure. The aim, however, is to think in BASIC I.D. terms to ensure thorough and comprehensive assessment and treatment coverage.

WHO MIGHT BENEFIT FROM THIS APPROACH?

Most clients are likely to show positive gains when receiving a broad-spectrum treatment in which salient issues are addressed. For example, a Dutch psychologist, Kwee (1984), organized a multimodal treatment outcome study on 84 hospitalized patients suffering from obsessive-compulsive disorders and extensive phobias, 90% of whom had received prior treatment without success. Over 70% of these patients had suffered from their disorders for more than 4 years. Multimodal treatment regimens resulted in substantial recoveries and durable 9-month follow-ups. This was confirmed and amplified by Kwee and Kwee-Taams (1994).

In Scotland, Williams (1988) in a carefully controlled outcome study compared multimodal assessment and treatment with less integrative approaches in helping children with learning disabilities. Clear data emerged in support of the multimodal procedures.

Follow-up studies that have been conducted since 1973 have consistently suggested that durable outcomes are in direct proportion to the number of modalities deliberately traversed (see Lazarus, 1989, 1997). Although there is obviously a point of diminishing returns, it is a multimodal maxim that *the more someone learns in therapy, the less likely he or she is to relapse.* To reiterate, it appears that lacunae or gaps in people's coping responses were responsible for many relapses.

CONTRADICTION OF THE TREATMENT

People in crisis require the therapist to focus immediately on the precipitating circumstances and events. There is often simply no time to dwell on the vicissitudes and nuances of the BASIC I.D. These cases have need of instantaneous relief from their untoward anxiety and depression. Less acute issues and much less dramatic problem areas may call for unimodal or bimodal interventions. For example, clients in a smoking cessation group, in terms of treatment adherence, are likely to respond better to structured methods of habit control than to a broad band of assessments and interventions. And when dealing with frankly psychotic (e.g., schizophrenic) individuals, or those who are in the manic state of a bipolar disorder, the first inroad should probably consist of supportive treatment and biopsychiatric interventions. When appropriate medications have taken effect, a multimodal treatment program may then be instituted to remedy excesses and deficits that may precipitate or aggravate the patient's initial or major complaints.

THEORY AND MECHANISM

The BASIC I.D. or multimodal framework rests on a broad social and cognitive learning theory (e.g., Bandura, 1977, 1986; Rotter, 1954) because its tenets are open to verification or disproof. Instead of postulating putative unconscious forces, social learning theory rests on testable developmental factors (e.g., modeling, observational learning, the acquisition of expectancies, operant and respondent conditioning, and various self-regulatory mechanisms). It must be emphasized that while drawing on effective methods from any discipline, the multimodal therapist does not embrace divergent theories but remains consistently within social-cognitive learning theory. The virtues of *technical eclecticism* (Lazarus, 1967, 1992; Lazarus, Beutler, & Norcross, 1992) over the dangers of *theoretical integration* have been emphasized in several publications (e.g., Lazarus, 1986, 1989, 1995; Lazarus & Beutler, 1993). The major criticism of theoretical integration is that it inevitably tries to blend incompatible notions and only breeds confusion.

TWO SPECIFIC MULTIMODAL PROCEDURES

Whereas multimodal therapists draw on the entire range of empirically supported methods, two procedures—bridging and tracking—are unique to this approach.

Bridging

Let's assume that a therapist is interested in a client's emotional responses to an event, saying, "How did you feel when your husband drank so much that he passed out at the party?" Instead of discussing her feelings, the client responds with defensive and irrelevant intellectualizations. "Well, it's not as if this happens every time we go out." The therapist persists: "Nevertheless, were you upset, or angry, or embarrassed?" The client, still avoiding the question, says that her husband works extremely hard and often looks for a release on the weekends.

It is likely to be counterproductive to confront the client and point out that she is evading the question and seems reluctant to face her true feelings. In situations of this kind, *bridging* is usually effective. First, the therapist deliberately tunes in to the client's preferred modality—in this case, the cognitive domain. Thus, the therapist explores the cognitive content. "So you see it as a simple need to relax and let go of tensions that arise during the week at work. Please tell me more." In this way, after perhaps a 5- to 10-min discourse, the therapist endeavors to branch off into other directions that seem more productive. "Tell me, while we have been discussing these matters, have you noticed any sensations anywhere in your body?" This sudden switch from Cognition to Sensation may begin to elicit more pertinent information (given the assumption that in this instance, Sensory inputs are probably less threatening than Affective material). The client may refer to some sensations of tension or bodily discomfort, at which point the therapist may ask her to focus on them, often with a hypnotic overlay: "Will you please close your eyes, and now feel that neck tension. [Pause.] Now relax deeply for a few moments, breathe easily and gently, in and out, in and out, just letting yourself feel calm and peaceful." The feelings of tension, their associated images and cognitions, may then be examined. One may then venture to bridge into Affect. "Beneath the sensations, can you find any strong feelings or emotions? Perhaps they are lurking in the background." At this juncture it is not unusual for clients to give voice to their feelings. "I am in touch with anger, fear, and sadness." When the

therapist begins *where the client is* and then bridges into a different modality, most clients then seem to be willing to traverse the more emotionally charged areas they had been avoiding.

Tracking the Firing Order

A fairly reliable pattern may be discerned in the way that many people generate negative affect. Some dwell first on unpleasant sensations (palpitations, shortness of breath, tremors), followed by aversive images (pictures of disastrous events), to which they attach negative cognitions (ideas about catastrophic illness), leading to maladaptive behavior (withdrawal and avoidance). This S-I-C-B firing order (Sensation, Imagery, Cognition, Behavior) may require a different treatment strategy from that employed with, say, a C-I-S-B sequence, an I-C-B-S, or yet a different firing order. Clinical findings suggest that it is often best to apply treatment techniques in accordance with a client's specific chain reaction. A rapid way of determining someone's firing order is to have him or her in an altered state of consciousness— deeply relaxed with eyes closed—contemplating untoward events and then describing their reactions.

ILLUSTRATIVE CASE

A brief case history should elucidate the procedural niceties of the points alluded to previously.

Leon, 26, a single white male, was in an executive training program with a large corporation. He was raised in an affluent suburb, did well at school, and graduated from college, but had tended to be rather obsessive-compulsive, prone to bouts of depression, and conflicted about his career options. After an initial session that consisted of the usual exploration of the client's current situation, some background information, and an inquiry into antecedent events and their consequences, Leon was asked to complete a Multimodal Life History Questionnaire (Lazarus & Lazarus, 1991) and bring it with him to the next session. Clients who comply tend to facilitate their treatment trajectory because the questionnaire enables the therapist rapidly to determine the salient issues across the client's BASIC I.D. Leon said that he was feeling too depressed to concentrate on answering the questionnaire; therefore, the therapist conducted a multimodal assessment.

A Step-by-Step Inquiry

B: What is Leon doing that is getting in the way of his happiness or personal fulfillment (self-defeating actions, maladaptive behaviors)? What does he need to increase and decrease? What should he stop doing and start doing?

A: What emotions (affective reactions) are predominant? Are we dealing with anger, anxiety, depression, or combinations thereof, and to what extent (e.g., irritation vs. rage; sadness vs. profound melancholy)? What appears to generate these negative affects—certain cognitions, images, interpersonal conflicts? And how does Leon respond (behave) when feeling a certain way? We discussed what impact various behaviors had on his affect and vice versa, and how this influenced each of the other modalities.

S: We discussed Leon's specific sensory complaints (e.g., tension, chronic lower back discomfort) as well as the feelings, thoughts, and behaviors that were connected to these negative sensations. Leon was also asked to comment on positive sensations (e.g., visual, auditory, tactile, olfactory, and gustatory delights). This included sensual and sexual elements.

I: Leon was asked to describe some of his main fantasies. He was asked to describe his "self-image." (It became evident that he harbored several images of failure.)

C: We explored Leon's main attitudes, values, beliefs, and opinions, and looked into his predominant shoulds, oughts, and musts. (It was clear that he was too hard on himself and embraced a perfectionistic viewpoint that was bound to prove frustrating and disappointing.)

I.: Interpersonally, we discussed his significant others; what he wanted, desired, and expected to receive from them; and what he, in turn, gave to them. (He was inclined to avoid confrontations and often felt shortchanged and resentful.)

D.: Despite his minor aches and pains, Leon appeared to be in good health and was health conscious. There were no untoward issues pertaining to his diet, weight, sleep, exercise, or alcohol and drug use.

The foregoing pointed immediately to three issues that called for correction: (1) His images of failure had to be altered to images of coping and succeeding. (2) His perfectionism needed to be changed to a generalized antiperfectionistic philosophy of life. (3) His interpersonal reticence called for an assertive modus vivendi wherein he would easily discuss his feelings and not harbor resentments. To achieve these ends, the techniques selected were standard methods—positive and coping imagery exercises, disputing irrational cognitions, and assertiveness training.

This straightforward case has been presented to demonstrate how the multimodal behavior therapy approach provided a template (the BASIC I.D.) that pointed to three discrete but interrelated components that became the main treatment foci. In a sense, the term *multimodal behavior therapy* is a misnomer because while the assessment is multimodal, the treatment is cognitive-behavioral and draws, whenever possible, on empirically supported methods. The main claim is that by assessing clients across the BASIC I.D. one is less apt to overlook subtle but important problems that call for correction, and the overall problem identification process is significantly expedited.

References

Bandura, A. (1977). *Social learning theory.* Englewood Cliffs, NJ: Prentice Hall.

Bandura, A. (1986). *Social foundations of thought and action: A social cognitive theory.* Englewood Cliffs, NJ: Prentice Hall.

Kwee, M. G. T. (1984). *Klinische multimodale gedragstherapie* [Clinical multimodal behavior therapy]. Lisse, Holland: Swets & Zeitlinger.

Kwee, M. G. T., & Kwee-Taams, M. K. (1994). *Klinishegedragstherapie in Nederland & vlaanderen* [Clinical behavior therapy in the Netherlands and other countries]. Delft, Holland: Eubron.

Lazarus, A. A. (1967). In support of technical eclecticism. *Psychological Reports, 21,* 415–416.

Lazarus, A. A. (1971). *Behavior therapy and beyond.* New York: McGraw-Hill.

Lazarus, A. A. (1976). *Multimodal behavior therapy.* New York: Springer.

Lazarus, A. A. (1986). Multimodal therapy. In J. C. Norcross (Ed.), *Handbook of eclectic psychotherapy* (pp. 65–93). New York: Brunner/Mazel.

Lazarus, A. A. (1989). *The practice of multimodal therapy.* Baltimore: Johns Hopkins University Press.

Lazarus, A. A. (1992). Multimodal therapy: Technical eclecticism with minimal integration. In J. C. Norcross & M. R. Goldfried (Eds.), *Handbook of psychotherapy integration* (pp. 231–263). New York: Basic Books.

Lazarus, A. A. (1995). Different types of eclecticism and integration: Let's be aware of the dangers. *Journal of Psychotherapy Integration, 5,* 27–39.

Lazarus, A. A. (1997). *Brief but comprehensive psychotherapy: The multimodal way.* New York: Springer.

Lazarus, A. A. (2000). Multimodal therapy. In R. J. Corsini & D. Wedding (Eds.), *Current psychotherapies* (6th ed., pp. 340–374). Itasca, IL: Peacock.

Lazarus, A. A., & Beutler, L. E. (1993). On technical eclecticism. *Journal of Counseling and Development, 71,* 381–385.

Lazarus, A. A., Beutler, L. E., & Norcross, J. C. (1992). The future of technical eclecticism. *Psychotherapy, 29,* 11–20.

Lazarus, A. A., & Lazarus, C. N. (1991). *Multimodal Life History Inventory.* Champaign, IL: Research Press.

Rotter, J. B. (1954). *Social learning and clinical psychology.* Englewood Cliffs, NJ: Prentice Hall.

Williams, T. A. (1988). *A multimodal approach to assessment and intervention with children with learning disabilities.* Unpublished doctoral dissertation, Department of Psychology, University of Glasgow.

Wolpe, J. (1958). *Psychotherapy by reciprocal inhibition.* Stanford, CA: Stanford University Press.

Wolpe, J., & Lazarus, A. A. (1966). *Behavior therapy techniques.* New York: Pergamon Press.

40 NONCONTINGENT REINFORCEMENT AS TREATMENT FOR PROBLEM BEHAVIOR

Timothy R. Vollmer and Carrie S. Wright

Noncontingent reinforcement (NCR) involves the time-based presentation of reinforcers. This treatment is used most often to reduce the frequency of operant behavior problems (Vollmer, Iwata, Zarcone, Smith, & Mazaleski, 1993). In time schedules, reinforcers are delivered on fixed-time (FT) or variable-time (VT) arrangements. Time schedules should not be confused with interval schedules. *Interval schedules,* such as fixed-interval (FI) and variable-interval (VI), are response-dependent schedules—they require a response in order for reinforcers to be delivered. On the other hand, *time schedules* (FT, VT) require no response; the reinforcers are delivered freely, regardless of whether a target behavior has occurred. Although the use of free reinforcers as a clinical intervention may seem counterintuitive at first blush, the procedure makes good sense upon closer inspection. Dozens of studies now support the clinical utility of NCR (see Carr et al., 2000, for a comprehensive review).

It is widely recognized that many severe behavior problems are maintained by inadvertent social reinforcement. For example, a child might engage in self-injurious behavior (SIB) because SIB produces attention from adult care providers (Iwata, Dorsey, Slifer, Bauman, & Richman, 1982/1994). By providing reinforcement independent of behavior, as in NCR, a dependency no longer exists between problem behavior and a known reinforcer. For example, the care provider might provide attention once every 5 min instead of providing attention following SIB (Vollmer et al., 1993). Thus, because the reinforcer is made available freely and frequently, the motivation to engage in problem behavior is reduced. In addition, the problem behavior no longer directly produces the reinforcer, so NCR contains extinction-like features.

Advantages of NCR include reduced negative side effects in comparison to extinction (Vollmer et al., 1998) and differential reinforcement (Vollmer et al., 1993), and ease of implementation in comparison to differential reinforcement. In clinical practice, the procedure is most commonly used as one component of a larger treatment package.

CONTRAINDICATIONS OF THE TECHNIQUE

The NCR procedure, in isolation, may not be the most appropriate intervention for individuals whose behavioral repertoire does not include appropriate alternative behavior. There is nothing explicit in the procedure for reinforcing adaptive

The work on this chapter was supported in part by a grant to the first author from the National Institute of Mental Health, grant number MH60643.

alternative behavior. However, some studies have shown that NCR can be combined with differential reinforcement to teach adaptive skills, such as communication (Goh, Iwata, & Kahng, 1999; Marcus & Vollmer, 1995). In other words, NCR should be viewed as one potential component of a larger treatment package that would include procedures for teaching adaptive skills.

Also, the successful application of NCR often requires good information about the operant function of the behavior problem. If an adequate functional analysis has not been or cannot be conducted, it is possible that NCR will be less effective. To date, all of the published studies on NCR included a functional analysis of behavior prior to beginning treatment. Little is known about the efficacy of the procedure in the absence of a functional analysis.

Although generally considered an easy-to-implement procedure, NCR can be labor intensive at the beginning of treatment. Most of the published studies showing positive effects involve rich schedules of reinforcement (e.g., continuous reinforcement) when treatment is first introduced. If a parent, teacher, or therapist does not have adequate resources to implement the procedure intensively at the outset, it may not be as effective. However, the schedule of reinforcement actually becomes very easy to implement once the schedule is thinned to something more manageable, such as FT 5 min.

Finally, if the behavior problem occurs at extremely high rates, the procedure may result in accidental reinforcement (Vollmer, Ringdahl, Roane, & Marcus, 1997). This happens because the delivery of the reinforcer continues to occur contiguously with the occurrence of behavior. Thus, the dependency between problem behavior and reinforcement is eliminated in fact, but a reinforcement contingency remains in place incidentally. There is a method to circumvent this problem, and that method will be discussed later in this chapter.

CONSIDERATIONS

The most important consideration in developing NCR treatments is to understand the operant function of the behavior prior to treatment. Un-

derstanding the operant function is best accomplished via functional analysis (Iwata et al., 1982/1994). It is outside the scope of this chapter to fully explain functional analysis procedures; however, it should be noted that a functional analysis involves systematically introducing particular consequences, such as attention, escape from instructional activity, and tangible items (e.g., toys, food) following occurrences of problem behavior. By intentionally presenting these consequences, the assessor can evaluate whether such events serve as reinforcers for problem behavior. Because functional analyses can require specialized skills and resources, at times a reasonable clinical judgment can be made about the operant function by conducting naturalistic observations of the behavior. In short, there must be some hypothesis about the reinforcers maintaining the problem behavior so that those reinforcers may be presented noncontingently during treatment. For example, if the problem behavior is maintained by (reinforced by) escape from instructional activity, escape can be presented on an FT schedule so that it is not longer contingent upon the occurrence of problem behavior (e.g., Vollmer, Marcus, & Ringdahl, 1995).

Although NCR is most commonly implemented by delivering the reinforcer identified via functional analysis, potent positive reinforcers of any sort can sometimes be used, even if they do not match the reinforcers maintaining problem behavior. For example, by use of potent tangible reinforcers such as food, demanding instructional situations may become less aversive to the individual receiving treatment, and therefore he or she may be less inclined to engage in escape behavior (Lalli et al., 1999). Also, through use of potent tangible reinforcers, behavior maintained by either attention or access to tangible items can be reduced because the individual is given something else to do (Fischer, Iwata, & Mazaleski, 1997). Most parents will recognize this sort of effect if they have ever given a toddler a favorite toy while they (the parents) finish some housework or pay bills (i.e., the noncontingent toy effectively competes with adult attention as reinforcement). Finally, because many behavior problems are maintained by automatic reinforcement (i.e., they are not socially reinforced), NCR in the form of attention, toys, or leisure activities can be used as a means of environmental enrichment. Research shows that environmental enrichment can decrease automatically reinforced behavior, presumably because it provides alternative sources of reinforcement (e.g., Horner, 1980).

The main reasons that one might select NCR as a treatment include the following: (1) Its effects typically occur rapidly; (2) it has been shown to produce fewer negative side effects than differential reinforcement of other behavior (DRO) and extinction; and (3) it is ultimately very simple to conduct. Most studies show that NCR effects are virtually immediate, insofar as the effects are evident within one experimental session (e.g., Hagopian, Fisher, & Legacy, 1994). Also, in one study, extinction-induced aggression was considerably lower in NCR versus DRO (Vollmer et al., 1993). In another study (Vollmer et al., 1998), extinction bursts were not seen with NCR but were consistently observed when a therapist implemented traditional extinction (i.e., when the therapist withheld the reinforcer that was maintaining problem behavior). The NCR procedure is ultimately easy to implement because the care provider does not need to see every instance of problem behavior in order to know when to deliver or not to deliver reinforcers. However, in DRO a therapist must reset a timer every time the problem behavior occurs. In NCR, the reinforcer is delivered at a set point in time no matter whether the problem behavior has occurred.

HOW DOES THE TECHNIQUE WORK?

Two processes, extinction and satiation, may be responsible for the decrease in responding observed during NCR. The decrease may be a result of *extinction* because the reinforcer is no longer delivered contingent on a response. *Satiation* may contribute to the effects because the reinforcer is made available freely and frequently (e.g., why bang your head to get attention when you are already getting lots of attention?). Another way to consider the effects of NCR is to examine the very nature of reinforcement. In NCR, the probability of obtaining a reinforcer is no greater given the occurrence of behavior than it would be given the nonoccurrence of behavior. Hence, a reinforcement effect is not expected and, therefore, the fre-

quency of the target response should be reduced (Catania, 1998).

STEP-BY-STEP PROCEDURES

Functional Analysis (Assessment)

When designing an intervention for problem behavior, it is important first to identify the functional reinforcer for that behavior (see Table 40.1). A functional analysis of problem behavior can be conducted using procedures similar to those described by Iwata et al. (1982/1994). Conditions are arranged to test hypotheses about the reinforcers maintaining problem behavior. Common test conditions include *attention, escape, tangible, alone,* and *play.* Typical functional analysis sessions last anywhere from 5 to 15 min, and several sessions of each condition should be conducted, usually in a multielement format (where sessions from each condition alternate either randomly or in some predesigned order). In the *attention* condition, the "therapist" acts as if his or her attention is diverted to some task such as reading or chatting with someone else. Problem behavior produces attention from the therapist. The purpose of the *attention* condition is to test whether attention reinforces problem behavior. In the *escape* condition, the therapist presents instructional demands to the participant. Problem behavior produces a brief break from the instructional activity (usually about 15–30 s). The purpose of the *escape* condition is to test whether escape reinforces problem behavior. In the *tangible* condition, the therapist "takes a turn" with some tangible item such as a toy, food, or beverage. Problem behavior produces access to the tangible item for about 30 s. The purpose of the *tangible* condition is to test whether tangible items

TABLE 40.1   Key Elements of NCR

Step	Description
Functional analysis	Identify reinforcers maintaining problem behavior.
Implementing a rich NCR schedule	Provide continuous (ideally) reinforcement for rapid suppression.
Thinning the NCR schedule	Use gradual increments.

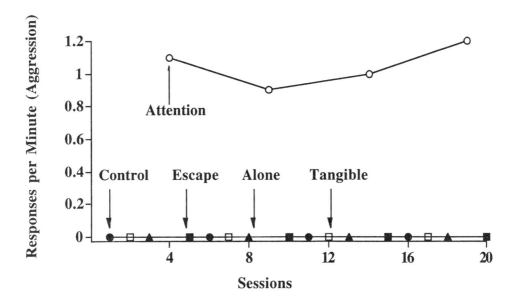

FIGURE 40.1   Hypothetical Functional Analysis Outcome

reinforce problem behavior. In the *alone* condition (usually used for self-injury or stereotypic behavior), there are no programmed contingencies for problem behavior. The purpose is to see if behavior persists even when the participant is alone. If so, the behavior is probably not socially reinforced (i.e., it is automatically reinforced). In the *play* condition, the participant receives a great deal of stimulation and attention, and no instructional demands are presented. Usually, low levels of problem behavior are observed in this condition, so it is used as point of comparison for the other condition. Overall, the idea of a functional analysis is to see which condition or conditions produce the highest levels of problem behavior.

A hypothetical functional analysis outcome is presented in Figure 40.1. In this example responses per minute of disruptive behavior (y axis) are graphed session by session (x axis). Disruption occurs only in the *attention* session. Results of this sort suggest that disruptive behavior is reinforced by attention. In this hypothetical case, attention should be used as the reinforcer during NCR (Vollmer et al., 1993). Alternatively, during times when noncontingent attention cannot be delivered, a highly preferred toy or leisure item could be made available noncontingently (Fischer et al., 1997).

If it is not practical to conduct the sort of functional analysis just described, the practitioner should at the very least conduct direct observations in the natural environment. These observations should be used to formulate a "best guess" about the reinforcers maintaining problem behavior.

NCR (First Variation)

After conducting the functional analysis, present the reinforcer known to maintain problem behavior on a very rich schedule. Ideally, the participant would have continuous access to the reinforcer. Thus, the participant has continuous access to attention, escape, or the tangible item, depending upon which reinforcer was shown to maintain problem behavior. This is a good starting point for very dangerous behavior because continuous access to the reinforcer usually produces an immediate suppression of behavior.

NCR (Second Variation)

After conducting the functional analysis, present a very potent tangible or social reinforcer during the context associated with problem behavior. For ex-

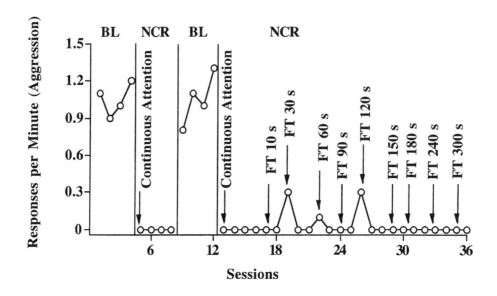

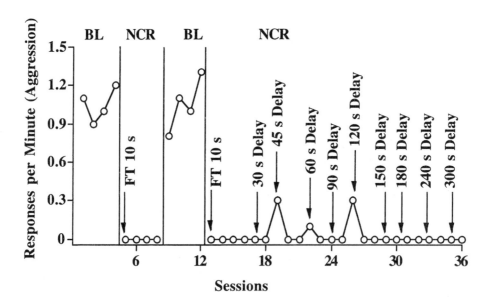

FIGURE 40.2   Example of NCR Schedule Thinning

ample, as treatment for escape behavior, juice could be made available continuously during instructional activity in order to reduce the aversiveness of instructional activity. Similarly, as treatment for attention-maintained behavior, a favorite toy could be made available to a child continuously when the adult must divert his or her attention (e.g., to pay bills, to talk on the telephone).

Schedule Thinning

Continuous access to reinforcement is sometimes both impractical (e.g., when the adult is busy) and undesirable (e.g., when a student should be engaged with schoolwork). Thus, the schedule of access to the reinforcer must be thinned systematically. A timer is useful for ensuring that reinforcement is delivered according to the schedule. Initially, reinforcement is provided on a rich schedule and faded to a thinner schedule as problem behavior remains at low rates. In order to thin the schedule, it is helpful to specify a criterion for fading out reinforcement. For example, clinicians may decide that two consecutive sessions with one or fewer instances of problem behavior is a sufficient criterion to slightly thin out the schedule of reinforcement.

Usually, the schedule is thinned incrementally, such as in 10-s units, until a more manageable schedule, such as FT 5 min, is obtained. In addition, it is important to thin the NCR schedule gradually. If an increase in problem behavior is observed when the schedule is thinned, it may be necessary to increase the schedule by smaller increments. An example of NCR schedule thinning is illustrated in Figure 40.2. Initially, continuous reinforcement is provided, resulting in a decrease in responding to zero. Eventually, the schedule is faded so that attention is provided every 5 min (FT 5 min) while problem behavior levels remain low.

WHEN NCR DOES NOT DECREASE PROBLEM BEHAVIOR

If high rates of problem behavior persist, consider the following possibilities: (1) The reinforcers maintaining problem behavior were not properly identified, (2) the NCR schedule was thinned too rapidly, or (3) the behavior is being reinforced inadvertently because of contiguous coupling, albeit incidental, with the reinforcer. To address (1), additional functional analyses or naturalistic observations should be conducted to ensure that all of the reinforcers maintaining problem behavior were identified. Frequently, problem behavior is reinforced by more than one type of consequence (e.g., Smith, Iwata, Vollmer, & Zarcone, 1993). To address (2), thin the schedule in smaller increments; perhaps using half the increments selected initially. To address (3), introduce a *momentary omission contingency* (Vollmer et al., 1997). That is, do not deliver the reinforcer at the scheduled interval if the problem behavior happens to occur at that moment. This will avoid the problem of accidental reinforcement because the re-

inforcer is never delivered at the moment the behavior occurs.

Further Reading

Iwata, B. A., Dorsey, M. F., Slifer, K. J., Bauman, K. E., & Richman, G. S. (1994). Toward a functional analysis of self-injury. *Journal of Applied Behavior Analysis, 27,* 197–209. (Reprinted from *Analysis and Intervention in Developmental Disabilities, 2,* 3–20, 1982)

Vollmer, T. R. (1999). Time-based schedules as treatment for severe behavior disorders. *Mexican Journal of Behavior Analysis, 25,* 85–103.

Vollmer, T. R., Iwata, B. A., Zarcone, J. R., Smith, R. G., & Mazaleski, J. L. (1993). The role of attention in the treatment of attention-maintained self-injurious behavior: Noncontingent reinforcement and differential reinforcement of other behavior. *Journal of Applied Behavior Analysis, 26,* 9–21.

References

Carr, J. E., Coriaty, S., Wilder, D. A., Gaunt, B. T., Dozier, C. L., Britton, L. N., Avina, C., & Reed, C. L. (2000). A review of "noncontingent" reinforcement as treatment for the aberrant behavior of individuals with developmental disabilities. *Research in Developmental Disabilities, 21,* 377–391.

Catania, A. C. (1998). *Learning* (4th ed.). Upper Saddle River, NJ: Prentice Hall.

Fischer, S. M., Iwata, B. A., & Mazaleski, J. L. (1997). Noncontingent delivery of arbitrary reinforcers as treatment for self-injurious behavior. *Journal of Applied Behavior Analysis, 30,* 239–249.

Goh, H., Iwata, B. A., & Kahng, S. (1999). Multicomponent assessment and treatment of cigarette pica. *Journal of Applied Behavior Analysis, 32,* 297–316.

Hagopian, L. P., Fisher, W. W., & Legacy, S. M. (1994). Schedule effects of noncontingent reinforcement on attention-maintained destructive behavior in identical quadruplets. *Journal of Applied Behavior Analysis, 27,* 317–325.

Horner, R. D. (1980). The effects of an environmental enrichment program on the behavior of institutionalized profoundly retarded children. *Journal of Applied Behavior Analysis, 13,* 473–491.

Iwata, B. A., Dorsey, M. F., Slifer, K. J., Bauman, K. E., & Richman, G. S. (1994). Toward a functional analysis of self-injury. *Journal of Applied Behavior Analysis, 27,* 197–209. (Reprinted from *Analysis and Intervention in Developmental Disabilities, 2,* 3–20, 1982)

Lalli, J. S., Vollmer, T. R., Progar, P. R., Wright, C., Borrero, J., Daniel, D., Barthold, C. H., Tocco, K., & May, W. (1999). Competition between positive and negative reinforcement in the treatment of escape behavior. *Journal of Applied Behavior Analysis, 32,* 285–296.

Marcus, B. A., & Vollmer, T. R. (1995). Effects of differential negative reinforcement on disruption and compliance. *Journal of Applied Behavior Analysis, 28,* 229–230.

Smith, R. G., Iwata, B. A., Vollmer, T. R., & Zarcone, J. R. (1993). Experimental analysis and treatment of multiply controlled self-injury. *Journal of Applied Behavior Analysis, 26,* 183–196.

Vollmer, T. R., Iwata, B. A., Zarcone, J. R., Smith, R. G., & Mazaleski, J. L. (1993). The role of attention in the treatment of attention-maintained self-injurious behavior: Noncontingent reinforcement and differential reinforcement of other behavior. *Journal of Applied Behavior Analysis, 26,* 9–21.

Vollmer, T. R., Marcus, B. A., & Ringdahl, J. E. (1995). Noncontingent escape as treatment for self-injurious behavior maintained by negative reinforcement. *Journal of Applied Behavior Analysis, 28,* 15–26.

Vollmer, T. R., Progar, P. R., Lalli, J. S., Van Camp, C. M., Sierp, B. J., Wright, C. S., Nastasi, J., & Eisenschink, K. J. (1998). Fixed-time schedules attenuate extinction-induced phenomena in the treatment of severe aberrant behavior. *Journal of Applied Behavior Analysis, 31,* 529–542.

Vollmer, T. R., Ringdahl, J. E., Roane, H., S., & Marcus, B. A. (1997). Negative side effects of noncontingent reinforcement. *Journal of Applied Behavior Analysis, 30,* 161–164.

41 PAIN MANAGEMENT

Robert J. Gatchel and Richard C. Robinson

Research over the past three decades has clearly demonstrated the central importance of psychosocial factors in the perception and reporting of chronic pain and disability (Flor & Turk, 1984; Fordyce, 1976; Katon, Egan, & Miller, 1985; Sternbach, 1974). As early as 1959, Engel (1959) argued that the perception of pain is a psychological phenomenon. He also described personality characteristics that he hypothesized predisposed individuals to chronic pain. These characteristics included a history of defeat, significant guilt, unsatisfied aggressive impulses, and a propensity to develop pain in response to a real or imagined loss. Gatchel and Epker (1999) have provided an updated review of many of the psychosocial risk factors, but appropriately refute the "myth" that there is one particular "pain-prone personality."

Melzack and Wall's (1965) *gate control theory of pain* represented an important milestone by hypothesizing that central nervous system mechanisms provided the physiological basis for psychological involvement in pain perception. Specifically, these researchers theorized that a neurophysiological mechanism in the spinal cord, located in the dorsal horns, acted as a gate for pain signals and allowed for modulation from various sources. Thus, the gate control theory integrated peripheral stimuli with cortical variables, explaining the impact that mood states may have on pain perception. Expanding upon this, the *biopsychosocial model* combined social factors with the psychological and physiological components of pain. Turk and Rudy (1987) elaborated and refined Melzak and Wall's early assumptions by incorporating cognitive, affective, psychosocial, behavioral, and physiological elements into the chronic pain experience. Their research suggested that, as suffering increases, psychosocial factors play an increasingly significant role in the perpetuation of pain behavior and suffering.

Patients with chronic pain disorders typically present with concurrent psychiatric disorders that contribute to their pain, suffering, and disability. Therefore, one is often simultaneously addressing chronic pain and the host of painful feelings and distressing thoughts that accompany this condition. For example, Kinney, Gatchel, Polatin, Fogarty, and Mayer (1993) reported chronic low back pain (CLBP) patients experience more depression and had higher rates of substance abuse and personality disorders than the general population. Polatin, Kinney, Gatchel, Lillo, and Mayer (1993) also attempted to delineate the complex relationship between psychopathology and pain. Using the Structured Clinical Interview for the *Diagnostic and Statistical*

This chapter was supported in part by grants 2K02 MH01107, 2R01 MH46402, and R01 DE10713 from the National Institutes of Health.

Manual of Mental Disorders–III–Revised, Polatin and colleagues (1993) found that of 200 CLBP patients, 77% met lifetime diagnostic criteria for psychiatric disturbances. The most common diagnoses were Depression, Substance Abuse, and anxiety disorders. In addition, 51% of the patients met criteria for a personality disorder. Likewise, Gatchel, Polatin, Mayer, and Garcy (1994) examined 152 CLBP patients prior to undergoing an intensive 3-week interdisciplinary treatment program, and found that 90% of the CLBP patients met criteria for a lifetime Axis I diagnosis, the most prevalent diagnoses being Major Depression and Substance Abuse.

Gatchel (1996) clarified this complex relationship among pain, psychopathology, and personality by theorizing about the progression from acute to chronic pain. The psychosocial changes that occur as a person progresses from acute to chronic pain is referred to as a "layering of behavioral/psychological problems over the original nociception of the pain experience itself" (p. 34). This model is based on a three-stage progression, from acute to subacute to chronic disability, following the experience of pain as a result of an identifiable injury. Stage 1 encompasses the resulting emotional reactions (e.g., fear, anxiety, and worry) that arise as a consequence of perceived pain. Stage 2 begins when the pain persists past a reasonable acute time period. It is at this stage that the development or exacerbation of psychological and behavioral problems occurs. Gatchel notes that the form these difficulties take depends primarily on the premorbid personality and psychological characteristics of the individual (i.e., a *diathesis*), as well as current socioeconomic and environmental stressors. For instance, an individual with a tendency to become depressed may develop a depressive disorder in response to the economic and social *stress* of being unable to work as a result of pain (Gatchel & Turk, 1996). Such a diathesis-stress model has also been amplified by Weisberg and colleagues (Weisberg, Vittengle, Clark, Gatchel, & Garen, 2000). This complex interaction of physical and psychosocioeconomic factors leads to Stage 3 of the model: As the patient's life begins to totally and completely revolve around the pain as a result of the chronic nature of the problem, the patient begins to accept the sick role. By doing so, the patient is excused from normal responsibilities and social obligations, which may serve to reinforce the maintenance of the sick role.

KEY CONCEPTUAL FACTORS IN TREATMENT

Physical Deconditioning

Physical deconditioning, involving the progressive lack of use of the body, generally accompanies patients during their progression toward chronic disability. It produces a circular effect leading to increased mental deconditioning. The combined interaction of the symptoms negatively impacts the emotional well-being and self-esteem of an individual (Gatchel & Turk, 1996).

Pain versus Hurt

When patients engage in an activity that produces pain, they are likely to associate the pain with the initial hurt. This causes patients to fear and avoid pain and possible pain-producing situations. Unfortunately, pain often accompanies physical reconditioning and the additional steps needed in order to resume normal responsibilities and social obligations. Therefore, patients must be taught that hurt and harm are not the same (Fordyce, 1988).

Coping

The ways an individual manages and copes with general stressors helps who will become a chronic pain patient. Thus, assessment of coping styles and instructing patients on more adaptive coping skills is an important part of a cognitive behavioral approach to treatment. The Multidimensional Pain Inventory (MPI), formerly the West-Haven Yale Multidimensional Pain Inventory, developed by Kerns, Turk, and Rudy (1985), is one of the most widely used measures in the pain area. The MPI is a brief self-report instrument that examines the person's perception of pain and coping ability. The MPI helps to identify patients who have difficulty coping with their pain, and it can guide the implementation of pain reduction interventions. Turk and Rudy (1988) identified three coping styles, using a cluster analysis on the MPI scales with a heterogeneous group of chronic pain patients: *dysfunctional* (43%), *interpersonally distressed* (28%), and *adaptive copers* (29.5%). The dysfunctional group members reported that their pain, and the interference caused by their pain, was extreme. Patients in the interpersonally distressed group reported a lack of support, caring, and understanding from their family members and significant others. In contrast, individuals in the adaptive copers group reported high levels of activity and life control, as well as lower levels of pain intensity, perceived interference, and affective distress.

Catastrophizing

The role of catastrophizing in the prediction of chronic pain and disability has gained increased attention in recent years. Catastrophizing involves thinking negatively, and in an exaggerated fashion, about events and stimuli. This can be applied to how individuals perceive their pain or their ability to cope with their pain (Sullivan, Stanish, Waite, Sullivan, & Tripp, 1998). In one of the first studies to address this variable, Butler, Damarin, Beaulieu, Schwebel, and Thorn (1989) evaluated cognitive strategies and postoperative pain in a sample of general surgical patients, and they found that increased catastrophizing was associated with higher levels of postoperative pain intensity. Main and Waddell (1991) also looked at this variable and found a strong relationship between catastrophizing and depressive symptoms in a sample of low back pain patients. Furthermore, of the cognitive variables investigated by the authors, catastrophizing was determined to have the "greatest potential for understanding current low back symptoms" (Main & Waddell, p. 287). Fortunately, catastrophizing is amenable to and especially suited for cognitive-behavioral interventions.

COGNITIVE BEHAVIORAL THERAPY FOR CHRONIC PAIN

Turk and Gatchel (2002) succinctly describe five aims of cognitive behavior therapy (CBT) for chronic pain. The *first goal* is to help patients alter their perceptions of their pain, from something that is overwhelming to something that they can learn to manage. The *second goal* is to educate patients that CBT will provide them with the tools they need to manage their pain more adaptively. The *third goal* is to alter each patient's self-perception, from someone who is passive and helpless to someone who is active and has the ability to affect both self and environment. The *fourth goal* is to instruct patients on how to monitor thoughts, feelings, behaviors, and physiology so that they can develop and maintain an understanding of the relationship among these variables. Finally, the *fifth goal* is to teach patients to develop more adaptive responses to their chronic pain that can be used in a variety of settings, and that can be maintained over time.

With these goals in mind, treatment consists of four major components: (1) reconceptualization, (2) skills acquisition, (3) skills consolidation, and (4) generalization and maintenance (Turk & Gatchel, 2002). Each of the procedures that accompany these components will be briefly reviewed.

Reconceptualization

Reconceptualizing chronic pain has two major components. The first involves instructing patients on how to recognize problematic thoughts; the second is helping people restructure their thinking (a process termed *cognitive restructuring*). Using a pain diary that asks patients to record their pain and tension levels at various times throughout the day, as well as to record pain-eliciting situations, is the most common way to help patients identify maladaptive thoughts. Further, patients are asked to record their thoughts and feelings before, during, and after those times when their pain increases, as a way of identifying maladaptive thoughts such as "The pain is killing me" or "If it hurts, I must be making it worse."

Once common negative thoughts have been identified, the therapist and the patient can work collaboratively to challenge the thoughts. This systematic questioning approach to previously unchallenged assumptions allows the patients to develop more objective, problem-solving, and therefore adaptive thoughts. For instance, a patient who thinks to herself, "I'll never travel again," can examine that thought objectively. It may be that the patient can travel, but that the physical cost of the pain would be unacceptable. However, with relaxation training, the cost of the pain could be decreased so that traveling is not something to be feared. Notice that the thought is not simply converted to a positive, Pollyana-ish thought, but to one that is more objective, active, and adaptive. Alteration of perceptions and long-standing beliefs does not happen during the sessions; rather, it happens when the patients practice more adaptive coping thoughts in their environment. When positive affective and behavioral changes occur, the therapist continuously draws the patients' attention to their accomplishments in an attempt to increase self-efficacy and reinforce adaptive change.

Skills Acquisition

Skills acquired in CBT for chronic pain can be roughly divided into self-regulatory skills and stress-management skills. *Self-regulatory skills* are techniques that allow patients to alter their physiological functioning in a manner that can decrease their pain, such as reducing muscle tension of autonomic arousal. The most common self-regulatory skills are relaxation training, distraction, self-hypnosis, and biofeedback. *Stress-management skills* entail teaching effective communication, planning, and time management strategies, as well as providing patients with a systematic approach to problem solving. Figure 41.1 lists the skills that are often taught. It is important to note that the skills listed do not differ from the skills used in other CBT protocols that have been described in this volume.

Problem solving

Relaxation (including progressive muscle relaxation and autogenic training)

Cognitive coping skills training

Attention diversion or distraction

Biofeedback

Imagery

Pacing

Communication skills

FIGURE 41.1   Common Skills Acquired in CBT for Chronic Pain

Two skills that are listed that may not be as recognizable to other CBT clinicians are attention diversion and pacing. With regard to *attention diversion,* also referred to as *distraction techniques,* the goal is to help the patient focus on other thoughts or feelings that are unrelated to his or her pain. One can easily imagine different distraction techniques, such as reading, conversing with a friend, or watching television.

Pacing is a deceptively simple-sounding concept that, in practice, can be challenging for patients without proper guidance and practice. The notion is that chronic pain patients will slowly begin to exercise and engage in physical activity that will increase adaptive beliefs and self-efficacy. The goal of pacing is for individuals to learn to be physically active to meet reasonable predetermined goals, rather than engaging in activity until the pain has overwhelmed them. For instance, if a patient can mow the yard for 30 min before his or her back begins to hurt, the patient may be instructed to mow the yard in 15 min increments.

Skill Consolidation

In the *skill consolidation* phase patients continue to practice, refine, and rehearse the new skill they have acquired. Having the patient practice with the therapist in session, as well as beginning to have the patient more fully integrate the skill in his or her environment outside therapy, becomes increasingly important. Practitioners of CBT will often have patients imagine using the skill in different situations, or will role-play with the patient various different problems that may occur.

Generalization and Maintenance

Cognitive behavior therapy for chronic pain should not be thought of as a one-time treatment that leads to a definitive cure. It provides people with the tools to manage their pain, so that it has an appreciable impact on their ability to enjoy those things in their lives that the patients perceive as important. For CBT to be truly effective, patients must continue to practice even when they have completed their course of therapy. Follow-up appointments at 3- to 6-month intervals, or on an as-needed basis, insure that the patient's gains are maintained and reinforce the progress they have made. It should be noted that Marlatt and Gordon have written extensively on the issue of relapse prevention, and their ideas are easily translatable to pain patients (e.g. Marlatt, 1996). That is to say, preparing the patient for inevitable setbacks does not make them more likely to occur. Instead, patients learn to reframe a setback as a temporary, manageable, and typical part of recovery. If a patient's pain flares up and the patient has stopped practicing his or her relaxation skills, then the patient is well prepared to engage in objective examination of any irrational negative thoughts. Patients can begin to take the necessary steps to retrain their bodies to relax without interference from thoughts that the situation is "hopeless."

A SESSION-BY-SESSION GUIDE TO A TYPICAL COURSE OF TREATMENT

In this section we have compiled a prototypical 12-week course of CBT for a chronic pain patient.

Assessment

A multimodal assessment should occur prior to the patient's starting treatment. During the assessment process, it is also critical to explain to patients that you are interested in all the ways that pain has impacted their lives, and that you are not trying to prove that their pain is fake or that they are "crazy" for having pain that has not resolved.

Session 1

As with all CBT protocols, the first session is used to establish rapport and provide the rationale for the procedures to be employed. The general concepts noted earlier (e.g., the gate control theory of pain) are explained and the idea that learnable skills can be of aid is introduced. Typically, the session concludes with instruction in diaphragmatic breathing and assignment of homework, including daily logs and material about managing pain.

Session 2

Each subsequent session begins with a review of the last session, and a review of the homework. In Session 2, relaxation training and its rationale are presented.

Session 3

This session focuses on how to identify and incorporate relaxation training in everyday situations that produce stress (as identified by review of the pain diary). The patient is asked to schedule brief relaxation periods prior to those particularly stressful situations.

Session 4

The rationale for distraction techniques is provided to the patient. Three distraction techniques are trained: (1) focusing on physical surroundings, (2) counting backward slowly, and (3) focusing on auditory stimuli. An example of each technique is provided, and the patient is asked to practice.

Session 5

The rationale for pleasant activity scheduling is provided to the patient. Examples are described to the patient, and possible barriers to engaging in the pleasant activity are reviewed.

Session 6

A step-by-step pleasant activity scheduling plan is introduced. These steps include creating a balance between unpleasant and pleasant behaviors, planning ahead, setting specific goals, rewarding oneself for achieving goals, and checking one's progress toward one's overall goals.

Session 7

The rationale for cognitive therapy is provided in this session. Patients are taught about irrational negative thoughts. Homework is assigned to help patients recognize when they are having these irrational, negative thoughts.

Session 8

Instructions are provided for changing irrational thoughts and self-instructional training. Patients are taught methods to change irrational thoughts, such as developing more rational alternative thoughts. The question "What evidence do you have for that?" is repeatedly posed to patients. Self-statements to deal with pain are also taught to the patient. Self-statements are broken down into four categories, including preparing, beginning, during, and after. These statements include, "I may have to move a little slower, but I can still go shopping," or "My pain is flaring up, but it will soon pass."

Session 9

Methods for improving assertiveness are introduced in this session. A plan to improve social skills and assertiveness is developed with the patient, and it includes developing a personal problem list, monitoring assertiveness, practice with assertive imagery, transfer from imaginary to real life, and evaluating progress.

Session 10

A rationale is provided for using newly developed social skills. Points that are stressed during this session often include the fact that it is important to have the opportunity to interact with other people, and that inadequate reward occurs when social activities are no longer rewarding.

Session 11

Strategies for maintaining treatment gains are reviewed in this session. Points that are stressed during this session include reviewing material already covered; review of what has been achieved; integrating what has been learned and incorporated into life; monitoring level of pain and tension on a regular basis; and examining possible "pitfalls" and solutions to them.

Session 12

The major theme of this session is "making a life plan." Points that are stressed during this session include maintaining one's gains, planning effectively, and spelling out long-term goals.

CONCLUSION

Cognitive behavior therapy for chronic pain incorporates techniques that are common for any CBT intervention. The slight adjustments to treatment involve educating patients about how psychosocial factors influence their pain. In addition, activity pacing and distraction are other techniques that are frequently used with chronic pain spatients; they may not be as frequently used with non–chronic pain patients. Unfortunately, chronic pain has a ripple effect, and very few areas of a person's life are not impacted when his or her pain is severe enough, and when it has lasted for a long period of time. However, the techniques learned in CBT have a ripple effect as well, and they frequently impact areas of a person's life that are outside the treatment's immediate focus. Of course, it is also extremely important that therapists working with chronic pain patients have a thorough understanding of the biopsychosocial approach to pain assessment and treatment because of the often complex interaction among physical, psychological, and socioeconomic factors that are underling pathophysiology and pain behaviors (cf. Gatchel & Turk, 1996).

References

Butler, R. W., Damarin, F. L., Beaulieu, C., Schwebel, A. L., & Thorn, B. E. (1989). Assessing cognitive coping strategies for acute postsurgical pain. *Psychological Assessment, 1,* 41–45.

Engel, G. L. (1959). "Psychogenic" pain and the pain-prone patient. *American Journal of Medicine, 26,* 899–918.

Flor, H., & Turk, D. C. (1984). Etiological theories and treatment for chronic back pain: I. Somatic models and interventions. *Pain, 19,* 105–121.

Fordyce, W. (1976). *Behavioral methods of control of chronic pain and illness.* St. Louis, MO: Mosby.

Fordyce, W. E. (1988). Pain and suffering: A reappraisal. *American Psychologist, 43,* 276–283.

Gatchel, R. J. (1996). Psychological disorders and chronic pain: Cause-and-effect relationships. In R. J. Gatchel & D. C. Turk (Eds.), *Psychological ap-*

proaches to pain management: A practitioner's hand-book (pp. 33–54). New York: Guilford Press.

Gatchel, R. J., & Epker, J. T. (1999). Psychosocial predictors of chronic pain and response to treatment. In R. J. Gatchel & D. C. Turk (Eds.), *Psychosocial factors in pain: Critical perspectives* (pp. 412–434). New York: Guilford Press.

Gatchel, R. J., Polatin, P. B., Mayer, T. G., & Garcy, P. D. (1994). Psychopathology and the rehabilitation of patients with chronic low back pain disability. *Archives of Physical Medicine and Rehabilitation, 75*(6), 666–670.

Gatchel, R. J., & Turk, D. C. (Eds.). (1996). *Psychological approaches to pain management: A practitioner's hand-book.* New York: Guilford Press.

Katon, W., Egan, K., & Miller, D. (1985). Chronic pain: Lifetime psychiatric diagnoses and family history. *American Journal of Psychiatry, 142,* 1156–1160.

Kerns, R., Turk, D., & Rudy, T. (1985). The West-Haven Yale Multidimensional Pain Inventory. *Pain, 23,* 345–356.

Kinney, R. K., Gatchel, R. J., Polatin, P. B., Fogarty, W. J., & Mayer, T. G. (1993). Prevalence of psychopathology in acute and chronic low back pain patients. *Journal of Occupational Rehabilitation, 1993,* 95–103.

Main, C. J., & Waddell, G. (1991). A comparison of cognitive measures in low back pain: Statistical structure and clinical validity at initial assessment. *Pain, 56,* 287–298.

Marlatt, G. A. (1996). Taxonomy of high-risk situations for alcohol relapse: Evolution and development of a cognitive-behavioral model. *Addiction, 91*(Suppl.), S37–S49.

Melzack, R., & Wall, P. D. (1965). Pain mechanisms: A new theory. *Science, 50,* 971–979.

Polatin, P. B., Kinney, R. K., Gatchel, R. J., Lillo, E., & Mayer, T. G. (1993). Psychiatric illness and chronic low-back pain. The mind and the spine—Which goes first? *Spine, 18*(1), 66–71.

Sternbach, R. A. (1974). *Pain patients: Traits and treatment.* New York: Academic Press.

Sullivan, M. J., Stanish, W., Waite, H., Sullivan, M., & Tripp, D. A. (1998). Catastrophizing, pain, and disability in patients with soft-tissue injury. *Pain, 77,* 253–260.

Turk, D. C., & Gatchel, R. J. (Eds.). (2002). *Psychological approaches to pain management* (2nd ed.). New York: Guilford Press.

Turk, D. C., & Rudy, T. E. (1987). Towards a comprehensive assessment of chronic pain patients. *Behavioral Research and Therapy, 25,* 237–249.

Turk, D., & Rudy, T. E. (1988). Toward an empirically derived taxonomy of chronic pain patients: Integration of psychological assessment data. *Journal of Consulting and Clinical Psychology, 56,* 233–238.

Weisberg, J. N., Vittengle, J. R., Clark, L. A., Gatchel, R. J., & Garen, A. A. (2000). Personality and pain: Summary and future directions. In R. J. Gatchel & J. N. Weisberg (Eds.), *Personality characteristics of patients with pain.* Washington, DC: American Psychological Association.

42 PARENT TRAINING

Kevin J. Moore and Gerald R. Patterson

Behavioral treatment for out-of-control children began in the late 1960s. It particularly emphasized the idea that the problem did not reside in the child; rather, it was in the social environment. Changing the aggressive child meant changing the environment that he or she lived in. The strategy that emerged was focused on training the parents (family members) to alter the contingencies they provided for both deviant and prosocial child behaviors.

Four different groups contributed to the development of these new procedures. S. Bijou played a key role during the early stages through his influence first on R. Hawkins and later on the Kansas parent trainers such as A. Christensen. Bijou also supported the Eugene, Oregon, group that included S. Eyeberg, S. Johnson, G. Patterson, and J. Reid. A third group at the Portland, Oregon, Medical School centered around C. Hanf, who produced such outstanding students as R. Forehand, C. Webster-Stratton, and R. Barkley. The fourth group, at Tennessee, consisted of R. Wahler and, for example, such productive students as J. Dumas. The general procedures that eventually became parent training (PT) were worked out over a series of meetings and exchanges of papers during the late 1960s and early 1970s.

We would like to thank Peter Sprengelmeyer for reading a draft of this chapter and providing useful suggestions. Support for this chapter was provided by Grants No. R37 MH 37940 and RO1 MH 54257 from the Antisocial and Other Personality Disorders Program, Prevention, Early Intervention, and Epidemiology Branch, National Institute of Mental Health (NIMH), U.S. Public Health Service (PHS); RO1 HD 34511 from the Center for Research for Mothers and Children, National Institute of Child Health and Human Development, U.S. PHS; RO1 MH 60195 and RO1 MH 38318 from the Child and Adolescent Treatment and Preventive Intervention Research Branch, DSIR, NIMH, U.S. PHS; and P30 MH 46690 from the Prevention and Behavioral Medicine Research Branch, NIMH, U.S. PHS.

THEORY

Observational data collected in homes and classrooms suggested that children's aggression was surprisingly functional (i.e., it worked; Patterson, Littman, & Bricker, 1967). Similarly, family interactions in homes showed that coercive child behaviors were very effective in manipulating aversive exchanges among family members. Also, these families provided little if any support for prosocial child behaviors. The parents were observed to be ineffective in such parenting practices as discipline (limit setting), encouragement (contingent positive), monitoring, involvement, and family problem solving. It was assumed that the parenting practices controlled the contingencies.

It was 25 years before it was possible to show that observation-based measures of the relative rate of reinforcement for coercive behaviors predicted children's observed rates of deviant behavior a week later (Snyder & Patterson, 1995). In another study, the relative rate of reinforcement observed in family interaction predicted the future likelihood of police arrest and out-of-home placement (Snyder, Schrepferman, & St. Peter, 1997).

The findings from several longitudinal studies strongly supported the assumed relationship between parenting skills and antisocial behavior (Forgatch, Patterson, & Ray, 1996; Patterson, Reid, & Dishion, 1992). Structural equation models were used to examine these relationships. Multimethod and multiagent indicators specified both the parenting practices and child outcomes. Now, 20 years later, parenting practices are widely accepted as being causally related to child antisocial outcomes.

More recent research literature emphasizes the important role played by positive reinforcers supplied by deviant peers for deviant behavior (Patterson, Dishion, & Yoerger, 2000). The programmatic studies by Dishion and his colleagues showed that the relative rate of reinforcement for deviant talk predicted criminal activity several years later (Dishion, Spracklen, Andrews, & Patterson, 1996). The influence of deviant peers seems to begin in the elementary grades with marked acceleration during early adolescence. The outcome seems to be reflected primarily in covert forms of antisocial behavior.

Furthermore, findings from many longitudinal studies have shown reliable correlations between early-onset delinquency (arrest prior to age 14) and later criminal careers. The data also showed that this trajectory may begin as early as age 2 or 3 years (Patterson, 1996; Shaw, Keenan, & Vondra, 1994).

Thus, the contingency or social learning theory stipulates that prevention should begin at an early age and should involve procedures that improve parenting practices. The outcomes should include both reduced rates of antisocial behavior and reduced contacts with deviant peers.

INTERVENTION

In the early 1970s and 1980s, a series of small-scale studies employed randomized trials and observation data to test the hypothesis that training in parenting skills was associated with significant reductions in observed deviant child behavior (Bry, 1982; Patterson, Chamberlain, & Reid, 1982; Walter & Gilmore, 1973; Wiltz & Patterson, 1974). The strongest evidence for the effectiveness of PT with younger antisocial children is to be found in the programmatic studies by Webster-Stratton (1984, 1990) and Webster-Stratton and Hammond (1997). There is now a sufficient number of randomized trial studies to merit systematic reviews of this literature. Reviewers consistently conclude that interventions based upon PT procedures produce reliable reductions in antisocial behavior (Kazdin, 1997; Kazdin & Weisz, 1998; Serketich & Dumas, 1996; Southam-Gerow & Kendall, 1997).

Cases referred for treatment typically require an average of 20 hours of professional time (including telephone calls and school visits). The procedures seem more effective with younger children 4 to 8 years old, as compared to older and adolescent children. Findings show that treatment failures are more likely for socially disadvantaged families and those with extremely depressed or antisocial parents. Parent training as a stand-alone treatment may be less effective for adolescent chronic delinquents. Studies that have attempted to treat these families using only PT have either met with no success (Henggeler, Melton, Brondino, Scherer, & Hanley, 1997), had limited success (Bank, Marlowe, Reid, Patterson, & Weinrott, 1991), or display such serious design flaws that their results are not interpretable. Alternatively, the Treatment Foster Care procedure put forward by Chamberlain and her colleagues (Chamberlain & Moore, 1998; Chamberlain & Reid, 1998) trains carefully selected foster parents to use PT concepts. They are effective with chronic offending adolescents. As the adolescent adapts to the highly structured environment, the child is returned to his or her home for brief periods, and the biological parents are trained to use PT procedures. The randomized trial shows significant reductions in police referrals for the members of the experimental group. Additional studies are now underway.

PARENT TRAINING PROCEDURES

Behavioral PT's primary treatment targets are to decrease coercive child behavior, primarily child noncompliance, and to increase the relative rates of reinforcement for prosocial behaviors. There are several reasons for having noncompliance be a main treatment target. First, child noncompliance is the most frequent referral complaint; second, noncompliance is involved in the largest percentage of negative parent-child interactions; third, children with compliance problems often teach parents, teachers, and siblings and peers not to attempt interactions with them where cooperation is the preferred behavior; and fourth, noncompliant children are often noncompliant across settings (e.g., home, school, neighborhood). Finally, the category of noncompliance subsumes most of the behaviors of the children with disruptive behavior who are referred for treatment. Common noncompliant referral behaviors include arguing, teasing, yelling, whining, complaining, temper tantrums, talking back, profanity, running off, noncompletion of chores, lying, stealing, ignoring directives or requests, not engaging in or completing homework assignments, physically resisting, destroying property, screaming, defiance, and disrupting others' activities.

The steps of PT are as follows: (1) observing and defining behavior; (2) use of reinforcement to encourage prosocial behavior, including the use of shaping to teach new behavioral repertoires (e.g., the skilled use of contingency management systems or token economies); (3) the use of mild punishment (e.g., time out from reinforcement, loss of privileges, and small work chores), the reduction of verbal reprimands, and the use of unambiguous directives; (4) generalization of the skills to school-related behaviors, including homework, to other community-based settings (e.g., the use of time-out procedures in public places and monitoring the child's whereabouts) and to anticipate future behavioral problems or developmental transitions (or both) where parenting practices are likely to need adjustment and new skills developed (e.g., entering middle school and the increasing freedom from direct adult observation and increasing peer involvement that accompanies these types of childhood transitions).

As part of the consent for treatment procedures, parents are instructed in the basic social learning principles about how children learn to act in particular ways. Parents are taught that they are the primary socializing agent of their children, that they have the most power and opportunity to change the problematic behavior of their children, and that children learn though encouragement and limit setting. Parents are taught that encouragement teaches children what they should do and limit setting teaches children what they should not do. Parents are also instructed in the "coercion cycle" (discussed earlier) and told that a primary focus of the training will be learning skills and strategies to avoid these problematic coercive cycles.

After consent is obtained, there is a clinical interview with one or both parents, direct observation and coding of parent-child interactions in the home and in the clinic, and the collection by phone 3 to 5 times per week of a Parent Daily Report (PDR; a list of 12 to 31 problem behaviors; Forehand & McMahon, 1981; Patterson, Reid, Jones, & Conger, 1975). This idealized observational assessment, particularly when it occurs in the home, is not always cost efficient or logistically possible (Forehand & McMahon). Fortunately, studies have demonstrated that both clinic-based observational assessment and the PDR are related at high enough levels to observed behavior in the home to be clinically sufficient for the assessment and clinical monitoring of targeted behaviors (e.g., Patterson, 1982; Patterson & Fleischman, 1979; Patterson, Reid, Jones, & Conger, 1975; Peed, Roberts, & Forehand, 1977).

Once the PDR has been collected, the parent or parents are asked to rate the endorsed items so that the two to four most troublesome behaviors are clearly identified. At the same time, the prosocial opposites of these behaviors are identified, and operational definitions are developed. Most of the time, an initial prosocial target behavior will be compliance to adult directives, and we usually label this "minding" versus "not minding." If the child is old enough, a chore is another behavior that is added to the data collection chart. Parents are then taught how to observe and collect data on the child's performance of these behaviors.

During this first step, we also currently recommend that one or more of the common broad-band childhood assessment instruments (e.g., Child Behavior Checklist [CBC-L], Achenbach, 1991; Behavioral Assessment System for Children [BASC], Reynolds & Kamphaus, 1994) be administered to parents and, when appropriate, to teachers. Even though these instruments have their limitations, they allow PT clinicians to gain efficient knowledge of comorbidity, cross-setting behavioral problems, or problem areas that might become the focus of treatment once a reasonable level of compliance is established.

In addition to the components delineated previously, we have found that phone contacts help parents both initiate and develop consistency in the use of PT intervention procedures (particularly early in the intervention process). During these phone contacts, clinicians help parents problem-solve implementation roadblocks and provide encouragement and reinforcement for parents' initial attempts to apply the intervention procedures. To summarize this first step, the main clinical objectives are to collect assessment information in order to identify target behaviors and their social-environmental contexts; to develop a baseline; and to begin to help the parents parse the behavioral stream into less global, more concrete, and smaller interactional segments. The baseline data are also used to help ascertain change as the rest of the intervention steps are systematically taught to and applied by the parents.

Teaching parents to observe, pinpoint, and track their children's behavior is important because it helps them to see the interactional sequences that are involved in the development and maintenance of both positive and problematic child behaviors. It also begins to teach parents that they will be directly involved in the treatment process, and it moves the parents away from mentalistic conceptualizations of why their children perform either antisocial or prosocial behaviors. The initial tracking chart usually includes only two problem behaviors and their prosocial opposites (e.g., not-minding vs. minding).

The next step involves teaching parents how to use contingent positive reinforcement to encourage appropriate behavior and to teach new prosocial behaviors. As part of this step, the clinician works with the parents to develop a written contingency plan for how the performance of developmentally appropriate prosocial behaviors will be reinforced. Usually, the criterion for the child's access to the reinforcer is specified and added to the tracking chart. The concept of reinforcement is carefully defined for the parents, and the powerful effects that attention (as a reinforcer) can have in the development and maintenance of problem behavior is discussed. Parents are then taught to place the majority of their attention on the prosocial behaviors they want their child to perform though the use of contingent praise, social reinforcement, and a contingency system. Examples of these contingency systems are readily available and range from very simple minding or not-minding charts for very young children (Forehand & McMahon, 1981; Patterson, 1975; Webster-Stratton, 2000) to sophisticated token economies for older children and adolescents (e.g., Barkley, Edwards, & Robin, 1998; Chamberlain & Mihalic, 1998; Patterson & Forgatch, 1987).

During this step, two additional skills are emphasized: (1) teaching the parents not to use verbal reprimands (nattering) and (2) teaching the use of clear and unambiguous directives (e.g., "Please take out the garbage by 5:30," vs. "Would you take the garbage out when you have a chance?"). In order to shape the parental behavioral repertoires emphasized in this step, and in other steps of behavioral PT, role-playing, modeling (live and videotaped), and in vivo feedback are clinical techniques used extensively.

In addition to these concepts and strategies, we have found it clinically useful to teach parents who lack them to develop parent-child routines they can use during critical periods of the day that have been identified as periods where bursts of child problem behaviors occur (Goodenough, 1931, as cited in Patterson, 1982). Behavioral problems do not occur at a consistent rate throughout the day but rather occur in bursts. Diurnal variations strongly suggest that these bursts occur at predictable times throughout the day. The periods of day were 7:30 A.M., 11:30 A.M., 5:30 P.M., and 8:30 P.M. and correspond to the times of the day when three things are occurring: (1) transitions, including biological state transitions, are taking place; (2) compliance demands are occurring at high frequency; and (3) parents are multitasking such things as meals and their own transitions. It is our experience, both as parents and as parent trainers, that if predictable routines (including encouragement and limit-setting procedures) can be established and reinforced during these times of the day, parents can significantly reduce rates of problematic child behavior and household stress and tension.

During this step, the clinician's task is to help parents to become competent in the use of a daily contingency management system where appropriate behavior and compliance are consistently reinforced. For most families, this system is just an expansion of the tracking chart, where incentives or privileges are earned contingent on the child's earning a certain number of points, stickers, or smiley faces for appropriate behavior. A rule of thumb that we use is that the child should be earning the agreed upon incentive or privilege 70 to 75% of the time. If not, the criterion is too high and needs to be adjusted. If age appropriate for the child, parents are also taught how to negotiate with their child for behavioral changes using individual contingency contracts. These contracts are sometimes used as an adjunct to an ongoing contingency system or as a stand-alone strategy.

The next step is teaching parents to use effective limit-setting techniques. This step is taught after parents have become firm with the use of positive reinforcement and incentives. It is important to note that it is our clinical experience and that of others (e.g., Barkley, 1987; Forehand & McMahon, 1981) that if limit-setting techniques and skills are taught before parents are firm with the reinforcement and encouragement techniques, they will drop out of treatment prematurely. With regard to limit setting, a primary goal of the clinician is to teach parents that limit setting is a teaching method and not a method whereby pain and suffering are necessary for children to learn to behave. Thus, parents are taught that limit setting works best when it is applied immediately and consistently, is used early in a sequence of problem behavior or episode of noncompliance, and is of short duration.

The primary limit-setting techniques that are taught to parents in this step are the use of time-out from reinforcement, privilege removal, and small work chores. It is commonly necessary in this step first to help the parents develop a clear set of 5 to 10 house rules that are behaviorally defined, written down, and posted. There are many examples of time-out procedures (e.g., Barkley, 1987; Becker, 1971; Christopherson, 1990; Forehand & McMahon, 1981; Patterson, 1975b) and clinicians using PT procedures must become familiar with and highly competent in the use of this procedure, including the use of backup consequences if time-out is refused. For training clinicians and parents to become competent with this skill, we like to use the procedure and description of its application contained in Patterson (1975a) because it is thorough and offers enough examples of how to manage common child and adult behaviors that have been shown to be problematic to the effectiveness of this technique.

In addition, the effectiveness of time-out (see Chapter 64, this volume) is enhanced by a social environment that is affectively upbeat and where there is a consistent probability of the child's receiving positive reinforcement. Although many skills taught in the previous steps help parents to develop a reasonably positive family environment, in families that have children with high rates of noncompliance, the development of a positive environment often needs to be explicitly taught. Christopherson (1990) presents a useful strategy for teaching parents this set of skills that he has called "Time In."

The other primary limit-setting skill that parents are taught to use is response-cost techniques, such as loss of privileges. This technique has a wide range of application. For example, response cost can be part of the contingency system whereby the child does not obtain enough points or tokens to gain access to privileges, such as later bedtime, riding his or her bike, or watching television. Parents are also taught how to remove access to privileges for refusing to go to a time-out and breaking rules. As children age, we also teach parents to use small, 5- to 10-min work chores (e.g., emptying a dishwasher, wiping down a mirror, etc.) as limit-setting consequences.

During the last step of PT, parents are taught that their contingency program needs to be "worked" (e.g., changed, progress assessed, some behaviors dropped and others added, etc.) so that the parents are more likely to develop and generalize the parenting skills to new behaviors and situations. This final stage then involves generalizing the skills developed to monitoring the child's educational performance (see Chapter 29, this volume), time away from home (e.g., monitoring friends, whereabouts, etc.), and the management of the child's behavior in other public settings. During this step, parents are taught how to tie home and school together by getting i nformation concerning school performance and behavior. This is done primarily though the use of a school card that goes between home and school on a daily basis. The use of a school card is usually tied into the daily contingency management system being used in the home, whereby the child earns or loses points based on teacher-reported performance and behavior. Depending on the particular circumstances and skill level of the parents, it is sometimes necessary for the clinician to go to a school meeting with the parents to establish the school card system. Parents are also taught to anticipate and manage problem behaviors that occur in public places, including how to use time-out in public places. For example, time-out may not be appropriate, and parents are taught how to place a child in time-out immediately upon returning home. Throughout this stage, parent trainers remain alert for behaviors that the parents can generalize their skills to include, encouraging parents to continue to identify behaviors they want to change, to record the effectiveness of their interventions on these behaviors, and to fine tune their home and school contingency programs.

CAVEAT

Even though on the surface PT appears to be an easy set of skills to develop in clinicians and teach to parents, our experience over the past 30 years strongly suggests the opposite. That is, considerable clinical acumen ("soft clinical skills"; Patterson & Chamberlain, 1988) is necessary to effectively treat children and families within a behavioral PT approach, and this is particularly true for clinic-referred children and their families. We strongly recommend that clinicians attempting to use this treatment method for the first time have significant training and supervision by clinicians experienced in the use of these techniques.

References

Achenbach, T. M. (1991). *Child Behavior Checklist–Cross-Informant Version.* (Available from Thomas Achenbach, PhD, Child and Adolescent Psychiatry, Department of Psychiatry, University of Vermont, 5 South Prospect Street, Burlington, VT, 05401).

Bank, L., Marlowe, J. H., Reid, J. B., Patterson, G. R., & Weinrott, M. R. (1991). A comparative evaluation of PT for families of chronic delinquents. *Journal of Abnormal Child Psychology, 19,* 15–33.

Barkley, R. A. (1987). *Defiant children: A clinician's manual for parent training.* New York: Guilford Press.

Barkley, R. A., Edwards, G. H., & Robin, A. L. (1999). *Defiant teens: A clinician's manual for assessment and family intervention.* New York: Guilford Press.

Becker, W. C. (1971). *Parents are teachers: A child management program.* Champaign, IL: Research Press.

Bry, B. H. (1982). Reducing the incidence of adolescent problems through prevention/intervention: One and five year follow-up. *American Journal of Community Psychology, 10,* 265–276.

Chamberlain, P., & Mihalic, S. F. (1998). *Multidimensional treatment foster care.* In D. S. Elliott (Series Ed.), *Book eight: Blueprints for violence prevention.* Boulder, CO: Institute of Behavioral Science, University of Colorado.

Chamberlain, P., & Moore, K. J. (1998). A clinical model for parenting juvenile offenders: A comparison of group care versus family care. *Clinical Psychology and Psychiatry, 3,* 375–386.

Chamberlain, P., & Reid, J. B. (1998). Comparison of two community alternatives to incarceration for chronic juvenile offenders. *Journal of Consulting and Clinical Psychology, 66,* 624–633.

Christopherson, E. R. (1990). *Beyond discipline: Parenting that lasts a lifetime.* Kansas City: Westport Publishers.

Dishion, T. J., Spracklen, K. M., Andrews, D. W., & Patterson, G. R. (1996). Deviancy training in male adolescent friendships. *Behavior Therapy, 27,* 373–390.

Forehand, R., & McMahon, R. J. (1981). *Helping the noncompliant child: A clinician's guide to parent training.* New York: Guilford Press.

Forgatch, M. S., Patterson, G. R., & Ray, J. A. (1996). Divorce and boys' adjustment problems: Two paths with a single model. In E. M. Hetherington & E. A. Blechman (Eds.), *Stress, coping, and resiliency in children and families* (pp. 67–105). Mahwah, NJ: Erlbaum.

Goodnough, F. L. (1931). *Anger in young children*. Minneapolis: University of Minnesota Press.

Henggeler, S. W., Melton, G. B., Brondino, M. J., Scherer, D. G., & Hanley, J. H. (1997). Multisystemic therapy with violent and chronic juvenile offenders and their families: The roles of treatment fidelity in successful dissemination. *Journal of Consulting and Clinical Psychology, 65*, 821–833.

Kazdin, A. E. (1997). Parent management training: Evidence, outcomes, and issues. *Journal of American Academy of Child and Adolescent Psychiatry, 36*, 1349–1356.

Kazdin, A. E., & Weisz, J. R. (1998). Identifying and developing empirically supported child and adolescent treatments. *Journal of Consulting and Clinical Psychology, 66*, 19–36.

Patterson, G. R. (1975a). *Families: Applications of social learning to family life*. Champaign, IL: Research Press.

Patterson, G. R. (1975b). Multiple evaluations of a parent training program. In T. Thompson (Ed.), *Applications of behavior modification: Proceedings of the first international symposium on behavior modification* (pp. 299–322). New York: Academic Press.

Patterson, G. R. (1982). *A social learning approach: Vol. 3. Coercive family process*. Eugene, OR: Castalia.

Patterson, G. R. (1996). Some characteristics of a developmental theory for early onset delinquency. In M. F. Lenzenweger & J. J. Haugaard (Eds.), *Frontiers of developmental psychopathology* (pp. 81–124). New York: Oxford University Press.

Patterson, G. R., & Chamberlain, P. (1988). Treatment process: A problem at three levels. In L. C. Wynne (Ed.), *State of the art in family therapy research: Controversies and recommendations* (pp. 189–223). New York: Family Process Press.

Patterson, G. R., Chamberlain, P., & Reid, J. B. (1982). A comparative evaluation of parent training procedures. *Behavior Therapy, 13*, 638–651.

Patterson, G. R., Dishion, T. J., & Yoerger, K. (2000). Adolescent growth in new forms of problem behavior: Macro- and micro-peer dynamics. *Prevention Science, 1*, 3–13.

Patterson, G. R., & Fleischman, M. J. (1979). Maintenance of treatment effects: Some considerations concerning family systems and follow-up data. *Behavior Therapy, 10*, 168–185.

Patterson, G. R., & Forgatch, M. S. (1987). *Parents and adolescents living together, part 1: The basics*. Eugene, OR: Castalia.

Patterson, G. R., Littman, R. A., & Bricker, W. (1967). Assertive behavior in children: A step towards a theory of aggression. *Monographs of the Society for Research in Child Development, 32*(5), 1–43.

Patterson, G. R., Reid, J. B., & Dishion, T. J. (1992). *A social interactional approach: Vol. 4. Antisocial boys*. Eugene, OR: Castalia.

Patterson, G. R., Reid, J. B., Jones, R. R., & Conger, R. E. (1975). *A social learning approach: I. Families with aggressive children*. Eugene, OR: Castalia.

Peed, S., Roberts, M., & Forehand, R. (1977). Evaluation of the effectiveness of a standardized parent training program in altering the interaction of mothers and their non-compliant children. *Behavior Modification, 1*, 323–350.

Reynolds, C., & Kamphaus, R. (1994). *Behavioral Assessment System for Children*. (Available from American Guidance Service, 4201 Woodland Road, Circle Pines, MN, 55014).

Serketich, W. J., & Dumas, J. E. (1996). The effectiveness of behavioral parent training to modify antisocial behavior in children: A meta-analysis. *Behavior Therapy, 27*, 171–186.

Shaw, D. S., Keenan, K., & Vondra, J. I. (1994). Developmental precursors of externalizing behavior: Ages 1 to 3. *Developmental Psychology, 30*, 355–364.

Snyder, J. J., & Patterson, G. R. (1995). Individual differences in social aggression: A test of a reinforcement model of socialization in the natural environment. *Behavior Therapy, 26*, 371–391.

Snyder, J., Schrepferman, L., & St. Peter, C. (1997). Origins of antisocial behavior: Negative reinforcement and affect dysregulation of behavior as socialization mechanisms in family interaction. *Behavior Modification, 21*, 187–215.

Southam-Gerow, M. A., & Kendall, P. C. (1997). Parent-focused and cognitive-behavioral treatments of antisocial youth. In D. Stoff, J. Breiling, & J. D. Maser (Eds.), *Handbook of antisocial behavior* (pp. 384–394). New York: John Wiley & Sons.

Walter, H., & Gilmore, S. K. (1973). Placebo versus social learning effects in parent training procedures designed to alter the behaviors of aggressive boys. *Behavior Therapy, 4*, 361–371.

Webster-Stratton, C. (1984). Randomized trial of two parent training programs for families with conduct-disordered children. *Journal of Consulting and Clinical Psychology, 52*, 666–678.

Webster-Stratton, C. (1990). Long-term follow-up of families with young conduct problem children:

From preschool to grade school. *Journal of Clinical Child Psychology, 19,* 144–149.

Webster-Stratton, C. (2000). *The incredible years training series.* Washington, DC: U.S. Department of Justice, Office of Justice Programs, Office of Juvenile Justice and Delinquency Prevention. (GPO no. 0718-A-09, Document # J 32.10:IN 2).

Webster-Stratton, C., & Hammond, M. (1997). Treating children with early-onset conduct problems: A comparison of child and parent training interventions. *Journal of Consulting and Clinical Psychology, 65,* 93–109.

Wiltz, N. A., Jr., & Patterson, G. R. (1974). An evaluation of parent training procedures designed to alter inappropriate aggressive behavior of boys. *Behavior Therapy, 5,* 215–221.

43 ENHANCING PERCEIVED SELF-EFFICACY: GUIDED MASTERY THERAPY

Walter D. Scott and Daniel Cervone

Research on perceived self-efficacy dates to the 1970s, its origin being the landmark paper of Bandura (1977). Bandura had observed that participant modeling treatments for phobics seemed to engender psychological change that was widespread. Therapy altered not only clients' autonomic arousal to threats, but their sense of self. Bandura reasoned that these self-perceptions might not be epiphenomenal, but causal. The basic tenet of self-efficacy theory (Bandura, 1977) was that people's appraisals of their own capabilities to execute actions to cope with challenging environments are proximal determinants of affective arousal, cognitive processing, and motivation. This idea proved enormously generative, with extensive lines of research in the subsequent years verifying that self-efficacy perceptions causally contribute to human development, adjustment, and achievement (Bandura, 1997; Cervone & Scott, 1995; Stajkovic & Luthans, 1998).

Self-efficacy theory should be understood as one component of the broader social-cognitive theory of personality functioning (Bandura, 1986; also see Cervone & Shoda, 1999). In social-cognitive analyses, personality and individual differences are analyzed in terms of cognitive and affective mechanisms through which people interpret events, develop skills, reflect on themselves, and plan courses of action. Self-efficacy processes, then, constitute only one in a spectrum of social-cognitive determinants of experience and behavior. Efficacy beliefs, however, take on particular significance because they both influence behavior directly and influence other psychological variables of significance. For example, the goals people adopt of tasks are based partly on their subjective appraisals of their efficacy for performance. Efficacy beliefs affect skill development in that people who doubt their capabilities may fail to undertake activities that inherently build skills. Research on perceived self-efficacy converges with other lines of work involving control beliefs (e.g., Skinner, 1995) in showing that subjective perceptions of personal control and efficacy contribute to personal development.

The established links between self-efficacy perceptions and emotion and action suggest, of course, that perceived self-efficacy is a valuable target for therapeutic change. People who come to believe that they can master challenges may experience less anticipatory anxiety and engage in activities in a more vigorous, persistent, and ultimately successful manner. The challenge, then, is to identify types of psychosocial interventions that might boost self-efficacy perceptions.

Self-efficacy theory (Bandura, 1977, 1997) is

particularly valuable in this regard, in that it analyzes not only the consequences of high versus low self-efficacy beliefs but their causes. Bandura (1977) has provided a taxonomy of the types of experiences that can alter efficacy beliefs. These include people's subjective interpretations of their own emotional and physiological states; exposure to verbal persuasion; observation of others' success and failure (i.e., modeling); and first-hand, enactive performance experiences. The last of these is generally found to be the most reliable.

In guided mastery therapy, the primary goal of the therapist is to foster a subjective sense of mastery or self-efficacy. This approach has been applied mainly to the treatment of simple phobias and Agoraphobia (Williams, 1992). For these conditions, guided mastery therapy has been found to boost self-referent beliefs and eradicate avoidant behavior more rapidly and more powerfully than do other performance-based treatments such as exposure therapies and systematic desensitization (Williams, 1990, 1995; Williams & Cervone, 1998). Research on simple phobias (Bandura, Adams, & Beyer, 1977) and Agoraphobia (Williams, Dooseman, & Kleifield, 1984) reveals that guided mastery interventions enable clients to perform the vast majority of behavioral acts that they had originally been incapable of performing.

WHO MIGHT BENEFIT FROM THIS TECHNIQUE

So far, guided mastery treatment has been developed and evaluated for a diversity of phobias, including Agoraphobia, Social Phobia, and simple phobias. For each of these conditions, there is strong support for the effectiveness of guided mastery therapy (see Bandura, 1997; Williams, 1992). Although guided mastery therapy has not yet been applied or evaluated outside anxiety problems, the role of self-efficacy beliefs in mood disorders, substance abuse, health habits, stress reduction, and athletic performance has been clearly documented (Bandura). Therefore, we would expect that mastery-based interventions targeting self-efficacy beliefs in these domains would be effective as well.

CONTRAINDICATIONS OF THE TREATMENT

The effectiveness of guided mastery therapy depends on the client's ability to attribute personal mastery as the reason for behavioral success. To the extent that other factors interfere with this cognitive process, which is critical, the success of guided mastery interventions is likely to be limited. For instance, guided mastery interventions may be inappropriate for a client who has elected psychotropic medication as a long-term component of his or her treatment regimen. Ingesting psychotropic medications provides a compelling and competing attribution for performance success. Other, more obvious contraindications include psychosis, which impairs the ability both to execute performances to one's full potential and to make meaningful mastery attributions. Finally, it is important to note that we currently know very little about the way that frequently occurring comorbid conditions impact the effectiveness of guided mastery approaches to phobias. For instance, phobic disorders often co-occur with mood disorders. In such cases, although perhaps not contraindicated, special care is likely to be required in the delivery of guided mastery therapy (e.g., increasing motivation to attempt activity exercises, and carefully attending to and challenging dysfunctional attributional processes, to name a few).

HOW DOES THE TECHNIQUE WORK?

Guided mastery therapy works by enhancing people's self-efficacy. Research using diverse methodologies, including structured questionnaires and thought-sampling techniques, suggest that thoughts about personal efficacy are the key mediator of behavior and behavioral change in successful Agoraphobia and Simple Phobia treatment interventions (Bandura, 1997; Williams, Kinney, Harap, & Liebmann, 1997; but cf. Hoffart, 1995, 1998). Even when alternative cognitive mediators, such as anticipatory anxiety, outcome expectations, and perceived danger, are statistically controlled, self-efficacy perceptions continue to predict reductions in anxiety and phobic behaviors. Indeed, self-efficacy appraisals have been found to be superior even to past treatment behavior in predicting treatment outcome.

STEP-BY-STEP PROCEDURES

The key focus for guided mastery therapy is therefore to provide an enabling environment in which the client is able to achieve a high degree of self-efficacy for the relevant performance domain. Behavioral success does not automatically stamp in a sense of confidence. Nor does the sheer amount of time that one is exposed to the feared stimuli. Rather, the successful reduction of fear and avoidance requires that the exposure exercises lead to a sense of confidence that one can competently cope with the feared object. Therefore, the therapist must ensure that people not only expose themselves to feared stimuli, nor that they experience only objective success, but that they subjectively attribute their exposure and success to their own efforts and skills. Although exposure and guided mastery approaches share some features, this key distinction of guided mastery therapy regarding the importance of quickly instilling mastery perceptions leads to a number of therapeutic innovations.

In the guided mastery approach, therapists take a more active helping role so that they are able to rapidly promote performance success and attributions of mastery. In addition to providing support and encouragement, a number of strategies are utilized to facilitate mastery. Many of these interventions are conducted outside the therapy office, in field settings. Early on in treatment, the therapist utilizes a variety of modeling interventions to demonstrate the feared activity for the client (see Chapter 36, this volume). Various modeling strategies are employed, including enactive modeling, symbolic modeling, and joint participation of the therapist with the client in the activity. These modeling strategies are pursued with the goal of enabling the client to perform at a high level as quickly as possible. Then the activity is broken down into graded, manageable subtasks that the client can perform alone with a good probability of success. Tasks can be made easier in a number of ways to insure mastery. Exposure time can be reduced. Protective performance aids may be utilized. And modeling can be

TABLE 43.1   Guided Mastery Therapy Steps and Related Procedures

Step	Procedures
Modeling	Enactive modeling Symbolic modeling Joint participant modeling
Graded task performance	Graded time exposure Protective mastery aids
Identification and removal of safety rituals and aids	
Self-directed mastery experiments	

used at difficult points. However, when the client feels a high degree of efficacy, all of these aids are withdrawn. In addition, any safety rituals or aids that the client uses to cope with the performance are identified. The therapist then has the client execute the performance without relying on coping strategies so that a robust and generalized sense of self-efficacy is obtained. The final stage involves identifying self-directed mastery experiments that the client pursues outside of therapy. We will now review these guided mastery interventions in more detail (see also Table 43.1).

Modeling

Modeling is used extensively in guided mastery therapy. In *enactive modeling,* the therapist behaviorally demonstrates the relevant performance. In *symbolic modeling,* the therapist offers verbal guidance or displays the relevant performance using video or film. Early in treatment, both enactive and symbolic modeling procedures are used to provide some guidance to clients in performing the specific feared task. They are also used throughout treatment to fine-tune performances and to assist clients with more challenging aspects of performance. In both forms of modeling, the therapist should strive to enact or describe very specific activities, usually the most problematic aspects of the performance.

Participant modeling is another modeling technique employed by guided mastery therapists. This involves the therapist's performing the feared activity with the client. Joint performance of an activity with a therapist has several advantages. First, the therapist can provide a reassuring presence. Studies have shown that this type of presence itself can reduce anxiety reactions. In addition, participant modeling is extremely useful for correcting problematic aspects of a client's performance. When a person is in the midst of performing a feared activity, he or she is usually quite attentive to such corrective modeling interventions.

Often in these participant modeling situations, the therapist employs a combination of both enactive and symbolic modeling strategies. For instance, the following enactive and symbolic modeling instructions might be offered to a height phobic as he or she attempts to lean over a rail looking down several stories:

> *Therapist:* Try to touch the railing here with your left hand. Good, you can touch it with your fingertips, so now see if you can touch it with the palm of the hand, like this [therapist models performance with client]. That's fine, now try to see if you can touch it with the palm of the hand, like this [again therapist models performance with client]. Very good, now can you also grab the railing with your right hand? That's a little difficult just now, so instead just touch it with your fingers. Good, now try to grasp it. Don't hold your breath; you can do this and breathe at the same time. Ok, can you grab it with both hands? Great, now you have to get your legs and body closer to the rail. Try to move your left foot a little closer and straighten your legs if you can. Square your shoulders with the railing. All right, you're doing very well. (Williams, 1990, pp. 101–102)

Graded Task Performance

Robust beliefs in personal efficacy are most thoroughly instilled through first-hand mastery experiences (Bandura, 1997). The personal experience of mastery is difficult to deny, even among individuals who typically doubt their performance capabilities. Consequently, after modeling, guided mastery therapists utilize graded task assignments. These procedures are quite similar to the graded task performance techniques described elsewhere (e.g., Beck, Rush, Shaw, & Emery, 1979) with some distinctive components. The basic idea is to get clients attempting those performances they fear. However, to the

client, the entire performance is feared and appears overwhelming. Therefore, the therapist breaks the performance down into subtasks that the client perceives as more manageable.

In the guided mastery approach, the therapist should strive to identify subtasks that the client believes can be accomplished with extra effort and persistence. Using a self-efficacy scale with the standard anchors of 0–100, this translates into performance subtasks that the client generally rates in the range of 20–50. To increase client's efficacy levels, participant modeling can be used extensively. After accomplishing a subtask, clients typically experience a significant increase in self-efficacy, which leads to greater persistence and effort on subsequent subtasks. Graded task assignment continues until the entire performance sequence is mastered.

Special attention is given to those situations in which clients fail to adequately perform a given subtask. In these cases, the therapist guides clients so that they attribute the failed performance to the size of the task demand. Then an easier subtask is selected. To boost client's efficacy sufficiently so that they attempt the easier performance with good effort and persistence, the therapist can employ more extensive enactive, symbolic, and participant modeling techniques. Finally, on some occasions, the client's major difficulty with a performance may lie with a specific skill required as part of the entire performance. In such cases, the therapist can have the client focus on and master that particular skill prior to proceeding to the overall performance.

In defining subtasks, the therapist utilizes a number of strategies for manipulating the difficulty of the performance so that is within the client's perceived ability level. One strategy involves graduating the amount of time that participants engage in the performance. For instance, an initial subtask might have a height phobic hold the rail and look over a balcony for a period of 5 s. Once this subtask is mastered, the duration can be increased first to 10 s, next to 30 s, then to 1 min, and so on.

Another strategy involves providing a number of protective mastery aids to enable the client to achieve performance mastery. Often these are direct physical aids provided by the therapist. For instance, a therapist might hold the client's arm as they walk over a feared bridge. A dog might be restrained with a leash as a dog phobic makes initial approaches. Of course, each of these protective aids is gradually withdrawn once these performances are mastered so that a robust, flexible, and more generalized sense of mastery is developed. However, these protective aids are useful initially for enabling the client to quickly attain a high level of performance and mastery. The more severe the phobia, the more these protective aids are utilized.

Identify and Remove Safety Rituals and Aids

Clients often use a number of safety rituals to cope with feared activities. For instance, clients may tense themselves to cope with approaching a high balcony. They may drive only in the slow lane to deal with their fear of driving in traffic. They may negotiate a grocery store by following a specific and circumscribed path. Although such coping strategies may help the client to cope with these fears, they limit the development of a sense of mastery that is both robust and resilient. The problem is that without these aids, clients doubt their abilities. And these self-doubts limit their ability to perform.

In guided mastery therapy, explicit attention is given to the presence of such coping aids. Clients are asked to tell the therapist about any special techniques, behaviors, or rituals that they use to help themselves cope with the feared performance. Then the therapist encourages the client to perform the task without relying on these safety rituals and aids. The goal is to promote a robust sense of efficacy that will last and that will generalize outside the treatment setting. Unless such safety rituals and aids are identified, and the client is given full opportunities to perform the activity without relying on them, it is likely that any therapeutic gains will be highly specific and highly transient.

Self-Directed Mastery Experiments

The final phase of guided mastery therapy has the client functioning essentially as his or her own guided mastery therapist. The client is taught the principles of guided mastery therapy and works collaboratively with the therapist to identify homework assignments (see Chapter 32, this volume). These homework assignments are designed with the goal of increasing both the proficiency and the flexibility of the previously feared performance. *Proficiency* means that assignments are executed outside therapy and the client performs without relying on aids or special rituals. *Flexibility* means that activities are chosen that require the client to perform the task in a variety of different ways. Although the therapist helps to specify these assignments initially, the client executes them outside the therapy context, either with a significant other or alone. The goal is for the client to continue applying these guided mastery therapy principles independently after formal therapy has concluded.

References

Bandura, A. (1977). Self-efficacy: Toward a unifying theory of behavioral change. *Psychological Review, 84,* 191–215.

Bandura, A. (1986). *Social foundations of thought and action.* Englewood Cliffs, NJ: Prentice Hall.

Bandura, A. (1997). *Self-efficacy: The exercise of control.* New York: Freeman.

Bandura, A., Adams, N. E., & Beyer, J. (1977). Cognitive processes mediating behavior change. *Journal of Personality and Social Psychology, 35,* 125–139.

Beck, A. T., Rush, A. J., Shaw, B. F., & Emery, G. (1979). *Cognitive therapy of depression.* New York: Guilford Press.

Cervone, D., & Scott, W. D. (1995). Self-efficacy theory of behavioral change. In W. O'Donohue & L. Krasner (Eds.), *Theories of behavior therapy* (pp. 349–383). Washington, DC: American Psychological Association.

Cervone, D., & Shoda, Y. (1999). Social-cognitive theories and the coherence of personality. In D. Cervone & Y. Shoda (Eds.), *The coherence of personality: Social-cognitive bases of consistency, variability, and organization* (pp. 3–33). New York: Guilford Press.

Hoffart, A. (1995). A comparison of cognitive and guided mastery therapy of Agoraphobia. *Behaviour Research and Therapy, 33,* 423–434.

Hoffart, A. (1998). Cognitive and guided mastery therapy of Agoraphobia: Long-term outcome and mechanisms of change. *Cognitive Therapy and Research, 22,* 195–207.

Skinner, E. A. (1995). *Perceived control, motivation, and coping.* Thousand Oaks, CA: Sage.

Stajkovic, A. D., & Luthans, F. (1998). Social cognitive

theory and self-efficacy: Going beyond traditional motivational and behavioral approaches. *Organizational Dynamics, 26,* 62–74.

Williams, S. L. (1990). Guided mastery treatment of Agoraphobia: Beyond stimulus exposure. In M. Hersen, R. M. Eisler, & P. M. Miller (Eds.), *Progress in behavior modification* (Vol. 26, pp. 89–121). Newbury Park, CA: Sage.

Williams, S. L. (1992). Perceived self-efficacy and phobic disability. In R. Schwarzer (Ed.), *Self-efficacy: Thought control of action.* Washington, DC: Hemisphere Publishing.

Williams, S. L. (1995). Self-efficacy, anxiety, and phobic disorders. In J. E. Maddux (Ed.), *Self-efficacy, adaptation, and adjustment: Theory, research, and application* (pp. 69–107). New York: Plenum Press.

Williams, S. L., & Cervone, D. (1998). Social cognitive theory. In D. Barone, M. Hersen, & V. B. Van Hasselt (Eds.), *Advanced personality* (pp. 173–207). New York: Plenum Press.

Williams, S. L., Dooseman, G., & Kleifield, E. (1984). Comparative effectiveness of guided mastery and exposure treatments for intractable phobias. *Journal of Consulting and Clinical Psychology, 52,* 505–518.

Williams, S. L., Kinney, P. J., Harap, S. T., & Liebmann, M. (1997). Thoughts of agoraphobic people during scary tasks. *Journal of Abnormal Psychology, 106,* 511–520.

44 POSITIVE ATTENTION

Stephen K. Bell, Stephen R. Boggs, and Sheila M. Eyberg

Positive attention (PA) is a technique used frequently in parent training in which parents are taught to respond to desirable child behaviors with positive social feedback. From a behavior analytic perspective, determining whether attention is positive for a particular child and equating it with positive reinforcement would require a functional assessment of its effect on the frequency or duration of the behavior preceding the positive attention. For the purposes of this chapter, however, we define *positive attention* as a general class of positive verbal and nonverbal adult responses intended as social reinforcers for desirable child behavior. Praise is an example of verbal PA and is perhaps the most common form of PA discussed in parent training. Hugging a child is an example of nonverbal PA.

Early research on PA, conducted largely in school settings, supported its utility in increasing cooperative play (Hart, Reynolds, Baer, Brawley, & Harris, 1968), study behavior (Hall, Lund, & Jackson, 1968), attention to task (Kazdin, 1973; Kazdin & Klock, 1973), compliance (Goetz, Holmberg, & LeBlanc, 1975), and cleanliness behavior (Miller, Brickman, & Bolen, 1975). Most of the research supporting the effectiveness of parental PA is found in the behavior modification literature and has involved children with devel-

opmental disabilities (e.g., Herbert & Baer, 1972) and behavior problems (e.g., Knight & McKenzie, 1974; McDonald, 1977).

In parent training programs, PA is typically used in conjunction with active ignoring of negative child behaviors. *Active ignoring* requires the parent to withdraw all social feedback from the child when negative behavior is occurring. By responding with PA to a child's positive behaviors and ignoring the child's negative behaviors, a parent creates a situation of *differential social attention*, which provides clear guidance for the child and allows the child to learn how to obtain the parents' attention in ways that will result in increasingly positive interactions for both the child and the parent. When positive attention is directed to child behaviors that are incompatible with targeted problem behaviors, the problem behaviors may decrease in frequency as they are replaced with the more rewarding positive behaviors.

ADVANTAGES OF THE TECHNIQUE

An important advantage of using PA in parent training is that parents almost uniformly consider this technique the most acceptable method of behavior management (Jones, Eyberg, Adams, & Boggs, 1998; Kazdin, French, & Sherick, 1981). A second advantage of PA is its easy accessibility for use as a social reinforcer in the natural environment. It is a convenient management technique that parents may use in most situations when they are with the child. A third advantage of PA is that behaviors sustained by social reinforcers are more likely to generalize from the family to other contexts, such as the school, where similar behavioral consequences are likely to occur. Forehand (1987) suggested that PA may function in an interactive manner with other behavior management techniques such that its influence on child behavior is optimized, a notion that has received some empirical support (Budd, Green, & Baer, 1976; Wahler, 1969).

LIMITATIONS OF THE TECHNIQUE

Some studies have questioned the effectiveness of differential social attention for reducing noncompliant behavior (Herbert et al., 1973; Roberts, 1985; Roberts, Hatzenbuehler, & Bean, 1981). For example, Herbert et al. found that differential parental attention led to an increase in negative child behavior for four of six children. The adverse effect was maintained over many sessions and was replicated in a reversal design. More recently, in a series of studies investigating maternal praise, Roberts (1985) concluded that praise alone might not serve a reinforcement function for compliance in clinic-referred children. Forehand (1987) reviewed results from both intervention and nonintervention studies and reached the similar conclusion that using rewards is not a sufficient intervention to produce behavior change reliably in noncompliant children.

It is highly unlikely that PA alone, or even in combination with active ignoring, is sufficient to treat young children with disruptive behavior disorders. The utility of PA is in its potential for *increasing* behaviors. Families of children with clinically significant disruptive behavior come to parent training with a constellation of problem behaviors that need to be *decreased*. To decrease negative child behavior, PA works by increasing incompatible behaviors that serve a similar func-

tion for the child and can therefore replace the negative behaviors. Thus, to treat the broad class of disruptive behavior, PA is used to increase a broad class of acceptable behavior. Positive attention will be effective only to the extent that it can provide more reinforcement (attention) than the child receives for disruptive behavior.

WHO MIGHT BENEFIT FROM PA?

Positive attention is a technique that may be useful in any situation where the goal is to increase the frequency of a behavior that is responsive to social consequences. Positive attention has long been used effectively in treatments for children with developmental delays, both to increase skills of daily living and as one component of treatments to address behavior problems (Herbert & Baer, 1972). The technique is also an established component of most empirically supported treatments for children with disruptive behavior disorders (Brestan & Eyberg, 1998; Pelham, Wheeler, & Chronis, 1998). The effectiveness of PA has been demonstrated in parent training programs addressing the behavior problems of children in physically abusive families (Balachova, Funderburk, Chaffin, & Silovsky, 2001; Lutzker & Rice, 1984), and recent studies incorporating parents into the treatment of children with anxiety disorders have provided encouraging results (Pincus, Choate, Eyberg, & Barlow, in press; Silverman, 2001).

HOW DOES PA WORK?

Positive attention with active ignoring works through the mechanism of differential social reinforcement. A number of contextual variables may influence the effectiveness of PA in parent-child interactions, however, such as the nature of the PA itself. The form of the PA will influence its effectiveness because the various forms of attentional stimuli are not functionally equivalent for an individual child. For example, Piazza et al. (1999) described a case in which positive touch (i.e., tickling), but not praise, served as a reinforcer for changing the behavior of a child with developmental delays and Oppositional Defiant Disorder. With a kindergarten sample, Kamins and Dweck (1999) found that children who received *process* praise (e.g., "You must have tried really hard") showed more persistence than children who received *person* praise (e.g., "You are a good girl") for working on a puzzle.

PA IN PARENT-CHILD INTERACTION THERAPY

In this section, we illustrate the application of PA in parent-child interaction therapy (PCIT; Bell & Eyberg, 2002; Eyberg & Boggs, 1998), a behavior therapy program for young children with disruptive behavior and their parents. In PCIT, the therapist teaches the parent to use PA with active ignoring during the first phase of treatment, called the *child-directed interaction (CDI)* phase. During the CDI, parents use differential social attention to shape their child's behavior and to establish a strong parent-child bond that will serve as a foundation for the disciplinary strategies that are introduced in the second phase of treatment. During the second phase, called the *parent-directed interaction (PDI)* phase, parents learn to give effective commands for desirable child behaviors and to provide consistent consequences in the form of labeled praise for compliance and time-out from positive reinforcement/PA for noncompliance. In each phase of treatment, CDI and PDI, parents attend one teaching session in which the therapist demonstrates the skills of the interaction and provides the rationales for their use. Following the teaching session, the parents and child attend coaching sessions together. During coaching sessions, the therapist observes from an observation room and actively coaches the parent in the use of the skills via a bug-in-the-ear device while the parent interacts with the child in the playroom.

FUNCTIONAL ANALYSIS IN PCIT

Because there are many forms of PA and varying targeted disruptive behaviors in PCIT, an ongoing functional analysis is key to the success of PA in this treatment program. A *functional analysis* is a detailed assessment of the antecedents and consequences of a behavior that may be used to determine what shapes and maintains it. Although the clinical setting allows for much less control of the specific antecedent and consequent events surrounding disruptive behaviors than would a laboratory, the reinforcing function of certain forms of PA (e.g., parental praise) for most children has been established empirically and clinically over many years. These forms of PA are therefore structured into treatment, and the functional analysis involves ongoing therapist and parent observations that fine-tune and informally assess the effectiveness of the individual applications of PA that are used in treatment.

STEP-BY-STEP PROCEDURES

When introducing differential social attention in the CDI teaching session, the therapist helps the parent to understand the behavioral principles underlying PA and active ignoring and how these techniques work in tandem to change the frequency of broad classes of positive and negative child behavior. The therapist emphasizes the power of the parent's attention—both positive and negative—to increase child behaviors. The therapist also stresses the importance of increasing the *positive opposites* of the negative child behaviors so that the child learns new behaviors to replace the old (disruptive) ones that were used to obtain parental attention. The therapist teaches the parents the *PRIDE* skills, which represent the major forms of PA that parents will use in CDI play sessions to increase the child's prosocial behavior and create or strengthen a positive parent-child attachment. The skills include *P*raising the child's positive behaviors, *R*eflecting the child's appropriate talk, *I*mitating the child's acceptable play behaviors, *D*escribing the child's positive actions, and showing *E*nthusiasm in interactions with the child.

In the CDI teaching session, each skill is taught by defining it and giving examples that apply to the specific family (e.g., attending to positive opposites of the problem behaviors of greatest concern to the parent). The therapist then models the skill for the parents with the child (if present) or an adult (co-therapist or parent) playing the child's role. Finally, the therapist engages the parent in a role-play in which the parent uses the skill with the therapist playing the child and presenting increasingly challenging situations for the parent. At the end of the teaching session, the therapist gives the parent a handout that lists the skills and provides examples. The parent is asked to practice the CDI each day in 5-min *special time* sessions with the child at home. In the following sections, we highlight some of the strategies that therapists use in teaching the specific PRIDE skills to the parents.

Praise

Praise is described as giving a compliment to the child that labels for the child exactly what he or she did that was positive, so the child can learn to repeat the behavior to receive praise again (e.g., "You're doing a nice job of keeping your hands to yourself"). By praising specific behaviors, parents increase the frequency of those behaviors. Praise also leads to increased self-esteem and may add warmth to the interaction. A useful exercise to help some parents learn to use praise strategically is to provide them a list of praise stems (e.g., "You're doing a nice job of _____"; "I like the way you are _____"; "Thank you so much for _____") and ask them to practice finishing the sentences with positive opposites that would be helpful for the child. During coaching sessions, the therapist can point out each time the child repeats behaviors that the parents have earlier praised, which may increase parent self-efficacy and lead to further praise by the parent.

Reflection

Reflection is described as repeating or paraphrasing what the child says. A reflection rewards the child for talking to the parent nicely and demonstrates that the parent is really listening to what the child says. In addition, reflecting the child's words may improve the child's speech and language by rephrasing sentences in a clearer way than the child expressed them. For example, if the child said, "You don't got that red thing on," the parent might say, "I don't have the chimney on top

yet." For parents, the most difficult part of learning to reflect is learning not to ask questions, such as, "The red one?" in response to their child's verbalizations. Rather than serving as a form of PA, questions have a high potential for being perceived by a child as critical. During coaching sessions, parents are encouraged to reflect everything that the child says (unless it is inappropriate). The resulting increase in parent-child conversation is an important method of improving the child's social skills.

Imitation

Imitation involves watching the child's activity and engaging in similar behaviors, with similar toys, next to the child. As therapy progresses, an oppositional child will gradually allow the parent to play with the same toy (e.g., build on the same house or draw a picture together). The therapist describes to the parent how imitating the child's behavior not only conveys approval of the child's activities and leads the child to seek increased positive interaction with the parent but may also lead to an increase in the child's imitation of the parent (Roberts, 1981). Many parents of disruptive children do not know how to play with their children. For these parents, understanding that they can learn simply by watching the child play and doing the same thing (when the child is behaving appropriately) is helpful. Through imitation, parents can teach their children turn-taking and other important social skills that are often lacking in children with disruptive behavior disorders. During coaching, therapists can help parents avoid shifting their attention away from the child's activity to their own and can gradually shape interactive play as the child becomes less angry and begins to trust the parent.

Behavioral Description

A *behavioral description* is a statement that describes for the child what he or she is doing (e.g., "Now you're drawing the other tree just the same size"). The therapist explains that behavioral descriptions convey approval of the child's activities. During coaching, therapists help parents learn to select the particular aspect of the child's behavior that they most value to describe, because what they describe will occur more often. Thus, a parent would be encouraged to describe *persistence* in a task for child who has a low frustration tolerance. (e.g., "You're sticking right with that until you get it," rather than simply, "You're looking again for where that piece fits"). As long as the child's play is acceptable, the parent must resist any temptation to suggest that it could be better. For example, even though a parent might wish that the child were building a straighter tower, the parent should ignore that aspect of the play and instead focus on something positive (e.g., "You are choosing pretty red blocks for your tower"). If the parent were to express disapproval of any child behavior, even subtly in tone of voice, the therapist would quickly remind the parent to ignore that behavior. If the behavior in question were not inappropriate, the therapist would also reframe the parent's perception while coaching ("Tim's tower is a little wobbly, but not bad for a 3-year-old! Describe the colors he chose for his tower").

Enthusiasm

Enthusiasm is a quality that parents must add to any form of PA they give in response to their child's positive behavior. Positive words delivered with a bland or apathetic emotional tone are unlikely to function as social reinforcers, especially with young children. Parents who are socially reserved sometimes suggest that expressing enthusiasm during the play does not feel genuine. Therapists will acknowledge these feelings and note that enthusiasm becomes more natural as the parents grow more comfortable with the other skills. Therapists will also vigilantly point out the child's positive response to parental enthusiasm during their play and will comment on how natural it sounds when that is the case. A substantial minority of parents of children with disruptive behavior disorders have clinically significant depression. For these parents, in particular, the therapist must model enthusiasm with the child and provide frequent feedback during coaching about the child's emotional and behavioral responses when the parent expresses genuinely enthusiastic PA.

ACTIVE IGNORING

In conjunction with PA for desirable behavior, active ignoring is used to reduce undesirable attention-seeking behaviors such as yelling, sassing, whining, and playing roughly with toys. The therapist re-emphasizes that any attention, positive or negative, can increase the behavior it follows. The first time the parent must use ignoring, the therapist coaches the parent to explain to the child that he or she will not pay attention to the child during their special time unless the child is playing nicely. After that, during active ignoring the parent avoids any verbal or nonverbal attention (e.g., laughing, frowning, reprimanding) in response to negative child behavior. As soon as the child stops the negative behavior, the parent returns to using PA. This contrast highlights for the child the differences between parental responses to positive versus negative behavior.

ACHIEVING PARENTAL COMPETENCE IN USING PA

One of the keys to achieving parental competence in PA is behavioral coding of the parent-child interaction during the first 5 min of each session. These data are used to determine the PA skills that will be the focus of coaching during the session, and they are charted each week to review the progress with the parents and enable them to determine what should be the focus of their CDI sessions at home during the week. The second key to achieving parental competence in PA is the active, directive coaching of the parent in session with the child. The coaching allows for immediate feedback to parents on their skills and enables the therapist to observe the effects of various forms of PA on different problem areas. It also enables the therapist to intervene in problem areas on the spot. A final key to success is structuring treatment as performance-based rather than time-limited. In PCIT, families do not move to the second phase of treatment until the CDI skills are mastered, and they continue in treatment until the parents have mastered both the CDI and PDI skills and the child's behavior is within normal limits.

References

Bell, S. K., & Eyberg, S. M. (2002). Parent-child interaction therapy. In L. VandeCreek, S. Knapp, & T. L. Jackson (Eds.), *Innovations in clinical practice: A source book* (Vol. 20, pp. 57–74). Sarasota, FL: Professional Resource Press.

Balachova, T., Funderburk, B., Chaffin, M., & Silovsky, J. (2001). *Tracking changes in abusive parents' ratings of their children's behavioral problems during PCIT.* Paper presented at the Second Annual Parent-Child Interaction Therapy Conference, Sacramento, CA.

Brestan, E. V., & Eyberg, S. M. (1998). Effective psychosocial treatments of conduct-disordered children and adolescents: 29 years, 82 studies, and 5,272 kids. *Journal of Clinical Child Psychology, 27,* 180–189.

Budd, K. S., Green, D. R., & Baer, D. M. (1976). An analysis of multiple misplaced parental social contingencies. *Journal of Applied Behavior Analysis, 9,* 459–470.

Eyberg, S. M., & Boggs, S. R. (1998). Parent-child interaction therapy for oppositional preschoolers. In C. E. Schaefer & J. M. Briesmeister (Eds.), *Handbook of parent training: Parents as co-therapists for children's behavior problems* (2nd ed., pp. 61–97). New York: Wiley.

Forehand, R. (1987). Parental positive reinforcement with deviant children: Does it make a difference? *Child and Family Behavior Therapy, 8,* 19–25.

Goetz, E. M., Holmberg, M. C., & LeBlanc, J. M. (1975). Differential reinforcement of other behavior and noncontingent reinforcement as control procedures during the modification of a preschooler's compliance. *Journal of Applied Behavior Analysis, 8,* 77–82.

Hall, R. V., Lund, D., & Jackson, D. (1968). Effects of teacher attention on study behavior. *Journal of Applied Behavior Analysis, 1,* 1–12.

Hart, B. M., Reynolds, N. J., Baer, D. M., Brawley, E. R., & Harris, F. R. (1968). Effect of contingent and non-contingent social reinforcement on the cooperative play of a preschool child. *Journal of Applied Behavior Analysis, 1,* 73–76.

Herbert, E. W., & Baer, D. M. (1972). Training parents as behavior modifiers: Self-recording of contingent attention. *Journal of Applied Behavior Analysis, 7,* 33–38.

Herbert, E. W., Pinkston, E. M., Hayden, M. L, Sajwaj, T. E., Pinkston, S., Cordua, G., & Jackson, C. (1973). Adverse effects of differential parental attention. *Journal of Applied Behavior Analysis, 6,* 15–30.

Jones, M. L., Eyberg, S. M., Adams, C. D., & Boggs, S. R. (1998). Treatment acceptability of behavioral interventions for children: An assessment by mothers of children with disruptive behavior disorders. *Child and Family Behavior Therapy, 20,* 15–26.

Kamins, M. L., & Dweck, C. S. (1999). Person versus process praise and criticism: Implications for contingent self-worth and coping. *Developmental Psychology, 35,* 835–847.

Kazdin, A. E. (1973). The effects of vicarious reinforcement on attentive behavior in the classroom. *Journal of Applied Behavior Analysis, 6,* 71–78.

Kazdin, A. E., French, N. H., & Sherick, R. B. (1981). Acceptability of alternative treatments for children: Evaluations by inpatient children, parents, and staff. *Journal of Consulting and Clinical Psychology, 49,* 900–907.

Kazdin, A. E., & Klock, J. (1973). The effect of nonverbal teacher approval on student attentive behavior. *Journal of Applied Behavior Analysis, 6,* 643–654.

Knight, M. F., & McKenzie, H. S. (1974). Elimination of bedtime thumb sucking in home settings through contingent reading. *Journal of Applied Behavior Analysis, 7,* 33–38.

Lutzker, J. R., & Rice, J. M. (1984). Project 12-Ways: Measuring outcome of a large in-home service for treatment and prevention of child abuse and neglect. *Child Abuse and Neglect, 8,* 519–524.

McDonald, J. E. (1977). Parent training in positive reinforcement and extinction to effect a decrease in noncompliant child behavior. *Journal of the Association for the Study of Perception, 12,* 16–21.

Miller, R. L., Brickman, P., & Bolen, D. (1975). Attribution versus persuasion as a means for modifying behavior. *Journal of Personality and Social Psychology, 31,* 430–441.

Pelham, W. E., Jr., Wheeler, T., & Chronis, A. (1998). Empirically supported psychosocial treatments for Attention-Deficit Hyperactivity Disorder. *Journal of Clinical Child Psychology, 27,* 190–205.

Piazza, C. C., Bowman, L. G., Contrucci, S. A., Delia, M. D., Adelinis, J. D., & Goh, H. L. (1999). An evaluation of the properties of attention as reinforcement for destructive and appropriate behavior. *Journal of Applied Behavioral Analysis, 32,* 437–449.

Pincus, D. B., Choate, M. L., Eyberg, S. M., & Barlow, D. H. (in press). Treatment of young children with Separation Anxiety Disorder using parent-child interaction therapy. *Cognitive and Behavioral Practice.*

Roberts, M. C. (1981). Toward a reconceptualization of

the reciprocal imitation phenomenon: Two experiments. *Journal of Research in Personality, 15,* 447–459.

Roberts, M. W. (1985). Praising child compliance: Reinforcement or ritual? *Journal of Abnormal Child Psychology, 13,* 611–629.

Roberts, M. W., Hatzenbuehler, L. C., & Bean, A. W. (1981). The effects of differential attention and time-out on child noncompliance. *Behavior Therapy, 12,* 93–99.

Silverman, W. (2001). Treating anxiety disorders in children: Key therapeutic principles and procedures. *Psychotherapy Bulletin, 36,* 10–14.

Wahler, R. G. (1969). Oppositional children: A quest for parental reinforcement control. *Journal of Applied Behavior Analysis, 2,* 159–170.

45 PROBLEM-SOLVING THERAPY

Arthur M. Nezu, Christine Maguth Nezu, and Elizabeth Lombardo

Problem solving is the overt, self-directed, cognitive-behavioral process by which a person attempts to identify adaptive solutions for stressful problems. Problem-Solving Therapy (PST) helps individuals cope more effectively with such problems by teaching them various skills. Effective coping can involve altering the nature of the problem (e.g., overcoming obstacles to a goal), changing one's reactions to the problem (e.g., accepting that a goal cannot be reached), or both. Overarching goals of PST include (1) decreasing the negative impact (e.g., emotional distress) related to the experience of both major (e.g., a divorce) and minor (e.g., loss of one's wallet) life events and problems; (2) increasing one's ability to cope more effectively with such problems; and (3) minimizing the likelihood of similar problems from occurring in the future.

Problems can be single events (e.g., obtaining a loan from a bank), a series of related problems (e.g., continuous arguments with a spouse), or chronic situations (e.g., major chronic illness, such as cancer). They can originate from the environment (e.g., interpersonal difficulties) or within the person (e.g., conflicting goals). Situations become problems when an effective response is required in order for the person to cope adaptively but such a response is not immediately available or identifiable due to the presence of various obstacles.

Such obstacles can include ambiguity, unpredictability, conflicting demands, deficient skills, or lack of resources.

PROBLEM-SOLVING PROCESS

According to D'Zurilla and Nezu (1999), problem-solving outcomes in the real world are hypothesized to be largely determined by two general, but partially independent, processes: (1) problem orientation and (2) problem-solving style (previously termed *problem-solving proper*). *Problem orientation* is a person's cognitive-emotional set, comprising a group of relatively stable generalized thoughts and feelings concerning problems in living, as well as one's ability to successfully resolve them. It can be either *positive* (e.g., viewing problems as opportunities to benefit in some way; perceiving oneself as able to solve problems effectively), which serves to enhance subsequent problem-solving efforts; or *negative* (e.g., viewing problems as a major threat to one's well-being; becoming immobilized when problems occur), which functions to inhibit attempts to solve problems.

Problem-solving style refers to various cognitive-behavioral activities aimed at coping with stressful problems. They can be either adaptive, leading to successful problem resolution, or dysfunctional, leading to negative consequences such as psychological distress. *Rational problem solving* is the constructive style geared to identify an effective solution to the problem and involves the systematic application of various specific adaptive problem-solving tasks (e.g., gathering information, generating alternative solutions, monitoring the consequences of an implemented solution). In addition, two dysfunctional problem-solving styles have been identified: (1) *impulsivity/carelessness* (i.e., impulsive, hurried, and incomplete attempts to solve a problem) and (2) *avoidance* (i.e., avoiding problems, procrastinating, and depending on others to solve one's problems).

In essence, through various didactics, role-plays, training exercises, and homework assignments, PST is geared to (1) increase one's positive problem orientation, (2) foster one's rational problem-solving style, (3) decrease one's negative problem orientation, (4) minimize one's tendency to be impulsive or careless, and (5) minimize one's tendency to avoid problems.

WHO CAN BENEFIT FROM PST?

In the literature, PST has been effectively applied as the sole intervention to a wide range of psychological problems, including Depression, suicidal ideation and behaviors, Schizophrenia, emotional problems of primary care patients, Social Phobia, behavioral problems of adults with mental retardation, substance abuse, and behavioral disorders of children. It has been used to improve the quality of life of patients with various medical problems, such as cancer, hypertension, head injuries, and arthritis. PST has also been combined with other cognitive-behavioral strategies for the treatment of Borderline Personality Disorder, marital and family problems, HIV-AIDS risk behaviors (e.g., unsafe sex), and parent-adolescent conflict. PST has also been applied as a maintenance strategy to enhance the effects of other treatment approaches for weight loss. Researchers have used PST to enhance the ability of individuals to serve as effective caregivers of persons with cancer, Alzheimer's Disease, dementia, adults with spinal cord injuries,

and children with behavior problems. PST has also been applied to enhance normal individuals' coping and stress management skills, to decrease vocational indecision, and to enhance social skills among shy young adolescents.

CONTRAINDICATIONS

Because PST has been found to help individuals representing wide arrays of both cognitive abilities (e.g., ranging from intellectually normal adults to persons with mild to moderate mental retardation) and psychological difficulties (e.g., ranging from normal college students to adults with Schizophrenia), it would appear that few contraindications for this intervention exist at present. Based on the authors' clinical experience, PST would not be recommended as the sole intervention for clinically significant anxiety disorders, such as simple phobias or Obsessive-Compulsive Disorder.

EVIDENCE FOR THE EFFICACY OF PST

With regard to the conceptual underpinnings of PST, a large number of studies have found problem-solving effectiveness and psychological distress and dysfunction to be significantly related. Such converging findings have emerged from investigations using varying research designs and differing measures of problem solving. For example, some studies have looked at simple correlations between measures of distress and problem solving, whereas others have looked at differences in problem solving between reliably diagnosed patient groups (having, e.g., Major Depressive Disorder, Post-Traumatic Stress Disorder). Further, several studies have found problem solving to serve as a significant moderator of the relationship between stress and distress (such as depression and anxiety)—that is, *at similar levels of high stress*, effective problem solvers are less depressed and anxious than ineffective problem solvers.

A large number of controlled outcome studies (as indicated in "Who Can Benefit from PST?") have found PST to be an effective cognitive-behavioral intervention for a variety of psychological disorders (see D'Zurilla & Nezu, 1999, for an overview of the outcome literature). In particular, a series of studies by Nezu and his colleagues have found PST to be especially effective in treating Major Depressive Disorder (e.g., Nezu, Nezu, & Perri, 1989) and in improving the quality of life of adult cancer patients (Nezu, Nezu, Friedman, Faddis, & Houts, 1998).

STEP-BY-STEP GUIDE

Although PST involves teaching individuals specific skills, similar to other CBT approaches, it should be conducted within a therapeutic context. Because PST does focus on skill building, it can easily be misunderstood by the novice therapist that it only entails a teaching process. However, it is important for the problem-solving therapist to be careful not to (1) conduct PST in a mechanistic manner; (2) focus only on skills training and not on the patient's emotional experiences; (3) deliver a canned treatment that does not address the unique strengths, weaknesses, and experiences of a given patient; and (4) assume that PST focuses only on superficial problems, rather than on more complex interpersonal, psychological, existential, and spiritual issues (if warranted). Thus, in addition to teaching the patient certain techniques to better cope with problems, effective PST requires the therapist to be competent in a variety of other assessment and intervention strategies, such as fostering a positive therapeutic relationship, assessing for complex clinical problems, modeling, behavioral rehearsal, assigning homework tasks, and appropriately providing corrective feedback.

Prior to training the specific PST components, the therapist should present an overall rationale describing the purpose, goals, and specific components of PST, emphasizing how it can be helpful to the unique circumstances of a given patient. Part of this rationale includes the notion that the experience of stressful events and difficult problems often leads to emotional distress and various behavioral problems. Moreover, PST is geared to teach people some new skills, as well as to help them to apply previously acquired problem-solving skills to new problems and stressful situations. An emphasis is also provided in the ra-

tionale that the goal of effective problem solving may not always lead to changes in the situation itself (i.e., problem-focused goals), but can also encompass cognitive or emotional changes, such as acceptance, increased tolerance, and decreases in emotional reactions to unchangeable events (i.e., emotion-focused goals). Structurally, PST training can be broken into three major foci: (1) training in problem orientation, (2) training in the four specific rational problem-solving skills (problem definition and formulation, generation of alternatives, decision making, solution implementation and verification), and (3) practice of these skills across a variety of real-life problems.

Training in Problem Orientation

Training in problem orientation (PO) is geared to foster (1) positive self-efficacy beliefs, (2) acceptance of the notion that it is normal to experience a wide range of problems in life, (3) the ability to identify problems accurately when they occur, and (4) the ability to minimize the likelihood that negative emotional reactions lead to impulsive or avoidant reactions. To achieve such objectives, PO training can include several different techniques, as described in the following section.

Reverse-Advocacy Role-Play

According to this strategy, the problem-solving therapist pretends to adopt a particular belief about problems (i.e., ones that tend to reflect a negative orientation) and asks the patient to provide reasons that belief is irrational, illogical, incorrect, or maladaptive. Such beliefs might include the following statements: "Problems are not common to everyone; if I have a problem, that means I'm crazy." "All my problems are caused by me." "There must be a perfect solution to this problem." At times when the patient has difficulty generating arguments against the therapist's position, the counselor then adopts a more extreme form of the belief, such as "No matter how long it takes, even if it takes forever, I will continue to try to find the perfect solution to my problem." This procedure is intended to help individuals identify alternative ways of thinking and then to dispute or contradict previously held negative beliefs with more adaptive perspectives. Moreover, this task permits the individual to provide arguments in his or her own words against previously expressed maladaptive thoughts. Also encouraged are homework assignments geared to reinforce such learning, such as providing counterarguments to other negative problem orientation beliefs (e.g., "People can't change;" "Most people don't have problems") not specifically addressed in session.

ABC Method of Constructive Thinking

With this technique, patients are taught to view emotional reactions from the "ABC" perspective, where A = the *a*ctivating event (such as a problem), B = *b*eliefs about the event (including what people say to themselves), and C = the emotional and behavioral *c*onsequences. In other words, how individuals *feel* and *act* often are products of how they *think*. Using a current problem, the PST therapist can use this procedure to diagnose negative self-talk and thoughts that are likely to lead to distressing emotions for a given patient. Such cognitions often include highly evaluative words, such as "should" and "must," catastrophic words used to describe non-life-threatening events, and phrases that tend to be overgeneralizations (e.g., "Nobody understands me!"). By examining one's self-talk, the patient can learn to separate realistic statements (e.g., "I wish . . .") from maladaptive ones (e.g., "I must have . . .") as they pertain to problems in living. The patient can also be given a list of positive self-statements that can be used to substitute for or help dispute the negative self-talk (as in the reverse-advocacy role-play strategy). These can be placed on an index card that can be carried throughout the day or posted in a visible place to remind the individual to use this strategy in real life. A useful homework assignment associated with this strategy would involve having the patient identify which negative thoughts were involved at times when he or she became emotionally distressed.

Visualization

As a means of enhancing patients' optimism, this technique is used to help them create the experience of successful problem resolution in their mind's eye and vicariously experience the reinforcement to be gained. Visualization in this context requests individuals to close their eyes and imagine that they have successfully solved a current problem. The focus is on the end point—not on how one got to the goal, but rather on the feelings of having reached the goal. To foster this, additional questions include "How would your life be different with this problem solved?" "How would you be feel about yourself, having solved this problem?" The central goal of this strategy is to have patients create and experience their own positive consequences related to solving a problem as a motivational step toward enhanced self-efficacy. In essence, it helps create a visual image of the light at the end of the tunnel.

Identifying Problems When They Occur

The purpose of this technique is to help normalize the experience of problems by discussing the wide range of possible problems that people in general can experience. The therapist can use existing problem checklists or create handouts that contain various categories of potential problems (e.g., work, relationships, sex, career) as a springboard to discuss this issue, as well as to begin to assess for the specific problems that a given patient is currently experiencing. In order to foster an individual's ability to recognize a problem, patients are taught to *use feelings as cues* (i.e., negative physical and emotional reactions) that a problem exists. In other words, rather than labeling their negative emotions as "the problem," they are instructed to conceptualize such emotions as a signal that a problem exists and then to observe what is occurring in their environment in order to recognize the real problem that is causing such emotions. Once such feelings as depression, anger, muscle tension, nausea, or anxiety arise, the patient is then instructed to use the mnemonic "STOP and THINK" as a means of inhibiting avoidance or impulsive problem-solving behavior. A handout containing a visual depiction of a stop sign with this message can be helpful for patients to place in their environment (e.g., on the refrigerator or bathroom mirror) as an important reminder. The "think" aspect of this phrase refers to the use of the four specific rational problem-solving skills described later. In addition, PST emphasizes that combining emotions and rational thinking (rather than relying solely on only one of these areas) leads to "wisdom," which represents effective real-life problem solving.

Training in Problem Definition and Formulation

The importance of this first rational problem-solving skill can be expressed in the age-old proverb "A problem well-defined is a problem half solved." In other words, with a clear understanding of what is wrong, one can then make attempts to make circumstances right. *Problem definition and formulation (PDF)* includes (1) gathering information about the problem, (2) objectively and concisely defining the problem, (3) separating facts from assumptions, (4) identifying the features that make the situation problematic, and (5) setting realistic goals.

In an effort to gain a comprehensive understanding of the problem, patients are instructed to ask *who, what, where, when,* and *how* in order to gather important facts about a problem. Suggesting that the patient take on the role of detective, investigator reporter, or scientist can foster such efforts. When describing problems, patients are trained to separate *assumptions* (e.g., "I'm no good") from *facts* (e.g., "I did poorly on this one exam"), as well as to use clear and unambiguous language (e.g., "I feel sad when I think about my father's death, which then makes me feel like giving up," vs. "I feel all screwed up!"). In addition, patients are taught to identify why a given situation is a problem (i.e., to ask, "What are the obstacles to goal attainment?" "What are the conflicting goals that make this a problem?") and to break larger problems into smaller ones in order to be able to articulate reasonably achievable goals.

Similar to all of the remaining problem-solving skills, training in PDF includes (1) therapist modeling of appropriate responses, (2) in-session practice of the skills, (3) therapist feedback of the patient's responses, and (4) relevant homework assignments. With regard to PDF, homework can include written descriptions of a current problem using the guidelines learned during this training.

Training in Generation of Alternatives

Patients are instructed to use various brainstorming principles to foster creativity and flexibility and to minimize the tendency to react to stressful problems in previously maladaptive habitual ways. These principles include (1) the *quantity principle* (i.e., the more solution ideas that are identified, the more likely it is to develop an effective solution), (2) the *deferment-of-judgment principle* (i.e., refrain from evaluating solutions until a comprehensive list is generated), and (3) the *strategies-tactics principle* (i.e., ideas can be conceptualized as both general strategies and as a variety of tactics or steps to carry out each of the strategies). If patients have difficulty developing such a list, they are instructed to combine ideas, modify existing ideas, identify how a role model (e.g., a personal hero) may approach a similar problem, or use visualization. If severe emotional distress (e.g., anxiety) interferes with one's ability to be creative, the therapist may wish to engage in relaxation training. Generation-of-alternatives (GoA) homework assignments would include having the patient generate a comprehensive list of possible solution ideas with regard to the well-defined problem or problems emanating from the PDF training.

Training in Decision Making

Decision making (DM) involves conducting a cost-benefit analysis with regard to the previously generated list of solutions as a means of identifying highly effective ones. Here, patients are instructed first to assess the likelihood that a given solution will actually solve the problem (i.e., the *likelihood of success*), and then to assess the likelihood that they can actually carry it out in an optimal manner (i.e., the *likelihood of implementation*). Second, they are taught to identify various positive and negative consequences related to each solution that are *personal* (effects on themselves), *social* (effects on family, coworkers, neighbors, etc.), *short term,* and *long term.* Next, using a simple rating scale, such as –3 (extremely negative) to +3 (extremely positive), each of these criteria is then appraised. These ratings are then used as guidelines to evaluate the overall effectiveness for each alternative. Because most problems in real life are likely to be complex, patients are generally taught to combine various effective ideas into an overall solution plan. Effective solution plans are defined as those that not only lead to successful problem resolution (i.e., that achieve the relevant problem-solving goals), but increase the likelihood of subsequent positive consequences and minimize the probability of related negative consequences. Relevant homework at this stage would entail conducting a detailed cost-benefit analysis of the various alternatives previously generated for a problem that the patient is currently experiencing.

Training in Solution Implementation and Verification

This final rational problem-solving skill involves actually implementing the solution plan and then evaluating the effectiveness of the outcome. Specific components of solution implementation and verification (SIV) include (1) carrying out the solution plan, (2) monitoring its outcome, (3) evaluating its effectiveness, and (4) troubleshooting whether the solution is unsuccessful versus engaging in self-reinforcement if the problem is resolved. Initially, in an effort to enhance motivation and decrease avoidance, the patient is instructed to conduct another cost-benefit analysis, this one assessing the advantages and disadvantages of *implementing versus not implementing* a solution plan. Visualization can be used to increase a patient's self-efficacy related to executing the solution, identifying and overcoming obstacles, and increasing the effectiveness of solution implementation. In addition, if relevant, the patient can practice, via role-playing, actually carrying out the chosen solution plan.

With regard to the "verification" aspect of this skill, patients are taught to assess the success or effectiveness of a given implemented solution plan by gathering relevant data to compare the actual to the desired outcome. If they are similar (i.e., if the problem-solving goals are being achieved), patients are encouraged to reward themselves for their efforts. If the problem is not adequately resolved, individuals are taught to recycle back through each of the rational problem-solving steps in order to identify what went wrong ("Was the problem not well defined?" "Were the goals unrealistic?" "Was the solution plan not carried out optimally?" "Were not enough solution ideas generated?" etc.). Relevant homework assignments can include practice in carrying out the solution plan, developing a procedure to measure the impact of the implemented plan (e.g., a simple rating scale), troubleshooting through each of the four rational problem-solving skills, or engaging in self-reinforcement (e.g., going to a favorite restaurant, purchasing a new article of clothing) if the problem becomes resolved.

Supervised Practice

After the majority of training has occurred, the remainder of PST should be devoted to practicing the newly acquired skills and applying them to a variety of stressful problems. As the 13th-century Persian poet Saa'di stated, "However much thou art read in theory, if thou hast no practice, thou art ignorant." This quote is to suggest that the more a patient applies these skills to various problem situations, the better he or she becomes at overall problem resolution. Beyond actually solving stressful problems, continuous in-session practice serves three additional purposes: (1) the patient can receive professional feedback from the therapist, (2) increased facility with the overall PST model can decrease the amount of time and effort necessary to apply the entire model with each new problem, and (3) practice fosters maintenance and generalization of the skills.

The number of practice sessions required after formal PST training often is dependent upon the competency level a patient achieves and on the actual improvement in his or her overall quality of life. Of the research protocols that have found PST to be an effective CBT intervention, the number of included sessions have ranged from 8 to 12 sessions.

In addition to focusing on resolving and coping with current problems, these practice sessions should also allow for *future forecasting*, whereby the patient is encouraged to look at a future goal or event (e.g., anticipated geographic move, request for promotion, contemplation of raising a family) and anticipate where potential problems might arise in order to apply such skills in a preventive manner. Continuous application of these skills is encouraged, for as the poet Emily Dickinson stated, "Low as my problem bending, another problem comes."

References

D'Zurilla, T. J., & Nezu, A. M. (1999). *Problem-solving therapy: A social competence approach to clinical intervention* (2nd ed.). New York: Springer.

Nezu, A. M., Nezu, C. M., Friedman, S. H., Faddis, S., & Houts, P. S. (1998). *Helping cancer patients cope: A problem-solving approach.* Washington, DC: American Psychological Association.

Nezu, A. M., Nezu, C. M., & Perri, M. G. (1989). *Problem-solving therapy for depression: Theory, research, and clinical guidelines.* New York: Wiley.

46 PUNISHMENT

David P. Wacker, Jay Harding, Wendy Berg, Linda J. Cooper-Brown, and Anjali Barretto

Behavioral reduction procedures, such as punishment (e.g., Azrin & Holz, 1966; Iwata, 1988) and extinction (Iwata, Pace, Cowdery, & Miltenberger, 1994; Lerman & Iwata, 1996), have been discussed extensively in the literature. Punishment can be defined on the basis of its application (Catania, 1998), its operations (Catania), and its functional relationship to the target behavior (Iwata, Pace, Dorsey, et al., 1994). Relative to application, we can describe how a behavior resulted in punishment (e.g., tantrumming led to a reprimand or placement in a time-out area). Relative to operation, we can describe the effect that punishment had on behavior (e.g., time-out reduced the child's tantrums). Relative to function, we can describe how a punishment procedure was matched (Iwata, Pace, Dorsey, et al., 1994) to the reinforcer maintaining problem behavior (time-out from parental attention reduced the child's attention-maintained tantrum behavior). As discussed by Catania (1998), the differences in these definitions relate to how explicitly we are describing the response-consequence relation. At the application level, we are describing a sequence of events. At the operations level, we are describing the effects of a consequence on behavior. At the functional relations level, we are explaining why those effects occurred.

These levels of definition, from application to operation to function, provide increased clarity in clinical situations. For example, the statement that time-out should be used by parents for tantrum behavior requires inferences about the function of the behavior (e.g., tantrums are maintained by positive reinforcement) and that the specific application (the specific manner by which it is applied) will reduce the rate of tantrums. These inferences, if left untested, can create confusion and overgeneralizations regarding the treatment and can result in countertherapeutic effects. Confusion can occur, for example, if a parent implements a treatment as specified and target behavior remains unchanged. It is now unclear what adjustments to the treatment are needed because the difficulty may be the specific application of the treatment or that the treatment itself is not punishing. This lack of effect on behavior may lead the parent to make overgeneralizations about the treatment (e.g., "Time-out does not work for tantrums") or about the behavior (e.g., "My child's tantrums do not respond to punishment"). These types of overgeneralizations may hamper future attempts at treatment. Countertherapeutic treatment can occur when the application of treatment reinforces target behavior. Countertherapeutic treatments occur for several reasons, with at least some related to the function of problem behavior. For example, if tantrums are maintained by negative reinforcement in the form of escape from demands or avoidance of a care provider, then removal to a time-out area may reinforce or strengthen the problem behavior (i.e., may function as a negative reinforcer). By specifying both the applications and operations of the procedure, and the functions of target behavior, we can avoid a wide range of clinical problems.

THE OPERATION OF PUNISHMENT

According to Azrin and Holz (1966), *punishment* is defined as the delivery of a consequence of behavior that reduces the future probability of the behavior. This generic or minimal (Azrin & Holz) definition leaves much unspecified but adequately describes the operation of punishment. To determine when or under what conditions a given application will be effective, we also need to specify the relation of punishment to ongoing reinforcement (Catania, 1998), including the function of target behavior (Iwata, Dorsey, Slifer, Bauman, & Richman, 1982/1994). The relation of punishment to reinforcement identifies the range of applications (procedural variability) that will be effective. Ideally, reinforcement would be delivered only for a wide range of appropriate behavior but never for problem behavior (see Chapter 23, this volume). In this case, punishment may not need to be a critical component of the treatment package. In other cases, problem behavior will continue to be strengthened by the delivery of reinforcement and punishment may need to be applied at a more intense (e.g., more consistent, more immediate, more severe) level.

THE FUNCTION OF PROBLEM BEHAVIOR

The function of problem behavior identifies the functional class of punishment applications that is likely to be most effective (see Chapters 27 and 28, this volume). Thus, if problem behavior occurs to gain adult attention, then consequences that reduce the presence of attention are likely to be effective and consequences that increase the amount of attention are contraindicated. Punishment techniques, like extinction and reinforcement techniques, must be specified in relation to the function of target behavior. For this reason, it is important to identify the function of problem

behavior prior to the selection of treatment. When the function (maintaining reinforcer) is known, then that reinforcer can be withheld (via extinction or punishment) contingent on problem behavior and provided contingently for adaptive behavior.

EFFECTIVENESS OF PUNISHMENT

The effectiveness of punishment has been reported in both the basic and the applied literatures for over 30 years (Azrin & Holz, 1966). When combined with reinforcement and extinction procedures, punishment can have immediate and substantial effects on target behaviors that do not respond to reinforcement treatments (e.g., Wacker et al., 1990). Surprisingly few negative side effects have been reported in the applied literature, perhaps because reductive procedures are almost always combined with reinforcement procedures (Lerman & Iwata, 1996), and very few examples of corporal punishment are reported in the applied literature. Thus, the decision to use punishment often is based more on practical (e.g., the need to quickly reduce a target behavior) and emotional (e.g., a care provider's perceptions about a particular application) considerations than on its overall merits. (See Alberto & Troutman, 1999, and Miltenberger, 2001, for a more comprehensive discussion of common applications of punishment and the ethical issues related to the use of punishment.) We agree with Iwata (1988), who characterized the use of punishment as a default treatment. By *default treatment*, Iwata was referring to punishment as evolving from a failure to produce desired behavior via reinforcement procedures. Punishment is often needed when we either have failed to identify reinforcers or are unable to control the delivery of those reinforcers sufficiently to increase alternative, adaptive behaviors. When the selection of punishment procedures is based on the function of problem behavior and is related to the ongoing reinforcement for both problem and alternative behavior, punishment procedures can be highly effective in suppressing behavior.

When it has been determined that a punishment procedure is warranted, several factors related to the delivery of the punisher will influence its effectiveness in suppressing behavior

(Miltenberger, 2001). In general, the effectiveness of punishment will be enhanced if the punisher follows problem behavior immediately and is contingent on the target behavior (follows every occurrence of problem behavior). Of equal importance is that alternative, adaptive behavior is reinforced in an immediate and contingent manner.

IDENTIFYING FUNCTIONAL TREATMENTS

In most cases, identifying the function of target behavior is a two-step process. First, we conduct a descriptive assessment based on interview, survey, or observation. This assessment, which is a type of antecedent-behavior-consequence (ABC) assessment (Bijou, Peterson, & Ault, 1968), is used to formulate hypotheses about the reinforcers maintaining target behavior and the consistency with which those reinforcers are delivered. We then formally test the hypotheses via either an extended (Iwata et al., 1982/1994) or a brief (Northup et al., 1991) functional analysis, depending on the setting: extended in homes and brief in outpatient clinics. Based on the results of these assessments, we provide a selection of intervention options to care providers that always includes differential reinforcement and may include punishment.

CASE EXAMPLES

In the following three case examples, we provide a summary of this approach in two settings (home and outpatient clinics) with two subgroups of young children (with and without developmental disabilities) and with different functions (positive and negative reinforcement) of target behavior.

Case Example of Korey

The Behavioral Pediatrics Clinic (Cooper et al., 1992) is an outpatient clinic that serves children ranging in age from 12 months to 9 years who are referred for behavioral concerns. A behavioral assessment is conducted as follows:

1. Initial information is obtained via school records, a parent questionnaire, behavior rat-

ing scales, and records from local service providers (e.g., counselors, social workers).
2. A phone call is made to the parents several days before the appointment to conduct an ABC interview. Based on the records and interview, hypotheses are formed regarding the variables maintaining target behavior.
3. A brief functional analysis is conducted by the parent with coaching from clinic staff.
4. A treatment plan is developed, and the treatment is practiced by the parent in clinic.

Korey was a 2-year-old boy with overall development within normal limits. Problem behaviors included self-injury (biting himself, scratching his face), aggression (biting, hitting his mother), tantrums, and noncompliance with requests. We hypothesized that Korey's problem behavior was maintained by positive reinforcement (attention from his mother).

During the brief functional analysis, Korey was observed interacting with his mother via a video camera mounted in the examination room. Prior to each analysis condition, Korey's mother briefly left the examination room, and she was given instructions regarding the activities to present to Korey and the consequences to provide for his appropriate and problem behaviors. Each condition lasted 5 min.

Problem behavior occurred only in the attention condition, not when playing or working with his mother. In the attention condition, Korey's mother was instructed to read a magazine while seated in a chair away from Korey. She was instructed to ignore him while he played but to provide attention (e.g., "Don't do that") when he engaged in target behavior. His target behavior quickly diminished when he was provided with noncontingent attention and escalated when attention was contingent on target behavior.

We recommended a treatment package that consisted of a positive reinforcement component to increase appropriate behavior and a punishment component to reduce target behavior. The positive reinforcement component consisted of functional communication training (Carr & Durand, 1985; see Chapter 28, this volume): Korey was taught to say "please" to gain access to his mother's attention. The punishment component consisted of a brief, nonexclusionary time-out from reinforcement for episodes of problem behavior. Korey's mother looked away from him until problem behavior did not occur for several seconds. Immediately following time-out, Korey's mother provided opportunities for Korey to gain her attention using appropriate communication. Thus, the emphasis was on teaching and reinforcing appropriate communication to increase adaptive behavior, and punishment was used to augment the positive reinforcement component.

Case Example of Annie

The Biobehavioral Outpatient Service (Northup et al., 1991) is a weekly, multidisciplinary clinic for persons with developmental disabilities who engage in severe problem behaviors such as self-injury, aggression, and destruction. The same assessment steps used in the Behavioral Pediatrics Clinic are used in this clinic.

Annie was a 2-year-old girl with severe developmental delays who received all nutrition via a gastrostomy tube. Annie was referred for assessment and treatment of self-injury (head banging and hand biting), aggression (scratching and hitting), and tantrums. Annie's mother reported that these behaviors occurred primarily during demands such as diaper changes, tube feedings, and so on. Our hypothesis was that problem behavior was maintained by escape from demands. Annie also had very limited play skills, and when she was given a toy, she often threw it or tossed it aside. The primary goals of intervention were to decrease problem behavior and to increase adaptive behavior (e.g., communication and play skills).

A brief functional analysis was conducted to test the effects of gaining adult attention and escaping nonpreferred activities as possible reinforcers for engaging in more severe forms (self-injury and aggression) of the target behavior. No problem behavior occurred during the test for attention but did occur throughout the escape condition. More mild problem behavior also occurred during free play when Annie threw her toys. These results suggested that severe problem behavior was maintained by escape from demands.

A functional communication training (FCT) package was developed for Annie that included three components: (1) reinforcement, (2) escape extinction, and (3) response cost. Each treatment

session began with Annie's mother presenting a demand to Annie. Reinforcement involved teaching Annie to press a microswitch that played a prerecorded message to request a break from the demand. Pressing the microswitch was an appropriate response that Annie could use to escape the task demands for a brief period (e.g., 20 to 30 s). Problem behavior within the context of demands resulted in escape extinction; the demand remained in place, and toys were withheld until the appropriate response occurred. The purpose of escape extinction was to prevent Annie from gaining access to the reinforcer (escape) by engaging in problem behavior. If Annie engaged in problem behavior during the break (e.g., threw her toys), a response cost was implemented. Response cost involved the immediate removal of the toys (loss of potential positive reinforcers) and presentation of the task demand (loss of negative reinforcer).

Case Example of Jon

Jon was a participant in a National Institutes of Health research project (Wacker, Berg, & Harding, 2000) that provides in-home behavioral assessment and treatment to young children with developmental and behavioral disorders. Jon was 2 years 11 months old and was diagnosed with Disruptive Behavior Disorder (not otherwise specified) and expressive language delays. Severe problem behaviors included aggression (e.g., biting, hitting, kicking, and pinching), property destruction (e.g., throwing items), and noncompliance. All assessment and treatment procedures were conducted in Jon's home on a weekly to monthly basis for 1 hour.

A behavioral assessment was conducted as follows: (1) Jon's mother recorded episodes of problem behavior during 30-min intervals throughout the day for 1 week on an ABC recording form. (2) Following completion of this written record, Jon's parents were interviewed to clarify concerns and to formulate initial hypotheses regarding environmental events that might be related to the occurrence of problem behavior. (3) Problem behavior was hypothesized to be related to a variety of social contexts (attention, tangibles, and demands); and (4) an extended functional analysis was conducted across multiple test conditions during 5-min sessions over a

2-week period. The results showed that problem behavior was elevated during attention, tangible, and escape conditions, but remained at zero or near-zero levels during the free-play condition. The occurrence of more severe problem behavior occurred at consistently high levels only during the escape condition. Thus, Jon's problem behavior appeared to be maintained by multiple social functions, with severe problem behavior most likely to occur during demands.

Treatment consisted of functional communication training to teach Jon to follow his mother's instructions and to mand appropriately when he wanted a break from tasks to play with his mother and preferred toys. Jon's treatment was matched to the results of his functional analysis, which indicated that his problem behavior was maintained by both escape from demands (negative reinforcement) and access to attention and preferred toys (positive reinforcement). An investigator modeled the procedures initially, provided prescriptive feedback to Jon's mother during subsequent sessions on a weekly basis for 3 months, and then provided feedback on a monthly basis for an additional 3 months.

During treatment probes, Jon had access to preferred toys and his mother's attention for 1 min before she presented him with the task. His mother then used hierarchical prompts to guide Jon in completing the task. First, his mother provided a verbal prompt (e.g., "Put the red block on top of the green block"). Then she modeled the behavior. If Jon completed the task, his mother provided praise. She then produced a picture card with the word "play" printed on it, and said, "Tell me what you want to do." Initially, Jon's mother used hand-over-hand guidance to assist Jon in touching the card to request "play." This physical guidance was always accompanied by his mother saying the word "play" ("Oh, you want to *play*. Thank you for telling me"). After touching the card, Jon was allowed to play with his mother and preferred toys for 1 min, at which time his mother presented him with a new task. Thus, Jon received positive reinforcement (attention and toys) for complying with his mother's request and for communicating appropriately.

If Jon engaged in mild problem behavior (e.g., whined or said "No"), his mother kept the task in front of Jon and reminded him to "do your work

and then you can play." This form of escape extinction procedure was often successful in getting Jon to complete the request and, thus, to gain an opportunity to mand for preferred toys. However, if Jon's behavior became more severe, his mother implemented a nonexclusionary time-out procedure blended with escape extinction. Jon was given no verbal attention and was not allowed to have any toys. Thus, in this treatment package, each function of Jon's problem behavior was matched to a treatment component, with one component involving punishment.

CONCLUSION

In each case example, the combination of reinforcement for adaptive behavior (i.e., mands) and punishment for problem behavior produced rapid reductions in problem behavior and gains in adaptive responding. In the third case example, treatment effects were also shown to be maintained over several months. This function-based approach to treatment increases the likelihood of developing an effective treatment plan while reducing the inadvertent reinforcement of

---

1. Conduct a descriptive assessment that identifies possible antecedent-response and response-reinforcer relations. One example is to conduct an ABC assessment via interview, recording form, or direct observation.

2. Conduct a brief or extended functional analysis to identify the function of target behavior.

3. Match all treatment components (reinforcement, extinction, punishment) to the hypothesized (descriptive) or identified (functional analysis) function of behavior. Make sure that the treatment package is internally consistent, meaning that all components are compatible.

4. Base the use of punishment on care provider preference. Some care providers have strong opinions (both pro and con) regarding the use of punishment applications. If no preference is indicated, we usually begin treatment with extinction and reinforcement components and then use punishment as a default technique.

5. Base the application of punishment on descriptive information obtained about the probability of ongoing reinforcement for problem behavior and the availability of alternative responses that can receive reinforcement.

FIGURE 46.1   Key Elements of Function-Based Punishment Procedures

problem behaviors. The key elements of applying punishment procedures that are matched to the function of target behavior are provided in Figure 46.1.

Further Reading

Cooper, L., Wacker, D., Thursby, D., Plagmann, L., Harding, J., Millard, T., & Derby, M. (1992). Analysis of the effects of task preferences, task demands, and adult attention on child behavior in outpatient and classroom settings. *Journal of Applied Behavior Analysis, 25*, 823–840.

Iwata, B., A., Dorsey, M. F., Slifer, K. J., Bauman, K. E., & Richman, G. S. (1994). Toward a functional analysis of self-injury. *Journal of Applied Behavior Analysis, 27*, 197–209. (Reprinted from *Analysis and Intervention in Developmental Disabilities, 2*, 2–30, 1982.)

Wacker, D. P., Berg, W. K., Harding, J. W., Derby, K. M., Asmus, J. M., & Healy, A. (1998). Evaluation and long-term treatment of aberrant behavior displayed by young children with disabilities. *Journal of Developmental and Behavioral Pediatrics, 19*, 260–266.

References

Alberto, P. A., & Troutman, A. C. (1999). *Applied behavior analysis for teachers* (5th ed.). Columbus, OH: Prentice-Hall.

Azrin, N. H., & Holz, W. C. (1966). Punishment. In W. K. Honig (Ed.), *Operant behavior: Areas of research and application* (pp. 380–447). New York: Appleton-Century-Crofts.

Bijou, S. W., Peterson, R. F., & Ault, M. H. (1968). A method to integrate descriptive and experimental field studies at the level of data and empirical concepts. *Journal of Applied Behavior Analysis, 1*, 175–191.

Carr, E. G., & Durand, V. M. (1985). Reducing behavior problems through functional communication training. *Journal of Applied Behavior Analysis, 18*, 111–126.

Catania, A. C. (1998). Consequences of responding: Aversive control. In *Learning* (4th ed., pp. 88–110). Upper Saddle River, NJ: Prentice Hall.

Cooper, L., Wacker, D., Thursby, D., Plagmann, L., Harding, J., Millard, T., & Derby, M. (1992). Analysis of the effects of task preferences, task de-

mands, and adult attention on child behavior in outpatient and classroom settings. *Journal of Applied Behavior Analysis, 25*, 823–840.

Iwata, B. A. (1988). The development and adoption of controversial default technologies. *The Behavior Analyst, 11*, 149–157.

Iwata, B., A., Dorsey, M. F., Slifer, K. J., Bauman, K. E., & Richman, G. S. (1994). Toward a functional analysis of self-injury. *Journal of Applied Behavior Analysis, 27*, 197–209. (Reprinted from *Analysis and Intervention in Developmental Disabilities, 2*, 2–30, 1982.)

Iwata, B. A., Pace, G. M., Cowdery, G. E., & Miltenberger, R. G. (1994). What makes extinction work: An analysis of procedural form and function. *Journal of Applied Behavior Analysis, 27*, 131–144.

Iwata, B. A., Pace, G. M., Dorsey, M. F., Zarcone, J. R., Vollmer, T. R., Smith, R. G., Rodgers, T. A., Lerman, D. C., Shore, B. A., Mazaleski, J. L., Goh, H.-L., Cowdery, G. E., Kalsher, M. J., McCosh, K. C., & Willis, K. D. (1994). The functions of self-injurious behavior: An experimental-epidemiological analysis. *Journal of Applied Behavior Analysis, 27*, 215–240.

Lerman, D. C., & Iwata, B. A. (1996). Developing a technology for the use of operant extinction in clinical settings: An examination of basic and applied research. *Journal of Applied Behavior Analysis, 29*, 345–382.

Miltenberger, R. G. (2001). *Behavior modification: Principles and procedures* (2nd ed.). Belmont, CA: Wadsworth/Thomson Learning.

Northup, J., Wacker, D., Sasso, G., Steege, M., Cigrand, K., Cook, J., & DeRaad, A. (1991). A brief functional analysis of aggressive and alternative behavior in an outclinic setting. *Journal of Applied Behavior Analysis, 24*, 509–522.

Wacker, D. P., Berg, W. K., & Harding, J. (2000). *Functional communication training augmented with choices*. Washington, DC: Department of Health and Human Services, National Institute of Child Health and Human Development.

Wacker, D., Steege, M., Northup, J., Sasso, G., Berg, W., Reimers, T., Cooper, L., Cigrand, K., & Donn, L. (1990). A component analysis of functional communication training across three topographies of severe behavior problems. *Journal of Applied Behavior Analysis, 23*, 417–429.

47 RAPID SMOKING

Elizabeth V. Gifford and Deacon Shoenberger

Recent reports estimate that about 25% of adults over 18, or 48 million Americans, are smokers (Centers for Disease Control and prevention [CDCP], 2000). Ninety-five percent of them report a desire to quit (Fisher, Haire-Joshu, Morgan, Rehberg, & Rost, 1990). Many smokers who indicate a desire to quit actually attempt quitting, as evidenced by the CDCP's (1993) report that 46% of adult daily smokers made a serious quit attempt (quitting for 1 day) in the previous year. These efforts are generally unsuccessful, as less than 6% of those surveyed were able to maintain abstinence for a single month (CDCP, 1993), and only 2.5% were permanently successful.

Smoking-related mortality is responsible for approximately 20% of all deaths in the United States (CDCP, 1993). Smoking is the single largest preventable cause of death in this country (CDCP, 2000). In 1990 alone, the CDCP estimates that smoking resulted in 5,048,740 years of potential life lost (2002). Quitting smoking is a matter of life and death. Thus there are few interventions behavioral clinicians can perform that will have a more meaningful impact on the lives of their patients. Indeed, clinicians are constantly seeking successful interventions for their cigarette-smoking clients. For those who have tried and failed to quit using other methods (see United States Department of Health and Human Services [USDHHS], 2000, for complete practice guidelines), rapid smoking is a powerful procedure with a well-supported track record.

The theoretical background for rapid smoking is well established. *Rapid smoking therapy* is an aversive conditioning procedure through which the pairing of gustatory cues with aversive internal consequences (e.g., nausea) is thought to produce conditioned responding. For example, after aversive conditioning patients experience increases in heart rate when exposed to the taste of cigarettes posttreatment (Zelman, Brandon, Jorenby, & Baker, 1992). This conditioned responding is thought to result in long-lasting taste aversion to cigarettes (Tiffany, Martin, & Baker, 1986).

Aversion treatment for smoking was developed in response to reported successful treatment of alcoholism (Bandura, 1969; Cautela, 1967) and sexual deviance (Feldman & MacCulloch, 1965) with aversive conditioning techniques. Wilde (1964) was the first to generalize these techniques to the treatment of smoking, using an apparatus that blew warm, smoky air into smokers' faces as they smoked. Further research eventually refined the technique to allow for the use of the cigarettes themselves as the aversive stimulus (Resnick, 1968; Lichtenstein, Harris, Birchler, Wahl, & Schmal, 1973). Other methods of aversion therapy include rapid puffing (without inhaling), smoke holding, and smoke satiation; however, these modified versions are not as effective (see Shwartz, 1987).

Initial studies of rapid smoking as a therapeutic intervention for smoking cessation were performed in the mid-1960s. Early studies reported 60–70% long-term follow-up abstinence rates when using rapid smoking techniques alone. For example, Resnick (1968) reported that instructing college students to smoke at a rate 2 to 3 times that of their normal rate for 1 week prior to a quit attempt resulted in 63% abstinence at 4 month follow-up as compared to 20% abstinence in controls.

One of the most prolific researchers into the efficacy of rapid smoking as an effective intervention for smoking cessation has been Ed Lichtenstein. Lichtenstein and colleagues performed numerous evaluations of rapid smoking in the early 1970s with extremely successful outcomes, showing 6-month follow-up abstinence rates of 60–70% (Schmal, Lichtenstein, & Harris, 1972; Lichtenstein et al., 1973; Lichtenstein & Rodrigues, 1977). As stated previously, these researchers also presented data suggesting that complicated mechanisms were not necessary to induce an aversive response to smoking. Early research using an apparatus similar to that used by Wilde (1964) showed no difference between groups treated with the smoke-blowing procedure in combination with rapid smoking and those treated solely with a rapid smoking protocol (both groups maintained 60% abstinence at 6-month follow-up). These findings provided justification for rapid smoking protocols using cigarettes as the aversive stimulus as an effective stand-alone intervention (Lichtenstein et al., 1973).

Most of the research studies that demonstrated rapid smoking's efficacy predate current standards for smoking cessation research. For example, many of these studies were small and used patients' self-report of smoking outcomes without biochemical confirmation. Later research has also demonstrated successful outcomes; for example, Hall, Sachs, Hall, and Benowitz (1984) found 50% quit rates at 2-year follow up, using biochemical verification of participant's self-reports (however, the number of participants, $N = 18$, was small).

Other, even more recent outcome studies of rapid smoking have not matched the abstinence rates of the first studies on rapid smoking (although the outcomes are similar to those of other treatments). For example, Fiore and colleagues (2000) report quit rates of 19–20% at 1-year follow-up in a meta-analysis of recent (1990s) research on rapid smoking. There could be a number of reasons for the differences in outcome, but it is important to note that these studies did not use the original methods used by Lichtenstein and colleagues. Later studies of rapid smoking have restricted or controlled the number of sessions, utilized group instead of individual treatment, added additional components, or had clients undergo rapid smoking treatment at home (Hall et al., 1984). One conclusion is that rapid smoking is most effective when conducted according to the full-scale original research protocols. Indeed, basic behavioral principles suggest that conditioning must be thoroughly accomplished for treatment effects to hold, and it is quite possible that modified protocols either fail to achieve conditioning or produce an attenuated version.

Though deviations from the original method may have resulted in less impressive outcomes, in many cases rapid smoking has been successfully combined with other techniques. In recent studies rapid smoking protocols have generally been imbedded in multicomponent programs, particularly in combination with behavioral counseling (Erickson, Tiffany, Martin, & Baker, 1983). In a study examining outcomes of varying levels of rapid smoking and coping skills training, Tiffany and colleagues (1986) found that subjects who received full-scale rapid smoking in combination with full-scale coping skills training were more likely to remain abstinent at 6-month follow-up than subjects treated with reduced variations of the two components. This study showed 6-month follow-up abstinence rates of 59% for the full-scale treatment subjects, consistent with outcomes of the original research.

Similarly, Barber (2001) found rapid smoking to be effective when used in combination with a hypnotic intervention, as 39 of 43 patients reported abstinence at 6-month and 3-year follow-up. These and other studies (Zelman et al., 1992) provide evidence for the effectiveness of rapid smoking protocols in combination with other psychosocial strategies, though again, research using the original methods used by Lichtenstein and colleagues appears to have provided the most successful outcomes. Quite recently, Stitzer and colleagues found that rapid smoking is efficacious at reducing cravings in individuals relapsing to smoking post posttreatment, although these immediate reductions in craving did not predict reductions in smoking (Houtsmuller & Stitzer, 1999). However, this study used a different population (people relapsing immediately after treatment), and again, the protocols differed substantially from those previously developed by Lichtentstein or Hall and their colleagues.

WHO MIGHT BENEFIT FROM THIS TECHNIQUE

Rapid smoking has been shown to be safe for healthy subjects, but it is also associated with some risk. Rapid smoking calls for the ingestion of large amounts of nicotine in a short period of time in order to induce mild nicotine intoxication and concomitant aversive conditioning. Rapid smoking does present the potentially fatal risk of nicotine toxicity, though research has shown the incidence to be extremely rare (see Lichtenstein, in Hauser, 1974). Nonetheless, it is essential to evaluate the health of the patient and all current medications before beginning a rapid smoking treatment. Because of the challenging nature of the protocol, rapid smoking is recommended after multiple other treatment efforts have failed. These initial treatment efforts should include front-line treatments such as cognitive behavioral therapy and nicotine replacement therapy.

CONTRAINDICATIONS

For patients on medication or with any medical issues, it is advised that rapid smoking be undertaken by a physician or under medical supervision (Hall & Hall, 1987). Rapid smoking should always be performed under the supervision of an experienced clinician and with particular emphasis on cessation of smoking before loss of consciousness or vomiting. It is important to note that the unique risk factors associated with rapid smoking therapy constitute a serious potential danger to pregnant women.

OTHER DECISIONS IN DECIDING TO USE OR NOT TO USE RAPID SMOKING

Because rapid smoking has been shown to elevate heart rate and blood pressure and to increase respiratory rate (Hall, Sachs, & Hall, 1979), there has been particular concern about the efficacy and safety of rapid smoking in patients with various cardiovascular diseases. Hall and colleagues (1984) found that rapid smoking could be safely conducted without medical monitoring in smokers with mild to moderate cardiopulmonary disease. These researchers determined that abnormal heart rate elevations during rapid smoking were less frequent than abnormal heart rate elevations during exercise or sexual intercourse, and that blood nicotine levels were well below lethal levels. While this study provides encouraging results, the authors caution that smokers with cardiovascular disease should consult a physician when engaging in rapid smoking therapy if they are taking certain medications (including beta blockers, digoxin, or diuretics), if they have congestive heart failure, if they have an artificial pacemaker, if they have difficulty breathing while performing daily activities and while sleeping, and if they wheeze when breathing. According to Hall and Hall (1987):

> Cautious therapists may not wish to carry out rapid smoking on patients with cardiopulmonary disease unless the therapist is in a medical setting. The probability of a recurrent myocardial infarction in this population is greater no matter what the patient's activity. If enough patients with cardiac disease underwent rapid smoking, by chance alone a small percentage would have a heart attack during treatment. (Sachs, Hall, Pechack, & Fitzgerald, 1979, p. 311)

A physician should evaluate any patient presenting with one or more risk factors for serious cardiovascular disease before engaging in rapid smoking therapy.

HOW DOES THE TECHNIQUE WORK?

As mentioned previously, aversive cessation techniques rely on basic associative conditioning: Replace the pleasurable associations of smoking with overwhelmingly negative associations. The success of this procedure therefore depends on the perceived noxiousness of the experience. These negative sensations must be maintained at high levels within and across multiple sessions. Both provider and patient need to be highly motivated and explicitly willing to tolerate an unpleasant and possibly distressing experience (empathically uncomfortable and distressing in the case of the provider). As in any smoking treatment, a strong relationship with the client enhances the likelihood of completing treatment.

Providing the patient with a rationale and a detailed description of possible and expected symptoms is extremely important in rapid smoking procedures. An accurate description of the aversiveness of the procedure is required both for informed consent, and because the patient's full attention on the noxious symptoms is required for conditioning. Rapid smoking is highly effective if, and only if, conditioning is accomplished. Patients should be informed that they will experience notable discomfort that may include nausea, lightheadedness, burning throat or eyes, tingling of the extremities, and headache. They should be warned that vomiting and fainting are possible, though they should stop smoking before these occur. The most difficult hurdle in rapid smoking is completing treatment. This should be discussed openly with the patient, and strategies to facilitate adherence (i.e., what are the possible barriers and how would they solve them?) should be incorporated into the treatment plan.

Along with the rapid smoking procedure, cognitive behavioral or supportive counseling (or both) for smoking cessation is recommended. At minimum, the following steps should occur. First, patients should discuss their upcoming quit attempt with the people in their lives and attempt to elicit support. Their quit date is the first day of rapid smoking. Failing success in eliciting active support, the clients should attempt to elicit agreement not to smoke in the house or in their presence, and not to offer them cigarettes. Second,

patients should be informed that drinking alcohol is highly linked to relapse, and cessation from alcohol is strongly recommended. Third, additional individualized risk factors should be discussed in detail: Where does the patient smoke now? When? Which situations are triggers? Which feelings? Strategies for coping with these high-risk feelings and situations should be discussed, and patients should be encouraged to (1) alter the triggers (e.g., cleaning out and putting candy in the ashtray in the car, not keeping cigarettes anywhere in the house, throwing away all their ashtrays, etc.), (2) develop coping strategies for when these situations are not avoidable (e.g., relaxation exercises, breathing, distraction, thinking about their grandchildren, etc.), and (3) escape from high-risk situations whenever possible (see Antonuccio, 1993, for a useful patient handbook and description). A minimum of two to three sessions should occur before the intensive rapid smoking protocol is implemented.

STEP-BY-STEP PROCEDURES

The following protocol comes from Hall and Hall (1987). After the therapist has fully informed the patient, developed the plan, established a high level of rapport, and provided initial support or coping skills training, the rapid smoking phase of treatment begins. Rapid smoking requires some preparation, including recording a looped tape with 6-s cues for inhaling and developing a checklist of negative symptoms for the patient to fill out during rest sessions. An emesis basin should also be present, both in case of vomiting and as a prop to enhance the suggestion of aversive levels of nausea (R. Hall, personal communication, May, 2002). Patients should bring one pack of cigarettes and matches, after having removed all other cigarettes from their home environments.

The setting in which the procedure will take place is important. Because the aversive sensations must be fully experienced, patients should be explicitly discouraged from using distraction (some patients can distract so successfully that they do not experience the rapid smoking as aversive; R. Hall, personal communication, May, 2002). The setting should provide as few distracting stimuli as possible. It is preferable to perform the procedure indoors in a closed and uninteresting room, with patients facing a blank wall. Even where public health regulations refuse to allow patients to smoke indoors, outdoor settings should be arranged to offer as little distraction as possible (e.g., in a loading-area doorway facing the cement wall).

As rapid smoking commences, patients are instructed to inhale the smoke from their regular brand of cigarette every 6 s until they feel unable to continue. They should be encouraged to continue to the point that they feel they are about to vomit or become severely light-headed. While they are rapid smoking, the practitioner should regularly encourage them to concentrate on the aversive symptoms they are experiencing as a result of smoking. Once they reach the point that they can no longer tolerate another inhalation, they are permitted to rest briefly (approximately 5 min), during which time they should fill out the sheet detailing their aversive symptoms. This serves as another means of maintaining focus on the unpleasant symptoms, as well as a way for the clinician to monitor their experience. Even during the rest period, the therapist should continue to point out the relationship between these symptoms and smoking. After the rest period, the patient should resume on the same schedule of one puff per 6 s. A minimum of two trials must occur during each session and more are advisable if patients can tolerate them. At the end of the final trial, they should report experiencing maximum levels of unpleasantness (i.e., a 10 on a 10-point scale).

After their final rest, they should be asked to sit and close their eyes and recall the unpleasant aspects of the experience they just went through. While recalling the sensations they should attempt to focus on amplifying and intensifying the negative experience and feelings. After they return home, if they experience the urge to smoke they should be encouraged to recall the aversive experiences as much as possible in order to help them resist the urges.[1]

According to Hall and Hall (1987), patients must agree not to smoke between sessions. Although they will not want to smoke immediately after the first session, cravings will probably return after the first session and patients should be told to expect this. The sessions should be spaced as closely as possible on an intensive schedule. For example, if beginning on a Monday, sessions should continue on Tuesday, Wednesday, Friday, and the following Monday. After the first five meetings patients may select the intervals between sessions; these intervals should be based on the amount of time they feel confident they can remain quit. Most studies have limited the number of sessions to 12 for no scientific reason, though it is unusual for patients to want to continue to participate for this long.

CONCLUSION

Rapid smoking is a powerful treatment for smoking cessation, perhaps the most powerful psychosocial treatment currently available. A recent meta-analysis evaluating psychosocial treatments identified that odds ratios and quit rates were higher for rapid smoking than for any other treatment: 2.0 (1.1, 3.5) and 19.9 (11.2, 29.0), respectively (USDHHS, 2000). Nonetheless, in recent years it has been infrequently practiced (USDHHS). This is probably due to the fact that, by definition, rapid smoking is an aversive procedure for both patients and practitioners. If the treatment is to be successful, the conditioning experience must be difficult.

The counterpoint to the difficulty of the protocol is the urgency of the need for powerful smoking-cessation treatments. The truth about the current state of smoking treatment is that the best we have to offer is usually not enough. Smoking is a life or death matter for those who will acquire cancer of the lung, kidney, pancreas, larynx, or cervix; chronic lung and heart disease; or pneumonia; and for the children of smoking mothers. For those who have repeatedly tried and failed to quit smoking, rapid smoking may be their best last chance.

---

1. Please note that R. Hall recommends that patients refrain from driving themselves home after a session, as some have reported feeling "foggy" afterward (Hall & Hall, 1987, p. 312).

Further Reading

Hall, S. M., & Hall, R. G. (1987). Treatment of cigarette smoking. In J. A. Blumenthal & D.C. McKee (Eds.), *Applications in behavioral medicine and health psychology: A clinician's source book* (pp. 301–323). Sarasota FL: Professional Resource Exchange.

Fiore, M. C., Bailey, W. C., Cohen, S. J., Dorfman, S. F., Goldstein, M. G., Gritz, E. R., Heyman, R. B., Roberto Jaen, C., Kottke, T. E., Lando, H. A., Mecklenburg, R. E., Dolan Mullen, P., Nett, L. M., Robinson, L., Stitzer, M. L., Tommasello, A. C., Villejo, L., Wevers, M. E., Baker, T., Fox, B. J., & Hasselblad, V. (2000). *Treating tobacco use and dependence: Clinical practice guideline.* Public Health Service. Rockville, MD: U.S. Department of Health and Human Services.

References

Antonuccio, D.O. (1993). *Butt out, the smoker's book: A compassionate guide to helping yourself quit smoking, with or without a partner.* Saratoga, CA: R & E Publishers.

Bandura, A. (1969). *Principles of behavior modification.* New York: Holt, Rinehart, & Winston.

Barber, J. (2001). Freedom from smoking: Integrating hypnotic methods and rapid smoking to facilitate smoking cessation. *The International Journal of Clinical and Experimental Hypnosis, 49*(3), 257–265.

Cautela, J. R. (1967). Covert sensitization. *Psychological Record, 20,* 459–468.

Centers for Disease Control and Prevention. (1993). Cigarette smoking–attributable mortality and years of potential life lost: United States, 1990. *Morbidity and Mortality Weekly Report, 45,* 588–590.

Centers for Disease Control and Prevention. (2000). State-specific prevalence of current cigarette smoking among adults and the proportion of adults who work in a smoke-free environment: United States, 1999. *Morbidity and Mortality Weekly Report, 49*(43);978–982.

Center for Disease Control and Prevention. (2002). MMWR: Cigarette smoking–attributable mortality and years of potential life lost: United States, 1990. *Morbidity Mortality Weekly Report,48*(43), 993–996.

Erickson, L. M., Tiffany, S. T., Martin, E. M., & Baker, T. B. (1983). Aversive smoking therapies: A conditioning analysis of therapeutic effectiveness. *Behavior Research and Therapy, 21,* 595–611.

Feldman, M. P., & MacCulloch, M. J. (1965). The application of anticipatory avoidance learning to the treatment of homosexuality: I. Theory, techniques, and preliminary results. *Behavior Research and Therapy, 2,* 165–183.

Fiore, M. C., Bailey, W. C., Cohen, S. J., Dorfman, S. F., Goldstein, M. G., Gritz, E. R., Heyman, R. B., Roberto Jaen, C., Kottke, T. E., Lando, H. A., Mecklenburg, R. E., Dolan Mullen, P., Nett, L. M., Robinson, L., Stitzer, M. L., Tommasello, A. C., Villejo, L., Wevers, M. E., Baker, T., Fox, B. J., & Hasselblad, V. (2000). *Treating tobacco use and dependence: Clinical practice guideline.* Public Health Service. Rockville, MD: U.S. Department of Health and Human Services.

Fisher, E. B., Haire-Joshu, D., Morgan, G. D., Rehberg, H., & Rost, K. (1990). Smoking and smoking cessation. *American Review of Respiratory Disorders, 142,* 702–720.

Hall, S. M., & Hall, R. G. (1987). Treatment of cigarette smoking. In J. A. Blumenthal & D.C. McKee (Eds.), *Applications in behavioral medicine and health psychology: A clinician's source book* (pp. 301–323). Sarasota FL: Professional Resource Exchange.

Hall, R. G., Sachs, D. P. L., & Hall, S. M. (1979). Medical risk and therapeutic effectiveness of rapid smoking. *Behavior Therapy, 10,* 249–259.

Hall, R. G., Sachs, D. P., Hall, S. M., & Benowitz, N. L. (1984). Two-year efficacy and safety of rapid smoking therapy in patients with cardiac and pulmonary disease. *Journal of Consulting and Clinical Psychology, 52*(4), 574–581.

Hauser, R. (1974). Rapid smoking as a technique of behavior modification: Caution in selection of subjects. *Journal of Consulting and Clinical Psychology, 42,* 625–626.

Houtsmuller, E. J., & Stitzer, M. L. (1999). Manipulation of cigarette smoking through rapid smoking: Efficacy and effects on smoking behavior. *Psychopharmacology, 142,* 149–157.

Lichtenstein, E., Harris, D. E., Birchler, G. R., Wahl J. M., & Schmahl, D. P. (1973). Comparison of rapid smoking, warm, smoky air, and attention placebo in the modification of smoking behavior. *Journal of Consulting and Clinical Psychology, 40,* 92–98.

Lichtenstein, E., & Rodrigues, M. P. (1977). Long-term effects of rapid smoking treatment for dependent smokers. *Addictive Behaviors, 2,* 109–112.

Resnick, J. H. (1968). Effects of stimulus satiation on the overlearned maladaptive response of cigarette smoking. *Journal of Consulting and Clinical Psychology, 32,* 500–505.

Sachs, D. P., Hall, R. G., Pechacek, T. F., & Fitzgerald, J. (1979). Classification of risk-benefit issues in rapid smoking. *Journal of Consulting and Clinical Psychology, 47*(6), 1053–1060.

Schmal, D. P., Lichtenstein, E., & Harris, D. E. (1972). Successful treatment of habitual smokers with warm, smoky air and rapid smoking. *Journal of Consulting and Clinical Psychology, 38,* 105–111.

Shwartz, Jerome L. 1987. *Review and evaluation of smoking cessation methods: The United States and Canada, 1978–1985.* National Cancer Institute: U. S. Department of Health and Human Services, Public Health Service, National Institutes of Health, 1987. NIH Publication No. 87–2940.

Tiffany, S.T., Martin, E. M., & Baker, T. B. (1986). Treatments for cigarette smoking: An evaluation of the contributions of aversion and counseling procedures. *Behavior Research and Therapy, 24*(4), 437–452.

U.S. Department of Health and Human Services (2000). Reducing tobacco use: A report of the Surgeon General (Rep. No. 29). Atlanta, GA: Author.

Wilde, G. J. S. (1964). Behavior therapy for addicted cigarette smokers. *Behavior Research and Therapy, 2,* 107–110.

Zelman, D. C., Brandon, T. H., Jorenby, D. E., & Baker, T. B. (1992). Measures of affect and nicotine dependence predict differential response to smoking cessation treatments. *Journal of Consulting and Clinical Psychology, 60*(6), 943–952.

48 RELAPSE PREVENTION

Kirk A. Brunswig, Tamara Penix Sbraga, and Cathi D. Harris

Relapse prevention (RP) is a varied program of cognitive-behavioral techniques that evolved as a calculated response to the longer term treatment failures of other therapies. It was conceived not as an alternative to those interventions, but as a supplemental tool that would make a variety of treatments, particularly for addictive behaviors, more effective. Relapse prevention is aimed at enabling clients to readily recall and utilize core treatment information when it is needed following the termination of formal treatment.

Relapse prevention was not originally concerned with all of the phases of treatment. It did not address the precontemplation, contemplation, preparation, and action stages of intervention, but instead focused on the maintenance phase of treatment. Relapse prevention was originally conceived as an answer to the problem of maintaining initial gains when treatment sessions are discontinued. Arguably, this is the most difficult challenge for any client. Without the structure and accountability of therapy and the support of a therapist or group, treatment gains are likely to wane over time. Relapse prevention provides a strategy to meet the challenge of not engaging in old behaviors.

WHO MIGHT BENEFIT

In the short period of time since its introduction, RP has evolved in numerous directions. In many venues, it is used as it was originally designed, as a booster treatment. However, its scope has expanded. It is no longer viewed as solely a supplemental intervention strategy, but is now being applied and utilized as a full program of treatment in areas such as risky sexual behaviors, overeating, and sexual offending. Relapse prevention is also emerging as a bona fide theory of compulsive habit patterns and the processes of relapse. It has been applied for a variety of treatment targets, typically for problems often viewed as issues of self-control, such as alcohol abuse, nicotine use, eating-related difficulties (overeating, self-restriction), and undercontrolled sexuality (e.g., sexual offending, sexual "addiction," and sexual harassment). Thus, for clients with problems in these domains, RP may be a beneficial intervention. Furthermore, RP will likely be the treatment of choice for clients presenting with problems of sexual misbehavior (e.g., sexual harassment and sexual offending, risky sexual behavior). It will also likely be the preferred treatment for clients presenting with "habit" or "self-control" problems (e.g., substance abuse) and, in addition, it continues to be a maintenance program for a variety of other interventions, including cognitive behavior therapy (CBT) for depression, anxiety, and substance abuse.

INDICATIONS AND CONTRAINDICATIONS

Relapse prevention should not be used in areas in which there is little empirical support for its utility (unless of course, as part of a research effort), or in areas in which there may be an existing treatment with empirical support. For example, while RP may serve as a useful booster for Obsessive-Compulsive Disorder, exposure and response prevention should be the primary interventions. Likewise, teaching avoidance strategies might be contraindicated for other anxiety disorders, such as Agoraphobia. For these problems, the clients typically already have a "relapse prevention" plan in place for the avoidance, management, and escape from feared stimuli or situations. However—and this point highlights some of the confusing aspects of RP—in terms of avoidance-based maladaptive coping, there may be utility in applying an RP analysis of cues, triggers, cognitive distortions, and high-risk situations to inform exposure-based interventions (e.g., family conflict as a cue that leads to a high-risk situation of isolation for the agoraphobic client).

Other Factors to Consider

Relapse prevention should also be avoided when the client's ability to recall historical data or to verbally process new information is impaired (e.g., in cases of mental retardation or developmental delay, organic injury, etc.), due to RP's reliance on verbal processing. There may be other media through which RP instruction could occur, although the effectiveness of alternative approaches has not been thoroughly evaluated. While significant numbers of developmentally delayed sex offenders are receiving treatment, RP is often a small element in a comprehensive treatment program (compare Haaven & Coleman in Laws, Hudson, & Ward, 2000).

THEORETICAL BASES

Alan Marlatt and Judith Gordon developed RP as a response to their concerns over the steadily plummeting survival of treatment gains once clients discontinued treatment if no further intervention was implemented. Their observations revealed that treatment, with all of its costs and benefits, was attenuated over time. Clients who responded to a variety of treatments for addictive behaviors could expect to reach abstinence, only to probabilistically lose control of the target behaviors again following the cessation of treatment. Thus, the primary assumption of RP evolved—it is problematic to expect the effects of a treatment that is designed to moderate or eliminate an undesirable behavior to endure beyond the termination of treatment for a number of reasons. Treatments typically involve an intense but limited period of time during which clients are brought into contact with new influences or experiences, information, and contextual components that aid in creating changes in their behaviors. In addition, therapy includes accountability and a regular dose of treatment that is given reliably over a period of time. The interaction between consistency and dose changes over the course of treatment and into aftercare. Once accountability and dose elements are significantly reduced or removed after the client has reached treatment goals and treatment is terminated, the client must learn to implement the skills and knowledge learned in a new context in an old context with little or no assistance. In fact, clients often enter environments in which their demonstration of treatment gains may be punished. Generalizing the skills to varied situations poses a significant challenge, and many treatment failures are the result.

There are reasons to presume that once treatment is discontinued a problem will reemerge as time passes. Factors such as returning to an old environment that elicited and previously maintained the problem behavior; forgetting the skills, techniques, and information taught during therapy; and a decrease in motivation may all lead to a return to pretreatment levels of the problem behavior. In 1995 Laws wrote of findings supporting this presumption. Hunt, Barnett, and Branch

(1971) found that within one year of ending treatment more than 80% of clients would resume the undesired behavior (treatment failure), and that two-thirds of these relapses would occur in the first 3 months. These and similar findings supported Marlatt's conclusion that a supplemental treatment was needed specifically for the maintenance of the gains that were acquired during the original treatment period. The original treatments were effective, but were not lasting. Marlatt sought to increase their longevity.

Marlatt and colleagues believed that treatment failures could be analyzed in order to discover internal and external variables that increased risk for relapse. They further reasoned that by knowing items such as situational factors, mood states, and cognitions, therapists could identify and target individualized risk factors for ongoing attention. The RP model proposes that at the conclusion of treatment a client feels self-efficacious about eliminating the unwanted behavior, and that this perception of self-efficacy stems from learned and practiced skills. Over time the client contacts internal and external risk factors or high-risk situations that threaten the client's self-control, and consequently his or her perception of self-efficacy. If the client has adaptive coping skills to adequately address the internal and external challenges to control, the client will not relapse. However, if his or her skills are not sufficient to meet the challenge, a lapse or relapse may occur (this will be described in greater detail later). In response to a resumption of the target behavior at some level, the client either increases attempts to implement adaptive coping skills or fails to cope effectively and engages in the undesirable behavior because it provides immediate gratification. Marlatt's supposition that the targets of intervention are cognitions and behaviors that are collectively referred to as *coping skills* is embedded within this framework. Marlatt and colleagues' treatment therefore employs cognitive-behavioral techniques to improve the retention, accessibility, and implementation of adaptive coping responses following the termination of treatment.

TREATMENT COMPONENTS

Laws (1995) outlined the principle components that serve as the foundation of RP. They are as follows:

- Identification of a maladaptive behavior
- A process of change defined by commitment and motivation
- Behavioral change and maintenance of behavior change
- Identification of *lapses* (single instances of the maladaptive behavior) and *relapses* (complete violation of the self-imposed abstinence rules) or a return to pretreatment behavior
- Lifestyle balance between obligatory and self-selected behaviors
- Recognition of the ideographic aspects of the maladaptive behavior
- Recognizing and planning behavioral responses for high-risk situations

In practice, RP identifies pathways to high-risk situations and how to cope effectively with pathway elements and high-risk situations in order to prevent or stop the unwanted target behavior. The goals of identification and effective coping are met through predicting and anticipating high-risk situations; identifying and challenging cognitive distortions, seemingly irrelevant decisions, and the abstinence-violation effect; and combating the problem of immediate gratification through contingency management. Therapists using RP as a model in which a full treatment program is embedded also include skills training components, such as social skills and coping skills. It is hypothesized that clients may not have learned the requisite skills to cope effectively in a given situation; therefore skills training often supplements RP. For other problems, functional assessment may indicate other skill deficits or behavioral excesses that work to maintain the maladaptive coping response that is the target of RP. Adjunctive treatment techniques are often employed within an RP framework to address these needs.

PROCEDURES

When implementing relapse prevention the client is first assisted in identifying his or her high-risk situations and the thoughts, feelings, and behaviors that give rise to each one. In the RP model, the problem behavior is seen as one element of a pattern (behavioral chain or maladaptive life cycle) in which an often distal trigger or cue sets a chain of internal and external behaviors in motion. Cognitive distortions, seemingly irrelevant decisions, the problem of immediate gratification, and the abstinence violation effect work to "speed the client along" toward a high-risk situation. Such situations are determined by an analysis of past displays of the undesirable behavior and accounts of tempting situations.

In addition to identifying the high-risk elements of the behavior chain, the client is assisted in employing appropriate self-control responses (interventions), which were acquired through treatment. These interventions can be implemented at any point in the behavior chain, ideally before the client reaches a high-risk situation at the end of the chain. Appropriate self-control responses are those behaviors that lead to avoidance of, management in, escape from, and debriefing after facing a high-risk situation. Typically, the client will prepare these avoid-escape-control responses in anticipation of contacting the fairly inevitable high-risk situation. For example, if a sexual offender finds himself fantasizing about a young child, he may, through treatment, learn to avoid triggers that lead to those thoughts, to "urge surf" during the fantasy (see Chapter 67, this volume), to distract himself to interrupt (escape from) the deviant fantasy, and then to journal about the event to perhaps modify his response strategies for the future.

Identifying High-Risk Situations

This component involves the ideographic assessment of high-risk situations. The client and clinician work together to identify the situations in which the client has previously engaged in problematic behavior and those situations in which the client is likely to engage in problematic behavior in the future. One technique often used requires the client to describe the thoughts, feelings, and behaviors that occurred before, during, and after each relevant instance of the undesired behavior. This data set can then be used to discern repeated elements that can be identified as precursors of high-risk situations and reinforcers of losses of control. The client will be asked to generate a list of situations that are low-risk, and what aspects of those situations differentiate them from high-risk situations. The treatment focus is to train clients to recognize themes and commonalties in their high-risk situations so that they can generalize the ability to assess level of risk in novel situations. The therapist works with clients to ensure that they are realistic in their assessment of the level of risk in a variety of hypothetical situations.

Identifying Cognitive Distortions

Another component of RP is the identification and challenging of *cognitive distortions*—self-statements that operate as permission-givers for engaging in offensive behaviors, and that function to bring the client from trigger or cue to a high-risk situation. Clients typically view these statements as both accurate representations of the world and adequate justifications for engaging in the unwanted behavior. Examples of cognitive distortions can be seen in Steen's (2001) *The Adult Relapse Prevention Workbook*, as well as the Brunswig and O'Donohue (2002) *Relapse Prevention for Sexual Harassers*. Some common cognitive distortions are victim blaming, entitlement, minimizing, rationalizing, projection, magnification, victim stance, catastrophizing, overgeneralizing, all-or-nothing, negative bias, positive bias, and personalization. Jenkins-Hall (1989; in Laws, 1989) describes the steps for changing cognitive distortions as (1) identifying the thoughts that lead to maladaptive behavior, (2) analyzing the validity and utility of the thoughts, and (3) using an intervention designed to change the cognitive distortions into more adaptive cognitions. The therapist first assists the client in developing alternative interpretations for his or her initial thoughts. The client is then asked to evaluate whether the past thinking made it easier to commit the problematic behavior and begins to develop skills to analyze the logic behind certain types of thinking. Finally, the client is assisted in disputing and challenging his or her thoughts in therapy and generalizing these skills to the natural environment. With respect to RP, clients are assisted in examining how cognitive distortions affect the prevention of relapses and are aided in challenging their thinking as it relates to the above elements of RP. Some of these distortions function similarly for many clients and are described next. Table 48.1 outlines points to consider in the various steps of relapse prevention.

Seemingly Irrelevant Decisions

Seemingly irrelevant decisions (SIDs; also called *seemingly unimportant decisions,* or SUDs) are those behaviors that might not lead directly to high-risk situations but are early in the chain of decisions that place the client in those situations. For example, if the client reports being more likely to engage in the problematic behavior after drinking, a SID would be agreeing to attend a luncheon with a coworker who is known to drink alcohol heavily at lunch. Lunching with the coworker is not the high-risk situation. However, the introduction of alcohol is likely to increase the individual's potential for getting into a high-risk situation.

In addressing SIDs, the therapist works with the client to determine the types of decisions that lead to high-risk situations. Once the client can identify many potential SIDs, he or she learns and practices effective coping strategies or interventions. The therapist works with the client to ensure that the generated solutions and skills are adequate and appropriate. In addition, therapists may also role-play situations with the client to allow the client a chance to practice the intervention skills in a hypothetical high-risk situation.

Problem of Immediate Gratification

In the problem of immediate gratification, or PIG, individuals acting in such a way as to receive immediate positive consequences will often suffer larger, more aversive consequences at a later date. However, there is a disconnect between pursuing the immediate positive reinforcement and considering future negative consequences of doing so. Sexual offenders offer a good example. Many will often offend against a victim to immediately gratify or reduce negative feelings or experiences with little thought for the long-term consequences of such behavior. Offending, or the problematic behavior, is a quick fix to feeling better.

Psychoeducational approaches that teach the client how to create a *decision matrix* are often employed to combat the PIG. This approach is similar to pros and cons, seen in motivational interviewing, among others. The therapist assists the client in developing the matrix, which is a concise, written representation of the positive and negative outcomes for engaging or not engaging in the problematic behavior (c.f. Brunswig & O'Donohue, 2002), and then in assigning probabilities (0.0 to 1.0) that each outcome will actually occur. This is done in both an immediate and a short-term frame of reference. The therapist challenges any unrealistic or improbable outcomes until the client is able to generate more realistic ones. The therapist then directs the client to analyze past situations in which he or she engaged in the problematic behavior, and to compare the immediate gratifications against the long-term consequences. Clients are then encouraged to utilize this decision matrix when encountering novel situations. Many sessions may be dedicated to role-playing situations to habituate this process. Moreover, many clients carry a small version of the decision matrix with them to have it available in case they contact a high-risk situation and freeze.

Abstinence Violation Effect

The abstinence violation effect (AVE) occurs when a client fails to cope effectively in a high-risk situation, lapses, and then views the lapse as so severe that he or she may as well fully *re*lapse. The reasoning recognizes a small failure, focuses on it as evidence that behavioral control is not possible, and indulges the desire for the immediate positive reinforcement that comes with enacting the problem behavior. For example, the overeater may have an AVE when thinking, "One slice of cheesecake is a lapse, so I may as well go all-out and have the rest of the cheesecake." The individual's belief is that, having violated the rule of abstinence, he or she may as well get the most out of the lapse, resulting in relapse.

Treatment here involves describing and predicting the AVE and working with the client to learn alternative coping skills to use when a lapse occurs, such that the client is more confident in responding appropriately to lapses on any point in the behavior chain. This also affords an opportu-

TABLE 48.1   Major Components in Relapse Prevention

	Major Task	Summary of Important Points
Step 1	Identification of lapses and relapses	• *Lapses* are occurrences of the problem behavior in the context of a behavior reduction or elimination plan (e.g., the smoking of a cigarette for the tobacco-cessation client).
		• *Relapse* is the return to baseline or pretreatment levels of the occurrence of the problem behavior (e.g., returning to a pack-a-day habit for the tobacco-cessation client).
		• The "acceptability" of lapses and relapses is dependent upon the behavior (e.g., sexual offenders may have more consequences for a relapse than the smoker).
		• This relative "acceptability" requires an idiographic assessment of the client's problem behavior—what it is, what it looks like, how it works for the client (functional assessment), and how the client and support group will recognize it as it happens.
		• There is no set limit to the time required for this or other intervention tasks described later. This aspect of RP is one of the features that make a somewhat nebulous amalgam of techniques difficult to encapsulate as a uniform intervention.
Step 2	Identification of high-risk situations	• Analyze all relevant previous occurrences of the problem behavior in terms of thoughts, feelings, and behaviors—before (triggers), during, and after these occurrences. This can be done by constructing a 3 × 3 grid, with the demonstration of the problem behavior being the cell of behavior-during.
		• Look for similarities across affect, cognitions, and behaviors that tend to co-occur reliably with the problem behavior.
		• For example, a common emotion that occurs before an act of sexual offending is *feeling discounted*—for that client, any situation in which he has felt or would be likely to feel discounted would be considered a high-risk situation.
		• High-risk situations can be *internal* (affect, cognitions), *external* (victim types, locations), or *interactive* (given certain internal conditions, external conditions may make an occurrence of the problem behavior more likely).
		• Work with the client to identify and monitor the before-during-after of any high-risk situation encountered while in treatment to assist in generalization for aftercare.
		• Develop a *dynamic problem-chain*, the chain of behaviors that probabilistically lead to lapse or relapse (e.g., asking what emotional and cognitive settings or events set up what decisions and behaviors that place the client in a situation in which he or she is likely to lapse or relapse).
		• *Interventions* focus on the avoidance of, management in, escape from, and debriefing after high-risk situations.
Step 3	Identify and track disinhibitors (cognitive distortions, SIDs, the AVE, and the PIG)	• Identify the relevant cognitive distortions and SIDs with your client.
		• Homework: Assign the client the task of monitoring the occurrences of the cognitive distortions and SIDs encountered on a daily basis.
		• Use techniques such as analyzing the validity and utility of the thoughts, developing alternative interpretations, directing the client to dispute and challenge his or her own thoughts, and other similar Rational Emotive Behavior Therapy, CBT, and cognitive therapy techniques.
		• Address the PIG through decision matrices and decisional balances.
		• Discuss the AVE, since a peril predicted can be addressed more thoughtfully than an unanticipated peril.
Step 4	Plan alternative behaviors	• Build upon the self-monitoring effect by having clients keep track of their occurrences of SIDs, cognitive distortions, high-risk situations, lapses, and AVE.
		• Use psychoeducation to instruct or enhance alternative behaviors that may meet the intended function of the problem behavior (e.g., for the social-skills-deficient sexual harasser who uses inappropriate verbal behavior to enlist social attention, provide instruction and practice on prosocial conversation skills).

continued

TABLE 48.1 *Continued*

Major Task	Summary of Important Points
	• Use psychoeducation to instruct or enhance distress tolerance skills for "hanging in there" when the client is presented with a desire to engage in the problem behavior or to reduce the aversive qualities of the withdrawal symptoms for not engaging in the problem behavior.
	• Use psychoeducation to instruct or enhance interventions for each intermediary step in the behavioral chains described previously. For example, work with the client to have practical and useful interventions for triggers, SIDs, and cognitive distortions, and for the avoidance of, management in (distress tolerance), escape from, and debriefing of high-risk situations. Interventions can occur at any point in the behavioral chain.
	• The creation of a *relapse prevention plan* is a dynamic and iterative process in which the triggers, distortions, high-risk situations, and interventions are planned for, documented, and debriefed on after their occurrence. While some clients have often presented voluminous plans (one has even presented his in a collection of three-ring binders!) the plan that can accompany clients everywhere they go will often be more likely to be used.

nity for the client to anticipate the AVE and include interventions for that AVE as a part of the relapse prevention plan. This is done through practice sessions in which the client and therapist identify lapse situations and practice the implementation of intervention skills. It must be emphasized to the client that lapses are to be expected and can be handled if planned for in advance. Clients who recognize that lapses are normal and expected are less likely to use a minor instance of the behavior as a rationale to relapse.

Planning for Lapses and Utilizing a Support Group

As indicated earlier, clients should be informed that lapses are to be expected and can be handled when they are anticipated. To plan for lapses the client should know how he or she would handle and intervene in situations in which the client feels at risk for engaging in the problematic behavior. This is referred to as the development of a *relapse prevention plan*. The client will need to have a plan that outlines strategies for avoiding, managing, escaping, and debriefing high-risk situations; for recognizing and intervening in cognitive distortions, SIDs/SUDs, the PIG, and the AVE; for seeking help from an identified support group should the need arise after therapy; and for modifying the relapse prevention plan based on feedback and on the successes and failures of the plan. One way to do this is for the client to learn and practice all of the requisite skills beforehand and continually review and update

the relapse prevention plan. In addition, the client can be assisted in developing cue cards, which can be used to refresh and prompt the client on his or her relapse prevention strategies as needed.

Maintenance and Aftercare

Eventually there is a gradual reduction of the role of therapy and therapist in the client's life. To enhance the gains made in therapy, as well as to assist the client in the implementation of his or her relapse prevention plan, sessions are often faded from bi-weekly to monthly and then to bi-monthly in order to provide the client time and opportunity to generalize new skills with support, accountability, and assistance in revising the relapse prevention plan if necessary. Because many of the problems addressed with RP are enduring behavior problems, practitioners employing RP typically inform each client that he or she will struggle with the problem for life and will likely never be "cured." To combat this and assist in the maintenance of problem-free behavior, sessions may continue annually for years. The purpose of these sessions is to act as boosters to the primary therapy and to assist the client in updating and reviewing the relapse prevention plan with the knowledge gained through experience. New triggers for old behaviors inevitably appear. Constant revision keeps the relapse prevention plan fresh and useful.

As with any therapeutic intervention, therapists are obligated to design a plan for aftercare. Relapse prevention is no exception. While the goal of RP is the prevention of the occurrence of problematic behavior, the client's lifestyle must also be addressed for the most effective process of change. The RP model speculates that lifestyle imbalance—that is, a lack of balance between positive and negative activities—is a major contributor to succumbing to potential losses of control. Therefore, the development of positive addictions or positive alternative behaviors is also emphasized. Positive alternatives are healthy behaviors and hobbies (e.g., reading, bowling, fly fishing) in which the client can engage without experiencing adverse consequences. It is crucial that the therapist work to avoid recommending previously paired triggers and positive alternatives (e.g., bowling, for the smoker who smoked while bowling) as those alternatives may work as conditioned triggers for the problem behavior. Prior to the fading of sessions, the therapist assists the client in identifying and getting involved in enjoyable alternative activities that support the developed relapse prevention plan.

CONCLUSION

Relapse prevention, summarized in Figure 48.1, was designed as an elegant booster shot. It was not intended to be a stand-alone treatment for any of the problems for which it has been used. There seems to be some recognition in the fields in which it is used that alone, it is not an adequate treatment. It does not naturally address change; it addresses the maintenance of change. Relapse prevention is consequently supplemented by other cognitive and behavioral techniques that are hypothetically linked to, or have demonstrated efficacy in, treating the problem behavior (e.g., see chapter 31, "Harm Reduction," in this volume). Therefore, each incarnation of the approach is different and as a result, an RP program is often difficult to identify by its techniques. We have presented the stripped-down model, which is unlikely to be encountered. However, it is important to recognize these core elements, particularly as efforts turn to empirically validating the use of RP for its variety of purposes. Com-

- Relapse prevention (RP) is a variety of cognitive-behavioral techniques designed to maintain the longevity of addiction and self-control treatment gains.
- Relapse prevention involves identifying the thoughts, feelings, and behaviors that lead to high-risk situations and coping effectively with them in order to prevent or stop a loss of self-control.
- Identifying and managing high-risk situations, cognitive distortions, seemingly irrelevant decisions (SIDs), the problem of immediate gratification (PIG), the abstinence violation effect (AVE_, and lifestyle imbalances are core points of intervention.
- Relapse prevention necessitates learning, practicing, and implementing difficult control skills throughout a lifetime. An evolving relapse prevention plan supports the generalizability of these efforts over time and changing contexts.

FIGURE 48.1 Major Elements of Relapse Prevention (RP)

parison of treatment programs that are identified as RP programs, but which include many different elements, almost ensures the obfuscation of its effectiveness in treating problems of self-control.

Further Reading

Brunswig, K. A., & O'Donohue, W. (2002). *Relapse prevention for sexual harassers*. New York: Kluwer Academic/Plenum Publishers.

Laws, D. R. (Ed.). (1989). *Relapse prevention with sex offenders*. New York: Guilford Press.

Laws, D. R., Hudson, S. M., & Ward, T. (Eds.). (2000). *Remaking relapse prevention with sex offenders: A sourcebook*. Thousand Oaks, CA: Sage.

Marlatt, G. A., & Gordon, J. R. (Eds.). (1985). *Relapse prevention*. New York: Guilford Press.

References

Brunswig, K. A., & O'Donohue, W. (2002). *Relapse prevention for sexual harassers*. New York: Kluwer Academic/Plenum Publishers.

Hunt, W. A., Barnett, L. W., & Branch, L. G. (1971). Relapse rates in addiction programs. *Journal of Clinical Psychology, 27*, 455–456.

Jenkins-Hall, K. A. (1989). The decision matrix. In D. R. Laws (Ed.), *Relapse prevention with sex offenders* (pp. 159–166). New York: Guilford Press.

Laws, D. R. (Ed.). (1989). *Relapse prevention with sex offenders*. New York: Guilford Press.

Laws, D. R. (1995). A theory of relapse prevention. In W. O'Donohue & L. Krasner (Eds.), *Theories of behavior therapy: Exploring behavior change* (pp. 445–474). Washington, DC: American Psychological Association.

Laws, D. R., Hudson, S. M., & Ward, T. (Eds.). (2000). *Remaking relapse prevention with sex offenders: A sourcebook.* Thousand Oaks, CA: Sage.

Marlatt, G. A. (1998). *Harm reduction: Pragmatic strategies for managing high-risk behaviors.* New York: Guilford Press.

Marlatt, G. A., & Gordon, J. R. (Eds.). (1985). *Relapse prevention.* New York: Guilford Press.

Sandberg, G. G., & Marlatt, G. A. (1991). Relapse prevention. In D. A. Gravlo & R. I. Shader (Eds.), *Clinical manual of dependence.* Washington, DC: American Psychiatric Press.

Steen, C. (2001). *The adult relapse prevention workbook.* Brandon, VT: Safer Society Press.

Ward, T., & Hudson, S. (1996). Relapse prevention: A critical analysis. *Sexual Abuse: A Journal of Research and Treatment, 8,* 177–199.

49 RELAXATION

Kyle E. Ferguson

Relaxation comes in many forms. Yoga, meditation, diaphragmatic breathing (see Chapter 11, "Breathing Retraining" in the present volume), hypnosis, guided imagery, Tai Chi, and Lamaze are common examples. In the empirical literature one review examined 12 scientific journals representing a nine-year span (1970–1979) and revealed 26 distinct referenced approaches (Hillenberg & Collins, 1982). Sleep disturbance, headache, hypertension, asthma, problematic alcohol usage, hyperactivity, and various forms of anxiety were some of the problems targeted for intervention. Accordingly, relaxation is not monolithic, either in the techniques employed or the problem areas for which it is applied. Due to its widespread use, some go so far as to call relaxation the "aspirin" of behavioral medicine (Russo, Bird, & Masek, 1980).

This chapter opens with a discussion of several key developments in relaxation training. Of these, a specific type of training method called *behavioral relaxation training and assessment (BRT)* is discussed at length (Poppen, 1988, 1998; Raymer & Poppen, 1985). Who might benefit from this form of training, contraindications of its use, and purported mechanisms underlying the technique are dealt with first. The remainder of the chapter provides step-by-step guidelines in teaching BRT to clients.

KEY DEVELOPMENTS IN RELAXATION TRAINING

Progressive Relaxation

Edmund Jacobson pioneered relaxation training early in the 20th century, while working on his dissertation at Harvard University (Carlson & Bernstein, 1995). For his dissertation Jacobson examined the effects of relaxation on the startle response. These fledgling ideas eventually culminated into two classic texts—one titled "You Must Relax" (1934), written for the layperson, and one titled "Progressive Relaxation" (1938), written for the professional audience.

Progressive relaxation involves a muscular tense-release procedure targeting dozens of muscle groups. It generally requires 30 to 50 sessions and several hours of daily practice over many days to master the technique. The following are the three principle components of progressive relaxation training:

(1) The subject relaxes a group, for instance, the muscles that bend the right arm. . . . (2) He learns one after the other. . . . With each new group he simultaneously relaxes such parts as have received practice previously. (3) As he practices from day to day . . . he progresses toward a habit of repose . . . a state in which quiet is automatically maintained. (Jacobson, 1934, p. 54)

By "quiet" Jacobson is referring to reductions in neuromuscular tension, verifiable through electromyography (EMG; Jacobson, 1938), and "quieting the nerves"—automatically shutting off mental activity, including worry (Jacobson, 1934, p. 33ff.). And the extent to which clients achieve "quiescence" usually leads to beneficial health outcomes. Reportedly, Jacobson (p. 417ff.) successfully treated insomnia, anxiety, stuttering, asthma, facial spasms, tremor, functional tachycardia (rapid heartbeat), and a host of other disorders using progressive relaxation. Indeed, his success in treating such intractable conditions paved the way for empirically driven relaxation techniques.

Systematic Desensitization

Wolpe adopted and streamlined progressive relaxation as a method of counterconditioning "neurotic-anxiety response habits" (1990, p. 150; see "Systematic Desensitization" Chapter 62, this volume). The muscular tense-release procedure, even after being abbreviated, induced a state of deep relaxation as clients progressed through a fear hierarchy, from less fearful to more fearful mental imagery. Wolpe (1958) called this procedure *systematic desensitization*. Insofar as clients remained in a deep state of relaxation it was believed to reciprocally inhibit and thus weaken learned anxiety habits (Wolpe, 1976). Ultimately, through this manner of systematic counterconditioning the anxiety response would no longer be elicited in the presence of stronger feared stimuli, as exposure increased over time.

Systematic desensitization was a milestone in the advancement of behavior therapy and, collaterally, streamlining Jacobson's labor intensive technique also marked a key development (O'Donohue, Henderson, Hayes, Fisher, & Hayes, 2001). Wolpe's abbreviated and more practical version of progressive relaxation made this technique accessible to a wider audience. Wolpe's (1985) version took about four to six sessions versus 30 to 40, and required only 15 min at any given time, not hours. Moreover, clients could achieve a level of mastery practicing only 15 to 20 min daily for far fewer days. Although data were not collected, one can assume that the requirement of several hours of daily practice using the technique originally conceived by Jacobson would have drastically lowered patient compliance.

Standardization of Progressive Relaxation

Another milestone in behavior therapy was the standardization of relaxation training. In 1973 Bernstein and Borkovec published a manual on progressive relaxation training, standardizing relevant aspects of the training situation. Among other points, physical properties of the "consultation room" (e.g., low ambient noise, proper lighting, etc.; p. 17), the client's chair (e.g., well-padded recliner providing complete support; p. 17), and detailed therapist's scripts (e.g., rationale and training scripts; p. 19ff.) were included in the manual. The manual even went so far as to describe to the reader "what words or phrases to avoid" (e.g., ". . . it is best to delete any reference which might possibly cause the client anxiety or embarrassment"; p. 52) and to alert him or her about clients' "strange or unfamiliar feelings" (p. 49ff.) that sometime manifest during training. As far as the basic procedure is concerned, the following is the training sequence by which clients are taught to tense and release the various muscle groups (p. 25):

1. Dominant hand and forearm
2. Dominant biceps
3. Nondominant hand and forearm
4. Nondominant biceps
5. Forehead
6. Upper cheeks and nose
7. Lower cheeks and jaws
8. Neck and throat
9. Chest, shoulders, and upper back
10. Abdominal or stomach region
11. Dominant thigh
12. Dominant calf
13. Dominant foot
14. Nondominant thigh
15. Nondominant calf
16. Nondominant foot

Since the publication of Bernstein and Borkovec's (1973) manual there have been scores of studies that used their standardized procedures (see Carlson & Hoyle, 1993, for a recent review). As an extension of Jacobson's earlier work, this standardized protocol has been used in treating a variety of different psychological and stress-related conditions. The disorders targeted for intervention were simply those for which tension played a major role in clients' presenting complaints (e.g., benign headaches, insomnia, gastrointestinal disorders).

Behavioral Relaxation Training and Assessment

Many clients have difficulties with progressive relaxation. For some, tensing is contraindicated. Clients with lower back pain, tension headaches, myofacial pain, temporomandibular disorder (TMD), and arthritis are cases in point. When muscles are sore and possibly spasming from splinting or bracing, tensing those affected areas can trigger shooting pain over and above clients' extant pain (e.g., throbbing, burning, tingling, pounding, etc.). On the other hand, some clients simply cannot "let go" once they have tensed a particular muscle group. Both of these limitations of progressive muscle relaxation led to the development of BRT (Poppen, 1998).

Work in BRT began in the early 1980s. While attempting to teach progressive relaxation to "pre-delinquent boys," Roger Poppen and his graduate student Don Schilling found that their clients were able to tense the various muscle groups but had difficulties releasing that tension (Poppen, personal communication, June 21, 1997). As a solution to this problem Schilling directly taught some of the relaxed postures that were to result from the tense-release cycle of progressive relaxation—he simply had the boys try to "look relaxed" (Poppen, 1998, p. 40). As it turned out, the boys not only looked relaxed but reported feelings of relaxation while emitting the behaviors. Out of these observations Schilling and Poppen (1983) derived a list of 10 specific relaxed behaviors and developed an assessment instrument to evaluate clients' proficiency in these, called the *Behavioral Relaxation Scale (BRS)*. The behaviors and activities included in the BRS are body, head, eyes, mouth, throat, shoulders, hands, feet, breathing, and quiet (i.e., no vocalizations or respiratory sounds; Shilling & Poppen, 1983). More details of this assessment device will be taken up later in the chapter. These 10 items are the core targets for BRT (Poppen, 1988, 1998; Raymer & Poppen, 1985).

Since its inception nearly two decades ago BRT has been used in managing a variety of different problems, including chronic headache (Michultka, Poppen, & Blanchard, 1988), recurrent seizures (Kiesel, Lutzker, & Campbell, 1989), ataxic tremor (Guercio, Chittum, & McMorrow, 1997), anxiety (Lindsay, Fee, Michie, & Heap, 1994), and aggression (Lundervold, 1986). Its primary assessment instrument, the BRS, has been validated (Norton, Holm, & McSherry II, 1997; Poppen & Maurer, 1982) and the effects of BRT have been shown to generalize outside of training settings (Poppen, Hanson, & Ip, 1988). BRT can be taught individually or in a group format (see Lindsay & Baty, 1989). Most important, nearly all clients, even those with severe intellectual or mental disabilities (e.g., Mental Retardation, Developmental Disabilities, acquired brain injuries, Schizophrenia, Hyperactivity Disorder, Dementia) can learn the techniques without undue effort (Poppen, 1998).

WHO MIGHT BENEFIT FROM THE TECHNIQUE

Relaxation training is seldom used on its own. It is usually combined with other procedures (e.g., biofeedback) and employed as part of a treatment package (e.g., stress management programs; see Chapter 61, this volume). Clients most likely to benefit from relaxation training are those for whom cognitive, autonomic, or muscular overarousal has become maladaptive—to the point of interfering with therapeutic progress or compromising their quality of life. Relaxation training may also be useful in the following:

- *Preparing patients for surgery.* Patients are usually anxious when they have to undergo invasive medical and surgical procedures (Horne, Vatmanidis, & Careri, 1994). When combined with preoperative psychoeducational programs, relaxation training has been associated with fewer postoperative hospital days, reduced postsurgical complications, and a reduction in medication use (Ludwick-Rosenthal & Neufeld, 1988).
- *Teaching clients how to cope with chronic pain.* Long after an injury has healed, individuals with chronic pain often try to avoid experiencing pain by way of bracing and tensing the surrounding areas of the injury site. This coping

style, however, actually exacerbates pain due to overtaxing the skeletal-muscular system (Hanson & Gerber, 1990). Relaxation training can be used as a coping strategy to break this muscle-tension-pain cycle (Linton, 1994; Poppen et al., 1988).

- *Reducing the frequency of migraine attacks.* Migraine is linked to arousal of the sympathetic branch of the autonomic nervous system (Sacks, 1992). Clients who are taught (via relaxation training) to regularly warm their hands to approximately 95° F tend to have fewer migraine attacks relative to clients who fail to meet or exceed this therapeutic threshold (Blanchard, 1992). Relaxation works best as a prophylactic through preventing the initial vasoconstrictive reaction, not as an abortive strategy.

CONTRAINDICATIONS

While relaxation has produced beneficial outcomes for most clients, for a minority of people relaxation elicits negative reactions. Called *relaxation-induced anxiety (RIA),* it has been documented in the literature using several forms of relaxation training including meditation, biofeedback, and progressive relaxation (Heide & Borkovec, 1983). Anecdotally, several of the reported negative side effects are intense restlessness, trembling, pounding heart, shivering, and profuse perspiration (Carrington, 1977). In one study, Edinger and Jacobson (1982) sent out a mail survey to 116 behavior therapists that used relaxation training. Of 17,542 of their clients, it was estimated that approximately 3.5% experienced negative side effects of relaxation—"intrusive thoughts" and "fear of losing control" being the most common reactions; and "disturbing sensory experiences" and "depersonalization" being some of the least common (p. 138). Chronically tense or anxious clients are particularly prone to RIA (Heide & Borkovec, 1984).

Mark and Nancy Schwartz (1995, p. 292) recommend the following as a means of minimizing the effects of RIA:

1. Inform clients that they might experience thoughts and sensations that seem unusual or bizarre. Tell them that these are normal signs of relaxation and to let these happen.
2. Especially for those clients who appear anxious, let them know that they should expect intrusive thoughts early on, and that this is normal.
3. Relaxation should be discussed in the context of increased control rather than diminished control.
4. Explain to clients that people usually become better at relaxation when they exert less effort rather than more effort—avoid using words like "try"—and that relaxation is "letting go" (see Hayes & Wilson's [1994, p. 297] "polygraph metaphor," a thought experiment demonstrating that one cannot force relaxation).
5. The therapist should use a different form of relaxation should the foregoing recommendations fail. When using a bodily focus type (e.g., progressive relaxation), switch to a cognitive approach (e.g., autogenic training). Conversely, when using a cognitive focus type, switch to a bodily approach. *Seldom do clients continue experiencing RIA after switching to a different form of relaxation.*

HOW DOES THE TECHNIQUE WORK?

Discrimination Training

There are two primary goals in relaxation training. The first goal is teaching clients how to discriminate between feelings of relaxation and psychophysiological arousal. This is achieved by having clients notice the sensations as they systematically relax targeted areas of their bodies. Ideally, once clients become proficient in this discrimination skill set they will be able to recognize when they are and are not relaxed, outside the therapeutic context. Insofar as clients become aware of relaxation—or stress-related internal cues—they are more likely to let themselves relax when approaching stressful situations (coping response) or, more distally, to use relaxation as a preventive measure (e.g., working it into their daily routines). Of course, in the absence of generalization probes or generalization training one would not know for certain whether these skills extend beyond the therapist's office (see Stokes & Baer, 1977, a classic article detailing generalization strategies).

Self-Control Training

The second goal of relaxation training is teaching clients how to evoke the relaxation response as a means of self-control (Benson, 1975; Kazdin, 1989). The *relaxation response,* among other things (cognitive-behavioral processes), is activating the parasympathetic branch of the autonomic nervous system (ANS). Parasympathetic activation is concerned with "slowing down the organism"— it is "restorative in nature" (Asteria, 1985, p. 38). With parasympathetic activation there is a slowing of heart rate (and myocardial responsiveness), increased blood flow to the extremities, pupilary constriction, and better delivery of respiratory gases throughout the body (Benson, 1975).

Because the autonomic system works in an all-or-nothing manner when the parasympathetic branch (or most of the system) is activated, it suppresses sympathetic arousal (Asteria, 1985). Sympathetic arousal triggers the fight-or-flight response, or what Selye called the "Alarm Reaction" (1974, p. 38ff.). Contrary to the functions of the parasympathetic branch, activating the sympathetic branch "speeds up the organism." Heart rate increases along with metabolism, and organs not required in protecting the organism (e.g., digestive system) are suppressed (Asteria). Chronic sympathetic arousal is believed to play a role in: cardiovascular disease, gastrointestinal and genitourinary problems, compromised immune functioning, Panic Disorder, Generalized Anxiety Disorder, Social Phobia, and Post-Traumatic Stress Disorder, among many others (Sullivan, Kent, & Coplan, 2000).

With that as background, let us turn next to a discussion of the procedures (summarized in Table 49.1) used in teaching BRT to clients.

STEP-BY-STEP PROCEDURES

Step 1: Setting

The training room should be quiet and calm—try eliminating as many distractions as possible

TABLE 49.1   Keys to Relaxation Training

1. Ensure that clients are comfortable before commencing with training.
2. Provide a solid rationale for relaxation training.
3. Assess relaxation using standardized assessment procedures.
4. The behaviors and activities targeted for training are breathing, body, head, shoulders, mouth, throat, hands, feet, quiet, and eyes.
5. During training, label, describe, and model the 10 postures.
6. Have clients imitate the therapist during training— provide corrective feedback when necessary.
7. Instruct clients during training to notice the sensations they feel as they relax the body, head, mouth, and so on.
8. Graph cumulative performance at the end of each session.
9. Assign homework after every session and monitor whether clients actually do it.
10. Teach cue-controlled relaxation to better ensure response generalization.

(Benson, 1975, p. 159). A small fan usually produces enough white noise to mask conversations outside, the sound of footsteps in the hallway, and so on. Also turn off the ringer on the telephone.

Use a recliner, one that provides total support for most clients (Bernstein & Borkovec, 1973). Make adjustments accordingly to accommodate clients' body types. For example, if clients are of smaller stature, in which case the recliner is too big, use pillows to provide additional support (e.g., under the knees and elbows). These adjustments are almost always necessary when working with small children. Clients of larger stature (e.g., over 6 ft tall) may require an ottoman, should the recliner fail to support their feet.

Client should dress comfortably, in loose-fitting clothing. Have clients remove their glasses, watches, bracelets, and the like. Clients should be neither too hot nor too cold in the training milieu. Use a space heater or gentle fan if necessary.

Step 2: Rationale

Providing a good rationale is an important strategy in motivating clients (also in increasing treatment compliance; Schwartz, 1995b). In presenting the rationale, (1) review clients' problematic behavior; (2) discuss how relaxation is a better functional alternative (e.g., as a coping strategy to reduce tension-arousal); (3) provide an overview of the procedures (without being too specific, thus contaminating the initial assessment) and what clients should expect while learning the techniques (Poppen, 1998, pp. 71–72; include Schwartz & Schwartz's [1995, p. 292] recommendations mentioned earlier); (4) emphasize the fact that the therapist serves mainly as a coach in relaxation training, and that most of the benefit comes from clients' practicing on their own; (5) explain that the ultimate aim of relaxation training is teaching self-management— it's the therapist's goal (as far as relaxation training is concerned) to become obsolete as soon as clients become proficient in this area. Discuss the rationale using language commensurate with clients' education and intellectual functioning.

Sample relaxation rationale script:
. . . relaxation training consists of learning to sequentially . . . relax various groups of muscles all through the body, while at the same time paying very close and careful attention to the feelings of . . . relaxation . . . in addition to teaching you how to relax, I will also be encouraging you to learn to recognize and pinpoint tension and relaxation as they appear in everyday situations . . . You should understand quite clearly that learning relaxation skills is very much like learning any other kind of skill such as swimming, or golfing, or riding a bicycle; thus in order for you to get better at relaxing you will have to practice doing it just as you would have to practice other skills. It is very important that you realize that . . . relaxation training involves learning on your part; there is nothing magical about the procedures. I will not be doing anything *to* you; I will merely be introducing you to the technique and directing your attention to various aspects of it, such as the presence of certain feelings in the muscles. Thus, without your active cooperation and regular practicing of the things you will learn today, the procedures are of little use . . . The goal of . . . relaxation training is to help you learn to reduce muscle tension in your body far below your adaptation level at any time you wish to do so . . . Do you have any questions about what I've said so far? (Answer any questions about the rationale behind relaxation training but defer questions about specific procedures until after

you have covered the material to follow. (Bernstein & Borkovec, 1973, pp. 19–20, italics in original)

Step 3: Assessment

Before commencing with the initial assessment, have clients sit quietly for a few minutes. After allowing clients to get acclimated, using the BRS form (see Figure 49.1), ask clients to rate their state or degree of relaxation. Use the following Self-Report Rating Scale[1] (always show clients the scale when assessing their self-report—*never rely on clients' memory of the items*).

1. Feeling deeply and completely relaxed throughout my entire body
2. Feeling very relaxed and calm
3. Feeling more relaxed than usual
4. Feeling relaxed as in my normal resting state
5. Feeling tension in some parts of my body
6. Feeling generally tense throughout my body
7. Feeling extremely tense and upset throughout my body

Subsequent to taking clients' self-report measures, instruct them to relax on their own for the next few minutes while the trainer sees how they relax. Avoid using language that suggests that clients' performance is being evaluated during the initial assessment. Use the BRS form to measure the 10 behaviors and activities already mentioned. A detailed description of these will be taken up shortly.

Assessment observation periods should be no less than 5 min, total. Observation periods are broken down into 1-min blocks. On the BRS form these columns are labeled 1 through 10. Each

1. Another self-report measure that is especially useful when employing systematic desensitization or exposure and response prevention is the *subjective unit of disturbance (SUD)* scale (Wolpe & Lazarus, 1966, p. 73). Have the client think of the most distressing experience in his or her life. This event is assigned the number 100. Next, have the client think of the most relaxing experience in his or her life. This event is assigned the number 0. The remaining items in the fear hierarchy are then assigned numbers that fall somewhere along this continuum (i.e., between 0 and 100).

Breathing Baseline: _____   Overall Assessment: (–) = Unrelaxed   (+) = Relaxed

	1		2		3		4		5		6		7		8		9		10		Total
Breathing	-	+	-	+	-	+	-	+	-	+	-	+	-	+	-	+	-	+	-	+	
Quiet	-	+	-	+	-	+	-	+	-	+	-	+	-	+	-	+	-	+	-	+	
Body	-	+	-	+	-	+	-	+	-	+	-	+	-	+	-	+	-	+	-	+	
Head	-	+	-	+	-	+	-	+	-	+	-	+	-	+	-	+	-	+	-	+	
Eyes	-	+	-	+	-	+	-	+	-	+	-	+	-	+	-	+	-	+	-	+	
Mouth	-	+	-	+	-	+	-	+	-	+	-	+	-	+	-	+	-	+	-	+	
Throat	-	+	-	+	-	+	-	+	-	+	-	+	-	+	-	+	-	+	-	+	
Shoulders	-	+	-	+	-	+	-	+	-	+	-	+	-	+	-	+	-	+	-	+	
Hands	-	+	-	+	-	+	-	+	-	+	-	+	-	+	-	+	-	+	-	+	
Feet	-	+	-	+	-	+	-	+	-	+	-	+	-	+	-	+	-	+	-	+	

Score %

Pre-Observation Self-Rating:
Relaxation: 1   2   3   4   5   6   7

Post-Observation Self-Rating:
Relaxation: 1   2   3   4   5   6   7

FIGURE 49.1   The Behavioral Relaxation Scale Score Sheet (reproduced from Poppen, 1998; permission granted by the author)

block is further broken down into three intervals: a 30-s interval to measure breathing, a 15-s interval to observe the nine behaviors on the BRS, and the remaining 15 s to record responses (Poppen, 1998, p. 49).

Breathing

Baseline breathing rate is taken during the first assessment. The baseline breathing rate is the standard by which further breathing rates are evaluated (Poppen, 1998, p. 53). Commencing with the first observational block (ideally, using a stopwatch that does not beep), begin counting breaths when the client inhales. One breath equals an inhalation-exhalation cycle. Stop counting breaths after the initial 30 s for each observation block. If the client is exhaling at that point, count the breath, even if he or she has not fully exhaled—do not count it as a breath if the client is inhaling. Ignore all other behavior during the breathing interval. Mark an X in the box corresponding to breathing on the BRS whenever breathing is interrupted with a snort, sneeze, sniffle, sigh, yawn, cough, and so on.

In calculating the baseline breathing rate, add up the overall frequency of breathing responses and divide by the number of observational blocks—always round up decimals. Do not include those intervals in which breathing was interrupted. On subsequent training days breathing rates are calculated the same way. Should those rates fall below the baseline rate then these are considered "relaxed." During the recording interval, for the 15 s remaining in the observation block write in the breathing frequency and circle the "+" or "–" to denote "relaxed" or "unrelaxed" breathing, respectively. Of course, the therapist does not indicate whether breathing is relaxed or unrelaxed during the initial assessment. A "+" or "–" also denotes "relaxed" or "unrelaxed" postures for the remaining items.

During the next 15 s scan the client's body, observing the remaining nine items. Again, as with the breathing interval, hold off recording responses until the final 15 s of the observation block. Below are the scoring criteria for the remaining items, indicated on the BRS.

Quiet

- *Relaxed:* The client is not making any sounds.
- *Unrelaxed:* The client makes noise such as talking, humming, burping, giggling, grunting,

snorting, sneezing, snoring, sniffling, sighing, whistling, yawning, coughing, and so on.

Body

- *Relaxed:* The shoulders, hips, and feet are in alignment, around midline (Poppen, 1998, p. 43). The body is supported by the recliner with no movement. Chest or abdominal movement resulting from breathing is, however, acceptable.
- *Unrelaxed:* (1) moving the torso or shifting the body weight; (2) positioning shoulders, hips, and feet out of alignment; (3) moving the limbs (e.g., knee jerk; exclude the hands and feet, which are scored separately); (4) positioning of the back, legs, or buttocks so they are not supported by the recliner.

Head

- *Relaxed:* The head is supported by the chair, lying still. The nose is in midline with the body. The chin does not drop into the chest or point up. *If one were to fasten a piece of string to the person's nose and attach it to the floor, the string would bisect the sternum and belly button.*
- *Unrelaxed:* (1) The head is not supported by the chair; (2) the head is moving; (3) the nose is out of midline; (4) the head is tilted up, down, or to the left or right.

Eyes

- *Relaxed:* The eyelids are closed. The lids have a smooth appearance and the eyes are still.
- *Unrelaxed:* (1) The eyelids are open; (2) the lids are wrinkled from squeezing the lids together; (3) the eyes or lids are moving.

Mouth

- *Relaxed:* The teeth are apart by about 1/3 to 1 in. There is no movement in the jaw region and the tongue is lying still.
- *Unrelaxed:* (1) The teeth or lips are together; (2) the teeth are more than an inch apart; (3) the jaw or tongue is moving; (4) the client is smiling or yawning.

Throat

- *Relaxed:* The throat is not moving. (Have the client breathe in through the nose and out through the mouth to prevent the throat from drying, which elicits swallowing. Should the client have problems with this breathing pattern, have him or her lightly press the tip of the tongue behind the top front teeth. This will impede airflow through the mouth.)
- *Unrelaxed:* The throat or muscles in the neck are moving.

Shoulders

- *Relaxed:* Shoulders are rounded (from letting go of tension) and do not lean to one side or the other. Taking breathing into consideration, there is no additional movement.
- *Unrelaxed:* (1) Shoulder shows movement not attributable to breathing; (2) one shoulder is higher than the other; (3) shoulders are shrugged, thus losing their rounded appearance.

Hands

- *Relaxed:* The hands are resting still in the lap or arms of the chair, palms down, fingers in a claw-like fashion. The fingers are resting on the pads, slightly splayed, and there is a small arch under the palm. A pencil should pass easily under the apex of the arch without touching the hand.
- *Unrelaxed:* (1) The hands or fingers are moving; (2) the hands are not supported or are otherwise out of position; (3) the fingers are curled into a fist; (4) the palms are flat.

Feet

- *Relaxed:* The legs are comfortably straight, lying still, roughly shoulder-width apart, with a slight bend at the knee, the feet fall limp to either side creating a 60° to 90° angle between them.
- *Unrelaxed:* (1) The feet (including the toes) show movement; (2) legs are crossed or knees are pulled toward the chest; (3) feet create more or less than a 60° to 90° angle.

Step 4: Behavioral Relaxation Training

BRT sessions usually take roughly a half hour, including assessment and training (Poppen, 1998, p. 72). BRT entails teaching clients the 10 behaviors on the BRS form. Although the 10 items may appear to be a lot for clients to take in, most clients can learn behavioral relaxation during the first session.

Each item on the BRS is taught by first (1) labeling the posture (or activity), followed by (2) giving a description of what it is and what it is not (i.e., relaxed and unrelaxed postures). Next, the therapist (3) provides a demonstration of relaxed and unrelaxed postures (modeling: "Let me demonstrate how you relax your hand . . . this is how you aren't supposed to relax your hand . . ."); then (4) asks the client to imitate the relaxed posture and (5) provides corrective feedback when necessary (e.g., "Not quite right, like this . . ."). Use manual guidance when clients are not responding to verbal instruction, but only as a last resort (Poppen, 1998, p. 74). Each item is introduced successively, one at a time, building upon the mastery of previous skills. Once clients are in the correct posture instruct them to notice the sensations as they relax that body part or are engaged in one of the relaxed activities (e.g., *quiet* and *breathing*).

If a client is working on the fifth item and loses the second, for example, provide corrective feedback for the posture that fell out of relaxation. Accordingly, corrective feedback is always based on cumulative performance. Work through each of the items in the following order: breathing,[2] body, head, shoulders, mouth, throat, hands, and feet.

Step 5: Ongoing Assessment

Following the first day of BRT, at the beginning of each subsequent session have clients relax using their newly acquired relaxation skills. Assess performance using the same procedures as in the initial assessment (Step 3). After 5 min of observation, provide corrective feedback if the therapist notices unrelaxed behavior.

Data gathered from ongoing evaluations reflect the extent to which clients practice these skills at other times, outside of the therapist's of-

fice (an indirect measure of generalization). Should clients perform poorly on the BRS, they may not be practicing on their own. Given that home practice is crucial to relaxation training, always address this issue when clients are not adhering to the program. *Contingency contracting* works well in reestablishing clients' motivation, even for seemingly intractable cases (see Chapter 19, "Contingency Management" in the present volume).

FURTHER CONSIDERATIONS

- Monitor the intake of vasoactive foods and beverages (e.g., caffeine, tyramine, monosodium glutamate, alcohol), as these are known to aggravate and trigger some physical symptoms—especially for those individuals who suffer from migraine and Raynaud's disease (Block & Schwartz, 1995).

- Graphing performance helps reinforce the notion that many clients can quickly attain a high level of mastery. Most importantly, clients are more likely to employ these skills when they feel confident in their abilities.

- Audiotape sessions to increase compliance and conserve time (see Schwartz, 1995c, for full details in making relaxation tapes).

- Assign homework asking clients to try out as many of the postures as possible in a variety of different situations. For example, while seated in a classroom students can relax the mouth and throat, remain quiet, engage in diaphragmatic breathing, relax the shoulders and head, and position the nonwriting hand in a clawlike manner (see Poppen, 1998, pp. 88–91, for modified BRT, called *upright relaxation training (URT)* and *mini-relaxation*). The more practice clients get in applying and adapting these skills to new settings, the greater the generalization gradient (Stokes & Baer, 1977).

- Another generalization strategy is to train clients in cue-controlled relaxation (Smith, 1990, p. 76). *Cue-controlled relaxation* involves pairing a word or two-word phrase (e.g., "calm" or "let go") with the relaxation response. Simply have the client repeat this word while becoming increasingly relaxed. After frequent pairings of the word with relaxation, the client will eventually be able to evoke the relaxation re-

---

2. Teach diaphragmatic breathing (see Chapter 11, "Breathing Retraining" in the present volume). Begin by discussing the difference between this approach and thoracic breathing, with an emphasis on how the former is far more efficient at increasing oxygen intake and regulating arousal states. One therapeutic standard is slowing respiration to approximately 6–8 breaths per minute (3–4 during the 30-s BRS assessment interval); this is about half the typical rate for most people (Schwartz, 1995a, p. 249).

sponse by saying the word alone. For example, if the client is getting upset while standing in a checkout line or sitting in the dentist's chair, or while on an airplane about to take off, have him or her quietly say the cue word (while emitting as many of the 10 BRT behaviors as possible). Of course, for the word or phrase to remain powerful in evoking the relaxation response, the client must continue pairing it with relaxation—otherwise the word or phrase loses its influence.

References

Asteria, M. F. (1985). *The physiology of stress.* New York: Human Sciences Press.

Benson, H. (1975). *The relaxation response.* New York: Avon Books.

Bernstein, D. A., & Borkovec, T. D. (1973). *Progressive relaxation training: A manual for the helping professions.* Champaign, IL: Research Press.

Blanchard, E. B. (1992). Psychological treatment of benign headache disorders. *Journal of Consulting and Clinical Psychology, 60,* 537–551.

Block, K. I., & Schwartz, M. S. (1995). Dietary considerations: Rationale, issues, substances, evaluation, and patient education. In M. S. Schwartz & Associates (Eds.), *Biofeedback: A practitioner's guide* (2nd ed., pp. 211–247). New York: Guilford Press.

Carlson, C. R., & Berstein, D. A. (1995). Relaxation skills training: Abbreviated progressive relaxation. In W. T. O'Donohue & L. Krasner (Eds.), *Handbook of psychological skills: Clinical techniques and applications* (pp. 20–35). Boston: Allyn & Bacon.

Carlson, C. R., & Hogle, R. H. (1993). Efficacy of abbreviated progressive muscle relaxation training: A quantitative review. *Journal of Clinical and Consulting Psychology, 61,* 105–106.

Carrington, P. (1977). *Freedom in meditation.* New York: Doubleday-Anchor.

Edinger, J. D., & Jacobson, R. (1982). Incidence and significance of relaxation treatment side-effects. *The Behavior Therapist, 5,* 137–138.

Guercio, J., Chittum, R., & McMorrow, M. (1997). Self-management in the treatment of ataxia: A case study in reducing ataxic tremor through relaxation and biofeedback. *Brain Injury, 11,* 353–362.

Hansen, R. W., & Gerber, K. E. (1990). *Coping with chronic pain: A guide to patient self-management.* New York: Guilford Press.

Hayes, S. C., & Wilson, K. G. (1994). Acceptance and commitment therapy: Altering the verbal support for experiential avoidance. *The Behavior Therapist, 17,* 289–303.

Heide, F. J., & Borkovec, P. D. (1983). Relaxation-induced anxiety: Paradoxical anxiety due to relaxation training. *Journal of Consulting and Clinical Psychology, 51,* 171–182.

Heide, F. J., & Borkovec, P. D. (1984). Relaxation-induced anxiety: Mechanisms and theoretical implications. *Behaviour Research and Therapy, 22,* 1–12.

Hillenberg, J. B., & Collins, F. L., Jr. (1982). A procedural analysis and review of relaxation training research. *Behaviour Research and Therapy, 20,* 251–260.

Horne, D. J., Vatmanidis, P., & Careri, A. (1994). Preparing patients for invasive medical and surgical procedures: II. Using psychological interventions with adults and children. *Behavioral Medicine, 20,* 15–21.

Jacobson, E. (1934). *You must relax: A practical method of reducing the strains of modern living.* New York: McGraw-Hill.

Jacobson, E. (1938). *Progressive relaxation: A psychological and clinical investigation of muscular states and their significance in psychological and medical practice.* Chicago: University of Chicago Press.

Kazdin, A. E. (1989). *Behavior modification in applied settings* (4th ed.). Pacific Grove, CA: Brooks/Cole.

Kiesel, K. B., Lutzker, J. R., & Campbell, R. V. (1989). Behavioral relaxation training to reduce hyperventilation and seizures in a profoundly retarded epileptic child. *Journal of the Multihandicapped Person, 2,* 179–190.

Lindsay, W. R., & Baty, F. J. (1989). Group relaxation training with adults who are mentally handicapped. *Behavioural Psychotherapy, 17,* 43–51.

Lindsay, W. R., Fee, M., Michie, A., & Heap, I. (1994). The effects of cue control relaxation on adults with severe mental retardation. *Research in Developmental Disabilities, 15,* 425–437.

Linton, S. J. (1994). Chronic back pain: Integrating psychological and physical therapy. *Behavioral Medicine, 20,* 101–104.

Ludwick-Rosenthal, R., & Neufeld, R. W. J. (1988). Stress management during noxious medical procedures: An evaluative review of outcome studies. *Psychological Bulletin, 104,* 326–342.

Lundervold, D. (1986). The effects of behavioral relaxation and self-instruction training: A case study. *Rehabilitation Counseling Bulletin, 30,* 124–128.

Michultka, D., Poppen, R., & Blanchard, E. B. (1988). Relaxation training as a treatment for chronic headaches in an individual having severe developmental disabilities. *Biofeedback and Self-Regulation, 13,* 257–266.

Norton, M., Holm, J. E., & McSherry, W. C., II. (1997). Behavioral assessment of relaxation: The validity of a behavioral rating scale. *Journal of Behavior Therapy and Experimental Psychiatry, 28,* 129–137.

O'Donohue, W. T., Henderson, D. A., Hayes, S. C., Fisher, J. E., & Hayes, L. J. (2001). A history of the behavioral therapies. In *A history of the behavioral therapies: Founders' personal histories* (pp. xi–xxii). Reno, NV: Context Press.

Poppen, R. (1988). *Behavioral relaxation training and assessment.* New York: Pergamon Press.

Poppen, R. (1998). *Behavioral relaxation training and assessment* (2nd ed.). Thousand Oaks, CA: Sage.

Poppen, R., Hanson, H., & Ip, S. V. (1988). Generalization of EMG biofeedback training. *Biofeedback and Self-Regulation, 13,* 235–243.

Poppen, R., & Maurer, J. (1982). Electromyographic analysis of relaxed postures. *Biofeedback and Self-Regulation, 7,* 491–498.

Raymer, R. H., & Poppen, R. (1985). Behavioral relaxation training with hyperactive children. *Journal of Behavior Therapy and Experimental Psychiatry, 16,* 309–316.

Russo, D. C., Bird, B. L., & Masek, B. J. (1980). Assessment issues in behavioral medicine. *Behavioral Assessment, 2,* 1–18.

Sacks, O. (1992). *Migraine* (rev. and exp.). Berkeley: University of California Press.

Schilling, D. J., & Poppen, R. (1983). Behavioral relaxation training and assessment. *Journal of Behavior Therapy and Experimental Psychiatry, 14,* 99–107.

Schwartz, M. S. (1995a). Breathing therapies. In M. S. Schwartz & Associates (Eds.), *Biofeedback: A practitioner's guide* (2nd ed., pp. 248–287). New York: Guilford Press.

Schwartz, M. S. (1995b). Compliance. In M. S. Schwartz & Associates (Eds.), *Biofeedback: A practitioner's guide* (2nd ed., pp. 184–207). New York: Guilford Press.

Schwartz, M. S. (1995c). The use of audiotapes for patient education and relaxation. In M. S. Schwartz & Associates (Eds.), *Biofeedback: A practitioner's guide* (2nd ed., pp. 301–310). New York: Guilford Press.

Schwartz, M. S., & Schwartz, N. M. (1995). Problems with relaxation and biofeedback: Assisted relaxation and guidelines for management. In M. S. Schwartz & Associates (Eds.), *Biofeedback: A practitioner's guide* (2nd ed., pp. 288–300). New York: Guilford Press.

Selye, H. (1974). *Stress without distress.* New York: J. B. Lippincott.

Smith, J. C. (1990). *Cognitive-behavioral relaxation training: A new system of strategies for assessment and treatment.* New York: Springer.

Stokes, T. F., & Baer, D. M. (1977). An implicit technology of generalization. *Journal of Applied Behavior Analysis, 10,* 349–367.

Sullivan, G. M., Kent, J. M., & Coplan, J. D. (2000). The neurobiology of stress and anxiety. In D. I. Mostofsky & D. H. Barlow (Eds.), *The management of stress and anxiety in medical disorders* (pp. 15–35). Boston: Allyn & Bacon.

Wolpe, J. (1958). *Psychotherapy by reciprocal inhibition.* Stanford, CA: Stanford University Press.

Wolpe, J. (1976). *Theme and variations: A behavior therapy casebook.* New York: Pergamon Press.

Wolpe, J. (1990). *The practice of behavior therapy* (4th ed.). New York: Pergamon Press.

Wolpe, J., & Lazarus, A. A. (1966). *Behavior therapy techniques: A guide to the treatment of the neuroses.* New York: Pergamon Press.

50 RESPONSE PREVENTION

Deborah A. Roth, Edna B. Foa, and Martin E. Franklin

INTRODUCTION

Response (ritual) prevention (RP) is an intervention of behavior therapy conceptualized as blocking avoidance or escape from feared situations. As such, it goes hand-in-hand with another behavioral intervention, *exposure* (see Chapters 33 and 34 in this volume). Exposure involves confronting situations, objects, and thoughts that evoke anxiety or distress because they are unrealistically associated with danger. By encouraging the individual to remain in the feared situation, RP allows the realization that the fear is unrealistic. This conceptualization has guided animal studies where fear extinction was achieved by blocking escape behavior (e.g., Baum, 1970), as well as the application of response prevention to clinical problems.

In its clinical application, *exposure and response (or ritual) prevention (EX/RP)* is most closely associated with the treatment of Obsessive-Compulsive Disorder (OCD), being used first by Meyer who titled his first (1966) publication on EX/RP "Modification of Expectations in Cases with Obsessional Rituals," thus implying that cognitive changes underlie the treatment. In a series of experiments, Rachman and his colleagues (see Rachman & Hodgson, 1980) demonstrated that exposure to cues that trigger obsessions in-

crease anxiety and discomfort and that ritualistic behavior led to a decrease in anxiety and discomfort. When patients were exposed to obsessional cues but were prevented from engaging in rituals, anxiety and discomfort decreased over time. When patients were then exposed to their obsessional cues again, the urge to ritualize had decreased as compared to the previous trial. This decrease in urge to ritualize did not occur if patients continued to engage in rituals in response to obsessional cues. These tenants form the premise of EX/RP—that patients are exposed to cues that lead to obsessions and are asked to refrain from engaging in rituals in order to learn that their anxiety will come down on its own and that the feared consequences do not occur. In other words, EX/RP serves to disconfirm beliefs, not only about anxiety itself, but also about what will happen if rituals are not performed.

Foa, Steketee, Grayson, Turner, and Latimer (1984) demonstrated the importance of using *both* exposure and ritual prevention in the treatment of OCD. In this study, patients with OCD were randomly assigned to receive either exposure alone, ritual prevention alone, or combined EX/RP. The component treatments seemed to have unique effects on OCD symptoms—ritual prevention led to reduction in compulsions and exposure led to reduction in the anxiety response to feared stimuli. Not surprisingly, then, the combined treatment was found to be superior to the component treatments, with patients in this group showing the greatest reductions in both anxiety and compulsions.

HOW EFFECTIVE IS EX/RP?

Following from these important studies, EX/RP has continued to be the treatment of choice for OCD, and furthermore, has been shown to be very effective. Foa and Kozak (1996), in a review of 12 outcome studies, reported that over 80% of people who complete EX/RP for OCD are deemed to be responders immediately posttreatment. Furthermore, EX/RP has been shown to have excellent long-term efficacy. In their review of 16 treatment outcome studies, Foa and Kozak reported that 76% of patients who completed EX/RP were deemed to be responders at an average follow-up time of 29 months.

In their review, Foa and Kozak (1996) examined data only from randomized clinical trials (RCTs), all of which have strict inclusion-exclusion criteria for participation. The design of such studies has led some to question whether treatments like EX/RP work with less carefully selected patients. Franklin, Abramovitz, Kozak, Levitt, and Foa (2000) explored this issue by looking at response rates among patients receiving EX/RP in an outpatient, fee-for-service clinic. These patients showed excellent response rates that were comparable to those seen in more carefully controlled RCTs.

Researchers have also examined the comparative efficacy of EX/RP versus medication in the treatment of OCD. Also of interest is whether there is an advantage to using a combined treatment. The research suggests that EX/RP is a superior treatment to medication alone for OCD. Foa and colleagues (in preparation) recently completed a study comparing EX/RP alone, clomipramine alone, and their combination. Patients who received either EX/RP or EX/RP and medication showed significantly more improvement on OCD symptoms than those who received medication alone (although all active treatments were superior to placebo). Similarly, in a study of treatments for pediatric OCD, de-

Haan, Hoogduin, Buitelaar, and Keijsers (1998) also found that EX/RP produced stronger therapeutic changes than clomipramine. Data from the Foa and colleagues (in preparation) study show that gains made with EX/RP are better maintained than are gains made with medication alone after treatment discontinuation. The study also suggests (in line with other OCD treatment outcome studies) that there is not a general advantage of combined medication and EX/RP for OCD over EX/RP monotherapy (Foa, Franklin, & Moser, 2002).

WHO MIGHT BENEFIT?

The efficacy of EX/RP for OCD has been demonstrated in children and adolescents (see March & Leonard, 1998), adults (see Foa, Franklin, & Kozak, 1998), and older adults (see Carmin, Pollard, & Ownby, 1999). Researchers have examined whether comorbidity negatively impacts treatment outcome. The presence of personality disorders is predictive of poor outcome in EX/RP (AuBuchon & Malatesta, 1994; Fals-Stewart & Lucente, 1993). In terms of Axis I disorders, comorbid Major Depression has garnered the most research attention. Abramowitz and colleagues (Abramowitz & Foa, 2000; Abramowitz, Franklin, Street, Kozak, & Foa, 2000) failed to find a linear relationship between level of depression and treatment outcome in OCD. Depression had an impact on treatment only at high levels of severity—patients with Beck Depression Inventory (BDI) scores greater than 30 were less likely to be treatment responders than patients with lower BDI scores. It is important to note, though, that even these severely depressed patients showed clinically significant reductions in OCD symptoms following EX/RP.

FREQUENCY AND DURATION OF SESSIONS

Historically, treatment for OCD has been quite intensive, often taking place in inpatient settings. More recently, clinicians have explored whether less intense treatments also produce good outcomes. Very few inpatient facilities for OCD exist, and even outpatient intensive treatment can be difficult to carry out both for the therapist and the patient. Our current OCD treatment protocol includes 17, twice-weekly, 2-hour sessions (generally two sessions of information gathering and treatment planning, and 15 sessions of EX/RP). We also offer an intensive treatment program that includes daily 2-hour sessions, lasting for 17 days in a row. At post-treatment evaluation, patients enrolled in the intensive treatment show a slight advantage over those enrolled in twice-weekly therapy, yet these differences disappear at follow-up (Abramowitz, Foa, & Franklin, 2003). Given the logistical difficulties of doing intensive treatment, both for clinicians and patients, twice-weekly treatment is certainly acceptable. At the current time, no studies have directly compared once-weekly treatment to twice-weekly or intensive treatment. It is certainly possible that once-weekly treatment would be effective for less severe (in terms of OCD symptoms and the presence of comorbid conditions) and more highly motivated patients (see Foa & Franklin, 1999), but this question should be explored empirically.

It is important in the treatment of OCD to have sessions of adequate duration. Prolonged, continuous exposure is more effective than short, interrupted exposure, and therefore sessions of at least 90 min are recommended. Our current treatment protocol includes sessions of 90 min to 2 hours, allowing for one in vivo exposure and one imaginal exposure (although this is adjusted depending on the idiosyncrasies of the patient's OCD). With longer exposures, patients will have the therapist's support with ritual prevention, affording an opportunity to see that anxiety and fear will decrease over time and to disconfirm their beliefs about what will happen if rituals are not performed. We treated a patient who became very uncomfortable if his hands felt dirty or "germy." He believed that if he did not wash his hands when they felt this way, he would feel more and more anxious and uncomfortable and that this feeling would never go away. Exposures with this patient included only a few minutes of walking through the clinic and touching items that were contaminated. For the remainder of the session, focus was placed on ritual prevention and helping the patient to see that as he continued to refrain from washing, his discomfort and anxious feelings subsided.

What patients do between treatment sessions is as important as what they do during treatment sessions. It is essential to remind patients that once they leave their sessions, they should resist the urge to undo what they have accomplished by engaging in rituals. Patients who are having difficulties with this often benefit from making a phone call to the clinician once they get home if the urge to ritualize is very strong. It is also important for patients who are enrolled in EX/RP to do homework on their own between sessions. In fact, one study found that compliance with homework assignments early in OCD treatment was the best predictor of treatment outcome (De Araujo, Ito, & Marks, 1996). Homework assignments should be planned at the end of each treatment session and should then be reviewed at the beginning of the next session. As treatment proceeds, patients should be encouraged to take a more active role in selecting homework assignments. Furthermore, clinicians should be alert to whether patients are generalizing what they learn in their sessions to situations that have not yet been targeted in treatment.

HOW IS EX/RP IMPLEMENTED?

The first step in implementing RP is for both the clinician and the patient to get a clear sense of the functional relationship between obsessions and compulsions. In conceptualizing OCD, clinicians have a clear sense of the distinction between obsessions and compulsions; for most patients, however, this distinction is not clear and perhaps not even something they have thought about. A good place to start with patients, then, is to provide them with definitions for obsessions and compulsions.

Obsessions are intrusive thoughts, images, or impulses that keep coming back to people and that do not make sense. An important point to get across to patients is that obsessions cause distress. Clearly, when people experience distress, they are motivated to get rid of it and this is where compulsions enter the OCD picture. *Compulsions* are behaviors or mental acts which people feel driven to perform and have difficulty resisting. Compulsions are meant to alleviate the distress brought on by obsessional thoughts or to prevent bad things from happening (e.g., patients with contamination obsessions wash their hands to prevent themselves from getting ill).

It is important to emphasize to patients that compulsions can be either overt behaviors, like hand-washing, or mental acts, like saying a prayer or counting up to a certain number. Some patients (and clinicians) do not recognize mental acts as compulsions, which can be highly problematic in treatment. The goal of treatment is to refrain from rituals, but *not* to stop obsessions. Attempting to push obsessions out of one's mind can actually have a paradoxical effect, increasing the frequency with which the thoughts subsequently occur (see Abramowitz, Tolin, & Street, 2001). Thoughts are not inherently problematic. Rather, it is what people do with their thoughts that maintain OCD symptoms over time.

Another key to the assessment process is identifying avoidance behaviors. While rituals are certainly meant to alleviate anxiety, they can also be time-consuming and embarrassing. People with OCD will sometimes attempt to avoid triggers that initiate the cycle of obsessions and compulsions. For example, a person who fears getting contaminated by food might never eat outside his or her own home, and a person who is worried about causing the house to catch fire by leaving the stove on might avoid ever turning the stove on in the first place. Getting a clear picture of avoidance patterns is also crucial to good treatment planning, since EX/RP will include exposure to cues that are being avoided and subsequent ritual prevention.

For some patients, the process of identifying obsessions, compulsions, and patterns of avoidance will be quite easy. For others, particularly those with mental rituals, the process is more challenging. We once treated a patient who came in to see us explaining that he was a "pure obsessional." He reported having a recurrent obsession in which a shark threatened to attack his girlfriend. The image of the shark swimming around his girlfriend in the water was very vivid and made him feel terrified as he sat in a boat helplessly looking on. The clinician who was assessing him asked him what he did in response to these feelings of terror and helplessness. The patient reported that he then saw an image of himself jumping into the water, battling the shark,

and rescuing his girlfriend. It became clear that he was not a pure obsessional at all—the obsessions involved the image of his girlfriend in danger; the compulsion involved the mental ritual of jumping into the water to save her. This distinction was crucial for treatment. In treatment, the patient was helped to focus on the obsessional content of the thought and resist the urge to engage in the mental compulsion. Once the association between the two thoughts was broken, the obsession gradually decreased in frequency and intensity.

The process of assessment is rounded out by having patients engage in self-monitoring (see Chapter 53, this volume). By increasing awareness, the process of self-monitoring gives patients a sense of the cues that trigger obsessions and how much time is being taken up by rituals in a typical day. It also helps patients to identify rituals of which they might not have even been aware. We recently treated a patient with contamination fears who in her initial session did an excellent job of describing her OCD symptoms. She came back in for her second session and reported that through self-monitoring, she had recognized an area that was causing significant problems for her that she had not even thought to mention at the last session. She noticed that her obsessional thoughts about germs and illness were at their worst after touching money and that these concerns triggered lengthy hand-washing rituals. This concern became a focus of treatment.

Once the initial assessment process is complete, patients are asked to begin ritual prevention. It is completely unrealistic to simply tell patients to stop engaging in rituals. If it were so simple to stop, they would have done so on their own. The best way to explain ritual prevention to patients is to place emphasis on the cognitive-behavioral model of OCD and on the functional relationship between obsessions and compulsions. Patients should be told that treatment involves exposing oneself to cues that trigger obsessive thoughts and the associated urge to ritualize, but to resist the urge to do so. The goal is to learn that anxiety decreases on its own without having to resort to rituals and that feared consequences are unlikely to happen. It is important to make clear that as long as patients acquiesce to that urge, the obsessional thoughts will be maintained over time. Given that obsessive thoughts are a source of distress, knowing that the thoughts should become less frequent and intense can be very motivating for patients. Of course, most patients also relish the idea of not having to engage in compulsions—even though this idea can be quite frightening. It can very useful to spend some time with patients picturing a life without OCD. Many will voice a desire to spend more time doing pleasurable things and less time doing rituals.

The importance of ritual prevention can be communicated to patients in a number of ways. It can be useful to talk about Foa and colleagues' influential 1984 study that was outlined previously. Many patients want to leave out aspects of the treatment (e.g., they will touch all sorts of contaminated things, as long as they can wash afterward) and this study emphasizes the importance of combining exposure *and* ritual prevention. Many patients also appreciate the use of metaphor. We sometimes use the example of the family dog begging for scraps at the dinner table. If the dog comes to one family member's chair and gets a nice bite of steak one night, he will likely visit that person again the following night. Each night that he gets a scrap, he will more strongly associate getting scraps with that person. If this generous family member suddenly decides to stop giving scraps to the dog, the dog will gradually stop begging at his chair. OCD works in much the same way—obsessions expect a response and for as long as they get the response they want (a ritual), they will continue to stick around. If they do not get what they want, though, they will eventually quiet down.

One of the most commonly asked questions that we are asked about EX/RP is whether complete ritual prevention is required right from the beginning of treatment. It is our sense that this goal is unrealistic for most patients. For some OCD patients, rituals occupy their entire day and it would be nearly impossible for them to simply stop engaging in all rituals from one day to the next. We saw a patient who maintained an extensive list of each behavior she engaged in during the day, from the exact order in which she changed her clothes, to when she washed her hands, to whether she used toilet tissue after going to the washroom. She feared contamina-

tion and worried that if she did not write down all her activities, she would either not do things properly or would forget whether she did them at all. These detailed lists usually filled about 12 pages of unlined paper each day. When ritual prevention was introduced, this patient balked and although she understood the rationale for complete RP, she refused to do it. Rather than lose the patient, we agreed to more gradual RP. Throughout treatment, she gradually reduced the length of her lists, eventually eliminating them completely. This patient's general style was to do things gradually at her own pace, and although this was frustrating for the clinician early on in treatment, the patient ended up doing extremely well.

Another commonly asked question is how to institute RP in people who have rituals in many different areas (e.g., washing, symmetry, checking). Some patients might be able to handle doing widespread RP right away. Others might be less overwhelmed if they can start with one focused area. In making this decision early on in treatment, clinicians should be mindful of the importance of giving their patients success experiences. If an overwhelming assignment is given early on in treatment, patients might feel as if they have failed and might see the prospect of living life without OCD as impossible. It is certainly better to initially assign a manageable RP task and use the success of that experience as a motivator for working on more difficult OCD symptoms. As therapy continues, it is essential that patients understand the principle of generalization. Particularly for complicated cases, there will not be time in therapy to tackle each OC symptom individually. Rather, patients should see that the principles of EX/RP can be applied to all OC symptoms and they must become comfortable working on difficult symptoms on their own. This is important in terms of long-term maintenance of gains since, once therapy ends, patients might experience recurrences of OC symptoms and might also develop new concerns. It is essential that they be able to apply the principles of EX/RP at these challenging times regardless of the nature of the symptoms.

Although clinicians should certainly be flexible about RP, they should clearly communicate to patients that complete RP is the goal of treatment and that they should develop a commitment to living life without OCD. It is important to recognize, however, that patients might violate RP rules and that they should see these violations as learning experiences, rather than as failures. This is particularly true early in treatment. When patients do engage in rituals, they should make a note of what happened and try to develop an awareness of what triggered the ritual. A pediatric patient that we treated found that he had the most difficulty resisting his rituals at night when he was tired. He was a very creative child, so we had him make a very artistic sign to put on his nightstand table reminding him to "boss back 'The Voice,'" which was what he called his OCD. We also purposefully integrated exposures into his nighttime routine so that he would get a lot of practice with RP at these challenging times.

As clinicians discuss the issue of RP violations with patients, it is essential that they establish a tone in the therapeutic relationship that encourages honesty. Patients should not feel that they need to hide violations. Rather, they should be encouraged to be open with the clinician about such occurrences and work collaboratively with the clinician to reduce the likelihood that violations will continue to occur in the future.

As therapy progresses, RP violations should become less frequent and clinicians should be more firm about the importance of this progression. When patients do engage in rituals, they should know to immediately re-expose themselves to the cue that triggered the urge to ritualize. For example, when individuals with contamination fears wash their hands after touching something they perceive to be contaminated, they should touch the object again and try again to resist the urge to ritualize. A "checker" who cannot resist the urge to check the locks repeatedly when leaving the house in the morning should be encouraged to open and lock the door again and then walk away without checking at all.

Finally, clinicians often wonder when to terminate OCD treatment. It is unrealistic to keep patients in treatment until they have *no* OCD symptoms. An important component of treatment is to help patients realize that they might continue to have some intrusive thoughts and urges to ritualize. The important issue is how patients handle these challenges. Patients will likely be ready to discontinue treatment when they recognize the importance of not suppressing obsessive thoughts and are able to refrain from ritualizing the great majority of the time. When they do slip, they should know to re-expose. Furthermore, as we mentioned earlier, it is important that patients know what to do if an old symptom starts to cause problems again or if a new concern arises. In short, we should feel confident sending patients away if they have the skills to be their own clinicians. As treatment progresses, it is essential to make patients comfortable in that role. Patients should take a more active role in designing exposures. If they come in to sessions with questions about how to deal with challenging situations, they should be encouraged to try to devise strategies on their own first before the clinician offers suggestions.

DEALING WITH RESISTANCE TO EX/RP

Some patients are very resistant to EX/RP. Given that this is the crux of the treatment, such resistance can put the therapy at a deadlock. Throughout this chapter, we have given some advice on making EX/RP palatable to patients, including doing gradual RP and not being punitive about RP violations. Setting a collaborative tone in the therapeutic relationship where both clinician and patient are working together to fight OCD (rather than the patient fighting the clinician) is absolutely essential to successful treatment.

Another excellent way to deal with resistance is to ask patients to articulate what they are afraid of. Often, they report being nervous about their feared consequences. It is best at these times to return to the model and to reiterate the rationale for EX/RP. It can also be comforting for patients to know that clinicians will not assign exercises that they would not do themselves. In fact, it is good clinical practice to do exposures along with the patient (e.g., sitting on the floor of the bathroom, eating a snack without first washing one's hands, etc.), particularly early in treatment. Finally, it can also be helpful to discuss with patients how they see their lives without OCD. The desire to return to work, to make more friends at school, or to take up a previously enjoyed hobby can serve as excellent motivation for doing difficult tasks.

One potential pitfall of returning to the model is that some patients will not accept the veracity of the treatment model. In this case, the patient's doubt can be reframed as a hypothesis to be tested. The clinician should allow the patient to feel doubt, but should encourage the patient to test out the belief that EX/RP will not work by giving it a good try. Clinicians can be supportive of the treatment approach by explaining that they have seen it work for many other patients, while being sympathetic to the patient's concerns that it might not work in his or her particular case.

Some patients are very compliant during treatment sessions, but have a difficult time applying what they have learned outside therapy. Many patients resist doing homework because they feel too anxious doing it without the support of the clinician. In this case, they can arrange for telephone contact with the clinician or secure the help of a trusted friend or family member. This support should gradually be faded to be sure that patients are not using other people as safety signals. This is simply another form of avoidance that will perpetuate the OCD over time. This concern should also be considered during treatment sessions. If it seems that the clinician is playing some sort of safety role, exposures can gradually be done without the clinician present.

Despite our best efforts, some patients simply refuse to engage in EX/RP. It might be that the cost of doing rituals fails to outweigh the benefit of not doing them. Simply put, patients sometimes come to treatment when they are not ready to change. When this is the case, it is often better to invite patients to come back to treatment when they are ready, rather than to have them stay in treatment and not have a success experience. Another option is to suggest that patients explore whether medication reduces their anxiety enough to make EX/RP seem more palatable.

OTHER APPLICATIONS OF EX/RP

Despite our emphasis here on the treatment of OCD, it is important to point out that EX/RP has been applied effectively to other disorders that bear some formal similarity to OCD, most notably Hypochondriasis (e.g., Visser & Bouman, 2001) and Body Dysmorphic Disorder (e.g.,

McKay, Todaro, Neziroglu, & Campisi, 1997). EX/RP has also been used in the treatment of eating disorders (e.g., Bulik, Sullivan, Carter, McIntosh, & Joyce, 1998) and substance use disorders (see Lee & Oei, 1993), based on the belief that anxiety can drive dysfunctional eating and substance use. For example, binge eating has been conceptualized as a way to escape from anxiety (e.g., see Polivy & Herman, 1993), and EX/RP can be used to help patients learn that they can face anxiety-provoking situations (regardless of whether they are related to food and eating or to other stressors) and experience a reduction in anxiety without needing to binge-eat. Finally, EX/RP has also been used in the treatment of disorders that are not characterized by difficulties with anxiety, including Pathological Gambling (Echeburua, Fernandez-Montalvo, & Baez, 2000) and Sexual Addiction (see Hollander & Wong, 1995). Given that the goal in EX/RP is anxiety reduction and the associated changes in erroneous anxiety-related cognitions, the value of the treatments for disorders that are best characterized as appetitive remains unclear.

References

Abramowitz, J. S., & Foa, E. B. (2000). Does Major Depressive Disorder influence outcome of exposure and response prevention for OCD? *Behavior Therapy, 31,* 795–800.

Abramowitz, J. S., Foa, E. B., & Franklin, M. E. (2003). Cognitive behavior therapy for Obsessive Compulsive Disorder: Effects of intensive versus twice-weekly sessions. *Journal of Consulting and Clinical Psychology, 71,* 394–398.

Abramowitz, J. S., Franklin, M. E., Street, G. P., Kozak, M. J., & Foa, E. B. (2000). Effects of comorbid depression on response to treatment for Obsessive-Compulsive Disorder. *Behavior Therapy, 31,* 517–528.

Abramowitz, J. S., Tolin, D. F., & Street, G. P. (2001). Paradoxical effects of thought suppression: A meta-analysis of controlled studies. *Clinical Psychology Review, 21*(5), 683–703.

AuBuchon, P. G., & Malatesta, V. J. (1994). Obsessive compulsive patients with comorbid personality disorder: Associated problems and response to a comprehensive behavior therapy. *Journal of Clinical Psychiatry, 55,* 448–453.

Baum, M. (1970). Extinction of avoidance responding

through response prevention (flooding). *Psychological Bulletin, 74*, 276–284.

Bulik, C. M., Sullivan, P. F., Carter, F. A., McIntosh, V. V., & Joyce, P. R. (1998). The role of exposure with response prevention in the cognitive-behavioural therapy for Bulimia Nervosa. *Psychological Medicine, 28*, 611–623.

Carmin, C. N., Pollard, A. C., & Ownby, R. L. (1999). Cognitive behavioral treatment of older adults with Obsessive-Compulsive Disorder. *Cognitive and Behavioral Practice, 6*, 110–119.

De Araujo, L. A., Ito, L. M., & Marks, I. M. (1996). Early compliance and other factors predicting outcome of exposure for OCD. *British Journal of Psychiatry, 169*, 747–752.

DeHaan, E., Hoogduin, K. A. L., Buitelaar, J. K., & Keijsers, G. P. J. (1998). Behavior therapy versus clomipramine for the treatment of Obsessive-Compulsive Disorder in children and adolescents. *Journal of the American Academy of Child and Adolescent Psychiatry, 37*, 1022–1029.

Echeburua, E., Fernandez-Montalvo, J., & Baez, C. (2000). Relapse prevention in the treatment of slot machine Pathological Gambling: Long-term outcome. *Behavior Therapy, 31*, 351–364.

Fals-Stewart, W., & Lucente, S. (1993). An MCMI cluster typology of obsessive-compulsives: A measure of personality characteristics and its relationship to treatment participation, compliance, and outcome in behavior therapy. *Journal of Psychiatric Research, 27*, 139–154.

Foa, E. B., & Franklin, M. E. (1999). Cognitive behavior therapy. In M. Hersen & A. S. Bellack (Eds.), *Handbook of comparative interventions for adult disorders* (pp. 359–377). New York: Wiley.

Foa, E. B., Franklin, M. E., & Kozak, M. J. (1998). Psychosocial treatments for Obsessive-Compulsive Disorder. In R. P. Swinson, M. M. Antony, S. Rachman, & M. A. Richter (Eds.), *Obsessive-Compulsive Disorder: Theory, research, and treatment* (pp. 258–276). New York: Guilford Press.

Foa, E. B., Franklin, M. E., & Moser, J. (2002). Context in the clinic: How well do CBT and medications work in combination? *Biological Psychiatry, 51*, 989–997.

Foa, E. B., & Kozak, M. J. (1996). Psychological treatment for Obsessive-Compulsive Disorder. In M. R. Mavissakalian & R. F. Prien (Eds.), *Long-term treatments of anxiety disorders* (pp. 285–309). Washington, DC: American Psychiatric Association Press.

Foa, E. B., Liebowitz, M. R., Kozak, M. K., Davies, S., Campeas, R., Franklin, M. D., Huppert, J. E., Kjernisted, K., Rowan, V., Simpson, H. B., Schmidt, A., & Tu, X. (in preparation). *Treatment of Obsessive-Compulsive Disorder by exposure and ritual prevention, clomipramine, and their combination: A randomized, placebo-controlled study.*

Foa, E. B., Steketee, G., Grayson, J. B., Turner, R. M., & Latimer, P. R. (1984). Deliberate exposure and blocking of obsessive-compulsive rituals: Immediate and long-term effects. *Behavior Therapy, 15*, 450–472.

Franklin, M. E., Abramowitz, J. S., Kozak, M. J., Levitt, J. T., & Foa, E. B. (2000). Effectiveness of exposure and ritual prevention for Obsessive-Compulsive Disorder: Randomized compared with nonrandomized samples. *Journal of Consulting and Clinical Psychology, 68*, 594–602.

Hollander, E., & Wong, C. (1995). Body Dysmorphic Disorder, Pathological Gambling, and sexual compulsions. *Journal of Clinical Psychiatry, 56* (Suppl. 4), 7–12.

Lee, N. K., & Oei, T. P. (1993). Exposure and response prevention in anxiety disorders: Implications for treatment and relapse prevention in problem drinkers. *Clinical Psychology Review, 13*, 619–632.

March, J. S., & Leonard, H. L. (1998). Obsessive-Compulsive Disorder in children and adolescents. In R. P. Swinson, M. M. Antony, S. Rachman, & M. A. Richter (Eds.), *Obsessive-Compulsive Disorder: Theory, research, and treatment* (pp. 367–394). New York: Guilford Press.

McKay, D., Todaro, J., Neziroglu, F., & Campisi, T. (1997). Body Dysmorphic Disorder: A preliminary investigation of treatment and maintenance using exposure with response prevention. *Behaviour Research and Therapy, 35*, 67–70.

Meyer, V. (1966). Modification of expectations in cases with obsessional rituals. *Behaviour Research and Therapy, 4*, 273–280.

Polivy, J., & Herman, C. P. (1993). Etiology of binge eating: Psychological mechanisms. In C. G. Fairburn & G. T. Wilson (Eds.), *Binge eating: Nature, assessment, and treatment* (pp. 173–205). New York: Guilford Press.

Rachman, S. J., & Hodgson, R. J. (1980). *Obsessions and compulsions*. Englewood Cliffs, NJ: Prentice-Hall.

Visser, S., & Bouman, T. K. (2001). The treatment of Hypochondriasis: Exposure plus response prevention vs. cognitive therapy. *Behaviour Research and Therapy, 39*, 423–442.

51 SATIATION THERAPY

Adrian H. Bowers

Satiation therapy dates back to the early 1960s and is predicated on behavioral theory. One of the first documented uses of satiation therapy was in the treatment of towel hoarding (Ayllon, 1963). Consequently, satiation therapy has been applied to a number of clinical problems, including specific types of hoarding (Forget, 1991), obsessional thoughts (Rachman, 1976; Rachman & Hodgson, 1980), auditory hallucination (Glaister, 1985), and in the treatment of sexual deviance (e.g., Johnston, Hudson, & Marshall, 1992; Laws, 1995; Laws & Marshall, 1991; Marshall, 1979; Marshall, Eccles, & Barbaree, 1991). Another connection to satiation therapy is found in early applications of behavioral theory. Although not grouped specifically under the heading of *satiation*, the techniques of negative practice and habituation have been used to treat habit disorders such as tics (Dunlap, 1932) and excessive eye blinking (Costello, 1963).

Ayllon (1963) described the treatment of an institutionalized woman that would obsessively collect towels and keep them in her room. The nurses reported an ongoing count of towels in her room to be between 19 and 29, despite continual verbal admonishments for towel collecting and continual removal of unneeded towels. At the beginning of treatment, nurses stopped removing towels and instead began to give towels to the woman one at a time (an average of 7 towels daily). By the third week of treatment an average of 60 towels a day were given to the woman. Nurses did not speak to the woman when ad-

ministering the towels and no explanation was given to the woman as to the change in towel policy. By week 13, roughly 625 towels were in the woman's room and she began to remove a few towels; at this point no new towels were placed in her room. Over the next few weeks the woman began to remove more and more towels from her room until, by week 26, a steady number of towels was maintained in her room—an average of 1 to 5 towels per week, well below pretreatment levels of 19 to 29 towels. Even more telling is the change in the verbal reactions of the woman to the continual towel offerings. The following is the progression of her statements throughout treatment: First week: "Oh, you found it for me, thank you"; second week: "Don't give me no more towels. I've got enough"; third week: "Take them towels away. . . . I can't sit here all night and fold towels"; fourth and fifth weeks: "Get these dirty towels out of here"; sixth week, after beginning to remove towels: "I can't drag any more of these towels, I just can't do it."

Clearly what was once reinforcing (an increased number of towels) soon became aversive with increasing exposure to the reinforcer (i.e., satiation). However, *satiation therapy* is a misnomer. A more apt description of the actual process is *over*-satiation therapy. Satiation is typically viewed as the levels of reinforcement that are obtained under free rein, such as that obtained by a rat on a free-feeding schedule. However, this is decidedly *not* what takes place in satiation therapy; rather, the subject is induced into obtaining more of the reinforcer than he or she would otherwise obtain. For example, the towel-hoarding woman was not allowed to obtain her optimal number of towels (as in Timberlake, 1995, and Allison, 1993) but was given more towels than she desired. This is a key element to satiation therapy, and perhaps the apt term of *over-satiation* should be at least remembered if not used when describing this therapeutic technique.

Satiation therapy has been used effectively to treat obsessive thoughts (Rachman, 1976; Rachman & Hodgson, 1980) by instructing the individual to repeat the obsessive thoughts or not avoid or suppress the obsessive thoughts (similar to the practice of overcorrection). Interestingly, Glaister (1985) reports successful treatment of an individual with auditory hallucinations by having the individual record the time of the speaking voice, the content, and how demanding the voice seemed on a 6-point scale. Treatment consisted of 85 half-hour homework assignments over 16 months of therapy (28 formal therapy sessions were used). Currently, the view of satiation as flooding to a stimulus (i.e., exposure) in order to habituate to the fear or anxiety associated with that stimulus, is an integral aspect of cognitive-behavioral treatment of obsessive-compulsive spectrum disorders that include techniques of exposure and response prevention (EX/RP, discussed in Chapter 50 in this volume). Readers should refer to empirically supported work in this area by such authors as Foa and Franklin (2001). Because satiation therapy in this context has been largely subsumed by EX/RP therapy, this chapter will focus on current applications of satiation therapy that maintain satiation as a distinct technique with ties to its historical and theoretical roots.

Currently, the main clinical area where satiation therapy is employed is in the treatment of sexual deviance. For example, satiation therapy has been used as a component of masturbatory reconditioning. Briefly, *masturbatory reconditioning* is based on a number of techniques designed to alter deviant sexual arousal by decreasing the reinforcement of deviant arousal or increasing the reinforcement of nondeviant arousal (or both). Satiation therapy is often a component of masturbatory reconditioning along with the techniques of thematic shift, fantasy alternation, and directed masturbation (Laws & Marshall, 1991). Specifically, satiation therapy in this context refers to exposure to the deviant stimulus fantasy at a level that exceeds the individual's hypothesized free-operant level of engagement with the stimulus fantasy (the individual may be instructed to masturbate while verbally repeating the deviant fantasy, or to verbally repeat the fantasy without masturbation).

EVIDENCE FOR THE EFFECTIVENESS OF SATIATION THERAPY

Although no large-scale studies have been conducted that utilize satiation therapy, a number of well-controlled ideographic case studies have been conducted that support the use of satiation therapy as a stand-alone technique or as an adjunctive technique in a treatment package. Furthermore, a review of the evidence suggests that satiation therapy and directed masturbation have more clear empirical support than such techniques as thematic shift and fantasy alternation (Laws & Marshall, 1991). More research is clearly needed to study each of the following: (1) client characteristics associated with favorable outcomes, (2) satiation therapy's mechanisms of action, (3) what clinical problems are most responsive to satiation therapy, (4) the effectiveness of satiation therapy versus that of other highly effective techniques (e.g., covert sensitization) for treating sexual deviancy, and (5) the duration of effects (i.e., the dose-response curve per dose of satiation). Although current use of satiation therapy has focused on the treatment of sexual deviance, a number of specific, widely disparate clinical problems may be found to respond to satiation therapy. Many other uses of satiation therapy may yet be discovered, considering its ease of use, potential for high client acceptability, and past successes.

WHO MIGHT BENEFIT FROM THIS TECHNIQUE

As previously discussed, individuals whose problems fall within the obsessive-compulsive spectrum disorders could benefit from satiation therapy, but their therapists should probably attempt to treat them with more traditional therapies such as EX/RP (Foa & Franklin, 2001) and acceptance-based techniques (Hayes, Wilson,

Gifford, Follette, & Strosahl, 1996) that are being incorporated into treatment of other anxiety-related disorders. However, satiation-based techniques are currently being used in the treatment of sexual deviates, and people with paraphilias or paraphilitic tendencies may benefit from satiation therapy. Although no large-scale studies have been conducted, satiation therapy as a stand-alone therapy or adjunctive technique has been used to treat numerous individuals with deviant sexual interests in controlled case studies (see Laws & Marshall, 1991; Marshall, 1979; Marshall & Lippens, 1977).

CONTRAINDICATIONS

Necessary prerequisites for satiation treatment include adequate motivation and an ability to concentrate on a particular topic (e.g., a deviant fantasy) for an extended period of time. Related to motivation, there are a number of concerns:

1. Individuals with deviant sexual interests may not be interested in changing these practices.
2. Individuals may not buy into the efficacy of the treatment. In fact, many individuals may view satiation therapy as a likely way of increasing deviant arousal and subsequently may lose motivation for the treatment.
3. Masturbatory reconditioning techniques that include actual masturbation may be a further barrier to motivation for some individuals. Overcoming shame and guilt associated with masturbating to deviant sexual fantasies may be a barrier for some individuals.

Providing individuals with a clear rationale as to the process of the treatment and its intended consequences may help with motivational problems and other concerns about the treatment.

OTHER DECISIONS IN DECIDING TO USE OR NOT USE SATIATION THERAPY

Treatment of sexual deviance should not be undertaken lightly, and there are considerable legal and ethical concerns related to satiation therapy and other masturbatory reconditioning techniques. Iatrogenic treatment effects have been noted with masturbatory reconditioning techniques (see Laws, 1985; Marshall, 1979); however, proper management of these occurrences has resolved these problems to baseline levels. Proper management includes being skilled in a number of techniques that are relevant to treating sexual deviance (e.g., satiation therapy, covert sensitization, directed masturbation, and aversive techniques). As Laws, an expert in the treatment of sexual deviance, notes, "We have seen many treatment failures, but we have never seen a treatment which made a sex offender more deviant" (1985, p. 43). Again, the caveat holds that what is meant by *treatment* is a comprehensive skills set of techniques related to the treatment of sexual deviance. Along these lines, the technique of covert sensitization has shown considerable effects for the treatment of sexual deviance and should be considered as a potential first-line treatment.

HOW DOES THE TECHNIQUE WORK?

At this time there is no definitive explanation as to how this technique works. However, there are a number of explanations that are reasonable and have theoretical support and some empirical backing. One of the earliest explanations relates to experimental findings that reinforcers lose their effect when an excessive amount of the reinforcer is made available. From comparative literature, the most common example is the decreases in behavior in such cases as bar pressing with a free-fed rat. Although this explanation is parsimonious, it is also descriptive solely of what occurs when an overabundance of a reinforcer is given to a subject—it does not describe how or why satiation works. A number of mechanisms of action of satiation therapy have been hypothesized, including (1) punishment or aversiveness related to boredom (verbal satiation) or the actual act of masturbating for a considerable amount of time (e.g., 1 hour) after reaching orgasm; (2) the possibility that explicit verbalization of fantasies may remove their reinforcing properties associated with their being forbidden and illicit, thereby reducing the arousal associated with them (Marshall, 1979); (3) Pavlovian or operant extinction; (4) Hullian conditioned inhibition (Laws, 1995). Another line of literature that has direct implications for mechanisms and prediction is behavioral economics and molar theories of behavior. These views relate to the entire system in which a reinforcement schedule occurs, whereby an upset in any particular reinforcement schedule will result in various changes of a reinforcer's strength (Allison, 1993; Timberlake, 1995).

STEP-BY-STEP PROCEDURES

Specifically, the described technique applies to verbal satiation therapy related to deviant sexual arousal. Please refer to Marshall (1979) for a description of satiation therapy for sexual deviance that includes masturbation as an active component.

1. *Consent.* Obtain informed consent from the patient. Issues to address in informing the client include the rationale for the treatment, likely effects of the treatment—both short-term and long-term—and a description of the procedures that will be used during therapy. Potential candidates may have concerns related to the embarrassment of covertly verbalizing their deviant fantasies. Furthermore, these fears may be related to the presence of a female therapist. Another concern may be that the procedure will increase levels of deviant sexual arousal. Explain to clients that deviant sexual arousal will be initially increased (several sessions), after which it will decrease.

2. *Therapeutic structure.* A number of variations are possible, but past use of verbal satiation has used the following structure: three weekly sessions in which the client continually covertly verbalizes fantasies for at least 30 min. Although no research has been conducted to determine the optimal time required for satiation for the majority of clients, based on past research designs 30 min is a reasonable guideline. Again, it is always better to aim for over-satiation as opposed to just meeting the mark of satiation based on the hypothesized mechanisms of action. Clues to possible appropriate satiation lengths may include clients demonstrating behaviors consistent with boredom or fatigue. Positive treatment effects are usually noted within 3 to 4 weeks. Some therapies have monitored progress by penile tumescence assessment once a month.

3. *Specifics.* Evidence suggests that the necessary components include (a) covertly verbalizing deviant fantasies for at least 30-min periods, (b) keeping the fantasy verbalization consistent and focused on sexual scenarios, and (c) verbalizing fantasies with few or no pauses. Related to this last specific, falling asleep has been noted on many occasions and should be monitored and prevented. Clients soon tire of this activity, yet some evidence suggests that this very boredom may be a mechanism of action (Marshall & Lippens, 1977). Laws (1995) noted a procedure to help prevent lapses of verbalization and falling asleep, which implemented a voice-operated relay (VOR) in the boom microphone of a headset worn by the client. If the client paused verbalizations for more than 5 s, the switch would close and a high-intensity sound would be emitted from the headset. This procedure enabled therapists not to have to monitor client verbalizations constantly. However, another concern is the content of the verbalizations. Therapists should consider continually monitoring or spot monitoring the content of client verbalizations to insure that verbalization is of a deviant fantasy nature.

4. *Apparatus.* Satiation without masturbation is a less demanding therapy and needs few laboratory materials. Therapists should consider using penile tumescence assessment, which could be outsourced. In session, the most crucial item is a tape recorder to record verbalizations for adherence. Therapists should also consider the use of a headset to record verbalizations and potentially use a VOR procedure.

5. *Self-management and relapse prevention.* Unfortunately, the treatment of sexual deviancy is an ongoing life process. Therapists should clearly state to clients that they will almost certainly not be cured by any particular treatment but rather will need continual treatment to maintain gains. Clients may be discouraged by this revelation but may find solace in framing treatment as a part of a healthy lifestyle that includes continual maintenance, much like the continual proper nutrition and exercise that

are needed for health benefits. Furthermore, incorporating the unpleasantness of treatment into the larger framework of the client's values (be it greater sexual intimacy with a partner or avoidance of the legal implications of their deviant actions) may be helpful for bolstering client resolve for continual self-management. Specifically, self-management may encompass homework assignments of satiation sessions conducted in a quiet, private place. Furthermore, the therapist should consider the use of relapse prevention (RP) techniques (see Chapter 48, this volume) in the maintenance of treatment gains (Laws, 1995).

Further Reading

Abel, G. G., & Rouleau, J. (1990). Male sex offenders. In M. E. Thase, B. A. Edelstein, & M. Hersen (Eds.), *Handbook of outpatient treatment of adults: Nonpsychotic mental disorders* (pp. 271–290). New York: Plenum Press.

Laws, D. R. (1995). Verbal satiation: Notes on procedure, with speculations on its mechanism of effect. *Sexual Abuse: A Journal of Research and Treatment, 7,* 155–166.

Marshall, W. L. (1979). Satiation therapy: A procedure for reducing deviant sexual arousal. *Journal of Applied Behavior Analysis, 12,* 377–389.

References

Allison, J. (1993). Response deprivation, reinforcement, and economics. *Journal of the Experimental Analysis of Behavior, 60,* 129–140.

Ayllon, T. (1963). Intensive treatment of psychotic behaviour by stimulus satiation and food reinforcement. *Behaviour Research and Therapy, 1,* 53–61.

Costello, C. G. (1963). The essentials of behavior therapy. *Canadian Psychiatric Association Journal, 8,* 162–166.

Dunlap, K. (1932). *Habits: Their making and unmaking.* New York: Liveright.

Foa, E. B., & Franklin, M. E. (2001). Obsessive-Compulsive Disorder. In D. H. Barlow (Ed.), *Clinical handbook of psychological disorders: A step-by-step treatment manual* (3rd ed., pp. 209–263). New York: Guilford Press.

Forget, J. (1991). L'élimination d'un comportement de ramassage de détritus par une technique de satiété. [The elimination of a trash collecting compulsion by a satiation technique.] *Science et Comportement, 21,* 40–48.

Glaister, B. (1985). A case of auditory hallucination treated by satiation. *Behavior Research and Therapy, 23,* 213–215.

Hayes, S. C., Wilson, K. G., Gifford, E. V., Follette, V. M., & Strosahl, K. (1996). Emotional avoidance and behavioral disorders: A functional dimensional approach to diagnosis and treatment. *Journal of Consulting and Clinical Psychology, 64,* 1152–1168.

Johnston, P., Hudson, S. M., & Marshall, W. L. (1992). The effects of masturbatory reconditioning with nonfamilial child molesters. *Behaviour Research and Therapy, 5,* 559–561.

Laws, D. R. (1985). Sexual fantasy alteration: Procedural considerations. *Journal of Behavior Therapy and Experimental Psychiatry, 16,* 39–44.

Laws, D. R. (1995). Verbal satiation: Notes on procedure, with speculations on its mechanism of effect. *Sexual Abuse: A Journal of Research and Treatment, 7,* 155–166.

Laws, D. R., & Marshall, W. L. (1991). Masturbatory reconditioning with sexual deviates: An evaluative review. *Advances in Behavior Research and Therapy, 13,* 13–25.

Marshall, W. L. (1979). Satiation therapy: A procedure for reducing deviant sexual arousal. *Journal of Applied Behavior Analysis, 12,* 377–389.

Marshall, W. L., Eccles, A., & Barbaree, H. E. (1991). The treatment of exhibitionists: A focus on sexual deviance versus cognitive and relationship features. *Behaviour Research and Therapy, 29,* 129–135.

Marshall, W. L., & Lippens, K. (1977). The clinical value of boredom: A procedure for reducing inappropriate sexual interests. *The Journal of Nervous and Mental Disease, 165,* 283–287.

Rachman, S. J. (1976). The modification of obsessions: A new formulation. *Behaviour Research and Therapy, 14,* 437–443.

Rachman, S. J., & Hodgson, R. J. (1980). *Obsessions and compulsions.* Engelwood Cliffs, N.J.: Prentice-Hall.

Timberlake, W. (1995). Reconceptualizing reinforcement: A causal-system approach to reinforcement and behavior change. In W. T. O'Donohue & L. Krasner (Eds.), *Theories of behavior therapy: Exploring behavior change* (pp. 59–96). Washington, DC: American Psychological Association.

52   SELF-MANAGEMENT

Lynn P. Rehm and Jennifer H. Adams

HOW DOES IT WORK?

The self-control model of depression (Rehm, 1977) was developed to integrate both cognitive and behavioral models of depression, provide a model to serve as a framework for depression research, and to serve as a structure for a therapy program that targets specific behavioral and cognitive deficits present in many individuals with depression (Rehm, 1985).

Kanfer's self-control model states that behavior directed toward long-term outcomes can be characterized as a three-stage feedback loop. When people want to change their behavior for a long-term outcome, they begin by self-monitoring the behavior; they compare this observed behavior to a standard in self-evaluation; and, based on the evaluation, they may reward or punish themselves in the self-reinforcement phase. The model assumes that people influence their own behavior as they might influence another person's behavior by applying contingent rewards or punishments.

Rehm's (1977) depression model suggests that people who are depressed or who are prone to depression have difficulty organizing their behavior around long-term goals, and that this difficulty can be described in terms of one or more of six deficits in self-control skills. These deficits include (1) selective attention to negative rather than positive information; (2) selective attention to immediate consequences of behaviors, as opposed to long-term consequences; (3) unrealistically high performance standards; (4) the use of a depresso-

genic attributional style— that is, the tendency to attribute failures to internal influences and successes to external influences or chance (see Chapter 5, "Attribution Change," in this volume); (5) the use of excessive self-punishment; and (6) the use of inadequate contingent self-reward to strengthen behavior toward long-term goals. When external reinforcements are absent, are lost, or are insufficient to maintain effortful behavior toward a goal, people with good self-control skills can manage their behavior to regain progress toward the same or a new goal. People who are prone to depression are at the mercy of external rewards and punishments and have difficulty maintaining behavior in their absence.

Self-management therapy (SMT) is a structured, manualized, cognitive-behavioral, group-format program for the treatment of depression that targets each of the skill deficits just identified. The program can be thought of in three ways. First, it is a program that systematically targets self-control components of depression and intervenes in each. Second, it is a program that teaches basic self-control skills in the context of depression. Third, in teaching self-control skills, the program can be thought of as teaching positive self-esteem. *Self-esteem* can be conceptualized not as a trait, but as a set of skills that people use to work toward goals.

Developed in a group therapy format, SMT has been successfully utilized with individuals as well. The group format, however, may impart additional benefits to the participants that are not available as part of the individual therapy experience. For example, the sharing of personal issues and concerns enables the participants to see that they are not alone in their experiences. Furthermore, the group members often provide support for one another, provide coping models, and challenge one another to meet their therapy-related goals (Rehm, 1985).

Self-management therapy, as it is currently implemented, is a 14-week program that meets for 1-1/2 hours each week. Twelve topic areas are discussed across the 14 weeks, with two additional weeks built in to allow for further review of topics as determined by the needs of the group members. Each session includes core elements, including a psychoeducational presentation, a discussion of the issues involved, written exercises, and weekly homework assignments. After the first session, each session begins with a review of the previous week's homework. The material and exercises are meant to target both the general deficits exhibited by many people with symptoms of depression, and the more specific concerns of the individual clients (Rehm, 1985).

EVIDENCE FOR THE EFFECTIVENESS OF SELF-MANAGEMENT THERAPY

Results of therapy outcome studies indicate that SMT is superior in reducing the severity, frequency, and duration of complaints common in those who meet the criteria for depression as compared to nonspecific therapies and to no-treatment and wait-list control conditions, and is equal to or superior to other forms of cognitive-behavioral therapy for depression (see Rehm, 1990, for a review). SMT has been investigated in a number of studies with adult outpatients by Rehm and his colleagues (Fuchs & Rehm, 1977; Kornblith, Rehm, O'Hara, & Lamparski, 1983; Rehm, Fuchs, Roth, Kornblith, & Romano, 1979; Rehm, Kaslow, & Rabin, 1987; Rehm et al., 1981) and by other psychotherapy researchers (Fleming & Thornton, 1980; Roth, Bielski, Jones, Parker, & Osborn, 1982; Rude, 1986; Thomas, Petry, & Goldman, 1987; Tressler & Tucker, 1980). The SMT program has been adapted for a variety of age ranges and populations, including renal dial-

ysis patients (Rogers, Kerns, Rehm, Hendler, & Harkness, 1982), veterans with Post-Traumatic Stress Disorder (PTSD; Rehm, 2001); psychiatric inpatients (Kornblith & Greenwald, 1982), psychiatric day-treatment patients (van den Hout, Arntz, & Kunkels, 1995), battered women (Bailey, Rehm, Martin, Holton, & Le, 1994), and both the elderly (Rokke, Tomhave, & Jocic, 1999, 2000) and children (Rehm & Sharp, 1996; Reynolds & Coats, 1986; Stark, Reynolds, & Kaslow, 1987).

INDICATIONS AND CONTRAINDICATIONS

SMT has been successfully employed with a wide variety of depressed patients. Participants must have a degree of motivation to complete a program that lasts 3 to 4 months and that includes homework. Dropouts are more common among people who seek treatment during an acute crisis. The program has been run with individuals having mild to severe levels of depression. Very severe depression may make it difficult for people to sustain the effort necessary for participation. Doing homework requires literacy, although we have had illiterate prisoners in the program who have kept self-monitoring logs as simple marks.

TOPIC-BY-TOPIC PROCEDURES

The following is an overview of the program. Interested therapists are encouraged to contact the first author to request a copy of the comprehensive therapist manual, which includes a step-by-step guide to each session, participant handouts, and visual aids (Rehm, 2001).

Topic I: Introduction, Depression, and Overall Rationale

At the start of the first session, the group leader reviews the parameters of group therapy and issues of confidentiality. Participants are given a binder in which they keep weekly handouts, in-session exercises, homework assignments, and the homework itself. By the end of the program they have assembled a set of materials that they may consult later to continue or to redo the program on their own.

Early in the first session, participants are asked to introduce themselves and say a few words about why they are seeking help and about their lives. The therapist guides this process by pointing out similarities among participants' concerns and encouraging discussion among participants. After these introductions, the therapist transitions into a presentation on the nature of depression. The therapist reviews the symptoms of depression in the categories of emotional, physical, cognitive, and behavioral symptoms. The therapist discusses the various forms and courses of depression.

The therapist then presents an overview and rationale for the therapy, emphasizing the psychoeducational nature of the group and the role of homework in the therapy process. The first homework assignment is to ask participants to monitor their moods daily, using a simple rating scale of 1 to 10 in which 1 represents the person's most depressed day ever and 10 represents his or her best day ever. It is stressed that the homework assignments are integral to the program, and will be reviewed each week.

Topic II: Self-Monitoring Positive Activities and Self-Statements

The first part of each session from this point on is devoted to reviewing the content of the previous session and the homework. Participants are encouraged to talk about any difficulties they may have had doing the assignment, and whether they noticed any pattern to their moods over the previous week. Participants are often surprised at the variability they see in their moods from one day to the next, which contrasts with their belief that every day is the same. The primary focus of this session is to present the idea that mood is influenced by behavior and thinking. Engaging in positive and rewarding activities is linked to positive mood and engaging in negative and punishing behavior is linked to negative mood. Thoughts that represent positive interpretations and evaluations of events lead to positive mood, whereas thoughts that involve pessimistic interpretations of events lead to negative mood. The concept that follows from this is that individuals can influence their own mood by their activities and by the thoughts they have about those activi-

ties. Mood cannot be influenced directly, but is influenced indirectly through changing behavior and thoughts. Mood can also be influenced biologically, as with antidepressant medications, but depression is not simply a biological process, despite much media attention to brain chemistry. It is important to acknowledge that the relationship is reciprocal. Mood also influences activity and thinking, in that being depressed leads to inactivity and negative thoughts. Attention plays a role in the development and maintenance of depression, in that persons who are depressed tend to selectively attend to negative events to the relative exclusion of positive events. The result is predominantly negative thoughts. The homework assignment that follows from these ideas it to record positive behaviors and thoughts (i.e., thought statements that have positive content relative to oneself) in the daily self-monitoring log, along with the day's mood. The therapist emphasizes the importance of recording all positive events and self-statements, even those that might seem trivial to the participant. Participants are given a list of potential positive activities and thoughts as a list of prompts to be reviewed if they are not noticing positive events each day.

Topic III: Mood and Events

At the following session the relationship between mood, on the one hand, and activities and thoughts, on the other, is reviewed along with the homework. Participants are asked whether there seemed to be a relationship between mood and activity; which activities most influenced mood; and whether they recorded any positive thoughts. The central activity of the session is an exercise in which participants graph their moods for the week and then, on the same graph, enter the number of positive activities and thoughts they had each day. In most cases the graphed lines are roughly parallel with common peaks and valleys. The graph demonstrates from the participants' own logs the relationship between events and daily mood. This is often very persuasive in convincing participants that they can get a handle on their moods by changing behavior and thoughts. For homework, participants continue to monitor their positive activities, positive thoughts, and moods.

Topic IV: Immediate versus Delayed Consequences

After completing the check-in procedures the therapist builds upon the ideas from the previous week by suggesting that all activities can have both positive and negative consequences, both immediately and after a delay. Working out may lead to feeling good, but also to stiffness. It may be uncomfortable immediately in the short term, but will lead to better health as a delayed, long-term outcome. Paper-and-pencil exercises are used to illustrate these ideas and to have participants practice identifying positive and negative, short- and long-term consequences of personal decisions, and the positive and negative thoughts that might be derived from each. When people are depressed they tend to focus on immediate consequences of their behavior and have difficulty thinking about the longer-term consequences. When a person is depressed it is particularly difficult to do things that have a long-term positive consequence, but are immediately boring or difficult. Homework for this session is to continue the self-monitoring assignment, and to identify and record at least one activity each day that represents engaging in a behavior that is difficult in the short term but has a high payoff in the long term. When such activities occur, each participant is also to record a positive thought reflecting the long-term consequence (e.g., "I will have a good result on my next cholesterol test because I am exercising").

Topic V: Attributions for Positive Events

After completing check-in procedures, the therapist presents the idea of a depressogenic attributional style. In this session the focus is on attributions for positive events. Depressed people tend to make attributions for positive events that are external, stable, and specific, rather than internal, stable, and specific. Essentially, depressed people tend not to take credit for personal successes and positive experiences and instead see them as caused by external, unreliable, and specific factors. Taking credit for a positive experience occurs when it is attributed to internal causes that represent stable, general characteristics of the person. These ideas are illustrated by a sequence of examples presented by

the therapist. The homework assignment is to continue to monitor positive events and mood, and to attempt to write at least one positive self-statement about a positive event that reflects an internal, stable, and specific attribution on a daily basis.

Topic VI: Causes of Negative Events or Failures

The primary goal of this session is to discuss depressogenic attributions made for negative events. People who are depressed tend to make internal, stable, and general attributions about negative events. The therapist's presentation is parallel to that for the previous topic. Examples are used to elicit depressed attributions for negative events and then to generate alternative explanations for the negative-event examples that are more external, unstable, and specific in nature. It is important to point out that attributions of causality are not entirely arbitrary, and that sometimes people do cause negative events. However, most events can be thought of as having multiple causes, and there are usually external causes for negative events as well. We are not encouraging people to take credit for everything positive that happens to them, nor to deny responsibility for any negative event. Instead, we are encouraging a more balanced and realistic view to replace the typically pessimistic view of most depressed people. For homework, participants are to continue monitoring positive events and mood, and to record at least one positive (external, unstable, and specific) self-statement about a negative event each day (e.g., "My friend didn't call today because she was too busy at work. I am sure that she will call me tomorrow").

Topic VII: Goal Setting

The presentation in this session is based upon the idea that difficulty in goal-setting and attainment is another facet of the development and maintenance of depression. Goals organize behavior, and lack of goal setting, or setting goals that are vague or unrealistic, is often characteristic of people who are depressed. Depressed persons often feel hopeless about achieving goals and focus on their distance from the goal rather than on steps that can be taken toward a goal. A goal-setting exercise in this session teaches basic behavioral ideas about goal setting. Goals should be stated positively (e.g., "I want to increase . . ."); they should be within the person's control and be realistically attainable; and, they should be concrete (it should be clear when the goal has been reached). Goals may be of short range (e.g., "Get groceries today"), medium range (e.g., "Complete my last semester in college"), or long range (e.g., "Save to buy sailboat"). Participants are asked to define a medium-range goal that they would like to work on over the next few weeks. Once the goal is defined, the participant writes sub-goals or specific behaviors that contribute to reaching the overall goal. For homework, each participant continues to monitor events and mood, and makes an effort to accomplish sub-goals that are then recorded as positive events. The idea is to practice working toward delayed consequences and paying attention to progress toward the goal. Participants may also redefine their goals or develop a second goal to work on.

Topic VIII: Rewards for Motivation

Goal setting is a central part of the program and discussion of progress and obstacles make up the beginning of subsequent sessions. After this discussion, the therapist talks about how rewards and punishments influence behavior and how people may administer rewards and punishments to themselves (e.g., "patting yourself on the back" or "kicking yourself"). The way we talk to ourselves can function as self-administered reward or punishment. Part of depression is little use of contingent self-administered reward to facilitate progress toward goals, and excessive use of self-punishment that inhibits progress toward goals. The goal of this session is to assist participants in creating a self-reward menu in order to enhance their ability to self-reward when engaging in positive behaviors. In this session the focus is on overt or tangible rewards. Participants are helped to develop a list that includes rewards that are (1) enjoyable, (2) of various magnitudes, and (3) freely available. Rewards may be either material in nature (e.g., a new book) or activities that are pleasant (e.g., going to a movie). For homework, in addition to monitoring behaviors and moods, participants are instructed to utilize their rewards contingently as motivators for engaging

in behaviors related to their more difficult sub-goals. Self-rewards are also positive activities to be recorded on the self-monitoring logs.

Topic IX: Rewards as Self-Statements

The goal of this session is to build upon the concepts of the previous week, and to introduce the idea of positive self-statements as rewards. Participants identify verbal self-rewards that (1) focus on accomplishments, (2) serve to strengthen a desirable behavior, and (3) allow for the development of positive self-evaluation and self-esteem. Participants are to modify the types of phrases they might use to praise others so that they can be said to themselves (e.g., "I did a great job!"). Participants write at least five self-statements that could serve as motivators for goal-directed behavior. For homework, in addition to monitoring behaviors and mood, participants should utilize positive self-statements as rewards for sub-goal behaviors and note the use of these self-statements on their self-monitoring logs. The intent is to have the depressed participant practice acknowledging progress toward a goal with a clear, positive self-statement.

Topic X: Assets List

A negative self-image is a component of depression. A negative view of oneself derives from the habit of attending to the negative, making negative attributions for positive and negative events, not seeing progress toward goals, and thus talking to oneself in primarily negative ways. *Self-image* can be thought of as the accumulated set of self-statements that the person makes each day. Since the program has the participants focus on positive events, positive delayed outcomes, nondepressed attributions, progress toward goals, and, positive self-statements, participants may now be ready to acknowledge their positive characteristics or traits—that is, the accumulation of positive observations about themselves. With these ideas in mind, the exercise in this session is to develop an assets list. Participants are asked to identify and write down at least five positive general statements that they can make about themselves (e.g., "I am loyal to my friends," or "I am good at carpentry"). Depressed people often find this process difficult and qualify or discount their positive qualities. Participants may almost need to be given permission to say out loud that they do have some positive qualities. The homework assignment associated with this topic is to note positive activities that are instances of their general positive statements about themselves and to record these thoughts on the log. They are also to add to their assets lists as they observe other positive qualities in themselves.

Topic XI: Review and Continuation

The goal of the final sessions are to help group participants assimilate and implement the knowledge that they have gained over the course of the group in order to facilitate long-term gains in functioning. In our earlier research trials of this program, participant feedback indicated that they felt they learned a lot but then were sent out on their own to use the program. We now add several sessions of review at the end of the program. These extra sessions can also provide for more flexibility in earlier parts of the program—if the therapist wants to spend an extra session on a topic, one fewer review session can be used while keeping the program a fixed length. These review sessions begin with a review of homework and discussion of what each person is doing regarding his or her goals. It is helpful for group members to share with one another strategies that they found particularly helpful in completing the different homework exercises, or to encourage group members to ask for assistance from one another in developing strategies to deal with particularly problematic issues. The therapist reviews each participant's progress and provides feedback with a review of various topics covered in the program that might be relevant. During the final session, participants are encouraged to continue to utilize their self-management skills in order to maintain the progress made during the group and to monitor their behaviors, self-statements, and mood. Participants are given extra copies of the self-monitoring log and other worksheets so that they may continue to work on the exercises on their own.

Further Reading

Rehm, L. P. (1977). A self-control model of depression. *Behavior Therapy, 8,* 787–804.

Rehm, L. P. (1985). A self-management therapy program for depression. *International Journal of Mental Health, 13*(3/4), 34–53.

Rehm, L. P. (1990). Cognitive and behavioral theories. In B. B. Wolman & G. Stricker (Eds.), *Depressive Disorder: Facts, theories, and treatment methods* (pp. 64–91). New York: Wiley.

Rehm, L. P., Wagner, A., & Tyndall, C. (2001). Mood disorders. In P. B. Sutker & H. E. Adams (Eds.), *Comprehensive handbook of psychopathology* (3rd ed., pp. 277–308). New York: Plenum Press.

References

Bailey, S., Rehm, L. P., Martin, H., Holton, H., & Le, N. (1994, April). *Self-management therapy for battered, depressed women.* Poster presented at the annual meeting of the Southwestern Psychological Association, Tulsa, OK.

Barlow, J. (1986). *A group treatment for depression in the elderly.* Unpublished doctoral dissertation, University of Houston, Houston, TX.

Fleming, B. M., & Thornton, D. W. (1980). Coping skills as a component in the short-term treatment of depression. *Journal of Consulting and Clinical Psychology, 48,* 652–655.

Fuchs, C. Z., & Rehm, L. P. (1977). A self-control behavior therapy program for depression. *Journal of Consulting and Clinical Psychology, 45,* 206-215.

Kornblith, S. J., & Greenwald, D. (1982, November). *Self-control therapy with depressed inpatients.* Paper presented at the meeting of the Association for the Advancement of Behavior Therapy, Los Angeles, CA.

Kornblith, S. K., Rehm, L. P., O'Hara, M. W., & Lamparski, D. M. (1983). The contribution of self-reinforcement training and behavioral assignments to the efficacy of self-control therapy for depression. *Cognitive Therapy and Research, 7,* 499-527.

Rehm, L. P. (1977). A self-control model of depression. *Behavior Therapy, 8,* 787–804.

Rehm, L. P. (1985). A self-management therapy program for depression. *International Journal of Mental Health, 13*(3/4), 34–53.

Rehm, L. P. (1990). Cognitive and behavioral theories. In B. B. Wolman & G. Stricker (Eds.), *Depressive Disorder: Facts, theories, and treatment methods* (pp. 64–91). New York: Wiley.

Rehm, L. P. (2001). *Self-management therapy for depression: Therapy manual and research protocol.* Houston, TX: Houston Veterans Administration Medical Center.

Rehm, L. P., Fuchs, C. Z., Roth, D. M., Kornblith, S. J., & Romano, J. (1979). A comparison of self-control and social skills treatments of depression. *Behavior Therapy, 10,* 429- 442.

Rehm, L. P., Kaslow, N. J., & Rabin, A. S. (1987). Cognitive and behavioral targets in a self-control behavior therapy program for depression. *Journal of Consulting and Clinical Psychology, 55,* 60-67.

Rehm, L. P., Kornblith, S. J., O'Hara, M. W., Lamparski, D. M., Romano, J.M., & Volkin, J. I. (1981). An evaluation of major components in a self-control therapy program for depression. *Behavior Modification, 5,* 459-490.

Rehm, L. P., & Sharp, R. N. (1996). Strategies in the treatment of childhood depression. In M. Reinecke, F. M. Dattilio, & A. Freeman (Eds.), *Comprehensive casebook on cognitive behavior therapy with adolescents* (pp. 103–123). New York: Guilford Press.

Rehm, L. P., Wagner, A., & Tyndall, C. (2001). Mood disorders. In P. B. Sutker & H. E. Adams (Eds.), *Comprehensive handbook of psychopathology* (3rd ed., pp. 277–308). New York: Plenum Press.

Reynolds, W. M., & Coats, K. I. (1986). A comparison of cognitive-behavioral therapy and relaxation training for the treatment of depression in adolescents. *Journal of Consulting and Clinical Psychology. 54*(5), 653–60.

Rogers, P. A., Kerns, R., Rehm, L. P., Hendler, E. D., & Harkness, L. (1982, August). *Depression mitigation in hemo-dialysands: A function of self-control training.* Paper presented at the meeting of the American Psychological Association, Washington, DC.

Rokke, P. D., Tomhave, J. A., & Jocic, Z. (1999). The role of client choice and target selection in self-management therapy for depression in older adults. *Psychology of Aging, 14*(1), 155–169.

Rokke, P. D., Tomhave, J. A., & Jocic, Z. (2000). Self-management therapy and educational group therapy for depressed elders. *Cognitive Therapy and Research, 24*(1), 99–119.

Roth, D., Bielski, R., Jones, M., Parker, W., & Osborn, G. (1982). A comparison of self-control therapy and combined self-control therapy and antidepressant medication in the treatment of depression. *Behavior Therapy, 13,* 133–144.

Rude, S. S. (1986). Relative benefits of assertion or cognitive self-control treatment for depression as a function of proficiency in each domain. *Journal of Consulting and Clinical Psychology, 54,* 390–394.

Stark, K. D., Reynolds, W. M., & Kaslow, N. J. (1987). A comparison of the relative efficacy of self-control therapy and a behavioral problem-solving therapy for depression in children. *Journal of Abnormal Child Psychology, 15*(1), 91–113.

Thomas, J. R., Petry, R. A., & Goldman, J. (1987). Comparison of cognitive and behavioral self-control treatments of depression. *Psychological Reports, 60,* 975–982.

Tressler, D. P., & Tucker, R. D. (1980, November). *The comparative effects of self-evaluation and self-reinforcement training in the treatment of depression.* Paper presented at the annual meeting of the Association for the Advancement of Behavior Therapy, New York, NY.

van den Hout, J. H., Arntz, A., & Kunkels, F. H. (1995). Efficacy of a self-control therapy program in a psychiatric day-treatment center. *Acta Psychiatrika Scandinavia, 92*(1), 25–9.

53 SELF-MONITORING AS A TREATMENT VEHICLE

Jennifer M. Heidt and Brian P. Marx

The technique of self-monitoring has its origins in behavioral assessment as a procedure in which clients were instructed to maintain a log in which they kept information regarding the duration, frequency, and severity of identified problem behaviors. Clinicians typically utilized the information yielded via a client's self-monitoring log as a first step in determining the ABC's—or antecedents, behaviors, and consequences—of a client's noted problem behaviors. Once determined, a clinician might use such information to develop intervention strategies. Additionally, such behavior logs were frequently used as a baseline against which future behavior logs (i.e., those that a client recorded throughout the course of treatment) would be compared in order to examine the degree of change accomplished in treatment of the problem behavior (Hayes, Nelson, & Jarrett, 1986).

Evidence for the effectiveness of self-monitoring as a treatment strategy in its own right began to accumulate in the early 1970s. Recognizing that the act of self-observation might have powerful effects on an individual's perception of his or her own behavior (e.g., clients frequently admit that they did not realize, prior to recording the frequency of a behavior, just how often they engaged in the behavior), researchers began to examine whether self-monitoring by itself could influence a client's previously identified problem behavior. McFall (1970) demonstrated that college students who monitored their desire to smoke decreased both the number of cigarettes smoked and the time spent smoking cigarettes. Frederickson (1975) used self-monitoring in the treatment of a 25-year-old woman with obsessive thoughts surrounding breast and stomach cancer. When the client simply monitored the frequency of her ruminative thoughts, they decreased rapidly from 13 to 2 per day. When asked to monitor her thoughts in a more detailed fashion (i.e., when the thoughts occurred, their specific content, etc.), the thoughts abated entirely, with no evidence of recurrence up to 4 months posttreatment. Harris (1986) used self-monitoring in a classroom setting in which four learning-disabled youths monitored whether they were paying attention whenever a sound was randomly played via a tape recorder (by indicating yes or no on a behavior log) as well as the number of words they had written during a particular work period. Self-monitoring improved the overall work performance of the youths in both conditions. Self-monitoring has also been shown to modify both the mood and daily activity of depressed subjects (Harmon, Nelson, & Hayes, 1980).

Success in the utilization of self-monitoring as an intervention has encouraged clinicians to incorporate the procedure into more comprehensive package treatments for various problems, including anxiety, depression, pain, overeating, and smoking. For example, Beck, Rush, Shaw, and Emery (1979) and Lewinsohn, Antonuccio,

Steinmetz, and Teri (1984) both incorporated self-monitoring techniques into their treatments for depression. Beck and colleagues' *multiple column technique* encourages the client to report as much information as possible regarding increases in dysphoria, including the date of occurrence, a brief description of the situation in which the increase occurred, the client's emotional reaction to the situation, the thoughts that occurred between the situation and the emotional reaction, and finally, a more adaptive, positive interpretation of the situation. Beck and colleagues have used the information derived from this process to more closely examine the evidence for distorted perceptions that may underlie depressive emotional reactions with clients and for use in cognitive restructuring procedures.

WHO MIGHT BENEFIT FROM THIS TECHNIQUE

In general, self-monitoring has wide applicability and is appropriate for both adults and children with a wide variety of psychopathology, including appetitive disorders, depression, anxiety, marital dysfunction, and various problem behaviors such as poor academic achievement and aggression. For example, Buxton, Williamson, Absher, and Warner (1985) used the procedure to graph caloric intake among individuals who overeat. Others have use the procedure to monitor daily intake of food and output of energy (in the form of exercise) in obese individuals (Coates & Thoresen, 1981; Gormally & Rardin, 1981), nicotine consumed by smokers (Abrams & Wilson, 1979; Shiffman, 1988), drinking and blood-alcohol levels in problem drinkers (Alden, 1988; Flegal, 1991; Sobell, Bogardis, Schuller, Leo, & Sobell, 1989), and academic behaviors in increasing academic performance and decreasing procrastination in individuals with low academic achievement (Green, 1982). Self-monitoring has also been used to examine and restructure maladaptive cognitions and monitor both situations in which anxiety arises and perceived level of anxiety (Basoglu, Marks, & Sengun, 1992; Hiebert & Fox, 1981; Rapee, Craske, & Barlow, 1990), to monitor emotional reactions to situational contexts among depressed individuals (Beck et al., 1979; Jarrett & Nelson, 1987), and to address in-ternalizing disorders in children (Beidel, Neil, & Lederer, 1991; Stark, Reynolds, & Kaslow, 1987). Finally, self-monitoring has been employed with individuals suffering from chronic illnesses to either self-regulate treatment, such as with Type II diabetes (Wing, Epstein, Norwalk, & Scott, 1988), or monitor the intensity of pain (Kerns, Finn, & Haythornthwaite, 1988).

CONTRAINDICATIONS

Due to the fact that self-monitoring is a relatively time-intensive task, one which requires a good deal of motivation on the part of the client, it may be less effective for individuals who either have extremely hectic schedules or have been entered into treatment by someone other than themselves (e.g., as with court-mandated therapy). Additionally, self-monitoring may not be appropriate for clients who present with particular types of problems. For example, Hollon and Kendall (1981) have noted that depressed clients may fail to engage in self-monitoring because they find the task at hand overwhelming or may not believe that such therapy can provide any help. Hollon and Kendall also noted caution in using the procedure with anxious clients who might balk at examining distressing cognitions and emotions in depth. In contrast, they suggest that obsessive or perfectionistic clients may spend entirely too much time monitoring their thoughts and actions in an attempt to produce perfect behavior logs.

Although self-monitoring may not be indicated for all clients, adapting various aspects of the self-monitoring task to the individual may increase motivation as well as the likelihood of engaging in the task. For example, adapting the type of log that is required to both a client's ability to self-monitor (e.g., for children, providing them with a structured log sheet that requires only that they mark off when certain events occur) and their particular problems or pathology (e.g., for obsessive clients, limiting the amount of time and detail that should be put into the task) may serve to address some of the client's difficulties with self-monitoring. For clients who may be less motivated, clinicians might consider involving them extensively in the analysis of the information gleaned from behavior logs, with the hope of making the client feel as though he or she has an active role in therapy, thereby increasing motivation. Clinicians may also attempt to improve a client's motivation by clearly delineating both the rationale behind the task (i.e., how self-monitoring would be helpful in treatment) and the specific detailed instructions to be followed.

OTHER DECISIONS IN DECIDING TO USE OR NOT TO USE SELF-MONITORING

A major issue often encountered in self-monitoring is that of *reactivity*. Although reactivity, or a change in the behavior being monitored, is of course the goal of the intervention, there are cases in which reactivity may cause an aspect of the problem to worsen rather than improve. Hollon and Kendall (1981) have noted that this sometimes occurs in clients who are monitoring negative affect, where self-monitoring of anxiety or depression may incur the mood state, causing increases in frequency, duration, or both (in contrast to this concern, see Harmon et al., 1980). In such cases, it is recommended that the clinician examine what in particular about the monitoring process is inciting such reactions in the client and incorporate this information into treatment. For example, depressed clients may report that monitoring their dysphoric states increases hopelessness, produces memories of previous depressive episodes, or increases rumination over past misfortunes. In such situations, the clinician should attempt to determine which aspects of monitoring the depressed state causes such distress and then use such information to adapt both self-monitoring and cognitive restructuring procedures (e.g., encouraging the client to focus on the present, record the present behavior and cognitions, and avoid rumination over prior events).

HOW DOES THE TECHNIQUE WORK?

Although there is evidence suggesting that self-monitoring may be an effective intervention for certain clients with various problem behaviors, the reasons for the efficacy of this treatment are not entirely understood. One hypothesis is that self-monitoring might provide important feedback to the client about various aspects of the problem behavior, such as when it is most likely to occur, how often it occurs, and how long it lasts in various conditions. Such detailed information regarding a behavior may help the client to recognize the sheer magnitude of the behavior (i.e., most clients remark that they did not realize how often they performed the behavior, nor how much of an effect it had on their daily activities prior to self-monitoring). Such feedback could serve as a wake-up call to the client, who may become strongly motivated to correct the problem. Additionally, clients learn when and in what situations the behavior is likely to occur, and can use this knowledge to help identify situations or aspects of situations to be more cognizant of or possibly avoid altogether in the future.

Another possible way in which self-monitoring works is that it may provide either reinforcing or aversive contingencies for the behavior of concern. For example, a client attempting to decrease the frequency of a given behavior (e.g., eating) may become encouraged (or discouraged) by the frequency rates recorded during self-monitoring and view such decreases (or increases) in problem behavior as a measure of his or her success in therapy. There is also some evidence that self-monitoring works much like an external cue or reminder (Hayes & Nelson, 1983).

STEP-BY-STEP PROCEDURES

There are six major steps involved in self-monitoring (see Table 53.1): presentation of the rationale underlying self-monitoring, discrimination of the target response, recording the target response, charting or graphing the target response, displaying the data collected, and analyzing the data collected (Thoresen & Mahoney, 1974).

Presentation of Rationale to Client

It is essential that the client understand the reasons behind using self-monitoring as a therapeutic device. The clinician should explain that self-monitoring is a tool that the client can utilize on his or her own, one that will provide informa-

TABLE 53.1   Steps of Self-Monitoring

Step	Relevant Questions
1. Presentation of rationale to client	Why is self-monitoring a good choice for this client and how will it be beneficial?
	Is the client's motivation great enough to input the effort required?
2. Discrimination of target response	What behavior is the client most intent on changing?
	How is the behavior operationalized?
	Is the client capable of discrimination (i.e., is guided practice required)?
3. Recording the target response	Does the client understand the concept of *systematic* recording?
	Will the recording precede or follow the behavior?
	What method will the client utilize in recording (diary, structured log sheet, wrist counter, etc.)?
4. Charting or graphing the target response	Can the client chart his or her progress on a weekly basis?
5. Displaying the data collected	Can the client display his or her progress charts in a public area as both personal and environmental reinforcement?
6. Analyzing the data collected	How do the client's collected data compare with goals set prior to treatment?
	How does the client feel about the progress to date (encouragement is essential)?

tion regarding target behaviors to both the clinician and the client and will help identify a variety of aspects surrounding the problem behavior, including the frequency, duration, and situations in which it is likely to occur. The client should be made aware that self-monitoring may require a great deal of effort and that his or her involvement (i.e., how much the client puts into the recording) in the process will likely determine how effective the treatment will be. The client should also be informed that observable change via self-monitoring typically takes 3 to 4 weeks and that he or she should not be discouraged if rapid change is not seen immediately. As discussed previously, such inclusion of the client in therapy is likely to increase motivation as it fosters the client's notion that she or he is actively involved in the change process.

Discrimination of Target Response

In order to accurately record instances of the target behavior, the client must be able to discriminate the target behavior from other behaviors. The first step in discriminating a target behavior is identifying which behavior the client should monitor. There is evidence that suggests that the selection of a target behavior can affect the results of self-monitoring (i.e., certain target behaviors may be better to self-monitor than others in a given situation). A good rule to employ in identi-

fying a target behavior is to focus on what behavior the client wants to change most.

Once a target behavior is selected, the clinician should practice discrimination with the client, offering specific examples of what qualifies as the target behavior and what does not. Initially, the client should monitor only one behavior to become familiar with the procedure. If no problems are encountered, additional behaviors can be added to the repertoire of those being monitored.

Recording the Target Response

There are a number of things to consider in recording the target response. The most important point for the client to understand is the need for systematic recording. Instructions must be clearly delineated such that the client knows when, where, and how to record responses. A major decision is whether the client should record an instance of behavior prior to engaging in the behavior (e.g., when the client has the urge to smoke or eat) or shortly after the behavior has been completed. Typically, prebehavior recording should be implemented in cases where the client is attempting to decrease an undesired behavior (such as smoking or overeating), whereas postbehavior recording may be more beneficial in cases where a client is trying to increase a desired behavior (such as self-assertion). Regardless of whether the recording is made before or after the behavior, self-monitoring is likely to be more effective when the recording occurs as temporally close to the behavior as possible. Delayed recording of behaviors has been shown to diminish the effectiveness of self-monitoring (Kanfer, 1980).

Another important decision in recording is the method the client will use, a factor largely determined by the nature of the target behavior and the elements about that behavior the client is hoping to change. If a client wants to monitor the frequency of a behavior that is typically of short duration, a wrist counter can be worn and the client can simply use the counter to record each instance of the behavior. If a client wants to monitor both the frequency and duration of a behavior, a stopwatch can be used in conjunction with a journal. Diaries are frequently employed in self-monitoring, particularly in situations where the target behavior is being monitored in great detail. In such cases, an individual can record all instances of the behavior in the diary, as well as any supplemental information, such as emotions and cognitions surrounding the target behavior. Daily log sheets are also employed in self-monitoring and can be very useful in structuring what needs to be recorded in a logical, systematic, easy-to-use fashion. Whatever method is decided upon, it is imperative that the client is comfortable with the system and that all questions be addressed prior to implementing the system in vivo. Because self-monitoring may work in part as a kind of reminder or cue (Nelson & Hayes, 1981), whichever method is selected should be reasonably salient.

Charting or Graphing the Target Response

Once the client has collected data for a given time period, the information regarding target behaviors should be translated into a chart or graph. A typical presentation is a line graph comparing aspects about the target behavior (e.g., frequency, duration) across days. For example, a client monitoring eating behavior could examine the number of calories consumed every day over the course of a week, graphing the number of calories on the vertical axis and the day of the week on the horizontal axis. Similarly, the same client conceivably would also be monitoring the amount of time spent exercising, making another graph of the duration of exercise on the vertical axis and the days of the week on the horizontal. Clients who are monitoring a number of behaviors are likely to be reinforced if all graphs yield consistent results that demonstrate behavior change in the desired direction, yet not overly discouraged if some graphs demonstrate improvement while others evidence a need to work on different areas.

Displaying the Data Collected

Displaying the client's graph in a public area is likely to serve a dual purpose. It can provide clients with a personal reminder of their hard work as well as what they have been able to accomplish, serving as a reinforcer for behavior change. Additionally, displaying the chart in a public arena increases both the social commitment to change and the possibility of reinforcement from others, such as a family member or coworker who may note the improvement and then compliment the client.

Analyzing the Data Collected

Feedback is an integral aspect of the self-monitoring technique. More specifically, self-monitoring is likely to be beneficial to the client both as a personal progress monitor and as a reinforcer; however, the clinician can aid greatly in the proper interpretation of various aspects of the data. For example, clients who do not see immediate, monumental improvement may become rapidly discouraged. It is the clinician's job to explain that the process of change often takes a long period of time and that constant improvement at every session (depicted as a perfect linear graph) is rare. Rather, seemingly minor improvements early on can be viewed as monumental in their own right, and mistakes or relapses are common and do not imply that treatment is doomed to failure. Clients should bring their charted data to weekly sessions with the clinician for analysis, feedback, and encouragement. The clinician should analyze and discuss the results with the client, comparing data collected to the goals agreed upon by both clinician and client prior to the initiation of treatment. Clients should also be encouraged to make such comparisons on their own outside the therapy sessions in order to further facilitate treatment.

Further Reading

Cormier, W. H., & Cormier, L. S. (1991). Self-management strategies: Self-monitoring, stimulus control, and self-reward. In *Interviewing strategies for helpers: Fundamental skills and behavioral interventions* (pp. 518–549). California: Brooks/Cole.

Thoresen, C. E., & Mahoney, M. J. (1974). *Behavioral self-control*. New York: Holt, Rinehart & Winston.

References

Abrams D. B., & Wilson, G. T. (1979). Self-monitoring and reactivity in the modification of cigarette smoking. *Journal of Consulting and Clinical Psychology, 47*, 243–251.

Alden, L. E. (1988). Behavioral self-management controlled-drinking strategies in a context of secondary prevention. *Journal of Consulting and Clinical Psychology, 56*, 280–286.

Basoglu, M., Marks, L., & Sengun, S. (1992). A prospective study of panic and anxiety in Agoraphobia with Panic Disorder. *British Journal of Psychiatry, 160*, 57–64.

Beck, A. T., Rush, A. J., Shaw, B. F., & Emery, G. (1979). *Cognitive therapy of depression*. New York: Guilford Press.

Beidel, D. C., Neal, A. M., & Lederer, A. S. (1991). The feasibility and validity of a daily diary for the assessment of anxiety disorders in children. *Behavior Therapy, 22*, 505–517.

Buxton, A., Williamson, D. A., Absher, N., & Warner, M. (1985). Self-management of nutrition. *Addictive Behaviors, 10*, 383–396.

Coates, T. J., & Thoresen, C. E. (1981). Behavior and weight changes in three obese adolescents. *Behavior Therapy, 12*, 383–399.

Cormier, W. H., & Cormier, L. S. (1991). Self-management strategies: Self-monitoring, stimulus control, and self-reward. In *Interviewing strategies for helpers: Fundamental skills and behavioral interventions* (pp. 518–549). California: Brooks/Cole.

Flegal, K. M. (1991). Agreement between two dietary methods in reported intake of beer, wine, and liquor. *Journal of Studies on Alcohol, 52*, 174–179.

Frederickson, L. W. (1975). Treatment of ruminative thinking by self-monitoring. *Journal of Behavior Therapy and Experimental Psychiatry, 6*, 258–259.

Gormally, J., & Rardin, D. (1981). Weight loss and maintenance and changes in diet and exercise for be-

havioral counseling and nutrition education. *Journal of Counseling Psychology, 28*, 295–304.

Green, L. (1982). Minority students' self-control of procrastination. *Journal of Counseling Psychology, 29*, 636–644.

Harmon, T. M., Nelson, R. O., & Hayes, S. C. (1980). Self-monitoring of mood versus activity by depressed clients. *Journal of Consulting and Clinical Psychology, 48*, 30-38.

Harris, K. R. (1986). Self-monitoring of attentional behavior versus self-monitoring of productivity: Effects on on-task behavior and academic response rate among learning- disabled children. *Journal of Applied Behavior Analysis, 19*, 417–424.

Hayes, S. C., & Nelson, R. O. (1983). Similar reactivity produced by external cues and self-monitoring. *Behavior Modification, 7*, 183-196.

Hayes, S. C., Nelson, R. O., & Jarrett, R. (1986). Evaluating the quality of behavioral assessment. In R. O. Nelson & S. C. Hayes (Eds.), *Conceptual foundations of behavioral assessment* (pp. 463-503). New York: Guilford Press.

Hiebert, B., & Fox, E. E. (1981). Reactive effects of self-monitoring anxiety. *Journal of Counseling Psychology, 28*, 187–193.

Hollon, S. D., & Kendall, P. C. (1981). In vivo assessment techniques for cognitive-behavioral processes. In P. C. Kendall & S. D. Hollon (Eds.), *Assessment strategies for cognitive- behavioral interventions* (pp. 319–362). New York: Academic Press.

Jarrett, R. B., & Nelson, R. O. (1987). Mechanisms of change in cognitive therapy of depression. *Behavior Therapy, 18*, 227–241.

Kanfer, F. H. (1980). Self-management methods. In F. H. Kanfer & A. P. Goldstein (Eds.), *Helping people change* (2nd ed., pp. 334–389). New York: Pergamon Press.

Kerns, R. D., Finn, P., & Haythornthwaite, J. (1988). Self-monitored pain intensity: Psychometric properties and clinical utility. *Journal of Behavioral Medicine, 11*, 71–82.

Lewinsohn, P. M., Antonuccio, D. O., Steinmetz, J. L., & Teri, L. (1984). *The Coping with Depression course*. Eugene, OR: Castalia.

McFall, R. M. (1970). Effects of self-monitoring on normal smoking behavior. *Journal of Consulting and Clinical Psychology, 35*, 135–142.

Nelson, R. O., & Hayes, S. C. (1981). Theoretical explanations for the reactive effects of self-monitoring. *Behavior Modification, 5*, 3-14.

Rapee, R. M., Craske, M. G., & Barlow, D. H. (1990).

Subject described fears of panic attacks using a new self-monitoring form. *Journal of Anxiety Disorders, 4,* 171–181.

Shiffman, S. (1988). Smoking behavior: Behavioral assessment. In D. M. Donovan & G. A. Marlatt (Eds.), *Assessment of addictive behaviors* (pp. 139–188). New York: Guilford Press.

Sobell, M. B., Bogardis, J., Schuller, R., Leo, G. I., & Sobell, L. C. (1989). Is self-monitoring of alcohol consumption reactive? *Behavioral Assessment, 11,* 447–458.

Stark, K. D., Reynolds, W. M., & Kaslow, M. J. (1987). A comparison of the relative efficacy of self-control therapy and a behavioral problem-solving therapy for depression in children. *Journal of Abnormal Child Psychology, 15,* 91–113.

Thoresen, C. E., & Mahoney M. J. (1974). *Behavioral self-control.* New York: Holt, Rinehart, & Winston.

Wing, R. R., Epstein, L. H., Norwalk, M. P., & Scott, N. (1988). Self-regulation in the treatment of Type II diabetes. *Behavior Therapy, 19,* 11–23.

54 SENSATE FOCUS FOR SEXUAL DYSFUNCTION

Lisa G. Regev

INTRODUCTION

Sensate focus is a key component in treating many types of sexual dysfunction. Masters and Johnson (1970) developed this technique to combat performance anxiety, the primary culprit of sexual problems. The couple is guided through a series of exercises that become progressively more anxiety provoking, analogous to the anxiety-mastering techniques proposed by Wolpe (1958) and Lazarus (1963). The couple begins with exercises imposing the least demand for sexual performance, such as nonsexual caressing while clothed, and moves through a hierarchy of increasingly demanding sexual activities over the course of treatment, eventually resulting in intercourse. During each of these exercises, they are taught to focus on the sensations they experience as their partner touches them, rather than engage in spectatoring (focusing on the adequacy of their performance). The receiver of sensate focus is also instructed to communicate specifically about the more and less enjoyable aspects of the interaction.

Sensate focus begins with a ban on intercourse until the exercises are successfully completed (Masters & Johnson, 1970). This serves two possible functions. One is to eliminate the anxiety-provoking thought that engaging in sensual touching may lead to intercourse. By banning intercourse, both partners can focus on the sensation instead of worrying about what will happen next. A second reason is that it allows the couple to start from scratch in building positive sexual experiences, rather than repeating problematic learned sexual patterns.

Sensate focus is one component within multi-component treatments for several sexual dysfunctions (Wincze & Carey, 2001). Other common ingredients of sex therapy include psycho-education, relaxation training (see Chapter 41, this volume), communication training, and directed practice (e.g., directed masturbation for Female Orgasmic Disorder, squeeze technique for Premature Ejaculation, or insertion of graded vaginal dilators for Vaginismus).

WHO MIGHT BENEFIT FROM SENSATE FOCUS

Sensate focus is the primary treatment component for individuals presenting with arousal disorders (Male Erectile Disorder and Female Sexual Arousal Disorder). Performance anxiety is hypothesized to play a central role in preventing arousal. By teaching couples to focus on their bodily sensations without the demand for sex, they are more likely to become aroused (Masters & Johnson, 1970).

Sensate focus contributes to the treatment of other sexual problems as well. It is used in conjunction with other treatment components to alleviate problems of desire and orgasm (e.g.,

Heiman & LoPiccolo, 1988; Zeiss & Zeiss, 1978). It has also been used as one component in preventing relationship distress among premarital couples in the Prevention and Relationship Enhancement Program (PREP; Markman, Blumberg, & Stanley, 1993).

CONTRAINDICATIONS

Sex therapy is generally contraindicated when the problem is due to organic causes. Prior to initiating sex therapy, it is important to rule out possible physiological causes for the problem, including drug side effects (e.g., antidepressants, antihypertensives, anxiolytics, anti-ulcer medications, street drugs, and alcohol) and medical conditions (e.g., diabetes, hypogonadism, cancer, and menopause). Most sexual problems that result primarily from medication use are reversible once the drug is discontinued. In some cases, changing the dose or class of drug can reverse the sexual problem as well (Crenshaw & Goldberg, 1996). Individuals who suffer chronic medical illnesses that impact sexual functioning may benefit from sex therapy, particularly if they are willing to pursue more modest treatment goals (Schover, 2000). For example, sensate focus may facilitate improved sensual pleasure and intimacy with a partner even if sexual functioning cannot be improved.

OTHER DECISION FACTORS IN DECIDING TO USE OR NOT TO USE SENSATE FOCUS

Prior to beginning sex therapy, it is important to assess factors that may impede progress. For example, Sexual Aversion Disorder resulting from a sexual trauma may be difficult to treat without first treating the trauma (Kaplan, 1995). Hypoactive Sexual Desire Disorder resulting from severe marital discord may be difficult to treat without first attending to general relationship functioning. Sex therapy relies on trust, emotional intimacy, attraction, and communication. However, a history of sexual trauma or severe marital discord should not be assumed to preclude sex therapy. Enhancing a couple's sexual relationship may help establish intimacy and communication

(Regev, O'Donohue, & Avina, 2003). Clinical judgment plays a central role in determining appropriate action in these cases.

HOW DOES SENSATE FOCUS WORK?

Currently, no conclusive statements can be made about how sensate focus works. Masters and Johnson (1970) speculated that performance anxiety interferes with arousal. The fear of sexual inadequacy leads individuals to monitor their arousal, while dreading failure. Barlow (1986) explicated a model of sexual arousal, distinguishing between sexually functional and dysfunctional individuals. In contrast to sexually functional individuals, people with sexual dysfunctions tend to experience negative affect, underreport levels of arousal, and focus on the consequences of not performing when faced with demands for sexual performance (Beck & Barlow, 1986; Heiman & Rowland, 1983).

Sensate focus (in conjunction with a ban on intercourse) teaches individuals who suffer from arousal problems to focus on the pleasurable sensations of sexual contact, without worrying about their ability to perform. It is hypothesized that refocusing them on erotic cues will facilitate arousal and possibly orgasm. Additionally, by teaching individuals to focus on their sensations, men learn to identify their "point of inevitability" when learning to control their ejaculatory latency (see Chapter 57, "Squeeze Technique," in this volume) and women learn to identify their pleasure points when learning to reach orgasm (see Chapter 24 on "Directed Masturbation").

For individuals presenting with low desire, sensate focus may work for different reasons. One is that it requires couples to extend foreplay and reduce the demand for sex. By engaging in prolonged foreplay without the ultimate goal of intercourse, some couples rediscover sexual enjoyment and hence, increased desire to engage in sexual activity. Another reason is that sensate focus teaches couples to communicate their sexual preferences as they engage in the exercises. It is no longer taboo to talk about what feels good and what does not feel good sexually. Instead, it is a required aspect of the treatment. This newly developed skill in communicating sexual preferences is hypothesized to result in improved sexual interactions overall, which may lead to more desire to engage in sexual activity. Additionally, sensate focus provides another avenue for couples to engage in an intimate form of pleasant events. The exercises require couples to set aside time to be together intimately, which would be expected to enhance their general relationship functioning and their desire to be together. Additional research is needed to help clarify the process by which sensate focus works.

EVIDENCE FOR THE EFFECTIVENESS OF SENSATE FOCUS

In addition to evaluating *how* sensate focus works, future research is needed to establish *that* sensate focus works. Sensate focus is one element within a multicomponent treatment and little is known about its effectiveness in relation to other treatment components. The Masters and Johnson approach to treating sexual problems (which includes sensate focus, among other components) has been found to be generally effective (Clement & Schmidt, 1983; Everaerd & Dekker, 1985; Hartman & Daly, 1983; Matthews, et al., 1976).

When treating primary Female Orgasmic Disorder, sensate focus and ban on intercourse significantly increased women's level of enjoyment of sexual activity (Fichten, Libman, & Brender, 1983). However, women were more likely to gain orgasmic capacity when also treated with directed masturbation (Riley & Riley, 1978). This treatment package has also been used to effectively treat low desire in women (Hurlbert, White, Powell, & Apt, 1993). Incorporating sensate focus in a relationship distress prevention program proved effective in preventing sexual dissatisfaction 3 years later (Markman, Floyd, Stanley, & Storaasli, 1988).

Prohibiting intercourse prior to initiating sex therapy has generally gone unchallenged in the literature. Masters and Johnson's (1970) intensive 2-week training required couples to abstain from sex for a few days. Lipsius (1987) argued that rigidly adhering to the ban on intercourse in the extended treatment format may have detrimental effects, such as loss of spontaneity and erotic feelings, because the ban may last several weeks or even months. Instead, he proposed a more moderate prohibition, where couples are encouraged to refrain from intercourse. However, spontaneous sex is not forbidden. Communication of sexual preferences was found to be effective whether intercourse was banned or not (Takefman & Brender, 1984). Instead of banning intercourse, Riley and Riley (1978) prescribed sensate focus and instructed that intercourse should take place only after extended foreplay.

STEP-BY-STEP PROCEDURES

The following procedures are utilized in treating couples using the mainstream approach to sensate focus. This discussion will focus on treating a couple presenting with Male Erectile Disorder. However, this procedure may be adapted to be used for females or males (homosexual or heterosexual) presenting with a variety of sexual problems (as noted previously). Generally speaking, sessions last approximately 1 hour, once per week. Sessions consist of psychoeducation and instruction on exercises to be completed at home. Bibliotherapy with minimal therapist contact (varying from 10 min per week to four sessions over a 3-month period) has also been found to be effective when treating Premature Ejaculation and Female Orgasmic Disorder (van Lankveld, 1998).

Ban on Intercourse

The first step in sensate focus involves contracting with the couple to abstain from attempting sexual intercourse until they are instructed otherwise (usually after a few weeks). Couples are provided the following rationale: Sexual problems often stem from distracting thoughts during sexual activity or pressure to perform sexually. By banning intercourse, they will learn to focus on pleasurable sensations without worrying about the need to perform.

Sensate Focus I

Following the intercourse-ban contract, the couple is instructed to engage in relatively low-anxiety exercises. The exact form of the home-

TABLE 54.1   Sensate Focus: Step-by-Step Procedures

Step	Details
Ban on intercourse	
Negotiate form, number, and initiation of exercises	
Sensate focus I (example)	Relax (e.g., by taking a warm bath or meditating) Partners take turns caressing each other without touching breasts or genitals Focus attention on the sensations of caressing or being caressed Communicate what feels good
Sensate focus II (example)	Relax (e.g., by taking a warm bath or meditating) Partners take turns caressing each other, including breasts and genitals Focus attention on the sensations of caressing or being caressed Communicate what feels good If they become aroused (e.g., erection), pause until arousal subsides
Sensate focus III (example)	Relax (e.g., by taking a warm bath or meditating) Partners take turns caressing each other, including breasts or genitals Engage in intercourse without thrusting Focus attention on the sensations of caressing or being caressed Communicate what feels good If they are about to reach orgasm, pause until arousal subsides
Resume engaging in intercourse	Continue to focus on sensations Continue to communicate what feels good
Self-monitor	Problem-solve treatment noncompliance Modify progression of treatment based on couple's needs

work exercises will require negotiation and will vary from couple to couple. Usually, the couple is instructed to caress each other's bodies, excluding the breasts and genitals. However, some couples may begin with more basic exercises, such as holding hands or hugging in bed in the dark. It is important to stress that the exercises take place at a time and place that is relaxing and both partners should not feel rushed or distracted by other tasks.

An example of sensate focus I: The male is instructed to sensually caress the woman's back, while he concentrates on how it feels to touch her and the woman concentrates on how it feels to be touched. An emphasis is placed on the importance of each person's focusing on his or her own sensations. They are instructed to notice distracting thoughts and refocus their attention to their sensations. The woman is also instructed to communicate which touches feel good and to pay particular attention to sensitive spots. She is to guide his caresses through communication, while avoiding talking too much, as it can distract them from focusing on their sensations. She is then instructed to lie on her back as he caresses her top to bottom, excluding her breasts and vagina.

Again, they are to focus on their sensations as he caresses her. Once he has completed caressing her, she is to complete the same exercise caressing him, without caressing his penis.

The specifics of the exercise should be negotiated prior to initiation. This includes the exact form of the exercise, who will initiate, and the number of times they will practice the exercise prior to the next session. Four to seven times per week is typical—presumably, the more they practice, the faster they progress.

Sensate Focus II

Once the couple completes sensate focus I without feeling anxious (usually after 2 weeks), they progress to sensate focus II. This exercise is the same as that in sensate focus I but also includes stimulation of breasts and genitals. Couples are reminded that arousal is not the goal and that they are not to stimulate each other to the point of orgasm. In fact, if they do become aroused at this stage, they are to pause their caresses until the arousal subsides (e.g., if a man becomes erect while his partner caresses his penis, she is to pause her caresses until he becomes flaccid again). This emphasizes the notion that arousal is not the goal. Instead, both partners are to focus on the sensations and prevent their thoughts from wandering.

Sensate Focus III

Once couples complete sensate focus II without feeling anxious, they progress to sensate focus III. In this exercise, couples also engage in vaginal containment, whereby they are instructed to manually insert his flaccid penis into her vagina. Again, if he becomes aroused, they are to pause the exercise until his erection subsides. They are to continue to focus on the sensations of touching and being touched. Once they successfully complete sensate focus III and no longer feel anxious while engaging in the exercises, the ban on sexual intercourse is lifted. For couples presenting with an arousal disorder, the problem may be resolved at this point. For other sexual problems, these exercises are part of a larger treatment package.

Self-Monitoring

During the course of treatment, couples are asked to self-monitor their sexual activity (defined broadly) on a daily basis. For example, couples may be asked to identify the sexual activities they engaged in and rate their levels of enjoyment, anxiety, communication of preferences, and ability to focus on their bodily sensations. This provides information about treatment compliance, readiness to move to the next level of exercises, and possible barriers to progress. More specifically, it helps identify ways in which exercises should be modified and tailored to the couple's needs.

How to Avoid Common Problems

Couples practicing sensate focus may encounter a number of problems. Common problems include couples' failure to comprehend the task, noncompliance, and an inability to focus on their sensations. When practicing sensate focus, it is imperative that couples understand *how* sensate focus works. Generally, this may require repeated explanations. Specifically, it should be explained that (1) sensate focus requires couples to take small steps towards achieving the long-term goal of a more satisfying sexual relationship and (2) at this stage, they are asked to focus on their sensations. This may be challenging, as couples may be more interested in focusing on performance. It should be emphasized that sessions will not focus on erections or orgasms during these exercises.

When couples fail to complete their homework exercises, the barriers to completion should be explored. One common barrier occurs when couples are so anxious about engaging in particular sexual exercises that they find reasons to avoid them. If this is the case, it is possible that a particular exercise is too high on the couple's hierarchy of anxiety-provoking activities. Encouraging the couple to identify a less anxiety-provoking activity and incorporating it as the next step may be helpful in resolving this problem.

Couples frequently report difficulty maintaining focus on their bodily sensations during this exercise. When this occurs, it is helpful to reassure the couple that staying focused can be difficult, especially at first. They should also be instructed to notice their distraction without self-criticism and return their attention to their sensations. This process is analogous to the process outlined in Chapter 35, "Mindfulness," in this volume.

Further Reading

Leiblum, S. R., & Rosen, R. C. (Eds.). (2000). *Principles and practice of sex therapy* (3rd ed.). New York: Guilford Press.

O'Donohue, W., & Geer, J. H. (Eds.) (1993). *Handbook of sexual dysfunctions: Assessment and treatment.* Boston: Allyn & Bacon.

Wincze, J. P., & Carey, M. P. (2001). *Sexual dysfunction: A guide for assessment and treatment* (2nd ed). New York: Guilford Press.

References

Barlow, D. H. (1986). Causes of sexual dysfunction: The role of anxiety and cognitive interference. *Journal of Consulting and Clinical Psychology, 54,* 140–148.

Beck, J. G., & Barlow, D. H. (1986). The effects of anxiety patterns in erectile dysfunction. *Behaviour Research and Therapy, 24*(1), 19–26.

Clement, U., & Schmidt, G. (1983). The outcome of

couple therapy for sexual dysfunctions using three different formats. *Journal of Sex and Marital Therapy, 9,* 67–78.

Crenshaw, T. L., & Goldberg, J. P. (1996). *Sexual pharmacology: Drugs that affect sexual function.* New York: Norton.

Everaerd, W., & Dekker, J. (1985). Treatment of male sexual dysfunction: Sex therapy compared with systematic desensitization and rational emotive therapy. *Behaviour Research and Therapy, 22,* 114–124.

Fichten, C. S., Libman, E., & Brender, W. (1983). Methodological issues in the study of sex therapy: Effective components in the treatment of secondary orgasmic dysfunction. *Journal of Sex and Marital Therapy, 9*(3), 191–202.

Hartman, L. M., & Daly, E. M. (1983). Relationship factors in the treatment of sexual dysfunction. *Behaviour Research and Therapy, 21,* 153–160.

Heiman, J., & LoPiccolo, J. (1988). *Becoming orgasmic: A sexual and personal growth program for women* (2nd ed.). New York: Simon & Schuster.

Heiman, J. R., & Rowland, D. L. (1983). Affective and physiological sexual response patterns: The effects of instructions on sexually functional and dysfunctional men. *Journal of Psychosomatic Research, 27*(2), 105–116.

Hurlbert, D. F., White, L. C., Powell, R. D., & Apt, C. (1993). Orgasm consistency training in the treatment of women reporting hypoactive sexual desire: An outcome comparison of women-only groups and couples-only groups. *Journal of Behavior Therapy and Experimental Psychiatry, 24,* 3–13.

Kaplan, H. S. (1995). Sexual aversion disorder: The case of the phobic virgin, or an abused child grows up. In R. Rosen and S. Leiblum (Eds.), *Case studies in sex therapy* (pp. 65–80). New York: Guilford Press.

Lazarus, A. (1963). The treatment of chronic frigidity by systematic desensitization. *Journal of Nervousness and Mental Diseases, 136,* 272–278.

Lipsius, S. H. (1987). Prescribing sensate focus without proscribing intercourse. *Journal of Sex and Marital Therapy, 13* (2), 106–116.

Markman, H. J., Blumberg, S. L., & Stanley, S. M. (1993). *Prevention and Relationship Enhancement Program: Consultant's manual.* Unpublished treatment manual.

Markman, H. J., Floyd, F. J., Stanley, S. M., & Storaasli, R. D., (1988). Prevention of marital distress: A longitudinal investigation. *Journal of Consulting and Clinical Psychology, 56,* 210–217.

Masters, W., & Johnson, V. (1970). *Human sexual inadequacy.* Boston: Little, Brown.

Matthews, A., Bancroft, J., Whitehead, A., Hackmann, A., Julier, D., Bancroft, J., Gath, D., & Shaw, P. (1976). The behavioral treatment of sexual inadequacy: A comparative study. *Behaviour Research and Therapy, 14,* 427–436.

Regev, L. G., O'Donohue, W. T., & Avina, C. (2003). Treating couples with sexual dysfunction. In D. Snyder & M. Whisman (Eds.), *Treating difficult couples: Helping clients with coexisting mental and relationship disorders.* New York: Guilford Press.

Riley, A. J., & Riley, E. J. (1978). A controlled study to evaluate directed masturbation in the management of primary orgasmic failure in women. *British Journal of Psychiatry, 133,* 404–409.

Schover, L. R. (2000). Sexual problems in chronic illness. In S. Leiblum & R. Rosen (Eds.), *Principles and practice of sex therapy* (3rd ed., pp. 398–422). New York: Guilford Press.

Takefman, J., & Brender, W. (1984). An analysis of the effectiveness of two components in the treatment of Erectile Dysfunction. *Archives of Sexual Behavior, 13*(4), 321–340.

van Lankveld, J. J. D. M. (1998). Bibliotherapy in the treatment of sexual dysfunctions: A meta-analysis. *Journal of Consulting and Clinical Psychology, 66,* 702–708.

Wincze, J. P., & Carey, M. P. (2001). *Sexual dysfunction: A guide for assessment and treatment* (2nd ed). New York: Guilford Press.

Wolpe, J. (1958). *Psychotherapy by reciprocal inhibition.* Stanford, CA: Stanford University Press.

Zeiss, R. A., & Zeiss, A. M. (1978). *Prolong your pleasure.* New York: Pocket Books.

55 SHAPING

Kyle E. Ferguson

Behavioral repertoires are not always effective when applied to new environments or even to their current environments. A skill set acquired under one condition does not necessarily generalize to other settings, even when those settings are similar. In some cases, in the absence of direct instruction, the natural contingencies rapidly shape up or refine those skills until a person's repertoire becomes maximally effective in the new situation (Ferster & Skinner, 1957). Colloquially, the person gets acclimated to his or her new surroundings with minimal effort. We see this when someone begins a new job or a child transfers to a new school and fits right in after several weeks. Other times this is not the case, especially when one considers special populations (e.g., mentally impaired elderly, children with developmental disabilities, and survivors of acquired brain injury). The natural contingencies fail to bring appropriate responding under situational control and, in the absence of direct instruction, reinforcing circumstances for the individual become more remote and punishment more likely. As a case in point, some employees continue to experience an inordinate amount of difficulty no matter how hard they try in their new roles. In other words, these individuals lack the requisite skills to successfully function in these environments. Accordingly, when the appropriate response class (i.e., different behaviors producing similar outcomes) is absent from a person's repertoire, the class of responding must be shaped by contingencies carefully arranged by other people, and the contingencies must be programmed (Skinner, 1966).

This chapter opens with a technical definition of shaping. Several clinical case examples that use this technique are considered next. The chapter then discusses who might benefit from shaping, contraindications of the technique, other decisions in deciding to use or not to use shaping, and purported learning mechanisms underlying this approach. The remainder of the chapter provides step-by-step guidelines in using this technique.

DEFINITION OF SHAPING

Shaping is the differential reinforcement of successive approximations toward desired performance (Holland & Skinner, 1961; Martin & Pear, 1978; Miltenberger, 2001; Skinner, 1953). The reader should note that the term *reinforcement* has a dual meaning: As used in the previous definition, it is the *procedure* of presenting a reinforcing consequence after the target behavior occurs. The procedural aspect of the definition concerns what the therapist does in response to what the client does. The other meaning of the term denotes an increase in the rate of behavior (responding over time) as a *function* of its consequences (e.g., smiling when a person makes eye contact increases the duration of eye contact; Pierce & Epling, 1999). The functional aspect of the definition is more relevant to what the client is doing.

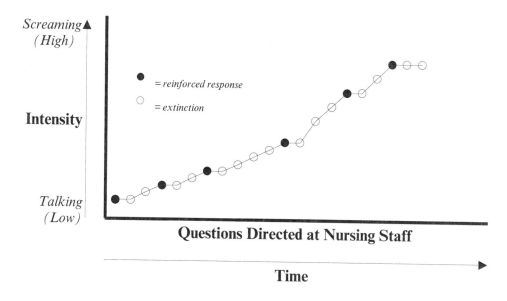

FIGURE 55.1

These data depict a functional relationship between reinforcer delivery on the part of nursing home staff and topographical characteristics of client communicative behavior. The abscissa (*x* axis) depicts perseverative questioning directed at nursing staff. Questions that resulted in reinforcement are represented by shaded-in circles. Questions that resulted in extinction (withholding of the reinforcer) are represented by open circles. The ordinate (*y* axis) depicts a continuum of communicative intensity from "talking" on one extreme (low) to "screaming" on the other (high).

That is to say, what is at issue is whether the client's behavior changes as a result of the shaping intervention.

The term *differential reinforcement* suggests that the reinforcer be delivered in a different way based on the current level of performance. Initially, the criterion is low. Any behavior that resembles the desired performance, even if it bears only a slight resemblance, is reinforced. Insofar as the current behavior increases over baseline levels (i.e., prior to implementing reinforcement), and the behavior maintains a steady rate for several minutes (or longer, for more complex behaviors), the reinforcer criterion is raised. Namely, a level of performance that once produced the reinforcer does not any longer. The reinforcer is withheld until the individual emits behavior that better approximates desired performance—the criteria become increasingly more stringent.

If one were to graph many demonstrations of differential reinforcement of successive approximations they would look similar to Figure 55.1. That is, the data would organize into stepwise patterns, like an ascending flight of stairs, alternating between the conditions of extinction and reinforcement.

CASE EXAMPLES

During the 1950s and 1960s many psychologists began applying the behavioral principles discovered in the learning laboratory to real-life settings. While these empirical regularities were based largely on work with nonhuman subjects, extending this technology to applied settings often produced dramatic clinical outcomes. Most notably, this technology of behavior worked well with individuals with extremely limited repertoires (e.g., those with mental retardation and severe psychiatric disturbances), whereas other approaches—namely, psychoanalytic and humanistic—were often of limited use.

In a classic study, Haughton and Ayllon (1965) examined the development of unusual and repetitive behaviors that appeared "meaningless" (p. 94). Their subject was a 54-year-old women diagnosed with Schizophrenia. She had been hospitalized for over 20 years. Using cigarettes as reinforcement, they shaped an arbitrary (and meaningless) response—"holding a broom while in an upright posture" (p. 96). To get her to do this they had one staff member hand her the broom while another handed her a cigarette. In just a few days their subject "developed a stereo-typed behavior of pacing while holding the broom" (p. 96).

Haughton and Ayllon's (1965) study demonstrates how abnormal behavior might develop through learning mechanisms. Their study also demonstrates the danger in ignoring environmental contingencies. The following quotation depicts the evaluation of one of two psychiatrists (naïve to the study):

> Dr. B's evaluation of the patient . . . Her constant and compulsive pacing holding a broom in the manner she does could be seen as a ritualistic procedure, a magical action. . . . Symbolism is a predominant mode of expression of deep seated unfulfilled desires and instinctual impulses. By magic, she controls others, cosmic powers are at her disposal and inanimate objects become living creatures. (Haughton & Ayllon, 1965, p. 97)

A young boy with autism was the subject of another classic study, conducted by Wolf, Risley, and Mees (1964). After having undergone cataract surgery their subject was required to wear glasses, which he vehemently refused to do. He would pull them off and throw them to the floor. This, of course, posed two problems. While not wearing his glasses made it almost impossible for him to see (first problem), what made matters worse was the fact that failing to wear his glasses increased the risk of irreversible blindness caused by retinal cell degeneration (second problem).

To get the boy to wear glasses, Wolf and his colleagues (1964) differentially reinforced closer approximations to the desired response (i.e., wearing them) using an edible reinforcer, food. During the initial stages of the shaping process, responses that only remotely approximated final performance were reinforced. These behaviors included simply touching the glasses and subsequently handling them.

Criteria for performance became increasingly more stringent. Earlier behaviors that had once resulted in reinforcement were put on extinction (no reinforcer followed responding), while more was required from the boy to obtain the reinforcer. For example, the subject was expected to bring the glasses within the proximity of his face and, ultimately, to put them on. To summarize the outcome of this study, the boy eventually got to the point where he routinely wore his glasses, becoming comfortable with them on for extended periods of time.

In a more contemporary case example, Jackson and Wallace (1974) used the principle of differential reinforcement in shaping the vocal intensity of a socially withdrawn 15-year-old girl diagnosed with mental retardation. Most notably, she had a condition known as *aphonia* (producing insufficient volume). As a means of shaping effective performance—increasing the volume of her voice—the clinicians used a voice-operated relay along with a decibel meter to accurately set performance criteria, provide continuous feedback, and automatically dispense the token reinforcer (exchangeable for books, beauty aids, photo albums, etc.).

Initially, criteria were set low with respect to the complexity of the words she was required to read (100 monosyllabic words) and the intensity with which the words were read (i.e., the relay device was set for maximum sensitivity). After she had emitted responses above the device's threshold, with a hit rate of approximately 80%, the sensitivity on the machine was decreased slightly. Hence, the subject was required to speak progressively louder to activate the reinforcer mechanism. Once her speech was shaped to normal intensity, researchers targeted word complexity—she was required to read polysyllabic words (one to five syllables). Eventually criteria and reinforcer density were stretched to five or six polysyllabic words spoken (within the range of normal intensity) per token.

It took about 100 sessions to reach target criteria, translating into several months of training. To summarize the outcome of this study, relative to baseline performance where the subject's voice was not any louder than background noise (the sound of an overhead fan), the volume of her voice was eventually shaped to that required for normal conversation. Remarkably, in part due to this intervention, the subject went from the special classroom to the regular classroom, and ultimately became gainfully employed as a waitress.

WHO MIGHT BENEFIT FROM THIS TECHNIQUE

Shaping is a versatile technique that can be used with any population and presenting problem where there is a skill deficit in the client's repertoire. The following list is just a small sample of published controlled studies that demonstrate its clinical utility:

- Increasing reading fluency and comprehension in 11- to 18-year-old boys with emotional disabilities (Miller & Polk, 1994)
- Teaching a problem-solving repertoire to adults with acquired brain injury (Foxx, Marchand-Martella, Braunling-McMorrow, & McMorrow, 1988)
- Establishing a toilet-training program for clients with mental retardation and developmental disabilities (Foxx & Azrin, 1973)
- Developing an early detection and prevention of breast cancer program (Saunders, Pilgram, & Pennypacker, 1986)
- Targeting children with autism to increase their social behavior, teach them to speak, and eliminate self-stimulation (Lovaas, 1977)
- Assertiveness training, targeting adults with chronic Schizophrenia (Bloomfield, 1973)
- Overcoming learned nonuse that develops after a stroke (Taub et al., 1993)
- Teaching motor skills to preschool children (Hardiman, Goetz, Reuter, & LeBlanc, 1975)
- Differentially reinforcing higher rates of speaking with a chronically depressed individual (Robinson & Lewinsohn, 1973)
- Reducing tremor caused by an acquired brain injury (Guercio, Ferguson, & McMorrow, 2001)

CONTRAINDICATIONS

Shaping is not contraindicated for most clients when used by therapists who are knowledgeable of the principles of learning. One of the dangers in the use of shaping by therapists who are not

knowledgeable is inadvertently shaping harmful behavior. Reinforcement increases the probability of any behavior that enters into the contingency. Accordingly, therapists must be careful not to deliver reinforcement right after the occurrence of problematic behavior that threatens the safety of the client or others.

OTHER DECISIONS IN DECIDING TO USE OR NOT TO USE THIS TECHNIQUE

The first question to ask in deciding whether to use a shaping program is whether performance problems are related to a skill deficiency or do problems lie in the person's environment (Mager & Pipe, 1984). Hypothetically, if someone offered the client $10,000 to engage in the activity, would he or she be able to do so? If not, chances are the problem is related to a skill deficit. In determining whether shaping is the best approach in skill training we then need to ask ourselves: Was the individual able to perform the activity earlier on? If so, the client needs some refresher training, not shaping. In these circumstances modeling the behavior or telling the client what to do (instructional control) are all that is required (Miltenberger, 2001). Does the client get enough opportunities to practice the skill? If not, employ booster sessions coupled with corrective feedback. Are environmental prompts called for? If so, checklists, posted signs, and reminders might alleviate the problem. Both of these—increasing opportunities for practice or ameliorating deficient antecedent control (prompts)—obviate shaping.

After ruling out rationales for alternative treatments we are more confident that a shaping program is in order. However, before actually implementing a program we also need to consider environmental factors related to performance. Technically, what is at issue is the contingencies of reinforcement relevant to the target behavior (Pierce & Epling, 1999).

When considering contingencies, performance deficits could also be attributed to environmental barriers. The first question to ask related to these influences is whether performance is punishing (Mager & Pipe, 1984). If this is the case, one should try decreasing the unpleasantness of the activity before employing another strategy (that is, if one has reason to believe that the client can already emit the behavior). Is nonperformance reinforcing? Along these lines, one cannot assume that clients are motivated to emit the target behavior. In emitting behavior incompatible with the target response (nonperformance), does the client evoke solicitous behavior from others? Does the client get to engage in a preferred activity? Does the social milieu promote or hinder effective performance (since not all work environments are task oriented)?

Finally, if the target behavior is not in the person's repertoire, and if one has reason to believe he or she can potentially emit the behavior with proper contingency management (i.e., differential reinforcement of successive approximations) and that other training strategies (e.g., modeling, prompting, instructional control) would be less effective, then one should try shaping.

HOW DOES THE TECHNIQUE WORK?

Shaping is conceptualized within an evolutionary framework (environmental selectionism; Skinner, 1990; Staddon & Simmelhag, 1971). While natural selection is the mechanism responsible for the evolution of species, contingencies of reinforcement (reinforcement and punishment) is the mechanism responsible for variations in operant behavior (Skinner, 1987).

When behavior is emitted it always varies topographically—no two responses are exactly the same. When responding looks almost identical from one moment to the next, what we are actually witnessing is average performance within certain dimensional parameters (Baum, 1994, pp. 64–65). For example, when we hear a familiar voice say "Hello" it varies each time in volume (e.g., louder if the speaker is farther away), pitch (e.g., a lower pitch when the person has a cold), speed (e.g., when the speaker is in a hurry), clarity (e.g., when the person has food in his or her mouth), and so on. Even though the speaker's voice varies in quality each time, it varies within normal limits—otherwise listeners would never be able to identify speakers by hearing alone.

Taking our "Hello" example, if one were to graph these data along some response dimension (e.g., pitch) it would likely result in a distribution similar to the one shown in Figure 55.2 (in this case, a normal distribution). Shaping works by reinforcing responses that vary toward one end of the response continuum. In this example the therapist sets the criterion a little higher than average. This, of course, places the behavior below the criterion on extinction (no reinforcement follows responding). Extinction produces increased variability in performance (Galbicka, 1994). The new reinforcement contingency is designed to select or capture extinction-induced behavior that meets or exceeds the criterion.

Once performance stabilizes, thus forming a new distribution (Distribution 2), the criterion is increased again and a new distribution is formed (Distribution 3). Once responding stabilizes (Distribution 3), the criterion is increased one last time (Distribution 4).

STEP-BY-STEP PROCEDURES

All effective shaping programs consist of the following components (summarized in Table 55.1): (1) selecting a target behavior, (2) assessing the current level of performance, (3) selecting the initial behavior, (4) selecting a reliable reinforcer, and (5) differentially reinforcing successive approximations (Alberto & Troutman, 1990; Baldwin & Baldwin, 1981; Cooper, Heron, & Heward, 1987; Foxx, 1982; Martin & Pear, 1978; Miltenberger, 2001; Sulzer-Azaroff & Mayer, 1991; Sundel & Sundel, 1993). The reader should note that these steps are arranged chronologically.

Step 1: Select a Target Behavior

The first step in developing a shaping program is to specify the instructional goal, or more precisely, the *target behavior* (Sulzer-Azaroff & Mayer, 1991). For it to be useful, the target behavior must be described in an objective, clear, and complete manner (Barlow & Hersen, 1984; Hawkins & Dobes, 1977).

An *objective* description refers only to the observable aspects of the target response. In other words, what does the target behavior look, sound, or feel like? Is it direct eye contact where both sets of eyes, the client's and other person's, are in alignment for over 20 s? Is it using the ap-

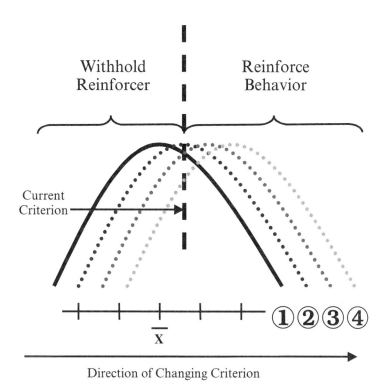

Withhold
Reinforcer

Reinforce
Behavior

Current
Criterion

X̄

① ② ③ ④

Direction of Changing Criterion

FIGURE 55.2

As criteria are gradually increased, distributions of responses centered around new means shift to the right. ②, ③, and ④ denote the changing distributions. Modeled after Baum's (1994) Figure 4.3, p. 65; and Galbicka's (1994) Figures 1 and 2, pp. 742–743.

propriate tone when making assertive requests— loud enough so that a person standing 10 feet away can hear everything? Is it a firm handshake with just enough pressure so that either person can't pull his or her hand away? While there is obvious flexibility in how the target behavior is described, objective definitions never reflect the intent of the person or internal processes that are believed to be relevant to the case (e.g., chemical imbalance). Descriptions referring to internal processes are unreliable.

A *clear* definition must be unambiguous, short, and to the point (parsimonious). Ideally, after reading the description of the behavioral target, any person with a ninth-grade education and unfamiliar with the case should be able to point it out when it is occurring. Observe, too, that clear definitions reduce the likelihood of inadvertently strengthening irrelevant behavior, thus making the shaping program more efficient

and increasing the chances of getting the behavior the therapist really wants (Sulzer-Azaroff & Mayer, 1991).

A *complete* definition must include all of the critical parts of the target behavior. Including all of its essential elements enables observers to discern when the target behavior begins and ends.

TABLE 55.1   Steps in Shaping

1. Select a target behavior

2. Assess the current level of performance

3. Select the initial behavior

4. Select reliable reinforcers

5. Differentially reinforce successive approximations using a Continuous Reinforcement schedule (FR1)

6. Once the client has reached the final criterion, by degrees, begin thinning out the Continuous Reinforcement schedule to an FR3 schedule, FR 6 schedule, etc.

Consider how one might treat someone with severe Claustrophobia who has to use an elevator daily (e.g., when showing potential business clients around), but becomes paralyzed by the mere thought of elevators. Going from one floor to at least the next floor might be the behavioral target. This definition would be considered complete because it necessarily entails approaching the elevator, pressing the up or down button, getting on, pressing the button for the next floor, and so on. Observers can easily discern whether the client actually rides the elevator successfully by waiting for him or her on another floor, in front of the elevator.

Step 2: Assess the Current Level of Performance

Once we have defined the target behavior and determined that shaping is the most appropriate intervention, we then have to come up with a way of measuring performance. Effective shaping programs use direct observational methods.

Direct observational methods are highly accurate and relatively simple to use. General points to consider in using a direct observational system are the following: When is behavior observed, for how long is the observation interval (e.g., in 1-min blocks or using spot checks), and what specific response dimensions are targeted (i.e., frequency, duration, topography, intensity; Bloom, Fischer, & Orme, 1995). Regarding the first point, one should observe the target behavior at times that best capture it. For example, if a child tends to tantrum on his or her way to school, then ideally observing the child at that time makes the most sense. Observing the child at other times wastes time.

As far as the observation interval is concerned, it depends on the target of interest. A more discrete behavior (with a clearly definable beginning and end) would call for shorter observational intervals, whereas more involved activities would necessitate longer observational intervals. The same can be said in determining what behavioral dimensions to measure. More discrete behaviors lend themselves to frequency (i.e., counting the number of responses or using rate, frequency/ time) and intensity measures (e.g., measuring voice tone with a decibel meter). For behaviors that are less transitory, use durational measure-

ment strategies that best capture the most important temporal dimensions of behavior (e.g., how long a child can sit in his or her desk before getting up; see Bloom, Fischer, & Orme, 1995, p 127ff., for details).

Step 3: Select the Initial Behavior

After deciding what measurement strategies to employ, the next step is figuring out where to begin the intervention. The best way of identifying where to start the shaping program is to observe the individual under natural conditions, in the context in which the target behavior is supposed to occur (Foxx, 1982). If this is not feasible, make an attempt at approximating what the therapist believes to be the most crucial variables of the natural conditions, under more artificial conditions (e.g., in the therapist's office as opposed to the client's residence).

In any event, under natural or analog conditions, try identifying what behaviors bear any resemblance to final performance. These are the behaviors the therapist will be targeting in ensuing steps, monitoring, reinforcing, and the like. This will be taken up in Step 6.

Step 4: Select Reliable Reinforcers

We move next to selecting reliable (positive) reinforcers. A *reinforcer* is any stimulus or event that increases the probability of the behavior that produces it (Pierce & Epling, 1999). Said differently, for a stimulus or event to function as a reinforcer we need to see a change in performance; namely, an increase in the frequency of responding. By contrast, when an event reliably follows behavior and we observe no change in frequency or actually see a behavioral reduction, then the event does not function as a reinforcer.

Identifying powerful reinforcers that can be delivered immediately, and for which the client does not readily satiate (i.e., gets bored with or loses interest), are crucial to the shaping program (Miltenberger, 2001; see the chapter on stimulus preference assessment in this volume). Powerful reinforcers will help maintain a high level of motivation in the client (Foxx, 1982).

In identifying reinforcers, if the client is articulate the therapist can simply ask him or her what he or she is willing to work for. However, in spite of what the client says, it is best to briefly test the purported reinforcers and see for yourself whether these produce the intended effects. If these do in fact work, use them. If these don't work, continue the search. For clients who are less articulate, the therapist should also ask them what they are willing to work for. Again, test these out—in some instances they will be accurate in identifying powerful reinforcers and in others they won't. The only way to know for certain what stimuli function as reinforcers is to actually observe a change in the frequency of responding following the repeated presentation of the stimuli, contingent on performance.

Reinforcers usually differ between people, and the same reinforcer may not increase the frequency of responding all of the time in the same individual. Take meat, for example: While meat reinforces the behavior of someone who enjoys meat (e.g., a person will drive across town for a well-prepared steak), meat will not reinforce the behavior of a vegetarian under most conditions (i.e., when the person isn't starving). By contrast, "Tofurky" may reinforce the purchasing behavior of the vegetarian most of the time, though not always. For instance, the vegetarian probably won't stock up on Tofurky several hours after eating a huge Thanksgiving meal of which Tofurky was the centerpiece.

It follows, therefore, that the greater the number of items on the reinforcer menu, the less likely satiation will become a problem in the program. Before proceeding to Step 5, be sure to have a well stocked armamentarium of reinforcers. Should any fail to function as reinforcing stimuli, at any given moment, employ another that has demonstrated efficacy.

Step 5: Differentially Reinforce Successive Approximations

After completing Steps 1 through 4 we are ready to begin shaping the client's behavior. Begin with the initial behavior as identified in Step 3 (Miltenberger, 2001). Deliver the reinforcer contingently every time the client emits the initial behavior. The reinforcer-to-response ratio should be 1:1. Technically, this is called a *continuous reinforcement schedule (CRF)* or a *fixed ratio (FR) schedule.*

These terms are used interchangeably throughout the shaping literature (Ferster & Skinner, 1957).

Once reliable performance has been achieved,[1] increase the criterion ever so slightly (again using a CRF schedule). The next approximation should require just a little more effort from the client. Bear in mind that if the therapist raises the criterion too high this will lead to what is called a "ratio strain" (Pierce & Epling, 1999). Simply, the client becomes frustrated and gives up trying. On the other end of the continuum, once a person has clearly mastered an approximation, move on quickly. Otherwise the contingencies will promote staying too long on each approximation that follows (Miltenberger, 2001).

While reinforcing responding at the next approximation, the therapist will undoubtedly see earlier behavior emerge. Do not reinforce old behavior—these behaviors are placed on extinction (i.e., no reinforcer follows responding). Reinforce only behavior that meets or exceeds the current criterion.[2] Continue using differential reinforcement of successive approximations, alternating between conditions of reinforcement (CRF schedule) and extinction. Eventually the target behavior will be reached, at which time the program shifts from behavioral acquisition to maintenance.

Maintenance refers to the extent to which responding persists under natural conditions (Sulzer-Azaroff & Mayer, 1991). To ensure that responding maintains after the program has been completed, gradually wean the client off of the reinforcer-rich FR1 schedule. By degrees, begin thinning out the FR1 schedule to an FR3 schedule (3 responses per reinforcer) or a variable ratio 3 schedule, VR3 (on average, every 3rd response

---

1. If the target behavior can be shaped up in one session, reliable performance might consist of a steady rate maintained for several minutes. If the target behavior will take more than one session, as a rule of thumb begin each ensuing session with the average criterion for performance derived from the previous session.
2. The exception to this rule is when a client has a run of failures at a given criterion. When this occurs you must lower the criterion and establish a run of successes before returning to the previously unsuccessful level. Establishing a behavioral momentum by backing up should push the client over such hurdles.

produces the reinforcer). Once performance is reliable, after several minutes thin the reinforcer density again to yet a leaner schedule of reinforcement, and so on (e.g., FR6, FR9, FR12, etc.). Do not rush this aspect of the program—take your time so as not to lose the target behavior.

CONCLUSION

When the appropriate response class is missing from a client's repertoire and other, potentially more parsimonious interventions can be ruled out, under carefully controlled conditions shaping can build new behaviors rapidly. How long it takes to shape a new behavior and the extent to which such programs are successful depends on whether the program is principle driven (not technique driven). Functionally oriented, principle-driven programs are inextricably tied to the learning principle of differential reinforcement of successive approximations. These are based on what the client actually does, not entirely on what everyone wants him or her to do. Effective shaping programs are thus tailor made for specific presenting problems. In other words, these adjust continuously in accord with the client's current level of performance. Of course, also in keeping with a principle-driven orientation, one must eventually abandon the program should it fail to produce desired results. Perhaps other techniques outlined in the present volume are more appropriate.

References

Alberto, P. A., & Troutman, A. C. (1990). *Applied behavior analysis for teachers: Influencing student performance* (2nd ed.). Columbus, OH: Charles E. Merrill.

Baldwin, J. D., & Baldwin, J. I. (1981). *Behavior principles in everyday life* (2nd ed.). Englewood Cliffs, NJ: Prentice Hall.

Barlow, D. H., & Hersen, M. (1984). *Single case experimental designs: Strategies for studying behavior change* (2nd ed.). New York: Pergamon Press.

Baum, W. M. (1994). *Understanding behaviorism: Science, behavior, and culture.* New York: HarperCollins.

Bloom, M., Fischer, J., & Orme, J. G. (1995). *Evaluating practice: Guidelines for the accountable professional* (2nd ed.). Boston: Allyn & Bacon.

Bloomfield, H. H. (1973). Assertiveness training in an outpatient group of chronic schizophrenics: A preliminary report. *Behavior Therapy, 4,* 277–281.

Cooper, J. O., Heron, T. E., & Heward, W. L. (1987). *Applied behavior analysis.* Columbus, OH: Merrill.

Ferster, C. B., & Skinner, B. F. (1957). *Schedules of reinforcement.* New York: Appleton-Century-Crofts.

Foxx, R. M. (1982). *Increasing behaviors of persons with severe retardation and autism.* Champaign, IL: Research Press.

Foxx, R. M., & Azrin, N. H. (1973). *Toilet training the retarded: A rapid program for day and nighttime independent toileting.* Champaign, IL: Research Press.

Foxx, R. M., Marchand-Martella, N. E., Martella, R. C., Braunling-McMorrow, D., & McMorrow, M. J. (1988). Teaching a problem-solving strategy to closed head-injured adults. *Behavioral Residential Treatment, 3,* 193–210.

Galbicka, G. (1994). Shaping in the 21st century: Moving percentile schedules into applied settings. *Journal of Applied Behavior Analysis, 27,* 739–760.

Guercio, J. M., Ferguson, K. E., & McMorrow, M. J. (2001). Increasing functional communication through relaxation and neuromuscular feedback. *Brain Injury, 15,* 1073–1082.

Hardiman, S. A., Goetz, E. M., Reuter, K. E., & LeBlanc, J. M. (1975). Primis, contingent attention, and training: Effects on child's motor behavior. *Journal of Applied Behavior Analysis, 8,* 399–409.

Haughton, E., & Ayllon, T. (1965). Production and elimination of symptomatic behavior. In L. Ullmann & L. Krasner (Eds.), *Case studies in behavior modification* (pp. 94–98). New York: Holt, Rinehart, & Winston.

Hawkins, R. P., & Dobes, R. W. (1977). Behavioral definitions in applied behavior analysis: Explicit or implicit. In B. C. Etzel, J. M. LeBlanc, & D. M. Baer (Eds.), *New directions in behavioral research: Theory, methods, and applications. In honor of Sidney W. Bijou* (pp. 167–188). Hillsdale, NJ: Erlbaum.

Holland, J. G., & Skinner, B. F. (1961). *The analysis of behavior: A program for self-instruction.* New York: McGraw-Hill.

Jackson, D. A., & Wallace, R. F. (1974). The modification and generalization of voice loudness in a fifteen-year-old retarded girl. *Journal of Applied Behavior Analysis, 7,* 461–471.

Lovaas, O. I. (1977). *The autistic child: Language development through behavior modification.* New York: Irvington.

Mager, R. F., & Pipe, P. (1984). *Analyzing performance problems or you really oughta wanna* (2nd ed.). Belmont, CA: Pitman.

Martin, G., & Pear, J. (1978). *Behavior modification: What it is and how to do it.* Englewood Cliffs, NJ: Prentice Hall.

Miller, B. L., Hou, C., Goldberg, M., & Mena, I. (1999). Anterior temporal lobes: Social brain. In B. L. Miller & J. L. Cummings (Eds.), *The human frontal lobes* (pp. 557–567). New York: Guilford Press.

Miller, A. D., & Polk, A. L. (1994). Repeated readings and precision teaching: Increasing reading fluency and comprehension in sixth through twelfth grade boys with emotional disabilities. *Journal of Precision Teaching, 1,* 46–66.

Miltenberger, R. G. (2001). *Behavior modification: Principles and procedures* (2nd ed.). Belmont, CA: Wadsworth.

Pierce, W. D., & Epling, W. F. (1999). *Behavior analysis and learning* (2nd ed.). Upper Saddle River, NJ: Prentice Hall.

Robinson, J. C., & Lewinsohn, P. M. (1973). Behavior modification of speech characteristics in a chronically depressed man. *Behavior Therapy, 4,* 150–152.

Saunders, K. J., Pilgram, C. A., & Pennypacker, H. S. (1986). Increased proficiency of research in breast cancer self-examination. *Cancer, 58,* 2531–2537.

Skinner, B. F. (1953). *Science and human behavior.* New York: Macmillan.

Skinner, B. F. (1957). *Verbal behavior.* New York: Appleton-Century-Crofts.

Skinner, B. F. (1966). The phylogeny and ontogeny of behavior. *Science, 153,* 1205–1213.

Skinner, B. F. (1987). *Upon further reflection.* Englewood Cliffs, NJ: Prentice Hall.

Skinner, B. F. (1990). Can psychology be a science of the mind? *American Psychologist, 45,* 1206–1210.

Staddon, J. E. R., & Simmelhag, V. L. (1971). The "superstition" experiment: A reexamination of its implications for the principles of adaptive behavior. *Psychological Review, 78,* 3–43.

Sulzer-Azaroff, B., & Mayer, G. R. (1991). *Behavior analysis for lasting change.* New York: Harcourt Brace College Publishers.

Sundel, S. S., & Sundel, M. (1993). *Behavior modification in the human services* (3rd ed.). Newbury Park, CA: Sage.

Taub, E., Miller, N. E., Novack, T. A., Cook, E. W., III, Fleming, W. D., Nepomuceno, C. S., Connell, J. S., & Crago, J. E. (1993). Technique to improve chronic motor deficit after stroke. *Archives of Physical Medicine and Rehabilitation, 74,* 347–354.

Wolf, M. N., Risley, T. R., & Mees, H. (1964). Application of operant conditioning procedures to the behavior problems of an autistic child. *Behaviour Research and Therapy, 1,* 305–312.

56 SOCIAL SKILLS TRAINING

Chris Segrin

Social skills training is a widely applied and effective treatment for a range of psychosocial problems that include Depression, Anxiety, Schizophrenia, loneliness, and marital distress, to name but a few. Perhaps one reason for the ubiquity of this technique in clinical contexts is that it is actually a collection of techniques aimed at improving the quality of people's interpersonal communication and relationships. For this reason, social skills training can take a variety of specific forms that can be tailored to the particular needs of the client.

Social skills involve the ability to communicate with other people in a fashion that is both appropriate and effective. *Appropriateness* indicates that the social behavior does not violate social and relational norms. Socially skilled behaviors are instrumentally effective; that is, they allow the actor to successfully achieve his or her goals in social situations. Socially skilled behavioral performances are a complex amalgamation of declarative and procedural knowledge; motivation; the ability to select among multiple behavioral response options; and at a most basic level, the ability to enact a particular social behavior.

Social skills training as a primary therapy for psychosocial problems or as an adjunct to other techniques has a long history with an efficacious track record. A number of narrative and meta-analytic reviews (e.g., Brady, 1984; Corrigan, 1991; Erwin, 1994; Taylor, 1996) show that social skills training is effective at increasing clients' social skills and at reducing their psychiatric symptoms. Most empirical tests indicate that social skills training is as effective in treating psychosocial problems as most other therapeutic techniques that are in vogue. Furthermore, clients often adhere to social skills training therapies more readily than some other therapies that have higher drop-out rates. Social skills training also appears to be more effective in outpatient (compared to inpatient) settings (Corrigan, 1991).

WHO WILL BENEFIT FROM SOCIAL SKILLS TRAINING

Social skills training is well suited to clients who are experiencing a psychosocial problem that is at least partly caused or exacerbated by interpersonal difficulties. These difficulties might include, for example, martial distress, low frequency of dating, a lack of close friends, insufficient social support, trouble initiating new relationships, strained relationships with coworkers, or impoverished social networks. Similarly, social skills training may be an effective adjunct to other therapeutic techniques when the psychosocial problem has collateral deleterious effects on clients' interpersonal relationships. For example, an individual with alcoholism is likely to experience troubled interpersonal relationships, regardless of what caused the problem drinking. Social skills training may be helpful for improving the quality of clients' communication with significant others and may help them to more effectively marshal social support in their time of distress. Because the majority of people who are afflicted with a psychosocial problem will have some interpersonal difficulties (Segrin, 2001), whether etiologic or consequential, social skills training has a very broad based applicability and utility. An especially attractive feature of social skills training is that it can be easily tailored to suit the client's particular needs. For instance, an adolescent who is having difficulty making new friends, but otherwise has satisfying interactions and relationships with family members and school teachers, might participate in a social skills training regime that is focused exclusively on how to effectively initiate conversation, invite others to participate in shared activities, show interest in other people, and so on.

CONTRAINDICATIONS

Notwithstanding the broad applicability of social skills training for treating many psychosocial problems, there are certain circumstances that will limit the effectiveness of the technique. Because social skills training relies heavily on learning processes, clients with profound learning disabilities are unlikely to benefit from more sophisticated forms of social skills training. Related prerequisites for social skills training include the ability to pay attention to the therapist or trainer for at least 15 to 90 min at a time, the ability to understand and follow instructions for appropriate and effective behaviors, and most importantly, a motivation to learn new, and improve or correct, existing social behaviors (Liberman, DeRisi, & Mueser, 1989). For this reason, clients with severe attention deficits or gross thought disorders may not respond as readily to social skills training. Also, those with low motivation to enhance their interpersonal relationships, such as people with antisocial personalities or catatonia, are unlikely to reap immediate benefits for social skills training. In such cases, psychotic symptoms, attention deficits, or maladaptive personalities need to first be brought under control or

addressed, after which social skills training may be more effective.

OTHER FACTORS IN DECIDING TO USE OR NOT TO USE SOCIAL SKILLS TRAINING

This technique demands a significant degree of skill on the part of the trainer. Social skills training has historically been offered by individuals whose backgrounds are as varied as the problems to which the technique is applied. More powerful effects for social skills training have been documented in those cases where the trainer was a practicing psychologist, as opposed to, say, a school teacher (Erwin, 1994). The decision to employ social skills training in the treatment of a psychosocial problem requires a frank and candid self-appraisal on the part of the practitioner. Ideally, the trainer would possess strong social skills and have a strong background in the rationale and application of the technique.

HOW DOES SOCIAL SKILLS TRAINING WORK?

The theoretical rationale behind social skills training can be described at two levels. In the most general sense, the technique is predicated on the assumption that improvements in people's social relationships will translate directly and immediately into improved quality of life. By teaching clients how to improve their social skills, it is believed that they will be able to have more satisfying, effective, and enjoyable interactions with other people. As we are inherently social animals, most people are predisposed to respond positively to such outcomes. What is particularly powerful about this assumption is that it is generally thought to operate regardless of whether the client's actual problem was caused by troubled interpersonal relationships. Even in cases where a psychosocial problem appears more attributable to biological, cognitive, or environmental (i.e., Schizophrenia or life stress) issues, there will be salutary effects pursuant to improving interpersonal communication and relationships through social skills training.

At a more specific level, the causal mechanisms underlying social skills training are essentially learning principles. In essence, the technique teaches clients new behaviors or appropriate modifications of existing behaviors. The new behaviors are aimed at producing positive reinforcement and diminishing the probability of punishing responses from the social environment. Indeed, this is how Libet and Lewinsohn (1973) actually define *social skill*. By emitting a greater proportion of behaviors that are positively reinforced by others (and a smaller proportion of behaviors that produce punishing responses from others) after social skills training, the client's overall sense of happiness, self-worth, and satisfaction is increased. There is also strong evidence to suggest that social skills training contributes to improved psychosocial functioning by reducing anxiety in social situations (Stravynski, Grey, & Elie, 1987).

STEP-BY-STEP PROCEDURES

As noted earlier, social skills training is actually a collection of techniques. Not all training programs utilize every one of these techniques, but the better-developed and more successful programs use most of them (see, e.g., Becker, Heimberg, & Bellack, 1987; Bellack, Mueser, Gingerich, & Agresta, 1997; Kopelowicz, Corrigan, Schade, & Liberman, 1998; Liberman et al., 1989). Many of the techniques presented in this section (and summarized in Table 56.1) can be successfully implemented in individual or group settings.

Assessment

Social skills training must start with an assessment phase. Because social skills training is a nonspecific technique, decisions invariably have to be made about what types of social skills to focus on during the training. Given the extensive and complex nature of social interaction skills, it is unwise to assume that all people in need of social skills training need of the same type of intervention. To proceed otherwise would create the potential for spending resources teaching skills that clients already possess, and missing skill areas in which clients genuinely need improvement.

The assessment of social skills can be carried out by a variety of methods (see Becker & Heimberg, 1988, and Meier & Hope, 1998, for reviews). One very popular and cost-efficient method is the use of *self-report instruments*. There are numerous popular and psychometrically sound instruments for assessing social skills as a trait-like entity, such as the Social Skills Inventory (Riggio, 1986, 1989), or for assessing social skills in particular interpersonal domains, such as the Interpersonal Competence Questionnaire (Buhrmester, Furman, Wittenberg, & Reis, 1988). There are an abundance of additional self-report instruments for assessing particular components or aspects of social skills, such as the Conflict Resolution Inventory (McFall & Lillesand, 1971) or the Dating and Assertion Questionnaire (Levenson & Gottman, 1978). In addition to self-reports, social

TABLE 56.1   Steps in Social Skills Training

Step	Description
Assessment	Determine the specific area of the client's social skills deficits through self-reports, behavioral observations, and/or third party assessments.
Direct instruction or coaching	Teach and explain the basis of effective and appropriate social behaviors to the client along with specific suggestions for how to enact such behaviors.
Modeling	Show the client models enacting appropriate social behaviors, and receiving positive reinforcements for doing so. The modeling of inappropriate behaviors along with critiques and explanations may also be helpful.
Role-playing	Encourage the client to practice certain social behaviors in a controlled environment, typically with the therapist and perhaps an assistant. Provide feedback to the client immediately after enacting the role-plays.
Homework assignments	Instruct the client to enact certain social behaviors in the real world. Start with easy behaviors and graduate to more complex ones. Debrief in the following session.
Follow-up	Reassess the client's social skills and calibrate as necessary where deterioration is noted.

skills can be effectively assessed through *behavioral observations*. While this ideally entails observation in naturalistic contexts, the use of staged role-plays with therapists and assistants has proven to be a useful mechanism of observing clients' enactment of skilled and unskilled social behaviors. A third method for the assessment of social skills involves the use of *third-party observers*. These might be spouses, teachers, parents, roommates, or friends of the client who can provide some information about how he or she behaves in various social situations. Ideally, the initial assessment phase in social skills training would employ the technique of triangulation by using multiple methods for assessing clients' social skills. The results of these assessments will then dictate the focal points of subsequent training.

Direct Instruction or Coaching

Once a determination has been made concerning appropriate targets for intervention via social skills training, a reasonable starting point would involve offering instructions on how to interact more effectively with other people. This can be achieved in a lecture format, small-group discussion, more casual one-on-one conversation, or even through video tapes and written manuals. Social skills training often commences with instructions about how to effectively use various communication behaviors, complete with a rationale for how and why the behaviors function as they do. Without any coaching or direct instruction there is a risk that clients will learn the behavior without also learning the reason for using it, and without learning when and why to use it. Explanation of how and why different behaviors are effective and appropriate is vital at this stage.

An example of direct instruction or coaching would be explaining the importance of showing interest in other people. The social skills trainer might start by stating that showing interest and paying attention to our conversational partners makes them feel valued. Further, most people respond very positively to others who make them feel worthwhile, valued, and cared for. The latter information provides an explanation for how and why showing interest in others works, and how it can be functional. In direct instruction and coach-

ing the trainer must explain how to enact the behaviors and how they work to create rewarding social interactions and relationships. The therapist might offer suggestions for how to show interest in other people, such as asking "How's it going today?" and then following up with another inquiry or a positive response to what the other person has to say. Similarly, the therapist might suggest that the client ask questions such as "How was your weekend?" or "What have you been up to lately?" Of course, it would be important to work on developing these conversation starters in more extended interactions in which the client responds appropriately to the discourse of his or her partner. These suggestions would be coupled with discussions and explanations of their effect on other people (e.g., making them feel valued, letting them know that other people care about them, and so on).

Modeling

Modeling figures prominently among the mechanisms by which humans acquire new behaviors (Bandura, 1977; see Chapter 36, this volume). Capitalizing on this phenomenon, most social skills trainers are inclined to include modeling as an important part of the overall training package. In fact, Liberman and colleagues (1989) argued that "the most effective way to teach complex social behavior is through modeling and imitation" (p. 102). Modeling can be presented either on videotape or in live depiction. The purpose of modeling is to demonstrate the effective, and sometimes ineffective, use of certain behaviors. People who have difficulty saying and doing certain things when in the presence of others are sometimes more comfortable doing so after seeing someone else perform the behavior first. For this reason modeling is an important and effective component of many social skills training programs.

There are several steps that social skills trainers can take to increase the likelihood of successful modeling and acquisition of new behaviors by the trainee (Bandura, 1977; Smith, 1982; Trower, 1995). First, multiple models demonstrating the same behavior, or the same model repeating the demonstration, will increase the potential for learning the behavior. Multiple models challenge the idea that only rare and super-capable people can perform the behavior. Second, the more similar the model is to the client in terms of sex, age, and other characteristics, the more likely the trainee is to imitate that model. Models that are similar to the target individual implicitly send the message that "people like us possess the qualities needed to perform this behavior." Third, models who are rewarded for their actions are more likely to be imitated. If the modeling can build in interaction with a second actor or confederate who rewards the model, the modeling process will be more effective. This is the cornerstone of observational learning: When we see people rewarded for performing a behavior, we are more likely to enact that behavior.

Modeling works because it gives people a template or guide for their own behavior. Bandura (1986) refers to this as "making the unobservable observable" (p. 66). People cannot observe their own behavior. However, the observation of others' behavior gives people a mental picture of how the behavior can and should be performed. The primary outcome of successful modeling is the production of perceived *response efficacy*. This is the feeling that "this task can be accomplished" or "there are things that can be done to solve this problem or accomplish this goal." Response efficacy is an important component in reducing anxiety in social situations. When people have no sense of response efficacy they may feel that the situation is hopeless and simply avoid it altogether. The use of models that are similar to the self also contributes to perceived *self-efficacy*. This is the feeling that "*I* can accomplish this task," or that "there are things that *I* can do to solve this problem or accomplish this goal." Modeling is an important source of perceived self-efficacy (Bandura, 1986, 1999).

Role-Playing

After appropriate behaviors have been clearly modeled, the next step often involves having the client enact the behavior in the context of a role-play. Coaching and modeling are passive techniques in which trainees absorb information presented by others. Role-playing, however, is literally an interactive learning technique that calls for production and practice of actual behavior. The purpose of role-playing is to have clients practice the desired behaviors in a controlled set-

ting where they can be observed and from which feedback and reinforcement can be offered.

Typically, role-plays are set up with a description of a fictitious scene that resembles the problematic situation in which new behaviors are desired. For example, in their social skills training with alcoholics, Foy and his colleagues had subjects role-play drink refusal (Foy, Miller, Eisler, & O'Toole, 1976). The scene was set up as follows: "You are at your brother's house. It is a special occasion and your whole family and several friends are there. Your brother says, 'How about a beer?'" (p. 1341). The therapist who played the role of the brother would also counter refusals from the subjects with statements such as "One drink won't hurt you." Clients were instructed to act as if they were actually in that situation.

The effective use of role-playing in social skills training must include more than the simple production and practice of behavior on the part of the trainee. It is vital that the trainer provide a detailed critique and abundant positive reinforcement for appropriate and desired behaviors. It is recommended that clients rerun the scene, performing it several times in order to produce the desired response (Liberman et al., 1989). Clients should be reminded that it is okay if things do not go well on the first try. The use of rewards for successful role-playing is predicated on the assumption that the behaviors that are positively reinforced are more likely to be repeated, hopefully in contexts outside the training environment. It is essential that there be proportionally more positive reinforcement than negative criticism (Trower, Bryant. & Argyle, 1978). The reward inherent in positive feedback can intensify motivation and effort. Negative criticism, on the other hand, can be discouraging if it is abundant and may inhibit subsequent attempts at performing the behavior. Trower and colleagues also note that feedback must emphasize effect rather than appearance. For example, it is better to tell a trainee, "You made me feel like you did not know what you were talking about" rather than "You looked confused." The emphasis on effect over appearance is predicated on the assumption that skilled behavior is ultimately a social perception that has to be created in others. Feedback following role-plays should also be detailed and specific, with a commentary on particular behaviors such as posture, vocal tone, eye contact, specific utterances, and so forth. Sometimes in group contexts, other clients are requested to offer feedback (a useful technique for getting them to practice social perception skills). One reason role-plays are such a useful part of social skills training is that they allow the client to practice the desired behaviors in a controlled setting, while also allowing the trainer to make observations and assessments of the client's progress.

Homework Assignments

Homework assignments call for in vivo practice of targeted behaviors. Homework assignments are not for the debutante in social skills training. Without successful training and verification of primary social skills through the techniques discussed earlier, homework assignments can set the client up for disaster. Of all the social skills training techniques, homework assignments require the highest level of existing skill on the part of the trainee. At the same time they have perhaps the highest potential for payoff in that the client puts into actual practice the skills learned in the training setting.

Homework assignments that are commonly employed in social skills training include things like asking directions from a bus driver, going to a business and asking for a job application, and calling up a friend and making a lunch date. Typically, homework assignments are graduated by difficulty, and easier tasks are assigned first. For example, a client might be asked to solicit information from the bus driver first, and then to make a lunch date with a friend after successfully completing other easy homework assignments.

Like role-plays, homework assignments often benefit from a debriefing during which the client and trainer discuss and critique the performances. Here again, praise and positive reinforcement are often used to enhance the effectiveness of the learning process. It has also been recommended that trainers appropriately prepare clients for the possibility of failures in future homework assignments (Liberman et al., 1989) and explain how people cannot realistically expect success in all of their social interactions. The goal of social skills training is simply to increase the probability of success in social interactions.

The adept trainer will capitalize on problems or failures that arise in the context of these homework assignments in order to highlight what went wrong and how it can be corrected. This learn-from-your-mistakes approach can be an effective component of homework assignments, so long as these interpersonal failures are not disproportionately represented in the trainee's experiences. Again, supportive feedback and encouragement are an important part of the analysis of interpersonal failures, if the trainee's motivation level and self-esteem are to be maintained.

Follow-Up

A thorough social skills training program must involve some form of follow-up. Social skills, like most other skills, will decay unless practiced somewhat diligently. There is little reason to believe that social skills training can be successfully accomplished via one-shot training procedures that teach skills and then send people out into the world with no follow-up. It is essential to monitor clients' successes and failures, with attempts to fine-tune their performances. Follow-up training may occur weeks or months after completion of the primary training regime, and often begins with a reassessment of clients' social skills. Depending upon the outcome of these reassessments, the trainer may offer refresher training procedures that could involve more coaching, role-plays, and homework assignments, for those areas that are still in need of improvement.

Further Reading

Bellack, A. S., & Hersen, M. (Eds.). (1979). *Research and practice of social skills training.* New York: Plenum Press.

Liberman, R. P., DeRisi, W. J., & Mueser, K. T. (1989). *Social skills training for psychiatric patients.* New York: Pergamon Press.

Segrin, C., & Givertz, M. (2003). Methods of social skills training and development. In J. O. Greene & B. R. Burleson (Eds.), *Handbook of communication and social interaction skills* (pp. 135–176). Mahwah, NJ: Lawrence Erlbaum.

References

Bandura, A. (1977). *Social learning theory.* Englewood Cliffs, NJ: Prentice Hall.

Bandura, A. (1986). *Social foundations of thought and action*. Englewood Cliffs, NJ: Prentice-Hall.

Bandura, A. (1999). Social cognitive theory of personality. In L. A. Perrin & D. P. John (Eds.), *Handbook of personality theory and research* (2nd ed., pp. 154–196). New York: Guilford Press.

Becker, R. E., & Heimberg, R. G. (1988). Assessment of social skills. In A.S. Bellack & M. Hersen (Eds.), *Behavioral assessment: A practical handbook* (3rd ed., pp. 365–395). New York: Pergamon Press.

Becker, R. E., Heimberg, R. G., & Bellack, A. S. (1987). *Social skills training treatment for depression*. New York: Pergamon Press.

Bellack, A. S., Mueser, K. T., Gingerich, S., & Agresta, J. (1997). *Social skills training for Schizophrenia: A step-by-step guide*. New York: Guilford Press.

Brady, J. P. (1984). Social skills training for psychiatric patients: II. Clinical outcome studies. *American Journal of Psychiatry, 141*, 491–498.

Buhrmester, D., Furman, W., Wittenberg, M. T., & Reis, H. T. (1988). Five domains of interpersonal competence in peer relationships. *Journal of Personality and Social Psychology, 55*, 991–1008.

Corrigan, P. W. (1991). Social skills training in adult psychiatric populations: A meta-analysis. *Journal of Behavior Therapy and Experimental Psychiatry, 22*, 203–210.

Erwin, P. G. (1994). Effectiveness of social skills training with children: A meta-analytic study. *Counselling Psychology Quarterly, 7*, 305–310.

Foy, D. W., Miller, P. M., Eisler, R. M., & O'Toole, D. H. (1976). Social-skills training to teach alcoholics to refuse drinks effectively. *Journal of Studies on Alcohol, 37*, 1340–1345.

Kopelowicz, A., Corrigan, P. W., Schade, M., & Liberman, R. P. (1998). Social skills training. In K.T. Mueser & N. Tarrier (Eds.), *Handbook of social functioning in Schizophrenia* (pp. 307–326). Boston: Allyn & Bacon.

Levenson, R. W., & Gottman, J. M. (1978). Toward the assessment of social competence. *Journal of Consulting and Clinical Psychology, 46*, 453–462.

Liberman, R. P., DeRisi, W. J., & Mueser, K. T. (1989). *Social skills training for psychiatric patients*. New York: Pergamon Press.

Libet, J., & Lewinsohn, P. M. (1973). The concept of social skill with special reference to the behavior of depressed persons. *Journal of Consulting and Clinical Psychology, 40*, 304–312.

McFall, R. M., & Lillesand, D. B. (1971). Behavioral rehearsal with modeling and coaching in assertion training. *Journal of Abnormal Psychology, 77*, 313–323.

Meier, V. J., & Hope, D. A. (1998). Assessment of social skills. In A. S. Bellack & M. Hersen (Eds.), *Behavioral assessment: A practical handbook* (4th ed., pp. 232–255). Needham Heights, MA: Allyn & Bacon.

Riggio, R. E. (1986). Assessment of basic social skills. *Journal of Personality and Social Psychology, 51*, 649–660.

Riggio, R. E. (1989). *Social skills inventory manual*. Palo Alto, CA: Consulting Psychologists Press

Segrin, C. (2001). *Interpersonal processes in psychological problems*. New York: Guilford Press.

Smith, M. J. (1982). *Persuasion and human action*. Belmont, CA: Wadsworth.

Stravynski, A., Grey, S., & Elie, R. (1987). Outline of the therapeutic process in social skills training with socially dysfunctional adults. *Journal of Consulting and Clinical Psychology, 55*, 224–228.

Taylor, S. (1996). Meta-analysis of cognitive-behavioral treatment for social phobia. *Journal of Behavior Therapy and Experimental Psychiatry, 27*, 1–9.

Trower, P. (1995). Adult social skills: State of the art and future direction. In W. O'Donohue & L. Krasner (Eds.), *Handbook of psychological skills training: Clinical techniques and applications* (pp. 54–80). Boston: Allyn & Bacon.

Trower, P., Bryant, B., & Argyle, A. (1978). *Social skills and mental health*. Pittsburgh: University of Pittsburgh Press.

57 SQUEEZE TECHNIQUE FOR THE TREATMENT OF PREMATURE EJACULATION

Claudia Avina

The squeeze technique was derived from Seman's (1956) stop-start technique and popularized by Masters and Johnson (1970). Both treatments require that males masturbate just prior to ejaculation and resume once the urge to ejaculate has dissipated. The difference between the two treatments is that in the squeeze technique, the male or his partner is required to squeeze the head of his penis to decrease his urge to ejaculate, while in the stop-start technique he is simply required to suspend sexual stimulation until his urge has decreased.

Masters and Johnson (1970) reported a remarkable posttreatment success rate of 97.8% for the squeeze technique in a sample of 186 men suffering from premature ejaculation over a span of 11 years. At the 5-year follow-up, a 2.7% failure rate was reported. To date, the dramatic results reported by Masters and Johnson (1970) have not been replicated in other studies (O'Donohue, Letourneau, & Geer, 1993). One obvious methodological difference between more recent studies and the work by Masters and Johnson is the inconsistency in outcome criteria. Masters and Johnson used the criterion of achieving partner satisfaction in 50% of coital attempts while others have compared posttreatment ejaculatory latency to baseline (Lowe & Mikulas, 1975). It has been suggested that the imprecision of the treatment criterion used by Masters and Johnson may have

inflated their results (O'Donohue et al., 1993). The work by Masters and Johnson has also been criticized for a lack of scientific rigor (O'Donohue et al., 1993; Zilbergeld & Evans, 1980).

Evaluating the effectiveness of the squeeze technique is problematic because treatment outcome studies commonly have either used mixed samples, used the squeeze technique in combination with other sex therapy approaches (Heiman & LoPiccolo, 1983; LoPiccolo, Heiman, Hogan, & Roberts, 1985), or failed to specify actual treatment practices (LoPiccolo et al.; Trudel & Proulx, 1987). In addition, the squeeze technique and the stop-start technique have been employed jointly or as equivalent treatments (Golden, Price, Heinrich, & Lobitz, 1978; Zeiss, 1978). The squeeze technique has also been used as part of a larger treatment package that involves other potentially active interventions such as CBT (Carey, 1998; Yulis, 1976) or systematic desensitization (Ince, 1973).

Empirical studies evaluating treatment outcomes with homogeneous samples of premature ejaculators and where the squeeze technique was one component of treatment have generally found significant improvements in ejaculatory latency (Lowe & Mikulas, 1975; Trudel & Proulx, 1987; Zeiss, 1978). The treatment packages in these studies were commonly composed of the squeeze technique, the stop-start technique, and sensate focus or communication skills. Lowe and Mikulas evaluated statistical differences between baseline and posttreatment latency, whereas Trudel and Proulx and Zeiss measured whether males met a criterion latency of more than 5 min. Golden and colleagues (1978) reported no significant differences of ejaculatory latency between the treatment and control group but did find that males in the treatment group were more satisfied with their orgasmic ability.

Treatment outcome studies using samples presenting with multiple sexual dysfunctions provide results that are difficult to interpret due to the practice of reporting improvements in sexual functioning for the entire treatment group (Clement & Schmidt, 1983; Everaerd & Dekker, 1985). It is difficult to discern how specific interventions impact specific problems. Studies that report improvements for premature ejaculation do so in terms of changes in length of foreplay and intercourse but not actual ejaculatory latency (Hartman & Daly, 1983; Heiman & LoPiccolo, 1983). Also, the small sample of men suffering from premature ejaculation (ranging from 2 to 21 subjects) in each of these studies provides inadequate evidence to make generalizations about treatment outcomes (Clement & Schmidt; Everaerd & Dekker; Hartman & Daly; Heiman & LoPiccolo; LoPiccolo et al., 1985).

The squeeze technique continues to be recommended as the psychological treatment for premature ejaculation (O'Donohue et al., 1993; Segraves & Althof, 1998). The lack of satisfactory data on the effectiveness of the squeeze technique can be more adequately accounted for by the lack of rigorous research than by deficiencies in the intervention. Yet it is not clearly understood why the squeeze technique works. It has been proposed that the squeeze technique may work because the procedure creates response extinction through a process of counterconditioning, teaches men to monitor arousal levels, and/or provides a greater frequency of sexual activity, thereby providing increased opportunities to learn ejaculatory control (LoPiccolo & Stock, 1986).

WHO MIGHT BENEFIT FROM THIS TREATMENT

As a treatment that helps individuals gain ejaculatory control, the squeeze technique will benefit males suffering from premature ejaculation. The *Diagnostic and Statistical Manual of Mental Disorders (fourth edition, text revision, or DSM-IV-TR;* American Psychiatric Association, 2000) diagnostic criteria define *premature ejaculation* as ejaculation resulting from minimal stimulation and before the person wishes it to occur (p. 554). In light of social pressure that the man is responsible for long-lasting intercourse, it is highly likely that healthy, sexually functioning males will experience ejaculation before they wish it to happen. The detection of the disorder should occur when there exists a consistent pattern of ejaculating quickly in the context of little stimulation, the pattern persists, and this behavior causes marked distress or interpersonal difficulty. The squeeze technique may be most appropriate for males who ejaculate too quickly because the behavior is a conditioned response (i.e., ending sexual activity quickly in order to avoid being discovered) or for males who lack a learning history of controlled ejaculatory latency during intercourse (i.e., ejaculating outside the vagina as a means of birth control).

CONTRAINDICATIONS

The squeeze technique is appropriate for males who suffer from a lack of ejaculatory control. However, currently there is no accepted standard for normal functioning in this domain, as the range of normative ejaculatory latency is fairly broad (O'Donohue et al., 1993). Recommended criteria include the lack of ability to control ejaculation for a sufficient amount of time to achieve partner satisfaction in at least 50% of coital attempts (Masters & Johnson, 1970) or ejaculating before a specified time criterion ranging from 1 to 10 min (Metz, Pryor, Nesvacil, Abuzzahab, & Koznar, 1997). The squeeze technique is expected to teach men ejaculatory control for approximately 15 to 20 min of sexual stimulation. The intervention may not be appropriate for males who can already control ejaculation for this length of time but still complain that they are ejaculating before the desired time or that they have not achieved sexual satisfaction with their partners. In these cases it may be more appropriate to provide psychoeducation about sexual functioning or to assess for problems in the sexual interactions between client and partner.

The problem of insufficient ejaculatory control may be a result of psychological factors, organic factors, or a combination. A medical evaluation should be consistently employed when a client complains of problems in sexual functioning. Administering the squeeze technique is not appropriate and potentially iatrogenic for individuals suffering from premature ejaculation that is largely due to a medical condition such as diabetes, prostatitis, urethritis, and urological disorders (Athanasiadis, 1998), or to organic factors such as trauma to the sympathetic nervous system and pelvic fractures (Athanasiadis, 1998).

OTHER FACTORS IN DECIDING TO USE OR NOT TO USE THE SQUEEZE TECHNIQUE

It is very possible that there will exist comorbid problems in males suffering from premature ejaculation. These individuals may be suffering from a different sexual dysfunction related to desire or arousal, as well as some other mental disorder such as Major Depression or Panic Disorder. In these instances, treatment providers should ascertain temporal order of the disorders when assessing the onset, context, and etiology of each sexual dysfunction or other disorder. One concern is that clients with underlying psychopathology may respond poorly to sex therapy (e.g., the squeeze technique; Avina, O'Donohue, & Regev, 2003). Another important issue is deciding on the appropriate treatment when premature ejaculation is the result of another disorder. Treatment providers must decide whether to (1) treat other mental disorders prior to implementing the squeeze technique, (2) implement the squeeze technique simultaneously with some other treatment, (3) treat only the other mental disorder, or (4) implement only the squeeze technique.

Although there does not appear to be a relationship between marital satisfaction and sexual dysfunction, except for problems of desire (Morokoff & Gillilland, 1993), it is not uncommon for committed partners to seek services for problems in sexual functioning (Heiman, Gladue, Roberts, & LoPiccolo, 1986; LoPiccolo et al., 1985; Masters & Johnson, 1970; Snyder & Berg, 1983). Sexual partners can experience anger, inadequate communication, distrust, or low levels of emotional closeness. Individuals in a committed relationship could also experience a fear of pregnancy, fear of losing control, or fear of contracting a sexually transmitted disease. Any one of these aspects could be detrimental to an individual's sexual functioning as they interfere with one's willingness and comfort in engaging in sexual intimacy. Avoidant and distant behaviors on behalf of the individual experiencing these factors may result in his or her partner's feeling insecure about his or her ability to sexually satisfy the other individual or distrustful of the individual's commitment to the relationship. The decision to implement the squeeze technique in the face of relationship problems should be made by determining the temporal order of the relationship and sexual difficulties, willingness of the couple to work on the diagnosed problem or problems, and the treatment that will likely lead to the most efficient and comprehensive positive outcomes (Jacobson & Margolin, 1979).

CLINICAL APPLICATION OF THE SQUEEZE TECHNIQUE

The squeeze technique can be employed by an individual or by his partner if his partner is willing to participate. The treatment involves providing psychoeducation about the ejaculatory process and a procedure for helping the individual gain ejaculatory control. Specifically, the treatment provider educates the individual about the two stages of ejaculation, involving involuntary contractions by the prostate gland and the discharge of seminal fluid (Masters & Johnson, 1970). This information is used to help the individual recognize different levels of arousal.

The individual is instructed to masturbate until a full erection is achieved and just prior to ejaculation. The individual is further instructed to stop masturbating at this point and squeeze the head of his penis with enough force that his urge to ejaculate halts almost immediately. Squeezing of the head of the penis is achieved using two fingers on the top and the thumb on the bottom of the coronal ridge (the dorsal side and frenulum of the penis) for approximately 3 to 4 s. Stimulation should resume about 10 to 30 s after the head of the penis has been released and once the urge to ejaculate has completely subsided. This process should be repeated at least three times prior to

Individual homework sessions should last approximately 15 to 20 min.

Apply the squeeze technique 3 to 4 times before ejaculating.

Begin employing the squeeze technique with manual stimulation first.

After achieving prolonged latency with manual stimulation exercises, proceed to intromission without thrusting.

After achieving prolonged latency with intromission without thrusting, proceed to intromission with thrusting.

Continue employing technique once a month for 6 to 12 months following treatment.

FIGURE 57.1   Step-by-Step Procedures of the Squeeze Technique

ejaculation. It is recommended that the client continue these exercises until he can delay his ejaculation for 15 to 20 min.

The individual's partner can be incorporated into this treatment by having the partner instead of the client carry out the manual stimulation and squeezing of the head of the client's penis. In order for the partner to carry out the technique successfully, the client will have to notify his partner when he is at the point just prior to ejaculation. It is important that the client-partner communication regarding when the male is at this point be clear, readily received, and acted on (McCarthy, 1989).

Once ejaculatory control is achieved with masturbation exercises, the squeeze technique may also include behavioral exercises between the client and his partner involving penile intromission. The couple is instructed to manually stimulate the penis until a full erection is achieved and then allow insertion of the penis without movement or pelvic thrusting. The client is instructed to concentrate on the sensations produced by this activity. When the client feels that he is about to ejaculate, the penis should be removed, the squeeze technique should be employed, and the penis should be reinserted. Similar to masturbation or manual stimulation exercises, this process should be repeated at least three times before ejaculation. As the client begins to gain ejaculatory control during intromission without movement, he will begin instructed to begin using pelvic thrusting. Once ejaculatory control is achieved during intromission without thrusting, his partner will be instructed to begin

using thrusting movements and the couple will be instructed to repeat the process of using the squeeze technique at least three times prior to ejaculation. The goal of the technique is to allow the male to gain ejaculatory control for 15 to 20 min during intercourse.

Masters and Johnson (1970) have suggested that after treatment is completed, the couple should (1) use the squeeze technique at least once a week with intercourse, (2) maintain a regular frequency of intercourse (this will depend on the individual couple's preferences), and (3) utilize the squeeze technique exercises using manual stimulation/masturbation for one 15- to 20-min session, once a month. It is recommended that ejaculatory control exercises continue for 6 to 12 months following treatment. It is also recommended that the squeeze technique be employed when there is a period of time (a few weeks) without sexual activity, thereby resulting in lack of opportunities for controlled ejaculation.

One final caveat should be pointed out regarding the expected success of this treatment. While the squeeze technique is administered in order to teach men ejaculatory latency, the goal should not be the length of latency but rather on the sexual pleasure experienced by the client and his partner (McConaghy, 1993; Wincze & Carey, 1991). Ejaculatory control is considered one component in achieving sexual satisfaction. Treatment providers should remain cognizant of other repertoire deficits in the client or his partner that may hinder sexual satisfaction and apply appropriate interventions as needed.

Further Reading

Masters, W., & Johnson, V. (1970). *Human sexual inadequacy*. Boston: Little, Brown.

Zeiss, R. A., & Zeiss, A. M. (1978). *Prolong your pleasure*. New York: Pocket Books.

References

American Psychiatric Association. (2000). Diagnostic and statistical manual of mental disorders (4th ed., text rev.). Washington, DC: American Psychiatric Association.

Athanasiadis, L. (1998). Premature ejaculation: Is it a biogenic or a psychogenic disorder? *Sexual and Marital Therapy, 13,* 241–255.

Avina, C., O'Donohue, W., & Regev, L. (2003). Psychological and behavioral counseling in the management of male sexual dysfunction. In F. Kandeel (Ed.), *Pathophysiology and treatment of male sexual and reproductive dysfunction.* New York: Marcel Dekker.

Carey, M. P. (1998). Cognitive-behavioral treatment of sexual dysfunctions. In V. E. Caballo (Ed.), *International handbook of cognitive and behavioural treaments for psychological disorders* (pp. 251–280). Kidlington, UK: Elsevier Science.

Clement, U., & Schmidt, G. (1983). The outcome of couple therapy for sexual dysfunctions using three different formats. *Journal of Sex and Marital Therapy, 9,* 67–78.

Everaerd, W., & Dekker, J. (1985). Treatment of male sexual dysfunction: Sex therapy compared with systematic desensitization and rational emotive therapy. *Behaviour Research and Therapy, 22,* 114–124.

Golden, J. S., Price, S., Heinrich, A. G., & Lobitz, W. C. (1978). Group vs. couple treatment of sexual dysfunctions. *Archives of Sexual Behavior, 7,* 593–602.

Hartman, L. M., & Daly, E. M. (1983). Relationship factors in the treatment of sexual dysfunction. *Behaviour Research and Therapy, 21,* 253–160.

Heiman, J. R., Gladue, B. A., Roberts, C. W., & LoPiccolo, J. (1986). Historical and current factors discriminating sexually functional from sexually dysfunctional married couples. *Journal of Marital and Family Therapy, 12,* 163–174.

Heiman, J. R., & LoPiccolo, J. (1983). Clinical outcome of sex therapy. *Archives of General Psychiatry, 140,* 94–101.

Ince, L. P. (1973). Behavior modification of sexual disorders. *American Journal of Psychotherapy, 27,* 446–451.

Jacobson, N. S., & Margolin, G. (1979). *Marital therapy: Strategies based on social learning and behavior exchange principles.* New York: Brunner/Mazel.

LoPiccolo, J., Heiman, J. R., Hogan, D. R., & Roberts, C. W. (1985). Effectiveness of single therapists versus cotherapy teams in sex therapy. *Journal of Consulting and Clinical Psychology, 53,* 287–294.

LoPiccolo, J., & Stock, W. E. (1986). Treatment of sexual dysfunction. *Journal of Consulting and Clinical Psychology, 54,* 158–167.

Lowe, J. C., & Mikulas, W. L. (1975). Use of written material in learning self-control of premature ejaculation. *Psychological Reports, 37,* 295–298.

Masters, W., & Johnson, V. (1970). *Human sexual inadequacy.* Boston: Little, Brown.

McCarthy, B. W. (1989). Cognitive-behavioral strategies and techniques in the treatment of early ejaculation. In S. R. Leiblum & R. C. Rosen (Eds.), *Priniciples and practice of sex therapy* (2nd ed., pp.141–167). New York: Guilford Press.

McConaghy, N. (1993). *Sexual behavior: Problems and management.* New York: Plenum Press.

Metz, M. E., Pryor, J. L., Nesvacil, L. J., Abuzzahab, F., Sr., & Koznar, J. (1997). Premature ejaculation: A psychophysiological review. *Journal of Sex and Marital Therapy, 23,* 3–23.

Morokoff, P. J., & Gillilland, R. (1993). Stress, sexual functioning, and marital satisfaction. *Journal of Sex Research, 30,* 43–53.

O'Donohue, W., Letourneau, E., & Geer, J. H. (1993). Premature ejaculation. In W. O'Donohue & J. H. Geer (Eds,), *Handbook of sexual dysfunctions: Assessment and treament* (pp. 303–334). Needham Heights, MA: Allyn & Bacon.

Segraves, R. T., & Althof, S. (1998). Psychotherapy and pharmacotherapy of sexual dysfunctions. In P. E. Nathan & J. M. Gorman (Eds.), *A guide to treatments that work* (pp. 447–471). New York: Oxford University Press.

Semans, J. H. (1956). Premature ejaculation: A new approach. *Southern Medical Journal, 49,* 353–358.

Snyder, D. K., & Berg, P. (1983). Determinants of sexual dissatisfaction in sexually distressed couples. *Archives of Sexual Behavior, 12,* 237–246.

Trudel, G., & Proulx, S. (1987). Treatment of premature ejaculation by bibliotherapy: An experimental study. *Sexual and Marital Therapy, 2,* 163–167.

Wincze, J. P., & Carey, M. P. (1991). *Sexual dysfunction: A guide for assessment and treatment.* New York: Guilford Press.

Yulis, S. (1976). Generalization of therapeutic gain in the treatment of premature ejaculation. *Behavior Therapy, 7,* 355–358.

Zeiss, R. A., (1978). Self-directed treatment for premature ejaculation. *Journal of Consulting and Clinical Psychology, 46,* 1234–1241.

Zilbergeld, R. B., & Evans, M. (1980). The inadequacy of Masters and Johnson. *Psychology Today, 14,* 29–43.

58 STIMULUS CONTROL

Alan Poling and Scott T. Gaynor

Stimulus control is present when a change in a particular property of a stimulus produces a change in behavior, such as an increase in the rate of occurrence of a particular response. In a general sense, a *stimulus* is a physical event. Changes in stimuli can be discrete, as when a particular person is either present or absent, or continuous, as when the intensity of a siren increases as a police car approaches. For example, the probability of a heroin abuser's making a request for the drug might be greater when a pusher is present than when he or she is absent; or the probability of a driver with a marijuana cigarette smoking the joint might decrease directly with the loudness of the siren. In the first case, stimulus control is *excitatory*. That is, behavior is more likely to occur in the presence of a particular stimulus than in its absence. *Inhibitory* stimulus control, where behavior is less likely to occur in the presence of a particular stimulus than in its absence, is evident in the second example.

Stimulus control does not refer to a particular therapeutic technique. Rather, the term describes relationships between antecedent stimuli and subsequent behaviors. Such relationships, which can be established through classical or operant conditioning, are of quintessential importance in cognitive behavior therapy. Many behavioral problems are to some extent stimulus control problems. For example, phobias involve exaggerated fear responses engendered by specific stimuli (e.g., spiders, crowds) or by thinking about those stimuli. Sexual fetishes are defined by sexual arousal educed by encountering or thinking about stimuli that do not evoke sexual arousal in most people. Reading problems are present when someone fails to react appropriately (e.g., make certain sounds) when presented with configurations of letters that constitute words. In fact, it is difficult to envision a behavior disorder that does not involve some degree of inappropriate stimulus control.

STIMULUS CONTROL AND CLASSICAL CONDITIONING

Not surprisingly, establishing, abolishing, or otherwise altering stimulus control is an important aspect of treating a wide range of behavior disorders. One general way in which stimulus control can be established or altered is through *classical* (or *respondent*) *conditioning*. In the context of classical conditioning, stimulus control is exercised by unconditional stimuli (USs), which reflexively elicit unconditional responses (URs). Stimulus control is also exercised by conditional stimuli (CSs), which are previously neutral stimuli that gain the capacity to elicit conditional responses (CRs) by virtue of being paired with USs in a particular way. In essence, for classical conditioning to occur, the probability of the US occurring must be higher shortly after presentation of the CS than at any other time. Most therapeutic applications that involve respondent conditioning entail altering stimulus control by a clinically relevant CS.

For example, CRs elicited by stimuli (CSs) that reliably precede delivery of any of a number of abused drugs (e.g., alcohol, cocaine, heroin), which serve as USs, can function as establishing operations (EOs) that increase the reinforcing effectiveness of the drug and increase the likelihood of behaviors that historically have produced it. The CRs also contribute to subjective urges or cravings for the drug. In this case, classical conditioning interacts with operant conditioning to contribute to drug use and abuse—EOs, established by classical conditioning, affect drug-seeking and drug-taking, which is operantly conditioned behavior (i.e., behavior primarily controlled by its consequences). For instance, the sight of a syringe by an intravenous heroin user may increase the momentary reinforcing effectiveness of heroin for that person and cause her or him to call someone from whom the drug has previously been obtained. This can occur even if the person has not used heroin for a protracted period and is not physically dependent on the drug.

The importance of classical conditioning in the genesis and treatment of drug abuse is emphasized in cue exposure therapy, which has gained considerable popularity in the past decade (e.g., Cunningham, 1998; Drummond, Tiffany, Glautier, & Remington, 1995). An important part of cue exposure therapy is exposing the client to stimuli that historically preceded drug delivery (CSs) under conditions where the drug (US) is not delivered. For example, a person who abuses alcohol would repeatedly see, hold, and smell her or his preferred adult beverage without taking a drink. With sufficient exposures, the capacity of the sight, smell, and feel of the beverage to elicit CRs that function as EOs would be abolished through the process of respondent extinction. The same process would be used to deal with the effects of other pre-drug stimuli, such as thinking about having a drink or entering a bar. The specific CSs that need to be dealt with will vary across clients and, as Cunningham points out, knowledge of how stimulus control of CRs is established and abolished is necessary to develop

effective therapies. He notes that removal of drug-related CSs, arranging extinction in multiple contexts, conditioned inhibition training, extinction reminder training, alternative outcome training, and outcome devaluation training can be useful adjuncts to respondent extinction. Each of these training procedures alters stimulus control in the context of classical conditioning.

STIMULUS CONTROL AND OPERANT CONDITIONING

Stimulus control also can be altered in the context of operant conditioning. One way to accomplish this is by arranging different consequences for a particular kind of behavior in the presence and absence of a stimulus (or stimulus class). That is, a particular response is reinforced in the presence of one stimulus, called a discriminative stimulus (S^D), and is not reinforced in the presence of another stimulus, called an S-delta (S^Δ). Under these conditions, the S^D comes to exercise excitatory stimulus control over responding. If conditions are arranged so that a particular stimulus (an S^D for punishment) is uniquely correlated with punishment, inhibitory stimulus control will be established.

Behavior therapists sometimes arrange differential reinforcement to establish appropriate stimulus-controlled behavior in their clients, especially in educational settings. Using a discrete-trials procedure to teach young people with autism to label objects accurately is a good example of this strategy. Here, on each trial, one of several possible objects would be presented to the child and he or she would be asked to label the object (e.g., the therapist might ask, "What is that?"). A correct response (e.g., saying "apple" when an apple was presented) would be reinforced (e.g., by delivering food or praise), whereas an incorrect response (e.g., saying "ball" when an apple was presented) would be followed by corrective feedback. If necessary, prompts would be provided to initiate responding (e.g., the therapist would tell the student, "Say 'apple'"). With repeated trials, accurate labeling would be established. Lovaas and his colleagues (e.g., McEachin, Smith, & Lovaas, 1993) have provided substantial evidence that early and extensive exposure to discrete-trials training programs greatly benefits people with autism.

In using any differential-reinforcement procedure to establish stimulus control, it is essential that participants learn to respond to relevant stimulus features (e.g., to the shape, not the color or size of the letter A) and that an appropriate degree of stimulus generalization is established. Stimulus generalization occurs when a novel stimulus evokes behavior similar to that controlled by an established S^D. In general, the degree to which the novel stimulus is physically similar to the S^D determines the degree of stimulus generalization. However, discrimination training using $S^Δs$ with features similar to the S^D can dramatically influence generalization.

In some cases, multiple physical dimensions define an S^D. For example, no single physical attribute defines the animals we call "dogs" or allows a person to label novel animals as "dogs" or "not dogs" with accuracy. In such cases, accurate labeling is established by presenting multiple examples and nonexamples of a class of stimuli (e.g., "dogs" and "not dogs") and arranging differential reinforcement in the presence of the two types of stimuli (e.g., reinforcing saying "dog" only when an example of this class of stimuli was presented). Such arrangements are used to develop concepts, which may be viewed as complex S^Ds.

In many clinical situations, functional assessment will reveal S^Ds that evoke inappropriate behaviors. For instance, delinquent behavior typically occurs more frequently in the presence of certain peers, who are S^Ds for such behavior, than in their absence. It is not surprising that teens with conduct disorders are often encouraged in therapy sessions to change peer groups. Avoiding contact with S^Ds that engender inappropriate responding, like avoiding exposure to CSs that have similar effects, can be a valuable component of therapy. In many instances, it is not possible to change naturally occurring contingencies of reinforcement, but it may be possible to teach a client to stay away from people who, or situations that, historically supported and may continue to support undesirable actions.

Altering a client's motivation to obtain the kind of reinforcer previously available in the presence of a particular S^D is another technique of potential therapeutic value. For instance, methadone

maintenance may reduce the momentary reinforcing value of heroin and make it less likely that a person will engage in drug-seeking behaviors in situations where such behaviors historically had been successful in producing the drug. To date, behavior therapists have not focused a great deal of attention on treatments that alter motivational variables, but attention to such treatments appears to be increasing with the growing acceptance of the EO concept of motivation (e.g., Iwata, Smith, & Michael, 2000).

RULES AND STIMULUS CONTROL

A second general way in which stimulus control can be established in the context of operant conditioning is by providing verbal humans with *rules,* which are statements that specify relations among stimuli and responses. Rules can establish inhibitory or excitatory stimulus control, even though there is no actual history of differential reinforcement in their presence of those stimuli. Therefore, they are not S^Ds, but they can function similarly. Moreover, rules can diminish sensitivity to consequences, thereby making it difficult to establish stimulus control. Thus, rules appear relevant to understanding and treating many psychopathological conditions (Hayes & Ju, 1998).

Hayes and his colleagues have developed a therapeutic approach, acceptance and commitment therapy (ACT), that is intended to overcome unhealthy forms of rule-governed behavior (Hayes, Strosahl, & Wilson, 1999). Special emphasis is placed on dealing with problematic derived stimulus equivalence relations. *Derived stimulus equivalence* occurs when a person learns, by direct experience with the stimuli or through other people's verbal descriptions, that stimulus B goes with A (A → B) and C goes with B (B → C). As a result of learning that A → B and B → C, symmetrical (A ← B, B ← C) and transitive (A ← → C) relations automatically emerge, although they were not specifically trained or described. The result is that stimuli A, B, and C become functionally equivalent. That is, they control the same behaviors. Such derived stimulus relations may be useful in understanding how many types of avoidance behavior emerge and are maintained despite the absence of a direct history of aversive consequences occurring in the presence of the avoided stimulus. For instance, imagine a child who has a history involving direct experiences with injections from a hypodermic needle, which the child found to be painful (i.e., the child would avoid them if possible). The child now overhears that "An insect bite is like a shot with a needle." Hearing such a statement will now endow the conceptual stimulus class of insects with similar stimulus functions as a needle. That is, the child may now respond in the presence of an insect with a classically conditioned response (increased heart rate) and operant escape response (running away), even though the insect may in fact be harmless and the child lacks any direct experience with insect bites of any real consequence. Also of note is that the conceptual stimulus class of insects and the needle share little to no physical similarity, so this would not appear a simple case of stimulus generalization. Although it is beyond our purposes to describe ACT, it is worth noting that the approach shows promise for reducing control by derived stimulus relations that occasion a variety of problematic avoidance responses.

Verbal interactions between a therapist and a client frequently are intended to alter the rules that the client generates and follows. Such interactions can constitute a valuable therapeutic technique, but it is important to realize that these activities are themselves influenced by their consequences. If there is nothing in a client's everyday social or nonsocial environment to support (i.e., reinforce) appropriate rule-governed behavior, then such behavior probably will not endure over long periods. In some cases, naturally occurring consequences in the client's everyday environment are sufficient to support appropriate behaviors that emerge. In other cases, however, contrived consequences may be needed. A significant problem in providing treatment for outpatients is arranging such consequences.

STIMULUS CONTROL BY THE CONSEQUENCES OF BEHAVIOR

Although stimulus control by definition involves relationships between antecedent events and behavior, the consequences of one's behavior in a so-

cial setting frequently serve as discriminative stimuli for subsequent responding. Reacting appropriately to such stimuli is an important part of daily social interactions. Imagine an adolescent girl from an authoritarian household where social praise is rarely provided for any kind of behavior, while social displeasure is readily displayed following most attempts at conversation or other social gestures. Such an environment essentially trains the teen to discriminate stimuli (e.g., facial features) that signal the availability of aversive social consequences (and to withhold behaviors that historically have produced such consequences), but gives her little exposure to stimuli associated with a high likelihood of affiliation. This type of history leaves her primed to discover that others also disapprove of her, but unlikely to recognize and react appropriately to signs of approval and liking from others. Therefore, she is unlikely to react appropriately in social settings.

If the teen has a fairly well developed repertoire of social skills, a reasonable therapeutic goal would be to facilitate the development of control of social approach responses by stimuli indicative of social affiliation and liking (smiles, greetings, invitations) and to decrease excessive sensitivity to potential signs of social displeasure. One might pursue this tack by focusing on instances of behavior that occur in the therapy session. For example, does the teen ever misinterpret the therapist's actions as signs of disappointment or displeasure? If so, this can be made an immediate focus of the therapy. For instance, the therapist can clarify the variables controlling his or her facial expressions (e.g., such as being in deep concentration) and block the client's escape and avoidance responses. Similarly, the therapist can help the teen recognize instances when he or she is showing genuine signs of interest, warmth, and caring in the therapy session, and emphasize the fact that these signs are to be valued and are indicative of appropriate behavior by the client. In essence, when such procedures are used, the therapist provides corrective differential reinforcement in vivo—during the therapy session (Kohlenberg & Tsai, 1991). The therapist initially would reinforce each occurrence of appropriate behavior. Over time, the schedule of reinforcement would become progressively more intermittent to approximate the consequences of behavior in the client's everyday environment.

As noted previously, however, therapists often attempt to engender changes in stimulus control through verbal means. For instance, the therapist may describe the client's tendency to see only the negative (to be under the control of stimuli that have signaled social punishment) and explain how this might have evolved and be maintained in the current environment. Then, the therapist might recommend a technique for changing stimulus control. For instance, the client may be taught social skills for initiating and maintaining conversations. As part of the skills training process, potential S^Ds (e.g., when another person says "hello," makes eye contact, or is smiling) and S^Δs (e.g., when the other person looks preoccupied, is in a rush, or is looking away) are described to the client. During the session the therapist and client may then conduct role-playing exercises to practice identification of relevant stimulus conditions for initiating a conversation. For homework, the therapist might recommend that the client conduct a behavioral experiment, where she is told to initiate conversations with several same-age peers who are not strongly negative toward her and then rate the success of her efforts. Because the necessary differential reinforcement cannot always be delivered in the therapy milieu, this is an attempt to try and place the client in situations in the natural social environment where differential consequences appear most likely to be provided.

CONCLUSION

The preceding example illustrates a number of points that should be kept in mind when trying to establish stimulus control through operant conditioning. First, stimulus dimensions that define the S^D and S^Δ should be described to verbal clients. Second, the consequences of target behaviors in the presence of the S^D and S^Δ should be described to such clients. Rules that specify relations among stimuli and responses may help to foster appropriate behavior. Third, artificially arranging differential reinforcement in the presence of the S^D and S^Δ may be necessary to establish appropriate stimulus control. Typically, each instance of appropriate behavior in the presence of the S^D is re-

inforced initially, with the schedule becoming more intermittent over time until real-life conditions are approximated. Fourth, when the S^D and S^Δ comprise classes of stimuli, which is usually the case in clinical situations, it is important to provide multiple examples and nonexamples of members of each class. Fifth, if individual members of the S^D and S^Δ classes differ in salience, begin training with an S^D and S^Δ that are maximally different from one another. Once stimulus control is well established, training can be extended to S^Ds and S^Δs that are more alike. Sixth, care must be taken to ensure that stimulus control established in a contrived setting generalizes to situations of everyday life. Such generalization cannot be assumed to occur automatically, and training especially designed to produce it often is required. Of course, establishing appropriate stimulus control may require additional considerations. Stimulus control is a large and complex topic that cannot be adequately covered in a short chapter such as this. A short chapter can, however, make the case that stimulus control is germane to the genesis and treatment of almost all forms of behavior disorders, and we have attempted to do so here. More detailed analyses, like those provided in the reference list, extend that case and offer useful suggestions for therapists. Figure 58.1 provides a useful summary of the main points of stimulus control.

---

1. Stimulus control is present when a change in a particular property of a stimulus produces a change in behavior, such as an increase in the rate of occurrence of a particular response.

2. Inappropriate stimulus control contributes to the genesis and maintenance of a wide range of behavior disorders.

3. Establishing, abolishing, or otherwise altering stimulus control is an important aspect of behavior therapy. Many therapeutic techniques affect stimulus control, although their actions may not commonly be construed in this way.

4. Stimulus control can be established or altered through either classical or operant conditioning.

5. Differential reinforcement is a powerful technique for establishing or altering stimulus control in the context of operant conditioning. Verbal rules, which specify relations among stimuli and responses, also can establish or alter stimulus control; such rules sometimes minimize an individual's sensitivity to the actual consequences of his or her behavior.

FIGURE 58.1   Key Points to Stimulus Control

References

Cunningham, C. L. (1998). Drug conditioning and drug-seeking behavior. In W. O'Donohue (Ed.), *Learning and behavior therapy* (pp. 518–544). Boston: Allyn & Bacon.

Drumond, D. C., Tiffany, S. T., Glautier, S., & Remington, B. (Eds.). (1995). *Addictive behavior: Cue exposure therapy and practice.* Chichester, England: Wiley.

Hayes, S. C., & Ju, W. (1998). Rule-governed behavior. In W. O'Donohue (Ed.), *Learning and behavior therapy* (pp. 374–391). Boston: Allyn & Bacon.

Hayes, S. C., Strosahl, K., & Wilson, K. G. (1999). *Acceptance and commitment therapy: An experiential approach to behavior change.* New York: Guilford Press.

Iwata, B. A., Smith, R. G., & Michael, J. (2000). Current research on the influence of establishing operations on behavior in applied settings. *Journal of Aplied Behavior Analysis, 33,* 411–418.

Kohlenberg, R. J., & Tsai, M. (1991). *Functional analytic psychotherapy: Creating intense and curative therapeutic relationships.* New York: Plenum Press.

McEachin, J. J., Smith, T., & Lovaas, O. I. (1993). Long-term treatment outcome for children with autism who received early intensive behavioral treatment. *American Journal on Mental Retardation, 97,* 359–372.

59 STIMULUS PREFERENCE ASSESSMENT

Jane E. Fisher and Jeffrey A. Buchanan

Stimulus preference assessment techniques are used for empirically identifying functional reinforcers. The concept of *stimulus preference assessment* was originally developed by Pace, Ivancic, Edwards, Iwata, and Page (1985) for the purpose of identifying potentially reinforcing stimuli for individuals with severe developmental disabilities. Identifying stimulus preferences in individuals with limited behavioral repertoires is a common challenge for behavior analysts. Stimulus preference assessment techniques emerged through recognition of the limitations in accuracy of nonempirical approaches to identifying functional reinforcers (e.g., through staff report). The procedures are used extensively with persons with developmental disabilities who have limited verbal abilities for communicating preferred objects or activities. They have also recently been employed with older adults with severe cognitive impairment (Fisher & Buchanan, 2000).

Since first described by Pace and colleagues (1985), several variations of stimulus preference assessment procedures have been reported in the literature (e.g., DeLeon & Iwata, 1996; Fisher et al., 1992). The basic procedure involves identifying a sample of potentially preferred stimuli for a particular client (e.g., based on the report of caregivers or informal observation) and then sequentially presenting the stimuli to the client singly, in pairs, or in groups while systematically recording the duration or frequency of the cli-

ents' touching or orienting to each stimulus. A *hierarchy of preference* is then generated based on the duration or frequency of the client's response to each stimulus. The client's preference is inferred based on the level of response, with more-preferred stimuli being associated with higher levels of responding. Following the development of the stimulus preference hierarchy, the contingent presentation of the stimuli ranked as highly preferred can be implemented to determine whether there is an increase in the target response indicating that the preferred stimuli are functional reinforcers (e.g., Piazza, Fisher, Hagopian, Bowman, & Toole, 1996). Variations in stimulus preference assessment procedure are described in the following sections.

ADVANTAGES OF THE TECHNIQUE

An important advantage of stimulus preference assessment procedures is that they involve direct sampling of a client's choice-behavior and the functional relationship between preferred stimuli and a target response. A second advantage involves their applicability for use with persons with severe impairments. They can be employed with clients with severely limited verbal or physical abilities, as they do not require a verbal or complex physical response (e.g., visual orientation to a stimulus can be used as the preference response for a client who is unable to speak or manipulate an object). Another advantage of stimulus preference procedures involves their utility for identifying potential reinforcing stimuli for persons with limited behavioral repertoires. Interventions targeting the strengthening of adaptive responses in this population can be facilitated by the efficient identification of potentially reinforcing stimuli.

WHO MIGHT BENEFIT FROM STIMULUS PREFERENCE ASSESSMENT

Stimulus preference assessment procedures are beneficial for clients with limited verbal abilities who cannot express their preferences through other forms of communication. The procedures have been found to be effective for individuals with severe levels of impairment, such as clients with severe or profound developmental disabilities (e.g., Fischer, Iwata, & Mazaleski, 1997; Fisher et al., 1992; Piazza et al., 1996) and with elderly persons with Alzheimer's disease with severe levels of impairment (Fisher & Buchanan, 2000).

OTHER FACTORS IN DECIDING TO USE OR NOT TO USE THE TECHNIQUE

For individuals with limited cognitive abilities and significant sensory and motor impairment, the levels of physical and sensory impairment should be taken into account when selecting a particular stimulus preference procedure. For instance, for individuals with severe levels of cognitive impairment (e.g., due to Alzheimer's disease), motor impairment (e.g., the person is confined to a wheelchair and is unable to propel the wheelchair independently), or sensory impairments (e.g., poor eyesight), versions of stimulus preference assessment that involve presentation of more than two stimuli at one time may be less effective. This issue is discussed in greater detail later in the chapter.

HOW DOES THE TECHNIQUE WORK?

The literature describes several variations of stimulus preference assessments that can be im-plemented with verbally impaired individuals. These include reinforcer surveys (e.g., Green et al., 1988), single-stimulus presentations (e.g., Pace et al., 1985), paired stimulus/forced choice presentations, and multiple-stimulus presentation assessments. We will, however, discuss only the latter two procedures because they have the greatest amount of empirical support as well as clinical utility.

Paired Stimulus Procedure

The paired stimulus (PS) procedure for conducting stimulus preference assessments was first described by Fisher and colleagues (1992) and is sometimes referred to as *forced choice assessment*. A PS assessment can be conducted using the following steps:

1. A list of potentially preferred stimuli must be generated. Generally, this list is constructed by interviewing caregivers familiar with the client or through informal direct observation of the client in the natural environment. The number of stimuli chosen depends on several factors, such as how many stimuli caregivers can identify, the accessibility of the identified stimuli, and the amount of time available to conduct the assessment (the more items chosen, the longer the assessment will take).
2. Construct a data sheet that includes a list of all pairs of stimuli to be presented. All stimuli should be paired with every other stimulus once, and the order of pairings should be randomized. For example, if there are a total of 5 stimuli, there should be a total of 10 pairs of stimulus presentations. In addition, the positioning of each stimulus should be counterbalanced such that each stimulus is presented on the client's left- and right-handed sides an equal number of times in order to control for placement effects.
3. Prior to beginning the procedure, allow the client to sample each stimulus for 30 s.
4. Place two stimuli from the list generated in Step 1 in front of the client. The literature recommends that items should be spaced about 0.7 m apart and both should be close enough to the client so he or she can touch or grab the stimuli.

5. When the client makes an approach response to one of the stimuli, provide the client access to the chosen stimulus for a brief period of time (i.e., about 5 s) and remove the other stimulus. An approach response may include touching the stimulus, gesturing to the stimulus, making eye contact, or making positive statements about the stimulus. Any attempts to grab both stimuli simultaneously should be blocked. Also, if the client does not approach either stimulus, allow access to each stimulus for 5 s and then repeat the paired presentation. If no approach response occurs, the trial is terminated.

6. Continue this process until all pairings have been presented to the client.

7. Calculate the percentage of time each stimulus was chosen when presented.

8. Organize data into a rank-ordered list of stimuli from most preferred to least preferred. The literature suggests that stimuli chosen at least 80% of the time are considered highly preferred and may be useful in treatment programs for strengthening behavior.

Multiple Stimulus without Replacement

The multiple stimulus without replacement (MSWO) procedure was first described by DeLeon and Iwata (1996). An MSWO assessment can be conducted using the following steps:

1. As with PS assessment procedures, the MSWO procedures begin by generating a list of potentially preferred stimuli based on caregiver reports or informal observation. The literature suggests that up to seven items can be used in a MSWO procedure. Using more than seven items may present practical difficulties in having enough space so that the client can have equal access to all stimuli simultaneously, particularly if some of the stimuli are large.

2. Construct a data sheet listing all stimuli.

3. Place all items in a straight line in random order. Items should be about 5 cm apart (farther apart if the items are larger).

4. Seat the client approximately 0.3 m from the stimulus array.

5. Instruct the client to select one of the items. Allow the client 30 s to make a selection.

6. Once the client selects an item, allow access to the stimulus for 30 s (or to completely consume the item if it is food or a beverage). Then, either remove the item from the immediate area or do not replace the item (if the item is edible). DeLeon and Iwata (1996) used physical contact with a stimulus as their definition of a selection. However, this definition can be expanded to include responses such as looking at, gesturing toward, touching, eating, or talking about the item.

7. Before the next trial, the remaining items should be rotated by taking the item at the left end and moving it to the right end. Then, shift all other stimuli to the left so that they are equally spaced on the table.

8. Continue this procedure until all items are selected. If during any trial the client does not select an item in the 30 s allowed, the procedure should be terminated and all other items recorded as "not selected."

9. The original study by DeLeon and Iwata (1996) suggested that the entire procedure should be repeated five times to provide adequate data concerning preferences and for identifying functional reinforcers. However, a study by Carr, Nicolson, and Higbee (2000) suggests that functional reinforcers can be identified if the procedures are repeated only three times. This shortened version of the MSWO procedure described by Carr and associates can be completed in less than 1 hour.

10. Calculate the percentage of times each stimulus was chosen during trials in which it was presented.

11. Create a rank-ordered list of stimuli from most preferred to least preferred.

It should be mentioned that a multiple stimulus assessment procedure *with* replacement has been used in the research literature (e.g., Windsor, Piche, & Locke, 1994). Although, it has been found that this procedure is less time consuming than the PS or MSWO procedures, there is a risk of false negatives (DeLeon & Iwata, 1996). False negatives are likely due to the fact that highly preferred items are chosen repeatedly because they are replaced after being chosen.

EVIDENCE FOR THE EFFECTIVENESS OF THESE PROCEDURES

Empirical evidence suggests that both of the PS and MSWO procedures successfully identify functional reinforcers. In evaluating the PS assessment procedure, Piazza and colleagues (1996) found that contingent presentation of stimuli ranked as highly preferred (i.e., ranked in the top 4 of 16 stimuli) during a PS assessment increased target responses (such as sitting in a chair or standing in a square) more effectively than those stimuli that were of middle or low preference. Fisher and colleagues (1992) also provide evidence that stimuli frequently chosen during a PS assessment could be used to strengthen behaviors such as in sitting in a chair or standing in a square.

DeLeon and Iwata (1996) provide evidence that the MSWO procedure also identifies functional reinforcers. These authors found that highly preferred items presented contingently upon target behaviors (e.g., placing blocks in a bucket, pressing a response panel) produced higher rates of responding when compared to baseline levels of responding.

Other studies have found that preferred stimuli can be used to reduce disruptive behaviors. For example, Fischer and colleagues (1997) presented a preferred stimulus (i.e., food) on a time-based schedule to two developmentally disabled individuals displaying self-injurious behavior. Although food was empirically determined not to function as a reinforcer for self-injurious behavior, noncontingent presentation of food produced reductions in this behavior. In addition, other studies have used different versions of stimulus preference assessment to reduce self-injurious behavior and destructive behaviors such as physical and verbal aggression (e.g., Fisher et al., 2000; Ringdahl, Vollmer, Marcus, & Roane, 1997).

WHEN TO CHOOSE ONE PROCEDURE OVER ANOTHER

As mentioned previously, the literature suggests that both the PS and MSWO procedures are able to identify stimuli that can serve as functional reinforcers. There are practical considerations, however, that may warrant selecting one procedure over another. For example, completion time may be an important factor, particularly in applied settings. In general, the literature indicates that the MSWO procedure can be completed in less than half the time required to complete the PS procedure when seven stimuli are used and each pairing is conducted five times (DeLeon & Iwata, 1996).

As mentioned earlier, the MSWO procedure can present difficulties when implemented with individuals with severe physical or cognitive impairments. For instance, when working with elderly individuals with severe dementia and impaired motor skills, several problems emerge. First, the large array of items may be several feet long, particularly if there are large items such as television monitors (for videos) or radios. If the individual is not able to ambulate independently, he or she may not have access to items that are farther away. This may result in biased selection of items within immediate view. Second, individuals with physical disabilities may not be able to make physical contact with the stimuli. When this is the case, selection responses should include visual orientation to or gesturing toward a stimulus. These less direct responses can be difficult responses to measure reliably when such a large array of items are presented at once. Third, a large array of stimuli may not be practical, particularly if stimuli include different types of videotapes or audiotapes. One could envision a situation where a client is presented with array of stimuli that includes a videotape playing, an audiotape playing, dolls, and food items all at once. This array of stimuli may be overwhelming for some clients, particularly those with severe dementia, and may result in disruptive behavior.

In sum, one must assess an individual's level of sensory, motor, and cognitive impairment before choosing a stimulus preference assessment procedure. For those with severe impairments, the PS assessment procedure may be more practical to implement because it is less overwhelming for the client and logistically easier for the therapist.

Further Reading

DeLeon, I. G., & Iwata, B. A. (1996). Evaluation of a multiple-stimulus presentation format for assessing reinforcer preferences. *Journal of Applied Behavior Analysis, 29,* 519–533.

Fisher, W., Piazza, C. C., Bowman, L. G., Hagopian, L. P., Owens, J. C., & Slevin, I. (1992). A comparison of two approaches for identifying reinforcers for persons with severe and profound disabilities. *Journal of Applied Behavior Analysis, 25,* 491–498.

References

Carr, J. E., Nicolson, A. C., & Higbee, T. S. (2000). Evaluation of a brief multiple-stimulus preference assessment in a naturalistic context. *Journal of Applied Behavior Analysis, 33,* 353–357.

DeLeon, I. G., & Iwata, B. A. (1996). Evaluation of a multiple-stimulus presentation format for assessing reinforcer preferences. *Journal of Applied Behavior Analysis, 29,* 519–533.

Fischer, S. M., Iwata, B. A., & Mazaleski, J. L. (1997). Noncontingent delivery of arbitrary reinforcers as treatment for self-injurious behavior. *Journal of Applied Behavior Analysis, 30,* 239–249.

Fisher, J. E., & Buchanan, J. A. (2000). *Distraction-based intervention for aggression in dementia patients.* Paper presented at the Association for the Advancement of Behavior Therapy, New Orleans.

Fisher, W., Piazza, C. C., Bowman, L. G., Hagopian, L. P., Owens, J. C., & Slevin, I. (1992). A comparison of two approaches for identifying reinforcers for persons with severe and profound disabilities. *Journal of Applied Behavior Analysis, 25,* 491–498.

Fisher, W. W., O'Conner, J. T., Kurtz, P. F., DeLeon, I. G., & Gotjen, D. L. (2000). The effects of noncontingent delivery of high- and low-preference stimuli on attention-maintained destructive behavior. *Journal of Applied Behavior Analysis, 33,* 79–83.

Green, C. W., Reid, D. H., White, L. K., Halford, R. C., Brittain, D. P., & Gardner, S. M. (1988). Identifying reinforcers for persons with profound handicaps: Staff opinion versus systematic assessment of preferences. *Journal of Applied Behavior Analysis, 21,* 31–43.

Pace, G. M., Ivancic, M. T., Edwards, G. L., Iwata, B. A., & Page, T. J. (1985). Assessment of stimulus preference and reinforcer value with profoundly retarded individuals. *Journal of Applied Behavior Analysis, 18,* 249–255.

Piazza, C. C., Fisher, W. W., Hagopian, L. P., Bowman, L. G., & Toole, L. (1996). Using a choice assessment to predict reinforcers' effectiveness. *Journal of Applied Behavior Analysis, 29,* 1–9.

Ringdahl, J. E., Vollmer, T. R., Marcus, B. A., & Roane, H. S. (1997). An analogue evaluation of environmental enrichment: The role of stimulus preference. *Journal of Applied Behavior Analysis, 30,* 203–216.

Windsor, J., Piche, L. M., & Locke, P. A. (1994). Preference testing: A comparison of two presentation methods. *Research in Developmental Disabilities, 15,* 439–455.

60 STRESS INOCULATION TRAINING

Donald Meichenbaum

The events of September 11, 2001, and their aftermath have highlighted the need to help individuals cope with stress. Whether the stress comes in the form of personal threats, uncertainties about the future, or loss (both material and spiritual), there is a need to bolster coping effectiveness. Stress inoculation training (SIT), developed in the 1980s as a form of cognitive behavioral intervention (see Meichenbaum, 1985, 1993), has been employed successfully in helping individuals cope with various forms of stress, including

1. Acute time-limited stressors such as medical examinations and surgery
2. Stress sequences that follow the exposure to traumatic events such as rape, or that require transitional adjustment due to the stress of job loss
3. Chronic intermittent stressors such as competitive athletic performance and ongoing evaluations
4. Chronic continual stressors such as the experience of medical conditions (e.g., chronic and intermittent pain) and psychiatric disorders (e.g., anxiety- and anger-related disorders), as well as the exposure to persistent occupational dangers such as police work, combat, nursing, and teaching

In short, SIT has been employed on both a preventative and a treatment basis with a broad array of individuals who have experienced stress responses.

WHO MIGHT BENEFIT FROM SIT?

A recent computer literature search revealed some 200 studies that have used SIT with varied populations. On a preventative basis, SIT has been used successfully with such populations as surgical patients, patients undergoing stressful medical examinations, hemodialysis patients, and various stressful occupational groups (flight attendants, soldiers, police officers, fire fighters, nurses, teachers, oil rig workers, and staff workers who work with developmentally delayed individuals), stepparents, parents of children who have cancer, and foreign students who have to deal with the stress of adjustment. On a treatment basis, SIT has been employed with medical patients, including patients with various forms of pain disorders, hypertension, cancer, ulcers, burns, AIDS, genital herpes, traumatic brain injury, and childhood asthma. With psychiatric patients, SIT has been used successfully with individuals (children, adolescents, adults) who have anger control problems; anxiety disorders such as Performance Anxiety, Dental Anxiety, phobias, and Post-Traumatic Stress Disorder (PTSD; e.g., rape victims and victims of sexual abuse); addictive disorders; and chronic psychiatric disorders. (For literature reviews see Maag & Kotlash, 1994; Meichenbaum, 1996, 2001; Saunders, Driskell, Johnston, & Salas, 1996.)

CONTRAINDICATIONS

Based on a review of the literature and on 25 years experience with SIT, there are no populations for whom SIT has been contraindicated. Rather, the ways in which SIT should be applied vary with each population, with the nature of the stress being experienced, and with the length of treatment. Foa and her colleagues (1999) raise a cautionary note about SIT's insufficiency in the treatment of rape victims. They found that with rape victims, gradual exposure-based treatment procedures were found to be more efficacious than SIT over a follow-up period. Thus, when the nature of exposure to the stressor is traumatic and explicit, specific interventions that focus on the impact and meaning of such stressful events may be an important addition to the SIT procedures or should be the focus of the primary treatment.

HOW DOES SIT WORK?

SIT is a broad-based cognitive-behavioral intervention that employs multicomponent training arranged in flexible, interlocking phases. The three phases are

1. A conceptual educational phase,
2. A skills acquisition and consolidation phase, and
3. An application phase.

SIT provides a set of procedural guidelines to be individually tailored to the needs and characteristics of each client or trainee and to the specific form of stress that is being experienced. SIT follows a set of general principles and the flexible application of accompanying clinical procedures, rather than being a set of canned interventions (see the step-by-step procedural guidelines discussed in the next section).

The treatment goals of SIT are to bolster clients' coping repertoires (intra- and interpersonal skills) and their confidence in being able to apply their coping skills in a flexible fashion that meets the appraised demands of the stressful situation. Stressors come in a variety of forms. Sometimes stressors lend themselves to change and can be altered or avoided, while other stressors are *not* changeable (e.g., irreversible loss, incurable illness).

SIT recognizes that some stressful situations do not lend themselves to direct-action problem-solving efforts, since solutions are not always readily attainable. In such instances, an emotionally palliative set of coping responses—such as acceptance, perspective taking, reframing, attention diversion, adaptive affective expression, and humor— may be employed. SIT highlights that there are no "correct" ways to cope. What coping efforts may work in one situation, or at one time, may not be applicable at other times.

A central concept underlying SIT is that of *inoculation*, which has been borrowed analogously from medicine and from social-psychological research on attitude change. The central notion is that bolstering an individual's repertoire of coping responses to milder stressors can serve to build skills and confidence in handling more demanding stressors. By means of gradual exposure, imagery rehearsal, and in-clinic and in situ rehearsal, a sense of mastery can be nurtured.

SIT adopts both a transactional view of stress and a strengths-based approach. From a transactional perspective, SIT highlights that in many instances the ability to cope most effectively with stress requires the need to alter, avoid, or minimize the effects of stressors by better managing the stress-engendering environment. For example, in dealing with medical stressors, SIT trainers can teach patients a variety of coping techniques, but they can also work to alter the ways in which doctors and hospitals interact with patients. With athletes, the focus of SIT may be on influencing the ways coaches relate to athletes, as well as teaching athletes to cope with performance anxiety. With rape victims, the focus of SIT is not only on helping individuals cope with the aftermath of trauma exposure, but also on learning how to alter the environmental stressors that reduce the impact of secondary victimization. Examples of the transactional nature of SIT were illustrated by Wernick (1983), who demonstrated the benefits of providing SIT to nurses who work on burn units in reducing the stress of burn patients; and by Deblinger and Heflin (1996), who demonstrated the benefits of using cognitive behavioral stress reduction procedures with the nonoffending parents of sexually abused children. Stress occurs in a context, and SIT therapists need to embrace such an ecologically sensitive treatment approach. See Meichenbaum and Jaremko (1983) for further examples of such transactionally based treatment approaches.

Second, SIT highlights that exposure to stressful events has the potential of making individuals, groups, and communities stronger and more resilient. There is a need to help individuals and groups access and employ naturally occurring intra- and interpersonal coping resources and social supports. SIT helps individuals deal with safety issues and the immediate and long-term sequelae of stress exposure. Other SIT treatment goals include the need to help individuals transform their distress and emotional pain into something meaningful that gives comfort and purpose to their lives. Issues of relapse prevention and ways to avoid revictimization also receive major attention (Meichenbaum, 1996).

The events of September 11 have taught us to appreciate and admire the coping efforts and courage that individuals and communities can muster in the face of horrific stressful events. SIT builds upon and supplements these coping efforts.

STEP-BY-STEP PROCEDURES

One of the strengths of SIT is its flexibility. SIT has been carried out with individuals, couples, and both small and large groups. The length of the SIT intervention has varied, being as short as 20 min for preparing patients for surgery to 40 sessions with psychiatric patients and patients with chronic medical conditions. In most instances, SIT consists of some 8 to 15 sessions, plus booster and follow-through sessions conducted over a 3- to 12-month period.

A Procedural Flow Chart of Stress Inoculation Training

Phase 1: Conceptual-educational

Phase 2: Skills acquisition, consolidation, and rehearsal

Phase 3: Application and follow-through

Phase 1: Conceptual-educational

- In a collaborative fashion, identify the determinants of the presenting clinical problem or the individual's stress concerns by means of (1) interview with the client and significant others, (2) the client's use of an imagery-based reconstruction of a prototypical stressful incident, and (3) psychosocial and behavioral assessments. Help the client to transform his or her description from global terms into behaviorally specific terms and learn how to disaggregate global stressors.
- Elicit the client's story or narrative accounts of stress and coping and collaboratively help the client identify coping strengths and resources. Help the client to appreciate the differences between changeable and unchangeable aspects of stressful situations and to collaboratively identify short-term, intermediate, and long-term goals.
- Have the client engage in self-monitoring in order to better appreciate how he or she may inadvertently, unwittingly, and unknowingly contribute to how stress reactions build and to better appreciate the interconnections between his or her feelings, thoughts, and behaviors and the reactions of others.
- Ascertain the degree to which coping difficulties arise from coping skills deficits, or whether such difficulties are the result of performance failures (e.g., maladaptive beliefs, feelings of low self-efficacy, negative ideation, secondary gains).
- Collaboratively develop a conceptualization of stress that highlights that stress reactions go through different phases (namely, preparing for the stressor, confronting the stressful situations, handling feelings of being overwhelmed, and reflecting on how the client's coping efforts went—sometimes they went well and sometimes not so effectively). The specific reconceptualization that is developed will vary depending upon the nature of the stressor.
- Debunk any myths concerning stress and coping.

Phase 2: Skills Acquisition, Consolidation, and Rehearsal

- Tailor skills training to the specific population and to the length of training.
- Ascertain the client's preferred mode of cop-

ing and how these coping efforts can be employed in the current situation. Consider what factors are blocking such coping efforts.

- Train problem-focused instrumental coping skills that are directed at the modification, avoidance, and minimization of the impact of stressors (e.g., problem-solving, assertiveness training, use of social supports).
- Train emotionally focused coping skills (e.g., perspective taking, emotion regulation, cognitive reframing).
- Have clients rehearse skills by means of imagery and behavioral practice.
- Build in generalization procedures. Consider possible barriers to using coping behaviors and ways to anticipate and address these possible obstacles.

Phase 3: Application and Follow-Through

- Encourage the application of coping skills to gradually more demanding stressful situations.
- Use relapse prevention procedures.
- Bolster the client's self-efficacy. Ensure that the client takes credit for improvement and offers self-attributions for change.
- Gradually phase out treatment and include booster and follow-through sessions.
- Involve significant others in the intervention plan.
- Have the client coach someone with a similar stressful situation. Put the client in a consultative role.
- Help the client restructure and reappraise environmental stressors, and when possible, alter them either individually or with the help of others.

Further Reading

Meichenbaum, D. (1985). *Stress inoculation training.* Elmsford, NY: Pergamon Press.

Meichenbaum, D. (1996). *Treating adults with Post-Traumatic Stress Disorder.* Waterloo, ON: Institute Press.

Meichenbaum, D. (2001). *Treating individuals with anger-control problems and aggressive behaviors.* Waterloo, ON: Institute Press.

Meichenbaum, D., & Deffenbacher, J. L. (1988). Stress inoculation training. *Counseling Psychologist, 16,* 69–90.

References

Deblinger, E., & Heflin, A. H. (1996). *Treating sexually abused children and their nonoffending parents: A cognitive-behavioral approach.* Thousand Oaks, CA: Sage.

Foa, E. B., Dancu, C., Hembree, E. A., Jaycox, L. H., Meadows, E. A., Street, G. D. (1999). A comparison of exposure therapy, stress inoculation training, and their combination for reducing Post-Traumatic Stress Disorder in female assault victims. *Journal of Consulting and Clinical Psychology, 67,* 194–200.

Maag, J., & Kotlash, J. (1994). Review of stress inoculation training with children and adolescents: Issues and recommendations. *Behavior Modification, 18,* 443–469.

Meichenbaum, D. (1985). *Stress inoculation training.* Elmsford, NY: Pergamon Press.

Meichenbaum, D. (1993). Stress inoculation training: A 20-year update. In R. L. Woolfolk & P. M. Lehrer (Eds.), *Principles and practices of stress management* (pp. 373–406). New York: Guilford Press.

Meichenbaum, D. (1996). *Treating adults with Post-Traumatic Stress Disorder.* Waterloo, ON: Institute Press.

Meichenbaum, D. (2001). *Treating individuals with anger-control problems and aggressive behaviors.* Waterloo, ON: Institute Press.

Meichenbaum D., & Jaremko, M. E. (Eds.). (1983). *Stress reduction and prevention.* New York: Plenum Press.

Saunders, T., Driskell, J. E., Johnston, J. H., & Salas, E. (1996). The effect of stress inoculation training on anxiety and performance. *Journal of Occupational Psychology, 1,* 170–186.

Wernick, R. L. (1983). Stress inoculation in the management of clinical pain: Applications to burn pain. In D. Meichenbaum & M. E. Jaremko (Eds.), *Stress reduction and prevention* (pp. 191–218). New York: Plenum Press.

61 STRESS MANAGEMENT

Aaron Kaplan and Ranilo Laygo

INTRODUCTION

Stress develops and is maintained through an interplay among biological, psychological, and social-environmental factors (referred to as a *biopsychosocial model* of stress). Illness may contribute to stress (Holmes & Rahe, 1967), and stress has been shown to suppress people's immune systems, thereby making them more susceptible to illness and disease (Kiecolt-Glaser & Glaser, 1991). Social relationships can cause stress (e.g., marriage or divorce) or can help an individual cope with stress (Bakal, 1992; Friedman & DiMatteo, 1989; Holmes & Rahe; Kiecolt-Glaser & Glaser). Furthermore, psychological factors (e.g., the person's interpretation of events) may contribute to a person's ability to cope with stress (Ellis, 1973; Lazarus, 1966).

Biological Factors

Hans Selye is known for his early research on stress (Selye, 1936, 1950). Selye observed that when an organism faces an environmental challenge, it responds in a predictable manner. He identified three stages that organisms go through when experiencing stress: alarm, resistance, and exhaustion. He called these stages the *general adaptation syndrome.*

In the first stage, the organism responds to a challenge by mobilizing its internal resources to fight the stressor. If exposure to the stressor continues, the organism adapts to the presence of the stressor and becomes more resistant to disease and illness. Over time, however, the organism's resistance will diminish as prolonged exposure to the stressor taxes its organ systems and their resources. In the final stage, resistance breaks down and the organism gradually becomes more susceptible to illness.

Since the 1930s, advances in endocrinology have allowed researchers to examine physiological events that relate to Selye's stage model. It is clear now that the structures and hormones involved in the hypothalamic-pituitary axis play a major role in a person's physiological response to stress and in the effects the stressor will have on the person's health.

When under stress, the human body responds by releasing several hormones. Cortisol is one hormone that causes an increase in blood sugar and the release of fatty acids, and slows inflammation of damaged tissue. These actions have positive effects during Selye's resistance stage; however, cortisol also suppresses immune function (Bakal, 1992; Munck & Guyre, 1991). Therefore, a person may become more susceptible to illness and disease as exposure to the stressor continues.

Social-Environmental Factors

Stressors can range from daily hassles (e.g., losing things, having too many things to do, having too little time to do things; Kanner, Coyne, Shaefer, & Lazarus, 1981) to ongoing stressors (e.g., financial concerns, beginning school, divorce; Holmes & Rahe, 1967). Events that are perceived as positive but involve major life changes, such as weddings, vacations, and moves, can also be a source of stress (Holmes & Rahe).

An individual's social world can be both a source of stress and a source of support. Clearly, strained work, family, or other social relationships can be sources of stress. In addition, the presence of supportive individuals in a person's life can provide emotional connection, assistance in problem solving, and other tangible assistance that may help a person cope with other life stressors (Cohen & Willis, 1985).

Psychological Factors

People differ with respect to how well they cope with stress. Because peoples' way of thinking can affect the way they feel (Ellis, 1973), those who use more adaptive cognitive coping strategies or appraisals of events may be better able to cope with stress (Carroll, 1992; Houston, 1977; Taylor, 1983). People also differ with respect to behavioral response to stress. For example, some individuals tend to engage in poor health practices when under stress (Cohen & Williamson, 1991).

WHO MIGHT BENEFIT FROM THIS TECHNIQUE

Stress management techniques described in this chapter have applicability to a broad range of patients across a variety of settings. Stress management may be used both as a primary focus of treatment and as adjunctive treatment for patients dealing with other significant problems in the biopsychosocial sphere.

CONTRAINDICATIONS

There are no contraindications for stress management in general. However, the therapist should consider the appropriateness of specific stress management techniques given a patient's comorbid illness (e.g., suggesting appropriate type and intensity of physical activity for a patient with coronary artery disease).

OTHER FACTORS IN DECIDING TO USE OR NOT TO USE STRESS MANAGEMENT

A patient suffering from a comorbid mental or physical illness may benefit from stress management. The therapist should make efforts to integrate stress management with the treatment plan for the primary illness. For example, a patient with chronic pain may benefit from learning stress management techniques as they relate to managing pain.

HOW DOES THE TECHNIQUE WORK?

Stress management works by teaching patients new skills to help them cope with stress. They learn to use behaviors and thoughts for coping during stressful situations. They also commit to making lifestyle changes that will lead to a better quality of life. The skills they learn are written in a straightforward stress management behavioral plan.

STEP-BY-STEP PROCEDURES

Stress management begins with a brief assessment of the patient's lifestyle, including areas of functioning that may cause or be impacted by stress. The patient is then presented with a psychoeducational overview of stress from a biopsychosocial perspective. Finally, strategies for making lifestyle changes and for coping with stress are discussed. The patient makes a concrete behavioral plan for implementing changes.

Assessment

Assessment should cover basic information regarding the patient's functioning in various domains, including health, daily responsibilities, and family and social functioning. The patient is also questioned about coping skills that he or she has found effective in the past so they may be mobilized in a behavioral plan (McCarthy, Lambert, & Brack, 1997). The following questions may prove helpful in gathering information about the patient's stress and areas of functioning.

Health

- What health concerns do you have? How do these contribute to your stress? How are these health concerns exacerbated by stress?
- What kind of and how much exercise or physical activity do you do?
- What are your diet and eating habits like?
- What is your pattern of cigarette, alcohol, and other drug use?

Daily Responsibilities

- How well do you think you are able to meet your daily responsibilities (including work, school, or other obligations)?
- What areas within these domains of functioning do you find satisfying and unsatisfying?

Family and Social Functioning

- What areas of family and social functioning do you find satisfying and unsatisfying?
- What areas of family and social functioning are causing you stress?

Coping Strategies

- What are some things that you do when you are feeling stressed that help you cope?
- What are some things you think or say to yourself when you are feeling stressed that help you cope?

Psychoeducation

The patient is presented with the biopsychosocial model of stress describing the relationship among biological and health factors, social-environmental factors, and psychological factors. Please refer to information presented in the introduction section.

It is important to emphasize how stress related to each sphere within the biopsychosocial model can impact the other spheres. Hans Selye's general adaptation syndrome is presented along with information about the hypothalamic pituitary axis. The patient learns that prolonged periods of stress can suppress immune functions and cause the person to become more prone to illness. Finally, patients learn that developing better coping thoughts and behaviors is a major focus of stress management.

Create a Behavioral Plan

The patient will create a behavioral plan listing straightforward and concrete strategies for reducing stress. In the beginning of treatment, the behavioral plan should include at least one lifestyle change, one coping behavior, and one coping thought. Strategies should be straightforward and concrete (e.g., stop and take deep breaths for 2 min when feeling stressed). Vague strategies should be avoided (e.g., get more exercise, eat better). The behavioral plan is viewed as a work in progress, and strategies may be changed or added to meet the patient's needs.

The behavioral plan should be written and placed conspicuously in the patient's environment as a reminder to the patient (see Robinson, 1996, for suggestions about creating individualized behavioral plans). Suggestions for lifestyle changes, coping behaviors, and coping thoughts are described next.

Lifestyle Changes

Lifestyle changes are meant to decrease stress and improve quality of life. Lifestyle changes should be consistent with the patient's interests and motivation. For example, some patients prefer not to do outdoor exercise, but (believe it or not) enjoy doing vigorous housework such as vacuuming and scrubbing.

Furthermore, if the patient already engages in positive lifestyle behaviors, these should be reinforced and enhanced. For example, if a patient already gets some exercise, the behavioral plan could include maintenance and improvement of that behavior (e.g., continue swimming after work Monday through Friday, and spending 15 min on the treadmill before swimming three days a week).

Exercise

Exercise is known to reduce stress (U.S. Public Health Service, 1979). In addition, regular exercise has other benefits such as improving mood, lowering blood pressure, controlling weight, decreasing anxiety, improving self-image, improving sleep, and increasing energy (see Carroll, 1992, for review).

Every patient is encouraged to engage in regular exercise. The therapist should help the patient identify an exercise schedule that is realistic given his or her needs and level of motivation. For some patients, the term *exercise* has negative connotations, so the term *physical activity* may be more acceptable. Whenever possible, it is suggested that the patient exercise in a manner that will be reinforcing and enjoyable. For example, one may choose to walk by the beach, or to go walking with friends or family.

Relaxation

Patients are encouraged to practice some form of relaxation. Techniques such as progressive muscle relaxation, guided visualization, and self-hypnosis are very useful and can be taught as part of stress management (see Davis, Eshelman, & McKay, 2000, and Chapter 41, this volume for a good description of relaxation techniques). Patients should plan to find an uninterrupted time to practice the technique at least once per day if possible. It is helpful if the patient uses a video- or audiotape to practice the relaxation exercise. Tapes can be purchased, or can be recorded by the therapist or patient. Other relaxation methods such as yoga and meditation may also be appealing to the patient. Classes may be available at local community centers and colleges.

Time Management

Patients are often overwhelmed with responsibilities and obligations that add stress to their lifestyles. Patients are encouraged to make at least one change in their schedules that will help make life more manageable. For example, the patient may commit to going to sleep and waking up an hour or so earlier. He or she may choose to cook enough servings of a meal in advance to last several days and cut down on food preparation time. The patient may decide to drop an activity from his or her schedule with an understanding that he or she can always start again when it will be more manageable.

Patients are also encouraged to break seemingly overwhelming tasks or responsibilities into smaller, manageable chunks. The therapist can help the patient learn to strategize around prioritizing smaller tasks so that the greater task is ultimately achieved.

Diet

People who are under stress engage in poor dietary habits (Wardle, Steptoe, Oliver, & Lipsey, 2000). They may not eat well-balanced meals and may eat at irregular times. We have found that many patients consume too much sugar, fat, and carbohydrates and not enough fruits, vegetables, and water. When possible, patients are encouraged to meet with a nutritionist for guidance on healthy eating habits.

Patients are encouraged to make at least one concrete change in their diets, such as drinking a glass of water with each meal, eating an extra serving of vegetables with lunch, or making one food substitution per day (e.g., replacing a scoop of rice with a vegetable). It often helps for patients to practice planning their meals in advance so they have more control over when and what they will eat.

Besides making changes in specific foods, patients are encouraged to make concrete changes in eating behavior (e.g., counting between bites to slow eating; eating at least a piece of toast or fruit in the morning; planning to eat at regular intervals during the day).

Substance Use

Substance use, such as alcohol and caffeine consumption and smoking, may increase when individuals are under stress (Conway, Vickers, Ward, & Rahe, 1981), and the effects of substance use in turn may cause stress. Patients who engage in these behaviors are encouraged to make concrete behavioral changes—for example, limiting drinking to weekends only, drinking only one cup of coffee in the morning and then switching to herbal tea the rest of the day; avoiding smoking within 2 hours of going to sleep. Of course, patients may also be encouraged to seek help in eliminating smoking, alcohol, or substance abuse.

Engage in Enjoyable Activities

Patients are encouraged to choose at least one enjoyable, stress-free activity and plan to do it at a regular interval. They may choose to engage in the activity with friends or family, which encourages positive social interaction.

Assertiveness Training

Many individuals experience stress around communicating and interacting with others (see Chapter 61, this volume). Assertiveness training can help people practice ways of expressing their wishes effectively while still respecting the needs and desires of others. Assertiveness training generally involves learning the differences among assertive, nonassertive, and aggressive communication styles (Lange & Jakubowski, 1976). Improved communication skills can help reduce stress related to interpersonal communication.

Coping Behaviors

Patients learn to implement concrete coping behaviors to deal with immediate stressors. Information gleaned from the assessment is used to target behavioral interventions. For example, if the patient indicates that much of his or her stress emanates from work, he or she should be encouraged to focus on coping behaviors in the work setting (e.g., taking a walk during the lunch break, or taking time out during the day at appropriate intervals). Coping behaviors should be individualized to meet the patient's preferences or needs. The patient may have indicated coping behaviors during the assessment that he or she finds useful. These should be included whenever possible in the behavioral plan.

Breathing

Patients learn and practice taking deep, regulated breaths from the diaphragm (see Chapter 11, this volume). Patients are encouraged to engage in the breathing for at least 2 min when feeling stressed.

Distraction

Patients may be taught to use techniques to distract themselves from excessive worry or rumination. They may use visual (e.g., looking at pictures), auditory (e.g., listening to music), or tactile (e.g., tapping) stimuli to distract themselves. They may also use visualization techniques as a means of distraction.

Time Out

Time out may be used to remove oneself from a stressful activity or situation. The patient should indicate in the behavioral plan what he or she plans to do during a time out (e.g., if stressed while studying I will either walk around campus one time or call a friend).

Coping Thoughts

Coping thoughts are used by patients to refute irrational thoughts, reframe cognitive distortions, and develop a more adaptive way of thinking. Coping thoughts are discussed and then rehearsed by the patient. They should be written in the behavioral plan.

Patients are taught the ABC model of thinking and emotion (Ellis, 1973; Chapter 14, this volume) and how one's thoughts or beliefs (B) related to a situation or antecedent (A) can affect one's mood as a consequence (C). Patients are also introduced to common cognitive distortions and irrational beliefs that may impact their emotional reactions to stressful events (Beck, 1967; Burns, 1990). It helps to have a handout for the patient regarding the ABC model, irrational beliefs, and cognitive distortions.

The patient may be asked, "What is a typical *stressful thought* you have during [event X] that may contribute to feeling stressed?" Patients are then coached to develop coping thoughts to use during typical stress provoking situations. These should be individualized to be consistent with the patient's cultural perspective or world view. The following are some typical, generic coping thoughts often found to be helpful: "I've been through this before and things turn out okay," "I can handle this—I've handled things like this before," "The only person I'm hurting when I worry about this is me," "It's not such a big deal." The patient may also identify cognitive distortions that he or she frequently uses and then develop alternative thoughts. Similar to coping *behaviors*, coping *thoughts* are written in the behavioral plan and the patient is encouraged to read and practice them regularly.

CONCLUSION

This chapter presents an approach to using cognitive and behavioral strategies in stress management. By learning to better cope with stress, it is hoped that one's overall quality of life will improve across the three spheres described in the biopsychosocial model.

Further Reading

Davis, M., Eshelman, E. R., & McKay, M. (2000). *The relaxation and stress reduction workbook.* Oakland, CA: New Harbinger.

Matheny, K. B., & McCarthy, C. J. (2000). *Write your own prescription for stress.* Oakland, CA: New Harbinger.

Robinson, P. (1996). *Living life well.* Reno, NV: Context Press.

References

Bakal, D. A. (1992). *Psychology and health* (2nd ed.). New York: Springer.

Beck, A. T. (1967). *Depression: Causes and treatment.* Philadelphia: University of Pennsylvania Press.

Burns, D. (1990). *Feeling good handbook.* New York: NAL/Dutton.

Carroll, D. (1992). *Health psychology: Stress, behavior, and disease.* London, UK: The Falmer Press.

Cohen, S., and Williamson, G. M. (1991). Stress and infectious disease in humans. *Psychological Bulletin, 109* (1), 5–24.

Cohen, S., & Willis, T. A. (1985). Stress, social support, and the buffering hypothesis. *Psychological Bulletin, 98*(2), 310–357.

Conway, T. C., Vickers, R. R., Jr., Ward, H. W., & Rahe, R. H. (1981). Occupational stress and variation in cigarette, coffee, and alcohol consumption. *Journal of Health and Social Behavior, 22,* 155–165.

Davis, M., Eshelman, E. R., & McKay, M. (2000). *The relaxation and stress reduction workbook.* Oakland, CA: New Harbinger.

Ellis, A. (1973). *Humanistic psychotherapy: The rational-emotive approach.* New York: Julian Press.

Friedman, H. S., & DiMatteo, M. R. (1989). *Health psychology.* Englewood Cliffs, NJ: Prentice Hall.

Holmes, T. H., & Rahe, R. H. (1967). The social readjustment rating scale. *Journal of Psychosomatic Research, 11,* 213–219.

Houston, B. K. (1977). Dispositional anxiety and the effectiveness of cognitive strategies in stressful laboratory and classroom settings. In C. D. Spielberger and I. G. Sarason (Eds.), *Stress and anxiety.* New York: Wiley.

Kanner, A. D., Coyne, J. C., Shaefer, C., & Lazarus, R. S. (1981). Comparison of two modes of stress management: Daily hassles and uplifts versus major life events. *Journal of Behavioral Medicine, 4*(1), 1–39.

Kiecolt-Glaser, J. K., & Glaser, R. (1991). Stress and immune function in humans. In R. Ader, D. L. Felten, & N. Cohen (Eds.), *Psychoneuroimmunology* (pp. 849–867). San Diego: Academic Press.

Lange, A. J., & Jakubowski, P. (1976). *Responsible assertive behavior: Cognitive-behavioral procedures for trainers.* Champaign, IL: Research Press.

Lazarus, R. S. (1966). *Psychological stress and the coping process.* New York: McGraw-Hill.

McCarthy, C. J., Lambert, R., & Brack, G. (1997). Structural model of coping, appraisals, and emotions after relationship breakup. *Journal of Counseling and Development, 76*(1), 53–64.

Munck, A., & Guyre, P. M. (1991). Glucocorticoids and immune function. In R. Ader, D. L. Felten, & N. Cohen (Eds.), *Psychoneuroimmunology* (pp. 849–867). San Diego: Academic Press.

Robinson, P. (1996). *Living life well.* Reno, NV: Context Press.

Selye, H. (1936). A syndrome produced by diverse nocuous agents. *Nature, 138,* 32.

Selye, H. (1950). *Stress* (1st ed.). Montreal: Acta.

Taylor, S.E. (1983). Adjustment to threatening events. *American Psychologist, 41,* 1161–1173.

U.S. Public Health Service (1979). *Healthy people: The surgeon general's report on health promotion and disease prevention.* Washington, DC: U.S. Government Printing Office.

Wardle, J., Steptoe, A., Oliver, G., & Lipsey, Z. (2000). Stress, dietary restraint, and food intake. *Journal of Psychosomatic Research, 48,* 195–202.

62 SYSTEMATIC DESENSITIZATION

Lara S. Head and Alan M. Gross

Systematic desensitization is an effective therapeutic treatment in the reduction of maladaptive anxiety (Wolpe, 1990). It is the process by which a person is induced into a deeply relaxed state and is presented with a series of graduated anxiety-evoking situations using imaginal (also known as in vitro) exposure. When anxiety is experienced during exposure, the image is terminated and a relaxed state is induced. With continued exposure to each situation, the person's level of anxiety weakens progressively, until the person no longer experiences anxiety in response to the aversive stimuli (Wolpe, 1958, 1990).

TYPES OF SYSTEMATIC DESENSITIZATION

In Vivo Desensitization

Similar to imaginal exposure in terms of procedure, in vivo desensitization utilizes a hierarchy of real-life anxiety-evoking situations that are presented to the client. While both are effective in isolation, imaginal and in vivo desensitization are often used together to facilitate transfer of skills. The client first successfully responds to anxiety-evoking situations using imaginal exposure and then confronts similar situations in a real-life setting (Wolpe, 1990).

Group Desensitization

Based on Wolpe's procedures, systematic desensitization using imaginal exposure is presented to a group of individuals with common anxiety-related difficulties. Administration of hierarchy items is typically determined by the progress rate of the slowest participating group member. Group desensitization can be especially useful for therapists treating multiple clients with similar phobias, allowing for cost- and time-effective intervention (Lazarus, 1961).

Self-Control Desensitization

Founded on Davison's counterconditioning model, the self-control desensitization process is regarded as a behavioral rehearsal procedure in which the client learns how to cope with anxiety during a series of anxiety-evoking situations using imaginal exposure. Rather than attempting to reduce anxiety caused by a specific scenario, the primary focus is to assist the client in identifying the physiological cues that indicate anxiety and then use the cues to help the client initiate relaxation to reduce the tension (Davison, 1968; Goldfried, 1971).

WHO MIGHT BENEFIT FROM THIS TECHNIQUE

Systematic desensitization is typically used in the treatment of anxiety and is considered the "first major practical application of behavioral principles in outpatient mental health" (St. Onge, 1995, p. 95; McGlynn, Mealiea, & Landau, 1981). It can be administered individually or in a group setting with equally effective results (Lazurus, 1961; Wolpe, 1990). While useful with persons experiencing generalized anxiety, systematic desensitization is most commonly used in treating persons with phobias where specific anxiety-evoking stimuli such as animals, insects, water, airplanes, and closed spaces have been identified. Systematic desensitization has also been used to treat Obsessive-Compulsive Disorder patients and patients with Agoraphobia (Foa, Steketee, & Ascher, 1980). However, therapists should evaluate each individual's symptoms for effective use of systematic desensitization. Other empirically supported treatments may be more appropriate given the client's primary problem.

Ideal systematic desensitization candidates have three or fewer phobias, demonstrate anxiety that is not the result of a lack of knowledge or skill regarding the stimuli, are able to demonstrate anxiety in response to imaginal exposure to anxiety-evoking stimuli, and with relaxation training are able to successfully relax (St. Onge, 1995). In addition, clients must also be able to develop a well-defined hierarchy of anxiety-evoking situations (Wolpe, 1990).

In vivo desensitization is effective with all age groups, but has proven most beneficial in the treatment of children with phobias or anxiety disorders. Children often do not have the visualization capabilities to implement imaginal exposure effectively (Ultee, Griffioen, & Schellekens, 1982).

CONTRAINDICATIONS

Three common difficulties are frequently cited as reasons a client may be unsuccessful in the systematic desensitization process: difficulty relaxing, poorly developed hierarchies, and difficulty visualizing images (Wolpe, 1990). If a client is unable to relax, additional practice may be needed. If the client feels uncomfortable being observed,

adjustments can be made to the relaxation script as well as to the room arrangement to help the client feel more comfortable (Foa et al., 1980). In terms of hierarchies, if the appropriate fears and anxieties are not addressed, the client may report little anxiety during exposure. Hierarchy revision may be needed to identify the appropriate anxiety-evoking stimuli. Or, if the client reports significant gaps in the anxiety levels of subsequent item presentations, hierarchy revision is needed to identify less anxiety-evoking items. Finally, clients must be able to visualize each item presentation clearly, and with adequate detail. If visualization difficulties occur, visualization training can be provided (Wolpe).

HOW DOES THE TECHNIQUE WORK?

Developed by Joesph Wolpe (1958), systematic desensitization was based on the principle of "reciprocal inhibition" (p. 71). Wolpe suggested that "If a response antagonistic to anxiety can be made to occur in the presence of anxiety-evoking stimuli so that it is accompanied by a complete or partial suppression of the anxiety response, the bond between these stimuli and the anxiety response will be weakened" (p. 71). While other responses incompatible with anxiety have been used, deep muscle relaxation remains the most commonly used and convenient anxiety inhibitor (Wolpe, 1961).

Contrary to Wolpe's suggestion that the effectiveness of systematic desensitization can be accounted for by reciprocal inhibition, Davison (1968) asserts that systematic desensitization is a *counterconditioning* process. Rather than inhibiting anxiety as Wolpe proposed, the presence of anxiety triggers physiological and behavioral cues that are used to prompt the implementation of replacement behaviors. Using this counterconditioning model, Goldfried (1971) developed *self-control desensitization* in which a person learns to cope with anxiety by recognizing bodily tension cues and using them to initiate relaxation in response to typically anxiety-evoking situations. Goldfried suggested that with practice, not only does the anxiety-evoking situation become less aversive, the person also learns to generalize these coping skills to other forms of anxiety.

Other theories have also been proposed as explanations for the success of systematic desensitization. Lader and Mathews (as cited in McGlynn et al., 1981) suggested that desensitization procedures result in *habituation* to the aversive stimuli. Anxiety is alleviated by increasing the frequency of sympathetic responses to aversive stimuli, which in turn encourages habituation. Wilson and Davison's theory (as cited in McGlynn et al., 1981) involving *extinction* posited that exposure to the stimuli (imagined or real-life) not followed by the anxiety-reinforcing element leads to extinction of fear responses. Finally, Wilkins's *cognitive-social reinforcement theory* (as cited in McGlynn et al., 1981) attributed systematic desensitization's success to five different elements: therapist expectations of improvement, positive reinforcement of client effort, concrete evidence of improvement, client control of aversive stimuli, and consistent focus on systematic desensitization as a learning process.

STEP-BY-STEP PROCEDURES FOR TRADITIONAL SYSTEMATIC DESENSITIZATION

Determining when to use systematic desensitization depends upon the individual and the problems being experienced. A complete behavioral analysis is suggested to identify anxiety-evoking stimuli and to determine the appropriateness of the anxiety given the actual level of danger (Wolpe, 1976; St. Onge, 1995). Consideration should also be given to ensure that no "cognitive misconceptions" exist (Foa et al., 1980, p. 40). If anxiety occurs as a result of a lack of knowledge about the situation or object, then correct information should be given and the client's level of anxiety reassessed. Phobic patients are typically aware that the fear they are experiencing in response to a particular object or situation is illogical (Foa et al.). Once systematic desensitization has been determined as an appropriate therapeutic treatment for the client, a three-step process (see Figure 62.1) unfolds:

1. Relaxation training
2. Development of graduated anxiety hierarchies
3. Presentation of hierarchy items while the client is in a deeply relaxed state (Wolpe, 1990)

1. Relaxation training
2. Development of graduated anxiety hierarchies
3. Imaginal exposure—presentation of hierarchy items while the client is in a deeply relaxed state

FIGURE 62.1   Key Elements of Systematic Desensitization

Step 1: Relaxation Training

Instruction in relaxation training involves teaching the client how to reduce tension in the body using a systematic procedure and assisting the client in its implementation (Wolpe, 1990; Chapter 49, this volume). Relaxation provides the client with the necessary antagonist that will serve to inhibit anxiety (Wolpe, 1958). In addition, relaxation serves as a calming mechanism, allowing the client to participate more readily in the imaginal exposure process by increasing the clarity of images sought (Levin & Gross, 1985). Relaxation training typically lasts approximately five to seven sessions, but more time may be needed depending upon the individual. The primary goal is *differential relaxation,* in which the client is able to relax completely muscles that are not being used during a given situation and reduce all unnecessary tension in pertinent muscles to a minimal degree (Wolpe, 1958, p. 135). Instruction focuses on teaching the client to recognize muscle tension by contracting and flexing muscles and then releasing that tension while focusing on the difference in body tension before and after muscle contraction (Wolpe, 1990). Different muscle groupings can be addressed during separate sessions using the following sequence: Session 1, arms; Session 2, head; Session 3, mouth; Session 4, neck and shoulders; Session 5, back, abdomen, and chest muscles; Session 6, lower body. However, relaxation training can be conducted in fewer sessions, according to the therapist's preference and client's progress.

During relaxation training, the client should be able to sit comfortably and concentrate with few distractions. Closing the eyes is encouraged but not a necessity. The therapist should speak softly when explaining instructions and presenting hierarchy items (St. Onge, 1995). The following relaxation script is provided for Session 1:

1. Take a deep breath, hold it (about 10 seconds). Hold it. Now, let go, feeling the release.

2. Stick your arms out and make a tight fist. Really tight. Feel the tension in your hands; notice the discomfort. I am going to count to three, and when I say "three," drop your arms and hands. One... Two... Three... Relax... Just let go... Notice the difference.

3. Raise your arms again, and bend your fingers back toward your body. Hold it. Now drop your arms and hands; just let go. Notice the sensations; feel the difference; feel the comfort.

4. Tense your forearms and upper arms by pressing your elbows down against the chair. Feel the tightness... Hold it. Now, relax. The muscles are letting go; your arms may even be getting warmer. Let your forearms really rest on a chair (or lap). Let go even more. [It is the act of relaxing these additional fibers that will bring about the greatest emotional effect.] Let the whole arm go limp, soft. Good. (St. Onge, 1995, pp. 100–101)

Each relaxation step lasts approximately 10 s, with 10- to 15-s pauses between each step. The entire relaxation process typically lasts about 25 min (St. Onge, 1995). Subjective units of discomfort (SUD) ratings (0–100 range) should be taken at the end of each relaxation session to determine the level of relaxation. Once the client is able to relax to a point of 0 or near 0 and an anxiety hierarchy has been developed, hierarchy item presentation can begin (Wolpe, 1990).

Step 2: Anxiety Hierarchy Development

Step 2 in the process of systematic desensitization is the formulation of a hierarchy of anxiety-evoking situations (Wolpe, 1990). Construction can be done concurrently with relaxation training and should be a collaborative effort on the part of the patient and therapist. Using information gathered from the client's history and clinical interview, as well as from any number of anxiety assessment tools, the therapist and client first identify a series of situations that cause the client maladaptive levels of anxiety. Daily logs completed by the client that record common behaviors and activities can be utilized to assist in item identification (Foa et al., 1980). Therapists can also use their personal observations of the client's behavior to determine additional anxiety-evoking scenarios that could be included in the hierarchy (Goldfried & Davison, 1994). Each situation should be specific and include sufficient detail to facilitate visualization (Goldfried & Davison). While many of the situations will have been previously experienced by the client, previous exposure is not a prerequisite. Situations must, however, be circumstances that would cause the client anxiety (Wolpe, 1990). Hierarchies typically include 10 to 20 items (St. Onge, 1995).

Once a list of situations has been devised, the client ranks the scenarios in order of aversiveness, with the most anxiety-evoking situation located at the top of the hierarchy (Wolpe, 1990). While some clients will construct only one hierarchy, many clients will be experiencing anxiety in response to a number of different stimuli. In these cases, multiple hierarchies may need to be constructed, each addressing related situations (Wolpe).

Step 3: Imaginal Exposure

Imaginal exposure is the final step in the systematic desensitization process (see Chapter 33, this volume). The client has been taught how to relax, has identified a series of anxiety-evoking situations, and is now ready to confront them. Each imaginal exposure session begins and ends with the client in a relaxed state. The client should report an SUD rating of 10 or less before beginning scene presentation (Wolpe, 1990).

Using verbal descriptions given by the client during the assessment process, a neutral scene is first presented by the therapist to serve as a control; it allows the therapist to assess the client's capacity to visualize clearly and determine if any obstacles exist that will hamper visualization (Wolpe, 1990, p. 172). The neutral scene, typically pleasurable in nature, will be utilized whenever the client experiences anxiety during the exposure process and can be returned to during relaxation periods. A signal, such as raising the index finger, should be used by the client to indicate that the scene image is clear. Once a clear image has been obtained, the client continues visualizing the scene for approximately 10 s, at which point the client is then asked to stop visualizing and an SUD rating is taken. The client is then returned to a relaxed state, with a reported SUD rating of 10 or less (Wolpe). The following script is provided (Wolpe, 1990, pp. 173–174).

"First I am going to help you to relax. When you are relaxed I will ask you to imagine certain scenes. Each time a scene becomes clear to you in your mind, let me know by raising your index finger . . . [Begin relaxation process] . . . Now you are feeling relaxed and calm. Imagine that you are sitting beside a clear blue lake. The sun is shining and a slight breeze is blowing. You feel so comfortable and relaxed. Fluffy white clouds are moving slowly overhead. [Watch the client for raised index finger, when indicated, allow visualization to continue for approximately 10 seconds] . . . Stop the scene. On a scale of 1 to 100, what is your SUD rating?"

The first hierarchy item is then presented in a similar fashion, using verbal descriptions of the anxiety-evoking situations. The client signals the therapist when the scene has been visualized clearly. Visualization continues for approximately 5 to 7 s, at which point the client is asked to terminate the scene, an SUD rating is taken, and the client is returned to a relaxed state. Additional presentations of the same scene continue until the SUD rating following visualization is 0 (Wolpe, 1990). Once a client has reported an SUD rating of 0 in response to a hierarchy item, the therapist can move on to the next item. Those scenes anticipated to create significant levels of anxiety can be initially presented for shorter periods of time, such as 2 to 3 s, with subsequent presentations of the same item increasing in length until the client tolerates a 5- to 7-s exposure period. The context of the image may also dictate the time length of visualization, with simple tasks requiring less exposure time (Wolpe).

During a typical 30-min exposure session, a client may be presented as many as three to four scene presentations, each ultimately yielding an SUD rating of 0. However, the number of items addressed in a single session and over the course of treatment will vary depending upon the progress of the client through the hierarchy. Each new session should begin with the most recent item to receive a zero SUD rating. Some reoccur-

rence of anxiety previously reported as 0 can occur. If so, the item should be presented again until the client reports a 0 anxiety level. The number of scene presentations will increase as the client's level of anxiety increases (Wolpe, 1990).

Following each session and especially during relaxation training, homework should be encouraged. This may include continued practice of relaxation techniques or in vivo exposure. Audio- and videotapes can be prepared by the therapist and given to the client to assist in these activities. However, the client should not attempt imaginal or in vivo exposure of a new hierarchy item without the therapist present (St. Onge, 1995).

Further Reading

McGlynn, F. D., Mealiea, W. L., Jr., & Landau, D. L. (1981). The current status of systematic desensitization. *Clinical Psychology Review, 1,* 149–179.

Wolpe, J. (1961). The systematic desensitization treatment of neuroses. *Journal of Nervous and Mental Disease, 132,* 189–203.

Wolpe, J. (1990). *The practice of behavior therapy* (4th ed.). New York: Pergamon Press.

References

Davison, G. C. (1968). Systematic desensitization as a counter-conditioning process. *Journal of Abnormal Psychology, 73,* 91–99.

Foa, E. B., Steketee, G. S., & Ascher, L. M. (1980). Systematic desensitization. In E. B. Foa & A. Goldstein (Eds.), *Handbook of behavioral interventions: A clinical guide* (pp. 38–91). New York: Wiley.

Goldfried, M. R. (1971). Systematic desensitization as training in self-control. *Journal of Consulting and Clinical Psychology, 37,* 228–234.

Goldfried, M. R., & Davison, G. C. (1994). *Clinical behavior therapy.* New York: Wiley.

Lazarus, A. A. (1961). Group therapy of phobic disorders by systematic desensitization. *Journal of Abnormal and Social Psychology, 63,* 504–510.

Levin, R. B., & Gross, A. M. (1985). The role of relaxation in systematic desensitization. *Behavior Research and Therapy, 23,* 187–196.

McGlynn, F. D., Mealiea, W. L., Jr., & Landau, D. L. (1981). The current status of systematic desensitization. *Clinical Psychology Review, 1,* 149–179.

St. Onge, S. (1995). Systematic desensitization. In M. Ballou (Ed.), *Psychological interventions: A guide to strategies* (pp. 95–115). Westport, CT: Praeger.

Ultee, C. A., Griffioen, D., & Schellekens, J. (1982). The reduction of anxiety in children: A comparison of the effects of systematic desensitization in vitro and systematic desensitization in vivo. *Behavior Research and Therapy, 20*, 61–67.

Wolpe, J. (1958). *Psychotherapy by reciprocal inhibition.* Stanford, CA: Stanford University Press.

Wolpe, J. (1961). The systematic desensitization treatment of neuroses. *Journal of Nervous and Mental Disease, 132*, 189–203.

Wolpe, J. (1976). *Theme and variations: A behavior therapy casebook.* New York: Pergamon Press.

Wolpe, J. (1990). *The practice of behavior therapy* (4th ed.). New York: Pergamon Press.

63 THINK-ALOUD TECHNIQUES

Gerald C. Davison and Jennifer L. Best

As your eyes glance over the text contained within the covers of this book, what thoughts are going through your mind? Is there an underlying theme to your cognitions? Are extraneous thoughts intruding as you read? Perhaps you are conscientiously poring over these pages with the sole purpose of extracting as much meaning from the text as possible. Perhaps something on a given page brings to mind a patient you are working with. Maybe you are silently talking back to the text, interjecting a running commentary or critique of what you are reading—or maybe you are reading more passively, with most of your mental resources devoted to thoughts such as what you had for lunch this afternoon, or reviewing the list of tasks you must finish in preparation for an upcoming professional conference.

With the advent of the cognitively-centered Zeitgeist within behavior therapy in the late 1960s (Bandura, 1969; Beck, 1967; Davison & Valins, 1969; Ellis, 1962; Mahoney, 1974; Mischel, 1968) came a burgeoning of methods for describing and analyzing the content of thought. These approaches fell primarily into two broad categories: endorsement techniques and production techniques (see Glass, 1993, for a review).

Endorsement techniques include self-report questionnaires such as the Fear of Negative Evaluation scale (FNE; Watson & Friend, 1969) and the Irrational Beliefs Test (IBT; Jones, 1968). Questionnaires contain a series of preassigned, exper-imenter-defined, or theory-driven statements. Participants are requested to endorse which items best apply and to what degree they reflect current, past or future thoughts, beliefs, and attitudes. Though endorsement methods require very little time and effort and they easily facilitate standardization procedures and the development of norms, they also constrain participants to define aspects of their thinking in terms of already established, a priori formulations.

Production methods include think-aloud (e.g., Genest & Turk, 1981), thought-sampling (e.g., Hurlburt, 1979; Klinger, 1978), thought-listing (e.g., Cacioppo & Petty, 1981), and video-mediated recall (e.g., Schwartz & Garamoni, 1986) protocols. Each of these procedures involves the participants either verbally reporting or creating a written record of what they are thinking or feeling. These more open-ended approaches allow study participants the freedom to describe their reactions rather than, as in endorsement methods, confining their responses to predetermined categories. Subsequently, the verbal productions are content-analyzed for the variables of interest.

Production methods tend to vary with respect to the context of recording (e.g., in an experimentally contrived laboratory situation versus in the participants' natural, day-to-day environments). Another point of divergence for production techniques is the type of stimulus medium (e.g., fictional or imaginal interpersonal vignettes presented via headphones or video monitor) used in the investigations (Glass, 1993).

Other important dimensions in the several cognitive assessment paradigms include the proximity of measurement to events of interest and the context dependence of thought recording. Endorsement measures typically rely on the individual's memory, with participants having to mentally survey their stores of retrospective accounts for thoughts and behaviors. Such measures of cognitive assessment also usually attempt to abstract general (vs. situationally diverse), enduring, emotional, cognitive, or behavioral tendencies. Production methods, in contrast, are often designed to characterize thinking in relation to specific situations relatively close to or concurrent with the experimental manipulation or task presented. For many thought-sampling studies, however, cognitions are randomly sampled throughout the day over several days (e.g., see Hurlburt, 1997, for a review). Thus events are naturally occurring as opposed to experimentally defined.

We turn now to a discussion of one type of production method, commonly referred to as think-aloud.

THINK-ALOUD METHODS OF
COGNITIVE ASSESSMENT

Think-aloud paradigms in particular have been a useful means of collecting thoughts in a variety of task situations and with various participant groups (see Genest et al., 1981, and Kendall & Hollon, 1981, for detailed reviews). Some of the earliest think-aloud studies were focused on determining the underlying mechanisms and thought processes associated with different aspects of academic performance among students at different age levels. Their findings may have important implications for designing effective prevention along with remediation interventions for students with learning disabilities.

For example, Randall and colleagues studied metacognitive processing in college students while performing a think-aloud task as they read (Randall, Fairbanks, & Kennedy, 1986). In other words, researchers wanted to learn more about how students attended to their own reading behaviors while actually reading. Reading comprehension difficulties were highlighted from the transcribed protocol analyses of the think-aloud data (e.g., how word substitutions affected interpretation of the material).

Another group of researchers used a think-aloud approach to examine cognition and metacognition among gifted, learning disabled, and average-performing middle school children while solving a series of math problems (Montague & Applegate, 1993). Verbalized self-talk while completing three mathematical word problems of increasing difficulty distinguished among the groups. In general, learning-disabled students tended to exhibit qualitatively different strategic processes during the task.

In addition to the study of learning disabilities, think-aloud methods have also been used extensively within the mental health literature. Think-aloud methodologies have been useful in the study of emotional reactions to social rejection (Craighead, Kimball, & Rehak, 1979); test anxiety in elementary school children (Fox, Houston, & Pittner, 1983); dysphoric college students (Conway, Howell, & Giannopoulos, 1991; Mayo & Tanaka-Matsumi, 1996); math-anxious college students (Blackwell, Galassi, Galassi, & Watson, 1985); adults with fear of snakes (Eifert & Lauterbach, 1987); and anxious elementary school children (Lodge, Tripp, & Harte, 2000).

The final portion of this chapter will very briefly introduce readers to a specific think-aloud paradigm that has been used in several investigations of interest to cognitive-behavioral theorists, scientists, and practitioners.

THE "ARTICULATED THOUGHTS IN SIMULATED
SITUATIONS" THINK-ALOUD COGNITIVE
ASSESSMENT PARADIGM

Among the think-aloud techniques introduced previously in this chapter is the *articulated thoughts in simulated situations (ATSS)* think-aloud approach of Davison and associates (Davison, Robins, & Johnson, 1983). ATSS is described as a research paradigm rather than as a specific procedure or assessment instrument because the various parameters of ATSS can take different forms depending on the purposes and practicalities of a particular experimental situation.

There are several basic features that define the ATSS paradigm. ATSS involves presenting study participants with multisegmented, imaginal vignettes or scenarios. During the course of an imagined situation, individuals think out loud at specified points interspersed between brief segments of the story. Participants are requested to pretend that the experimental scene is actually happening to them in the laboratory. Their think-aloud reports are transcribed for later content-analysis. The following are typical instructions for ATSS:

> In this study we are interested in the kinds of thoughts people have when they are in certain situations. Often, when people are going about their daily affairs, interacting with others, and so forth, they have a kind of internal monologue going through their heads, a constant stream of thoughts or feelings that reflect their reactions to something that is happening.
>
> What we'd like you to do is to play a part in a couple of situations we have taped. Your part will involve listening to situations and tuning in to what is running through your mind, and then saying these thoughts out loud. The tapes are divided into seven segments. At the end of each segment, there will be a tone, followed by a pause of 30 seconds, during which time we would like you to say out loud whatever is going through your mind. Say as much as you can until you hear another tone. Of course, there are no right or wrong answers, so please just say whatever comes to mind, without judging whether it seems appropriate or not. The more you can tell us the better.
>
> Try to imagine as clearly as you can that it is really you in the situation right now. Note that your task is not to speak back to any one of the voices on the tape as though you were having a conversation with one of them. Rather, you should tune in to your own thoughts and say them out loud. The microphones in front of you will enable us to tape your comments.

One taped scene in which the participant overhears two pretend acquaintances criticizing him or her includes the following segments.

First acquaintance: He certainly did make a fool of himself over what he said about religion. I just find that kind of opinion very closed-minded and unaware. You have to be blind to the facts of the universe to believe that. [30-second pause for subject's response]

Second acquaintance: What really bugs me is the way he expresses himself. He never seems to stop and think, but just blurts out the first thing that comes into his head.

ATSS data are content analyzed using a priori defined codes for the cognitive constructs under investigation. Continuous frequency counts or categorical present-absent counts comprise the traditional data reduction methods employed in ATSS studies.

There are distinct features that set ATSS apart from other think-aloud approaches as an experimental tool. First, ATSS has traditionally provided participants with imagined, audiotaped encounters versus scenarios shown on videotape[1] or in response to actual experimental tasks, such as contending with a series of math problems. This feature of ATSS permits participants to envision particularly meaningful images instead of having experimenter-generated images as the stimuli. It further provides not only the unique opportunity to study the interplay of thoughts, emotions, and behavioral intentions in situations that commonly occur; but also facilitates the chance to examine these interrelationships in unusual or rare events that might not be ethical or even possible to expose persons to in vivo.

Second, unlike think-aloud approaches that are truly online and therefore may interrupt task performance and attention, ATSS is pseudo-online. Participants alternate between hearing segments of the scenario unfold and verbalizing their thoughts. Third, ATSS relies less heavily on the memory of the participant than do think-aloud methods that require participants to think out loud directly after the entire experimental manipulation (e.g., after completing a problem

---

1. The ATSS *paradigm* per se does not preclude other modes of presentation of the complex social stimulus—for example, videotape or even virtual reality. Thus far in our lab and in independent research settings, however, audiotaped presentations have been quite effective.

set). Thoughts instead are articulated in response to smaller bits of information than if a vignette were presented to participants in full before they were instructed to think aloud. Thus, one can sample very nearly in the moment of experience instead of relying on participants' recollections of thinking during a prior experience.

In order for readers to obtain some idea of the breadth of ATSS investigations, results from selected studies employing ATSS methodology are briefly listed here. Those interested in a more detailed review of ATSS research are referred to two previously published ATSS review papers (Davison, Navarre, & Vogel, 1995; Davison, Vogel, & Coffman, 1997) and to the specific studies themselves.

1. The articulated thoughts of participants hearing the taped criticisms of two pretend acquaintances or the taped negative comments of a pretend teaching assistant about their term papers were more irrational than was their thinking aloud to a neutral tape (Davison, Feldman, & Osborn, 1984; Davison & Zighelboim, 1987).

2. Depressed patients from a psychiatric clinic and outpatients with other psychological disorders listened to a tape describing an outdoor barbecue, one that they had supposedly planned and on which it had rained. The articulated thoughts of the depressed participants were more distorted, as predicted by Beck's (1967) cognitive theory of depression, than those of the other nondepressed outpatients (White, Davison, Haaga, & White, 1992).

3. Socially anxious therapy patients articulated thoughts of greater irrational content (in line with Ellis' 1962 theory) than did nonanxious control participants (Bates, Campbell, & Burgess, 1990; Davison & Zighelboim, 1987).

4. Men with borderline hypertension and Type A behavior pattern verbalized more hostile thoughts than did men with Type B personality (Weinstein, Davison, DeQuattro, & Allen, 1986) and responded to social criticism with less self-supportive cognitions (Williams, Davison, Nezami, & DeQuattro, 1992).

5. Recent ex-smokers who relapsed within 3 months following ATSS demonstrated a greater tendency to articulate thoughts about smoking without prompting (Haaga, 1987) and expressed fewer negative expectations associated with smoking than did those who remained abstinent at 3-month follow-up (Haaga, 1988).

6. In a study that directly compared ATSS articulations to overt behavior, Davison, Haaga, Rosenbaum, Dolezal, and Weinstein (1991) found that verbalized expressions of positive self-efficacy were inversely related to behaviorally indexed speech anxiety; that is, the more anxiously participants behaved on a timed behavioral-checklist measure of public-speaking anxiety, the less capable they felt themselves to be while articulating thoughts in a stressful simulated speech-giving situation.

7. In a treatment outcome study comparing progressive muscle relaxation (PMR) and health education to health education alone, men with borderline hypertension articulated fewer hostile expressions at posttreatment in the PMR condition than in the health education condition (Davison, Williams, Nezami, Bice, & DeQuattro, 1991).

8. An ATSS investigation of maritally violent men found that ATSS variables distinguished between levels of marital aggression better than did questionnaire measures of dysfunctional thinking (Eckhardt, Barbour, & Davison, 1998). Marital violence was associated with, for example, more articulated hostile attributions, illogical thought content (e.g., dichotomous thinking), and demandingness and with fewer anger control statements than with men who were not maritally violent.

9. A recent ATSS study examining attitudes toward homosexuals and anti-gay hate crimes demonstrated that anti-gay attitudes predicted more articulated disapproval of the victim and support for the perpetrator during the hate crime scenario than in the non–hate crime condition (Rayburn & Davison, 2003).

CONCLUSION

Think-aloud typically provides an open-ended online response format, examines the potential contextual or situational influence on cognitive and emotional processing, and strives for ecological validity in stimulus design. Think-aloud techniques also exhibit notable convergent, predictive, and construct validity when pitted against, for example, self-report measures (e.g., see Davison et al., 1997).

On the other hand, a principal criticism of the think-aloud method (as well as other production methods) is the issue of reliability or replicability of findings. Although researchers allow participants to verbalize extensively what is on their minds, the data are analyzed with experimenter-defined, a priori codes for the information-processing variables of interest. Coded categories are rarely repeated in a large number of studies, either within or across research laboratories. Experimenter-devised codes for describing cognitive, affective, and behavioral processes may not be the most accurate representation of how the actual participants conceptualize their own thinking. However, despite their limitations, think-aloud techniques have clearly been demonstrated to be userful for studying cognitive, behavioral, and affective reactions in a wide range of academic and social situations.

References

Bandura, A. (1969). *Principles of behavior modification.* New York: Holt, Rinehart, & Winston.

Barlow, D. H. (1993). *Clinical handbook of psychological disorders* (2nd ed.). New York: Guilford Press.

Bates, G. W., Campbell, T. M., & Burgess, P. M. (1990). Assessment of articulated thoughts in social anxiety: Modification of the ATSS procedure. *British Journal of Clinical Psychology, 29,* 91–98.

Beck, A. T. (1967). *Depression: Clinical, experimental, and theoretical aspects.* New York: Harper & Row.

Blackwell, R. T., Galassi, J. P., Galassi, M. D., & Watson, T. E. (1985). Are cognitive assessment methods equal? A comparison of think-aloud and thought-listing. *Cognitive Therapy and Research, 9,* 399–413.

Cacioppo, J. T., & Petty, R. E. (1981). Social psychological procedures for cognitive response assessment: The thought-listing technique. In T. V. Merluzzi, C. R. Glass, & M. Genest (Eds.), *Cognitive assessment* (pp. 309–342). New York: Guilford Press.

Conway, M., Howell, A., & Giannopoulos, C. (1991). Dysphoria and thought suppression. *Cognitive Therapy and Research, 15,* 153–166.

Craighead, W. E., Kimball, W. H., & Rehak, P. J. (1979).

Mood changes, physiological responses, and self-statements during social rejection imagery. *Journal of Consulting and Clinical Psychology, 47,* 385–396.

Davison, G. C., Feldman, P. M., & Osborn, C. E. (1984). Articulated thoughts, irrational beliefs, and fear of negative evaluation. *Cognitive Therapy and Research, 8,* 349–362.

Davison, G. C., Haaga, D. A., Rosenbaum, J., Dolezal, S. L., & Weinstein, K. A. (1991). Assessment of self-efficacy in articulated thoughts: "States of mind" analysis and association with speech anxious behavior. *Journal of Cognitive Psychotherapy: An International Quarterly, 5,* 83–92.

Davison, G. C., Williams, M. E., Nezami, E., Bice, T. L., & DeQuattro, V. (1991). Relaxation, reduction in angry articulated thoughts, and improvements in borderline essential hypertension and heart rate. *Journal of Behavioral Medicine, 14,* 453–468.

Davison, G. C., Navarre, S. G., & Vogel, R. S. (1995). The articulated thoughts in simulated situations paradigm: A think-aloud approach to cognitive assessment. *Current Directions in Psychological Science, 4,* 29–33.

Davison, G. C., Robins, C., & Johnson, M. K. (1983). Articulated thoughts during simulated situations: A paradigm for studying cognition in emotion and behavior. *Cognitive Therapy and Research, 7,* 17–40.

Davison, G. C., & Valins, S. (1969). Maintenance of self-attributed and drug-attributed behavior change. *Journal of Personality and Social Psychology, 11,* 25–33.

Davison, G. C., Vogel, R. S., & Coffman, S. G. (1997). Think-aloud approaches to cognitive assessment and the articulated thoughts in simulated situations paradigm. *Journal of Consulting and Clinical Psychology, 65,* 950–958.

Davison, G. C., & Zighelboim, V. (1987). Irrational beliefs in the articulated thoughts of college students with social anxiety. *Journal of Rational-Emotive Therapy, 5,* 238–254.

Eckhardt, C. I., Barbour, K. A., & Davison, G. C. (1998). Articulated thoughts of maritally violent and nonviolent men during anger arousal. *Journal of Consulting and Clinical Psychology, 66,* 259–269.

Eifert, G. H., & Lauterbach, W. (1987). Relationships between overt behavior to a fear stimulus and self-verbalizations measured by different assessment strategies. *Cognitive Therapy and Research, 11,* 169–183.

Ellis, A. (1962). *Reason and emotion in psychotherapy.* Secaucus, NJ: Lyle Stuart.

Fox, J. E., Houston, B. K., & Pittner, M. S. (1983). Trait

anxiety and children's cognitive behaviors in an evaluative situation. *Cognitive Therapy and Research, 7,* 149–154.

Genest, M., & Turk, D. C. (1981). Think-aloud approaches to cognitive assessment. In T. V. Merluzzi, C. R. Glass, & M. Genest (Eds.), *Cognitive assessment.* New York: Guilford Press.

Glass, C. R. (1993). A little more about cognitive assessment. *Journal of Counseling and Development, 71,* 546–548.

Haaga, D. A. (1987). *Smoking schemata revealed in articulated thoughts predicts early relapse from smoking cessation.* Paper presented at the 21st Annual Convention of the Association for Advancement of Behavior Therapy, Boston.

Haaga, D. A. (1988). *Cognitive aspects of the relapse prevention model in the prediction of smoking relapse.* Paper presented at the 22nd Annual Convention of the Association for Advancement of Behavior Therapy, New York.

Hurlburt, R. T. (1979). Random sampling of cognitions and behavior. *Journal of Research in Personality, 13,* 103–111.

Hurlburt, R. T. (1997). Randomly sampling thinking in the natural environment. *Journal of Consulting and Clinical Psychology, 65,* 941–949.

Jones, R. G. (1968). *A factored measure of Ellis's irrational belief system with personality and maladjustment correlates.* Unpublished doctoral dissertation, Texas Technological College, Lubbock.

Kendall, P. C., & Hollon, S. D. (1981). Assessing self-referent speech: Methods in the measurement of self-statements. In P. C. Kendall & S. D. Hollon (Eds.), *Assessment strategies for cognitive-behavioral interventions.* New York: Academic Press.

Klinger, E. (1978). Modes of normal concious flow. In K. S. Pope & J. L. Singer (Eds.), *The stream of conciousness: Scientific investigations into the flow of human experience* (pp. 225–258). New York: Plenum.

Lodge, J. L., Tripp, G., & Harte, D. K. (2000). Think-aloud, thought-listing, and video-mediated recall procedures in the assessment of children's self-talk. *Cognitive Therapy and Research, 24,* 399–418.

Mahoney, M. J. (1974). *Cognition and behavior modification.* Cambridge, MA: Ballinger.

Mayo, V. D., & Tanaka-Matsumi, J. (1996). Think-aloud statements and solutions of dysphoric persons on a social problem-solving task. *Cognitive Therapy and Research, 20,* 97–113.

Mischel, W. (1968). *Personality and assessment.* New York: Wiley.

Montague, M., & Applegate, B. (1993). Middle school students' mathematical problem solving: An analysis of think-aloud protocols. *Learning Disability Quarterly, 16,* 19–32.

Randall, A., Fairbanks, M. M., & Kennedy, M. L. (1986). Using think-aloud protocols diagnostically with college readers. *Reading Research and Instruction, 25,* 240–253.

Rayburn, N., & Davison, G. C. (2003). Articulated thoughts about anti-gay hate crimes. *Cognitive Therapy and Research, 23,* 431–447.

Schwartz, R. M., & Garamoni, G. L. (1986). A structural model of positive and negative states of mind: Asymmetry in the internal dialogue. *Advances in cognitive-behavioral research and therapy, 5,* 1–62.

Watson, D., & Friend, R. (1969). Measurement of social-evaluative anxiety. *Journal of Consulting and Clinical Psychology, 33,* 87–104.

Weinstein, K. A., Davison, G. C., DeQuattro, V., & Allen, J. W. (1986). *Type A behavior and cognitions: Is hostility the bad actor?* Paper presented at the 94th Annual Convention of the American Psychological Association, Washington, DC.

White, J., Davison, G. C., Haaga, D. A. F., & White, K. (1992). Cognitive bias in the articulated thoughts of depressed and nondepressed psychiatric patients. *Journal of Nervous and Mental Disease, 180,* 77–81

Williams, M. E., Davison, G. C., Nezami, E., & DeQuattro, V. L. (1992). Articulated thoughts of Type A and B individuals in response to social criticism. *Cognitive Therapy and Research, 16,* 19–30.

64 TIME-OUT (AND TIME-IN)

Patrick C. Friman and Jack W. Finney

INTRODUCTION

Time-out (TO) is the most commonly used child disciplinary tactic in the United States. As a label, TO is an abbreviation of a longer label—time-out from positive reinforcement—first reported in basic science reports on animals in the 1950s (e.g., Ferster, 1958). As a procedure, TO involved either placing experimental animals in chambers devoid of access to activities with known reinforcing (i.e., motivating) properties (e.g., drinking, eating, wheel running, etc.) or eliminating such access in chambers where the animals had already been placed. In these basic experiments TO proved to be an extraordinarily powerful procedure with two particularly salient effects: (1) reducing the likelihood of future occurrences of the behavior that led to its administration, and (2) increasing the reinforcing properties of events that were eliminated or denied during TO. In more colloquial terms, TO reduced an experimental animal's interest in some behaviors while simultaneously increasing its interest in others.

The basic science reports on TO attracted the attention of applied researchers; in the early 1960s, the first reports showing the beneficial effects of TO on child misbehavior appeared and the dissemination of this now universally used procedure began (e.g., Wolf, Risley, & Mees, 1964). At present, a professional or popular book on child management techniques that does not include a section on TO would be hard to find (e.g., Christophersen, 1997; Forehand & McMahon, 1981). Unfortunately for readers searching for an optimal method for using TO, more variability than uniformity is found across the multitude of published descriptions. In this paper, we provide a synthesis of the published studies and descriptions, with special emphasis on teaching parents to use TO with children at home.

UNDERLYING PROCESSES

The fundamental process underlying the utility of TO involves how children derive meaning from the teeming multitude of events that compose their day-to-day lives, how they learn to exhibit appropriate and inappropriate behavior, or more generally, how they learn. Research on learning by several of the most eminent behavioral scientists of the 20th century (e.g., Bandura, Bijou, Skinner, Thorndike, Watson) shows that child learning largely results from the emergence of functional relations between what children do, what happened before they did it, and the change or contrast in experience generated by what they have done. Said slightly differently, child learning occurs as a function of repetition followed by changes or contrast in child experience. An important corollary of this position is that the number of repetitions necessary for children to make meaningful connections is governed by the amount of the experiential contrast that follows what they do. The more contrast, the fewer repetitions necessary for learning a meaningful relationship between a behavior, its antecedents, and its experiential consequences.

A major class of experientially unpleasant events for children involves those in which very little happens. In other words, children do not like situations in which nothing of interest is occurring and avoidance of such situations motivates a substantive portion of their behavior. From a theoretical perspective, "nothing" is hard to define. From an empirical perspective it can be hard to document. But from a procedural perspective, experiences involving nothing, not much, or very little can be arranged, and related arrangements compose the first important dimension of effective TO.

The second (and equally) important dimension of TO involves a severe restriction on the child's capacity to make something happen or to change the experience of nothing into an experience of something interesting. In other words, situations in which there is nothing going on and little or nothing that can be done about it are aversive for children. After placing a child in a situation with nothing going on (i.e., in TO), the next step is to narrow the range of responses that result in escape from TO to include only appropriate behavior (e.g., quiet acceptance).

In addition to reducing the likelihood of behavior it follows (because children will avoid it), TO also increases the reinforcing properties of events that were denied during its implementation, the primary one of which for children is parental attention. Thus, immediately following TO, parents are in possession of a powerful commodity (i.e., attention) that can be used to teach their child appropriate alternatives to the behavior that led to TO.

EVIDENCE OF EFFECTIVENESS

As might be expected, given the early line of basic research rapidly leading to rigorously documented successful application (e.g., Wolf et al., 1964), there is a long line of applied research showing that TO is an effective method for managing a broad range of misbehavior in children. A

much-abbreviated sample of empirically documented successes includes routine misbehavior (e.g., Mathews, Friman, Barone, Ross, & Christophersen, 1987), disruptive behavior disorders (Kavale, Forness, & Walker, 1999) and clinically exotic habits (e.g., trichotillomania; Blum, Barone, & Friman, 1993). A particularly informative early review traced the systematic replication of TO as it evolved from a basic science preparation to a regularly reported treatment application (Johnston & Pennypacker, 1980).

CONTRAINDICATIONS

From a conceptual perspective, TO appears to be a generically effective, basically harmless reductive procedure because it merely involves strategic diminishment of preferred events. From a procedural perspective, however, TO can be complicated and it is contraindicated in some cases. Chief among them are those involving the possibility of self-harm or the probability of excessive stimulation if children are left unattended. Timeout is also not appropriate for children whose lives are impoverished in terms of human contact; marked by neglect, abuse, or inappropriate out-of-home placement; or who are ill. Additionally, TO is not appropriate for children whose misbehavior is motivated primarily by social avoidance. Time-out can be useful to establish a cooling-off period for older children (i.e., older than 7 years) faced with disciplinary action, but probably should not be the only disciplinary method employed.

THE ROLE OF TIME-IN

As indicated, the fundamental basis for the utility of TO is that children learn through repetition with experiential contrast and thus, in order for TO to be effective, children must be in situations the removal from which generates nonpreferred contrast. If nothing preferred was occurring prior to a TO, the possibility for experiential contrast during a subsequent TO is reduced and thus the possibility of learning following TO is also reduced. Conversely, if engagement, fun, or affection is abundant prior to a TO, the possibility for nonpreferred experiential contrast during a subsequent TO is increased and correspondingly the possibility of learning following TO is also increased. Therefore, prior to using TO, it is necessary to establish a high degree or level of time-in (TI; Solnick, Rincover, & Peterson, 1977). Heuristically, TI can be thought of as the functional opposite of TO. Time-out is a procedure that minimizes preferred experience and is used in response to inappropriate child behavior. Time-in is a procedure that maximizes preferred experience (e.g., physical affection, parental participation in child activities, etc.) and is used in response to appropriate child behavior. There are many ways to establish TI, several of which we will describe here.

Physical Affection

The general goal of TI is to increase children's enjoyment of their own lives. At the simplest level of application, TI involves the provision of frequent and consistent physical affection when children are engaged in acceptable behavior. One way to prescribe this is to instruct parents to increase the number of times they touch their child affectionately by at least 50 discrete times a day. This does not mean that parents have to extensively hold and cuddle their child; rather, it merely means that whenever children are within reach parents should reach out and provide 1 or 2 seconds of physical affection (e.g., by patting them on the shoulder, ruffling their hair, etc.). Frequent touching is particularly beneficial when children are involved in boring, effortful, onerous, or distracting activities. Additionally, physical affection with children can be more powerful if it is supplied nonverbally. Questioning, commenting, or even praising, although enhanced by being paired with physical affection, can diminish the central message (e.g., I love you) carried by the affection itself.

Letting Them Help

Children may not like to do their own chores but they often do like to help as parents work on parent projects. With a little creativity, a parent can readily arrange for the child to provide some real or apparent assistance with whatever task the parent is currently undertaking (e.g., sweep-

ing small corner of kitchen, holding the dustpan, turning on the garden hose, etc.). Allowing children to help can be rewarding for children because it suggests they can make valuable contributions to the parent and it also sets the occasion for parents to acknowledge and praise the help provided.

Catching Them Being Good

Even flagrantly misbehaving children exhibit some appropriate behavior, yet, for a variety of reasons (e.g., when a high rate of misbehavior obscures the good behavior) adults often fail to acknowledge it much. Training parents to be at least as observant of and positively responsive to appropriate behavior as they are observant of and critical toward inappropriate behavior will naturally increase the amount of TI in a child's life (e.g., Christophersen, 1997).

Second- and Third-Hand Compliments

Sometimes direct compliments have limited potency because their delivery is ineffective (e.g., insincere) or their meaning has been contaminated by the parent-child interactions that preceded them (e.g., praise following a power struggle may suggest the child has lost). However, when compliments about the child are shared with a second person and then are either overheard or delivered to the child by the other person, they can be a very effective means of increasing TI (e.g., Ervin, Miller, & Friman, 1996).

Special Time

One way to ensure a modicum of TI is to have parents provide each of their children a small amount of special time (e.g., 5–15 min) that the child determines how to use (e.g., piggyback rides, talking). The time should be delivered every day the children and parents are home together (even on days when children have misbehaved).

Miscellaneous

There are many other ways of establishing TI (e.g., games, family meetings, outings, etc.) and they are limited only by the imaginations of the therapist and parent and by the resources in the home. Although it is not necessary for parents to conduct a TI procedure immediately prior to a TO, the therapist should ensure that parents are frequently using TI procedures prior to prescribing TO.

USING TIME-OUT

Where?

The central difficulty for the therapist teaching parents about TO is to communicate that it is a condition, not a location. Thus, although a barren locked room can provide TO, it is entirely unnecessary (and usually inhumane) to use one for that purpose. The key components of TO are major reductions in children's access to preferred events and their methods for changing the situation. The most preferred events in a child's life are social contact with others and engagement with entertaining objects (e.g., toys, games, television), and thus these are the preferred events to which access is curtailed in TO. Confining children to their room can accomplish these goals, but so, too, can confining them to a seated position anywhere in the home (e.g., on a chair in the dining room) or out of the home (e.g., on a bench at the park). Relying solely on bedrooms can inconvenience parents (e.g., when bedrooms are on a different floor than the location of the infraction), whereas the goal of TO is to strategically inconvenience misbehaving children. Children confined to their rooms may also find ways to amuse themselves and thus diminish the nonpreferred aspect of TO. Also, if children are in their rooms crying out or yelling with no response from the parent, the children may not know whether they are being ignored or just not being heard. When children are crying out and yelling and their parents are well within visual and auditory range, it is clear to the children that they are being ignored and this knowledge activates the second functional dimension of TO, a dramatic limitation on the child's capacity to control the situation. Thus the bedroom can be used as a backup for TO but probably should not be the primary location for its implementation. Generally, an adult-sized

1. Determine whether TO is an appropriate approach to discipline or whether it is contraindicated (e.g., because of illness, impoverished home life, potential for abuse, etc).

2. Help parents generate a variety of ways to establish time for their child.

3. Help parents identify the most typical child behaviors for which TO will be used.

4. Help parents identify a variety of places for TO to be used (e.g., chair, corner, front step).

5. Review with parents the importance of consistent use of TO.

6. Instruct parents in the actual use of TO, including

   • What is said to the child before TO (e.g., specific and brief)

   • What is said to the child during TO (i.e., nothing).

   • What is said to the child after he or she has become calm and quiet (e.g., are you ready to get up now?)

   • What to do if the child leaves TO before time is up

   • What do when TO is over (e.g., practice desired behavior)

7. Instruct parents when to contact therapist for additional help (e.g., if something unusual happens or if no results are produced).

FIGURE 64.1   Steps to Prescribing Time-Out

chair located near but not within the center of activities in the house is best. Larger chairs are more difficult for children to leave and thus reduce child attempts at escape. Locating the chair near central activities makes parental vigilance easier and makes what the child has temporarily lost more apparent. Figure 64.1 summarizes the steps to TO that are discussed in this chapter.

What If Children Refuse To Go to Time-Out?

This problem can be avoided by physically guiding children to TO rather than instructing them to go. Using an instruction sets the occasion for defiance or noncompliance, whereas using guidance obviates these concerns. Use of guidance is also a clear demonstration that the parent has taken control of the interaction.

For What Behavior?

Parental discipline of children is the primary method by which children are acculturated and trained to exhibit civilized conduct. Most children do not automatically or spontaneously generate the behaviors that compose such conduct.

Rather, they emit approximations in response to the unfolding events of their lives. Shaping these approximations into fully expressed exemplars of civilized conduct requires teaching, the success of which is dependent on response repetition followed by experiential contrast. Time-out provides the kind of contrast that teaches children that the behavior that preceded its administration is unacceptable. It also increases the value of parental attention, denied during TO, which increases a parent's subsequent capacity to reinforce appropriate child behavior. Therefore, TO should be used for any behaviors that parents feel are unacceptable, or more generally, for any instance where the parent may be tempted to raise his or her hand or voice to the child. To make matters simpler, unacceptable child behaviors can be divided into three categories: dangerous, defiant, and disruptive. As a general rule, TO should always follow dangerous or defiant behavior. Because disruption is an inevitable dimension of child behavior, however, much of it can be ignored. But disruption can also either be a target for TO or the target of a command (e.g., "Go in your room and do that"), compliance with which should be followed by praise and noncompliance with which should be followed by TO.

What To Say Before and During Time-Out

Although language is the primary tool most adults use to teach children, absent the experiential changes discussed here it actually is not very powerful, especially for young children. In the act of discipline involving TO, therefore, it is best to say very little. A rule of thumb is to use one or two words for every year of child life to label the infraction and then take the child to TO and say no more.

How Long Should Time-Out Last?

Clinic lore and a variety of child behavior manuals assert TO should last 1 min for every year of child age. This rule was the product of efficiency, not empirical research. That is, it was easy to remember but it has not been empirically evaluated. Generally, exit from TO should be contingent upon child behavior, not the passage of time. Departure from TO is typically a highly preferred event and thus it has power to strengthen the be-

havior preceding it. Therefore, departure should be allowed when the child has accepted TO as indicated by the exhibition of quiet and composed behavior (i.e., when behaviors such as crying, pleading, and bargaining have stopped). A version of the clinic lore assertion can then be used. Specifically, once children in TO are quiet and composed they should not be required to remain there any longer than 1 min for every year of age. Acceptance can be tested merely by asking the child if he or she would like to get out of TO. If the child says "yes" in an acceptable tone of voice, departure is allowed. If the child says "no," nothing at all, or anything that is tonally or semantically unacceptable, TO should continue.

Clinic lore also asserts timers should be used. They are unnecessary but if they are used one critical rule should be borne in mind. The timer is for the parent, not the child. That is, the timer is to be used to remind parents how long the child has been in TO, not to show children in TO the rate at which time is passing. While in TO children would typically prefer to know that rate, but in TO preferences are held to a minimum and thus the timer is not used for them.

What To Do About Misbehavior in Time-Out

Children will inevitably misbehave while in TO, especially in the early stages of teaching it to them. The cardinal rule is that adult responses to children in TO are *always nonverbal*. Between the instruction to go to TO and the parental inquiry about whether the child would like to leave TO, adults should say *nothing*. All misbehavior exhibited while children remain in TO should be ignored and this includes profanity, insults, removing clothes, and even spitting. There are two reasons for ignoring this behavior. First, TO involves a severe restriction on child preferences and children angry about being placed in TO would prefer that the parent respond to them, so this preference should not be granted. Second, TO increases the reinforcing properties of events denied during its administration, one of which is parent response to the child. Thus, if the parent responds to gross misbehavior during TO, even if the parental response is negative, there is a heightened probability that behavior will be exhibited in the future (i.e., learned).

Perhaps the most difficult challenge involves children who repeatedly leave TO prior to being granted permission to do so. The simplest method for contending with these unexcused departures is simply to physically (and nonverbally) return children to TO repeatedly until they surrender to the process. There are also several mild forms of physical restraint that can be used. One involves using a chair with sides (arms) for TO and placing an arm across the sides and near or against the child's lap in a fashion that approximates a seat belt. Another involves using a chair with a gap in the backside through which a parent can grasp the back of a child's pants and gently hold when escape is attempted. Or the child's bedroom can be used as a backup TO location when children are highly resistant.

What To Do After Time-Out

Contrary to clinic lore and most child behavior manuals, it is unnecessary and usually unproductive to lecture children on what they did that led to TO (Blum, Williams, Friman, & Christophersen,1995). As indicated previously, messages about discipline should be very brief. Additionally, the assertion that that such messages should be revisited thoroughly after TO is based on the widely held but mistaken assumption that children primarily learn from what they hear or are told. Consistent with our assertion that children learn through repetition with experiential contrast, following TO, children should be given multiple opportunities to practice acceptable alternatives to the behaviors that led to TO. The easiest form of practice is to issue several simple commands and to praise and appreciate any child compliance, and conversely, to use another TO as a consequence for noncompliance. If defiance or noncompliance led to TO, a related instruction should inaugurate the practice session. The reasons for using parental instructions for post-TO practice are straightforward. Diminished instructional control is a major component of most child misbehavior and practice complying with simple parental instructions followed by appropriate consequences strengthens this critical skill. Additionally, a parent's ability to effectively teach children to follow instructions is increased after TO due to the increased value of parental attention resulting from the TO.

CONCLUSION

Children learn through repetition with experiential contrast, and thus good discipline will provide detectable contrast. Yelling or spanking can serve this purpose but there are multiple problems associated with their use. Time-out is much more subtle but it can serve the purpose very well if three conditions are met: (1) sources of social interaction and preferred child experiences are restricted, (2) the child's inappropriate attempts to terminate TO are ignored outright, and (3) the child's life was generally interesting and fun before TO was imposed. In other words, to be effective TO must minimize child preferences and must occur in a generalized context called TI.

Further Reading

Blum, N., Williams, G., Friman, P. C., & Christophersen, E. R. (1995). Disciplining young children: The role of reason. *Pediatrics, 96*, 336–341.

Christophersen, E. R. (1997). *Little people.* Kansas City, KS: Overland Press.

Forehand, R., & McMahon, R. J. (1981). *Helping the noncompliant child.* New York: Guilford Press.

Friman, P. C., & Blum, N. J. (2003). Behavioral pediatrics: Therapy for child behavior problems presenting in primary care. In M. Hersen & W. Sledge (Eds.), *Encyclopedia of psychotherapy* (pp. 379–399). New York: Academic Press.

References

Blum, N. J., Barone, V. J., & Friman, P. C. (1993). A simplified behavioral treatment for trichotillomania in the young child. *Pediatrics, 91*, 993–995.

Blum, N., Williams, G., Friman, P. C., & Christophersen, E. R. (1995). Disciplining young children: The role of reason. *Pediatrics, 96*, 336–341.

Christophersen, E. R. (1997). *Little people.* Kansas City, KS: Overland Press.

Ervin, R., Miller, P., & Friman, P. C. (1996). Feed the hungry bee: Using positive peer reports to improve the social interactions and acceptance of a socially rejected girl in residential placement. *Journal of Applied Behavior Analysis, 29*, 251–253.

Ferster, C. B. (1958). Control of behavior in chimpanzees and pigeons by time out from positive reinforcement. *Psychological Monographs, 72,* (8, whole no. 461).

Forehand, R., & McMahon, R. J. (1981). *Helping the noncompliant child.* New York: Guilford Press.

Friman, P. C., & Blum, N. J. (2003). Behavioral pediatrics: Therapy for child behavior problems presenting in primary care. In M. Hersen & W. Sledge (Eds.), *Encyclopedia of psychotherapy,* (pp. 379–399). New York: Academic Press.

Kavale, K. A., Forness, S. R., & Walker, H. M. (1999). Interventions of oppositional defiant disorder and conduct disorder in the schools. In H. C. Quay and A. E. Hogan (Eds.), *Handbook of disruptive behavior disorders* (pp. 441–454). New York: Kluwer.

Johnston, J. M., & Pennypacker, H. S. (1980). *Strategies and tactics of human behavioral research.* Hillsdale, NJ: Lawrence Erlbaum.

Mathews, J. R., Friman, P. C., Barone, J. V., Ross, L. V., & Christophersen, E. R. (1987). Decreasing dangerous infant behavior through parent instruction. *Journal of Applied Behavior Analysis, 20,* 165–170.

Solnick, J. V., Rincover, A., & Peterson, C. R. (1977). Some determinants of the reinforcing and punishing effects of timeout. *Journal of Applied Behavior Analysis, 10,* 415–424.

Wolf, M. M., Risley, T. & Mees, H. (1964). Application of operant conditioning procedures to the behavior problems of an autistic child. *Behavior Research and Therapy, 1,* 305–312.

65 TOKEN ECONOMY

Patrick M. Ghezzi, Ginger R. Wilson, Rachel S. F. Tarbox, and Kenneth R. MacAleese

Ayllon and Azrin's (1965, 1968) pioneering work in the 1960s with psychiatric patients at Anna State Hospital in Illinois led to the development of the token economy. The rest is history, and today there are volumes of research articles, literature reviews, books and book chapters on the token economy.

Our purpose for this chapter is to offer a set of guidelines for practitioners to follow when designing and maintaining a token economy for an individual or group of individuals. We underscore 'guidelines' to call attention to the fact that as with any other deliberate, systematic behavior management technique, a token economy is always tailored for a particular individual, whether alone or in a group. There is no "one size fits all" token economy, and for that reason we encourage practitioners to use the guidelines as starting points for managing behavior in their own token economy.

WHO MIGHT BENEFIT FROM A TOKEN ECONOMY

All modern textbooks on applied behavior analysis (e.g., Kazdin, 1994; Miltenberger, 2001; Sulzer-Azaroff & Mayer, 1991) give examples of the benefits of a token economy with people as diverse as the mentally retarded, prisoners, drug and alcohol abusers, geriatric patients, students, classroom teachers, and outpatient children and adults. Similarly, the settings in which token economies have been applied range from hospitals, prisons, and community mental health facilities to day-care centers, classrooms, nursing homes, and households.

In theory, there is no limit to the number of settings or participants in a token economy. Nor is there any limit, in theory, to the number of behaviors that may be targeted for change. There are practical limits, however, that each practitioner must consider in the light of his or her own unique circumstances.

CONTRAINDICATIONS AND OTHER CONSIDERATIONS IN DECIDING WHETHER TO USE A TOKEN ECONOMY

Most of us know how an economy works. We know that our pay depends on performing the tasks our jobs entail, that our pay is money, typically, and that we can exchange the money we earn for whatever goods and services are available and affordable to us. As it turns out, this relationship among tasks, receiving payment for performing them, and using money to buy things is at the center of all modern economic systems. It is also at the center of a token economy.

While knowing how an economy works in

one's own life may be necessary, it is insufficient preparation for designing and managing an economy for someone else. For starters, what will the person be paid to do, and when and where will they do it? What will they be paid, and how and when will they get paid? What can they buy with their pay, and how much will it cost them for whatever it is they wish to buy? These are just a few of the many and often vexing questions that must be answered, both when designing a token economy and while managing one over time.

As with any economic system, a token economy affects people in powerful and sometimes unexpected ways. People may become irritated or angry over what they have to do; when, where, and why they have to do it; how much they get paid; and how much things cost. Some may even try to sabotage the economy by forging, stealing, or trading tokens. The people responsible for designing and managing a token economy must be alert to problems of that sort, and must be willing and able to change tasks, alter pay rates, adjust costs, or tighten security as needed to ensure the success of the economy.

The fact that a token economy requires a great deal of planning, monitoring, and modifying discourages many professionals from using it as a means to manage a person's behavior. That is a good reaction, for the most part, because behavior can ordinarily be managed in much easier ways. The child who seldom helps around the house may need nothing more than timely encouragement or an occasional reward for taking out the trash, feeding the dog, or watering the plants. If that fails to increase helping around the house, then perhaps more consistent or sincere encouragement or more frequent or valuable rewards are needed. The point is that it is always best to manage behavior simply, naturally, and conveniently. A token economy has none of those characteristics, and thus should be regarded as a treatment option only when other, less cumbersome interventions have failed to produce the desired results.

HOW A TOKEN ECONOMY WORKS

A token economy takes full advantage of the fact that behavior is affected by its consequences.

Consequences that follow a given behavior and that result in an increase in the tendency for that behavior to recur on the next similar occasion are termed *positive reinforcers*. The tokens in a token economy act as positive reinforcers for the behavior, or behaviors, that precede and produce them. By themselves, tokens do not ordinarily act as positive reinforcers. That action must be established by literally backing up the tokens with objects or events that already act as reinforcers. The relation among behavior, tokens, and back-up reinforcers constitute the internal workings of a token economy.

STEP-BY-STEP PROCEDURES

Presented herein (and summarized in Table 65.1) are eight guidelines for designing and managing a token economy. Keep in mind that the guidelines are starting points, and that each one will have to be tailored to each participant's specific circumstances, whether alone or in a group.

Step 1: Define the Target Behavior

It is important to clarify exactly what behavior is, and what it is not. In the most simple terms, behavior is what a person says or does. Things people say or do are stated as verbs or action words. "Please," "thank-you," and "excuse me" are actions, as are kicking, running, climbing, and reading. A person does not say or do a bad attitude, laziness, or stubbornness. Terms of that sort must be translated into the observable, concrete actions or behaviors to which they refer.

One approach to defining behavior as observable actions is to think in terms of what a person says or does that leads someone to say, for example, that the person is lazy or stubborn, or has a bad attitude. The lazy child may be called thus because he seldom takes out the trash, feeds the dog, or mows the lawn. The stubborn teenager may refuse to clean her room or obey her curfew, while the student with a bad attitude may never study or complete his homework assignments.

The reason for defining behavior is straightforward: The sole purpose of designing and maintaining a token economy is to change a person's behavior. Knowing exactly what behavior, or behaviors, will be targeted for change is therefore critical to that purpose. Clear, concise, and easy-to-understand definitions are preferred over vague or ambiguous definitions or definitions that are subject to change or interpretation. Indeed, arguments over whether a behavior has occurred ordinarily center on imprecise or capricious definitions. Disputes may be avoided by making sure that everyone agrees on what does and does not constitute the target behavior. When disputes occur, be prepared to clarify or revise the definition of the target behavior in question.

Some token economies have a penalty component, technically termed a *response cost.* It is essentially a punishing consequence for inappropriate or undesirable behavior: When the offending behavior occurs, reinforcers—the tokens in a token economy—are taken away immediately. The intended effect is to reduce or eliminate future occurrences of the behavior to which the response-cost penalty applies. The inappropriate or undesirable behavior targeted for reduction or elimination in this way must be clearly and unambiguously defined and distinguished from the appropriate or desirable behavior that will be increased or established by other, more positive means.[1]

Step 2: Specify the Setting

Because a person's behavior is always a matter of time and place, it is important to be clear on exactly when and where the token economy will and will not operate. The teacher who uses a token economy to increase the rate at which a student solves simple subtraction problems is restricting the economy to a certain activity (arithmetic) and probably to a certain place (a desk), and perhaps as well to a certain time of the day (say, morning). The teacher may decide to expand or contract the time and place that the token economy operates, and may even suspend the token economy for a while, for example, to see how

accurate her student performs on the subtraction problems without the token economy in place. Whatever the case, make sure to specify the time and place that the token economy will and will not operate.

Step 3: Select Tokens

The tokens in a token economy are just that—tokens. Technically, they are *conditioned reinforcers* that are to a token economy what money is to an economy more generally. The best tokens are durable, inexpensive to make or buy, and easy to handle and store.

A token economy can be an easy mark for counterfeiters and other saboteurs. It is always good practice to make it impossible for unauthorized persons to duplicate tokens. (Points or stars on a sheet of paper, poker chips, and the like should be used with caution, as these and similar other tokens are fairly easy to find, make, or copy.) It is also good practice to preempt a related problem: stealing tokens. This can be prevented by using tokens, for example, that are color coded by days of the week or that bear the name or initials of the person to whom the tokens belong. If subversive activities occur, then consequences must be in place to discourage the person responsible from making the same or a similar mistake in the future. Steps must be taken as well to prevent others from behaving in ways that undermine the token economy.

Step 4: Identify Back-Up Reinforcers

By themselves, tokens, like money, have no value. Tokens gain in value, as does money, when they can be used to buy an assortment of things and activities. The things and activities that tokens buy, and that literally back up the tokens, are called *back-up reinforcers,* or simply *back-ups.*

It is vital to the success of a token economy to back up the tokens with tangible things and activities. The challenge is to identify exactly what those things and activities are for a particular person. Fortunately, there are ways to do that, with each way more or less tailored for the person for whom the token economy is created. For example, with typically developing children and adults, it may be sufficient simply to ask them

---

1. A restriction on the length of this chapter prevents us from any further discussion of response cost. The context is here, however, for the careful reader to see how a response-cost component might be used (and abused) in a token economy.

what they would like to work toward. With children and adults with delays or deficiencies in their behavior development, it may be necessary either to interview a parent or caregiver or to conduct what is termed a *reinforcer preference assessment* in order to identify their own unique, individually effective back-ups.

Whatever the method used to identify back-ups, keep in mind, first, that people will ordinarily work for tokens in exchange for the things that they normally enjoy doing, such as snacking, watching television, listening to music, or talking on the phone; and second, that people will work even harder for the things that they do not ordinarily do but would enjoy doing, such as staying up late, going to the movies, spending the night with a friend, or using the family car.

Step 5: Determine a Schedule of Token Reinforcement

The matter of determining a schedule of token reinforcement raises two questions: (1) How many tokens should be given for appropriate or desirable behavior? and (2) how often should tokens be given? The answer to the first question is, it depends. That is, the amount of tokens a person earns by performing any one of a number of target behaviors depends on the relative merit or importance that is attached to each behavior. This is a personal judgment, one that is ordinarily made by those who design and manage the token economy.

As to how often token should be given, the general rule is that the more frequent a behavior occurs, the fewer tokens are earned. The reciprocal rule—less-frequent behavior earns more tokens—also applies. It is also important to make sure that the person earns enough tokens to make it worth his or her while in terms of being able to exchange tokens for back-ups.

In the early phases of the token economy, it is best to present tokens immediately following each and every occurrence of a target behavior. However, sometimes a target behavior should occur only under certain circumstances. The parents of a child who identify taking out the trash as a target behavior may find that their child takes out the trash several times a day without regard to how much trash is in the container. Avoid-

ing those sorts of problems is usually a matter of specifying the conditions under which tokens may and may not be earned.

The practice of giving tokens for all occurrences of a target behavior may eventually be relaxed. By "relaxed" we mean that once a target behavior is occurring regularly and appropriately, tokens may be given intermittently, say, after every third or fourth instance of the behavior (ratio, or response-based, token reinforcement) or after every minute or so of continuously performing the behavior (interval, or time-based, token reinforcement). Either way, the main advantage of this practice follows from the finding that intermittently reinforced behavior is more durable and persistent than is behavior that is always or continuously reinforced. Put another way, it is possible, and often desirable, to get a person to do more with less frequent or fewer reinforcements.

The move from continuous to intermittent token reinforcement must be made with care. "Lean" the schedule slowly or gradually, and be alert for undesirable changes in either or both the quantity and quality of the target behavior. Parents may move their child too quickly, for example, from earning one token for every 5 min spent studying to earning one token for every 30 min spent studying. Under the strain of suddenly having to work longer or harder for the same token amount, the child may become inattentive or careless, or may simply stop studying altogether. Gradual increases in the amount of time or the number of times a target behavior occurs before a token is earned should prevent that sort of undesirable change from occurring.

Giving tokens on an intermittent basis has the practical advantage of having to keep only a relatively small number of tokens on hand to dispense. It has the advantage, too, of keeping the number of tokens that a person earns or can save relatively low. This becomes important when faced with the challenge of making sure that tokens keep their value.

Tokens may lose their value when there are too many, or too few, tokens in circulation. When a person earns as many or more tokens than are needed to exchange for a back-up, there is no reason for that person to continue working and earning additional tokens. Similarly, when a person cannot earn the tokens that are needed to exchange for a back-up, there is no reason for that person to continue or even to begin to work for it. These problems relate, respectively, to the admonition that there be no millionaires (so to speak) or impoverished persons in a token economy. Preventing or remediating problems of that sort is often a matter of establishing an appropriate exchange rate for the token economy.

Step 6: Establish an Exchange Rate

The *exchange rate* in a token economy specifies exactly how many tokens are needed to buy exactly how much or how many of the things and activities constitute the back-ups. Determining the cost in tokens of each back-up is therefore an integral and ongoing part of a token economy.

One way to establish an exchange rate is to begin by determining the maximum number of tokens that a person can earn, say, in one day. With that figure in hand, set the cost for each back-up according to these guidelines: (1) The most preferred or highly valued back-up should be expensive, but not so expensive that the person will never earn enough tokens for an exchange. (2) The least preferred or lowest valued back-up should be inexpensive, but not so inexpensive that the person can quickly or easily earn enough tokens for an exchange. (3) Moderately preferred or valued back-ups should be at the median, neither too expensive or too inexpensive.

To illustrate how an exchange rate might be established, suppose that Janice, a typically developing preadolescent, can earn a maximum of four tokens each day for performing four after-dinner kitchen chores. If Janice's most preferred back-up for the moment is a one-night weekend sleepover at her girlfriend's house, then the cost for that back-up might be set at four tokens, meaning that she must do all four of her chores in one day in exchange for spending the night at her friend's house. A back-up with momentarily less value, say, a ride to school one morning, might cost one token, meaning that she must do at least one of her four chores in a day, for instance, loading and starting the dishwasher. With this rate, the number of tokens Janice earns is proportional both to the amount of work she must do to earn tokens and to the cost of the back-ups.

Step 7: Establish a Place and Time to Exchange Tokens

It is important to be clear on the time and place that tokens can be exchanged for back-ups. As to time, exchanges should occur frequently in the early stages of the token economy, when the rules of the system are being learned and the reinforcing value of the tokens in relation to their back-ups are being established. Later stages may enforce less-frequent exchanges.

Increasing the time between earning tokens and exchanging them for back-ups is often a worthy goal, one that capitalizes on the increase in the value of the back-ups that ordinarily occurs when a person has infrequent access to them. The main advantage of this practice is that it encourages a person to continue earning tokens between exchanges. An added benefit is that as tokens are being earned between exchanges, praise, attention, approval, and other consequences that typically or naturally accompany or follow the target behavior may acquire reinforcing properties. Providing natural consequences in addition to tokens is especially important when the eventual goal is to prepare a person to return to a token-free environment.

A convenient place or location where a person can go to exchange tokens for back-ups must also be determined. The arrangement may be formal or informal. A "store" at the back of a classroom displaying back-ups and their prices and staffed at set times by the teacher's aide who collects tokens, dispenses back-ups, and records exchanges is a far more formal arrangement than, say, a parent's sit-down with her two children in the living room to handle the day's exchanges. Whether formal or informal, it is important to decide where exchanges will take place, and, wherever that place may be, to have the back-ups, and their costs, available and in plain sight.

Step 8: Keep Records

At a minimum, objective records should be kept continuously on (1) the number of tokens earned by a person for each and every target behavior; (2) the number of tokens a person exchanges at any one time; (3) exactly what back-ups were purchased, and when; and (4) the token cost of the

TABLE 65.1   Guidelines for Designing and Managing a Token Economy

1. Define the behaviors targeted for change in clear, concise, unambiguous action words.

2. Specify the setting or settings in which the token economy will and will not operate.

3. Select tokens that are durable, inexpensive, easy to handle and store, and hard to forge.

4. Identify back-ups that are effective for each person.

5. Determine a schedule of token reinforcement for each target behavior.

6. Establish an exchange rate for tokens and back-ups.

7. Decide when and where tokens may be exchanged for back-ups.

8. Keep continuous records on tokens earned and exchanges made by each person.

back-ups. Records of which target behaviors are on what schedule of token reinforcement should also be kept. Records on other aspects of the token economy should be kept as well, as needed, to ensure that the token economy is being properly and efficiently administered, and most important, to ensure that the token economy is maximally effective in producing and maintaining significant behavioral gains.

Table 65.1 contains the eight guidelines for designing and managing a token economy. Use the table as a checklist, making sure that each guideline is in place for the duration of the token economy.

Further Reading

We recommend studying the research on the token economy, both while designing a token economy and while managing one over time. In addition to the surveys presented in modern textbooks in applied behavior analysis, books by Ayllon and Azrin (1968), Kazdin (1977), and Leitenberg (1976) are especially helpful resources. The books also contain a wealth of references to specific applications of a token economy, for example, to children in a classroom setting. Research on specific populations and settings are invaluable sources for guidance on how practitioners can best design and manage token economies to suit their own particular circumstances.

References

Ayllon, T., & Azrin, N. H. (1965). The measurement and reinforcement of behavior of psychotics. *Journal of the Experimental Analysis of Behavior, 8,* 357–383.

Ayllon, T., & Azrin, N. H. (1968). *The token economy: A motivational system for therapy and rehabilitation.* New York: Appleton-Century-Crofts.

Kazdin, A. E. (1977). *The token economy: A review and evaluation.* New York: Plenum.

Kazdin, A. E. (1982). The token economy: An evaluative review. *Journal of Applied Behavior Analysis, 15,* 431–445.

Kazdin, A. E. (1994). *Behavior modification in applied settings.* Pacific Grove, CA: Brookes/Cole.

Leitenberg, H. (1976). *Handbook of behavior modification and behavior therapy.* Englewood Cliffs, NJ: Prentice-Hall.

Miltenberger, R. G. (2001). *Behavior modification: Principles and procedures.* Belmont, CA: Wadsworth.

Sulzer-Azaroff, B., & Mayer, G. R. (1991). *Behavior analysis for lasting change.* Fort Worth, TX: Holt, Rinehart, & Winston.

66

TREATMENT OF INSOMNIA: THE USE OF COGNITIVE-BEHAVIORAL TECHNIQUES

Henry J. Orff, Michael T. Smith,Carla Jungquist, and Michael L. Perlis

BACKGROUND

Insomnia affects a staggering number of people. Approximately 5 to 35% of the population of the United States report sleep disturbance problems at some point in their lives (Ford & Kamerow, 1989; Gallup Organization, 1995; Mellinger, Balter, & Uhlenhuth, 1985) and approximately 10 to 15% of the U.S. population, more than 27 million people, suffer from persistent insomnia (Ancoli-Israel & Roth, 1999). The day-to-day cost of insomnia is not limited to fitful sleep. Insomnia is, as one might expect, associated with diminished quality of life, poorer work performance, and increased absenteeism. Insomnia is also associated with increased vulnerability for medical conditions (Wingard & Berkman, 1983), psychiatric disorders, risk for automobile accidents, and increased health care utilization (Kupperman, Lubeck, & Mazonson, 1995).

Given the personal and societal costs of insomnia, it follows that this is a disorder that should be aggressively treated. Fortunately, there are a variety of cognitive and behavioral interventions that are empirically validated and target insomnia as a clearly defined disease entity.

THE COGNITIVE-BEHAVIORAL MODEL OF INSOMNIA

The cognitive-behavioral model, as originally put forth by Spielman and colleagues (Spielman, Caruso, & Glovinsky, 1987), posits that insomnia occurs acutely in relation to both trait and precipitating factors. Thus, an individual may be prone to insomnia due to trait characteristics, but experiences actual episodes because of precipitating factors. The acute insomnia becomes subchronic when it is reinforced by maladaptive coping strategies. These strategies, in turn, result in conditioned arousal and chronic insomnia (e.g., Spielman et al.). A graphic for this model is presented in Figure 66.1.

Trait factors extend across the entire biopsychosocial spectrum. Biological factors include hyperarousal or hyper-reactivity. Psychological factors include worry or the tendency to be excessively ruminative. Social factors, although rarely a focus at the theoretical level, include such things as the bed partner's keeping an incompatible sleep schedule or social pressures to sleep according to a nonpreferred sleep schedule. Precipitating factors, as the name implies, are acute occurrences that constitute life stress events.

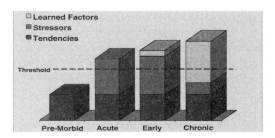

FIGURE 66.1   The Nature of Insomnia Over Time

Source: Adapted from Spielman, Caruso, & Glovinsky (1987).

When an insomnia episode is initiated there are a variety of maladaptive strategies that individuals adopt in the attempt to get more sleep. Research and treatment have focused on two in particular: excessive time in bed and the practice of staying in bed while awake. Excessive time in bed refers to the tendency of patients with insomnia to go to bed earlier and/or to get out of bed later. Such changes are enacted in order to increase the opportunity to get more sleep. These behaviors, however, lead to decreased sleep efficiency. That is, when the opportunity to sleep exceeds basal ability to generate sleep, the consequence is more frequent (and longer) awakenings. The practice of staying in bed while awake, as with the prior strategy, is enacted to increase the opportunity to get more sleep. In addition, the practice is often adopted under the rationale that staying in bed is at least restful. While it is a seemingly reasonable behavior, staying in bed while awake leads to an association of the bed and bedroom with arousal, not sleepiness and sleep. That is, when confronted with stimuli that are typically associated with sleep, they elicit arousal responses via classical conditioning. The two maladaptive behaviors are likely to occur concurrently and promote one another. Excessive time in bed increases the likelihood that the individual will be awake while in bed. Being awake while in bed increases the likelihood that the individual will attempt to get more sleep by increasing sleep opportunity. The end result is conditioned arousal during the traditional sleep period and chronic insomnia.

The Spielman model of insomnia has received a fair amount of empirical support and the therapies that are derived from its principles appear to be effective, both in comparison to placebo conditions (Murtagh & Greenwood, 1995) and compared to pharmacologic interventions (Smith et al., 2002).

WHO MIGHT BENEFIT FROM THIS TREATMENT

Cognitive-behavioral treatments can be employed with patients who are classified as having primary insomnia. As well, individuals with secondary insomnia may also benefit from cognitive-behavioral-style treatments. This then raises the question, "How is insomnia defined?"

The American Psychiatric Association's nosology (the *Diagnostic and Statistical Manual of Mental Disorders, fourth edition*, or *DSM-IV*; APA, 1994) includes a formal diagnosis of Primary Insomnia under the category of dyssomnias. The dyssomnias include problems of initiating or maintaining sleep or of excessive sleepiness characterized by disturbances associated with the amount, quality, timing, or perception of sleep. The *DSM-IV* diagnostic criteria for Primary Insomnia (307.42) requires the following: (1) the predominant complaint of difficulty in initiating or maintaining sleep, or nonrestorative sleep, for at least 1 month; (2) that the sleep disturbance (or associated daytime fatigue) causes clinically significant distress or impairment in social, occupational, or other important areas of functioning; (3) that the sleep disturbance does not occur exclusively during the course of another sleep disorder (e.g., narcolepsy, breathing-related sleep disorder, circadian rhythm sleep disorder, or a parasomnia, etc.); and (4) that the disturbance is not due to the direct physiological effects of a substance (e.g., a drug of abuse, a medication) or another psychiatric or general medical condition.

The American Academy of Sleep Medicine uses its own nosology (International Classification of Sleep Disorders, or ICSD; ASDA, 1991). Within this classification system the *DSM-IV* definition of "primary" insomnia is further refined. Of the three subtypes of insomnia (Psychophysiological, Sleep State Misperception, and Idiopathic Insomnia.), two are classified based on the factors that are thought to contribute to the occurrence and/or severity of the disorder (Psychophysiological Insomnia and Idiopathic Insomnia). The remaining subtype (Sleep State Misperception) is reserved for a small subset of patients who have an extreme discrepancy between their subjective report of insomnia and traditional polysomnographic findings, which demonstrate normal sleep macrostructure (architecture).

Psychophysiological Insomnia, as characterized by the ICSD, is a disorder of somaticized tension and learned sleep-preventing associations that leads to difficulties initiating and/or maintaining sleep, excessive daytime fatigue, and complaints of impaired daytime function (e.g., concentration and memory difficulties).

Sleep State Misperception Insomnia (SSMI) is a disorder in which the complaint of insomnia and/or nonrestorative sleep occurs without objective evidence of a sleep disturbance. Complaints of poor sleep in these individuals appear to be clinically genuine, yet polysomnographic (PSG) or actigraphic measures of sleep do not reveal sleep-continuity or sleep-architecture disturbances. This condition, unlike that of Psychophysiologic Insomnia, requires PSG or actigraphic measures to establish the diagnosis.

Idiopathic Insomnia is a lifelong and unremitting inability to obtain adequate sleep that is presumably due to an abnormality of the neurological control of the sleep-wake system. Idiopathic insomnia usually is present at birth and necessarily by early childhood. This disorder may be due to heritable neurochemical imbalances within the ascending reticular activating system (arousal), the raphe nuclei, and/or the medial forebrain areas.

Most classification schemes (regardless of the type of insomnia) do not specify criteria for (1) how much wakefulness (prior to desired sleep onset or during the night) is considered abnormal, (2) how little total sleep must be obtained to fall outside the normal range, or (3) how frequently these difficulties must occur to be considered pathologic. With respect to how much wakefulness, most clinicians and investigators consider 30 or more minutes to fall asleep and/or 30 or more minutes of wakefulness after sleep onset to represent the threshold between normal and abnormal sleep. With respect to how much sleep, many are reluctant to fix a value for this pa-

rameter. In part, establishing such a value is difficult because representing what is pathological with one number is too confounded by factors like age, prior sleep, and the individual's basal level of sleep need. As well, such values can be misleading as it is also possible that an individual can experience profound sleep initiation or maintenance problems in the absence of sleep loss. For those who are inclined to set minimums, most specify that the amount of sleep obtained on a regular basis be equal to or less than either 6.5 or 6.0 hours per night. Finally, there is also no fixed benchmark for frequency. Most investigators require that the subjects experience problems on three or more nights per week, but this may have more to do with increasing the odds of studying the occurrence of the disorder in laboratory than an inherent belief that less than three nights per week is normal.

OTHER ISSUES TO CONSIDER IN MAKING A DIFFERENTIAL DIAGNOSIS OF INSOMNIA

As noted previously, it is also important to distinguish primary insomnia from secondary insomnia in the clinical evaluation of the patient. As a secondary disorder or as a symptom of other disorders, the inability to fall asleep or stay asleep, or the tendency to awaken early in the morning, may be related to a variety of factors including primary medical or psychiatric conditions, drug use or abuse, or other extrinsic or intrinsic sleep disorders. A careful clinical history is required to determine if any of these factors may account for the patient's symptoms. Typical medical exclusions include untreated or unstable gastrointestinal disorders (e.g., gastroesophageal reflux disease, or GERD), cardiopulmonary disorders (e.g., heart disease), and neuroendocrine disorders (e.g., estrogen deficiency). Typical psychiatric exclusions include untreated or unstable affective or anxiety disorders. Typical drug use or abuse exclusions include the use of medications and recreational drugs that have insomnia as a direct effect or as a withdrawal effect. Typical sleep-disorder exclusions include other intrinsic sleep disorders (e.g., sleep apnea), circadian rhythm disorders (e.g., shift-work sleep disorder), and extrinsic sleep disorders (e.g. inadequate sleep hygiene).

While most investigators are willing to make the distinction between primary and secondary insomnia, some have suggested that insomnia should not be defined as a separate disorder and that it is, in fact, always secondary to other disorders. This position carries with it the implication that if the parent disorder is treated, the secondary insomnia will resolve. While this has not been put to a clear empirical test, clinical experience suggests that while medical and psychiatric disorders may precipitate insomnia, the sleep initiation and maintenance problems often persist after the parent conditions are stable or resolved.

THE TREATMENT OF INSOMNIA

In general there are three main types of therapy that can be employed, from a behavioral standpoint, to deal with chronic insomnia (in order of priority): stimulus control, sleep restriction, and sleep hygiene therapies. These therapies and the session-to-session clinical regimen are described next.

Standard Therapy: Sleep Restriction, Stimulus Control, and Sleep Hygiene

Stimulus Control Therapy

Stimulus control therapy is considered to be the first-line behavioral treatment for chronic Primary Insomnia and therefore should be prioritized accordingly (Chesson et al., 2000; Chapter 56, this volume). Stimulus control instructions limit the amount of time patients spend awake in bed or the bedroom and are designed to decondition presleep arousal. Typical instructions include the following: (1) keep a fixed wake time 7 days per week, irrespective of how much sleep you get during the night; (2) avoid any behavior in the bed or bedroom other than sleep or sexual activity; (3) sleep only in the bedroom; (4) leave the bedroom when awake for approximately 15 to 20 min; (5) return only when sleepy. The combination of these instructions reestablishes the bed and bedroom as

strong cues for sleep and entrains the circadian sleep-wake cycle to the desired phase.

Sleep Restriction

Sleep estriction therapy (SRT) requires patients to limit the amount of time they spend in bed to an amount equal to their average total sleep time. In order to accomplish this, the clinician works with the patient to (1) establish a fixed wake time and (2) decrease sleep opportunity by prescribing a later bedtime. Initially, the therapy results in a reduction in total sleep time, but over the course of several days, results in decreased sleep latency, and decreased wake time after sleep onset. As sleep efficiency increases, patients are instructed to gradually increase the amount of time they spend in bed. In practice, patients roll back their bedtime in 15-min increments, given sleep diary data that show that on the prior week the patient's sleep was efficient (85% or more of the time spent in bed was spent asleep [total sleep time/time in bed]). This therapy is thought to be effective for two reasons. First, it prevents patients from coping with their insomnia by extending sleep opportunity. This strategy, while increasing the opportunity to get more sleep, produces a form of sleep that is shallow and fragmented. Second, the initial sleep loss that occurs with SRT is thought to increase the pressure for sleep, which in turn produces quicker sleep latencies, less wake after sleep onset, and more efficient sleep. It should be noted that the treatment has a paradoxical aspect to it. Patients who report being unable to sleep are in essence being told to sleep less. Such a prescription needs to be delivered with care and compliance must be monitored. Sleep restriction should typically be limited to no less than 5 hours of sleep opportunity. As well, sleep restriction is contraindicated in patients with histories of mania or seizure disorder, because it may aggravate these conditions.

Sleep Hygiene

Sleep hygiene requires that the clinician and patient review a set of instructions that are geared toward helping the patient maintain good sleep habits (see Table 66.1). It should be noted that sleep hygiene instructions are not helpful when provided as a monotherapy (Lacks & Morin,

TABLE 66.1   Sleep Hygiene Instructions

Instruction	Rationale
1. Sleep only as much as you need to feel refreshed during the following day.	Restricting your time in bed helps to consolidate and deepen your sleep. Excessively long times in bed lead to fragmented and shallow sleep. Get up at your regular time the next day, no matter how little you slept.
2. Get up at the same time each day, 7 days a week.	A regular wake time in the morning leads to regular times of sleep onset, and helps to set your biological clock.
3. Exercise regularly.	Schedule exercise times so that they do not occur within 3 hours of when you intend to go to bed. Exercise makes it easier to initiate sleep and deepen sleep.
4. Make sure your bedroom is comfortable and free from light and noise.	A comfortable, noise-free sleep environment will reduce the likelihood that you will wake up during the night. Noise that does not awaken you may nonetheless disturb the quality of your sleep. Installing carpeting and insulated curtains, and closing the door, may help.
5. Make sure that your bedroom is at a comfortable sleep temperature during the night.	Excessively warm or cold sleep environments may disturb sleep.
6. Eat regular meals and do not go to bed hungry.	Hunger may disturb sleep. A light snack at bedtime (especially carbohydrates) may help sleep, but avoid greasy or heavy foods.
7. Avoid excessive liquids in the evening.	Reducing liquid intake will minimize the need for nighttime trips to the bathroom.
8. Cut down on all caffeine products.	Caffeinated beverages and foods (coffee, tea, cola, chocolate) can cause difficulty falling asleep, awakenings during the night, and shallow sleep. Even caffeine consumed early in the day can disrupt nighttime sleep.
9. Avoid alcohol, especially in the evening.	Although alcohol helps tense people fall asleep more easily, it causes awakenings later in the night.
10. Be aware that smoking may disturb sleep.	Nicotine is a stimulant. Try not to smoke during the night when you have trouble sleeping.
11. Don't take your problems to bed.	Plan some time earlier in the evening for working on your problems or planning the next day's activities. Worrying may interfere with initiating sleep and produce shallow sleep.
12. Train yourself to use the bedroom only for sleeping and sexual activity.	This will help condition your brain to see bed as the place for sleeping. Do not read, watch TV, or eat in bed.
13. Do not *try* to fall asleep.	This only makes the problem worse. Instead, turn on the light, leave the bedroom, and do something different like reading a book. Don't engage in stimulating activity. Return to bed only when you are sleepy.
14. Put the clock under the bed or turn it so that you can't see it.	Clock watching may lead to frustration, anger, and worry, which interfere with sleep.
15. Avoid naps.	Staying awake during the day helps you to fall asleep at night.

Note: This list includes the usual practices described as good sleep hygiene, but it also includes some principles subsumed under *Stimulus Control Therapy, Sleep Restriction Therapy,* and *Relaxation.*

1992) and might be even less helpful when provided as written instructions that are not tailored to the individual or are cast in absolute terms. With respect to the former, providing patients with a handout (especially without an explanation of the clinical science behind the issues) undermines patient compliance. With respect to the latter, sleep hygiene instructions have within them several absolute dictums (e.g., "Avoid caffeinated products" and "Do not nap"). Both of these instructions are too simple. For example, caffeine may be used to combat some of the daytime sequale of insomnia and withdrawal from the substance, if timed appropriately, may actually enhance subjects' ability to fall asleep more quickly. Napping may be useful to sustain high levels of daytime function and performance. Such a compensatory strategy, however, should only be allowed provided that time to bed is delayed.

STEP-BY-STEP PROCEDURES

Session 1: Clinical Evaluation and 2-Week Baseline

During this session, the patient's sleep complaints are reviewed with the clinician responsible for treatment and the patient is instructed to keep a sleep diary for a baseline period of 2 weeks. All subjects are carefully instructed on how to complete this measure. Diaries can be commenced simultaneously with treatment for other existing conditions or in conjunction with sleep medication usage. Note that Session 2 is scheduled 2 weeks after Session 1; all other sessions are scheduled at 1-week intervals.

Session 2: Sleep Restriction and Stimulus Control Therapy

Baseline sleep diary data are reviewed. This information sets the parameters for sleep restriction therapy and guides the patient toward the treatment to be prescribed. The standard approach is interactive and didactic. The patient and the clinician evaluate the data together. After reviewing the data and identifying basic assumptions, most patients easily deduce what might represent a good counterstrategy. The primary assumption most patients identify is what we call the *positive correlation fallacy:* the more time in bed, the more sleep one will get. When the patient has identified one or more components of therapy, the clinician explains in detail the rationale and procedures for sleep restriction and stimulus control therapy (discussed previously).

Session 3: Sleep Hygiene and Sleep Restriction Therapy Adjustments

As with all sessions, sleep diary data are reviewed and charted. The upward titration process is begun and sleep hygiene instructions are reviewed by having the patient read aloud the various imperatives and the corresponding rationales. After the patient and the clinician have identified the relevance of the issue, the clinician reviews in more detail the basic concepts and related clinical research. The amount of, and manner in which, information is presented varies according to patient interest.

Session 4: Sleep Restriction Therapy Adjustments

Sleep diary data are reviewed and charted. Upward titration continues.

Session 5: Sleep Restriction Therapy Adjustments and Cognitive Restructuring

Sleep diary data are reviewed and charted. Upward titration continues. In this session, a Barlow-style approach to decatastrophization (Barlow, 1992) procedure is used. The clinician should address the perception of dire consequences from sleep loss, using a form of cognitive restructuring. This involves reviewing the worst possible outcome scenarios and exploring the mismatch between the certainty that there will be negative outcomes and the frequency with which such events actually occur.

Session 6: Sleep Restriction Therapy Adjustments

Sleep diary data are reviewed and charted. Upward titration continues.

Session 7: Sleep Restriction Therapy Adjustments

Sleep diary data are reviewed and charted. Upward titration continues.

Session 8: Relapse Prevention

This last session is largely psychoeducational. The clinician reviews (1) the question of how insomnia gets started and the strategies that maintain poor sleep, and (2) the strategies that are likely to abort an extended episode of insomnia.

ADJUNCTIVE OR ALTERNATIVE THERAPIES

In addition to these principal behavioral techniques, there are also several adjunctive therapies that may prove helpful to the patient and can be included in the treatment plan: relaxation training, phototherapy, and cognitive therapy.

Relaxation Training

Different relaxation techniques target different physiological systems. *Progressive muscle relax-*

ation is used to diminish skeletal muscle tension. *Diaphragmatic breathing* is used to make breathing slower and shallower and resembles the form of breathing, interestingly, that naturally occurs at sleep onset. *Autogenics training* focuses on increasing peripheral blood flow. Most practitioners select the optimal relaxation method based upon which technique is easiest for the patient to learn, which is most consistent with how the patient manifests arousal, and which technique is not contraindicated by medical conditions (e.g., progressive muscle relaxation might not be an ideal choice for patients with certain neuromuscular disorders).

Phototherapy

There is substantial empirical evidence that bright light has antidepressant and sleep-promoting effects. The sleep-promoting effects of bright light may occur via several mechanisms, including shifting the circadian system; enhancement of the amplitude of the circadian pacemaker, promoting wakefulness during the day and sleep at night; or indirectly, via its antidepressant effects. In practice, bright light is used to shorten or lengthen the diurnal phase of the patient's day. In the case where the patient's insomnia has a phase delay component (i.e., the patient prefers to go to bed late and wake up late) bright light exposure in the morning for a period of time may enable the patient to feel sleepy at an earlier time in the evening. In the case where the patient's insomnia has a phase advance component (i.e., the patient prefers to go to bed early and wake up early) bright light exposure after dark may enable the patient to stay awake later and wake up later. It is generally assumed that phototherapy has no significant side effects, but this is not always the case. Mania may be triggered by bright light in patients not previously diagnosed with Bipolar Disorder. Other side effects include insomnia, hypomania, agitation, visual blurring, eye strain, and headaches. Individuals with eye-related problems or who are at risk for such conditions such as diabetes should consult an eye care specialist prior to initiating light therapy.

Cognitive Therapy

Several forms of cognitive therapy for insomnia have been developed. Some have a didactic focus (Morin, 1993), others use paradoxical intention (Shoham-Salomon & Rosenthal, 1987), and others use a form of cognitive restructuring (Buysse & Perlis, 1996). While the approaches differ in procedure, all are based on the observation that patients with insomnia have negative thoughts and beliefs about their condition and its consequences. Helping patients challenge the veracity of these beliefs is thought to decrease the anxiety and arousal associated with insomnia.

TECHNIQUES FOR DEALING WITH CLIENT NONCOMPLIANCE

Cognitive behavior therapy (CBT) techniques for insomnia can be challenging for both the client and the practitioner. This may be particularly true early in the therapeutic process as the client will be asked to accept a difficult regimen of behavioral change and concomitant sleep deprivation. Sleep loss alone may try the patience of a client and this makes compliance with any therapeutic modality a problematic issue. There are, however, some strategies (most based in clinical experience) that may enhance the likelihood of a successful clinical outcome. Examples of these techniques include the following:

1. *Good "salesmanship" (a motivational approach to therapy)*. There is no more important a method than the demonstration of a good knowledge base regarding (in general) sleep medicine and (in specific) the principles behind the behavioral interventions. Patients will often have challenging questions regarding the procedures. Clear and compelling explanations go a long way toward gaining patient trust and compliance. Sharing information about the clinical efficacy and effectiveness of treatment can often be powerful in obtaining compliance.

2. *A Socratic versus pedantic approach to patient education*. It is also important to educate and work with the client throughout the treatment process. Whenever possible, clients should be

led to answers that they "discover" rather than being told the concepts or what to do. This process will reduce patient resistance, particularly in reactant patients or in patients that are not treatment naive.

3. *Realistic goal setting.* It is of great importance for the therapist to understand the goals of the client and determine whether and how they can be realistically met. Such evaluation of the client should include a discussion of life circumstances, since it would be unwise to start a client through treatment at a time when personal situations may make compliance an issue. It also important to make clients aware from the very first session that CBT will be difficult and that they will get worse before they get better.

4. *A scientific approach to treatment.* Finally, it may be helpful to keep graphs of client progress throughout treatment. Rewarding clients by showing them their progress graphically from week to week makes the process more tangible and has the effect of proving to clients that the treatment is working and that they are gaining control over their problem and achieving success.

EFFICACY OF COGNITIVE-BEHAVIORAL TREATMENT STRATEGIES

As for the clinical efficacy of the behavioral approach, there is clear evidence that the treatment modality is effective and that the clinical gains are comparable to those produced by hypnotics. When behavioral treatments are employed and sleep hygiene instructions followed, very good long-term results have been obtained in the improvement of sleep for those who suffer from chronic sleep problems (Murtagh and Greenwood, 1995). In a recent meta-analysis (Morin, Culbert, & Schwartz, 1994), a 32 to 41% improvement in sleep was observed when using behavioral strategies. Sleep latency was reduced by 39 to 43%, number of awakenings was reduced by 30 to 73%, duration of awakenings was reduced by 46%, and total sleep time was increased by 8.0 to 9.4%. In real numbers this amounted to patients falling asleep 24 to 28 min sooner, experiencing 0.5 to 1.2 fewer awakenings during the night, and

getting about 30 to 32 more minutes of sleep at night. These outcomes are comparable to the gains that can be obtained with medication, and in the case of sleep initiation difficulties may actually be superior to pharmacotherapy (Smith et al., 2002).

CONCLUSION

Sleep is thought to be essential to many vital processes, including, but not limited to, physiologic restoration, immune system function, memory consolidation, and mood. Without good quality and quantity sleep, the careful balance that exits in these many complex systems is susceptible to dysregualtion.

Insomnia represents one of the more ubiquitous forms of sleep disturbance. Unfortunately, despite its prevalence and associated negative sequelae, only a small fraction of patients seek out treatment or have access to behavioral sleep medicine specialists This is especially unfortunate given the existence of multiple forms of effective therapy. We hope the material presented in this chapter highlights the need to treat insomnia, provides health care professionals with information on the techniques employed by behavioral sleep medicine specialists, and presents enough information so as to allow clinicians to decide whether to refer patients to a specialist or to seek specific training in this form of CBT treatment. While this chapter provides a good introduction to the CBT of insomnia, the chapter cannot provide a good substitute for mentored clinical experience. We would like to encourage those interested in developing an expertise in the CBT treatment of insomnia to seek out additional training in behavioral sleep medicine through accredited fellowship and CME programs.

Further Reading

Hauri, P. (1991). *Case studies in insomnia.* New York: Plenum Publishers.

Morin, C. M. (1993). *Insomnia: Psychological assessment and management.* New York: Guilford Press.

Perlis, M., & Lichstien, K. (Eds.). (In press). *Treating sleep disorders: The principles and practice of behavioral sleep medicine.* Philadelphia: Wiley.

Reference List

American Psychiatric Association. (1994). *Diagnostic and statistical manual of mental disorders* (4th ed.). Washington, DC: American Psychiatric Association.

American Sleep Disorders Association. (1991). *The international classification of sleep disorders: Diagnostic and coding manual.* Rochester, MN.: American Sleep Disorders Association.

Ancoli-Israel, S., & Roth, T. (1999). Characteristics of insomnia in the United States: Results of the 1991 National Sleep Foundation survey. *Sleep, 22*(Suppl 2), S347-S353.

Barlow, D. H. (1992). Cognitive-behavioral approaches to Panic Disorder and Social Phobia. *Bulletin of the Menninger Clinic, 56*(2 Suppl A), A14–28.

Buysse, D. J., & Perlis, M. L. (1996). The evaluation and treatment of insomnia. *Journal of Practicing Psychology and Behavioral Health, 2,* 80–93.

Chesson, A., Jr., Hartse, K., Anderson, W. M., Davila, D., Johnson, S., Littner, M., Wise, M., & Rafecas, J. (2000). Practice parameters for the evaluation of chronic insomnia. An American Academy of Sleep Medicine report. Standards of Practice Committee of the American Academy of Sleep Medicine. *Sleep, 23*(2), 237-241.

Ford, D. E., & Kamerow, D. B. (1989). Comments to "Epidemiologic study of sleep disturbances and psychiatric disorders: An opportunity for prevention?" *Journal of the American Medical Association, 262,* 1479-1484.

Gallup Organization. (1995). *Sleep in America.* Princeton, NJ: Gallup Organization.

Kupperman, M., Lubeck, D. P., & Mazonson, P. D. (1995). Sleep problems and their correlates in a working population. *Journal of General Internal Medicine, 10,* 25–32.

Lacks, P., & Morin, C. M. (1992). Review of "Recent advances in the assessment and treatment of insomnia." *Journal of Consulting and Clinical Psychology, 60,* 586–594.

Mellinger, G. D., Balter, M. B., & Uhlenhuth, E. H. (1985). Insomnia and its treatment: Prevalence and correlates. *Archives of General Psychiatry, 42,* 225–232.

Morin, C. M. (1993). *Insomnia: Psychological assessment and management.* New York: Guilford Press.

Morin, C. M., Culbert, J. P., & Schwartz, S. M. (1994). Nonpharmacological interventions for insomnia: A meta-analysis of treatment efficacy. *American Journal of Psychiatry, 151,* 1172–1180.

Murtagh, D. R., & Greenwood, K. M. (1995). Identifying effective psychological treatments for insomnia: A meta-analysis. *Journal of Consulting and Clinical Psychology, 63,* 79–89.

Shoham-Salomon, V., & Rosenthal, R. (1987). Paradoxical interventions: A meta-analysis. *Journal of Consulting and Clinical Psychology, 55,* 22–28.

Smith, M. T., Perlis, M. L., Park, A., Smith, M. S., Pennington, J., Giles, D. E., & Buysse, D. J. (2002). Comparative meta-analysis of pharmacotherapy and behavior therapy for persistent insomnia. *American Journal of Psychiatry, 159,* 5–11.

Spielman, A., Caruso, L., & Glovinsky, P. (1987). A behavioral perspective on insomnia treatment. *Psychiatric Clinics of North America, 10,* 541–553.

Wingard, D., & Berkman, L. (1983). Mortality risk associated with sleeping patterns among adults. *Sleep, 6,* 102–107.

67 URGE SURFING

Andy Lloyd

Of the many barriers to a productive and healthy life that people face, urge control may be one of the most daunting (Baumeister, Heatherton & Tice, 1994). Giving in to temptation, whether it is to drugs, irresponsible spending, or infidelity, can have broad negative implications for clients. Many skills have been developed to address such problems within the domain of addictions and habit control. Abstinence-based approaches (e.g., Alcoholics Anonymous), relapse prevention techniques, and urge management techniques (Marlatt & Gordon, 1985) are widely used with clients suffering from addictions. This chapter focuses on urge management, in particular, the skill known as *urge surfing*. Urge surfing has been demonstrated to be an effective component of cognitive behavioral treatment packages (Copeland, Swift, Roffman, & Stephens, 2001). Teaching the client how to urge surf can play an instrumental role in the client's ability to resist the temptations the urge is directed toward (e.g., drinking, smoking, infidelity, etc.).

Urge surfing is a cognitively based urge management technique. In general, urge surfing involves teaching the client a collection of closely related strategies to cope with and overcome urges to behave in ways (e.g., to smoke) that are counter to their therapeutic goals. Clients are taught to treat urges as though they were like waves in the ocean. Urges come on, grow in intensity, and eventually subside just like ocean waves. Moreover, like waves, urges tend to be brief. They do not grow and grow until the client has to do something before they will go away. Urges go away on their own. The only way that urges get stronger is to give in to them. The more an individual acquiesces to urges, the more frequent and strong they may become. Each time an urge is resisted through urge surfing, the urge has been beaten and subsequent urges become less frequent and less intense.

Although urge surfing has elements that can be understood as being avoidance based, it is fundamentally an acceptance strategy. Urge surfing can be viewed as an avoidance skill when the client is most successful with the distraction components of the skill. Clients who are skilled at thinking about something else when an urge strikes, or at engaging in an incompatible behavior when the urge strikes (Azrin & Nunn, 1977), may successfully ride out the urge without fully experiencing its severity. To do this is to avoid fully experiencing the urge. Despite this observation, urge surfing is fundamentally an acceptance skill (see Hayes, Strosahl, & Wilson, 1999, for an example of a prominent acceptance-based intervention strategy). Urge surfing does not combat the urge in order to make it go away. Rather, clients are taught how to fully experience the urge in a different way—that is, to experience the urge for what it is: brief, nonlethal, of relatively predictable course, and most important, defeatable.

CLINICAL POPULATIONS

Urge surfing has been widely used with clients suffering from alcohol and drug dependencies (Copeland, Swift, Roffman, & Stephens, 2001), but its principles could easily be applied to other clinical domains where self-control skills are relevant (e.g., sexual behavior, financial excesses, etc.). It is typically used as a component of larger treatment packages (e.g., Copeland et al.), but there is no clear reason to believe that it could not be used as a stand-alone skill applied to a wide variety of client problems involving the detrimental effects of urges. The skill is readily understandable when delivered along with the ocean-wave metaphor and it can easily be taught within the confines of a 50-min therapy session.

People tend to be their weakest in the face of urges during periods of negative emotional arousal (Prochaska, Norcross, & DiClemente, 1994). These times are referred to as *high-risk situations.* Despite positive therapeutic gains (e.g., abstinence from smoking for many days or weeks), clients are likely to struggle with urges and may experience a lapse or relapse. A *lapse* is defined as an individual, circumscribed event that runs counter to the goal of abstinence. A person who "breaks down" and smokes a cigarette after 2 months of abstinence, but does not pick up the habit again, is said to have experienced a lapse. A *relapse* is defined as a more robust return to the behavior that the client wants to abstain from. A person who gradually starts to smoke again following a period of abstinence has experienced a relapse. Approximately 35% of relapses take place during periods of negative emotional arousal (Prochaska, Norcross, & DiClemente). It is during such situations that urges seem to get the best of us. Clients are more prepared to face these urges utilizing their newly developed urge-surfing skills if they are aware that they are in high-risk situations. Prochaske and colleagues also found that certain cognitive errors lead to relapse:

- Overconfidence (e.g., "I'll have no problem quitting smoking. I've gone a day without cigarettes and it will be a breeze from here on out.")
- Inappropriate self-testing (e.g., "If I keep a

pack of cigarettes with me at all times, then I can truly prove I am strong enough to quit.")
- Self-blaming (e.g., "My drinking ran my family away and ruined my job. It has already ruined my life. What do I have to gain from quitting now?")

These attitudes set the client up for failure in a number of ways. First, by thinking that they've beaten the habit, clients are setting themselves up for a potentially severe letdown when they experience urges for that habit. Second, clients are unnecessarily placing themselves in high-risk (or "trigger") situations by testing themselves with access to cigarettes, alcohol, and so on. Finally, clients are admitting to failure before they even try to quit by selectively focusing on the costs already incurred by the habit they are trying to break. Therapists need to be aware of these and similar thoughts being expressed by clients so that they can be dealt with constructively.

In addition to the beliefs just expressed, Chiauzzi (1989) identified several personality traits that may contribute to client relapse:

- Perfectionism (e.g., the client may not be able to handle small setbacks and failures while struggling with the addiction)
- Dependency (e.g., the client may return to the apparent comfort of the habit when others are pushing him or her to change)
- Passive-aggressiveness (e.g., the client may blame others and drive them away)
- Self-centeredness (e.g., the client may not be willing to admit that he or she has a problem that needs to be dealt with)
- Rebelliousness (e.g., the client may resent or resist those who offer help)

URGE SURFING STEP-BY-STEP

There are four basic steps to urge surfing. Although more or less emphasis can be placed on each of the steps, it is important to cover each one of them at least briefly. The basic components of urge surfing can be taught within a single session. Once the skill is taught, the client can then continue to self-monitor his or her urges, or the skill can be further developed by spending session time discussing the client's urges and his or her reactions to them. The four basic steps to urge surfing are

1. Describing the skill of urge surfing.
2. Assessing the client's high-risk urge situations with him or her.
3. Developing a clear understanding of how the client experiences his or her urges.
4. Challenging the client's irrational assumptions that typically occur during the urge.

Each of these four steps will be described in detail so that the skill of urge surfing can be taught by the practitioner who reads this chapter.

Step 1: Describing Urge Surfing

For the client who is suffering, and giving in to, his or her urges, it is important to begin by emphasizing that urges are natural biological reactions to an addiction or strong habit. There is nothing wrong or bad about experiencing urges, and their presence does not point to a character flaw or weakness on the part of the client. More or less time can be spent normalizing the presence of urges and validating the uncomfortable feelings they bring about.

Next, the therapist should spend time describing both the costs associated with giving into the urges and the basic phenomenology of urges. One cost associated with giving into urges is that the urges don't go away, and they may become more frequent and even intense. Another, more evident, cost associated with giving in to urges involves the very behaviors the client is working to reduce (e.g., drug dependence and its costs to quality of life). Every time the client gives in to the urge to, say, smoke a cigarette, he or she is not living in a valued way. These points should be explained to the client in common-sense terms.

Experiencing an urge is an aversive condition. If this were not the case, then few people would have difficulty overcoming urges. Again, it is important to validate the client's claims regarding the difficulty of dealing with the urges. This creates a context within which rapport can develop. For a client who is struggling with urges, any therapist comment to the effect that "Your urges aren't that bad, and you should be able to easily deal with them" may contribute to the client's belief that he or she is just too weak to handle the urges. Such negative self-efficacy beliefs may already be implicated in the client's difficulty with urges, and it is counter to the goals of urge surfing to contribute in any way toward such beliefs.

Although urges can be difficult to withstand, it should be stressed to the client that urges are like waves. Instead of getting worse as time goes by urges actually gradually decrease in intensity. It is in this way that urges are like waves and the client can view him- or herself riding out the wave. Urges typically last only a few minutes, and rarely more than 10 minutes. People tend to give in to their urges before they ever get a chance to experience their gradual decrease in intensity. In the experience of some people, urges simply do not go away until they are defeated, so to speak, when the individual gives in to them. These individuals are giving in to the urges right away. This is another reason that it is important to validate the client's experiences with urges. For many clients, the very idea that urges subside after time is simply untenable because they have experienced so many urges without ever noticing this phenomenon.

Step 2: Assessing High-Risk Urge Situations

It is important to identify the situations that typically trigger urges for the client. This step facilitates a discussion of urges, affording client and therapist the opportunity to clear up any questions and confusion regarding the client's urges. Have the client develop a list of urge triggers. A client who is trying to quit smoking cigarettes, for example, may experience urges after meals, while driving or drinking, or when with friends who smoke. Developing an urge trigger list may help the client to avoid such situations. Drawing the client's attention to trigger situations can help him or her avoid making seemingly irrelevant decisions (SIDs) that lead him or her into the situations in the first place.

After a list of trigger situations has been developed the therapist should help the client develop an easy-to-remember and simple list of strategies to avoid trigger situations, or to distract when such situations are unavoidable.

Step 3: Experiencing Urges

Have the client create a detailed description of how he or she experiences urges. This can be done in session or in vivo. While experiencing an urge the client should sit in a comfortable position with feet flat on the floor, take some deep breaths, turn his or her attention inward, and focus on where in the body the urge is being experienced. The urge may be experienced in the chest, the stomach, or just about anywhere else in the body. Have the client simply notice the urge as it is experienced. Does it stay in one area of the body or does it move around to different places?

Have the client describe the urge in as many terms as possible. For example, does the urge feel like a tingling sensation, a burning sensation, maybe a pressure? If the urge feels like a pressure, then what kind of pressure? Is it a constant pressure, like a vice is being closed, or is it a pulsating pressure, like a heartbeat? If the urge changes body locations, have the client describe what it feels like when it changes. Instruct the client to use descriptive words while he or she attends to the urge as it grows in intensity and then slowly goes away. This is urge surfing.

Two important goals have been accomplished at this point, and you will likely want to discuss these with the client. First, the client has successfully urge surfed. That is, the client has resisted an urge even though the urge was confronted directly. By describing the urge, where it is felt, how it changes, and so on, the client has fully experienced the urge without having given in to it. One of the experiential differences between the way that urges were previously experienced and how they are experienced by the client while urge surfing might be attributable to an experiential shift from what Mischel (1996) referred to as "hot" to "cold" thoughts.

Hot thoughts are thoughts that focus on desirable qualities of objects such as the sweet, sugary taste associated with eating a cookie or the relaxing, euphoric state brought about by smoking a cigarette. Hot thoughts are consummative thoughts. *Cold thoughts,* on the other hand, are thoughts that focus on the neutral, purely de-scriptive qualities of objects, such as the round shape and brown color of a cookie, and the stick-like shape and cost of a cigarette. Cold thoughts are nonconsummative thoughts. In this sense when a client urge surfs he or she can be said to be thinking about the desired object in a different way.

Some clients may express surprise at how easily they resisted the urge in this way, and even more surprise at just how quickly the urge subsided. For some clients this experience will mark the first time that they can recall having experienced an urge going away naturally because they had previously "defeated" their urges by giving in to them. The purpose of urge surfing is to teach the client to experience the urge directly and wait it out. By focusing on the physical sensations of the urge and keeping track of how these sensations change and gradually subside over time, the client is attending to the cold aspects of the urge rather than the hot aspects of the desired object. The more the client practices this skill the more evidence, in the form of personal experience, the client will have to support the claim that urges are, in fact, brief and capable of being dealt with.

Step 4: Challenging Irrational Thoughts

After the client has successfully engaged in urge surfing for a short time it might be necessary to check in with him or her to determine what kinds of thoughts are accompanying the urges. It is important to remind the client that giving in to urges only makes them stronger. It is like starting a storm at sea that makes the waves more frequent and strong. To defeat the urges the client has to surf them out.

Ask the client to report whether the urges are successfully being surfed and, if so, how they may be changing in duration, frequency, and intensity. The client may experience a moderate increase along any one of these three dimensions if he or she has never maintained abstinence from the behavior or substance they are trying to abstain from. If this happens, the client may start to question his or her dedication to abstinence or ability to abstain, or may even the claim that the urges will eventually subside. These thoughts need to be dealt with because they can provide an obstacle to the client's abstinence. A number of approaches can be used to maintain client compliance with the therapeutic goals:

- Discuss the client's original decision to abstain from using.
- Discuss the benefits of abstaining.
- Remind the client that he or she has successfully surfed an urge and that it can be done again, maybe even with less difficulty.
- Remind the client that the urges only get stronger when they are given in to.

Sometimes this is not enough. Clients may express skepticism regarding their potential success. Maybe the client believes that his or her experience is far worse than the normal person's experience at dealing with urges, saying that, for example, "For them it was easy, but I am really hooked." If this is the case, then straightforward cognitive restructuring procedures can be applied.

The client can be asked to provide evidence that he or she really is more hooked than other addicts. Discussing the fact that other addicts who have successfully quit had to go through the same difficult situations can help reorient the client to his or her original valued therapy goals.

Clients may complain that the urges are just too horrible to endure despite what others may have gone through to kick the habit. Again, the therapist can challenge such statements by asking, "And what's so bad about a few minutes of discomfort?" The therapist can also simply have the client create a pro-and-con list for the habit.

Likely, the only pro on the list will be the avoidance of the uncomfortable urges that come with it.

References

Azrin, N. H., & Nunn, R. G. (1977). *Habit control in a day (stuttering, nail biting, and other nervous habits)*. New York: Pocket Books.

Baumeister, R. F., Heatherton, T. F., & Tice, D. M. (1994). *Losing control: How and why people fail at self-regulation*. New York: Academic Press.

Chiauzzi, E. (1989). Breaking the patterns that lead to relapse. *Psychology Today*, (December), 18–19.

Copeland, J., Swift, W., Roffman, R., & Stephens, R. (2001). A randomized controlled trial of brief cognitive-behavioral interventions for Cannabis Use Disorder. *Journal of Substance Abuse Treatment*, 21(2), 55–64.

Hayes, S. C., Strosahl, K. D., & Wilson, K. G. (1999). *Acceptance and commitment therapy: An experiential approach to behavioral change*. New York: Guilford Press.

Larimer, M. E., Palmer, R. S., & Marlatt, G. A. (1999). Relapse prevention: An overview of Marlatt's cognitive-behavioral model. *Alcohol Research and Health*, 23(2), 151–160.

Marlatt, G. A., & Gordon, J. R. (1985). *Relapse prevention*. New York: Guilford Press.

Mischel, W. (1996). From good intentions to willpower. In P.M. Gollwitzer & J. A. Bargh (Eds.), *The psychology of action: Linking cognition and motivation to behavior* (pp. 197–218). New York: Guilford Press.

Prochaska, J. O., Norcross, J. C., & DiClemente, C. C. (1994). *Changing for good*. New York: William Morrow.

68 VALIDATION PRINCIPLES AND STRATEGIES

Kelly Koerner and Marsha M. Linehan

Empathy is the platform for all therapeutic intervention (Bohart & Greenberg, 1997). A related but distinct concept also important in psychotherapy is validation. Whereas empathy is the accurate understanding of the world from the client's perspective, *validation* is the active communication that the client's perspective makes sense (i.e., is correct). To validate means to confirm, authenticate, corroborate, substantiate, ratify, or verify. To validate, the therapist actively seeks out and communicates to the client how a response makes sense by being relevant, meaningful, justifiable, correct, or effective. Validating an emotion, thought, or action requires *empathy*, an understanding of the particular or unique significance of the context from the other person's perspective. However, validation adds to this the communication that the emotion, thought, or action is a valid response. Were the client to ask, "Can this be true?" empathy would be understanding the "this" whereas validation would be communicating "yes."

WHO MIGHT BENEFIT FROM VALIDATION

All clients may benefit from validation, but validation may be essential for the success of change-oriented strategies with those who are particularly emotionally sensitive and prone to emotional dysregulation (Linehan, 1993). It may also be especially beneficial in working with disoriented elderly individuals (Feil, 1992). Precise and specific validation may be most indicated when much of the client's responding is dysfunctional or disoriented but where the therapist's corrective feedback about this may produce a client who is less collaborative and open to learning and, in effect, more dysfunctional.

In general, validation is used to balance change, increase verbal and nonverbal communication, prevent or decrease withdrawal, provide feedback and strengthen self-validation, strengthen clinical progress, and strengthen the therapeutic relationship. Feil (1992) suggests that with the old-old, validation can also be used to help the individual justify continuing to live. In nearly all situations, the therapist may usefully validate that the client's problems are important, that a task is difficult, that emotional pain or a sense of being out of control is justifiable, and that there is wisdom in the client's ultimate goals, even if not by the particular means he or she is currently using. Similarly, it is often useful for the therapist to validate the client's views about life problems and beliefs about how changes can or should be made. Unless the client believes that the therapist truly understands the dilemma (e.g., exactly how painful, difficult to change, or important a problem is) he or she will not trust that the therapist's solutions are appropriate or adequate, and collaboration and consequently the therapist's ability to help the client change will be limited.

However, helping clients change often requires invalidating, rather than validating, the client's important self-constructs, emotional avoidance, and other responses incongruent with achieving his or her long-term goals. When the client says, "I can't stand this emotional pain," the therapist's interventions are versions of, "Yes, you can," which encourages the experience and acceptance of painful emotions without avoidance or maladaptive responses to emotional pain. Yet, it is a normal psychological process for emotional arousal to occur when significant goals are blocked and important self-constructs are disconfirmed. When feedback is inconsistent with important self-constructs, consequent arousal and the sense of being out of control result in both failure to process new information and intense effort to gain control.

Therefore, helping clients change often requires intervening in a manner that modulates emotional arousal so that work on the therapeutic task continues. The therapist must simultaneously align with the client's goals and self-constructs without reinforcing dysfunctional behavior, without evoking such emotional reactivity that the therapeutic task is derailed, and without dropping a focus on needed change. Validation strategies add needed balance to change procedures. Validation is a therapeutic "yes, but," when combined with change strategies so that the therapist simultaneously communicates why something could not be otherwise yet must change. When the client says, "I can't stand it!" the therapist says "Yes, I know the pain is excruciating and seems unendurable, but I think we can go a little bit further."

Validation is also used to balance pathologizing that both clients and therapists are prone to do. Clients often have learned to treat their own valid responses as invalid (as stupid, weak, defective, or bad). Similarly, therapists also have learned to view normal responses as pathological. Validation strategies balance this by requiring the therapist to search for the strengths, normality, or effectiveness inherent in the client's responses whenever possible and by teaching the client to self-validate. Even patently invalid behavior may be valid in terms of being effective.

Cutting one's arms in response to overwhelming emotional distress makes sense given that it often produces relief from unbearable emotions: It is an effective emotion regulation strategy.

WHAT TO VALIDATE

Validate the valid. Note that

> . . . validation means the acknowledgement of that which is valid. It does not mean the "making" of something valid. Nor does it mean validating that which is invalid. The therapist observes, experiences and affirms but does not create validity. That which is valid preexists the therapeutic action. (Linehan, 1997, p. 356)

Validation functions as reinforcement—what you validate you will see more of.

To determine how a response is valid (or invalid), consider three ways it could be valid (Linehan, 1997). A response is valid if it is (1) relevant and meaningful; (2) well-grounded or justifiable in terms of facts, logical inference, or generally accepted authority; or (3) an appropriate or effective means to obtain one's ultimate goals. In other words, something can be valid in terms of current context (i.e., empirical facts, consensual agreement), antecedents (i.e., previous events), or consequences (i.e., effective for immediate or ultimate goals). During a psychotherapy session, it is invalid to fall asleep, refuse to talk, or change topics whenever problem solving is broached. The behavior is not relevant to the therapeutic task at hand. When a client says she hates herself, hatred might be both relevant and justifiable if the person violated her own important values (e.g., had deliberately harmed another person out of anger). The response of self-hatred may be relevant and justifiable, yet at the same time ineffective because it is incompatible with the balanced problem solving required to keep oneself from doing the hateful behavior again. Or say, for example, you've forgotten some fact that is important to a client without being aware you have done so. As the conversation continues, the client becomes overly cheery and stops saying anything of substance about the topic. When you wonder aloud about the change in mood and depth of the conversation, the client airily dismisses your concern. The client's response may be valid in terms of past learning history (understandable if her cultural background prohibits drawing attention to another's failings or directly expressing irritation about them) or current circumstances (if your tone is defensive or accusatory and it's logical to infer you won't be open to the feedback). But her response may be simultaneously invalid in that it may be ineffective to her long-term goals if her response fails to prompt any examination or correction in your behavior that hurt her feelings or if you need the fact in order to be most helpful to her. In short, look at context, antecedents, and consequences of the response. Does the response make sense in light of empirical facts, previous events, current context, logic, or consensual agreement? Is it compatible with the client's long-term goals? If yes, then the behavior is valid.

All behavior is valid in some way. Coming to a party at 5:00 P.M. that doesn't start until 8:00 P.M. may be invalid in that it is based on an incorrect belief about when the party starts, but it would be a valid response to an incorrectly stated invitation for 5:00 P.M. Even extremely dysfunctional behavior may be valid in terms of historically making sense—all of the factors needed for the behavior to develop have occurred: therefore, how could the behavior be other than it is?

CONTRAINDICATIONS AND FACTORS IN DECIDING TO USE OR NOT TO USE VALIDATION

The only true contraindication is that therapists should not validate invalid behavior. That is, the therapist does not want to validate responses that are dysfunctional and incompatible with progress toward the agreed-upon therapeutic goals. Because validation by definition functions as reinforcement, the therapist should be aware of what he or she is implicitly or explicitly validating and respond differentially to valid and invalid responses. Particularly with clients who are highly sensitive to emotional cues (e.g., individuals who tend to respond in an angry or extremely despairing manner to perceived threat), the therapist may become more and more careful in what he or she says in order to avoid setting off the cli-

ent's reaction. But this means that the client does not change. In fact, emotional sensitivity and intensity (e.g., anger or despair) are inadvertently made more likely (negatively reinforced) as the therapist withdraws a focus on change. In other words, the client's emotional response may gradually shape the therapist out of using effective change-oriented strategies that increase painful emotions. Validation can provide the balm for both therapist and client to negotiate through change procedures.

HOW DOES THE TECHNIQUE WORK?

Validation likely works via a number of processes. Validation may function as self-verification. A compelling series of research studies by Swann and his colleagues (Swann, 1984, 1987, 1992, 1997; Swann & Ely, 1984; Swann, Griffin, Predmore, & Gaines, 1987; Swann, Hixon, Stein-Seroussi, & Gilbert, 1990; Swann, Pelham, & Chidester, 1988; Swann & Read, 1981a, 1981b; Swann & Schroeder, 1995; Swann, Stein-Seroussi, & Giesler, 1992) suggests that verification of one's self-view, all other things being equal, will serve as a general reinforcer for most individuals. People will work to obtain feedback, even if negative, that is consistent with important self-constructs and views (a process called *self-verification*). It is a normal psychological process for emotional arousal to occur when significant goals are blocked and important self-constructs are disconfirmed. When feedback is inconsistent with important self-constructs, consequent arousal and the sense of being out of control result in both failure to process new information and intense effort to gain control. Validation, on the other hand, reduces arousal and the sense of being out of control and thereby increases learning and collaboration.

In contrast, it may be that the most important function of validation is that it communicates to the individual that he or she is understood and that this sense of being understood is critical to trusting a therapist sufficiently to collaborate. From this viewpoint, it is not the nonverification of the individual's self-constructs that is so important but rather the misunderstanding of the problems, needs, goals, and capabilities of the client. Whichever position is borne out by future research, both offer insight into the function of validation in psychotherapy.

EVIDENCE FOR THE EFFECTIVENESS OF VALIDATION

Preliminary work by Fruzzetti and colleagues (Fruzzetti, 2000; Fruzzetti & Rubio, 1998) indicates that the addition of validation training for partners facilitates better individual outcomes. The evidence for the usefulness of validation comes primarily from a logical extension of basic research on corrective feedback and the power of expectancies.

STEP-BY-STEP PROCEDURES

Step 1: Know Thy Client

Know thy client—and know thy psychopathology and normal psychology literatures. Be aware of what is valid and invalid for the specific client. Does the response move the client toward his or her immediate or ultimate goals? If so, the response is valid. Remember that a response can be both valid and invalid simultaneously. Constantly be aware of the client's current emotional arousal and how this is affecting the ability to process new information, and balance change and validation accordingly.

Step 2: Validate the Valid, Invalidate the Invalid

Be specific about what you are validating. For example, a case manager who has come to ignore repeated requests by a client to become his own payee because the client typically injudiciously spends the money, hears another impassioned request but ignores it completely as if it were irrelevant. Dismissiveness invalidates both the valid and invalid aspects of the request. Differential responding would require validating the valid (the wisdom of the ultimate goal of independence) while invalidating the invalid (e.g., insisting that an adequate plan to correct the mishandling of money be in place before making the change). The same behavior can be both valid and invalid. Of course, the case manager's ignoring of the re-

quests is also both valid and invalid: valid in the sense of being justifiable based on the client's mishandling of money, but invalid to the extent that it ignores the client's normative desire to control his own money and work toward greater independence.

To validate emotional responses, encourage emotional expression, teach emotion observation and labeling, read the client's emotions, and directly validate emotions (e.g., "feeling sad makes sense"). To validate behavioral responses, teach behavioral observation and labeling skills. Identify self-imposed demands or unrealistic standards for acceptable behavior and use of guilt, self-berating, or other punishment strategies (identify the *should*). Counter the *should* (i.e., communicate that all behavior is understandable in principle). Accept the *should* (i.e., respond to the client's behavior nonjudgmentally and discover whether there is truth to the *should* when phrased as "should in order to . . ."). Validate the client's disappointment in his or her own behavior. To validate cognitive responses, elicit and reflect thoughts and assumptions, find the "kernel of truth" in the client's cognitions, acknowledge the client's intuitive ability to know what is wise or correct, and respect the client's values. To validate the person's ability to attain desired goals, assume the best, encourage, focus on strengths, contradict or modulate external criticism, and be realistic in assessment of capabilities. To invalidate the invalid, be descriptive and nonjudgmental, articulating how the response does not make sense either in terms of antecedents or consequences.

Step 3: Validate at the Highest Possible Level

Remember that actions speak louder than words. Linehan (1997) has described six levels of validation. While all levels are important, higher levels are viewed as more important and at times crucial.

At each level, do not rely solely on explicit verbal validation. Acting and responding as if the client's responses are valid is often both required and more powerful than verbal validation. In other words, if you were trapped at a fourth-floor window of a burning building, and a firefighter showed interest, accurately reflected your distress, understood better than you your terror, and genuinely communicated how it made sense with both your learning history and current circumstances for you to be on the verge of a panic attack, it would still be insufficient! Putting the fire out is what you need and this functional validation, responding to the client's experience as valid (and therefore compelling), is essential. Verbal validation alone, when in fact functional validation is required, is one of the most therapist-like of errors. Avoid it.

- *Level 1: Listen with complete awareness, be awake.* Listen and observe in an unbiased manner, communicate that the client's responses are valid by listening without prejudging. For example, the case manager hears the client's request to become his own payee without construing it solely in terms of the mismanagement of money.
- *Level 2: Accurately reflect the client's communication.* Communicate understanding by repeating or rephrasing, using words close to the client's own without added interpretation.
- *Level 3: Articulate unverbalized emotions, thoughts, or behavior patterns.* Perceptively understand what is not stated but meant without the client's having to explain things.
- *Level 4: Describe how the client's behavior makes sense in terms of past learning history or biology.* Identify the probable factors that caused the client's response. For example, to a client who constantly seeks reassurance that therapy "is going okay," the therapist might validate by saying, "Given the unpredictability of your parents, it makes sense to have the feeling of waiting for the other shoe to drop and seek reassurance."
- *Level 5: Actively search for the ways that the client's behavior makes sense in the current circumstances and communicate this.* Find the ways a response is currently valid, whenever possible, and remember not to rely only on verbal validation. For example, say you were walking to a movie theater with a friend who'd been raped in an alley, you proposed that you take a shortcut through an alley so that you wouldn't be late for the movie, and your friend said she did not want to because she was afraid. Saying, "Of course you're afraid, you were raped in an alley, how insensitive of me" would be a Level-4 validation. Saying, "Of

course you are afraid, alleys are dangerous, let's walk around" would be a Level-5 validation. When you can find a Level-5 validation (and search like a fiend for it), use it rather than a Level 4. So, for example, with the client seeking reassurance, the therapist might search for ways that he or she is communicating ambivalence or in some other way cueing the client's response, so that seeking reassurance is sensible, even if the history of unpredictable parents were known. Validating in terms of the past when in fact there are aspects in the current situation prompting the response is experienced as extremely invalidating. For example, if a client is angry that his therapist is rigid about adjusting the therapy payment in the face of his unexpected layoff and difficulty finding new work (and in fact the therapist is decidedly and unreasonably inflexible), it is to be expected that the client would become angrier if the therapist attempted to validate by beginning with how the client's response is understandable given how withholding and rigid his father was.

- *Level 6: Be radically genuine.* Act in a manner that communicates respect for the client as a person and an equal, more than the person as client or disorder. Play to the person's strengths rather than to fragility, in a manner comparable to how you'd offer help to a treasured colleague or loved one. Whereas levels 1 to 5 represent sequential steps in validation of a kind, Level 6 represents both changes in level as well as in kind, in which the therapist validates the individual rather than any particular response or behavioral pattern. As Rogers has described this radically genuine stance:

> He is without front or façade, openly being the feelings and attitudes which at the moment are flowing in him. It involves the element of self-awareness, meaning that the feelings the therapist is experiencing are available to his awareness, and also that he is able to live these feelings, to be them in the relationship, and able to communicate them if appropriate. It means that he comes in to a direct personal encounter with his client, meeting him on a person-to-person basis. It means he is being himself, not denying himself. (Rogers & Truax, 1967, p. 101).

1. Know thy client. Know what responses are normative, abnormal, and in line with the client's ultimate therapeutic goals.

2. Validate the valid; invalidate the invalid. Be specific, precise, and differentially respond to strengthen emotional, behavioral, and cognitive responses in line with the client's ultimate therapeutic goals.

3. Validate at the highest possible level. Remember, actions speak louder than words. Listen with complete awareness; accurately reflect; articulate the unverbalized; describe how responses make sense in terms of the past or preferably current circumstances. Be radically genuine.

4. Actively validate early in therapy; fade to normal levels over time.

FIGURE 68.1   Keys to Validation

Step 4: Actively Validate Early in Therapy; Fade to Normal Levels of Validation over Time

Finally, while empathy and functional validation should remain high throughout therapy, the active verbal validation to provide corrective feedback or balance pathologizing should be faded from an initially high level to normative level. (For a summary of the steps of validation, see Figure 68.1).

Further Reading

Linehan, M. M. (1993). Validation. In *Cognitive behavioral therapy for Borderline Personality Disorder* (pp. 221–249). New York: Guilford Press.

Linehan, M. M. (1997). Validation and psychotherapy. In A. Bohart & L. Greenberg (Eds.), *Empathy reconsidered: New directions in psychotherapy* (pp. 353–392). Washington, DC: American Psychiatric Association.

References

Bohart, A., & Greenberg, L. (Eds.). (1997). *Empathy reconsidered: New directions in psychotherapy*. Washington, DC: American Psychiatric Association.

Feil, N. (1992). *Validation: The Feil method*. Ohio: Edward Feil.

Fruzzetti, A. E. (2000). *The role of validation in individual psychopathology, relationship quality, and treatment*. Symposium paper presented at the 34th annual convention of the Association for the Advancement of Behavior Therapy, New Orleans, LA.

Fruzzetti, A. E., & Rubio, A. (1998). *Observing intimacy: Self-disclosure and validation reciprocity and its impact on relationship and individual well-being*. Symposium paper presented at the 32nd annual convention of the Association for the Advancement of Behavior Therapy, Washington, DC.

Greenberg, L. S. & Paivio, S. C. (1997). *Working with emotions in psychotherapy*. New York: Guilford Press.

Linehan, M. M. (1993). Validation. In *Cognitive behavioral therapy for Borderline Personality Disorder* (pp. 221–249). New York: Guilford Press.

Linehan, M. M. (1997). Validation and psychotherapy. In A. Bohart & L. Greenberg (Eds.), *Empathy reconsidered: New directions in psychotherapy* (pp. 353–392). Washington, DC: American Psychiatric Association.

Rogers, C. R., & Truax, C. B. (1967). The therapeutic conditions antecedent to change: A theoretical view. In C. R. Rogers (Ed.), *The therapeutic relationship and its impact* (pp. 97–108). Madison: University of Wisconsin Press.

Swann, W. B. (1984). Quest for accuracy in person perception: A matter of pragmatics. *Psychological Review, 91*, 457–477.

Swann, W. B. (1987). Identity negotiation: Where two roads meet. *Journal of Personality and Social Psychology, 53*, 1038–1051.

Swann, W. B. (1992). Seeking "truth," finding despair: Some unhappy consequences of a negative self-concept. *Current Directions in Psychological Science, 1*, 15–18.

Swann, W. B. (1997). The trouble with change: Self-verification and allegiance to the self. *Psychological Science, 8*, 177–180.

Swann, W. B., & Ely, R. J. (1984). A battle of wills: Self-verification versus behavioral confirmation. *Journal of Personality and Social Psychology, 46*, 1287–1302.

Swann, W. B., Griffin, J., Predmore, S. C, & Gaines, B. (1987). The cognitive-affective crossfire: When self-consistency confronts self-enhancement. *Journal of Personality and Social Psychology, 52*, 881–889.

Swann, W. B., Hixon, J. G., Stein-Seroussi, A., & Gilbert, D. T. (1990). The fleeting gleam of praise: Cognitive processes underlying behavioral reactions to self-relevant feedback. *Journal of Personality and Social Psychology, 59*, 17–26.

Swann, W. B., Pelham, B. W., & Chidester, T. R. (1988). Change through paradox: Using self-verification to alter beliefs. *Journal of Personality and Social Psychology, 54*, 268–273.

Swann, W. B. & Predmore, S. C. (1985). Intimates as agents of social support: Sources of consolation or despair? *Journal of Personality and Social Psychology,* *49,* 1609–1617.

Swann, W. B., & Read, S. J. (1981a). Acquiring self-knowledge: The search for feedback that fits. *Journal of Personality and Social Psychology, 41,* 1119–1128.

Swann, W. B., & Read, S. J. (1981b). Self-verification processes: How we sustain our self-conceptions. *Journal of Experimental and Social Psychology, 17,* 351–372.

Swann, W. B., & Schroeder, D. G. (1995). The search for beauty and truth: A framework for understanding reactions to evaluations. *Personality and Social Psychology Bulletin, 21,* 1307–1318

Swann, W. B., Stein-Seroussi, A., & Giesler, R. B. (1992). Why people self-verify. *Journal of Personality and Social Psychology, 62,* 392–401.

69

WORKING WITH IMPLOSIVE (FLOODING) THERAPY: A DYNAMIC COGNITIVE-BEHAVIORAL EXPOSURE PSYCHOTHERAPY TREATMENT APPROACH

Donald J. Levis and Adam R. Krantweiss

The theory and treatment technique of implosive therapy (IT) was developed in 1959 by Thomas G. Stampfl. London (1964) was the first to describe this approach in print. Stampfl, however, was reluctant to publish his theory until clinical research confirmed that the technique was non-harmful and effective (Stampfl & Levis, 1967). Implosive therapy was designed as a relatively short-term behavioral approach applicable to a wide variety of psychopathology, including the treatment of psychotic behavior. Stampfl's technique was the first to systematically apply the principle of direct experimental extinction to treatment that combined the use of both an in vivo and imagery mode to present previously conditioned aversive stimuli. Implosive therapy can be characterized as a dynamic cognitive-behavioral exposure approach to treatment. The technique is sometimes referred to in the literature (Levis & Hare, 1977) as flooding or a response prevention approach to treatment. The term *implosion,* which is borrowed from physics, reflects the abruptness and depth of the cues that are represented with the consequent intense anxiety reaction. Stampfl's approach is unique in its ability to integrate areas of psychology, in its res-

olution of the neurotic paradox, and its ability to reduce complex behavior to basic principles of experimental psychology.

To fully comprehend the diversity and power of this approach, it is essential for the practitioner to comprehend the underlying learning theory supporting this treatment technique. Since detailed reports of Stampfl's theory have been presented elsewhere, only a cursory review will be provided here (Boudwyns & Shipley, 1983; Levis, 1980, 1981, 1985, 1987, 1989, 1991, 1995; Stampfl, 1970, 1983, 1987, 1991; Stampfl & Levis, 1967, 1969, 1973, 1976).

IMPLOSIVE THEORY

Stampfl viewed maladaptive behavior as a learned response that is considered to be an end product of antecedent aversive conditioning. The theoretical learning model adapted by Stampfl is primarily based on an extension to the area of psychopathology of O. H. Mowrer's two-factor theory of avoidance learning (Mowrer, 1947, 1960). In theory, the learning of maladaptive behavior can be separated into two different response categories. The first involves the conditioning of an aversive emotional state, which is based on the well-established laws of classical conditioning. Fear and other emotional aversive conditioning result from the simple contiguity of pairing of nonemotional stimulation in space and time with an inherent primary aversive event producing pain, fear, frustration, or severe deprivation. Following sufficient repetition, the nonemotional stimulus acquires the capability of eliciting the aversive emotional state. Most importantly, Stampfl believes the conditioning events of patients involve multiple complex sets of stimuli that comprise both external and internal aversive stimuli that are encoded in long-term memory. Thus, the assumption is made that central state constructs such as images, thoughts, and memories function as conditioned stimuli, which represent the major controlling stimulation maintaining psychopathology (Levis, 1995; Stampfl, 1970).

Emotional conditioning is also viewed as a secondary source of drive, possessing both motivational and reinforcing properties that set the stage for the learning of the second response class, avoidance or escape behavior. This second response class is governed by the laws of instrumental learning. Avoidance and escape behavior are learned by the organism in an attempt to prevent, remove, or reduce the aversive state elicited by the presence of conditioned emotional stimuli. In theory, any response that achieves this objective is, in turn, reinforced by the resulting reduction in this aversive state. The more effective the avoidance response is in achieving this objective, the greater the amount of reinforcement. The conceptualization of clinical symptoms and maladaptive behavior as avoidance behavior is a central component of IT theory.

From the foregoing analysis it would follow that because patients' symptoms occur in the absence of any primary reinforcement, their symptoms should eventually undergo an extinction effect. Clinical evidence exists that this is true for some cases, but for other cases, patients' symptoms appear to persist for years. Freud (1936) first raised this issue of sustained symptom maintenance, and Mowrer (1948) labeled it the "neurotic paradox." More specifically, the paradox is why neurotic behavior is at one and the same time

self-defeating and yet self-perpetuating instead of self-eliminating. To provide a resolution of this paradox, Stampfl extended Solomon and Wynne's (1954) conservation of anxiety hypotheses, which basically states that any part of the conditioned stimulus (CS) complex that is not exposed will maintain its aversive properties until full exposure results in an extinction effect. Stampfl postulated that the eliciting set of cues triggering symptoms' onset are backed by a multiple network of unexposed CS cues stored in long-term memory. These cues are believed to be ordered in a sequential or serial arrangement according to their accessibility along a dimension of stimulus intensity, with the more aversive cues being least accessible. As the initial set of cues undergoes an extinction effect from repeated exposure, it is replaced with another, more aversive, set of cues, which secondarily reconditions the first set of cues reinstating symptom occurrence. This process continues to repeat itself, resulting in the maintenance of symptomatology over long periods of time until each set of cues encoded in the serial arrangements is fully extinguished (for a more detailed presentation of this important theoretical contribution along with the supporting experimental evidence, see Levis, 1991, 1995; Levis & Brewer, 2001; Stampfl, 1987, 1991).

OVERVIEW OF THE THERAPEUTIC EXTENSION OF IMPLOSIVE THEORY

The implementation of this well-established principle of experimental extinction is straightforward in a laboratory setting, where the CS cues eliciting avoidance responding are known conditions and therefore easily reproducible. However, the contingencies of the conditioning history of a patient upon first contact are unknown. Despite the fact that it is difficult, if not impossible, to specify the aversive conditioning events with exact precision, it is feasible, as Stampfl noted, for a trained clinician following a few diagnostic interviews to locate key stimuli associated with the problem areas of the patient. Once these are located it is not difficult to formulate a hypothesis as to the type of traumatic events that may have contributed to the client's behavior. Of course, these initial hypotheses must be conceived as only first approximations of the original conditioning sequences, but it is quite possible that they incorporate a number of the more significant avoided components. As therapy progresses it is usually possible to obtain additional information as to the validity of these cues and to generate new hypotheses. A key advantage of the IT technique is that it is an operational treatment procedure, in that confirmation or disconfirmation of a hypothesized cue area is determined by whether or not the presentation of the material elicits a strong emotional response. The assumption is made that the stronger the overt emotional response obtained, the greater the support is for the continual presentation of the cue area until extinction is obtained. The technique is also a feedback approach in that the therapist has the added advantage of being able to alter or restructure a given hypothesis by focusing on the patient's reported associations to the stimuli being presented and incorporating them into the development of additional hypotheses. Thus, the therapist can produce a chain of associations that not only releases new unexposed fear cues but also frequently results in the decoding of an actual traumatic memory. However, knowledge of the actual historical conditioning events is not required, because the technique is based on the premise that if the anxiety-eliciting hypotheses are close to the actual event, the principle of generalization of extinction should produce an extinction effect.

In an attempt to aid the therapist in the selection, classification, and ordering of cues to be presented, Stampfl (1970) suggested the use of a four-cue category system. These cue categories can be conceptualized in terms of a progression along a continuum that ranges from extremely concrete and physical cues at one end to more hypothetical and dynamic cues at the other end. These cue categories are as follows: (1) *symptom-contingent cues*, or those environmental cues that are correlated until the elicitation of symptom onset; (2) *patient reportable, internally elicited cues*, the thoughts, feelings, and physical sensation that the patient reports experiencing while engaging in the problematic behavior; (3) *unreportable cues*, which are hypothesized to be related to reportable internally related cues (e.g., feeling of loss of control); and (4) *hypothesized dynamic cues*, which are cues associated with death, the afterlife, sexual fear, or primary process thoughts.

WHO MIGHT BENEFIT FROM THE TECHNIQUE

As noted earlier, IT was designed to be applicable to the treatment of a wide variety of psychopathology, including the treatment of psychotic behavior. Not only have the underlying theoretical principles incorporated by IT received strong experimental support at the animal, human, and clinical level of analysis, but experimental support has also been obtained for Stampfl's clinical technique and that of related CS exposure therapies. Outcome studies of exposure therapy in the 1970s (Levis & Hare, 1977) and the 1980s (Levis & Boyd, 1985) were supplemented by even more supporting research in the 1990s. Experimental support for the clinical use of exposure therapy exists for the following nosologies: phobic behavior, Agoraphobia, panic attacks, depression, obsessive-compulsive behavior, Post-Traumatic Stress Disorder, and psychotic behavior. Numerous case reports of the successful use of exposure therapy also exist for the treatment of a variety of other nosologies.

CONTRAINDICATION OF THE TREATMENT

Although no experimental data exist for the contraindication of use of this technique, it is essential in order for the technique to be effective that the patient be willing to cooperate in the technique's administration. Although the vast majority of patients willingly participate, occasionally the initial fear level of a given patient may be so strong that cooperation is not obtained, requiring the use of an alternate or modified technique. It is also critical for the technique's effectiveness that the procedure elicit emotional responding. Although the technique has been readily used with patients on psychotropic medication, it is possible that some medication especially designed for the treatment of psychotic symptoms may result in the blocking or retardation of emotional responding. Prior to the start of treatment, all patients are instructed to have a physical exam to insure that the technique will not exacerbate an existing medical condition. Concerns in this area should be coordinated with the patient's medical doctor. Finally, data do not exist for the use of this technique in cases of Substance Abuse, psychopathic behavior, or sexual predation.

OTHER ISSUES IN DECIDING TO USE OR NOT USE AN EXPOSURE-BEHAVIORAL APPROACH

Despite the strong experimental support for the clinical efficacy of exposure-based technique, considerable resistance to its use still exists. It may prove beneficial to review some of the concerns that have been raised in the past and that have emerged during our experience when training new therapists in the technique. Historically concerns were initially expressed by behavior therapists who objected to Stampfl's inclusion of dynamic cues because of their psychoanalytic implications. This objection persisted despite the finding that these cues were often reported to be present in the thoughts of the patients and that such cues were readily interpreted within a behavioral learning theory framework. Interestingly, many IT therapists report that the use of dynamic cues frequently produces the greatest clinical gains. A second concern, which still emerges with new therapists, centers on the fear that the elicitation of a high level of affect with a patient may produce a harmful effect or create a psychotic reaction. This hypothesis was directly tested with hospitalized patients who manifested a low degree of ego-strength and was disconfirmed (Boudwyns, 1975; Boudwyns & Levis, 1972; Boudwyns & Wilson, 1972; Hogan, 1966). These data, combined with the survey study of Shipley & Boudwyns (1983) and over 40 years of successful therapeutic use, have empirically put this concern to rest. The final resistant point encountered relates to the therapist's own avoidance of presenting to patients anxiety-eliciting cues involving such content areas as rejection, anger, sex, guilt, shame, and fears of loss of control. The clinical gains achieved from the use of this technique quickly extinguish this concern.

Patients, on the other hand, report that they stay in treatment because the treatment rationale makes sense to them, they recover quickly from each session, they can see the changes in their lives, and they like the fact that they are trained in how to use the technique between sessions, which gives them a sense of control over their fears. The overall attrition and noncompliance rate of patients exposed to IT is very low, with missing of sessions being rare.

HOW DOES THE TECHNIQUE WORK?

Implosive therapy and related exposure therapies base their treatment effectiveness on the established laws of direct experimental extinction, the repeated presentation of aversive stimuli that elicit symptom behavior in the absence of any aversive reinforcement. Laboratory and clinical evidence strongly confirms that procedures that prevent or block the occurrence of the avoidance behavior or repeatedly present the aversive complex of stimuli that elicit symptomatic behavior, to result in a rapid unlearning (extinction) of both the eliciting emotional state and the resulting avoidance behavior. These manipulations at first result in the elicitation of a strong emotional response, which is followed by an equally strong extinction effect, relegating the aversive eliciting stimuli to a neutral state devoid of its motivational properties. Clinical evidence supports the contention that therapeutic cognitive restructuring take place following the process of emotional extinction.

A STEP-BY-STEP PROCEDURAL OUTLINE OF IMPLOSION THERAPY

The following sections describe the steps that make up the process of IT.

Stimulus Mode of Conditioned Stimulus Presentation

The execution of the principle of experimental extinction is achieved by representing, reinstating, or symbolically reproducing in the absence of physical pain those conditioned cues responsible for motivating and maintaining the patient's symptomatology. In those cases in which the CS patterns being avoided involve discrete external stimuli, in vivo exposure to those cues can be pre-

TABLE 69.1   Key Steps in IT and Related Exposure Therapies

1. Performing in-depth pretreatment diagnostic interview
2. Formulating a treatment plan
3. Presenting a treatment rationale
4. Using first-session instructional set
5. Executing effective treatment scenes

sented by encouraging the patient to confront the phobic object directly (e.g., a snake) or by directly blocking the patient's symptoms (e.g., hand washing in a case of obsessive-compulsive behavior). If the therapeutic decision is made to present only in vivo cues, the procedure outlined by Foa and Tillmanns (1980) can be adopted. However, most IT therapists adopt both an in vivo and an imagery mode of CS presentation. The advantage of presenting in vivo cues in imagery is that they can be combined with the presentation of symptom-related internal cues, such as those cues and events associated with guilt, anger, and fears of rejection, pain, punishment, and loss of control. Thus, the imagery mode enhances the ability of the therapist to expose the patient to a variety of stimuli (visual, auditory, and tactile) hypothesized to be links to the original conditioning history.

In-Depth Interviewing

The first task of the therapist is to identify as accurately as possible those conditioned aversive stimuli that are presumed to mediate the emotional responses (e.g., anxiety, anger, rejection, depression) that are determinants of the symptoms and problems of the client. To achieve this objective, two or three 1-hour sessions are conducted with the patient in an ordinary office or therapy room. The key question that constantly guides the therapist is "What cue areas do the patient's symptoms prevent from full exposure?" The diagnostic workup should include not only a thorough analysis of the situational cues surrounding the onset of each symptom reported by the patient but also a thorough review of the individual's family, sexual, religious, cultural, and medical history. Early memories of aversive events with family members should be solicited,

as well as any reccuring nightmares or other such material that may aid the therapist in an attempt to restructure the life-history conditioning events. Careful notes are taken listing both internal stimuli (images, thoughts, and impulses) and external stimuli (stimuli associated with public events; e.g., phobic objects, social situations, parental arguments, etc.). Experience indicates that rapport can be facilitated by skillfully discussing difficult areas of sexuality, expression of anger, or thoughts of suicide. To maximize the obtainment of information it is important to raise these "base-rate" questions in a manner that implies that the therapist assumes such conflicts exist. The administration of global personality inventories like the Minnesota Multiphasic Personality Inventory (MMPI-2) also has been shown to be useful.

Formulating a Treatment Plan

Following the interview phase and the classification of the obtained material into hypothesized cue areas, a treatment plan is developed by the therapist. Cue areas hypothesized by the therapist to be maintaining symptoms are then integrated by the therapist into scenes along a dimension from the least to the most anxiety eliciting. This serial cue hierarchy can then be incorporated into Stampfl's four cue categories previously outlined.

Presenting the Treatment Rationale

It is helpful to first provide a simple explanation to the patient of the underlying avoidance model of conditioning and the role the serial CS hypothesis plays in maintaining the patient's symptomatology. Next a treatment rationale is presented:

> "Before we actually start the treatment procedure, I would like to take a little time and describe to you the rationale behind the technique we are going to use. First, let me ask you a question. If you were learning to ride a horse and you fell off, what would your instructor have you do? [The usual answer given is to get back on the horse.] Exactly, and if you didn't your fear might increase and generalize not only to the surrounding stimuli but might even back up to the entrance of the stable. By forcing yourself to be exposed to what you are afraid of, you can

overcome your fears. Let me try another example. Have you ever been frightened by a horror movie? If you have and you stayed to see the movie over and over again, it is unlikely by the tenth showing you would have any fear of the situation. It is the same situation that confronts a young medical intern who, upon seeing his or her first operation, faints from horror at the sight of an open chest. However, with continual exposure to such operations, the fear is overcome. The technique we are going to use follows the same basic principle of extinction. You will be asked to imagine various scenes in imagery that are designed to elicit anxiety. Repeating the scene many times will reduce or extinguish your fear level. Your fears are learned, and they can be unlearned by confronting them directly in imagery. Images can't hurt you in reality. Do you have any questions?"

"Neutral" Imagery Training

Approximately 20 minutes should be set aside at the end of the last diagnostic interview to assess the patient's imagery ability. The purpose of such training is to allow the therapist to establish a crude baseline for the patient's ability to imagine various sensory modalities (e.g., visual, auditory, tactile) and to establish the therapist as the director of the scenes. Such neutral imagery may include watching TV, walking down a street, eating a meal, and the like. Details of the scenes should be fully described (e.g., facial expressions), and scenes should be designed not to elicit any anxiety.

First Implosive Session

The first IT session is initiated during the third or fourth session. After a few minutes of conversation, the patient is asked to play out various scenes presented by the therapist. A typical instructional set is provided by the following excerpt:

"Your task is much like that of an actor (actress). You will be asked to play the part of yourself and to portray certain feelings and emotions in imagery. Like an actor (actress) you are to 'live' the scenes with genuine emotions and affect. I (the therapist) will direct the scene. You will be asked to close your eyes

and follow the scenes in imagery. Please put yourself in the scene as best as you can and imagine the events I describe as clearly as possible. The scenes, like movies, do not necessarily involve real events. You only have to believe or accept the scenes as real when you are visualizing them. The greater the level of affect you can experience, the greater the benefits received. Do you have any questions before we start?"

In order to circumvent resistance, it is important that the therapist make little or no attempt to secure admission from the patient that the content of the scene actually applies to the patient. It is usually convenient to begin the first session by incorporating relevant material reported by the client (e.g., symptom contingent cues, active memory of a traumatic experience, or a frequently recurring dream). It is useful to develop a scene slowly, allowing the client sufficient time to formulate a relatively good image by having him or her to describe context cues (setting cues). The relevant material within a scene can be played over and over again even though other features of the scene are changing. A given scene is usually terminated after some diminution in anxiety is noted. Never stop a scene in the middle of a given theme—always complete the sequence. Following the last scene in the session, allow at least 10 minutes to pass to insure that the patient's anxiety level is back to normal. When patients are asked to open their eyes, the anxiety level elicited usually returns to baseline within 5 minutes. Repetition is a critical component of IT, and each scene presented within a session should be repeated at least once. To facilitate the extinction process at the end of each session, the patient is assigned homework, which involves repeating the scenes administered during the session for at least a 20-minute period daily until the next session.

The therapist's attitude and method of scene presentation play an important role. The more sensitive and empathetic the therapist is in understanding the client's problem, the better able the therapist is to present the scene material. The therapist should try to feel the role being played. By varying the vocal inflection at appropriate places, the therapist can produce a greater effect. The more involved and dramatic the therapist becomes in describing a given scene, the more realistic the scene becomes, and the easier it is for the client to participate.

Dealing with Resistance and Defenses

Cooperation on this patient's part is essential for maximum effects to be obtained. The skills of the therapist are critical in this regard. Because of the nature of the material being presented, resistance should be expected. When encountered three strategies can be adapted. The first is to override or overpower the resistance directly. For example, it is common for a patient to say "It is not true." The therapist's response is "Whether it's true or not, just imagine it." If the patient says, "I can't see that," the therapist's response is "Yes, you can see it." If this direct approach doesn't work after several minutes of pressure, the second strategy of circumventing the patient's defenses can be used. This can be achieved by changing the content of the scene to a lesser anxiety-arousing level. After a while the therapist can return to the more anxiety-eliciting material previously awarded. The third strategy involves "imploding" the defense directly. For example, if the patient says, "I can't do this, it will make me worse or I will lose control," the therapist's response is to have the patient close his or her eyes and describe an IT scene in which the patient, as a function of coming to therapy, loses control and ends up in the back ward of a mental hospital, to remain there for the rest of his or her life. The first author's experience has been that this scene never fails to work and that after one repetition the patient readily goes back to working on the scene where the defense materialized.

Session Spacing and Treatment Duration

It should be clear from this discussion that a given therapy session cannot necessarily be held to the usual 50-minute session. The therapist must be flexible in this regard. If a session of 50 minutes is allotted for scenes to be presented, allow half an hour between patients. Some sessions have run 2 or 3 hours, some 20 minutes. The desired spacing between sessions is also unknown. Usually, one meeting a week is scheduled, but more frequent visits have also produced good effects. Duration of treatment clearly varies with the individual case. Symptom removal has occurred following one session, and usually reduction in symptomatology is obtained after 10 to 15 sessions.

However, with more difficult cases involving multiple problem or problems of long standing, more time may be needed to obtain significant gains. Longer periods of treatment are also needed when the defense structure of the patient is strong and the therapist finds it difficult to evoke much anxiety. (For a more detailed discussion of the procedure steps, see Levis, 1980.)

References

Boudwyns, P. A. (1975). Implosive therapy and desensitization therapy with inpatients: A five-year follow-up. *Journal of Abnormal Psychology, 84,* 159–160.

Boudwyns, P. A., & Levis, D. J. (1975). Autonomic reactivity of high and low ego-strength to repeated anxiety eliciting scenes. *Journal of Abnormal Psychology, 84,* 682–692.

Boudwyns, P. A., & Shipley, R. H. (1983). *Flooding and implosive therapy.* New York: Plenum.

Boudwyns, P. A., & Wilson, A. E. (1972). Implosive therapy and densensitization therapy using free-association in the treatment of inpatients. *Journal of Abnormal Psychology, 79,* 259–268.

Foa, E. B., & Tillmanns, A. (1980). The treatment of obsessive-compulsive neurosis. In A. Goldstein & E. B. Foa (Eds.), *Handbook of behavioral interventions: A clinical guide* (pp. 416–500). New York: John Wiley & Sons.

Freud, S. (1936). *The problems of anxiety* (H. A. Bunker, Trans.). New York: Norton.

Hogan, R. A. (1966). Implosive therapy in the short-term treatment of psychotics. *Psychotherapy: Theory, Research, and Practice, 3,* 25–31.

Levis, D. J. (1980). Implementing the technique of implosive therapy. In A. Goldstein & E. B. Foa (Eds.), *Handbook of behavioral interventions: A clinical guide* (pp. 92–151). New York: John Wiley & Sons.

Levis, D. J. (1981). Extrapolation of two-factor learning theory of infrahuman avoidance behavior to psychopathology. *Neuroscience and Biobehavioral Review, 5,* 355–370.

Levis, D. J. (1985). Implosive theory: A comprehensive extension of conditioning theory of fear/anxiety to psychopathology. In S. Reiss & R. R. Bootzin (Eds.), *Theoretical issues in behavior therapy* (pp. 49–82). New York: Academic Press.

Levis, D. J. (1987). Treating anxiety and panic attacks: The conflict model of implosive therapy. *Journal of Integrative and Eclectic Psychotherapy, 6*(4), 450–461.

Levis, D. J. (1989). The case for a two-factor theory of avoidance: Do non-fear interpretations really offer an alternative? In S. B. Klein & R. R. Mowrer (Eds.), *Contemporary learning theories* (pp. 227–277). Hillsdale, NJ: Erlbaum.

Levis, D. J. (1991). A clinician's plea for a return to the development of nonhuman models of psychopathology: New clinical observations in need of laboratory study. In M. R. Denny (Ed.), *Fear, avoidance, and phobias: A fundamental analysis* (pp. 395–427). Hillsdale, NJ: Erlbaum.

Levis, D. J. (1995). Decoding traumatic memory: Implosive theory of psychopathology. In W. O'Donohue & L. Krasner (Eds.), *Theories of behavior therapy* (pp. 173–207). Washington, DC: American Psychological Association.

Levis, D. J., & Boyd, T. L. (1985). The CS exposure approach of implosive therapy. In R. M. Turner & L. M. Ascher (Eds.), *Evaluation of behavior therapy outcome* (pp. 56–94). New York: Springer.

Levis, D. J., & Brewer, K. E. (2001). The neurotic paradox: Attempts by two-factor fear theory and alternative avoidance models to resolve the issues associated with sustained avoidance responding in extinction. In R. R. Mowrer & S. B. Klein (Eds.), *Handbook of contemporary learning theories* (pp. 561–597). Hillsdale, NJ: Erlbaum.

Levis, D. J., & Hare, N. (1977). A review of the theoretical rationale and empirical support for the extinction approach of implosive (flooding) therapy. In M. Hersen, R. M. Eisler, & P. M. Miller (Eds.), *Progress in behavior modification IV* (pp. 300–376). New York: Academic Press.

London, P. (1964). *The modes and morals of psychotherapy.* New York: Holt, Rinehart & Winston.

Mowrer, O. H. (1947). On the dual nature of learning: A re-interpretation of "conditioning" and "problem-solving." *Harvard Educational Review, 17*, 102–148.

Mowrer, O. H. (1948). Learning theory and the neurotic paradox. *American Journal of Orthopsychiatry, 18*, 571–610.

Mowrer, O. H. (1960). *Learning theory and behavior.* New York: John Wiley & Sons.

Shipley, R. H., & Boudwyns, P. A. (1983). Flooding and implosive therapy: Are they harmful? *Behavior Therapy, 11*, 503–508.

Solomon, R. L., & Wynne, L. C. (1954). Traumatic avoidance learning: The principle of anxiety conservation and partial irreversibility. *Psychological Review, 61*, 353–385.

Stampfl, T. G. (1970). Implosive therapy: An emphasis on covert stimulation. In D. J. Levis (Ed.), *Learning approaches to therapeutic behavior change* (pp. 182–204). Chicago: Aldine.

Stampfl, T. G. (1983). Exposure treatment for psychiatrists? *Contemporary Psychology, 28*, 527–529.

Stampfl, T. G. (1987). Theoretical implications of the neurotic paradox as a problem in behavior theory: An experimental resolution. *The Behavior Analyst, 10*, 161–173.

Stampfl, T. G. (1991). Analysis of aversive events in human psychopathology: Fear and avoidance. In M. R. Denny (Ed.), *Fear, avoidance and phobias* (pp. 363–393). Hillsdale, NJ: Erlbaum.

Stampfl, T. G., & Levis, D. J. (1967). The essentials of implosive therapy: A learning theory based on psychodynamic behavioral therapy. *Journal of Abnormal Psychology, 72*, 496–503.

Stampfl, T. G., & Levis, D. J. (1969). Learning theory: An aid to dynamic therapeutic practice. In L. D. Eron & R. Callahan (Eds.), *Relationship of theory to practice in psychotherapy* (pp. 85–114). Chicago: Aldine.

Stampfl, T. G., & Levis, D. J. (1973). Implosive therapy. In R. M. Jurjevich (Ed.), *Direct psychotherapy: 28 American originals* (pp. 83–105). Coral Gables, FL: University of Miami Press.

Stampfl, T. G., & Levis, D. J. (1976). Implosive therapy: A behavioral therapy. In J. T. Spence, R. C. Carson, & J. W. Thibaut (Eds.), *Behavioral approaches to therapy* (pp. 86–110). Morristown, NJ: General Learning Press.

AUTHOR INDEX

SUBJECT INDEX